MW00962744

THE

CAREER

DIRECTORY

2000 EDITION

Edited by:
Richard W. Yerema

MEDIACORP CANADA INC.
TORONTO

Here's What Reviewers Are Saying About The Career Directory...

"The Career Directory is an excellent resource for first-time job seekers and those looking for entry-level positions. Well indexed by company name and functional speciality"
Canada Employment Weekly

"A valuable reference guide for job seekers"
The Toronto Star

"The Career Directory is a user-friendly resource, easy to use and informative. It is an excellent career search resource"
Guidance & Counselling

"The Directory is an affordable and essential book for job hunting and career planning in Canada"
The Aquinian, St. Thomas University

"It is easy-to-use, an excellent source, and is necessary for anyone who wants to break into the job market"
The Underground, University of Toronto

"While written for new graduates seeking employment, it is useful for career-changers or students considering educational programs who want to foresee potential areas and types of employment. Also new Canadians with training from foreign institutions have found this book useful"
Career Action News, Toronto Centre for Career Action

"Students intending to look for summer or full-time work
later this year will find a valuable resource in The Career Directory"
The Toronto Star

"For those looking for that first job upon graduation
or even a summer job, this book could prove invaluable"
The Lance, University of Windsor

"Finding a job is the formidable hurdle facing university graduates
and others these days. These books offer information and
advice that could help"
The Star Phoenix, Saskatoon

"It can also help you determine whether a company is right
for you even before you walk in the door"
Eye On Toronto, CFTO - CTV

"An excellent source of pertinent information"
Toronto Career Directory User

"A truly informative directory"
London Career Directory User

"Helps one make sense of what occupations are available for what
degrees, what prospective companies are actually looking for,
and valuable contact names within various corporations"
The Lexicon, York University

Thoughts and Thanks

An acknowledgement to the incredible power of paddles, pucks and pedals... and the unique characteristics of the borg titanium implants. Also, an overdue thank you to all of those people who have helped in the transformation back to my true mental age. Hhmmm...

As always, thank you and good luck to the readers of this directory. I sincerely hope that it helps drop you on the right portage to the next 40 years!

Richard Yerema
ry@mediacorp2.com

The Career Directory
Mediacorp Canada Inc.
P.O. Box 682, Station "P"
Toronto, Ontario
M5S 2Y4

Telephone   (416) 964-6069
Fax   (416) 964-3202

E-mail   info@mediacorp2.com
Web Site   http://www.mediacorp2.com

© 2000 Mediacorp Canada Inc. All rights reserved. No part of this publication may be reproduced, stored in a retrieval system, or transmitted, in any form or by any means, electronic, mechanical, photocopying, recording, or otherwise, without the prior written permission of the publisher. The information contained in this publication has been compiled from primary sources we believe to be reliable; while every effort has been made to ensure the accuracy of this publication, we assume no liability for errors or omissions. THE CAREER DIRECTORY is a trade mark of Mediacorp Canada Inc.

To purchase the information in this directory on disk or in label format, telephone (416) 964-6069.

ISBN 0-9681447-8-0. 9th Edition. First edition: 1992.

Printed in Canada by Webcom.

TABLE OF CONTENTS

Continues...

TABLE OF CONTENTS
(Continued)

THE STORY OF THE CAREER DIRECTORY...

The story of *The Career Directory* is one of the true legends of Canadian publishing. In the summer of 1989, two University of Toronto graduates had become frustrated in their search for work related to their studies. Through the course of their job searches, they were unable to find a good source of objective information about employers interested in hiring recent graduates.

Richard Yerema, the writer of the two, put together a looseleaf listing of all the employers he discovered that were hiring new graduates. The listings were short and to the point — just a few words about what each employer did, the academic fields they were interested in, and Richard's own assessment of how to best get a job there. A few dozen interesting employers were listed.

Richard's friends learned what he was working on and soon started asking if they could "borrow" his looseleaf listings for their own job searches. In turn, their friends began asking where they could get such information. Then it occurred to Richard that maybe researching and writing these looseleaf listings was a full-time job in itself — and so *The Career Directory* was born.

The first edition in 1991 was thin (by today's standards), but became an instant hit at campus career centres and bookstores. Over the years, the book has helped thousands of jobseekers get started on their careers. Now in its 9th annual edition, *The Career Directory* now includes profiles of over 1,000 employers and is Canada's best-selling career book.

While the size and scope of *The Career Directory* have expanded, its purpose hasn't — the book remains a trusted and objective source of information about employers that are interested in hiring people from particular academic backgrounds. Within its pages, you'll find valuable and unique information that will help you focus your job search and tap the potential of the hidden job market. Painstakingly compiled from thousands of interviews and questionnaires, this information allows you to "look inside" an employer to assess whether they are a suitable match for your qualifications.

All the information in the book is presented in a user-friendly format. *The Career Directory* has no tables, abbreviations or codes to decipher. The 2000 Edition is the largest to date and represents a significant expansion in the book's coverage. In addition to updated and expanded listings for returning employers, this year's edition includes more new employers than ever before.

HOW TO USE THIS DIRECTORY

This directory is a guide for job-seekers interested in finding Canadian employers that recruit people with particular educational backgrounds. You can use this book to find:

✔ Employers that recruit full-time employees with your educational background;

✔ Employers in a particular industry;

✔ Employers in a particular region of the country;

✔ Employers that participate in co-op work/study programs; and

✔ Employers that offer summer jobs.

The information in this directory is compiled from thousands of listing forms sent to employers and interviews conducted with human resource managers and recruiters.

To use this directory, start with the **Educational Index**. Locate your degree or diploma (e.g. Bachelor of Arts, Bachelor of Engineering, Community College Diploma) in the Table of Contents (p. 5). Then turn to that section and find the particular field of study that applies to you (e.g. Bachelor of Arts in Journalism, Bachelor of Engineering in Aerospace, Community CollegeDiploma in Nursing). The companies listed below your degree or diploma are your primary targets for full-time employment.

Next, go back to the starting point for your degree or diploma. At the top of each section are employers that hire people with your degree or diploma, but have not specified a field of study. (Their field of study is listed as "General".) These employers are your secondary targets for full-time employment.

Once you have identified your primary and secondary targets, go the **Employer Listings** to find out more information on the employers. Each employer listing provides:

• A brief overview of the company's operations, including the number of employees.

• Full contact information, including the employer's human resources contact, mailing address, telephone and fax numbers, email address and website.

• The average starting salary.

HOW TO USE THIS DIRECTORY
(Continued)

- A rating on the company's potential for career advancement.

- A rating on the benefits offered.

- The academic qualifications desired, including degree, diploma and field of study.

- The non-academic skills desired.

- Information on whether co-op or summer employment opportunities are available.

- The preferred method for initial contact by job-seekers (e.g. send resume, call, apply online).

The information in each listing will allow you to make informed decisions about which employers are best suited to your qualifications and career objectives.

Besides the Educational Index, there are four useful topical indexes located after the employer listings. The **Industry Index** lets you find all the employers in a particular business or line of work that may interest you. The **Geographic Index** lists the employers by province. The **Co-Op** Index shows all the employers that participate in co-op work/study programs. And the **Summer Job Index** lists all the employers that traditionally offer summer positions for students.

A final word is in order about the scope of this directory. Don't be disheartened if you have qualifications that are superior to those listed by employers, or are not exactly what the employer has specified. Always write the employer and inquire whether positions for people with your particular qualifications are available. This directory should be seen as a starting point for your job search, not a replacement for your own hard work and research. The aim of this book is to point you in the right direction, but the journey is up to you.

Education Index

BACHELOR OF ARCHITECTURE

BACHELOR OF ARCHITECTURE - LANDSCAPE

BACHELOR OF ARTS - GENERAL

BACHELOR OF ARTS - ARCHEOLOGY

BACHELOR OF ARTS - BUSINESS

BACHELOR OF ARTS - CRIMINOLOGY

BACHELOR OF ARTS - ECONOMICS

BACHELOR OF ARTS - ENGLISH

BACHELOR OF ARTS - FRENCH

BACHELOR OF ARTS - LANGUAGES (OTHER)

BACHELOR OF ARTS - MUSIC

BACHELOR OF ARTS - PHILOSOPHY

BACHELOR OF ARTS - POLITICAL SCIENCE

BACHELOR OF ARTS - PSYCHOLOGY

BACHELOR OF ARTS - PUBLIC RELATIONS / COMMUNICATIONS

BACHELOR OF ARTS - RECREATION STUDIES

BACHELOR OF ARTS - SOCIAL WORK

BACHELOR OF ARTS - SOCIOLOGY

BACHELOR OF ARTS - URBAN GEOGRAPHY

BACHELOR OF COMMERCE - GENERAL

BACHELOR OF COMMERCE - ACCOUNTING

BACHELOR OF COMMERCE - FINANCE

BACHELOR OF COMMERCE - HOTEL/FOOD SERVICES

BACHELOR OF COMMERCE - HUMAN RESOURCES

BACHELOR OF COMMERCE - INFO SYSTEMS/IS

BACHELOR OF COMMERCE - MARKETING

BACHELOR OF COMMERCE - PUBLIC ADMINISTRATION

BACHELOR OF EDUCATION - GENERAL

BACHELOR OF EDUCATION - ADULT

BACHELOR OF EDUCATION - EARLY CHILDHOOD

BACHELOR OF EDUCATION - INTERMEDI-ATE SENIOR (7-12)

BACHELOR OF EDUCATION - JUNIOR INTERMEDIATE (4-10)

BACHELOR OF EDUCATION - PHYSICAL & HEALTH

BACHELOR OF EDUCATION - PRIMARY JUNIOR (0-6)

BACHELOR OF EDUCATION - SPECIAL NEEDS

BACHELOR OF ENGINEERING - GENERAL

BACHELOR OF ENGINEERING - AEROSPACE

BACHELOR OF ENGINEERING - AGRICULTURAL

BACHELOR OF ENGINEERING - ARCHITECTURAL/BUILDING

BACHELOR OF ENGINEERING - BIOMEDICAL ELECTRONICS

BACHELOR OF ENGINEERING - AUTOMATION/ROBOTICS

BACHELOR OF ENGINEERING - BIOTECHNOLOGY

BACHELOR OF ENGINEERING - CHEMICAL

BACHELOR OF ENGINEERING - CIVIL

BACHELOR OF ENGINEERING - COMPUTER SYSTEMS

BACHELOR OF ENGINEERING - ELECTRICAL

BACHELOR OF ENGINEERING - ENGINEER-ING PHYSICS

BACHELOR OF ENGINEERING - ENVIRON-MENTAL/RESOURCES

BACHELOR OF ENGINEERING - FOOD PROCESSING

BACHELOR OF ENGINEERING - FOREST RESOURCES

BACHELOR OF ENGINEERING - GEOLOGICAL

BACHELOR OF ENGINEERING - INDUSTRIAL CHEMISTRY

BACHELOR OF ENGINEERING - INDUSTRIAL DESIGN

BACHELOR OF ENGINEERING - INDUSTRIAL ENGINEERING

BACHELOR OF ENGINEERING - INSTRU-MENTATION

BACHELOR OF ENGINEERING - MARINE

BACHELOR OF ENGINEERING - MATERIALS SCIENCE

BACHELOR OF ENGINEERING - MECHANICAL

BACHELOR OF ENGINEERING - METAL-LURGY

BACHELOR OF ENGINEERING - MICRO-ELECTRONICS

BACHELOR OF ENGINEERING - MINING

BACHELOR OF ENGINEERING - PETRO-LEUM/FUELS

BACHELOR OF ENGINEERING - POLLUTION TREATMENT

BACHELOR OF ENGINEERING - POWER/HYDRO

BACHELOR OF ENGINEERING - PRODUCTION/MANUFACTURING

BACHELOR OF ENGINEERING - PULP & PAPER

BACHELOR OF ENGINEERING - SURVEYING

BACHELOR OF ENGINEERING - TELECOM-MUNICATIONS

BACHELOR OF ENGINEERING - TRANSPORTATION

BACHELOR OF ENGINEERING - WATER RESOURCES

BACHELOR OF ENGINEERING - WELDING

BACHELOR OF LAWS - GENERAL

BACHELOR OF SCIENCE - ACTUARIAL/ STATISTICS

BACHELOR OF SCIENCE - AGRICULTURE/ HORTICULTURE

BACHELOR OF SCIENCE - AUDIOLOGY

BACHELOR OF SCIENCE - BIOLOGY

BACHELOR OF SCIENCE - CHEMISTRY

BACHELOR OF SCIENCE - COMPUTER SCIENCE

BACHELOR OF SCIENCE - DENTISTRY

BACHELOR OF SCIENCE - ECOLOGY

BACHELOR OF SCIENCE - ENVIRONMENTAL

BACHELOR OF SCIENCE - FORESTRY

BACHELOR OF SCIENCE - GEOGRAPHY

BACHELOR OF SCIENCE - GEOLOGY

BACHELOR OF SCIENCE - HEALTH SCI-ENCES

BACHELOR OF SCIENCE - METALLURGY

BACHELOR OF SCIENCE - METEOROLOGY

BACHELOR OF SCIENCE - MICROBIOLOGY

BACHELOR OF SCIENCE - NURSING

BACHELOR OF SCIENCE - NUTRITION

BACHELOR OF SCIENCE - OCCUPATIONAL THERAPY

BACHELOR OF SCIENCE - OCEANOGRAPHY

BACHELOR OF SCIENCE - PHARMACY

BACHELOR OF SCIENCE - PHYSICS

BACHELOR OF SCIENCE - PHYSIOTHERAPY

BACHELOR OF SCIENCE - PSYCHOLOGY

BACHELOR OF SCIENCE - SPEECH PATHOLOGY

BACHELOR OF SCIENCE - TEXTILES

BACHELOR OF SCIENCE - ZOOLOGY

CERTIFIED GENERAL ACCOUNTANT - GENERAL

CERTIFIED GENERAL ACCOUNTANT - FINANCE

CERTIFIED MANAGEMENT ACCOUNTANT - GENERAL

CERTIFIED MANAGEMENT ACCOUNTANT - FINANCE

CHARTERED ACCOUNTANT - GENERAL

CHARTERED ACCOUNTANT - FINANCE

COMMUNITY COLLEGE - GENERAL

COMMUNITY COLLEGE - ACCOUNTING

COMMUNITY COLLEGE - ADVERTISING

COMMUNITY COLLEGE - AGRICULTURE/ HORTICULTURE

COMMUNITY COLLEGE - AIRCRAFT MAINTE- NANCE

COMMUNITY COLLEGE - AMBULANCE/ EMERGENCY CARE

COMMUNITY COLLEGE - ANIMAL HEALTH

COMMUNITY COLLEGE - ANIMATION

COMMUNITY COLLEGE - ARCHITECTURAL TECHNICIAN

COMMUNITY COLLEGE - AUDIO/VISUAL TECHNICIAN

COMMUNITY COLLEGE - AUTOMOTIVE MECHANIC

COMMUNITY COLLEGE - BUSINESS ADMINISTRATION

COMMUNITY COLLEGE - CAD/CAM/ AUTOCAD

COMMUNITY COLLEGE - CARPENTRY

COMMUNITY COLLEGE - CHILD CARE/ EDUCATION

COMMUNITY COLLEGE - COMMUNICATIONS / PUBLIC RELATIONS

COMMUNITY COLLEGE - COMPUTER SCIENCE

COMMUNITY COLLEGE - COOKING/CHEF TRAINING

COMMUNITY COLLEGE - DENTAL ASSIST-ANT

COMMUNITY COLLEGE - DENTAL HYGIEN-IST

COMMUNITY COLLEGE - DIETICIAN/NUTRI-TION

COMMUNITY COLLEGE - ELECTRONICS TECHNICIAN

COMMUNITY COLLEGE - ENGINEERING TECHNICIAN

COMMUNITY COLLEGE - FACILITY MANAGEMENT

COMMUNITY COLLEGE - FASHION ARTS/ DESIGN

COMMUNITY COLLEGE - FINANCIAL PLANNING

COMMUNITY COLLEGE - FORESTRY

COMMUNITY COLLEGE - FUNERAL SERVICES

COMMUNITY COLLEGE - GRAPHIC ARTS/ DESIGN

COMMUNITY COLLEGE - HEALTH SCIENCES (OTHER)

COMMUNITY COLLEGE - HEALTH/HOME CARE AIDE

COMMUNITY COLLEGE - HEAVY EQUIPMENT

COMMUNITY COLLEGE - HOSPITALITY

COMMUNITY COLLEGE - HUMAN RESOURCES

COMMUNITY COLLEGE - HVAC SYSTEMS

COMMUNITY COLLEGE - INFORMATION SYSTEMS

COMMUNITY COLLEGE - INSURANCE

COMMUNITY COLLEGE - JOURNALISM

COMMUNITY COLLEGE - LABORATORY TECHNICIAN

COMMUNITY COLLEGE - LEGAL ASSISTANT

COMMUNITY COLLEGE - MARINE ENGINEERING

COMMUNITY COLLEGE - MARKETING/ SALES

COMMUNITY COLLEGE - MASSAGE THERAPY

COMMUNITY COLLEGE - MUSIC

COMMUNITY COLLEGE - NUCLEAR MEDICINE

COMMUNITY COLLEGE - NURSING RN

COMMUNITY COLLEGE - NURSING RNA/RPN

COMMUNITY COLLEGE - OFFICE ADMINIS- TRATION

COMMUNITY COLLEGE - ORTHOTICS/ PROSTHETICS

COMMUNITY COLLEGE - OTHER TRADES

COMMUNITY COLLEGE - PHOTOGRAPHY

COMMUNITY COLLEGE - PLUMBER

COMMUNITY COLLEGE - PODIATRY

COMMUNITY COLLEGE - PURCHASING/ LOGISTICS

COMMUNITY COLLEGE - RADIATION THERAPY

COMMUNITY COLLEGE - RADIOLOGY

COMMUNITY COLLEGE - REAL ESTATE SALES

COMMUNITY COLLEGE - RECREATION STUDIES

COMMUNITY COLLEGE - REHABILITATION

COMMUNITY COLLEGE - RESPIRATORY THERAPY

COMMUNITY COLLEGE - SECRETARIAL

COMMUNITY COLLEGE - SECURITY/EN-FORCEMENT

COMMUNITY COLLEGE - SOCIAL WORKER/ DSW

COMMUNITY COLLEGE - TOOL & DIE / MACHINIST / MILLWRIGHT

COMMUNITY COLLEGE - TRAVEL/TOURISM

COMMUNITY COLLEGE - TV/RADIO ARTS/ BROADCAST

COMMUNITY COLLEGE - ULTRASOUND TECHNICIAN

COMMUNITY COLLEGE - UPHOLSTERY

COMMUNITY COLLEGE - URBAN PLANNING

COMMUNITY COLLEGE - WELDING

MASTER OF ARTS - GENERAL

MASTER OF BUSINESS ADMINISTRATION - ACCOUNTING

MASTER OF BUSINESS ADMINISTRATION - FINANCE

MASTER OF BUSINESS ADMINISTRATION - HUMAN RESOURCES

MASTER OF BUSINESS ADMINISTRATION - INFORMATION SYSTEMS/IS

MASTER OF BUSINESS ADMINISTRATION - MARKETING

MASTER OF BUSINESS ADMINISTRATION - PUBLIC ADMINISTRATION

MASTER OF EDUCATION - GENERAL

MASTER OF EDUCATION - ADULT

MASTER OF EDUCATION - PHYSICAL & HEALTH

MASTER OF EDUCATION - SPECIAL NEEDS

MASTER OF ENGINEERING - GENERAL

MASTER OF ENGINEERING - AEROSPACE

MASTER OF ENGINEERING - ARCHITECTURAL/BUILDING

MASTER OF ENGINEERING - BIOMEDICAL ELECTRONICS

MASTER OF ENGINEERING - BIOTECHNOLOGY

MASTER OF ENGINEERING - CHEMICAL

MASTER OF ENGINEERING - CIVIL

MASTER OF ENGINEERING - COMPUTER SYSTEMS

MASTER OF ENGINEERING - ELECTRICAL

MASTER OF ENGINEERING - ENGINEERING PHYSICS

MASTER OF ENGINEERING - ENVIRONMENTAL/RESOURCES

MASTER OF ENGINEERING - FOOD PROCESSING

MASTER OF ENGINEERING - FOREST RESOURCES

MASTER OF ENGINEERING - GEOLOGICAL

MASTER OF ENGINEERING - INDUSTRIAL CHEMISTRY

MASTER OF ENGINEERING - INDUSTRIAL DESIGN

MASTER OF ENGINEERING - INDUSTRIAL ENGINEERING

MASTER OF ENGINEERING - MATERIALS SCIENCE

MASTER OF ENGINEERING - MECHANICAL

MASTER OF ENGINEERING - METALLURGY

MASTER OF ENGINEERING - MICROELECTRONICS

MASTER OF SCIENCE - MATERIALS SCIENCE

MASTER OF SCIENCE - MATHEMATICS

MASTER OF SCIENCE - METALLURGY

MASTER OF SCIENCE - MICROBIOLOGY

MASTER OF SCIENCE - NURSING/HEALTH ADMINISTRATION

MASTER OF SCIENCE - NUTRITION

MASTER OF SCIENCE - OCCUPATIONAL THERAPY

MASTER OF SCIENCE - PHARMACY

MASTER OF SCIENCE - PHYSICS

MASTER OF SCIENCE - PHYSIOTHERAPY

MASTER OF SCIENCE - PSYCHOLOGY

MASTER OF SCIENCE - SPEECH PATHOLOGY

Employer Listings

3M CANADA COMPANY
PO Box 5757
London, ON N6A 4T1

Tel.	519-451-2500
Fax	519-452-6502
Website	www.3m.com

3M Canada Company is part of a global corporation manufacturing and selling more than 50,000 diverse products. The company serves the consumer/office, industrial, automotive, aerospace, electronics, health care, safety and security markets. 3M Canada Company was established in 1951 as one of 3M's first international subsidiaries. 3M Canada's head office is in London. Manufacturing is carried on in London, and at seven other plants located in Brockville, Havelock, Perth and Toronto, Ontario and Morden, Manitoba. Sales offices are located in major cities across the country and customers are supported by a national service network. 3M Canada employs over 2,000 employees across the country. Graduates most likely to be hired come from the following academic areas: Bachelor of Arts (Economics), Bachelor of Science (General, Biology, Chemistry, Computer Science, Physics), Bachelor of Engineering (Chemical, Electrical, Mechanical, Computer Systems, Materials Science), Bachelor of Commerce/Business Administration (General, Finance, Information Systems, Marketing), Master of Business Administration (General), Master of Engineering (Chemical, Mechanical, Electrical) and Doctorate (Related Fields). Graduates are hired to occupy Technical Service, Engineering, Sales, Marketing and Customer Service positions. Highly motivated along with excellent interpersonal and communication skills are listed as desirable non-academic qualifications. Company benefits and the potential for advancement are both rated as excellent. The average annual starting salary falls within the $35,000 to $52,000 range. The most suitable method for initial contact by those seeking employment is to mail a resume with a covering letter. 3M Canada Company does hire a limited number of summer students annually. *Contact:* Human Resources Operations.

724 SOLUTIONS INC.
4101 Yonge Street, Suite 702
Toronto, ON M2P 1N6

Tel.	416-226-2900
Fax	416-226-4456
Email	info@724solutions.com
Website	www.724solutions.com

724 Solutions Inc. conceives, designs and delivers Internet software applications enabling "anytime, anywhere, anyway" access to trusted banking, investment and lifestyle services. 724 has partnered with Bell Mobility and the Bank of Montreal to provide the technology infrastructure for "Veev", which is a new service that gives consumers immediate, secure and easy access to information and financial institutions they know and trust. The software enables financial institutions to deliver banking, brokerage and information content on a wide variety of internet access devices. Graduates most likely to be hired come from the following academic areas: Bachelor of Science (Computer Science), Bachelor of Engineering (Computer Systems, Telecommunications), Master of Science (Computer Science) and Community College Diploma (Computer Science). Graduates would occupy Senior Designer/Architect, Security Architect, Software Developer, Database Architect/Analyst, Systems Specialist, QA Analyst, Internet Application Developer, Project Manager and Business Development and Sales positions. Team player, entrepreneurial spirit, experience in a finan-cial institution (or related experience), and the ability to work irregular and varied hours are all listed as desirable non-academic qualifications. Company benefits are rated as industry standard. The potential for advancement is listed as being excellent. The average annual starting salary falls within the $55,000 to $60,000 range. The most suitable method for initial contact by those seeking employment is to apply through the company's website. 724 Solutions Inc. does hire summer and co-op work term students. *Contact:* Sally Dakin, Human Resources Manager.

A.G. SIMPSON COMPANY LIMITED
675 Progress Avenue
Toronto, ON M1H 2W9

Tel.	416-438-6650
Fax	416-438-6533
Website	www.agsimpson.com

A.G. Simpson Company Limited is an OEM supplier of automotive stampings and assemblies. Headquartered in Scarborough, the company has been supplying to the automotive industry for over 50 years. In addition to the Scarborough location the company has Canadian based manufacturing facilities in Oshawa, Windsor, Oakville and Cambridge, and American based facilities in Sterling Heights, Michigan, Dickson, Tennessee, Troy, Michigan and Earth City, Missouri. A.G. Simpson Company Limited employs 500 people at this location and a total of 3,500 people in Canada. Graduates most likely to be hired come from the following academic areas: Bachelor of Arts (Economics, Psychology), Bachelor of Science (Computer Science, Environmental, Metallurgy), Bachelor of Engineering (General, Chemical, Materials Science, Metallurgy, Pollution Treatment, Automation/Robotics, Computer Systems, Instrumentation, Microelectronics, Mechanical, Industrial Design, Industrial Production, Welding, Resources/Environmental), Bachelor of Commerce/Business Administration (Accounting, Finance, Human Resources, Information Systems, Marketing), Chartered Accountant, Certified Management Accountant, Certified General Accountant, Master of Business Administration (Accounting, Finance, Human Resources, Information Systems, Marketing), Community College Diploma (Accounting, Business, Communications, Facility Management, Financial Planning, Human Resources, Marketing/Sales, Purchasing/Logistics, Secretarial, Security, CAD/CAM/Autocad, Computer Science, Electronics Technician, Engineering Technician, Laboratory Technician, Nursing RN) and High School Diploma. Graduates would occupy Process Engineer, Q.C. Technician, Production Planning, Tooling Engineer, etc. positions. Previous work experience in automotive stamping and QS9000 work environments are both listed as desirable non-academic qualifications. Company benefits are rated as excellent. The potential for advancement is listed as being good. The average annual starting salary falls within the $35,000 to $40,000 range. The most suitable method for initial contact by those seeking employment is to mail a resume with a covering letter. *Contact:* Human Resources.

A-1 SERVICE GROUP
201 Spinnaker Way, Unit 12
Concord, ON L4K 4C6

Tel.	905-669-4095
Fax	905-669-3769
Email	resume_hr@iname.com
Website	www.a1-servicegroup.com

A-1 Service Group installs and services pedestrian traffic counting systems, POS/Data and electrical systems for shopping centers and retail stores. The company has been installing and servicing pedestrian traffic counters for many years and today has one of the largest installed client bases in North America and is continuing to expand rapidly. A-1 Service Group provides site surveys, shared installations, turn key installations, software installation, training and a full preventive maintenance program to ensure each installation's trouble free operation. The company employs approximately 40 people at this location. Graduates most likely to be hired come from the following academic areas: Bachelor of Engineering (Electrical, Construction, Telecommunications) and Community College Diploma (Electronics Technician). Previous work experience in the electric and data systems installation field, retail and shopping centre industry knowledge and the ability to travel are all listed as desirable non-academic qualifications. Company benefits are rated as industry standard. The potential for advancement is listed as being excellent. The most suitable methods for initial contact by those seeking employment are to mail, fax or e-mail a resume with a covering letter, or through the company's website. *Contact:* Olga Webster, Administrative Assistant.

ABB CANADA
860 Harrington Court
Burlington, ON L7N 3N4

Tel. 905-639-8840
Fax 905-639-8639
Email .... michelle.catherwood@ca.abb.com
Website .... www.abb.ca

ABB Canada, Burlington - Process Automation, formerly Elsag Bailey (Canada) Inc., supplies process control systems, services and instrumentation products to a broad section of the industrial process and utility markets in Canada and overseas. ABB Canada, Burlington - Process Automation is a branch of ABB Canada, headquartered in St-Laurent, Quebec. ABB Canada is a domestic leader serving customers in the automotive, chemical, oil and gas, mining and metals, pulp and paper and utility markets. ABB Canada is in turn a member of ABB Group, based in Zurich, Switzerland. ABB Group is a global engineering and technology company serving customers in electrical power generation, transmission, distribution, automation, oil, gas, petrochemicals, industrial products, contracting and financial services. ABB employs 200,000 people in over 100 countries. ABB Canada employs 3,500 people in 45 centres from coast to coast. ABB Canada, Burlington - Process Automation employs a total of 300 people. Graduates most likely to be hired come from the following academic areas: Bachelor of Science (Computer Science, Mathematics), Bachelor of Engineering (General, Chemical, Electrical, Mechanical, Computer Systems, Instrumentation, Petroleum/Fuels, Pulp and Paper), Bachelor of Commerce/Business Administration (Accounting, Finance) and Community College Diploma (Accounting, Business, CAD/CAM/Autocad, Computer Science, Electronics Technician). Graduates would occupy Technician - Sales and Service and Engineering - Sales, Engineering, and Marketing positions. Team player, strong communication skills, good negotiating skills, well organized, customer focused and an ability to meet deadlines are all listed as desirable non-academic qualifications. The most suitable method for initial contact by those seeking employment is to mail a resume with a covering letter. ABB Canada, Burlington - Process Automation does hire summer and co-op work term students. *Contact:* Human Resources.

ABB CANADA
200 Chisholm Drive
Milton, ON L9T 5E7

Tel. 905-875-4500
Fax 905-875-4649
Email .... roy.w.kendall@abb.ca
Website .... www.abb.ca

ABB Canada, Milton is involved in the manufacturing of switchgear equipment. ABB Canada, Milton is a branch of ABB Canada, headquartered in St-Laurent, Quebec. ABB Canada is a domestic leader serving customers in the automotive, chemical, oil and gas, mining and metals, pulp and paper and utility markets. ABB Canada is in turn a member of ABB Group, based in Zurich, Switzerland. ABB Group is a global engineering and technology company serving customers in electrical power generation, transmission, distribution, automation, oil, gas, petrochemicals, industrial products, contracting and financial services. ABB employs 200,000 people in over 100 countries. ABB Canada employs 3,500 people in 45 centres from coast to coast. ABB Canada, Milton is ISO 9001 registered company and employs a total of 100 people. Graduates most likely to be hired come from the following academic areas: Bachelor of Engineering, Bachelor of Commerce/Business Administration, Chartered Accountant and Community College Diploma (General). Graduates would occupy Engineering Technologist, Production Planner and Accountant positions. Company benefits are rated as industry standard. The potential for advancement is listed as excellent. The average annual starting salary is competitive within the industry. The most suitable method for initial contact by graduates seeking employment is to mail a resume with a covering letter. ABB Canada, Milton does hire summer students. *Contact:* Human Resources Manager.

ABB CANADA
134 Norfinch Drive
Toronto, ON M3N 1X7

Tel. 416-667-9800
Fax 416-667-9816
Website .... www.abb.ca

ABB Canada, Toronto - I & C Division designs, develops and manufactures industrial type measuring devices and process instrumentation systems. Products include a wide range of both smart and conventional products to manage process mediums such as liquids, gases and slurries. ABB Canada, Toronto - I & C Division is a branch of ABB Canada, headquartered in St-Laurent, Quebec. ABB Canada is a domestic leader serving customers in the automotive, chemical, oil and gas, mining and metals, pulp and paper and utility markets. ABB Canada is in turn a member of ABB Group, based in Zurich, Switzerland. ABB Group is a global engineering and technology company serving customers in electrical power generation, transmission, distribution, automation, oil, gas, petrochemicals, industrial products, contracting and financial services. ABB employs 200,000 people in over 100 countries. ABB Canada employs 3,500 people in 45 centres from coast to coast. Graduates most likely to be hired at this location come from the following academic areas: Bachelor of Engineering (Mechanical, Chemical, Electrical) and Community College Diploma (Instrumentation Electronics). Graduates would occupy Service Technician, Sales Engineer, Systems Engineer, Calibration Technician and Project Manager positions. Reliable, dependable, ingenuity, a sense of urgency and a good work attitude are all listed as desirable non-academic qualifications. Company benefits are rated above average. The potential for advancement is listed as excellent. The average annual starting salary falls within the $25,000 to $30,000 range. The most suitable method for initial contact by graduates seeking employment is to mail a resume with a covering letter. ABB Canada, Toronto - I & C Division does hire summer students, depending on the workload at that particular time (please inquire first). *Contact:* Human Resources.

ABB CANADA

201 Woodlawn Road West
Guelph, ON N1H 1B8

Tel. 519-822-2120
Fax 519-837-4625
Website .... www.abb.ca

ABB Canada, Guelph manufactures small and specialty power transformers as well as operating a transformer repair facility for the utilities and industrial markets. ABB Canada, Guelph is a branch of ABB Canada, headquartered in St-Laurent, Quebec. ABB Canada is a domestic leader serving customers in the automotive, chemical, oil and gas, mining and metals, pulp and paper and utility markets. ABB Canada is in turn a member of ABB Group, based in Zurich, Switzerland. ABB Group is a global engineering and technology company serving customers in electrical power generation, transmission, distribution, automation, oil, gas, petrochemicals, industrial products, contracting and financial services. ABB employs 200,000 people in over 100 countries. ABB Canada employs 3,500 people in 45 centres from coast to coast. ABB Canada, Guelph is ISO 9001 registered and employs a total of 260 people. Graduates most likely to be hired come from the following academic areas: Bachelor of Engineering (Electrical, Mechanical), Community College Diploma (CAD/CAM/Autocad, Carpentry, Engineering Technician) and High School Diploma. Graduates would occupy Design Engineer, Drafting Designer, Insulation Manufacturer, and Power Transformer Winder, Assembler, and Tanker positions. Innovative, initiative, team work and good customer service skills are all listed as desirable non-academic qualifications. Company benefits are rated above average. The potential for advancement is listed as excellent. The average annual starting salary falls within the $45,000 to $50,000 range. The most suitable method for initial contact by those seeking employment is to fax a resume with a covering letter. *Contact:* Ken Dietz, Human Resources Manager.

ABC GROUP

110 Ronson Drive
Toronto, ON M9W 1B6

Tel. 416-246-9886
Fax 416-246-1780
Email .... abchr@abcgrp.com
Website .... www.abcsaleseng.com

ABC Group is a Tier 1 automotive supplier of blow and injection moulded parts and assemblies to the original equipment manufacturers including General Motors, Ford and Chrysler. The company boasts one of the most diverse product lines in the automotive industry, including fuel tanks, spoilers, interior/exterior trim and many custom accessories. The ABC Group's reputation for product innovation related to interior, exterior and under-the-hood automotive systems is internationally recognized. In addition to the company's international automotive operations, the ABC Group also supplies to packaging, commercial and industrial markets worldwide. There are 150 employees at this location, a total of 3,500 employees in Canada and a total of 5,000 employees worldwide. Graduates most likely to be hired come from the following academic areas: Bachelor of Engineering (General, Chemical, Electrical, Mechanical, Automation/Robotics, Industrial Design, Industrial Engineering, Industrial Production, Instrumentation), Bachelor of Commerce/Business Administration (General, Accounting, Finance, Human Resources), Certified Management Accountant, Certified General Accountant, Master of Business Administration (General, Accounting, Finance, Human Resources), Master of Engineering (Mechanical) and Community College Diploma (Accounting, Business, Human Resources, Secretarial, CAD/CAM/Autocad, Engineering Technician, Tool and Die, Machinist, Welding, Laboratory Technician). Graduates would occupy Project Engineer, Process Engineer, Program Manager, Plant Manager, Design Engineer, Robotic Engineer, Quality Engineer, Controls Engineer, CAD Operators, Plant Controllers and Accounting Coordinator positions. A willingness to learn and perform duties as required are both listed as desirable non-academic qualifications. Company benefits are rated as industry standard. The potential for advancement is listed as excellent. The average annual starting salary falls within the $40,000 to $45,000 range. The most suitable methods for initial contact by those seeking employment are to mail, fax or e-mail a resume with a covering letter, or through on-campus recruitment programs (see your campus career centre for details). ABC Group does hire summer and co-op work term students. *Contact:* Scott Smith, Recruiter, Human Resources Department.

ACART

171 Nepean Street, Suite 600
Ottawa, ON K2P 0B4

Tel. 613-230-7944
Fax 613-232-5980
Email .... results@acart.com
Website .... www.acart.com

Acart is a full service advertising agency with its headquarters in Ottawa. The agency is wholly Canadian-owned and has successfully operated with continuous growth over the past 19 years. Presently, Acart employs 55 permanent staff, many of whom have won national and international awards in recognition of their excellent design and communications skills. Graduates most likely to be hired come from the following academic areas: Bachelor of Arts (Journalism), Bachelor of Commerce/Business Administration (General, Marketing), Master of Business Administration (Marketing) and Community College Diploma (Advertising, Graphic Arts, Journalism, Photography, Television/Radio Arts). Depending upon their particular skill level, graduates would occupy Client Service, Creative Service, New Media and Production Service positions. Positive attitude, competent, hard working, creative, able to use time efficiently and good listening skills are all listed as desirable non-academic qualifications. Company benefits are rated as industry standard. The potential for advancement is listed as being excellent. The average annual starting salary falls within the $20,000 to $25,000 range. The most suitable methods for initial contact by those seeking employment are to mail a resume with a covering letter, or by applying through the company's website. Acart does hire summer and co-op work term students. *Contacts:* John Westbrook, Client Services or John Sterarsinic, Creative Services.

ACCOUNTMATE (CANADA) INC.
5225 Berri Street, Suite 304
Montreal, QC H2J 2S4

Tel.	514-495-8446
Fax	514-495-8415
Email	info@accountmate.ca
Website	www.accountmate.com

AccountMate (Canada) Inc. is a leading developer of advanced, integrated accounting solutions. AccountMate (Canada) Inc. is a subsidiary of Novato, California based AccountMate Software Corporation, established in 1984. The company's flagship product line is the Visual AccountMate series of accounting software, which includes Windows 95/NT-based, MS SQL Server and AS/400-based packages, as well as the widely used AccountMate Professional and Premiere. All products are designed for the small to mid-sized business and divisions of Fortune 1000 corporations. The company has over 100,000 installations serving 200 industries worldwide. In addition, AccountMate is an IBM Developer partner and a Microsoft partner. There are 14 employees at this location and a total of 100 employees worldwide. Graduates most likely to be hired come from the following academic areas: Bachelor of Science (Computer Science) and Community College Diploma (Accounting, Secretarial). Graduates would occupy Analyst Programmer and Administrative positions. Computer smart and accounting knowledge for technical support are listed as desirable non-academic qualifications. Company benefits and the potential for advancement are both rated as excellent. The average annual starting salary falls within the $25,000 to $30,000 range. The most suitable method for initial contact by those seeking employment is to e-mail a resume with a covering letter. AccountMate (Canada) Inc. does hire co-op work term students. *Contact:* Renée Fortin, Operations Manager.

ACCUCAPS INDUSTRIES LIMITED
2125 Ambassador Drive
Windsor, ON N9C 3R5

Tel.	519-969-5404
Fax	519-969-5022
Email	hr1@accucaps.com
Website	www.accucaps.com

Accucaps Industries Limited is a manufacturer of soft gelatin capsules for the pharmaceutical, OTC, health and nutritional, cosmetic and recreational markets. The company has experienced rapid growth and has been recognized as one of "Canada's 50 Best Managed Private Companies". Accucaps employs a total of 280 personnel. Graduates most likely to be hired come from the following academic areas: Bachelor of Science (Chemistry, Computer Science, Microbiology), Bachelor of Engineering (Chemical, Mechanical), Bachelor of Commerce/Business Administration (General, Accounting, Finance, Human Resources, Information Systems, Marketing), Certified Management Accountant, Community College Diploma (Accounting, Administration, Business, Human Resources, Information Systems, Marketing/Sales, Purchasing/Logistics, Computer Science, Engineering Technician, Tool and Die, Machinist, Laboratory Technician) and High School Diploma. Innovative, strong team skills and good communication skills are listed as desirable non-academic qualifications. Company benefits are rated above average. The potential for advancement is listed as excellent. The average annual starting salary falls within the $30,000 to $35,000 range. The most suitable method for initial contact by those seeking employment is to mail a resume with a covering letter. Accucaps Industries Limited does hire summer and co-op work term students. *Contact:* Human Resources Department.

ACRES INTERNATIONAL LIMITED
500 Portage Avenue, 6th Floor
Winnipeg, MB R3C 3Y8

Tel.	204-786-0171
Fax	204-786-2242
Email	winnipeg@acres.com
Website	www.acres.com

Acres International Limited is a leading North American consulting engineering, planning and management company. Established in 1924, the firm undertakes projects in the power, transportation and urban infrastructure, mining and heavy industrial sectors. From offices across Canada, the United States and project offices worldwide, Acres carries out assignments for public utilities, private developers, industry, governments and major foreign aid financing institutions. Assignments have been completed in over 110 countries. Acres has over 750 staff comprised of engineers, scientists, economists, technical and administrative personnel. With its head office located in Toronto, Acres International Limited established the Winnipeg office in 1965 and has been providing services to clients in mid-Canada since 1945. Today, the Winnipeg office employs over 80 specialists in the provision of a full range of services for hydroelectric power and water resources developments, general engineering for industry, and environmental studies for clients throughout Manitoba, Saskatchewan and northwestern Ontario. Hydroelectric engineering skills, developed in Manitoba, have been applied to major projects in Uganda and Mexico. Graduates most likely to be hired at the Winnipeg office come from the following academic areas: Bachelor of Engineering (Civil, Electrical, Mechanical, Environmental/Resources, Geological Engineering, Industrial Design, Industrial Engineering, Mining, Power/Hydra, Pulp and Paper, Transportation, Water Resources). Graduates would occupy Technologist and Engineer-in-Training positions. Reliability, flexibility, team player and good leadership skills are all listed as desirable nonacademic qualifications. Company benefits are rated above average. The potential for advancement is listed as being good. The average annual starting salary falls within the $30,000 to $35,000 range. The most suitable method for initial contact by those seeking employment is mail a resume with a covering letter. Acres International Limited, Winnipeg does hire summer and co-op work term students. *Contact:* Brenda Robertson, Human Resources.

AD OPT TECHNOLOGIES INC.
3535 Queen Mary Road, Suite 650
Montreal, QC H3V 1H8

Tel.	514-345-0580
Fax	514-345-0422
Email	hum-res@ad-opt.com
Website	www.ad-opt.com

AD OPT Technologies Inc. specializes in software planning programs which provide optimal planning solutions for problems requiring complicated mathematical solutions, such as the monthly and daily scheduling of airline crews. The company's software applications can be easily integrated to fit the scheduling requirements of virtually any ERP system. AD OPT customers include Swissair, Federal Express, Northwest Airlines, Delta Airlines, TWA, Air Canada, Nav Canada, Canadian Regional Airlines, Air Transat, UPS, the U.S. FAA, DFS and Sabena Airlines. The company employs more than 70 experts in scheduling, operations research and computer engineering, while maintaining strong ties with world renowned university research centres dedicated to optimisation. Graduates most likely to be hired come from the following academic areas: Bachelor of Science (Computer Science, Mathematics), Bachelor of Engineering (Computer Systems) and Master of Science (Mathematics, Operations Research). Graduates would occupy Software Developer, Programmer-Analyst and Project Manager positions. Bilingual (French/English), team oriented, strong work ethic, initiative, dynamic, results oriented and autonomous are all listed as desirable non-academic qualifications. Company benefits are rated above average. The most suitable methods for initial contact by those seeking employment are to fax or e-mail a resume with a covering letter, or via the company's website. *Contact:* Domenica Fiori, Human Resources Manager.

ADACEL TECHNOLOGIES (CANADA) LIMITED
7900, boul Taschereau
Brossard, QC J4X 1C2

Tel.	450-672-3888
Fax	450-672-1114
Email	careers@AdacelCanada.com
Website	www.adacelcanada.com

Adacel Technologies (Canada) Limited is recognized for its industry-leading advances in research and development, innovative software, outstanding technology and powerful international strategic alliances. Adacel Technologies (Canada) Limited is a wholly-owned subsidiary Adacel Technologies, based in Melbourne, Australia. Since commencing operations in 1987, Adacel has developed a wide range of information systems with applications in markets as diverse as air traffic management, telecommunications, simulation and training systems. Adacel Technologies Limited is recognized for its ability to develop high-quality, innovative software and systems solutions tailored to the demanding operational environment of air traffic management, and for meeting the simulation and training requirements of air traffic controllers. Adacel Technologies (Canada) Limited employs a total of 40 people while Adacel employs over 160 people worldwide. Graduates most likely to be hired come from the following academic areas: Bachelor of Science (Computer Science), Bachelor of Engineering (Electrical, Aerospace, Computer Systems, Microelectronics), Bachelor of Commerce/Business Administration (Accounting, Human Resources, Marketing), Chartered Accountant, Certified Management Accountant, Certified General Accountant, Master of Business Administration (Marketing), Master of Engineering (Electronics, Computer Science) and Community College Diploma (Computer Animation, Computer Science, Electronics Technician). Company benefits are rated as excellent. The potential for advancement is listed as being good. The average annual starting salary falls within the $30,000 to $100,000 range, depending upon the position. The most suitable methods for initial contact by those seeking employment are to mail, fax or e-mail a resume with a covering letter, or via the company's website. Adacel Technologies (Canada) Limited does hire summer and co-op work term students. *Contacts:* Richard Grenier or Ian Keiller.

ADDICTIONS FOUNDATION OF MANITOBA, THE
1031 Portage Avenue
Winnipeg, MB R3G 0R8

Tel.	204-944-6200
Fax	204-786-7768
Email	hr@afm.mb.ca
Website	www.afm.mb.ca

The Addictions Foundation of Manitoba (AFM) is a provincial crown agency providing a a broad range of services relating to alcohol, drug and gambling problems. Substance abuse and gambling prevention, education and treatment programs, and impaired driver services are available across the province through the agency. The AFM also provides many youth programs in accordance with its mandate to provide counselling, education, prevention and research with regards to the problems associated with addictions. Graduates most likely to be hired come from the following academic areas: Bachelor of Arts (Psychology, Social Work), Bachelor of Education (Adult), Bachelor of Commerce/Business Administration (Accounting) and Community College Diploma (Accounting). Graduates would occupy Rehabilitation Counsellor and Secretarial positions. Adaptable, confident, enthusiastic, leadership skills, patient, productive, professional, good writing skills, analytical, dependable, flexible, logical, personable, communicative, responsible, persuasive, organized, innovative and diplomatic are all listed as desirable non-academic qualifications. Company benefits and the potential for advancement are both rated as excellent. The average annual starting salary falls within the $25,000 to $30,000 range. The most suitable method for initial contact by those seeking employment is to mail a resume with a covering letter. The Addictions Foundation of Manitoba occasionally hires students for summer and co-op work terms. *Contact:* Personnel Manager.

ADM MILLING COMPANY
950 Mill Street
Montreal, QC H3C 1Y4

Tel.	514-846-8500
Fax	514-933-3802
Website	www.admworld.com

ADM Milling Company is involved in the milling of wheat into flour and is a division of Archer Daniels Midland Company. Headquartered in Decatur, Illinois, Archer Daniels Midland Company is a major international company with processing, storage, transportation and sales offices worldwide. ADM Milling currently has over 70 facilities ranging throughout the United States, Canada, Central America and the Caribbean, and is constantly taking steps to increase its presence in both foreign and domestic markets. The company maintains five manufacturing facilities in Canada. Graduates most likely to be hired come from the following academic areas: Bachelor of Science (Chemistry), Bachelor of Engineering (Electrical, Mechanical), Bachelor of Commerce/Business Administration (Accounting, Finance, Marketing), Certified Management Accountant, Certified General Accountant and Community College Diploma (Accounting, Administration, Business, Marketing/Sales, Secretarial, Electronics Technician, Engineering Technician, Mechanic, Laboratory Technician). Graduates would occupy R&D Technician, QC Technician, Junior Engineer, Accountant, and Sales and Marketing Representative positions. Enthusiasm, flexibility, adaptability and a desire to learn are all listed as desirable non-academic qualifications. Company benefits are rated above average. The potential for advancement is listed as average. The average annual starting salary falls within the $20,000 to $25,000 range. The most suitable method for initial contact by those seeking employment is to mail a resume with a covering letter. *Contact:* Human Resources.

ADP CANADA
3250 Bloor Street West, 16th Floor
Toronto, ON M8X 2X9

Tel.	416-248-3200
Fax	416-248-3326
Email	adphr@idirect.ca
Website	www.adp.com

ADP Canada provides payroll and related services to Canadian businesses. There are more than 400 employees at this Canadian head office location, a total of 1,500 across Canada and more than 30,000 employees worldwide. Other Canadian locations include Halifax, Montreal, Winnipeg, Edmonton, Calgary and Vancouver. The parent company, ADP is based in Roseland, New Jersey. Graduates most likely to be hired come from the following academic areas: Bachelor of Science (Computer Science), and Bachelor of Commerce/Business Administration (Accounting, Finance, Human Resources, Information Systems, Marketing), Chartered Accountant, Certified Management Accountant, Certified General Accountant, Master of Business Administration (Accounting, Finance, Human Resources, Information Systems, Marketing) and Community College Diploma (Accounting, Administration, Business, Communications, Financial Planning, Human Resources, Marketing/Sales, Secretarial). Graduates would occupy Accountant, Sales, Information Systems, Client Services, Computer Operations, PC Support, Applications Development, Programming and Administrative Assistant positions. Applicants should possess a client service orientation. Company benefits are rated above average. The potential for advancement is listed as excellent. The average annual starting salary falls within the $25,000 to $30,000 range. The most suitable method for initial contact by those seeking employment is to mail a resume with a covering letter. ADP Canada has temporary work available through their busy season, between November and February. *Contact:* Human Resources.

ADVANCED CONCEPTS CENTRE, LOCKHEED MARTIN CORPORATION
3001 Solandt Road
Kanata, ON K2K 2M8

Tel.	613-599-3280
Fax	613-592-4111
Email	acc.solutions@lmco.com
Website	www.lmco.com/acc

Advanced Concepts Centre / ACC helps clients use current leading-edge information technologies to achieve particular business goals faster and more efficiently. ACC is part of Integrated Business Solutions, the commercial IT services arm of Lockheed Martin Corporation. Lockheed Martin is an international professional services organization that partners with customers to develop and deploy business process and information technology solutions. ACC has helped its customers from industries such as manufacturing, telecommunications, insurance, banking, finance and retail, leverage ACC's capabilities in object technology, data warehousing, enterprise-wide work flow solutions, imaging, internet technologies and project management, to strengthen their business strategy through their technology investment. With more than 200 instructor-led training courses available in on-site forums or public/open enrollment courses throughout North America and around the world, the ACC has developed an evolved approach that guarantees that every program is focused, effective and enjoyable. There are 9 professionals at this location, a total of 15 in Canada and more than 200 worldwide. Graduates most likely to be hired come from the following academic areas: Bachelor of Science (Computer Science), Bachelor of Engineering (Computer Science), Bachelor of Commerce/Business Administration (Information Systems), Master of Business Administration (Information Systems), Master of Science (Computer Science, Information Systems), Master of Engineering (Computer Science, Information Systems) and Doctorate (Computer Science, Information Systems). These graduates would occupy positions as Instructors, Consultants and Mentors with 10 plus years industry experience. Entrepreneurial and self-motivated are listed as desirable non-academic qualifications. Company benefits are rated above average. The potential for advancement is listed as excellent. The average annual starting salary falls in the $60,000 plus range. The most suitable methods for initial contact by those seeking employment are to fax a resume with a covering letter, or through the company's website. *Contact:* Staffing Manager.

Advanced Microwave Technologies

ADVANTECH, ADVANCED MICROWAVE TECHNOLOGIES INC.
657 Orly Avenue
Dorval, QC H9P 1G1

Tel.	514-420-0045
Fax	514-420-0055
Email	nebeng@advantech.ca
Website	www.advantech.ca

Advantech, Advanced Microwave Technologies Inc. specializes in designing, manufacturing and marketing solid state power amplifiers and related subsystems for the telecommunications industry. The company's products are used worldwide in point-to-point microwave systems, satellite earth-stations, VSAT terminals as well as for PCS, MMDS and LMCS/LMDS applications. In 1999, the Québec Chamber of Commerce awarded Advantech the 1999 "Mercure" in the research and development category for its innovative and dynamic approach to research and development. The company was sponsored by the Business Development Bank of Canada for this award. Advantech employs at total of 125 people. Graduates most likely to be hired come from the following academic areas: Bachelor of Engineering (Electrical, Industrial Engineering, Industrial Production/Manufacturing, Microwave Telecommunications), Bachelor of Commerce/Business Administration (Marketing), Master of Engineering (Electrical, Microwave Telecommunications), Doctorate of Engineering (Electrical, Microwave Telecommunications) and Community College Diploma (Electronics Technician). Graduates would occupy Radio Frequency Engineer, Industrial Engineer, Components Engineer, Project Manager (with a military background), Digital Signal Processing Engineer, Manufacturing Manager, Product Manager, Technical Sales Representative and Radio Frequency Technician positions. Team player, creative, self motivated, results oriented and able to work in a deadline driven environment are all listed as desirable non-academic qualifications. Company benefits are rated as industry standard. The potential for advancement is listed as excellent. The average annual starting salary falls within the $35,000 to $40,000 range. The most suitable methods for initial contact by those seeking employment are to fax or e-mail a resume with a covering letter. Advantech, Advanced Microwave Technologies Inc. does hire summer students. *Contact:* Gabrielle Neben, Human Resources.

AEC INFOCENTER INC.

25 Imperial Street, Suite 210
Toronto, ON M5P 1B9

Tel.	416-489-9000
Fax	416-489-3201
Email	mark@aecinfo.com
Website	www.aecinfo.com

AEC InfoCenter Inc. is an online business resource dedicated to the architectural, engineering, construction and home building industries. Staffed by industry professionals, the InfoCenter assembles and provides resource material relevant to the daily business needs of construction industry professionals. The company employs 19 people at this location and a total of 21 people worldwide. Graduates most likely to be hired come from the following academic areas: Bachelor of Science (Computer Science), Bachelor of Commerce/Business Administration (General, Human Resources, Marketing, Public Administration), Master of Business Administration (General, Marketing) and Community College Diploma (Advertising, Business, Marketing/Sales, Office Administration, Secretarial). Graduates would occupy Secretary, Administrative Assistant, Marketing Assistant, Marketing Manager, IT Technician and Human Resources positions. Team player, energetic, previous work experience and a willingness to learn are all listed as desirable non-academic qualifications. Company benefits are rated above average. The potential for advancement is listed as being excellent. The average annual starting salary falls within the $20,000 to $50,000 range and ultimately depends on the position being considered. The most suitable method for initial contact by those seeking employment is to fax a resume with a covering letter. AEC InfoCenter Inc. does hire summer students and occasionally hires co-op work term students. *Contacts:* Mit Rowe, IT Technician; Sheryl Nightingale, Secretary, Administration or Mark Nightingale, Marketing, Business.

AEROINFO SYSTEMS INC.

13351 Commerce Parkway, Suite 1373
Richmond, BC V6V 2X7

Tel.	604-214-8700
Fax	604-214-8701
Email	personnel@aeroinfo.com
Website	www.aeroinfo.com

AeroInfo Systems Inc. specializes in delivering business process automation solutions to the air transportation industry. The company provides information technology to support the planning and accomplishment of aircraft maintenance and engineering processes. AeroInfo's products and services are based on open standards defined by the Air Transport Association (ATA), the Federal Aviation Administration (FAA) and the International Standards Organization (ISO). The company's detailed industry knowledge, steady customer focus and effective use of advanced technologies provide measurable benefits to some of the world's largest commercial carriers including United Airlines, Northwest Airlines, Canadian Airlines and Air Canada. AeroInfo employs a total of 20 people at the Richmond location. Graduates most likely

to be hired come from the following academic areas: Bachelor of Science (Computer Science), Bachelor of Engineering (Computer Systems), Master of Business Administration (Information Systems) and Community College Diploma (Computer Science). Graduates would occupy Software Developer (Java/Unix/Corba), Technical Sales, Systems Architect, and Project Leader positions. A good sense of humour, attention to detail, results oriented, strong work ethic, consistent and organized work habits, and above average time management skills are all listed as desirable non-academic qualifications. Company benefits are rated above average. The potential for advancement is listed as excellent. The average annual starting salary falls within the $45,000 to $50,000 range. The most suitable method for initial contact by those seeking employment is to e-mail a resume with a covering letter. *Contacts:* Fred Rego, VP Airline Services or Don Konrad, Manager, Administration & Finances.

AETERNA LABORATORIES INC.

1405 boul du Parc-Technologique
Quebec, QC G1P 4P5

Tel.	418-652-8525
Fax	418-652-0881
Email	aeterna@aeterna.com
Website	www.aeterna.com

AEterna Laboratories Inc. is the third most important medical biotechnology company in Quebec and one of the ten largest in Canada. The company conducts research to develop and market innovative products that contribute to the well-being of the population. AEterna operates on a worldwide scale by establishing strategic alliances, at selected times in product development, with companies in the pharmaceutical, nutritional and cosmetic fields. The activities of AEterna are concentrated into two divisions, the Biopharmaceutical Division and the Cosmetics and Nutrition Division. The Biopharmaceutical Division has a diversified program to develop a new class of treatments to control a number of diseases complicated by the formation of new blood vessels. The products developed by AEterna based on the angiogenesis inhibitor AE-941 target such diseases as solid tumor cancers, psoriasis, age-related muscular degeneration (AMD), rheumatoid arthritis and osteoarthritis. The Cosmetics and Nutrition Division supports the Biopharmaceutical Division. Through the marketing of nutritional supplements and active ingredients, this division helps AEterna finance part of the development of antiangionenic therapies. AEterna employs a total of 123 people at this location. Graduates most likely to be hired come from the following academic areas: Bachelor of Science (Biology, Chemistry, Computer Science, Microbiology, Nursing, Pharmacy), Bachelor of Engineering (Chemical, Civil, Industrial Engineering, Industrial Production/Manufacturing), Bachelor of Commerce/Business Administration (Accounting, Finance, Human Resources, Marketing), Chartered Accountant, Certified Management Accountant, Master of Business Administration (General, Finance, Human Resources, Marketing), Community College Diploma (Accounting, Human Resources, Marketing/Sales, Secretarial, Computer Science, Laboratory Technician, Nursing RN) and High School Diploma. Leadership skills, a high level of motivation, team spirit, autonomy and a scientific spirit are all listed as desirable non-academic qualifications. Company benefits and the potential for advancement are both rated as excellent. The most suitable methods for initial contact by those seeking employment are to mail, fax or e-mail a resume with a covering letter. AEterna Laboratories Inc. does hire summer students. *Contacts:* Yvon Carrier, Human Resources Department or Luc Dupont, Executive Vice President.

AETNA LIFE INSURANCE COMPANY OF CANADA
79 Wellington Street West
PO Box 120, Aetna Tower, TD Centre
Toronto, ON M5K 1N9

Tel.	416-864-8000
Fax	416-864-8549
Website	www.aetna.ca

Aetna Life Insurance Company of Canada provides group life insurance, group health insurance, individual life insurance, and individual disability insurance. The company has been offering Canadians financial security through superior insurance products and related services for more than a century. Graduates most likely to be hired come from the following academic areas: Bachelor of Science (Actuarial, Computer Science, Health Sciences, Mathematics, Nursing, Psychology), Bachelor of Commerce/Business Administration (Accounting, Finance, Marketing, Information Systems), Chartered Accountant, Certified Management Accountant, Certified General Accountant, Master of Business Administration (Accounting, Finance, Marketing, Information Systems), Community College (Accounting, Administration, Advertising, Business, Communications, Facility Management, Insurance, Marketing, Purchasing/Logistics, Secretarial, Human Resources, Journalism, Law Clerk, Security/Law Enforcement, Computer Science, Dental Assistant, Nursing RN/RNA) and High School Diploma. Graduates would occupy a wide variety of positions in many functional areas. Team player, customer service oriented, computer skills, integrity and excellent verbal and communication skills are all listed as desirable non-academic qualifications. Company benefits are rated as excellent. The potential for advancement is listed as being good. The most suitable methods for initial contact by those seeking employment are to mail, fax or e-mail a resume with a covering letter, or through the company's website at www.aetna.ca. Aetna Life Insurance Company of Canada does hire summer and co-op work term students. *Contact:* Human Resource Services.

AGF MANAGEMENT LIMITED
TD Bank Tower, PO Box 50
Toronto, ON M5K 1E9

Tel.	416-367-1900
Fax	416-865-4189
Email	resume@agf.com
Website	www.agf.com

AGF Management Limited is one of Canada's oldest and most broadly diversified wealth management companies with assets under management in excess of $5 billion. Founded in 1957, the company is an independent Canadian owned company, and is listed on the Toronto Stock Exchange. AGF's head office is in Toronto with branch offices located in Oakville, Montreal, Vancouver and Halifax. AGF employs 400 people at the Toronto location and a total of 650 people in Canada. Graduates most likely to be hired come from the following academic areas: Bachelor of Arts (English, French, Journalism, Languages), Bachelor of Science (Actuarial, Computer Science, Mathematics), Bachelor of Engineering (Electrical, Computer Systems), Bachelor of Commerce/Business Administration (General, Accounting, Finance, Information Systems), Chartered Accountant, Certified Management Accountant, Certified General Accountant, Master of

Business Administration (Accounting, Finance, Information Systems, Marketing) and Community College Diploma (Accounting, Administration, Business, Human Resources, Information Systems, Secretarial, Journalism). Graduates would occupy Financial Analyst, Client Administration Representative, Client Service Representative, Marketing Coordinator, Systems Administrator, Application Developer, Accountant and Copywriter positions. Customer service skills, team player, flexible, computer skills, analytical and excellent communication skills are all listed as desirable non-academic qualifications. Company benefits and the potential for advancement are both rated as excellent. The average annual starting salary falls within the $25,000 to $30,000 range. The most suitable methods for initial contact by those seeking employment are to mail, fax or e-mail a resume with a covering letter. AGF Management Limited does hire summer and co-op work term students. Most hiring for work terms occurs between October and April. *Contact:* Manager, Recruitment and Development.

AGRA INC.
335 - 8th Avenue SW, Suite 1900
Calgary, AB T2P 1C9

Tel.	403-263-9606
Fax	403-263-9676
Email	info@agra.com
Website	www.agra.com

AGRA Inc. is an international engineering, construction, environment and technology corporation. The company employs approximately 5,000 people in 160 offices in 20 countries. This location is the corporate head office and employs approximately 30 people. Positions relating to AGRA's activities (other than those specified in this listing) are not available through this location. To inquire about other positions you must contact each subsidiary company directly (research at your campus placement centre). Graduates hired for positions at this location come from the following academic areas: Bachelor of Laws, Bachelor of Commerce/Business Administration (Accounting, Finance, Marketing), Chartered Accountant (Finance), Certified Management Accountant (Finance), Certified General Accountant (Finance), Community College Diploma (Administration, Secretarial) and High School graduates for support staff functions. Relevant work experience, a high energy level, excellent communication skills, outside interests and computer skills (Windows environment) are all listed as desirable non-academic qualifications. Company benefits are rated above average. The potential for advancement is listed as average. The average annual starting salary is dependent upon the position being considered. The most suitable method for initial contact by those seeking employment is to mail a resume with a covering letter. AGRA Inc. occasionally hires summer students at this location. *Contact:* Director of Human Resources.

AGRA MONENCO INC.
2010 Winston Park Drive, Suite 100
Oakville, ON L6H 6A3

Tel.	905-829-5400
Fax	905-829-5625
Website	www.agra.com

AGRA Monenco Inc. is an international engineering, procurement and construction management company specializing in the provision of complete solutions in the areas of process industries, electric power, infrastructure and systems technology. AGRA Monenco is a wholly-owned subsidiary of AGRA Inc., one of Canada's largest international engineering, construction and technology corporations. The company's stock is traded on the Toronto and Montreal stock exchanges under the trading symbol AGR. AGRA Inc. employs 7,000 people and operates 186 offices in 24 countries. AGRA Monenco Inc. employs 325 people at this location. Graduates most likely to be hired come from the following academic areas: Bachelor of Science (Computer Science, Environmental, Metallurgy), Bachelor of Engineering (General, Chemical, Civil, Electrical, Mechanical, Resources/Environmental), Bachelor of Commerce/Business Administration (Accounting, Information Systems), Master of Business Administration (Finance) and Community College Diploma (Administration, Human Resources, Purchasing/Logistics, Architecture/Drafting, CAD/CAM/Autocad, Computer Science, Engineering Technician, HVAC Systems). Graduates are hired for various positions relating to their academic backgrounds. Company benefits are rated above average. The potential for advancement is listed as being good. The average annual starting salary falls within the $30,000 to $35,000 range. The most suitable methods for initial contact by graduates seeking employment are to mail a resume with a covering letter, or through employee referrals. AGRA Monenco Inc. does hire summer and co-op work term students. *Contact:* Human Resources.

AIMTRONICS CORPORATION
6680 Campobello Road
Mississauga, ON L5N 2L8

Tel. 905-821-4313
Fax 905-821-4314
Email .... careers@aimtronics.com
Website .... www.aimtronics.com

Aimtronics Corporation provides complete electronics manufacturing services. The company has 30 years of business experience, over 250,000 square feet of manufacturing facilities in six North American locations. Facilities are located in Kanata, Brockville, Mississauga, Vancouver, Delta and Ogdensburg, New York. The company employs over 600 people. Graduates most likely to be hired come from the following academic areas: Bachelor of Science (Computer Science), Bachelor of Engineering (Electrical, Mechanical, Automation/Robotics, Industrial Engineering, Industrial Production/Manufacturing, Microelectronics), Community College Diploma (CAD/CAM/Autocad, Computer Science, Electronics Technician, Engineering Technician) and High School Diploma. Graduates would occupy Technician and Trainee positions related to the assembly of printed circuit boards. Aimtronics offers graduates an interesting and exciting environment designed to bring out the best in each individual. The company fosters a corporate culture that is built on solid principles and core values that include respect for the individual, honesty and integrity, collaboration and teamwork and the pursuit of excellence. Company benefits are competitive and rated as industry standard. The potential for advancement is listed as being good. The average annual starting salary falls within the $20,000 to $25,000 range. The most suitable methods for initial contact by those seeking employment are to mail, fax or e-mail a resume with a covering letter, or via the company's website. Aimtronics Corporation does hire co-op work term students. *Contacts:* Phil Toerink, Manufacturing Manager or Bereket Weldai, Test Engineering Manager.

AIR CANADA
PO Box 14000, Zip 264
Montreal, QC H4Y 1H4

Tel. 514-422-5000
Fax 514-422-5650
Website .... www.aircanada.ca

Air Canada is a full service international air carrier serving over 545 destinations around the world. In operation for over 60 years, Air Canada is Canada's largest airline. Graduates most likely to be hired come from the following academic areas: Bachelor of Science (Computer Science), Bachelor of Engineering (Aerospace), Bachelor of Commerce/Business Administration (Accounting, Finance, Information Systems, Marketing), Certified General Accounting and Master of Business Administration (Finance, Human Resources, Information Systems, Marketing). Good customer service skills, team player, positive attitude, flexibility and excellent communication and interpersonal skills are all listed as desirable non-academic qualifications. Company benefits are rated above average. The potential for advancement is listed as being good. The average annual starting salary falls within the $25,000 to $30,000 range. The most suitable method for initial contact by those seeking employment is to mail a resume with a covering letter. Air Canada does hire summer students on occasion. *Contact:* Carol Enright, Manager Staffing, Employment & Human Resource Programs.

AIR ONTARIO INC.
1000 Air Ontario Drive
London, ON N5V 3S4

Tel. 519-453-8440
Fax 519-453-8470
Website .... www.airontario.com

Air Ontario Inc. is a commercial airline providing regional service to destinations in Ontario, Quebec and the northeastern United States. Headquartered in London, Ontario, Air Ontario is a wholly-owned subsidiary of Air Canada, and one of four Air Canada connectors. Primarily serving business customers, the airline carries over one million passengers annually to 21 destinations throughout its operating area. Air Ontario's fleet of 21 Dash 8-100 series aircraft (seating 37 passengers), and 6 Dash 8-300 series aircraft (seating 50 passengers) enables the airline to offer premium commuter aircraft service. Air Ontario employs 150 people at this location and a total of 900 people in the company. Graduates most likely to be hired come from the following academic areas: Bachelor of Science (Computer Science), Bachelor of Engineering (Computer Systems), Bachelor of Commerce/Business Administration (Accounting, Finance, Human Resources, Information Systems, Marketing), Certified General Accountant, Master of Business Administration, Community College Diploma (Accounting, Advertising, Financial Planning, Human Resources, Marketing/Sales, Purchasing/Logistics, Secretarial, Travel/Tourism, Aircraft Maintenance) and High School Diploma. Graduates would occupy PC Support Trainer, Executive Secretary, Receptionist, Human Resources Officer, Payroll Assistant, Revenue Accounting Clerk, Accounts Payable Clerk, Assistant Controller, Supervisor Revenue Accounting, AME, AME Apprentice and Maintenance Supervisor positions. Customer service skills, positive attitude, enthusiasm, technical knowledge relating to job skills, good job fit/qualifications, flexibility and good communication skills are all listed as desirable non-academic qualifications. Company benefits are rated as excellent. The potential for advancement is listed as being good. The most suitable method for initial contact by those seeking employment is to mail a resume with a covering letter. Air Ontario Inc. does hire one or two summer students per season. *Contact:* Human Resources.

AIR PRODUCTS CANADA LTD.
2090 Steeles Avenue East
Brampton, ON L6T 1A7

Tel. 905-791-2530
Fax 905-791-6797
Website .... www.apci.com

Air Products Canada Ltd. is an industrial gas company involved in the manufacture, sale and distribution of industrial gas products. These include liquid products (LOX, LIN, LAR) used in their merchant business, cylinder products which are used primarily in their welding products supply and specialty gas business and onsite generation. Air Products Canada Ltd. is a division of Air Products and Chemicals, Inc. based near Allentown, Pennsylvania. Air Products and Chemicals, Inc. provides industrial gases and related equipment and services, and selected chemicals to a very diverse base of customers in the manufacturing, process, and service industries worldwide. The company and its affiliates have operations in over 30 countries and more than 17,000 employees. Air Products and Chemicals, Inc. is listed as one of the 500 largest corporations in the United States. Air Products Canada Ltd. employs 75 people at this location and a total of 375 in Canada. Graduates most likely to be hired come from the following academic areas: Bachelor of Science (Chemistry), Bachelor of Engineering (Chemical, Metallurgy, Civil, Mechanical, Welding), Bachelor of Commerce/Business Administration, Certified Management Accountant, Certified General Accountant, Master of Business Administration, Community College Diploma (Business, Secretarial, Welding) and High School Diploma. Graduates would occupy Applied Research Engineer, Development Engineer, Specialty Gas Sales, Welding Products Sales, Sales Representative, Inside Sales Representative, Clerk/Secretary and Customer Service Representative positions. Good interpersonal and communication skills, business aptitude, bilingual, flexible, and computer literacy are all listed as desirable non-academic qualifications. Company benefits are rated above average. The potential for advancement is listed as being good. The average annual starting salary falls within the $30,000 to $35,000 range. The most suitable method for initial contact by those seeking employment is to mail a resume with a covering letter. *Contact:* Human Resources Manager.

AIRPORT DEVELOPMENT CORPORATION
370 Queen's Quay West, 3rd Floor
Toronto, ON M5V 3J3

Tel. 416-260-2333
Fax 416-260-2347

Airport Development Corporation is an engineering, construction and land development firm. The company employs more than 10 people at this location. Graduates most likely to be hired come from the following areas: Bachelor of Engineering (Civil, Environmental), Bachelor of Architecture, Bachelor of Landscape Architecture and Community College Diploma (Business, Marketing/Sales, Secretarial, Engineering, Industrial Design). Graduates are hired to occupy Clerk, Draughtsperson, Architect and Accountant positions. Company benefits are rated above average. The potential for advancement is listed as being good. The most suitable method for initial contact by those seeking employment is to mail a resume with a covering letter. *Contact:* Controller.

AIT CORPORATION
1545 Carling Avenue, Suite 700
Ottawa, ON K1Z 8P9

Tel. 613-722-2070
Fax 613-722-2063
Email .... jobs@ait.ca
Website .... www.ait.ca

AIT Corporation designs and develops identification and security systems, including secure travel documents, passport issuance systems and passport readers. In addition, AIT designed and developed Rapid Eye, a remote telesurveillance system. The company employs approximately 85 employees at this location and a total of 100 employees worldwide. Graduates most likely to be hired come from the following academic areas: Bachelor of Science (Computer Science), Bachelor of Engineering (Electrical, Computer Systems), Certified General Accountant, Master of Science (Computer Science), Master of Engineering (Electrical) and Community College Diploma (Information Systems, Computer Science, Electronics Technician, Engineering Technician). Graduates would occupy Programmer, Technical Support, Electromechanical Draftsperson, Hardware Developer and Software Designer positions. The ability to work independently, good communication skills, relevant work experience, co-op work term experience, team player and good problem solving skills are all listed as desirable non-academic qualifications. Company benefits are rated as excellent. The potential for advancement is listed as being good. The average annual starting salary falls within the $40,000 to $45,000 range, depending upon experience. The most suitable method for initial contact by those seeking employment is to e-mail a resume with a covering letter. AIT Corporation does hire summer students, and co-op students throughout the year. *Contact:* Donna Burnett, Manager, Human Resources.

AJAX, PICKERING & WHITBY ASSOCIATION FOR COMMUNITY LIVING
36 Emperor Street
Ajax, ON L1S 1M7

Tel. 905-427-3300
Fax 905-427-3310

The Ajax, Pickering & Whitby Association for Community Living is a social service agency involved in supporting the participation of individuals in the life of the community. These are individuals who are disadvantaged by an impairment in ability to learn, generalize what is learned and transfer learning from one specific context to another. Support to an individual with such an impairment means the promotion of circumstances and conditions which minimize restrictions on people's lives, enhance their life long opportunities for effective and re-warding participation, enable people to gain more control over their own lives, enable people to build their own career and lifestyle at home and in leisure pursuits, and ensure security of the person in his/her home, and protect against imposed discontinuity of relationships with family and chosen people. The Association employs 150 people. Graduates most likely to be hired come from the following academic areas: Bachelor of Arts (Psychology, Recreation Studies), Bachelor of Science (Nursing, Psychology), Bachelor of Education (Special Needs), Community College Diploma (Nursing RNA) and Developmental Service Worker. Graduates would occupy the following positions: Counsellor and Support Worker (for developmentally delayed adult individuals) and Contract Support Worker (providing support to families and their handicapped family member). Excellent communication skills, maturity, commitment to the principles of the Association, experience, flexible regarding work hours, able to work independently, able to handle emergencies and a knowledge of community resources are all listed as desirable non-academic qualifications. Company benefits are rated above average. The potential for advancement is listed as average. The average annual starting salary falls within the $25,000 to $35,000 range. The most suitable method for initial contact by those seeking employment is to mail a resume with a covering letter. The Ajax, Pickering & Whitby Association for Community Living does hire summer students. *Contacts:* Human Resources Department or Residential Services Department or A.R.C. Industries (Vocational Department).

ALBERTA ALCOHOL AND DRUG ABUSE COMMISSION / AADAC
10909 Jasper Avenue, 6th Floor
Edmonton, AB T5J 3M9

Tel. 780-415-0377
Fax 780-427-1436
Website .... www.aadac.com

The Alberta Alcohol and Drug Abuse Commission / AADAC helps Albertans achieve lives free from the abuse of alcohol, other drugs and gambling. As an agency funded by the government of Alberta, AADAC's role is to promote people's independence and well being through increasing use of social, emotional, spiritual and physical resources, and to provide cost-effective, holistic alternatives to hospital-based and medical services. Founded in 1951 as the Alcoholism Foundation of Alberta to treat drinking problems, AADAC's name and mandate expanded to include other drugs in 1970. In 1994, AADAC also became responsible for addressing problem gambling. The Commission delivers services in four areas: Community Outpatient and Prevention Services, Crisis Services, Residential Treatment Services, and Research Information and Monitoring Services. Currently, AADAC employs 500 people in the province of Alberta. Graduates most likely to be hired come from the following academic areas: Bachelor of Arts (Psychology, Social Work, Sociology), Bachelor of Science (Nursing, Psychology) and Community College Diploma (Social Work/DSW, Nursing RN). Graduates would occupy Nurse or Addictions Counsellor positions. Company benefits are rated as industry standard. The potential for advancement is listed as being good. The average annual starting salary falls within the $35,000 to $40,000 range. The most suitable method for initial contact by those seeking employment is via telephone. The Alberta Alcohol and Drug Abuse Commission does hire summer students. *Contact:* Human Resource Consultants.

ALBERTA JUSTICE
9833 - 109 Street
1st Floor, Bowker Building, Human Resources
Edmonton, AB T5K 2E8

Tel. 780-427-0514
Fax 780-422-1330
Email .... reception.hr@just.gov.ab.ca
Website .... www.gov.ab.ca/just

Alberta Justice is the province of Alberta's department of justice. The department's mandate is to ensure equality and fairness in the administration of justice in Alberta. Alberta Justice employs 4,000 people. Graduates most likely to be hired come from the following academic areas: Bachelor of Arts (Criminology, Economics, Psychology, Sociology), Bachelor of Science (Chemistry, Computer Science, Nursing, Occupational Therapy), Bachelor of Laws, Bachelor of Commerce/Business Administration (Accounting, Finance, Human Resources, Information Systems), Chartered Accountant, Certified Management Accountant, Certified General Accountant, Doctorate (Medical Doctor) and Community College Diploma (Accounting, Administration, Business, Financial Planning, Human Resources, Secretarial, Legal Assistant, Law Enforcement, Corrections Worker, Computer Science, Laboratory Technician, Nursing RN, Radiology Technician). Graduates would occupy Clerical, Professional, Technical, Medical, Legal and Administrative positions. Related work experience, team player, enthusiasm, and good organization skills are all listed as desirable non-academic qualifications. Departmental benefits are rated above average. The potential for advancement is listed as being good. The average annual starting salary ranges widely, depending upon the class of position. The most suitable method for initial contact by those seeking employment is to mail a resume with a covering letter. Alberta Justice does hire summer students. *Contact:* Brian Sveinbjornson, Manager, Recruitment Classification and Employee Relations.

ALBERTA-PACIFIC FOREST INDUSTRIES INC.
PO Box 8000
Boyle, AB T0A 0M0

Tel. 780-525-8000
Fax 780-525-8423
Email .... gettyde@alpac.ca
Website .... www.alpac.ca

Alberta-Pacific Forest Industries Inc. operates the largest single-line kraft pulp mill in the world. The mill manufactures pulps that are widely used in many paper grades, including the prestigious wood-free coated and uncoated printing papers, lightweight and technical specialty papers, such as scripture paper, photographic paper, adhesive backing paper, cigarette plug and tube wrap, various tissue grades and many others. Alberta-Pacific began operations in 1991 and quickly established itself as an industry benchmark in terms of production, environmental performance, forestry research and ecosystem management. Originally, the Alberta government selected Alberta-Pacific from among several competitive bids based on its commitment to responsibly steward the forest management area, its environmentally advanced production process, plus strong aboriginal liaison and employment programs. Today, the company employs a total of 430 people. Graduates most likely to be hired come from the following academic areas: Bachelor of Science (Chemistry, Forestry), Bachelor of Engineering (Chemical, Mechanical, Forest Resources), Bachelor of Commerce/Business Administration (Accounting), Chartered Accountant, Certified Management Accountant, Certified

General Accountant and Community College Diploma (Accounting, Computer Science, Forestry). Good problem solving skills, mechanical aptitude, a high level of motivation, excellent interpersonal skills and the ability to adjust to change or adversity are all listed as desirable non-academic qualifications. Company benefits are rated above average. The potential for advancement is listed as being average. The average annual starting salary falls within the $40,000 to $45,000 range. The most suitable methods for initial contact by those seeking employment are to mail or fax a resume with a covering letter. Alberta-Pacific Forest Industries Inc. does hire summer and co-op work term students. *Contacts:* Derek Getty, Human Resources Consultant or Lyle Robideau, Human Resources Consultant.

ALBERTO-CULVER CANADA INC.
506 Kipling Avenue
Toronto, ON M8Z 5E2

Tel.	416-251-3741
Fax	416-251-3062
Website	www.alberto.com

Alberto-Culver Canada Inc. manufactures toiletries and household products. Products include Alberto European and VO5 hair care products, as well as Sugar Twin, Molly McButter and Mrs. Dash food products. Alberto-Culver Canada Inc. is a subsidiary of Aurora, Illinois based Alberto-Culver Company. Alberto-Culver Canada Inc. employs more than 100 people. Graduates most likely to be hired come from the following academic areas: Bachelor of Arts (Business), Bachelor of Commerce/Business Administration (Marketing, Finance), Certified Management Accountant (Finance, Accounting), Certified General Accountant, Master of Business Administration and Community College Diploma (Accounting). Employment opportunities for graduates exist as Assistant Product Managers, Sales Representatives, Accounting Clerks and General Office positions. Computer literacy is listed as a desirable non-academic qualification. Company benefits are rated as excellent. The potential for advancement is listed as being good. The average annual starting salary falls within the $20,000 to $25,000 range. The most suitable method for initial contact by those seeking employment is to mail a resume with a covering letter. Alberto-Culver Canada Inc. does hire summer students occasionally. *Contact:* Joan Madden, Administrator, Human Resources.

ALCATEL CANADA WIRE, A DIVISION OF ALCATEL CANADA INC.
140 Allstate Parkway
Markham, ON L3R 0Z7

Tel.	905-944-4300
Fax	905-994-4350
Website	www.alcatel.com

Alcatel Canada Wire, A Division of Alcatel Canada Inc. is part of Alcatel's global cables and components business. Alcatel builds next generation networks, delivering end-to-end voice and data communications solutions to established and new carriers, as well as enterprises and consumers worldwide. In the field of telecommunications and power cables, the company offers products, systems and services to meet the growing requirements of three main markets: infrastructure, industry and construction. Alcatel has 120,000 employees in more than 130 countries. Alcatel Canada Wire operates nine production facilities, a warehouse and numerous sales offices throughout Canada and the United States. There are 100 employees at this location, a total of 900 in Canada and a total of 1,500 in North America. Graduates most likely to be hired come from the following academic areas: Bachelor of Engineering (General, Chemical, Electrical, Mechanical, Computer Systems, Metallurgy), Bachelor of Commerce/Business Administration (Accounting, Finance, Human Resources, Information Systems, Marketing), Master of Business Administration (Accounting, Finance, Human Resources) and Community College Diploma (Marketing/Sales). Excellent communication skills, computer skills, goal oriented and a high energy level are all listed as desirable non-academic qualifications. Company benefits are rated above average. The potential for advancement is listed as being good. The average annual starting salary depends upon the candidates qualifications and previous experience. The most suitable methods for initial contact by those seeking employment are to mail or fax a resume with a covering letter. Alcatel Canada Wire Inc. does hire co-op work term students. *Contact:* Human Resources.

ALDO GROUP INC.
905 Hodge Street
St. Laurent, QC H4N 2B3

Tel.	514-747-2536
Fax	514-747-7993
Email	human_resources@aldogroup.com
Website	www.aldogroup.com

The Aldo Group Inc. is a Canadian leader in the fashion footwear industry. The group employs 500 people at this location and a total of 5,000 employees worldwide. Graduates most likely to be hired come from the following academic areas: Bachelor of Science (Computer Science), Bachelor of Commerce/Business Administration (General, Accounting, Finance, Marketing), Master of Business Administration (Marketing) and Community College Diploma (Advertising, Marketing/Sales, Secretarial, Fashion Arts, Graphic Arts, Architectural Technician, Information Systems). Bilingual, multilingual, dynamic, fashion orientation/awareness and a strong will to succeed are all listed as desirable non-academic qualifications. Company benefits and the potential for advancement are both rated as excellent. The most suitable method for initial contact by those seeking employment is to mail a resume with a covering letter. Aldo Group Inc. does hire co-op work term students. *Contact:* Human Resources.

ALL COMMUNICATIONS NETWORK OF CANADA CO. / ACN
2660 Argentia Road
Mississauga, ON L5N 5V4

Tel.	905-567-5005
Fax	905-567-0440
Website	www.acncanada.ca

All Communications Network of Canada Co. / ACN is a cooperative marketing company specializing in high quality telecommunications products and services. ACN is a cooperative marketing company focused on helping consumers save money on the telecommunications services that they are already using, such as long distance calling, paging and Internet services. ACN is a privately held corporation with offices and distribution centres in Canada, the United States and Europe. The company employs 106 people at this location and a total of 356 people worldwide. Graduates most likely to be hired come from the following academic areas: Bachelor of Arts (General), Bachelor of Science (General, Computer Science),

Bachelor of Engineering (General, Telecommunications), Bachelor of Commerce/Business Administration (General), Chartered Accountant, Community College Diploma (Accounting, Business, Communications/Public Relations, Marketing/Sales) and High School Diploma. Graduates would occupy Accounting Associate, Billing Analyst, Customer Care, IT Administrator and Commercial Service positions. Team player, good communication and organization skills and strong customer service skills are all listed as desirable non-academic qualifications. Company benefits are rated as industry standard. The potential for advancement is listed as being good. The average annual starting salary falls within the $35,000 to $40,000 range. The most suitable methods for initial contact by those seeking employment are to mail or fax a resume with a covering letter. All Communications Network of Canada Co. / ACN does hire summer students. *Contact:* Aileen Duncan, Human Resources Manager.

ALLAN CRAWFORD ASSOCIATES LTD. / ACA
5835 Coopers Avenue
Mississauga, ON L4Z 1Y2

Tel.	905-890-2010
Fax	905-890-1959
Email	barbr@aca.ca
Website	www.aca.ca

Allan Crawford Associates Ltd. / ACA is one of Canada's oldest and largest independent suppliers of high technology products and services. Established in 1959, ACA serves the Canadian market with market leading products and leading edge technology. The company's goal is to provide the quality of product knowledge, support and after sales service expected from a local manufacturer. In addition to Mississauga, ACA has locations in Montreal, Ottawa, Calgary and Vancouver. There are more than 50 employees at this location. Graduates most likely to be hired come from the following academic areas: Bachelor of Arts (General), Bachelor of Science (Chemistry, Computer Science, Physics), Bachelor of Engineering (General, Chemical, Civil, Systems, Environmental, Electrical, Industrial, Materials Science, Mechanical), Bachelor of Commerce/Business Administration (Accounting, Finance, Marketing, Information Systems), Master of Business Administration (Information Systems) and Community College Diploma (Computer Science, Electronic Technician, Engineering Technician, Mechanic). Graduates would occupy Sales Engineer and Sales Agent positions. Accordingly, a sales aptitude is listed as a desirable non-academic qualification. Company benefits are rated above average. The potential for advancement is listed as being good. The average annual starting salary falls within the $25,000 to $30,000 range. The most suitable method for initial contact by graduates seeking employment is to mail a resume with a covering letter. Allan Crawford Associates Ltd. does hire summer students. *Contact:* Operations Manager.

ALLCOLOUR PAINT LTD.
1257 Speers Road
Oakville, ON L6L 2X5

Tel.	905-827-4173
Fax	905-827-6487

Allcolour Paint Ltd. is involved in the manufacture of industrial paint and paint related products. There are 80 employees at this location, and a total of 84 employees in Canada. Graduates most likely to be hired come from the following academic areas: Community College Diploma (Administration, Secretarial) and High School

Diploma. Graduates would occupy Clerical positions. Company benefits are rated above average. The potential for advancement is listed as average. The average annual starting salary falls within the $25,000 to $30,000 range. The most suitable methods for initial contact by those seeking employment are to mail or fax a resume with a covering letter. Allcolour Paint Ltd. does hire summer students. *Contact:* Human Resources.

ALLELIX BIOPHARMACEUTICALS INC.
6850 Goreway Drive
Mississauga, ON L4V 1V7

Tel.	905-677-0831
Fax	905-677-9595
Website	www.allelix.com

Allelix Biopharmaceuticals Inc. is a leading Canadian biotechnology company. The company focuses on the discovery and development of biopharmaceutical products for tissue repair, immunological and inflammatory diseases. Allelix applies the latest advances in the scientific understanding of molecular and cellular biology to discover new approaches for the development of therapeutic products for these conditions. A subsidiary division focuses on bioinformatics and a sister company works in radiopharmaceutical research. Currently the company employs 180 people and continues to grow steadily. Graduates most likely to be hired come from the following academic areas: Bachelor of Science (General, Biology, Chemistry, Computer Science, Health Sciences, Microbiology, Pharmacy), Bachelor of Engineering (Chemical), Bachelor of Commerce/Business Administration (Finance, Marketing), Master of Business Administration (Finance, Marketing), Master of Science (Molecular Biology, Chemistry, Pharmacy), Doctorate (Molecular Biology, Biochemistry, Pharmacy) and Community College Diploma (Laboratory Technician). Graduates are hired to occupy Research and Development, Business Development, Finance and General Administration positions. Initiative, drive, a strong work ethic, creativity, research oriented and excellent communication skills are all listed as desirable non-academic qualifications. Company benefits are rated as excellent. The potential for advancement is listed as being good. The most suitable method for initial contact by those seeking employment is to mail a resume with a covering letter. *Contact:* Human Resources Department.

ALLIANZ CANADA
425 Bloor Street East, Suite 200
Toronto, ON M4W 3R5

Tel.	416-961-5015
Fax	416-961-8874
Website	www.allianz.ca

Allianz Canada provides automobile, home and business insurance as well as unique international capabilities, special risk and marine expertise. Allianz Canada is the Canadian subsidiary of German-based Allianz AG, a large multinational insurance organization operating in over 50 countries on five continents. Allianz Canada is found in all regions of Canada with office locations in Quebec, Ontario, Alberta and British Columbia. The company also services the Maritimes through a Managing General Agent. Allianz's services can be accessed through one of hundreds of independent insurance brokers who represent the Allianz Canada companies. Allianz Canada employs 250 people at this location and a total of 450 people in Canada. Graduates most likely to be hired come from the following academic areas: Bachelor of Arts (General, Economics), Bachelor of Science (General, Actuarial, Computer Science, Mathematics), Bachelor of Commerce/Business Administration (Accounting, Finance, Human Resources, Information Systems, Marketing), Chartered Accountant, Certified Management Accountant, Certified General Accountant, Master of Business Administration (Accounting, Finance, Human Resources, Information Systems, Marketing) and Community College Diploma (Accounting, Administration, Business, Human Resources, Information Systems, Insurance, Secretarial, Computer Science). Graduates would occupy entry level positions such as, Claims Clerk, Underwriting Clerk and Accounting Clerk. Team player, insurance experience and good communication skills are all listed as desirable non-academic qualifications. Company benefits and the potential for advancement are both rated as excellent. The average annual starting salary falls within the $20,000 to $25,000 range. The most suitable method for initial contact by those seeking employment is to mail a resume with a covering letter. *Contact:* Kerry Abbott, Human Resources Consultant.

ALLIED INTERNATIONAL CREDIT CORP.
11 Allstate Parkway, Suite 500
Markham, ON L3R 9T8

Tel. 905-513-3504
Fax 905-470-8155

Allied International Credit Corp. is a third party debt collections company. There are 260 employees at this location, a total of 310 in Canada and 440 employees worldwide. Graduates most likely to be hired come from the following academic areas: Bachelor of Arts (Psychology), Bachelor of Commerce/Business Administration (Finance), Community College Diploma (Business, Financial Planning, Secretarial, Legal Assistant) and High School Diploma. Graduates would occupy Collections Officer, Financial Negotiator, Secretary, Data Entry Clerk, Customer Service Representative, Payroll Clerk and Human Resources Assistant positions. Company benefits are rated as industry standard. The potential for advancement is listed as being good. The average annual starting salary falls within the $20,000 to $25,000 range. The most suitable methods for initial contact by those seeking employment are to mail or fax a resume with a covering letter. Allied International Credit Corp. does hire summer students. *Contact:* Carole Geroux, Consultant, Human Resources.

ALLSTATE INSURANCE COMPANY OF CANADA
10 Allstate Parkway
Markham, ON L3R 5P8

Tel. 905-477-6900
Fax 905-475-4924
Website .... www.allstate.ca

Allstate Insurance Company of Canada is a property and casualty insurance company. Activities include policy sales, claims administration, administration of current and renewal policies, writing and processing of new policies, accounting and collections and the development of new products. The company employs approximately 400 people at this location and a total of 1,200 people across Canada. Graduates most likely to be hired come from the following academic areas: Bachelor of Arts (Economics), Bachelor of Science (Actuarial, Computer Science, Mathematics), Bachelor of Commerce/Business Administration (Accounting, Finance, Marketing), Chartered Accountant, Certified General Accountant, Master of Business Administration (General, Accounting, Finance)

and Community College Diploma (Accounting, Business, Communications, Financial Planning, Insurance). Graduates would occupy Accountant, Underwriter, Programmer, and Supervisory and Customer Service positions. Initiative, team player, and good communication and problem solving skills are listed as desirable non-academic qualifications. Company benefits are rated above average. The potential for advancement is listed as being good. The average annual starting salary falls within the $25,000 to $30,000 range. The most suitable methods for initial contact by those seeking employment are to mail a resume with a covering letter, or by responding to positions advertised in major newspapers. *Contacts:* Tricia Biglow, Human Resources Manager or Mary Collins, Sr. Human Resources Representative.

AMCOR TWINPAK - NORTH AMERICA INC.
1255 route Transcanadienne, Bureau 210
Dorval, QC H9P 2V4

Tel. 514-684-7070
Fax 514-684-3128
Website .... www.twinpak.com

Amcor Twinpak - North America Inc. is a Canadian leader in plastic, paper and composite material packaging. Headquartered in Dorval, the company operates through a network of more than a dozen manufacturing facilities and sales offices across North America. There are 20 employees at this location, a total of 1,250 in Canada and a total of 1,441 employees in the company. Amcor Twinpak serves customers in the food and beverage, pharmaceutical, cosmetic and construction industries. Graduates most likely to be hired come from the following academic areas: Bachelor of Engineering (General, Chemical, Mechanical, Environmental/Resources, Industrial Chemistry), Bachelor of Commerce/Business Administration (General, Accounting, Finance, Human Resources, Information Systems, Marketing), Chartered Accountant, Certified Management Accountant, Certified General Accountant, Master of Business Administration (General, Marketing), Community College Diploma (Accounting, Administration, Human Resources, Information Systems, Secretarial, CAD/CAM/Autocad, Computer Science, Tool and Die, Machinist) and High School Diploma. Graduates would occupy Plant Engineer, Secretary, Accounting Clerk, Laboratory Technologist, Customer Service Representative, Sales Representative and Operator positions. Initiative, great communication skills, computer skills, team player, positive attitude, flexibility and a commitment to continuous learning are all listed as desirable non-academic qualifications. Company benefits are rated as excellent. The potential for advancement is listed as being good. The average annual starting salary falls within the $25,000 to $30,000 range. The most suitable methods for initial contact by those seeking employment are to fax or e-mail a resume with a covering letter. Amcor Twinpak - North America Inc. does hire summer and co-op work term students. *Contact:* Katherine Axiuk, Director of Human Resources.

AMDAHL CANADA LIMITED
12 Concorde Place, Suite 300
Toronto, ON M3C 3R8

Tel. 416-510-3111
Fax 416-510-3353
Website .... www.amdahl.com

Amdahl Canada Limited provides integrated computing solutions that meet the needs of many of the largest users of information technology in the world. The Amdahl portfolio includes hardware, software, and operational and consulting services that offer customers a choice in creating powerful technology-based information enterprises. Amdahl Canada Limited is a subsidiary of Sunnyvale, California based Amdahl Corporation, which in turn is a wholly owned subsidiary of Fujitsu Limited. Headquartered in Toronto, Amdahl Canada Limted also maintains locations in Quebec, Montreal, Ottawa, Mississauga, Calgary and Edmonton. Graduates most likely to be hired at the company's headquarters come from Bachelor of Commerce/Business Administration (General, Finance) programs. Graduates would be hired to occupy the position of Associate Account Executive. Company benefits are rated as excellent. The potential for advancement is listed as being good. The average annual starting salary falls within the $30,000 to $35,000 range. The most suitable method for initial contact by those seeking employment is to mail a resume with a covering letter. Amdahl Canada Limited does hire summer students, primarily for mail room positions. *Contact:* Human Resources Manager.

AMERICAN AIRLINES INC.
PO Box 6005, L.B. Pearson International Airport
Malton, ON L5P 1B6

Fax 905-612-0144
Website .... www.aa.com

American Airlines Inc. is an international scheduled airline transportation company, serving over 300 destinations worldwide. There are 125 employees at this location, a total of 500 in Canada and 100,000 employees worldwide. Graduates most likely to be hired come from the following academic areas: Bachelor of Arts (General), Bachelor of Commerce/Business Administration (General, Accounting, Marketing) and Community College Diploma (Administration, Business, Marketing/Sales). At this location, graduates would occupy entry level positions as Airport Passenger/Cargo Service Agents, as well as Passenger Sales and Marketing positions. Team player, flexible, enthusiastic and responsible are all listed as desirable non-academic qualifications. Company benefits are rated as industry standard. The potential for advancement is listed as average. The average annual starting salary for entry level positions falls within the $15,000 to $20,000 range. The most suitable method for initial contact by those seeking employment is to mail a resume with a covering letter. *Contact:* Human Resources/Administration.

AMERICAN EXPRESS CANADA INC. / AMEX
101 McNabb Street
Markham, ON L3R 4H8

Tel. 905-474-8000
Fax 905-474-8004
Website www6.americanexpress.com/canada

American Express Canada Inc. / Amex provides financial services including credit cards, travellers cheques and banking services. These include asset management, lines of credit, insurance and travel services. There are more than 2,500 employees at this location. Graduates most likely to be hired come from the following academic areas: Bachelor of Arts, Bachelor of Science, Bachelor of Laws, Bachelor of Commerce/Business Administration, Master of Business Administration (Marketing, Finance), Masters (General/Related) and Community College Diploma (Business/Finance). Graduates would occupy entry level positions in Marketing, Systems, Finance, Cus-

tomer Service and Administration. Company benefits and the potential for advancement are both rated as excellent. The average annual starting salary falls within the $30,000 to $35,000 range. The most suitable method for initial contact by graduates seeking employment is to mail a resume with a covering letter. American Express Canada Inc. does hire a limited number of summer and co-op work term students. *Contact:* Human Resources.

AMERICAN STANDARD INC.
1401 Dupont Street
Toronto, ON M6H 2B1

Tel. 416-536-1078
Fax 416-535-9760
Email .... morriss@amstd.com
Website .... www.americanstandard.com

American Standard Inc. is a major manufacturer of plumbing fixtures, fittings and bathroom accessories. The company is a wholly owned subsidiary of the publicly traded American Standard Companies Inc. (NYSE: ASD). The company is the world's largest producer of bathroom and kitchen fixtures and fittings and one of the world's largest producers of air conditioning and heating systems. It is also the leading producer of braking systems and electronic controls for heavy-duty buses and trucks in Europe. American Standard Inc. employs more than 250 people at this location. Graduates most likely to be hired come from the following academic areas: Bachelor of Engineering (General) and Community College Diploma (General/Related). Company benefits are rated as excellent. The potential for advancement is listed as being good. The average annual starting salary is dependent upon the level of position. The most suitable method for initial contact by graduates seeking employment is to mail a resume with a covering letter. *Contact:* Employee Relations.

AMJ CAMPBELL VAN LINES
6140 Vipond Drive
Mississauga, ON L5T 2B2

Tel. 905-670-7111
Fax 905-795-3786
Website .... www.yellowpages.ca/amjcampbell

AMJ Campbell Van Lines is the largest member of Atlas Van Lines, and is involved in the transportation of household goods and commercial products. Divisions include domestic and overseas moving, trade show, and the office moving division. There are approximately 350 employees at this location and more than 2,000 employees across Canada, including branches and franchises. Graduates most likely to be hired come from the following academic areas: Bachelor of Commerce/Business Administration, Master of Business Administration and Community College Diploma (Accounting, Administration, Business, Facility Management, Marketing/Sales, Secretarial). Hard working, team player and a great attitude are all listed as desirable non-academic qualifications. Company benefits are rated above average. The potential for advancement is listed as excellent. The average annual starting salary falls within the $25,000 to $30,000 range. The most suitable methods for initial contact by those seeking employment are to mail or fax a resume with a covering letter. AMJ Campbell Van Lines does hire summer and co-op work term students. Summer students are always in demand for moving positions. *Contact:* Lynda Quinnett, Human Resources.

AML WIRELESS SYSTEMS INC.

260 Saulteaux Crescent
Winnipeg, MB R3J 3T2

Tel.	204-949-2411
Fax	204-889-1268
Email	lrosney@amlwireless.com
Website	www.amlwireless.com

AML Wireless Systems Inc. develops, manufactures, markets and supports wireless electronic products for a broad range of applications for customers around the world. The company employs approximately 38 people. Graduates most likely to be hired come from the following academic areas: Bachelor of Science (Computer Science, Mathematics, Physics), Bachelor of Engineering (Electrical, Mechanical, Engineering Physics, Telecommunications), Bachelor of Commerce/Business Administration (Accounting, Finance, Human Resources, Marketing) and Community College Diploma (Accounting, Business, Financial Planning, Human Resources, Marketing/Sales, Office Administration, Secretarial). Graduates would occupy Applications Engineer, Sales/Marketing Representative, Test Technician, and Documentation Clerk (Autocad) positions. Company benefits are rated as excellent. The potential for advancement is listed as being good. The most suitable methods for initial contact by those seeking employment are to mail, fax or e-mail a resume with a covering letter. AML Wireless Systems Inc. does hire summer students. *Contact:* Lisa Rosney, Human Resources.

AMP OF CANADA LTD.

20 Esna Park Drive
Markham, ON L3R 1E1

Tel.	905-475-6222
Fax	905-474-5556
Email	jfrappie@amp.com
Website	www.amp.com

AMP of Canada Ltd. is a leading supplier of electronic connectors and interconnection systems. AMP of Canada Ltd. is a subsidiary of Harrisburg, Pennsylvania based AMP Incorporated. The company has locations around the world and over 40,000 employees worldwide. AMP of Canada Ltd. employs approximately 275 people at this location and a total of 330 people in Canada. Graduates most likely to be hired come from the following academic areas: Bachelor of Science (Computer Science), Bachelor of Engineering (Metallurgy, Mechanical), Bachelor of Commerce/Business Administration (Finance) and Master of Business Administration (Marketing). Graduates would occupy Sales Trainee, Administrative Trainee, and Manufacturing Engineer positions. Team oriented and good communication skills are both listed as desirable non-academic qualifications. Company benefits are rated as excellent. The potential for advancement is listed as being good. The average annual starting salary falls within the $30,000 to $35,000 range. The most suitable method for initial contact by those seeking employment is to mail a resume with a covering letter. AMP of Canada Ltd. does hire a limited number of summer students. *Contact:* Human Resources Department.

AMS MANAGEMENT SYSTEMS CANADA INC.

180 Elgin Street, Suite 1400
Ottawa, ON K2P 2K3

Tel.	613-232-7400
Fax	613-232-0324
Website	www.amsinc.com

AMS Management Systems Canada Inc. is a subsidiary of one of the world's leading business and information technology consulting firms, American Management Systems. AMS provides a full range of consulting services, including business re-engineering, systems integration, and systems development and implementation. An international presence in the IT consulting industry, AMS employs 8,500 consultants in 55 offices throughout North America and Europe. AMS Management Systems Canada Inc. was established in 1985, and has grown to over 225 employees supporting clients in Ottawa, Toronto and Montreal. The company partners with clients in the financial, telecommunications and government sectors to achieve breakthrough performance through the intelligent use of information technology. Graduates most likely to be hired come from the following academic areas: Bachelor of Science (Computer Science, Mathematics), Bachelor of Engineering (Electrical, Computer Systems, Industrial Engineering), Bachelor of Commerce/Business Administration (Finance, Information Systems), Master of Business Administration (Finance, Information Systems), Master of Science (Computer Science, Mathematics) and Master of Engineering (Electrical, Computer Systems, Industrial Engineering). Graduates would occupy IT Consultant positions, fulfilling a variety of roles such as Systems Analyst, Application Developer, Business Analyst and Programmer Analyst. Strong oral and written communication skills, team player, previous IT experience/exposure, strong problem solving skills and well-rounded interests are all listed as desirable non-academic qualifications. Company benefits and the potential for advancement both rated as excellent. The most suitable method for initial contact by those seeking employment is through on-campus recruitment initiatives (visit your campus career centre for details). AMS Management Systems Canada Inc. does hire students for summer and co-op work terms. *Contact:* AMS Canada - Recruiting.

ANDERSEN CONSULTING

185 The West Mall, Suite 500
Toronto, ON M9C 5L5

Tel.	416-641-5000
Fax	416-641-5074
Website	www.ac.com

Andersen Consulting is a $8.3 billion global management and technology consulting organization whose mission is to help its clients create their future. The organization works with clients from a wide range of industries to link their people, processes and technologies to their strategies. Andersen Consulting has approximately 65,000 people in 48 countries and maintains offices across Canada in Vancouver, Toronto, Etobicoke, Ottawa and Montreal. The Canadian practice employs over 1,300 talented professionals with skills in strategy, change management, process and technology consulting. Andersen Consulting's Canadian practice provides consulting services to clients in the communications and high-tech, government, products, resources, and financial services industries. Graduates most likely to be hired come from the following academic areas: Bachelor of Arts (Economics, Psychology), Bachelor of Science (Computer Science, Mathematics), Bachelor of Engineering (General, Chemical, Civil, Electrical, Mechanical, Aerospace, Automation/Robotics, Computer Systems, Engineering Physics, Environmental/Resources, Food Processing, Industrial Design, Industrial Engineering, Industrial Production/Manufacturing, Microelectronics, Power/Hydro, Pulp and Paper), Bachelor of Commerce/Business Administration (General, Accounting, Finance, Human Resources, Information Systems, Marketing, Public Administration), Master of Business Administration (General, Accounting, Finance, Human Resources, Information Systems, Marketing, Public Administration), Master of Arts (Psychology, Industrial Relations), Master of Science and Master of Engineering. Graduates would occupy Analyst positions in Strategy, Technology, Process and Change Management. Team player, good problem-solving skills, well rounded interests, strong communication skills, an ability to work hard, and an interest in travel are listed as desirable non-academic qualifications. Andersen Consulting offers a total learning environment, in which applicants are challenged to learn on their own, on the job in one of the industry's best training programs. Accordingly, company benefits are rated as above average and the potential for advancement is listed as excellent. The most suitable method for initial contact for those seeking employment is to apply through on-campus recruitment initiatives. *Contact:* See your campus career centre for details.

AON CONSULTING INC.
145 Wellington Street West, Suite 500
Toronto, ON M5J 1H8

Tel. 416-542-5531
Fax 416-542-5513
Website .... www.aon.com

Aon Consulting Inc. provides innovative solutions to assist clients in linking human resource strategies with business strategies. The company operates in the areas of health and benefits, retirement, human resources, change management, organizational communication, compensation and workers compensation. Aon Consulting Inc. is part of Aon Consulting Worldwide Inc., a subsidiary of the Aon Group, a global organization serving clients through 400 owned offices in 60 countries. The Canadian organization has 13 offices nationally and operates as Groupe-Conseil Aon Inc. in Quebec and Aon Consulting Inc. in the rest of Canada. There are 150 employees at this location and a total of 540 employees in Canada. Graduates most likely to be hired come from the following academic areas: Bachelor of Arts (General), Bachelor of Science (Actuarial, Mathematics), Bachelor of Laws, Bachelor of Commerce/Business Administration (Accounting, Finance, Human Resources, Information Systems), Chartered Accountant, Certified Management Accountant, Certified General Accountant, Master of Business Administration (Accounting, Finance, Human Resources, Information Systems) and Community College Diploma (Accounting, Administration, Human Resources, Secretarial). Graduates would occupy Pension Administrator, Secretary, Actuarial Analyst, Research Analyst, Financial Analyst, Accountant, Programmer, Pension Analyst, Benefits Analyst and Human Resources Analyst positions. Computer literacy, customer service skills, strong communication and organization skills, team player and previous consulting experience are all listed as desirable non-academic qualifications. The most suitable methods for initial contact by those seeking employment are to mail or fax a resume with a covering letter.

Aon Consulting hires actuarial students for co-op work term placements. *Contact:* Kathy Garicpy, Director of Human Resources.

APOTEX INC.
150 Signet Drive
Toronto, ON M9L 1T9

Tel. 416-749-9300
Fax 416-401-3828
Email .... recruit@apotex.ca
Website .... www.apotex.com

Apotex Inc. is the largest vertically integrated Canadian owned pharmaceutical company in the country with over 3,000 employees across the country. The company researches, develops, manufactures and distributes 176 quality medicines that also are exported to 115 countries. With a research budget of $70.2 million in 1998, Apotex was the 17th largest research and development spender for all companies in Canada. Graduates most likely to be hired come from the following academic areas: Bachelor of Science (Chemistry, Microbiology), Bachelor of Engineering (Electrical, Mechanical, Agricultural Engineering, Architectural/Building, Industrial, Industrial Production/Manufacturing), Bachelor of Commerce/Business Administration (Accounting, Finance, Human Resources, Information Systems, Marketing) and Community College Diploma (Human Resources, Marketing/Sales, Secretarial). Graduates would occupy Office Clerk, Administration, Accounting, Human Resource, Chemist, Biochemist, Microbiologist, Clinical Research and Industrial Engineer positions. Excellent communication and interpersonal skills, flexibility and the ability to work in a team are all listed as desirable non-academic qualifications. Company benefits and the potential for advancement are both rated as excellent. The average annual starting salary is dependent upon the position being considered. The most suitable methods for initial contact by those seeking employment are to mail or fax a resume with a covering letter. Apotex Inc. does hire co-op work term students. *Contact:* Human Resources - Recruiter.

APPLE CANADA INC.
7495 Birchmount Road
Markham, ON L3R 5G2

Tel. 905-513-5800
Fax 905-513-4291
Website .... www.apple.ca

Apple Canada Inc. is the Canadian sales and marketing subsidiary of Apple Computer Inc. based in Cupertino, California. Established in 1980 and headquartered in Markham, Apple Canada Inc. serves its customers through more than 450 channel partners and from offices across the country in Halifax, Quebec City, Montreal, Ottawa, Calgary, Edmonton, Vancouver and Victoria. Apple employs approximately 60 people at this location and a total of 100 people in Canada. Graduates most likely to be hired come from the following academic areas: Bachelor of Commerce/Business Administration (Accounting, Finance, Marketing), Master of Business Administration (General, Accounting, Finance, Marketing) and Community College Diploma (Marketing/Sales, Office Administration). Recent post-secondary graduates without job-related experience are not generally hired. Company benefits are rated as excellent. The potential for advancement is listed as being good. The most suitable methods for initial contact by those seeking employment are to mail a resume with a covering letter, or by applying through the company's website. Apple Canada Inc. occasionally hires summer and co-op work term students. *Contacts:* Lynne Jarjour, Human Resources Manager or Bethany Kopstick, Human Resources Specialist.

APPLIED DIGITAL ACCESS CANADA INC. / ADA
8644 Commerce Court, Imperial Square
Burnaby, BC V5A 4N6

Tel.	604-415-5917
Fax	604-415-5900
Email	bcg_careers@ada.com
Website	www.ada.com

Applied Digital Access Canada Inc. / ADA is a leading provider of systems, software and services to telecommunications service providers. ADA's products manage the performance, quality, reliability and availability of these networks. Benefits, which can be realized by the deployment of ADA products, include improved quality of service, increased productivity, and lower operating expenses. ADA targets all types of network operators, telecommunications service providers, internet service providers (ISPs), cable, cellular, and wireless providers. ADA's goal is to consistently meet and frequently exceed customer expectations, continually striving to improve the capability, quality and reliability of its products and services. The company employs 90 people in Canada, and a total of 300 people worldwide. ADA's headquarters is located in San Diego, California. Graduates most likely to be hired come from the following academic areas: Bachelor of Science (Computer Science, Mathematics), Bachelor of Engineering (Electrical), Bachelor of Commerce/Business Administration (Information Systems), Master of Science, Master of Engineering and Community College Diploma (Administration, Communications/Public Relations, Human Resources, Information Systems, Computer Science, Electronics Technician). Graduates would occupy Verification and Software Developer positions. Team player, require minimal guidance, enthusiastic and able to work on own initiative are all listed as desirable non-academic qualifications. Company benefits are rated above average. The potential for advancement is listed as being good. The average annual starting salary falls within the $40,000 to $45,000 range. The most suitable methods for initial contact by those seeking employment are to e-mail a resume with a covering letter, or by applying through the company's website at www.ada.com. Applied Digital Access Canada Inc. does hire students for summer and co-op work terms. *Contact:* Jennifer Rigal, Technical Recruiter.

AQUALTA
10065 Jasper Avenue, 20th Floor Capitol Square
Edmonton, AB T5J 3B1

Tel.	780-412-3414
Fax	780-412-7888
Website	www.aqualta.com

Aqualta is the third largest water distributor in Canada with pipelines spanning 2,800 kilometres. Aqualta's main responsibility is to provide high quality water to the citizens of Edmonton and 40 surrounding communities in Alberta. As part of this responsibility, the company manages two water treatment plants and the distribution system within the city boundaries. In order to maintain the infrastructure, Aqualta also manages capital projects which ensures that service disruptions are kept to a minimum and allows the company to maintain a very strong technological edge with its competitors. Aqualta also runs a full scale laboratory to ensure that water quality remains at its peak while researching the newest water treatment technologies. The company has entered into private and public partnerships in building and operating systems in other parts of western Canada. Presently, there are 273 permanent and 40 temporary (mostly seasonal) employees. Aqualta is a member of the EPCOR group of companies. EPCOR, based out of Edmonton, is the parent company of Edmonton Power, Aqualta and Eltec. EPCOR is governed by an independent board of directors and management team. The City of Edmonton is the sole shareholder of the EPCOR group, which was incorporated May 1, 1996. Graduates most likely to be hired come from the following academic areas: Bachelor of Science (Chemistry), Bachelor of Engineering (Civil, Environmental/Resources, Water Resources), Chartered Accountant, Certified Management Accountant, Master of Engineering (Environmental Sciences) and Community College Diploma (CAD/CAM/Autocad, Electrician, Engineering Technician, Instrumentation Technician, Laboratory Technician). Graduates would occupy Water Plant Director, Controller, Drafting Technician, Junior Engineer, Accountant, Engineering Technologist, Contract Inspector, Project Coordinator and Project Manager positions. Leadership skills, initiative, empowering of others, teamwork skills, adaptive to change and open communication skills are all listed as desirable non-academic qualifications. Company benefits are rated as industry standard. The potential for advancement is listed as being good. The average annual starting salary falls within the $25,000 to $30,000 range for clerical positions, $30,000 to $35,000 range for technical positions and $45,000 to $50,000 range for professional positions. The most suitable method for initial contact by those seeking employment is via telephone. Aqualta does hire students for summer and co-op work terms. *Contact:* Human Resources.

ARAMARK CANADA LTD.
811 Islington Avenue
Toronto, ON M8Z 5W8

Tel.	416-255-1331
Fax	416-255-7640
Website	www.aramark.ca

Aramark Canada Ltd., formerly Versa Services Ltd., is the largest contract service management company in Canada, providing services such as food, catering, cleaning, office management and vending services. These services are provided through four distinct market areas, including: Campus Services, Business Services, Healthcare Support Services and Sports & Entertainment Services. Aramark Canada Ltd. is a subsidiary of Philadelphia, Pennsylvania based Aramark, a global leader providing managed services. Aramark employs more than 150,000 people in 15 countries serving 15 million people at more than 500,000 locations around the world. Aramark Canada Ltd. employs more than 100 employees at this location and over 15,000 employees across Canada. Graduates most likely to be hired come from the following academic areas: Bachelor of Arts (General), Bachelor of Science (Computer Science, Health Sciences), Bachelor of Commerce/Business Administration (Accounting, Finance), Certified Management Accountant (Finance), Certified General Accountant (Finance), Community College Diploma (Business, Cooking, Hospitality, Human Resources, Food/Nutrition) and High School

Diploma. Related work experience, and good interpersonal and communication skills are listed as desirable non-academic qualifications. Company benefits are rated above average. The potential for advancement is listed as excellent. The average annual starting salary falls within the $20,000 to $25,000 range. The most suitable method for initial contact by those seeking employment is to mail a resume with a covering letter. Aramark Canada Ltd. does hire summer students. *Contact:* Human Resources.

ARBOR MEMORIAL SERVICES INC.
2 Jane Street
Toronto, ON M6S 4W8

Tel. 416-763-4531
Fax 416-763-8714
Email .... loverend@arbormemorial.com

Arbor Memorial Services Inc. owns cemetery properties, funeral homes and crematoria across Canada. The company employs over 1,600 people in Canada. Graduates most likely to be hired come from the following academic areas: Bachelor of Arts (General), Bachelor of Science (General, Horticulture), Bachelor of Engineering (Civil), Bachelor of Landscape Architecture, Bachelor of Commerce/Business Administration (Accounting, Human Resources, Information Systems, Marketing), Chartered Accountant, Certified Management Accountant, Certified General Accountant and Community College Diploma (Accounting, Administration, Business, Human Resources, Marketing/Sales, Secretarial, Architecture/Drafting, Horticulture, Computer Science, Funeral Services). Graduates would be hired to occupy Administrative Assistant/Clerical, Marketing Coordinator, Accounting Clerk, Property Manager, Sales Representative and Funeral Director positions. An adaptable and flexible approach to working, team player, problem solving abilities and entrepreneurial skills are all listed as desirable non-academic qualifications. Company benefits are rated above average. The potential for advancement is listed as being good. The average annual starting salary falls within the $25,000 to $35,000 range, and is commission based for sales positions. The most suitable methods for initial contact by those seeking employment are to mail, fax or e-mail a resume with a covering letter. Arbor Memorial Services Inc. does hire summer students to work primarily on the cemetery properties. In addition, co-op work term students are hired occasionally. *Contacts:* Michelle Gibbons, Human Resources; Dana Dramnitzke, Human Resources or Lori Overend, Human Resources.

ARCHITECTS CRANG AND BOAKE INC.
1 Valleybrook Drive
Toronto, ON M3B 2S7

Tel. 416-449-1203
Fax 416-449-4063
Email .... acbi@interlog.com

Architects Crang and Boake Inc. is an architectural design firm providing contract documents for construction purposes. The firm maintains offices in China, the United Arab Emirates, and in Toronto. There are 50 employees at this location, a total of 70 employees worldwide. Graduates most likely to be hired come from the following academic areas: Bachelor of Engineering (Architectural/Building), Bachelor of Architecture, Community College Diploma (CAD/CAM/Autocad) and High School Diploma. Recent graduates would occupy CADD Drafting Technician (architectural) and CADD Designer positions. Self-starter, able to travel, team player and coop-

erative are listed as desirable non-academic qualifications. Company benefits are rated as industry standard. The potential for advancement is listed as being good. The average annual starting salary falls within the $25,000 to $45,000 plus range, depending upon the experience of the applicant and the position being considered. The most suitable methods for initial contact by graduates seeking employment are to mail a resume with a covering letter, or via telephone. Architects Crang and Boake Inc. does hire summer students. *Contact:* Sheldon Ublansky.

ARCTIC CO-OPERATIVES LIMITED
1645 Inkster Boulevard
Winnipeg, MB R2X 2W7

Tel. 204-697-1625
Fax 204-697-1880

Arctic Co-operatives Limited provides a full range of business services to its member co-ops located throughout Canada's north. Services include, accounting, merchandise procurement, construction services, management advice and direction, and recruitment and benefits administration. The co-operative is owned and controlled by 42 member co-ops, and all member co-ops are aboriginally owned. Arctic Co-operatives Limited employs 55 people at this location, and a total of 90 people throughout the co-operative. Graduates most likely to be hired come from the following academic areas: Bachelor of Commerce/Business Administration (Accounting, Finance, Human Resources, Information Systems, Marketing) and Certified General Accountant. Graduates would occupy Auditor, Area Manager and Merchandise Manager positions. Knowledge of Aboriginal cultures is listed as a desirable non-academic qualification. Company benefits are rated above average. The potential for advancement is listed as average. The average annual starting salary falls within the $15,000 to $20,000 range. The most suitable method for initial contact by those seeking employment is to mail a resume with a covering letter. Arctic Co-operatives Limited does hire summer students. *Contact:* James Kaassen, Division Manager, Human Resources.

ARMTEC
15 Campbell Road, PO Box 3000
Guelph, ON N1H 6P2

Tel. 519-822-0210
Fax 519-822-1160
Website .... www.armtec.com

Armtec engineers, manufactures and markets products used in municipal, highway, industrial, mining and water resource construction products. Products include corrugated steel drainage pipes, guard rails for highways, retaining walls, field-assembled under passes and bridges, metal grating, water control gates and distribution of geotextiles. Armtec maintains Branch Office, Sales Office and Plant locations across Canada. There are approximately 250 employees across Canada. Graduates most likely to be hired come from the following academic areas: Bachelor of Engineering (Civil, Mechanical), Bachelor of Commerce/Business Administration (Accounting) and Community College Diploma (Accounting, Engineering). Graduates would occupy Junior Engineer, Engineering Technologist and Cost Accounting Clerk positions. Computer software knowledge, good verbal and written communications skills, interpersonal skills and relevant work experience are all listed as desirable non-academic qualifications. Company benefits are rated as excellent. The potential for advancement is listed as average. The average annual starting salary depends upon the position being considered. The most suitable method for initial contact by those seeking employment is to mail a resume with a covering letter. Armtec does hire a limited number of summer students, primarily for clerical and plant positions. In addition, Armtec occasionally hires engineering students for co-op work terms. *Contact:* Jan McEwin, Human Resources.

ARNOLD BROTHERS TRANSPORT LTD.
739 Lagimodiere Boulevard
Winnipeg, MB R2J 0T8

Tel.	204-257-6666
Fax	204-257-2213
Website	www.arnoldbr.com

Arnold Brothers Transport Ltd. is a line haul transportation company, providing full load service throughout Canada and the United States. Established in 1958, the company employs approximately 300 people at this location, and a total of 500 people in Canada. Graduates most likely to be hired come from the following academic areas: Bachelor of Commerce/Business Administration (General, Marketing), Chartered Accountant, Certified Management Accountant, Certified General Accountant and Community College Diploma (Accounting, Computer Science). Graduates would occupy Accounting Management/Supervision, General Accounting, Computer Programming, Computer Systems Maintenance, and Sales and Marketing Representative/Management positions. Past work experience, transportation background, self and time management skills, team oriented, detail and deadline oriented, proactive approach, reliable, dependable and good problem solving skills are all listed as desirable non-academic qualifications. Company benefits are rated as industry standard. The potential for advancement is listed as being good. The average annual starting salary is dependent upon the position being considered. The most suitable method for initial contact by those seeking employment is to mail a resume with a covering letter. Arnold Brothers Transport Ltd. does hire summer students. *Contact:* Human Resources.

ART GALLERY OF ONTARIO / AGO
317 Dundas Street West
Toronto, ON M5T 1G4

Tel.	416-977-0414
Fax	416-979-6689
Email	Human_Resources@ago.net
Website	www.ago.net

The Art Gallery of Ontario / AGO is Ontario's main art gallery and the eighth largest art museum in North America. The AGO's collection comprises more than 24,000 works representing 1,000 years of extraordinary European, Canadian, modern, Inuit and contemporary art. The gallery is funded by the Ontario Ministry of Citizenship, Culture and Recreation. Additional operating support is received from the Volunteers of the Art Gallery of Ontario, the City of Toronto, the Department of Canadian Heritage and The Canada Council. The AGO employs approximately 300 people involved in all gallery activities from the displaying of art to all associated administrative functions. Graduates most likely to be hired come from the following academic areas: Bachelor of Arts (Fine Art, History) and Community College Diploma (Food/Nutrition, Administration, Secretarial). Graduates would occupy clerical, secretarial, food service and educational positions. Company benefits are rated above average. The potential for advancement is listed as aver-

age. The average annual starting salary falls within the $25,000 to $30,000 range. The most suitable method for initial contact by those seeking employment is to mail a resume with a covering letter. The Art Gallery of Ontario does hire summer students through government programs. *Contact:* Director of Human Resources.

ARTSMARKETING SERVICES INC.
260 King Street East, Suite 500
Toronto, ON M5A 1K3

Tel.	416-941-9000
Fax	416-941-8989
Website	www.artsmarketing.com

Artsmarketing Services Inc. is an international marketing company that works exclusively with non-profit organizations throughout North America. Clients include major symphonies, theatres, operas, and ballet companies, as well as museums and public television stations. Graduates most likely to be hired come from the following academic areas: Bachelor of Arts (General, Economics, English, Fine Arts, Journalism, Music, Psychology, Arts Management, Theatre, Communications), Bachelor of Science, Bachelor of Education, Bachelor of Commerce/Business Administration (Finance, Public Administration, Marketing, Information Systems), Master of Business Administration (Accounting, Finance, Marketing, Information Systems), Master of Arts (Arts Management) and Community College Diploma (Administration, Advertising, Business, Communications, Marketing, Graphic Arts, Human Resources, Photography, Television/Radio Arts). Graduates who are hired will enter an extensive hands-on management training program. Following the successful completion of the training program, they are made Campaign Managers whose responsibilities include hiring, training and motivating a sales staff of 12 to 15 people. Listening skills, sense of humour, interpersonal and communication skills, problem solving abilities, leadership qualities, an arts background, ability to relocate, sales, telemarketing, managerial and fundraising experience are all listed as desirable non-academic qualifications. The potential for advancement is listed as excellent. Remuneration is commission based and may vary between $18,000 and $30,000 for the first year. The most suitable methods for initial contact by those seeking employment are to mail or fax a resume with a covering letter, or via telephone. *Contacts:* Ken Lampe, Director, Human Resources (x 226) or David Macdonald, Manager, Human Resources (x 239).

ASECO INTEGRATED SYSTEMS LTD.
635 Fourth Line, Unit 16
Oakville, ON L6L 5B3

Tel.	905-339-0059
Fax	905-339-3857
Email	aseco@istar.ca
Website	www.aseco.net

ASECO Integrated Systems Ltd. is an employee owned provider of consulting and systems integration services. The company's expertise is in providing manufacturing information and control systems, management information systems and their connectivity. Over the last ten years, ASECO has rapidly emerged as a leader in computer and control systems integration, manufacturing execution systems, control systems engineering, and custom software development. ASECO has been providing high quality consulting and integration services to clients such as Nabisco Ltd., Heinz USA, Ford Motor Company, DuPont, General Electric and Glaxo/Wellcome Pharmaceuticals throughout North America and Europe. Graduates most likely to be hired come from the following academic areas: Bachelor of Science (Computer Science), Bachelor of Engineering (Electrical, Computer Systems, Industrial Engineering, Industrial Production), Bachelor of Commerce/Business Administration (Information Systems) and Community College Diploma (Computer Science, Engineering Technician). Graduates would occupy Engineer-in-Training and Programmer Analyst positions. Previous co-op work experience, excellent written and oral communication skills and a willingness to travel are all listed as desirable non-academic qualifications. Company benefits are rated as industry standard. The potential for advancement is listed as excellent. The average annual starting salary falls within the $45,000 to $55,000 range. The most suitable methods for initial contact by those seeking employment are to mail, fax or e-mail a resume with a covering letter, or via the company's website. ASECO Integrated Systems Ltd. does hire summer and co-op work term students. *Contacts:* Diane Filippin, Human Resources or Robert Peters, President.

ASSOCIATES, THE
8500 Leslie Street, Suite 600
Thornhill, ON L3T 7P1

Tel. 905-709-8500
Fax 905-709-8457
Website .... www.theassociates.com

The Associates is a consumer loan company providing personal loans, mortgages, sales, finance, and private label credit cards. There are approximately 15 employees at this location, a total of 3,000 across Canada and 40,000 employees worldwide. Graduates most likely to be hired come from the following academic areas: Bachelor of Arts (General), Bachelor of Commerce/Business Administration and High School Diploma. Graduates would occupy Management Trainee, Customer Service Representative, Account Executive, Sales Representative and Clerical positions. Excellent organization and customer service skills, sales ability, good interpersonal and leadership skills, energy, initiative, flexibility, and strong oral and written communication skills are all listed as desirable non-academic qualifications. Company benefits and the potential for advancement are both rated as excellent. The average annual starting salary falls within the $25,000 to $30,000 range. The most suitable methods for initial contact by those seeking employment are to mail or fax a resume with a covering letter. The Associates does hire summer and co-op work term students. *Contact:* Human Resources Director.

ASSUMPTION LIFE
P.O. Box 160
Moncton, NB E1C 8L1

Tel. 506-853-6040
Fax 506-853-5428

Assumption Life is a mutual life insurance company which provides life insurance, disability insurance and annuity products, as well as pension plans and mortgage loans. The company's products are distributed through career officers, brokers and general agents, serving clients in the four Atlantic provinces, Quebec and Ontario. This location is the head office location for Assumption Life. The company employs a total of 200 people in Canada. Graduates most likely to be hired come from the following academic areas: Bachelor of Science (Actuarial, Computer Science, Nursing), Bachelor of Laws (Corporate), Bachelor of Commerce/Business Administration (General, Accounting, Finance, Information Systems, Marketing), Chartered Accountant, Certified General Accountant, Master of Business Administration (General) and Community College Diploma (Accounting, Communications/Public Relations, Information Systems, Insurance, Marketing/Sales, Secretarial, Nursing RN). Adaptable, creative, enthusiastic, leadership skills, professional, analytical, communicative, flexible, organized, dependable, initiative and good writing skills are all listed as desirable non-academic qualifications. Company benefits are rated above average. The average annual starting salary falls within the $20,000 to $30,000 range. The most suitable methods for initial contact by those seeking employment are to mail or fax a resume with a covering letter. Assumption Life does hire summer and co-op work term students. *Contact:* Rachelle Gagnon, Human Resources Consultant.

ATCO ELECTRIC
10035 - 105 Street, PO Box 2426
Edmonton, AB T5J 2V6

Tel. 780-420-7038
Fax 780-420-7594
Email .... hrgeneration@atcoelectric.com
Website .... www.apl.ca

ATCO Electric provides electric energy services to 164,000 customers, including homes, businesses, farms, oilfields and other resource industries. ATCO Electric (formerly Alberta Power Limited) is part of the Calgary based ATCO Group, one of Canada's premier corporations. ATCO Electric serves more than 200 communities, including villages, small to mid-sized cities, Native reserves and Metis settlements as well as two communities in Saskatchewan. ATCO's service area also includes 56 rural electrification associations. Geography, distance and climate present unique challenges to delivering power in the company's service area. This area covers almost two-thirds of the province and includes only 15 per cent of Alberta's population, but a large proportion of the province's natural resource wealth. Graduates most likely to be hired come from the following academic areas: Bachelor of Engineering (Electrical, Power, Mechanical, Industrial Design), Bachelor of Commerce/Business Administration (Accounting, Finance, Human Resources, Information Systems), Certified Management Accountant, Master of Business Administration (General, Finance, Human Resources), Master of Engineering (Mechanical, Electrical) and Community College Diploma (Accounting, Human Resources, Purchasing/Logistics, CAD/CAM/Autocad, Engineering Technician, Health Nurse/Wellness). The most suitable method for initial contact by those seeking employment is to mail a resume with a covering letter. *Contact:* Human Resources.

ATCO NOISE MANAGEMENT LTD.
1243 McKnight Boulevard NE
Calgary, AB T2E 5T2

Tel. 403-292-7804
Fax 403-292-7816
Email .... info@atconoise.com
Website .... www.atconoise.com

ATCO Noise Management Ltd. designs, supplies and constructs acoustic solutions for industrial customers. The company's full range of services include ambient noise surveys, regulatory reviews, preparation of acoustic specifications, budget pricing and post-construction testing.

ATCO has demonstrated its capabilities with a long list of customers in over 90 countries and in a number of major industrial markets, including: gas transmission, power generation, urban transportation, turbine testing, original equipment manufacturers, retrofit and industrial gas production. ATCO Noise Management Ltd. is a member of the Calgary based ATCO Group, one of Canada's premier corporations. ATCO Noise Management Ltd. employs more that 50 people. Graduates most likely to be hired come from the following academic areas: Bachelor of Engineering (Civil, Mechanical), Bachelor of Commerce/Business Administration (Accounting, Human Resources, Marketing) and Community College Diploma (Secretarial, Engineering Technician, HVAC Systems). Graduates would occupy Engineering Designer, Mechanical Engineer, Project Manager, Project Coordinator, Site Supervisor, Sales Representative, Accountant, Secretary and Clerk positions. Team player, the ability to "think on your feet" and common sense are all listed as desirable non-academic qualifications. Company benefits are rated above average. The potential for advancement is listed as being good. The average annual starting salary falls within the $55,000 to $60,000 range. The most suitable method for initial contact by those seeking employment is to mail a resume with a covering letter. ATCO Noise Management Ltd. does hire summer and co-op work term students. *Contacts:* Scott Roszell or Boris Rassin.

ATLANTIC PACKAGING PRODUCTS LTD.
111 Progress Avenue
Toronto, ON M1P 2Y9

Tel. 416-298-8101
Fax 416-297-2264

Atlantic Packaging Products Ltd. manufactures paper and plastic packaging products and recycled paper products. The company employs more than 100 people. Graduates most likely to be hired come from the following academic areas: Bachelor of Science (Chemistry), Bachelor of Engineering (Mechanical, Electrical), Bachelor of Commerce/Business Administration, Chartered Accountant, Certified Management Accountant and Community College Diploma (General/Related). Graduates would occupy Junior Engineering and Clerk positions. A high level of initiative and good verbal and written communication skills are listed as desirable non-academic qualifications. Company benefits are rated above average. The potential for advancement is listed as being good. The average annual starting salary falls within the $20,000 to $25,000 range. The most suitable methods for initial contact by those seeking employment are to mail or fax a resume with a covering letter, or via telephone. Atlantic Packaging Products Ltd. does hire summer students. *Contact:* Recruiter, Personnel.

ATLANTIS AEROSPACE CORPORATION
1 Kenview Boulevard
Brampton, ON L6T 5E6

Tel. 905-792-1981
Fax 905-792-7251
Email .... positions@atlantis.com
Website .... www.atlantis.com

Atlantis Aerospace Corporation is an international leader in the development of simulation and training devices, performance support software systems, and avionics testing equipment. As a leading Canadian design and engineering firm, Atlantis specializes in training and performance enhancement products for industry and government.

Founded in 1978, the company employs more than 200 people. Graduates most likely to be hired come from the following academic areas: Bachelor of Science (Computer Science, Physics), Bachelor of Engineering (General, Aeronautical) and Community College Diploma (Aircraft Maintenance, Computer Science, Electronics Technician). Graduates would occupy Simulation and Software Designer/Developer positions. Good communication skills, the ability to work in a team environment and a proven ability to plan for and meet deadlines are all listed as desirable non-academic qualifications. Company benefits are rated above average. The potential for advancement is listed as being good. The average annual starting salary falls within the $35,000 to $40,000 range. The most suitable methods for initial contact by those seeking employment are to mail or e-mail a resume with a covering letter. Atlantis Aerospace Corporation does hire summer students. *Contact:* Human Resources.

ATLAS SYSTEMS GROUP
10060 Jasper Avenue, 1650 Scotia Place
Edmonton, AB T5J 3R8

Tel. 780-426-4444
Fax 780-426-2233
Email .... Resume@atlas.ca
Website .... www.atlas.ca

Atlas Systems Group is a Canadian based consulting firm focused on providing information technology services. Focus areas include infrastructure management, project management, business analysis, business process design, integrated business applications implementations, and application systems design, development and support. The company's mission is to assist its clients in achieving their business objectives through the effective and efficient use of information technology. Atlas Systems Group was established in 1987 and today employs a total of 40 people. Graduates most likely to be hired come from the following academic areas: Bachelor of Science (Computer Science), Bachelor of Engineering (Computer Systems), Bachelor of Commerce/Business Administration (Information Systems), Certified Management Accountant, Certified General Accountant, Master of Business Administration (Information Systems), Master of Science (Computer Science), Master of Engineering (Computer Systems) and Community College Diploma (Accounting, Human Resources, Computer Science, Information Systems). Graduates would occupy Programmer, Programmer/Analyst, Systems Analyst, Business Analyst, Project Manager, ERP Implementation Specialist. Previous work experience, team player, self-initiative, flexible and an outgoing personality are all listed as desirable non-academic qualifications. Company benefits are rated as industry standard. The potential for advancement is listed as being good. The average annual starting salary falls within the $25,000 to $30,000 range. The most suitable method for initial contact by those seeking employment is to e-mail a resume with a covering letter. *Contact:* Human Resources.

ATOMIC ENERGY CONTROL BOARD / AECB
280 Slater Street, PO Box 1046, Station B
Ottawa, ON K1P 5S9

Tel. 613-955-5894
Fax 613-995-0390
Website .... www.gc.ca/aecb

The Atomic Energy Control Board / AECB's mission is to ensure that the use of nuclear energy in Canada does not pose undue risk to health, safety, security and the environment. This is accomplished by controlling the development, application and use of nuclear energy in Canada, and by participating on behalf of Canada in international measures of control. The AECB reports to Parliament through the Minister of Natural Resources. Established in 1946, the AECB employs approximately 360 people at this location and a total of 416 people across Canada. Graduates most likely to be hired come from the following academic areas: Bachelor of Science (Computer Science, Mathematics), Bachelor of Engineering (Electrical, Mechanical), Bachelor of Commerce/Business Administration (Accounting, Finance, Human Resources, Information Systems), Master of Science (Health Physicist), Master of Engineering (Nuclear Engineering) and Community College Diploma (Human Resources, Secretarial, Computer Science). Graduates would occupy Health Physicist, Reactor Physicist, Program Officer, Project Officer - at Nuclear Sites, and various professional and administrative positions in Finance, Human Resources, Information Systems and Training. At the Research Office graduates would occupy Scientific positions to regulate disposal of radioactive waste, Transport positions to regulate the transportation of radioactive materials and Inspector positions. Leadership ability, interpersonal skills, good communication skills, customer service skills, and an ability to work independently and within groups are all listed as desirable non-academic qualifications. The most suitable method for initial contact by those seeking employment is to mail a resume and covering letter. The Atomic Energy Control Board does hire summer students. *Contact:* Resourcing, Planning & Official Languages Services.

AVALON EAST SCHOOL BOARD
215 Water Street, Suite 601, Atlantic Place
St. John's, NF A1C 6C9

Tel. 709-758-2372
Website www.aesb.k12.nf.ca

Avalon East School Board operates local elementary and secondary schools. The board employs a total of 750 people. Graduates most likely to be hired come from the following academic areas: Bachelor of Arts (English, French, Geography, Graphic Arts, History, Languages, Music), Bachelor of Science (Biology, Chemistry, Computer Science, Geology, Geography, Mathematics, Physics), Bachelor of Education (General, Early Childhood, Primary Junior, Junior Intermediate, Intermediate Senior, Special Needs), Master of Arts (English, French, Geography, Graphic Arts, History, Languages, Music), Master of Science (Biology, Chemistry, Computer Science, Geology, Geography, Mathematics, Physics), Master of Education (General) and Community College Diploma (Accounting, Secretarial). Graduates would be hired to occupy Teacher, School Administrator, Student Assistant and Secretarial positions. Child centred, and excellent interpersonal and communication skills are listed as desirable non-academic qualifications. The average annual starting salary falls within the $25,000 to $30,000 range. The most suitable method for initial contact by those seeking employment is to mail a resume with a covering letter. The Avalon East School Board hires summer students in specialized areas (eg. French Immersion). *Contact:* Human Resources.

AVCO FINANCIAL SERVICES CANADA LIMITED
201 Queens Avenue
London, ON N6A 1J1

Tel. 519-672-4220
Fax 519-660-2652

Avco Financial Services Canada Limited provides a variety of financial services, including mortgages, revolving charges and sales contracts. Avco maintains over 225 branch locations across Canada employing a total of approximately 1,200 people. The head office, located in London, Ontario, provides human resources, marketing, product development, accounting, audit, legal, communication, and insurance services to the field. The company's international headquarters are located in Costa Mesa, California. Graduates most likely to be hired come from the following academic areas: Bachelor of Arts (Marketing), Bachelor of Commerce/Business Administration (Finance, Marketing) and Community College Diploma (Finance, Marketing) and Community College Diploma programs. Graduates would be hired to occupy related entry-level positions. Finance or marketing experience as well as sales or customer service experience are all listed as desirable assets. Company benefits are rated as excellent. The potential for advancement is listed as being good. The average annual starting salary depends upon the position being considered. The most suitable method for initial contact by graduates seeking employment is to mail a resume with a covering letter. *Contact:* Human Resources.

AVESTA SHEFFIELD INC.
2140 Meadowpine Boulevard
Mississauga, ON L5N 6H6

Tel. 905-567-9900
Fax 905-567-8302
Email .... vstamper@asnad.com
Website .... www.avestasheffield.com

Avesta Sheffield Inc., based in Stockholm, Sweden, is one of the world's largest stainless steel producers. The North American Division of Avesta Sheffield offers the widest range of premium-quality standard and special grade stainless steel product forms to the domestic and international market. The North American Division includes a division headquarters in Shaumburg, Illinois, four mills in the United States, the Canadian operation (based at this location), and a welding products subsidiary in New York. Stainless steel is Avesta's only product, therefore the company is committed to promoting and supporting its use, as well as being committed to long term mutually beneficial partnerships with more than 200 authorized stock distributors in the United States. In addition, Avesta serves a limited number of fabricators and end users in a wide variety of industries in the United States, Canada and Mexico. Avesta Sheffield employs 73 people at this location, a total of 143 people in Canada, and 7,500 worldwide. Graduates most likely to be hired come from the following academic areas: Bachelor of Science (Chemistry, Computer Science, Metallurgy), Bachelor of Engineering (Industrial Chemistry, Metallurgy, Pulp and Paper, Water Resources), Bachelor of Commerce/Business Administration (Accounting, Finance, Marketing), Master of Engineering (Metallurgy) and Community College Diploma (Marketing/Sales, Purchasing/Logistics, CAD/CAM/Autocad). Graduates would occupy Inside Sales, Warehouse, Materials Processing and Management positions in Sales, Finance and Purchasing. Team player, leadership skills, initiative, creativity, sales experience, an ability to learn, relationship building and negotiation skills are all listed as desirable non-academic qualifications. Company benefits are rated above average. The potential for advancement is listed as being good. The average annual starting salary falls within the $25,000 to $30,000 range. The most suitable method for initial contact by those seeking employment is to mail a resume with a covering letter. Avesta Sheffield Inc. does hire summer and occasionally co-op work term students. *Contact:* Victoria Stamper, Manager, Training & Development.

AVNET INTERNATIONAL (CANADA) LTD.
6705 Millcreek Drive, Unit 1
Mississauga, ON L5N 4R9

Tel. 905-812-4400
Fax 905-812-4426
Website .... www.hh.avnet.com

Avnet International (Canada) Ltd. is a Fortune 100 company involved in the distribution of electronic components, computers and peripherals. The majority of Avnet's staff are sales people. Avnet International (Canada) Ltd. is a division of Avnet Inc., a Fortune 500 company employing approximately 6,000 people worldwide. Avnet International (Canada) Ltd. employs 80 people at this location and a total of 160 people across Canada. Graduates most likely to be hired come from the following academic areas: Bachelor of Engineering (Computer Systems, Microelectronics), Bachelor of Commerce/Business Administration (Accounting, Human Resources, Marketing) and Community College Diploma (Administration, Business, Human Resources, Marketing/Sales, Computer Science, Electronics Technician, Engineering Technician). Graduates would occupy Inside Sales Representative, Administrative Assistant, Product Integration Technician, Human Resources Generalist, Credit and Collections Representative and Customer Service Representative positions. Previous work experience in distribution (specifically electronics and computers), a proactive approach and a willingness to learn are all listed as desirable non-academic qualifications. Company benefits are rated above average. The potential for advancement is listed as excellent. The average annual starting salary varies with the position. The most suitable method for initial contact by those seeking employment is to mail a resume with a covering letter. *Contact:* Human Resources Manager.

AVON CANADA INC.
5500 Trans-Canada Highway, PO Box 8000
Pointe-Claire, QC H9R 1B6

Tel. 514-630-5459
Fax 514-630-5480
Email .... nathalie.beaudoin.-.rh@avon.com
Website .... www.avon.ca

Avon Canada Inc. is a major manufacturer and the country's largest direct-seller of beauty and related products. Worldwide, Avon is the world's leading direct seller of beauty and related products. The company's products are sold in 131 countries including China, Latin America and Eastern Europe through more than 2.3 million Avon Independent Sales Dealers worldwide. Based in Pointe-Claire, Quebec, Avon Canada Inc. employs 700 people at this location, approximately 1,100 full and part-time associates, and is represented by over 55,000 Independent Sales Dealers in virtually every corner of Canada. Graduates most likely to be hired come from the following academic areas: Bachelor of Arts (Graphic Arts), Bachelor of Science (Computer Science), Bachelor of Engineering (Computer Systems, Industrial Production), Bachelor of Laws, Bachelor of Commerce/Business Administration (Finance, Human Resources, Marketing), Master of Business Administration, Community College Diploma (Administration) and High School Diploma. Graduates would

occupy Marketing Assistant, Industrial Engineer, Systems Analyst and Financial Analyst positions. Bilingualism, team player and flexibility are listed as desirable non-academic qualifications. Company benefits are rated above average. The potential for advancement is listed as excellent. The average annual starting salary falls within the $28,000 to $32,000 range. The most suitable method for initial contact by those seeking employment is to mail a resume with a covering letter. Avon Canada Inc. does hire summer students. *Contact:* Nathalie Beaudoin, Human Resources.

AXA INSURANCE
5700 Yonge Street, Suite 1400
Toronto, ON M2M 4K2

Tel. 416-218-4116
Fax 416-218-4174
Email .... hr@axa-insurance.ca
Website .... www.axa-insurance.ca

AXA Insurance (Canada) is part of the France Based AXA Group, the second largest insurer in the world, and active in over 60 countries on five continents. AXA Insurance serves Ontario, the Atlantic and Prairie provinces. The company markets a broad range of property/casualty insurance products through independent brokers. There are 215 employees at this location, and a total of 500 employees in Canada. The AXA Group employs 100,000 people worldwide. Graduates most likely to be hired come from the following academic areas: Bachelor of Arts (Criminology, Economics, History, Philosophy, Political Science, Psychology, Sociology), Bachelor of Science (Actuarial, Computer Science, Mathematics, Nursing, Occupational Therapy, Physiotherapy, Psychology), Bachelor Education (General), Bachelor of Commerce/Business Administration (General, Accounting, Finance, Information Systems), Certified Management Accountant, Certified General Accountant, Community College Diploma (Accounting, Business, Insurance, Secretarial, Nursing RN/RNA, Rehabilitation Therapy) and High School Diploma. Graduates would occupy Customer Service Representative, Claims Representative, Personal Lines Underwriter, Portfolio Analyst, Junior Accountant, and various clerical and support positions. Team player, initiative, customer relations skills, organized, excellent interpersonal skills, and an ability to adapt quickly to change are all listed as desirable non-academic qualifications. Company benefits are rated as industry standard. The potential for advancement is listed as being good. The average annual starting salary falls within the $25,000 to $30,000 range. The most suitable methods for initial contact by those seeking employment are to mail, fax or e-mail a resume with a covering letter, or via the company's website. AXA Insurance does hire a limited number of summer students. In addition, AXA also hires co-op work term students. *Contact:* Recruiter.

AXIA NETMEDIA CORPORATION
1040 - 7 Avenue SW, Suite 600
Calgary, AB T2P 3G9

Tel. 403-231-1709
Fax 403-508-7911
Email .... jobs@axia.com
Website .... www.axia.com

Axia NetMedia Corporation uses worldwide computer and telecommunications networks to develop and implement customer solutions for information exchange, communications and learning. The company employs 120 people at this location, a total of 375 in Canada and a total of 405 people worldwide. Graduates most likely to be hired come from the following academic areas: Bachelor of Arts (Communications, Fine Arts), Bachelor of Science (Computer Science), Bachelor of Engineering (Computer Systems), Bachelor of Commerce/Business Administration (Information Systems, Marketing), Chartered Accountant, Master of Business Administration (Marketing), Master of Science (Computer Science, Information Systems), Community College Diploma (Accounting, Communications/Public Relations, Marketing/Sales, Graphic Arts, Electronics Technician, Information Systems) and MCSE accreditation. Graduates would occupy Accountant, Marketing Director, Programmer, Net Media Producer, Designer, Art Director, Web Developer, Graphic Artist, Multimedia Specialist, Product Specialist and Knowledge Engineer positions. Innovative, initiative, energy, enthusiasm, focus, internet savvy, intellectual curiosity and success-driven are all listed as desirable non-academic qualifications. Company benefits are rated above average. The potential for advancement is listed as being excellent. The average annual starting salary falls within the $40,000 to $45,000 range. The most suitable methods for initial contact by those seeking employment are to fax or e-mail a resume with a covering letter, or via the company's website. Axia NetMedia Corporation does hire co-op work term students. *Contact:* Marion J. Wood, Director of Human Resources.

B.A. BANKNOTE
975 Gladstone Avenue
Ottawa, ON K1Y 4W5

Tel. 613-728-5854
Fax 613-728-1688

B.A. Banknote is a printer of securities products. A division of Quebecor Printing Inc., the company employs 155 people at this location, a total of 310 in Canada and 320 people worldwide. Graduates most likely to be hired come from the following academic areas: Bachelor of Arts (Economics, Graphic Arts), Bachelor of Science (Chemistry), Bachelor of Engineering (Pollution Treatment, Pulp and Paper), Bachelor of Commerce/Business Administration (General, Accounting, Finance, Human Resources, Information Systems, Marketing, Public Administration), Certified Management Accountant, Certified General Accountant, Master of Business Administration (Marketing, Public Administration) and Community College Diploma (Accounting, Administration, Business, Communications, Human Resources, Graphic Arts, HVAC Systems). Graduates would occupy Customer Service Representative, International Sales Representative, Laboratory Technician, Manager and Printing positions. Team player, flexible, creative and innovative are all listed as desirable non-academic qualifications. Company benefits and the potential for advancement are both rated as excellent. The average annual starting salary falls within the $20,000 to $25,000 range. The most suitable method for initial contact by those seeking employment is to mail a resume with a covering letter. *Contact:* Manager, Human Resources.

BABCOCK & WILCOX CANADA
581 Coronation Boulevard
Cambridge, ON N1R 5V3

Tel. 519-621-2130
Fax 519-621-2310
Email .... resume@pgg.mcdermott.com
Website .... www.babcock.com

Babcock & Wilcox Canada is a leader in nuclear and fossil-fuelled steam generation technology. The company's steam generation products convert water into steam using a variety of heat sources. The resulting steam is used by utilities to drive the generators that produce electricity, and in industrial power production for a variety of industrial processes. Based in Cambridge, Babcock & Wilcox Canada is a division of The Babcock & Wilcox Company, a wholly owned subsidiary of McDermott International, Inc. which is based in New Orleans. McDermott is a multinational corporation specializing in energy-related industries, such as offshore oil technology, marine construction and power generation. Babcock & Wilcox Canada employs 900 people at this location and a total of 950 in Canada. Graduates most likely to be hired come from the following academic areas: Bachelor of Arts (General, Economics, Journalism), Bachelor of Science (General), Bachelor of Engineering (Mechanical, Industrial Engineering, Metallurgy), Bachelor of Commerce/Business Administration (Accounting, Finance, Human Resources), Chartered Accountant, Certified Management Accountant, Certified General Accountant, Master of Business Administration (General), Community College Diploma (Accounting, Administration, Business, Communications, Human Resources, Purchasing/Logistics, Secretarial, Journalism, Legal Assistant, CAD/CAM/Autocad, Computer Science, Electronics Technician, Engineering Technician, Tool and Die, Machinist, Welding, Nursing RN/RNA) and High School Diploma. Graduates would occupy Trainee, Clerk, Technician, Engineering, Drafting, Marketing, Communications, Industrial, Personnel, Co-op, Accountant, Analyst, Proposal/Project Manager and Construction Site Manager positions. Good communication, negotiation, computer, team player, leadership and people management skills are all listed as desirable non-academic qualifications. Company benefits are rated above average. The potential for advancement is listed as excellent. The average annual starting salary falls within the $30,000 to $35,000 range. The most suitable methods for initial contact by those seeking employment are to mail or fax a resume with a covering letter. Summer students are hired, primarily co-op placements with high schools, colleges, and universities. *Contacts:* Gloria Majich, Manager, Staff Relations and Employment or Tom Thomas, Personnel Officer, Human Resources.

Baffin Regional Health
and Social Services Board

BAFFIN REGIONAL HEALTH AND SOCIAL SERVICES BOARD
PO Box 200
Iqaluit, NN X0A 0H0

Tel. 800-663-5738/867-979-7610
Fax 867-979-7404
Email .... brhbpers@nunanet.com
Website .... www.nunanet.com/~brhbfin

Baffin Regional Health and Social Service Board represents the interests of the people (predominately Inuit) served in the region, through the provision of health and social services. The board operates and controls programs established and funded by the government of the Northwest Territories. In addition to a 34 bed acute care hospital with diagnostic and support services in Iqaluit, the board operates 12 community health centres, provides regional health programs (dental, health, promotion, nutrition, environmental health), medivac services (air ambulance) and social services programs. The board employs a total of 300 people throughout the region. In addition to eligibility for NWTRNA registration, significant directly related nursing experience is vital for success. A Nursing Degree or advanced Nursing Diploma qualification are required for OR, Public and Community Health Assignments. Equivalencies are always considered. Graduates would occupy professional nursing opportunities in the hospital, urban public health office and home care service, and remote community health centres. Self-reliance, and a sense of adventure would be desirable character attributes. Baffin Regional Health and Social Services Board offers a competitive salary, Northern and other allowances, relocation and rental assistance (and the chance to find out all about amoutis and muktuk!). Accordingly, employee benefits are rated above average. The potential for advancement is listed as being good. The most suitable method for initial contact by those seeking employment is to fax a resume with a covering letter, or for further information visit the Board's website or phone toll free at 1-800-663-5738. Baffin Regional Health Board does hire co-op work term students. *Contact:* Keith Dennison, Director, Human Resources.

BAIN AND COMPANY

162 Cumberland Street, Suite 300
Toronto, ON M5R 3N5

Tel.	416-929-1888
Fax	416-929-3470
Website	www.bain.com

Bain and Company provides strategic management consulting services. Headquartered in Boston, Massachusetts, Bain and Company is one of the world's leading global strategy consulting firms. The firm serves clients through a network of 25 offices across 16 countries and five continents, all tightly integrated into an operational whole. Bain and Company employs more than 25 employees at this location. Graduates most likely to be hired come from the following academic areas: Bachelor of Commerce/Business Administration (General, Finance) and Master of Business Administration. Bachelor of Commerce/Business Administration graduates would occupy Associate Consultant positions, and Master of Business Administration graduates would occupy Consultant positions. Graduates should possess a strong record of achievement. Company benefits and potential for advancement are both rated as excellent. The most suitable method for initial contact by those seeking employment is to mail a resume, covering letter, and a copy of academic transcripts. Bain and Company does hire summer students, primarily Masters of Business Administration students from Harvard University, Stanford, and the University of Pennsylvania. *Contact:* Recruiting Coordinator.

BALLARD POWER SYSTEMS INC.

9000 Glenlyon Parkway
Burnaby, BC V5J 5J9

Tel.	604-454-0900
Fax	604-412-4747
Email	careers@ballard.com
Website	www.ballard.com

Ballard Power Systems Inc. is at the forefront of research, development and manufacture of the proton exchange membrane (PEM) fuel cell. Founded in 1979 under the name Ballard Research Inc. to conduct research and development in high energy lithium batteries, the company began developing PEM fuel cells in 1983. Today, these systems have evolved into pre-commercial prototypes proving the practicality of the Ballard Fuel Cell, and are widely viewed as viable alternatives to conventional technologies. Ballard's focus is now on working with its strategic partners worldwide to develop competitive products for mass markets by reducing cost and implementing high volume manufacturing processes. Ballard's strategic partners include DaimlerChrysler, Ford, GPU International Inc. (New Jersey), Alstom SA (France) and Ebara Corporation (Japan). There are 370 employees at this location, a total of 505 in Canada and a total of 600 employees worldwide. Graduates most likely to be hired come from the following academic areas: Bachelor of Science (Chemistry, Computer Science), Bachelor of Engineering (Chemical, Electrical, Mechanical, Engineering Physics, Industrial Design, Industrial Engineering, Industrial Production/Manufacturing), Bachelor of Commerce/Business Administration (Accounting, Finance, Human Resources, Information Systems, Marketing), Chartered Accountant, Certified Management Accountant, Master of Business Administration (General, Accounting, Finance, Human Resources, Marketing), Master of Science (Chemistry, Computer Science), Master of Engineering (Chemical, Industrial, Mechanical, Electrical), Community College Diploma (Accounting, Human Resources, Office Administration, Secretarial, Legal Assistant, Automotive Mechanic, CAD/CAM/Autocad, Computer Science, Electronics Technician, Engineering Technician) and High School Diploma. Team player, flexibility, adaptability and a high level of initiative are all listed as desirable non-academic qualifications. In addition, work term or co-op experience is regarded highly. Company benefits and the potential for advancement are both rated as excellent. The average annual starting salary falls within the $30,000 to $35,000 range. The most suitable methods for initial contact by those seeking employment are to mail or e-mail a resume with a covering letter, or by applying through the company's website. Ballard Power Systems Inc. does hire summer and co-op work term students. *Contacts:* Ken Cooper, Human Resources Specialist or Kelly Mertsch, Human Resources Specialist (Co-op Students).

BANFF CENTRE, THE

PO Box 1020, Station 19
Banff, AB T0L 0C0

Tel.	403-762-7546
Fax	403-762-6677
Email	Erin_Vant@banffcentre.ab.ca
Website	www.banffcentre.ab.ca

The Banff Centre is an unique Canadian institution playing a special role in the advancement of cultural and professional life. The centre is internationally recognized for its advanced work in the arts and management, and for developing and hosting conferences on contemporary issues. The Banff Centre employs approximately 550 people, and is divided into four main divisions: Centre for the Arts, Centre for Management, Centre for Conferences, and Centre for Mountain Culture. Graduates most likely to be hired come from the following academic areas: Bachelor of Arts (General, Journalism, Music), Bachelor of Engineering (Computer Systems), Bachelor of Education (Adult), Bachelor of Commerce/Business Administration, Master of Business Administration, Master of Arts

(Music, Dance, Visual Arts, Theatre Arts, Media), Master of Education (Adult, Career Development) and Community College Diploma (Accounting, Administration, Communications, Marketing/Sales, Cooking, Graphic Arts, Hospitality, Human Resources, Journalism, Photography, Recreation, Security/Enforcement, Computer Science). These graduates are hired for a broad range of positions, from entry level hospitality operations, to administrative and clerical, to program coordinators and supervisors, and finally to management level positions. Team player, strong customer service orientation, creative, hard working and innovative are all listed as desirable non-academic qualifications. The average annual starting salary falls within the $15,000 to $25,000 range for junior level positions. Company benefits and the potential for advancement are both rated as excellent. The most suitable methods for initial contact by those seeking employment are to mail a resume with covering letter, or via telephone. The Banff Centre does hire summer and co-op work term students, the number of positions varies from year to year. *Contacts:* Lisa Flierjans, Recruiting & Training Coordinator or Erin Vant, Administrative Assistant, Recruiting.

BANK OF MONTREAL
55 Bloor Street West, 5th Floor
Toronto, ON M4W 3N5

Tel.	416-927-7700
Fax	416-927-5772
Website	www.bmo.com

Bank of Montreal is Canada's first bank and one of the largest banks in North America. The Bank of Montreal is a retail bank, a commercial bank and an investment bank. Founded in 1817, the bank has grown into an organization with US$101 billion in assets and over 32,000 employees in Canada, the United States and around the world. Graduates most likely to be hired come from the following academic areas: Bachelor of Arts (General, Economics), Bachelor of Science (Computer Science, Mathematics), Bachelor of Engineering (Electrical, Computer Systems, Telecommunications), Bachelor of Commerce/Business Administration (Accounting, Finance, Human Resources, Information Systems, Marketing), Chartered Accountant, Master of Business Administration (Accounting, Finance, Human Resources, Information Systems, Marketing, Pubic Administration), Master of Arts (Economics), Master of Library Science, Master of Science (Computer Science), Master of Engineering (Computer Systems) and Community College Diploma (Accounting, Administration, Business, Human Resources). Students and graduates enjoy considerable job variation across the bank. Positions in Account Management, Information Technology, Capital Markets, Investment Banking, Financial Strategy, Human Resources, Legal Affairs, Branch Management, Customer Service, Financial Services, Business Processes, Accounting, Marketing and Communications are just a sample of what is available to "out-of-the-box" thinkers with a strong customer service orientation. The Bank of Montreal offers challenging career opportunities, backed by continuous professional development, with the facilities, mentoring and tools to "make it happen". The bank's flexible company benefits and potential for advancement are both rated as excellent. The most suitable methods for initial contact by those seeking employment are to mail or fax a resume with a covering letter, via on-campus recruitment initiatives (visit your campus career centre for details), or visit the bank's website for more information. The Bank of Montreal does hire summer and co-op work term students. *Contact:* Human Resources Division.

BANKERS TRUST, BT ALEX BROWN
Royal Bank Plaza, North Tower, Suite 1700
Toronto, ON M5J 2J2

Tel.	416-865-2206
Fax	416-865-1346
Email	hr.canada@bankerstrust.com

Bankers Trust, BT Alex Brown is a corporate investment banking firm providing global banking services. The company employs 70 people at this location, a total of 75 people in Canada and 26,000 people worldwide. Graduates most likely to be hired come from the following academic areas: Bachelor of Science (Actuarial, Mathematics), Bachelor of Engineering (General, Civil, Electrical, Environmental/Resources, Industrial Chemistry, Industrial Engineering), Bachelor of Commerce/Business Administration (Accounting, Finance, Marketing), Chartered Accountant, Certified General Accountant and Master of Business Administration (Finance). Graduates would occupy Corporate Financial Analyst, Credit Analyst and Controller Analyst positions. Company benefits are rated as excellent. The average annual starting salary is dependent upon the position being considered. The most suitable methods for initial contact by those seeking employment are to mail or fax a resume with a covering letter. Bankers Trust, BT Alex Brown does hire summer and co-op work term students. *Contact:* Kathryn Wash, Human Resources Manager.

BARR SHELLEY STUART
808 - 4th Avenue SW, Suite 720
Calgary, AB T2P 3E8

Tel.	403-269-1320
Fax	403-265-9997
Email	bss@cadvision.com

Barr Shelley Stuart provides accounting, consulting and financial services. Barr Shelley Stuart Chartered Accountants provide accounting, audit and tax accounting services. Barr Shelley Stuart Consultants provide human sources, marketing and entrepreneurial consulting services. The Tamarack Group, Corporate Finance is involved in mergers and acquisitions, business valuations, investor relations, financing and venture capital. Graduates most likely to be hired come from the following academic areas: Bachelor of Arts (Economics, English, Journalism), Bachelor of Science (Computer Science), Bachelor of Commerce/Business Administration (Accounting, Finance, Human Resources, Information Systems, Marketing), Chartered Accountant, Certified Management Accountant, Certified General Accountant, Community College Diploma (Accounting, Administration, Business, Facility Management, Human Resources, Marketing/Sales, Secretarial, Graphic Arts, Journalism) and High School Diploma. Graduates would occupy Chartered Accountant, CA Student, Junior Accountant, Intermediate Accountant, Senior Accountant, Staff Accountant, Human Resources Manager, Accounting Technician, Marketing Manager, Administrative Assistant, Clerk and Administrative positions. Team player, flexible, strong written and verbal communication skills, related work experience and excellent interpersonal skills are all listed as desirable non-academic qualifications. Company benefits are rated above average. The potential for advancement is listed as average. The average annual starting salary falls within the $25,000 to $30,000 range, depending upon position, skills and experience. The most suitable method for initial contact by those seeking employment is to mail a resume with a covering letter. Summer students are hired occasionally, depending upon the workload. *Contact:* Jane Grant, Human Resources Manager.

BAYCREST CENTRE FOR GERIATRIC CARE
3560 Bathurst Street
Toronto, ON M6A 2E1

Tel. .... 416-785-2500 ext 2732
Fax 416-785-2490
Email .... jobopps@baycrest.org
Website .... www.baycrest.org

The Baycrest Centre for Geriatric Care is a large chronic care, geriatric hospital and home for the aged. The centre provides care for the elderly that enriches their quality of life. Baycrest's programs take place on-site and in the home and are designed to meet both individual and family needs, and include counselling, education and referrals to clients and families. Baycrest is a fully affiliated teaching institution with the University of Toronto, with more than 500 students from universities, colleges, high schools and technical institutes receiving educational training at Baycrest each year. Over 130 Baycrest staff member are full, associate or assistant professors at the University of Toronto. The centre employs more than 1,000 people. Graduates most likely to be hired come from the following academic areas: Bachelor of Science (Nursing RN), Chartered Accountant, Master of Social Work, Master of Science (Nursing Administration) and Community College Diploma (Secretarial, Administration, Food/Nutrition Sciences). Company benefits are rated above average. The potential for advancement is listed as average. The most suitable method for initial contact by graduates seeking employment is to mail a resume with a covering letter. The Baycrest Centre for Geriatric Care does hire summer students through government grant programs. Contact: Employee Services.

BAYER INC.
77 Belfield Road
Toronto, ON M9W 1G6

Tel. 416-248-0771
Fax 416-248-1297
Email .... canada.corp.comm@bayer.com
Website .... www.bayer.ca

Bayer Inc., the Canadian subsidiary of the international group Bayer AG (Germany), is researched based with major businesses in life sciences and chemicals. Headquartered in Toronto, with a major manufacturing facility in Sarnia, Ontario, Bayer Inc. employs more than 2,200 people in Canada, whereas Bayer AG employs more than 150,000 people worldwide. Graduates most likely to be hired come from the following academic areas: Bachelor of Arts (Economics, French, Graphic Arts, Languages, Political Science, Psychology), Bachelor of Science (Actuarial, Agriculture, Biology, Chemistry, Computer Science, Environmental, Mathematics, Microbiology, Pharmacy, Psychology), Bachelor of Engineering (Chemical, Industrial Chemistry, Pulp and Paper, Computer Systems, Telecommunications), Bachelor of Commerce/Business Administration (Accounting, Finance, Human Resources, Information Systems, Marketing), Chartered Accountant, Certified Management Accountant, Certified General Accountant, Master of Business Administration (Accounting, Finance, Human Resources, Information Systems, Marketing), Master of Science (General, Health Sciences) and Community College Diploma (Accounting, Administration, Business, Communications, Financial Planning, Human Resources, Marketing/Sales, Purchasing/Logistics, Graphic Arts, Legal Assistant, Photography, Computer Science, Animal Health, Radiology Technician). The most suitable method for initial contact by those seeking employment is to mail a resume with a covering letter. Bayer Inc. does hire summer students. Contact: Human Resources Department.

BAYWOOD HOMES
250 Rimrock Road
Toronto, ON M3J 3A6

Tel. 416-633-7333
Fax 416-633-7491
Email .... baywood@baywoodhomes.com
Website .... www.baywoodhomes.com

Baywood Homes is a residential home builder with over a quarter of a century of experience. Baywood Homes is a family run company and has become a leader in the creation of communities in Southern Ontario. The company employs a total of 50 people at this location. Graduates most likely to be hired come from the following academic areas: Bachelor of Engineering (General, Electrical, Mechanical, Architectural/Building), Bachelor of Architecture, Bachelor of Commerce/Business Administration (General, Marketing, Public Administration), Master of Business Administration (Accounting) and Community College Diploma (Accounting, Advertising, Business, Communications/Public Relations, Real Estate Sales, Secretarial, Carpentry, Plumber). Graduates would occupy Sales and Marketing Coordinator, Sales and Marketing Assistant, Sales Agent, Sales Assistant, Estimator, Office Administrator, Secretary, Accountant, Project Manager, Site Supervisor and General Labour/Handyman positions. Excellent organizational, analytical and time management skills are all listed as desirable non-academic qualifications. Company benefits are rated as industry standard. The potential for advancement is listed as being excellent. The average annual starting salary falls within the $25,000 to $30,000 range. The most suitable method for initial contact by those seeking employment is to fax a resume with a covering letter. Baywood Homes does hire co-op work term students. Contact: Rose Morelli, Human Resources Coordinator.

BAZAAR & NOVELTY / STUART ENTERTAINMENT
301 Louth Street
St. Catharines, ON L2S 3V6

Tel. 905-687-1700
Fax 905-687-4129
Email .... bazaar@bingoking.com

Bazaar & Novelty is a multi-faceted manufacturing and distribution company specializing in the production of breakopen tickets, bingo paper and bingo ink markers. In operation for over 60 years, the company also specializes in the design, manufacture and supply of video lottery terminals, electronic bingo equipment and associated computerized gaming management systems. Bazaar & Novelty operates through a network of distribution centres coast to coast in Canada. Manufacturing facilities are located in British Columbia, Manitoba, Ontario, Nova Scotia and Newfoundland. In Ontario, Bazaar & Novelty's single largest market in North America, the company operates four corporate distribution centres in addition to its head office and manufacturing facility located in St. Catharines. In 1994, Bazaar & Novelty became a part of the US based Stuart Entertainment Group of Companies. The group provides products and services to state and provincial lotteries, tribal gaming enterprises, the charitable gaming industry, commercial casinos and the general public in North America and abroad. The company employs more than 2,000 employees. Bazaar & Novelty employs over 570 people in Canada. Graduates most likely to be hired come from the following academic areas: Bachelor of Science (Computer Science), Bachelor of Engineering (Industrial Production), Bachelor of Commerce/Business Administration (Accounting, Finance, Human Resources, Marketing), Chartered Accountant and Community College Diploma (Accounting, Administration, Advertising, Business, Purchasing/Logistics, Graphic Arts, Electronics Technician). Company benefits are rated above average. The potential for advancement is listed as being good. The average annual starting salary depends upon the position being considered. The most suitable methods for initial contact by those seeking employment are to mail or fax a resume with a covering letter. *Contact:* Human Resources Manager.

BCT.TELUS COMMUNICATIONS INC.
3777 Kingsway, 6th Floor
Burnaby, BC V5H 3Z7

Tel.	604-432-4435
Fax	604-435-5530
Email	empcentre@bctel.com
Website	www.bctel.com

BCT.TELUS Communications Inc. is the second largest communications company in Canada delivering a full range of services to millions of people and thousands of businesses. In 1999, Telus Communications (Alberta) and BC Tel (British Columbia) merged to form the second largest communications company in Canada and is committed to an aggressive national growth strategy that will offer full service communications solutions to customers across Canada. BCT.TELUS Communications Inc. employs 25,000 employees, operates one of the most advanced high speed networks in the world, maintains more than 4.5 million access lines and has offices in more than 100 centres throughout British Columbia and Alberta. The company has recently acquired two operations which expand their operations into eastern Canada and Dallas, Texas offering advertising and internet solutions and services. Graduates most likely to be hired come from the following academic areas: Bachelor of Science (Computer Science), Bachelor of Engineering (Electrical, Computer Systems, Telecommunications) and Bachelor of Commerce/Business Administration (General, Accounting, Finance, Marketing). Graduates would occupy Clerk, Trainee, Technician and Customer Service positions. Possessing previous work experience in a related field is a definite asset. The most suitable method for initial contact by those seeking employment is to mail a resume with a covering letter. BCT.TELUS Communications Inc. does hire summer students. *Contact:* Employment Centre.

BDH INC.
350 Evans Avenue
Toronto, ON M8Z 1K5

Tel.	416-255-8521
Fax	416-255-5985
Website	www.bdhinc.com

BDH Inc. is a manufacturer and distributor of chemical and pharmaceutical products. The company employs approximately 120 people. Graduates most likely to be hired come from the following academic areas: Bachelor of Science (Chemistry, Microbiology), Certified Management Accountant and Community College Diploma (Business, Sciences). Graduates would occupy Laboratory Technician, Accounting Clerk and Customer Service Representative positions. Previous experience in this industry is listed as a definite asset. Company benefits are rated as excellent. The potential for advancement is listed as being good. The most suitable method for initial contact by graduates seeking employment is to mail a resume with a covering letter. BDH Inc. does hire summer and co-op

work term students. *Contact:* Human Resources Department.

BDO DUNWOODY
National Office
33rd floor, Royal Bank Plaza, PO Box 32
Toronto, ON M5J 2J8

Tel.	416-865-0200
Fax	416-367-3912
Email	swilliams@national.bdo.ca
Website	www.bdo.ca

BDO Dunwoody is a public accounting and business consulting firm. With 76 office locations across Canada, BDO ranks as the eighth largest firm in the country as well as a member of the tenth largest international firm. Activities include audit, accounting, tax, insolvency, corporate recovery, merger and acquisitions, valuations, mediation and arbitration, litigation support and forensic accounting. The firm employs approximately 800 employees across the country. Graduates most likely to be hired come from the following academic areas: Bachelor of Commerce/Business Administration (Accounting), Master of Business Administration (Accounting) and Community College Diploma (Accounting). Graduates would occupy C.A. Student, Accounting Technician and Insolvency Technician positions. Company benefits and the potential for advancement are both rated as excellent. The average annual salary for an entry level position falls within the $25,000 to $32,000 range. The most suitable method for initial contact by those seeking employment in any Toronto region office is to mail a resume with a covering letter to the Toronto office (check website/yellow/white pages for the nearest office location). BDO Dunwoody does hire third year students majoring in accounting for summer positions at some office locations. *Contact:* Gary Wasylow.

BEARDEN ENGINEERING CONSULTANTS LTD.
4646 Riverside Drive, Suite 1
Red Deer, AB T4N 6Y5

Tel.	403-343-6858
Fax	403-343-2122
Email	bearden@telusplanet.net

Bearden Engineering Consultants Ltd. is an engineering consulting firm. The firm employs apporoximately 12 people and is involved in the complete planning, design and detailing of commercial buildings, community centres, curling and ice arenas, churches and funeral homes, restaurant and lounges, office buildings, apartments and row housing, motels and hotels, warehouses and industrial buildings and custom homes. In addition, the company is also involved in structural analysis, design and inspection of new and existing buildings or structures, frames, trusses, cranes and industrial applications, preserved wood foundations and building science studies. Graduates most likely to be hired come from the following academic areas: Bachelor of Engineering (Civil, Architectural/Building), Master of Engineering (Project Management) and Community College Diploma (Accounting, Administration, Secretarial, Architecture/Drafting, CAD/CAM/Autocad, Engineering Technician). Engineering and Technical graduates would occupy Structural Engineer, Architectural Technologist, Project Manager and Inspector positions. Team player, wide interests and clear long-term goals are listed as desirable non-academic qualifications. Company benefits are rated as industry standard. The potential for advancement is listed as average. The average annual starting salary falls within the $25,000 to $45,000 range. The most suitable method for initial contact by those seeking employment is to mail a resume with a covering letter. Bearden Engineering Consultants Ltd. does hire summer students. *Contacts:* Terry Bearden, President or Steve Chow, Partner.

BEAVER FOODS
493 Dundas Street, PO Box 5644
London, ON N6B 1W4

Tel. 519-679-2661
Fax 519-679-5740
Email .... info@beaverfoods.com
Website .... www.beaverfoods.com

Beaver Foods is the largest Canadian-owned contract food service management company. The company is a wholly owned division of Cara Operations Ltd., and currently employs over 7,000 people in over 1,100 food service units across Canada. This location is the home office, and the company maintains 11 other office locations across Canada. Graduates most likely to be hired come from the following academic areas: Bachelor of Science (Computer Science), Certified General Accountant and Community College Diploma (Accounting, Cooking/Chef, Hospitality, CAD/CAM/Autocad, Information Systems). Graduates would be hired to occupy Level 1 Programmer Analyst Trainee, Level 1 I.C. Support Analyst Trainee, Level 1 Technical Support Analyst Trainee, Baker, District Accountant, Unit Manager Trainee, Unit Cook, Unit Chef, CAD Operator/Design Layout, Secretary and Data Entry Operator positions. The ability to work in a team environment, strong interpersonal and organizational skills, a degree of mobility, creative, adaptive and proactive are all listed as desirable non-academic qualifications. Company benefits and the potential for advancement are both rated as excellent. The average annual starting salary depends upon the position being considered and the applicant's field of study. The most suitable methods for initial contact by those seeking employment are to mail a resume with a covering letter, or by applying through the company's website. Beaver Foods does hire summer students, with the number varying from year to year. Co-op work term students are hired for Accounting and IT placements. *Contact:* John Hodgson, Director, Training and Development.

BECKMAN INSTRUMENTS (CANADA) INC.
6733 Mississauga Road, Suite 604
Mississauga, ON L5N 6J5

Tel. 905-819-1234
Fax 905-819-1208

Beckman Instruments (Canada) Inc. sells and services life sciences and diagnostic instrumentation to research laboratories and diagnostic laboratories. There are more than 50 people employed at this location. Graduates most likely to be hired come from the following academic areas: Bachelor of Science (Life Sciences - Chemistry, Biology, Physics), Bachelor of Engineering (Electrical), Master of Science (Chemistry, Biology) and Community College Diploma (Electronics Technician). Graduates would occupy Sales Representative, Customer Service Representative and Service Technician positions. Laboratory experience and experience in the selling of lab equipment are listed as desirable non-academic qualifications. Company benefits are rated above average. The most suitable method for initial contact by graduates seeking employment is to mail a resume with a covering let-

ter. Beckman Instruments (Canada) Inc. does hire summer students. *Contact:* Human Resources.

BELL CANADA
700, rue de la Gauchetiere Ouest, 11 Sud 1
Montreal, QC H3B 4L1

Website .... www.bell.ca

Bell Canada markets a world class portfolio of products and services to more than seven million business and residence customers in Ontario and Quebec. Bell is the largest telecommunications operating company in Canada. The skilled and committed Bell team is comprised of approximately 38,000 employees on a corporate mission to be a world leader in helping people communicate and manage information. Graduates most likely to be hired come from the following academic areas: Bachelor of Engineering (Civil, Electrical), Bachelor of Commerce/Business Administration (Accounting, Finance, Information Systems) and Master of Business Administration (Finance, Information Systems, Marketing). Graduates should possess a good academic record, a high level of initiative, good communication skills, demonstrated leadership in extra curricular activities or through job experiences, be able to excel in a competitive environment characterized by constant change, function effectively as a team player and focus on exceeding customers' needs and expectations. Typical permanent and contract positions in the Toronto, Montreal and Ottawa areas include Project Manager and Business Analyst positions. Bell offers a competitive benefits package, comprehensive employee development programs and exciting career opportunities. Accordingly, company benefits and the potential for advancement are both rated as excellent. The average annual starting salary falls within the $35,000 to $40,000 range. The most suitable methods for initial contact by those seeking employment are to mail or e-mail (addresses specified on job postings) a resume with a covering letter, or through on-campus recruitment initiatives (see your campus career centre for details). Bell Canada does hire summer and co-op work term students. Bell is an equal opportunity employer. *Contact:* Management Recruiting, Resume Processing Centre.

BELL MOBILITY
2920 Matheson Boulevard East, 8th Floor
Mississauga, ON L4W 5J4

Tel. 905-282-4499
Fax 905-282-3071
Email .... careers@mobility.com
Website .... www.bellmobility.ca

Bell Mobility provides a range of wireless communications - cellular, paging, data, satellite, PCS and airline passenger communications - to over 2 million Canadians. The company is a subsidiary of BCE Mobile Communications Inc. Graduates are hired from the following academic areas: Bachelor of Arts (General), Bachelor of Science (General), Bachelor of Engineering (RF Technology), Bachelor of Commerce/Business Administration (Accounting, Finance, Information Systems, Marketing) and Community College Diploma (Accounting, Administration, Advertising, Business, Communications, Marketing/Sales, Secretarial, Computer Science, Engineering Technician). Highly motivated, team spirited, results oriented and possessing a customer service orientation are all listed as desirable non-academic qualifications. Company benefits and the potential for advancement are both rated as excellent. The average annual starting salary is dependent upon the position being considered. The most suitable methods for initial contact by those seeking employment are to mail or fax a resume with a covering letter. *Contact:* Human Resources.

BENCHMARK TECHNOLOGIES INC.
1682 West 7th Avenue, Suite 310
Vancouver, BC V6J 4S6

Tel.	604-731-8584
Fax	604-738-8625
Email	brianh@benchtech.com
Website	www.benchtech.com

Benchmark Technologies Inc. develops custom software solutions for mostly Fortune 5000 sized companies. The company consults and advises clients on appropriate technology, coding standards, database selection (as well as modeling and administration), tools selections, and systems configuration. Benchmark employs a total of 25 people. Graduates most likely to be hired come from the following academic areas: Bachelor of Science (Computer Science, Mathematics), Bachelor of Engineering (Computer Systems), Bachelor of Commerce/Business Administration (General, Information Systems), Master of Business Administration (General, Information Systems) and Community College Diploma (Computer Science, Information Systems). Graduates would occupy Junior Programmer/Analyst, Junior Systems Analyst and Software Engineer positions. High intelligence, creativity, flexibility, team player, love for learning, quick learner and relevant work experience are all listed as desirable non-academic qualifications. Company benefits are rated above average. The potential for advancement is listed as being good. The average annual starting salary falls within the $35,000 to $40,000 range, depending upon the experience of the applicant and the position being considered. The most suitable method for initial contact by those seeking employment is to e-mail a resume with a covering letter. *Contacts:* Brian Haley, Managing Partner or Peter Humphrys, Managing Partner.

BEST WESTERN WHEELS INN
615 Richmond Street, P.O. Box 637
Chatham, ON N7M 5J7

Tel.	519-351-1100
Fax	519-436-5541
Website	www.wheelsinn.com

Best Western Wheels Inn provides hospitality, restaurant, fitness and entertainment facilities. There are approximately 420 employees at this location. Graduates most likely to be hired come from the following academic areas: Bachelor of Arts (General, Recreation), Bachelor of Science (General), Bachelor of Engineering (General, Mechanical), Certified General Accountant, Community College Diploma (Accounting, Administration, Advertising, Business, Facility Management, Human Resources, Marketing/Sales, Secretarial, Cooking, Hospitality, Travel/Tourism, Massage Therapy) and High School Diploma. Customer service skills, related work experience, team player, loyalty, dependable and a positive attitude are all listed as desirable non-academic qualifications. Company benefits are rated as industry standard. The potential for advancement is listed as being good. The average annual starting salary falls in the $15,000 plus range, depending upon the position being considered. The most suitable methods for initial contact by those seeking employment are to mail a resume with a covering letter, via telephone, or by appointment for network pur-

poses. Best Western Wheels Inn does hire summer students. *Contact:* Human Resources.

BEST-SELLER INC.
3300 Chemin de la Cote-vertu, Bureau 203
Saint-Laurent, QC H4R 2B7

Tel.	514-337-3000
Fax	514-337-9290
Email	career@BestSeller.com
Website	www.BestSeller.com

Best-Seller Inc. provides a full range of Year 2000 compliant turnkey library automation solutions. These include the company's flagship software, PortFolio and Best-Seller NT, a new generation of web-based products using the latest in client-server technology and NT servers. The company's products are popular with public, special and academic libraries throughout North America and France. In 1996, Best-Seller Inc. celebrated its tenth anniversary of installing systems in libraries. In addition to the company's main office in Montreal, Best-Seller Inc. has recently opened an office in France to serve its European customers. The company employs a total of 43 people. Graduates most likely to be hired come from the following academic areas: Bachelor of Science (Computer Science, Documentation Librarians), Bachelor of Engineering (Computer Systems), Bachelor of Commerce/Business Administration (Accounting, Finance, Information Systems) and Community College Diploma (Computer Science, Information Systems). Graduates would occupy Programmer, Librarian, Technical Support, Hardware Specialist and Accounting positions. A minimum of three years work experience is listed as desirable non-academic qualification. Company benefits and the potential for advancement are both rated as excellent. The average annual starting salary falls within the $30,000 to $35,000 range. The most suitable method for initial contact by those seeking employment is to e-mail a resume with a covering letter. *Contact:* career@bestseller.com.

BETHANY CARE SOCIETY
1001 - 17 Street NW
Calgary, AB T2N 2E5

Tel.	403-284-0161
Fax	403-284-1232
Email	bethany2@cadvision.com

Bethany Care Society provides innovative healthcare delivery, housing, and lifestyle services to seniors and persons with disabilities. The society's leadership strength is founded on a rich history in the community since 1947, and a philosophy of care that emphasizes wellness, choice and independence. Bethany Care Society employs over 1,000 people in its facilities throughout southern Alberta. Graduates most likely to be hired come from the following academic areas: Bachelor of Science (Nursing, Occupational Therapy, Pharmacy, Physiotherapy), Bachelor of Commerce/Business Administration (Human Resources) and Community College Diploma (Dietitian/Nutrition, Health/Home Care Aide, Nursing RN/RNA, Rehabilitation Therapy). Graduates would occupy various healthcare positions relating directly to their designated professions. Good problem solving skills, energetic, team player, self-motivated, excellent communication skills and a desire to make a positive difference in someone's life are all listed as desirable non-academic qualifications. Full time employees are offered a comprehensive benefits package that is competitive in the health care industry. The potential for advancement is rated as average. The most suitable methods for initial contact by those seeking employment are to mail, fax or e-mail a resume with a covering letter. Bethany Care Society does hire summer students. *Contact:* Michael Stuart, Manager of Employment.

BEVERTEC CST INC.
191 The West Mall, Suite 309
Toronto, ON M9C 5K8

Tel.	416-695-7525
Fax	416-695-7526
Email	resumes@bevertec.com
Website	www.bevertec.com

Bevertec CST Inc. develops and implements innovative software solutions for the financial services, manufacturing, communications and transportation sectors, as well as federal, provincial and municipal government agencies. The company focuses on three core areas: I.T. Consulting, Software Solutions and Training. Established in 1981, Bevertec CST Inc. is based in Toronto and serves clients in Canada, the US, South America and Asia. Graduates most likely to be hired come from the following academic areas: Bachelor of Science (Computer Science). Possessing two to three years previous work experience is listed as a desirable non-academic qualification. Company benefits and the potential for advancement are both rated as excellent. The most suitable method for initial contact by those seeking employment is to e-mail a resume with a covering letter. *Contact:* Human Resources.

BIC INC.
155 Oakdale Road
Toronto, ON M3N 3W2

Tel.	416-742-9173
Fax	416-741-4965
Email	mparenti@bic.ca
Website	www.bicworld.com

BIC Inc. is a leading manufacturer and distributor of writing instruments, lighters, and razors. There are 75 employees at this location, a total of 120 in Canada and 10,000 employees worldwide. Graduates most likely to be hired come from the following academic areas: Bachelor of Commerce/Business Administration (Accounting, Finance, Human Resources, Information Systems, Marketing), Chartered Accountant, Certified Management Accountant, Certified General Accountant and Community College Diploma (Accounting, Business, Human Resources, Marketing/Sales, Purchasing/Logistics, Secretarial, Engineering Technician). Graduates would occupy Clerk, Secretary, Computer Programmer, Trade Analyst, Product Manager, Cost Analyst, Customer Service Representative, Inventory/Purchasing, Account Manager and Accounts Payable/Receivable positions. Adaptable, creative, responsible, analytical, personable, enthusiastic, professional, customer service focussed, team players, "out-of-the-box" thinker, an aptitude to learn other languages and adaptability are all listed as desirable non-academic qualifications. Company benefits are listed as excellent. The potential for advancement is rated as average. The average annual starting salary for entry level positions falls within the $25,000 to $30,000 range. The most suitable method for initial contact by those seeking employment is to mail a resume with a covering letter. BIC Inc. does hire summer students and co-op work term students for positions in Human Resources, Marketing, and Information Systems. *Contact:* Monica Parenti, Human Resources Manager.

BIOMIRA INC.
2011 - 94th Street
Edmonton, AB T6N 1H1

Tel.	780-450-3761
Fax	780-463-0871
Email	hr@biomira.com
Website	www.biomira.com

Biomira Inc. is a biotechnology firm dedicated to the development and commercialization of products to benefit patients with cancer. Products in development for cancer management include blood tests, imaging agents, and innovative, non-toxic approaches to therapy. The company employs approximately 164 people at this location, and a total of 234 people in Canada. Graduates most likely to be hired come from the following academic areas: Bachelor of Science (Chemistry, Microbiology, Medical Laboratory Sciences, Immunology, Pharmacology), Bachelor of Engineering (Biotechnology), Master of Science (Chemistry, Microbiology, Immunology, Pharmacology), Master of Engineering (Biotechnology), Doctorate (Chemistry, Microbiology, Immunology, Pharmacology) and Community College Diploma (Biological Sciences - Lab Option). Graduates would occupy Technician, Research Scientis, and Bioprocess Engineer positions. Previous lab experience, able to work under direction, attention to detail and good communication skills are all listed as desirable non-academic qualifications. Company benefits are rated as excellent. The potential for advancement is listed as being good. The average annual starting salary depends upon the candidate. The most suitable method for initial contact by those seeking employment is to mail a resume with a covering letter. Biomira Inc. hires summer students, generally from the province of Alberta. *Contact:* Irene Watson, Senior Human Resources Advisor.

BIRKS JEWELLERS INC.
1240 Phillips Square
Montreal, QC H3B 3H4

Tel.	514-397-2511
Fax	514-397-2455
Email	attallaa@birks.com
Website	www.birks.com

Birks Jewellers Inc. has been a retail industry leader and a provider of high-end jewellery and luxury gift items for over a century. The company's aim is to offer its customers across Canada a superior quality of service and merchandise. Presently, the company has 200 employees at this location and a total of 1,000 employees at 37 stores across Canada, as well as through 8 corporate sales locations in Canada and the United States. Graduates most likely to be hired come from the following academic areas: Bachelor of Commerce/Business Administration (General, Accounting, Finance, Human Resources, Information Systems, Marketing), Community College Diploma (Accounting, Administration, Business, Human Resources, Marketing/Sales) and High School Diploma. Graduates would be hired as Trainees for Store Management positions and Sales Associate positions. Self motivated, enthusiastic, customer service driven, team player and good communication skills are all listed as desirable non-academic qualifications. The most suitable method for initial contact by those seeking employment is to mail a resume with a covering letter. Birks Jewellers Inc. does hire summer students. *Contacts:* Mrs. A. Attalla, Manager, Human Resources or Mrs. M. Borsellino, Administrative Assistant, Human Resources.

BIWAY, A DIVISION OF DYLEX LIMITED
637 Lakeshore Boulevard West, Suite 330
Toronto, ON M5V 3L6

Tel.	416-586-1212
Fax	416-586-6948
Website	www.dylex.com/home.htm

BiWay, a division of Dylex Limited is Canada's leading community discount retailer. BiWay employs approximately 5,000 people in stores located in Ontario, New Brunswick, Nova Scotia, Newfoundland, and Prince Edward Island. Graduates most likely to be hired should possess a High School Diploma, while some level of post-secondary education is preferred for Management positions. Graduates would occupy Management Trainee and Sales Associate positions. Excellent communication skills, dynamic, driven, dedicated, thrive on challenges, previous retail experience, including fashion retailing, and good organizational and problem solving skills are all listed as desirable non-academic qualifications. Company benefits are rated above average. The potential for advancement is listed as excellent. The average annual starting salary is dependent upon the experience of the applicant and the position being considered. The most suitable methods for initial contact by those seeking employment are to mail or fax a resume with a covering letter to the Recruiting Manager at the head office, or the Store Manager at the desired Store location (check yellow/white pages for location nearest you). *Contacts:* Recruiting Manager (head office) or Store Manager (store locations).

BLAKE, CASSELS & GRAYDON
Box 25, Commerce Court West
Toronto, ON M5L 1A9

Tel.	416-863-2400
Fax	416-863-2653
Email	sg@blakes.ca
Website	www.blakes.ca

Blake, Cassels & Graydon is one of the leading business law firms in Canada with over 360 lawyers in Vancouver, Calgary, Toronto, Ottawa, London and Beijing. The firm employs approximately 700 people at this location. Graduates most likely to be hired come from the following academic areas: Bachelor of Laws and Community College Diploma (Legal Secretary, Law Clerk). Graduates would occupy Associate, Legal Secretary, Law Clerk, Accounting and Computer Systems positions. Highly motivated, positive attitude and excellent communication skills are listed as desirable non-academic qualifications. Company benefits are rated above average. The potential for advancement is listed as being good. The average annual starting salary falls within the $20,000 to $25,000 range. The most suitable methods for initial contact by those seeking employment are to mail a resume with a covering letter, or via telephone. Blake, Cassels & Graydon does hire summer students for Secretarial, Reception and Clerical help positions. *Contact:* Sue Gagliardi, Recruitment Co-ordinator.

BLOORVIEW MACMILLAN CENTRE
25 Buchan Court
Toronto, ON M2J 4S9

Tel.	416-494-2222
Fax	416-494-9985
Email	humanresources@bloorviewmacmillan.on.ca
Website	www.bloorviewmacmillan.on.ca

The Bloorview MacMillan Centre (Bloorview Site) provides rehabilitation services for children and young adults with physical disabilities. Children and young adults are medically referred for in-patient or out-patient services. The Bloorview MacMillan Centre is Ontario's largest facility for young people with disabilities and special needs, specializing in family-centred rehabilitation and habilitation, advocacy, education and research. Graduates most likely to be hired come from the following academic areas: Bachelor of Arts (Recreation Studies), Bachelor Science (Nursing, Nutritional Sciences, Occupational Therapy, Pharmacy, Physical Therapy), Bachelor of Education (Early Childhood ECE), Bachelor of Commerce/Business Administration (Accounting, Finance, Human Resources, Information Systems), Certified Management Accountant, Certified General Accountant, Master of Business Administration (Finance, Human Resources), Master of Arts (Journalism) Master of Social Work, Master of Science (Nursing, Health Administration, Speech Pathology), Master of Library Science, Doctorate (Psychology) and Community College Diploma (Human Resources, Secretarial, Nursing RPN, Respiratory Therapy). The most suitable method for initial contact by those seeking employment is to mail a resume with a covering letter. *Contact:* Human Resources.

BLOORVIEW MACMILLAN CENTRE
350 Rumsey Road
Toronto, ON M4G 1R8

Tel.	416-425-6220
Fax	416-424-3868
Email	humanresources@bloorviewmacmillan.on.ca
Website	www.bloorviewmacmillan.on.ca

The Bloorview MacMillan Centre (MacMillan Site) provides rehabilitation services for children and young adults with physical disabilities. Children and young adults are medically referred for in-patient or out-patient services. The Bloorview MacMillan Centre is Ontario's largest facility for young people with disabilities and special needs, specializing in family-centred rehabilitation and habilitation, advocacy, education and research. The centre employs more than 250 people at this location. Graduates most likely to be hired come from the following academic areas: Bachelor of Arts (Social Work), Bachelor of Science (Physiotherapy, Psychology, Nursing RN, Occupational Therapy), Bachelor of Engineering (Mechanical, Electrical, Biomedical), Bachelor of Education, Chartered Accountant (Finance), Master of Social Work, Master of Science (Speech Pathology), Doctorate (Psychology) and Community College Diploma (Recreation, Nursing RN/RNA, Dental Assistant). Previous related work experience, reliability, dedication and sensitivity are all listed as desirable non-academic qualifications. Company benefits are rated above average. The potential for advancement is listed as average. The most suitable method for initial contact by those seeking employment is to mail a resume with a covering letter. The Bloorview MacMillan Centre does hire summer students for mostly recreation and pool positions. *Contact:* Human Resources.

BOEING TORONTO, LTD.
PO Box 6013, Toronto AMF, Airport Road
Mississauga, ON L5P 1B7

Tel.	905-677-4341
Fax	905-673-4303
Website	www.boeing.com

Boeing Toronto, Ltd. manufactures and assembles airplane wings. The company employs a total of 1,600 people at this location, while Boeing employs a total of 220,000 employees worldwide. Graduates most likely to be hired come from the following academic areas: Bachelor of Arts (Political Science, Psychology), Bachelor of Science (Metallurgy), Bachelor of Engineering (Mechanical, Aerospace, Computer Science, Industrial Design, Industrial Engineering, Industrial Production/Manufacturing), Bachelor of Commerce/Business Administration (Accounting, Finance, Human Resources, Information Systems), Chartered Accountant, Certified Management Accountant, Community College Diploma (Accounting, Business, Human Resources, Purchasing Logistics, Secretarial, Automotive Mechanic, Engineering Technician, Information Systems, Tool and Die, Machinist, Millwright, Welding, Nursing RN) and High School Diploma. Graduates would occupy Clerk, Technician, Engineering Design, Computer Programming, Industrial Engineering and Trouble Shooting positions. Good problem solving skills, process focus, team player and an ability to make decisions are all listed as desirable non-academic qualifications. Company benefits are rated above average. The potential for advancement is listed as average. The average annual starting salary falls within the $30,000 to $35,000 range. The most suitable methods for initial contact by those seeking employment are to mail or fax a resume with a covering letter. Boeing Toronto, Ltd. does hire summer and co-op work term students. *Contacts:* Judy Bis or Anna-Maria Andreucci.

BOILER INSPECTION & INSURANCE CO. OF CANADA, THE
18 King Street East
Toronto, ON M5C 1C4

Tel. 416-363-5491
Email .... hr@biico.com
Website .... www.biico.com

The Boiler Inspection & Insurance Co. of Canada is a specialized market leader in boiler and machinery insurance. Believing in the value added concept of engineering and technical expertise in insuring risks, the company underwrites, inspects, advises, engineers, adjudicates claims, and assists customers in preventing losses. There are 87 employees at this location, and a total of 210 employees in Canada. Graduates most likely to be hired come from the following academic areas: Bachelor of Engineering (Mechanical), Bachelor of Commerce/Business Administration and Community College Diploma (Insurance). Graduates would occupy Customer Service Representative, Marketing Representative, Inspection Trainee and Claims Trainee positions. Computer interest and literacy, a transferable skill set, maturity and dependability are all listed as desirable non-academic qualifications. Company benefits are rated as excellent. The potential for advancement is listed as being good. The most suitable method for initial contact by those seeking employment is to mail a resume with a covering letter. The Boiler Inspection & Insurance Co. of Canada does hire summer students. *Contact:* Teresa Tos, Director, Human Resources & Public Relations.

BOMBARDIER AEROSPACE
123 Garratt Blvd.
Toronto, ON M3K 1Y5

Tel. 416-633-7310
Fax 416-375-7629
Website .... www.bombardier.com

Bombardier Aerospace is a manufacturer of the world's highest performing executive jets. The company employs approximately 5,000 people at this location. Graduates most likely to be hired come from the following academic areas: Bachelor of Arts, Bachelor of Science, Bachelor of Engineering, Bachelor of Laws, Bachelor of Education, Bachelor of Commerce/Business Administration, Chartered Accountant, Master of Business Administration and Community College Diploma (General/Related). The most suitable method for initial contact by graduates seeking employment is to mail a resume with a covering letter. *Contact:* Employment Office.

BONAR INC.
2360 McDowell Road
Burlington, ON L7R 4A1

Tel. 905-637-5611
Fax 905-637-1066
Email .... pdraper@lowandbonar.com
Website .... www.lowandbonar.com

Bonar Inc. is a leading North American manufacturer of plastic film and bags, paper multiwall bags, poly coated paper (used in packaging and masking), folding cartons and rotationally molded rigid plastic products. Bonar and its wholly-owned subsidiaries operate plants in Canada and the United States. The company's customer base includes chemical processors, lawn and garden suppliers, food processing companies, the mining industry, the construction industry and insulation manufacturers. Bonar emphasizes customer satisfaction and service along with quality assurance through an ongoing commitment to the Quality Management Institute's ISO 9000 Programs. Bonar Inc. is a subsidiary of Dundee, Scotland based Low and Bonar PLC. There are approximately 300 employees at this location, 750 in Canada and a total of 1,200 employees in North America. Graduates most likely to be hired come from the following academic areas: Bachelor of Engineering (Pulp and Paper, Mechanical, Industrial Production), Bachelor of Commerce/Business Administration (Accounting, Finance, Marketing), Master of Business Administration (Accounting, Finance, Marketing) and Community College Diploma (Accounting, Administration, Business, Marketing/Sales). Graduates would occupy Engineer Technician (QC), Sales and Service Coordinator, Sales Representative, Sales Trainee, Accounting Clerk, Junior Accountant, Secretary and Production Control positions. Company benefits are rated above average. The potential for advancement is listed as being good. The average annual starting depends upon the position and the applicant's experience. The most suitable method for initial contact by those seeking employment is to mail a resume with a covering letter. Bonar Inc. does hire summer students at some locations. *Contact:* Human Resources.

BONUS RESOURCE SERVICES CORP.
7506 - 43 Street, Suite #1
Leduc, AB T9E 7E8

Tel. 780-986-3070
Fax 780-986-8810

Bonus Resource Services Corp. provides oil well services, including well workover's and completions. There are approximately 200 employees at this location, a total 1,000 in Canada and a total of 1,100 employees worldwide. Graduates most likely to be hired come from the following academic areas: Bachelor of Commerce/Business Administration (Accounting, Finance), Certified Management Accountant, Master of Business Administration (Accounting, Finance), Community College Diploma (Accounting, Human Resources, Marketing/Sales, Purchasing/Logistics, Secretarial, Auto Mechanic, Electronics Technician, Welding) and High School Diploma. Graduates would occupy Clerk, Middle Management and a variety of Support positions. Previous work experience, team player, self-motivated, flexible and a good attitude are all listed as desirable non-academic qualifications. Company benefits are rated as excellent. The potential for advancement is listed as being good. The most suitable methods for initial contact by those seeking employment are to mail or fax a resume with a covering letter. Bonus Resource Services Corp. occasionally hires summer students. *Contact:* Janice L. Escaravage, Manager Human Resources.

BOT CONSTRUCTION LIMITED
1224 Speers Road
Oakville, ON L6L 2X4

Tel.	905-827-4167
Fax	905-827-0458

Bot Construction Limited is active in heavy civil engineering construction and development projects. This includes bridges, roadways, sewers, watermains, and major rock and earth excavations. There are 17 employees at this location and a total of 300 employees in Ontario. Graduates most likely to be hired come from the following academic areas: Bachelor of Engineering (Civil) and Community College Diploma (Engineering Technician). Graduates would occupy Contracts Co-ordinator, Estimator, Project Administrator, Project Engineer and Project Manager positions. A proven, solid work ethic, good references and an ambition to learn are all listed as desirable non-academic qualifications. Company benefits are rated as industry standard. The potential for advancement is listed as being good. The average annual starting salary falls within the $30,000 to $35,000 range. The most suitable method for initial contact by those seeking employment is to mail a resume with a covering letter. Bot Construction Limited does hire summer students. *Contact:* Human Resources.

BOWLERAMA LIMITED
28 Cecil Street
Toronto, ON M5T 1N3

Tel.	416-979-2142
Fax	416-979-0119
Website	www.bowlerama.com

Bowlerama Limited operates 17 bowling centres in southern Ontario, including 8 in Toronto. There are 15 Bowlerama employees at its head office with 125 permanent employees in the bowling centres. The company also employs approximately 300 part-time workers during the bowling season. Operational activities include bowling sales and services. Post-secondary education is not required for employment application. Graduates and non-graduates would apply for bowling centre Manager and Assistant Manager positions. The most suitable method for initial contact by graduates and non-graduates seeking employment is to mail a resume with a covering letter. Bowlerama Limited does hire summer students. *Contacts:* Harry Fine, Vice President or Ali Qureshi, Vice President, Finance.

BRAEMAR
637 Lakeshore Boulevard West
Toronto, ON M5V 3J7

Tel.	416-586-7475
Fax	416-586-7087
Website	www.braemar.com

Braemar is a retailer of ladies' clothing. In addition to the company's head office at this address, Braemar employs a total of 1,200 people across Canada in retail operations. Braemar is a division of Dylex Limited. Graduates most likely to be hired come from the following academic areas: Bachelor of Arts (General), Bachelor of Commerce/Business Administration (General, Accounting, Marketing, Public Administration) and Community College Diploma (Administration, Advertising, Business, Communications, Human Resources, Marketing/Sales, Hospitality). Graduates would occupy Administrative, Store Management, Financial, Sales Associates and Planning/Merchandise Assistant positions. Team oriented, initiative, enthusiastic, good communication skills, receptive to change, thorough, retail experience, computer skills and good leadership skills (for management positions) are all listed as desirable non-academic qualifications. Company benefits are rated above average. The potential for advancement is listed as excellent. The average annual starting salary falls within the $20,000 to $30,000 range. The most suitable method for initial contact by those seeking employment is to mail a resume with a covering letter. *Contact:* Christine Leskovar, Human Resources Co-ordinator.

BRANDON UNIVERSITY
270 - 18th Street
Room 337, Clark Hall/Original Building
Brandon, MB R7A 6A9

Tel.	204-728-9520
Fax	204-726-4573
Website	www.brandonu.ca

Brandon University, located in Manitoba's second largest city, provides quality post-secondary education. With an academic history reaching back 100 years, Brandon University received its own charter in 1967 and today has an enrollment of 2,650 students, a faculty of 170 and a total staff compliment of 400. Graduates most likely to be hired come from the following academic areas: Bachelor of Arts (General, Criminology, Economics, English, French, Geography, History, Journalism, Languages, Music, Philosophy, Political Science, Psychology, Recreation Studies, Sociology), Bachelor of Science (General, Biology, Chemistry, Computer Science, Geology, Geography, Mathematics, Physics, Zoology, Nursing, Psychology), Bachelor of Education (General, Early Childhood, Primary Junior, Junior Intermediate, Intermediate Senior, Physical/Health), Bachelor of Commerce/Business Administration, Chartered Accountant, Certified Management Accountant, Certified General Accountant, Master of Business Administration, Master of Arts, Master of Science, Master of Health Science, Doctorate and Community College Diploma (Business). Depending upon academic background and experience, graduates would occupy Lecturer, Assistant Professor, Professional Associate, Administrative Associate, Instructional Associate, Library Assistant, Technician, Computer Programmer and Accounting positions. Relevant work experience, particularly in an academic environment is a definite asset. Company benefits are rated above average. The potential for advancement is listed as being good. The average annual starting salary falls within the $30,000 to $35,000 range. The most suitable method for initial contact by those seeking employment is to mail a resume with a covering letter. Brandon University does hire summer students. *Contacts:* Mrs. Barbara M. Smith, Director, Human Resources or Mrs. Brenda Bull, Assistant, Human Resources.

BREWERS RETAIL INC.
1 City Centre Drive, Suite 1700
Mississauga, ON L5B 4A6

Tel.	905-949-0429
Fax	905-277-7533

Brewers Retail Inc. operates 440 Beer Store retail outlets and commercial delivery depots throughout Ontario. There are approximately 130 employees at this location and a total of 6,000 employees across the province. Graduates most likely to be hired come from the following academic areas: Bachelor of Arts (General, Economics, Urban Geography/Planning), Bachelor of Science (Computer Science), Bachelor of Commerce/Business Administration and Community College Diploma (Accounting, Administration, Advertising, Business, Human Resources, Marketing/Sales, Secretarial, Computer Science). Graduates would be hired to occupy a limited number of clerk or trainee positions in one of the company's field operations offices, located in major cities across Ontario, with the opportunity to become Store Manager within approximately two to three years from starting. A positive attitude, good work ethic, management potential and strong interpersonal skills are all listed as desirable non-academic qualifications. Company benefits are rated above average. The potential for advancement is listed as average. The most suitable methods for initial contact by graduates seeking employment are to mail or fax a resume with a covering letter. Brewers Retail Inc. does hire part-time staff in retail stores throughout the province. *Contact:* Recruiting & Personnel Services.

BRIGGS & STRATTON CANADA INC.
301 Ambassador Drive
Mississauga, ON L5T 2J3

Tel.	905-795-2632
Fax	905-795-8768
Website	briggsandstratton.com

Briggs & Stratton Canada Inc. is involved in the distribution of small engines and small engine parts. Briggs & Stratton Canada Inc. is a subsidiary of Milwaukee, Wisconsin based Briggs & Stratton Corporation. Briggs & Stratton Corporation is the world's largest producer of air-cooled gasoline engines for outdoor power equipment. The company designs, manufactures, markets and services these engines for original equipment manufacturers worldwide. Briggs & Stratton engines are incorporated into products for both the consumer market and industrial/commercial applications. Briggs & Stratton Canada Inc. employs approximately 35 people. Graduates most likely to be hired come from the following academic areas: Bachelor of Commerce/Business Administration (Accounting, Marketing), Chartered Accountant (Finance), Certified Management Accountant (Finance) and Community College Diploma (Accounting, Business, Marketing/Sales, Purchasing/Logistics, Secretarial). Graduates would occupy Accounting, Sales, Clerical and Secretarial positions. Good interpersonal and communication skills and hands-on mechanical abilities are listed as desirable non-academic qualifications. Company benefits are rated as excellent. The average annual starting salary falls within the $25,000 to $30,000 range. The most suitable method for initial contact by graduates seeking employment is to mail a resume with a covering letter. Briggs & Stratton Canada Inc. does hire summer students. *Contact:* Controller.

BRISTOL AEROSPACE LIMITED
PO Box 874
Winnipeg, MB R3C 2S4

Tel.	204-775-8331
Fax	204-774-0195
Email	balhr@bristol.ca
Website	www.bristol.ca

Bristol Aerospace Limited has over a half century of experience in design, development and manufacturing for the world aerospace community. The company is a leading Canadian and western Canada's largest aerospace company operating its 700,000 square foot plant and aircraft hangars in Winnipeg. Thirty kilometres north, Bristol operates Canada's only solid fuel propellant plant, the Rockwood facility. The company specializes in precision manufacture of aeroengine and aerostructure components and subsystems, offers a comprehensive range of repair and overhaul services for aircraft and components, participates in space science research through the provision of sounding rockets, payloads, and small satellites, and produces defence equipment such as air-to-ground rockets, booster motors and target training systems. Bristol Aerospace Limited is a subsidiary of Mississauga, Ontario based Magellan Aerospace Corporation. Graduates most likely to be hired come from the following academic areas: Bachelor of Science (Metallurgy), Bachelor of Engineering (Metallurgy, Electrical, Mechanical, Aerospace), Bachelor of Commerce/Business Administration (Finance), Chartered Accountant, Certified General Accountant and Community College Diploma (Aircraft Maintenance, Engineering Technician). Graduates would occupy Accounting Clerk, Design Engineer, Metallurgy Engineer, Electrical Engineer, Avionics Engineer, Production Planner, Avionics Technician/Mechanic, Aircraft Technician/Mechanic and Engineering Technologist positions. Company benefits are rated as excellent. The potential for advancement is listed as being good. The most suitable method for initial contact by those seeking employment is to mail a resume with a covering letter. *Contact:* Human Resources Department.

BRITISH COLUMBIA INSTITUTE OF TECHNOLOGY / BCIT
3700 Willingdon Avenue
Burnaby, BC V5G 3H2

Tel.	604-432-8384
Fax	604-434-8462
Email	hrassist@bcit.bc.ca
Website	www.bcit.bc.ca

British Columbia Institute of Technology / BCIT is a postsecondary institution offering a wide variety of career programs from pre-apprenticeship to degree levels. The institute employs approximately 1,500 people. Program profiles include Vocational Trades, Business, Computing and Academic Studies, Construction, Electrical and Electronic Technology, Health Sciences, Manufacturing, Mechanical and Industrial Technologies; Processing, Energy and Natural Resources; and Transportation. Graduates are hired from a broad range of academic disciplines for managerial and supervisory, instructional, instructional support, technical and administrative support and international opportunities. Remaining current with trends in particular industry, team player, flexible and excellent interpersonal, communication and leadership skills are all listed as desirable non-academic skills. Company benefits are rated as excellent. The potential for advancement is listed as being good. The average annual starting salary falls within the $25,000 to $60,000 plus range, depending on the position being considered. The most suitable methods for initial contact by those seeking employment are to mail, fax or e-mail a resume with a covering letter, by applying in person, or through the institute's website. BCIT is an equal opportunity employer and invites applications from all qualified men and women, persons with disabilities, aboriginals and members of visible minority groups. The institute does hire summer students. *Contact:* Human Resources.

BURGER KING RESTAURANTS OF CANADA INC.
401 The West Mall, 7th Floor
Toronto, ON M9C 5J4

Tel. 416-626-6464
Fax 416-626-6696
Website .... www.burgerking.com

Burger King Restaurants of Canada Inc. operates fast food restaurants throughout Canada. Each location employs approximately 40 people, including 3 managers per restaurant. Burger King seeks qualified candidates for Restaurant Management positions, which involve the following responsibilities: cost control, administration, training, food quality control, communications and scheduling. Graduates most likely to be hired come from the following academic areas: Bachelor of Arts (General), Bachelor of Commerce/Business Administration (Accounting, Finance, Human Resources, Information Systems, Marketing, Public Administration), Community College Diploma (Cooking, Hospitality) and High School Diploma. Applicants should possess experience in retail or the food industry, preferably in a management capacity. Company benefits are rated above average. The potential for advancement is listed as excellent. The average annual starting salary is dependent upon the position being considered, and the experience and education of the applicant. The most suitable method for initial contact by graduates seeking employment is to mail a resume with a covering letter to this address. Burger King Restaurants of Canada Inc. does hire summer students for general restaurant help only (contact individual Restaurant Manager). *Contacts:* Chantal Gignac, Regional Human Resources Manager or Brenda Marlowe, Regional Human Resources Manager.

BURGESS WHOLESALE LTD.
1172 Davis Drive
Newmarket, ON L3Y 4X7

Tel. 905-853-6544
Fax 905-853-5682
Website .... www.burgesswholesale.com/burgess.htm

Burgess Wholesale Ltd. is a food service distributor. The company sells directly to restaurants, hospitals and various institutional clients. Burgess maintains three state-of-the art facilities in Ontario, a modern fleet with multiple temperature controlled trucks, the latest in computer technology and over 5,000 of the most highly demanded products for the Ontario foodservice industry. A Division Of Sobey's Inc., Burgess Wholesale Ltd. provides a one-stop-shop opportunity for operators across Ontario. Burgess employs approximately 200 people at this location and a total of 400 people in Canada. Graduates most likely to be hired come from the following academic areas: Bachelor of Commerce/Business Administration (Finance, Human Resources, Information Systems, Marketing) and Community College Diploma (Business, Marketing/Sales, Purchasing/Logistics, Hospitality). Graduates would be hired to occupy entry level positions in Sales, Purchasing, Finance and Administration, Warehouse and Delivery, Information Systems and Human Resources. Ambition, solid work ethic, positive attitude,

and a willingness to offer long term commitment through advancement and relocation are all listed as desirable non-academic qualifications. Company benefits and the potential for advancement are both rated as excellent. The average annual starting salary falls within the $20,000 to $25,000 range. The most suitable method for initial contact by those seeking employment is to mail a resume with a covering letter. Burgess Wholesale Ltd. does hire summer students. *Contact:* Human Resources Manager.

BUSINESS DEPOT LTD.
30 Centurian Drive, Suite 106
Markham, ON L3R 8B9

Tel. 905-513-6116
Fax 905-513-7194
Email .... corpjobs@busdep.com
Website .... www.business-depot.com

Business Depot Ltd. is one of Canada's fastest growing retailers, operating 133 locations from coast to coast. In partnership with its parent company Staples, the company has 900 stores and is growing. In 1999 Business Depot Canada opened a new store every two weeks. Business Depot's first store was opened in 1991 in Concord, Ontario, and since then it has become Canada's leading retailer in office supply products, employing over 6,000 people. Store locations average 30,000 square feet, carry over 7,000 brand name products, and are conveniently located in high traffic areas. Graduates most likely to be hired come from the following academic areas: Bachelor of Arts (General, Economics, Political Science, Psychology, Recreation Studies, Sociology/Social Work), Bachelor of Engineering (Computer Systems), Bachelor of Commerce/Business Administration (General, Accounting, Finance, Human Resources, Information Systems, Marketing, Public Administration, Hospitality), Chartered Accountant, Certified Management Accountant, Certified General Accountant and Community College Diploma (Accounting, Administration, Advertising, Business, Communications/Public Administration, Facility Management, Human Resources, Information Systems, Marketing/Sales, Recreation Studies, Travel/Tourism). Graduates would occupy Executive Assistant, Category Specialist, Junior Technical Systems Analyst, Help Desk Support, Entry Level Human Resource, Graphic Artist, Programmer/Analyst, CAD Operator and Management positions. Retail or service related experience, team player, goal oriented, self-starter, quick learner, energetic, entrepreneurial spirit, leadership and excellent communication skills are all listed as desirable non-academic qualifications. With projected growth of 20 stores per year, Business Depot offers current and future associates excellent opportunities for personal and professional growth. Associates would utilize their management skills almost immediately, have the option to travel in Canada, apply their education and enhance their skills. Career positions offer an attractive and competitive compensation (the average annual starting salary falls within the $25,000 to $30,000 range, plus bonus) and benefits package. The most suitable methods for initial contact by those seeking employment are to mail, fax or e-mail a resume with a covering letter, quoting reference number CD-002. Business Depot Ltd. does hire co-op work term students. *Contacts:* Christine Arruda - Store Management Positions (carruda@busdep.com) or Joanne Taylor - Home Office Positions (corpjobs@busdep.com).

C-FER TECHNOLOGIES INC.
200 Karl Clark Road
Edmonton, AB T6N 1H2

Tel.	780-450-3300
Fax	780-450-3700
Email	d.zurawell@cfertech.com
Website	www.cfertech.com

C-FER Technologies Inc. has developed new technologies and processes for applications in the energy industry. These innovations have reduced costs, increased revenues, reduced risk, increased safety, and extended the life of wells and equipment in the field. The company holds patents and intellectual property rights to dozens of products and processes, including revolutionary Downhole Oil/Water Separation technology, PC-PUMP software, PIRAMID software and more. C-FER offers engineering expertise from the ground up, including project management, engineering economics, experimental design, risk and reliability engineering, limit states design, failure analysis/structural testing, investigative engineering, software development, computer modeling, solid mechanics, materials engineering and prototype design and manufacture. C-FER's world class laboratory services offer a powerful combination of testing and analysis tools designed to accommodate a vast range of research and testing requirements. With extensive review and development, testing and refining, the company has the know how to make solutions work in the real world. In business for over 15 years, C-FER employs 46 full-time and 10 part-time (summer, contract, co-op) employees at this location. The company also maintains an office location in Calgary. Graduates most likely to be hired come from the following academic areas: Bachelor of Science (Computer Science), Bachelor of Engineering (Civil, Electrical, Mechanical), Bachelor of Commerce/Business Administration (Accounting, Finance, Human Resources, Information Systems, Marketing), Master of Engineering, Doctorate of Engineering and Community College Diploma (Accounting, Business, Human Resources, Marketing/Sales, Secretarial, Electronics Technician, Engineering Technician). Graduates would occupy Engineer, Marketing, Salesperson, Secretary, Software Developer, Technologist, Accountant, and Human Resource positions. Team player, self-motivated, initiative and excellent communication skills are all listed as desirable non-academic qualifications. Company benefits are rated as excellent. The potential for advancement is listed as average. The average annual starting salary is dependent upon the position being considered. The most suitable method for initial contact by those seeking employment is to mail a resume with a covering letter. C-FER Technologies Inc. does hire co-op work term students. High School graduates are hired for summer positions, usually only one student per summer season. *Contact:* Diane Zurawell, Human Resources.

CAA INSURANCE COMPANY, ONTARIO
60 Commerce Valley Drive East
Thornhill, ON L3T 7P9

Tel.	905-221-4300
Fax	905-771-3447
Website	www.central.on.caa.ca

CAA Insurance Company, Ontario is one of Canada's leaders in automobile, insurance and travel related services. CAA's operations are carried out through three main operational areas, including the auto club, travel agency, and the insurance company. There are more than 100 employees at this location. Post-secondary education is not listed as a prerequisite for employment application.

Most entry-level positions are clerical and customer service in nature, requiring good customer service skills, knowledge of the city and a basic knowledge of North American geography. Company benefits are rated as excellent. The potential for advancement is listed as average. The average annual starting salary falls within the $15,000 to $20,000 range. The most suitable method for initial contact regarding employment opportunities is to mail a resume with a covering letter. CAA Insurance Company, Ontario does employ summer students to work from May to September. *Contact:* Recruiter.

CADABRA
1 Antares Drive, Suite 300
Nepean, ON K2E 8C4

Tel.	613-266-7046
Fax	613-226-5276
Email	hrmgr@cadabradesign.com
Website	www.cadabradesign.com

Cadabra is a leader in the development of physical synthesis tools, stretching the boundaries of automated design. Graduates working in the company's Research and Development Group, develop state of the art IC design automation tools. These graduates have experience in UNIX, C++, object oriented design methodologies, and in developing user friendly, intuitive GUI's. Graduates working with the company's Customer Team, design custom IC solutions and perform architectural optimization analysis on customer driven programs. In addition, these graduates participate in core product development, are lead users providing direct input into the tool design, aid customers in developing custom cell libraries, act as the front line in customer support, provide a liaison between customers and Cadabra, and actively participate in defining the product feature set. Graduates most likely to be hired come from the following academic areas: Bachelor of Science (Computer Science, Combinatories & Optimization, Mathematics) and Bachelor of Engineering (Electrical, Computer Systems, Systems Design, Engineering Physics). Graduates would occupy Software Designer/Developer and Applications Engineer positions. Fast, smart, flexible, an ability to drive creative solutions to complex engineering problems, and strong technical and interpersonal skills are all listed as desirable non-academic qualifications. The most suitable methods for initial contact by those seeking employment are to mail or e-mail a resume with a covering letter. Cadabra does hire summer and co-op work term students. *Contact:* Human Resources Manager.

CADILLAC FAIRVIEW CORPORATION LTD., THE
20 Queen Street West, 5th Floor
Toronto, ON M5H 3R4

Tel.	416-598-8200
Fax	416-598-8578
Email	staffing@cadillacfairview.com
Website	www.cadillacfairview.com

The Cadillac Fairview Corporation Limited is one of Canada's premier owners and operators of commercial real estate properties. Employed at this location are more than 250 people involved in the development of new projects through all phases of planning, financing, construction, leasing and management of completed properties. Graduates most likely to be hired come from the following academic areas: Bachelor of Arts (General, Economics, Urban Geography), Bachelor of Science (General, Computer Science, Mathematics), Bachelor of Commerce/Business Administration (Accounting, Finance, Marketing), Certified Management Accountant (Finance), Certified General Accountant (Finance), Master of Business Administration (Accounting, Finance, Marketing, Information Systems) and Community College Diploma (Architecture/Drafting, Computer Science, HVAC Systems). A positive attitude, team player and possessing related background experience are all listed as desirable non-academic qualifications. Graduates would occupy entry level clerk, analyst positions, etc. Company benefits and the potential for advancement are both rated as excellent. The most suitable method for initial contact by those seeking employment is to mail a resume with a covering letter identifying the type of position being sought. The Cadillac Fairview Corporation Limited does hire a limited number of summer students annually (approximately 6 to 12 students). *Contact:* Susan Henderson, Recruitment Coordinator, Personnel/Human Resources.

CAE ELECTRONICS LTD.
8585 Cote de Liesse, PO Box 1800
St-Laurent, QC H4L 4X4

Tel.	514-341-6780
Fax	514-340-5335
Email	hr@cae.ca
Website	www.cae.ca

CAE Electronics Ltd. is one of the world's leading advanced technology companies and one of Canada's foremost scientific systems and software enterprises. CAE applies sophisticated real-time computer based technology to large complex simulation, training, control and monitoring tasks across a broad spectrum of civil and military aviation, hydro and thermal power generation, transmission and distribution, air traffic management, maritime operations, space exploration and submarine detection systems. Founded in 1947, there are 3,600 employees at this location, a total of 4,000 in Canada and approximately 6,000 employees worldwide. Graduates most likely to be hired come from the following academic areas: Bachelor of Arts (Languages), Bachelor of Science (Mathematics, Physics), Bachelor of Engineering (Chemical, Electrical, Automation/Robotics, Computer Systems, Power, Telecommunications, Mechanical, Aeronautical, Marine), Bachelor of Commerce/Business Administration (Accounting, Finance, Human Resources, Information Systems, Marketing), Chartered Accountant, Certified Management Accountant, Certified General Accountant, Master of Business Administration (Accounting, Finance, Human Resources, Information Systems, Marketing), Master of Science, Master of Engineering, Community College Diploma (Accounting, Administration, Business, Marketing/Sales, Secretarial, Aircraft Maintenance, CAD/CAM/Autocad, Computer Science, Electronics, Engineering, HVAC Systems, Marine Engineering) and High School Diploma. Good communication skills, a willingness to learn, adaptability, flexibility, team player, innovative and creative are all listed as desirable non-academic qualifications. Company benefits are rated as excellent. The potential for advancement is listed as being good. The average annual starting salary falls within the $30,000 to $35,000 range. The most suitable methods for initial contact by those seeking employment are to mail, fax or e-mail a resume with a covering letter. CAE Electronics Ltd. does hire summer students. *Contacts:* Human Resources or Aurora Pietianiro, Group Leader.

CAE NEWNES
3550 - 45th Street SE, PO Box 8
Salmon Arm, BC V1E 4N2

Tel.	250-832-7116
Fax	250-804-4015
Email	dwight.guy@caenewnes.com
Website	www.caenewnes.com

CAE Newnes, a division of CAE Electronics Ltd., is North America's leading manufacturer of state-of-the-art, fully automated sawmill equipment. CAE Newnes employs over 500 skilled employees. Graduates most likely to be hired come from the following academic areas: Bachelor of Engineering (Electrical, Mechanical), Chartered Accountant, Certified General Accountant, Community College Diploma (Electronics Technician, Engineering Technician, Information Systems) and High School Diploma. Graduates would occupy Electrical Engineer, Mechanical Engineer, Technician and Technologist positions. Team player, a good attitude, conscientious and adaptable are all listed as desirable non-academic qualifications. Company benefits are rated above average. The potential for advancement is listed as being good. The average annual starting salary falls within the $35,000 to $40,000 range. The most suitable methods for initial contact by those seeking employment are to mail, fax or e-mail a resume with a covering letter. CAE Newnes does hire summer and co-op work term students. *Contact:* Valerie Worobec.

CALGARY BOARD OF EDUCATION, THE
515 Macleod Trail SE
Calgary, AB T2G 2L9

Tel.	403-294-8100
Fax	403-294-8333
Website	www.cbe.ab.ca

The Calgary Board of Education operates one of the largest school systems in Canada. The board is the second largest employer in the City of Calgary, employing over 9,000 staff and operating 219 schools. Graduates most likely to be hired come from the following academic areas: Bachelor of Arts (Journalism, Psychology), Bachelor of Science (Computer Science), Bachelor of Education (Early Childhood, Primary Junior, Junior Intermediate, Intermediate Senior) and Master of Business Administration (Finance). Graduates would occupy Teacher, Administrator, Computer Technology, Communications, Psychologist, Accountant, etc. positions. Company benefits are rated above average. The potential for advancement is listed as being good. The average annual starting salary falls within the $25,000 to $30,000 range. The most suitable method for initial contact by those seeking employment is to mail a resume with a covering letter. The Calgary Board of Education does hire summer students. *Contact:* Duncan Truscott, Superintendent, Employee Services.

CALGARY CENTRE FOR PERFORMING ARTS, THE
205 - 8th Avenue SE
Calgary, AB T2G 0K9

Tel.	403-294-7455
Fax	403-294-7457

The Calgary Centre for Performing Arts is an arts centre with a concert hall, four theatres, banquet and retail space. The company administrates the building, and operates as the landlord to the other resident companies. The centre's operations are divided into the following departments: Executive, Facility Management, Stage Production, Reception/Security, and Public Information and Programming. The centre employs 34 full-time and 100 part-time employees. Graduates most likely to be hired come from the following areas: Bachelor of Arts (General,

Criminology, Economics, English, Journalism, Languages, Music), Bachelor of Science (General, Computer Science), Bachelor of Engineering (General, Computer Systems), Bachelor of Commerce/Business Administration (Accounting, Finance, Marketing, Information Systems, Public Administration), Chartered Accountant, Certified Management Accountant, Master of Business Administration (Accounting, Finance, Marketing, Information Systems, Public Administration) and Community College Diploma (Accounting, Administration, Advertising, Business, Communications, Facility Management, Financial Planning, Human Resources, Marketing, Secretarial, Engineering Technician, HVAC Systems). Applicants would be considered for Director of Facilities, Director of Programming, Controller, Accounting Clerk, Stage Technician, Administrative Assistant, Front of House Coordinator, Building Operating Engineer, Utility Person, Catering Sales, Catering Coordinator, Communications Manager and Contract Administrator positions. Team player, a love of the arts and three to five years work experience are listed as desirable non-academic qualifications. Company benefits are rated as excellent. The potential for advancement is listed as average. The average annual starting salary falls within the $20,000 to $25,000 range. The most suitable method for initial contact by those seeking employment is to mail a resume with a covering letter. *Contact:* Cheryl Craiggs, Vice President, Finance Department.

CAMBIOR INC.
800, boul René-Levesque Ouest, Bureau 850
Montreal, QC H3B 1X9

Tel. 514-878-3166
Fax 514-878-0635
Email .... info@cambior.com
Website .... www.cambior.com

Cambior Inc. is an international diversified gold producer with operations, advanced development projects, and exploration activities in both North and South America. The company has more than 2,300 full time employees. Cambior hires university and college graduates with a Degree or Diploma in Science and Engineering (Mining, Geology, Metallurgy, Industrial Production, Instrumentation, Environment and Pollution Treatment), Commerce and Business Administration (Accounting, Finance, Human Resources and Actuarial Sciences) and Corporate and International Law. Successful candidates occupy positions as engineers, geologists, technicians, legal advisors and supervisors. Previous work experience, team player and dedication are listed as desirable non-academic qualifications. The average annual starting salary ranges between $35,000 and $40,000. Company benefits and the potential for advancement are considered excellent. Graduates interested in seeking permanent employment with the company should mail a resume or curriculum vitae and a covering letter to the Human Resources Department. Cambior Inc. also hires summer students. *Contact:* Roxanne Hugron.

CAMBRIDGE MEMORIAL HOSPITAL
700 Coronation Boulevard
Cambridge, ON N1R 3G2

Tel. 519-740-4920
Fax 519-740-4907
Website .... www.advertech.net/cmhf

Cambridge Memorial Hospital is a full-service, community based hospital providing primary and secondary health care, as well as offering acute and chronic care, full-time pre-hospital and emergency services, and a variety of ambulatory programs. The hospital assists in educational programs for employees and medical staff, and contributes to the education of health care providers through direct affiliations and indirect relationships with educational institutions. The hospital also participates in research that contributes to improved health and health care services, and contributes to health planning at the local, regional, provincial and national levels. The Cambridge Memorial Hospital employs approximately 1,200 people. Graduates most likely to be hired come from the following academic areas: Bachelor of Science (Nursing, Nutritional Sciences, Occupational Therapy, Pharmacy, Physical Therapy, Speech Pathology), Bachelor of Engineering (Biomedical Electronics) and Community College Diploma (Human Resources, Social Work, Dietician, Emergency Technician, Laboratory Technician, Nuclear Medicine Technician, Nursing RN/RNA, Radiology Technician, Respiratory Therapy, Ultrasound Technician). Company benefits are rated above average. The potential for advancement is listed as average. The average annual starting salary varies depending on the position being considered. The most suitable methods for initial contact by those seeking employment are to mail a resume with a covering letter, or via telephone. Cambridge Memorial Hospital does hire summer students. *Contact:* Human Resources.

CAMECO CORPORATION
2121 - 11th Street West
Saskatoon, SK S7M 1J3

Tel. 306-956-6400
Fax 306-956-6539
Email .... scott_tuttle@cameco.com
Website .... www.cameco.com

Cameco Corporation is the world's largest publicly traded uranium company and a growing gold producer. There are 250 employees at this location, a total of 1,450 employees in Canada and a total of 1,800 employees worldwide. Cameco operates and owns two-thirds of the world's two largest, high-grade uranium mines at Key Lake and Rabbit Lake in northern Saskatchewan. The company also obtains a share of production from the Crow Butte mine in Nebraska, and recently purchased about three-quarters of the Wyoming based, Highland operation. Cameco also maintains a controlling interest in both McArthur River and Cigar Lake, the two largest uranium projects under development in the world, located in northern Saskatchewan. The company also has refining and conversion plants in Ontario, at Blind River and Port Hope respectively. In addition, the company also mines gold in Saskatchewan as well as operates and owns one-third of the Kumtor gold project located in Kyrgyzstan in Central Asia. Graduates most likely to be hired come from the following academic areas: Bachelor of Science (Chemistry, Computer Science, Environmental, Geology, Metallurgy, Nursing), Bachelor of Engineering (Chemical, Industrial Chemistry, Metallurgy, Automation, Computer Systems, Instrumentation, Industrial Design, Fish/Wildlife, Mining, Water Resources), Bachelor of Commerce/Business Administration (Accounting, Finance, Human Resources, Information Systems, Marketing), Chartered Accountant, Certified Management Accountant, Certified General Accountant, Master of Business Administration (General, Finance), Master of Science (Chemistry), Master of Engineering (Chemical, Mechanical, Mining), Community College Diploma (Accounting, CAD/CAM/Autocad, Computer Science, Electronics, Engineering, Chemical Technician, Safety and Radiation Technician, Welding) and High School Diploma. Team player, adaptability, self-starter, previous work experience, adaptability, and good communication, problem-solving, decision making and leadership skills are all listed as desirable non-academic qualifications. Company benefits are rated as excellent. The potential for advancement is listed as being good. The most suitable method for initial contact for those seeking employment is to mail a resume with a covering letter. Cameco Corporation does hire summer students. *Contact:* Scott Tuttle, Supervisor, Staffing & Recruitment.

CAMI AUTOMOTIVE INC.
300 Ingersoll Street
Ingersoll, ON N5C 4A6

Tel.	519-485-6400
Fax	519-425-3100
Email	careers@cami.ca
Website	www.cami.ca

CAMI Automotive Inc. is a high volume, automotive manufacturing facility producing sub-compact cars and sport-utility vehicles for the worldwide market. Vehicle models produced include the Suzuki Swift, Pontiac FireFly, Chevrolet Metro, Suzuki Vitara and Chevrolet Tracker. CAMI is a joint venture between the Suzuki Motor Corporation and General Motors of Canada Ltd., and is a fast paced, team oriented full production operation comprised of stamping, welding, paint and assembly departments. Graduates most likely to be hired come from the following academic areas: Bachelor of Science (Computer Science), Bachelor of Engineering (Chemical, Electrical, Mechanical, Industrial Engineering), Bachelor of Commerce/Business Administration (Finance), Chartered Accountant, Certified Management Accountant, Certified General Accountant and Community College Diploma (Materials Management, Architectural Technician, Computer Science). Graduates would occupy Production Engineer positions in the Stamping, Assembly, Welding and Paint departments, as well as Finance, Material Planner and Production Systems Control positions. Excellent interpersonal, communication and organizational skills, self-motivated and good problem solving skills are all listed as desirable non-academic qualifications. Company benefits and the potential for advancement are both rated as excellent. The average annual starting salary is dependent upon the level of position and the experience of the candidate. The most suitable methods for initial contact by those seeking employment are to mail, fax or e-mail a resume with a covering letter. CAMI Automotive Inc. does hire co-op work term students. *Contact:* Staff Recruitment Team.

CAMPBELL SOUP COMPANY LIMITED
60 Birmingham Street
Toronto, ON M8V 2B8

Tel.	416-251-1131
Fax	416-253-8641
Website	www.campbellsoup.ca

Campbell Soup Company Limited is involved in the processing and marketing of food products. There are over 500 employees at this location. Graduates most likely to be hired come from the following academic areas: Bachelor of Science (General, Chemistry, Computer Science, Microbiology), Bachelor of Engineering (Civil, Industrial), Bachelor of Commerce/Business Administration (Finance, Marketing), Chartered Accountant and Master of Business Administration (Marketing). Graduates would occupy Marketing Assistant, Research Assist-

ant (Research and Development), Accountant, Computer Programmer and Systems Analyst positions. A compatibility with the organization, creative, personable, innovative, ambitious, team oriented and a high level of initiative are all listed as desirable non-academic qualifications. Company benefits are rated above average. The potential for advancement is listed as excellent. The average annual starting salary falls within the $35,000 plus range. The most suitable methods for initial contact by those seeking employment are to mail a resume with a covering letter, or via telephone. Campbell Soup Company Limited does hire summer students, depending upon the current need of the company. *Contact:* Human Resources.

CANADA 3000 AIRLINES LIMITED
27 Fasken Drive
Toronto, ON M9W 1K6

Tel.	416-674-0257
Fax	416-674-7225
Website	www.canada3000.com

Canada 3000 Airlines Limited provides reliable, affordable, air travel based on the needs of the leisure traveller. Founded in Toronto in 1988, the airline now has operating bases from coast to coast in all of Canada's major cities. Since its inception, Canada 3000 has demonstrated a steady growth and built a solid reputation, in both Canada and the many overseas markets in which it serves. The Airline employs 2,000 people worldwide. Graduates most likely to be hired come from the following academic areas: Bachelor of Commerce/Business Administration (General, Accounting, Finance) and Community College Diploma (Accounting, Information Systems, Marketing/Sales, Hospitality, Travel/Tourism, Aircraft Maintenance, Engineering Technician). Graduates would occupy Junior Clerk, Intermediate Accountant, Administrator, Sales Assistant, Reservation Sales Agent, Passenger Service Agent, Flight Attendant, Aircraft Maintenance Engineer/Technician and Information Systems Analyst positions. Motivated, task oriented, committed, flexible, travel familiarity and work experience are all listed as desirable non-academic qualifications. Company benefits are rated above average. The potential for advancement is listed as being good. The average annual starting salary falls within the $20,000 to $25,000 range. The most suitable method for initial contact by those seeking employment is to mail a resume with a covering letter. *Contact:* Director, Human Resources.

CANADA LIFE ASSURANCE COMPANY, THE
330 University Avenue
Toronto, ON M5G 1R8

Tel.	416-597-1456
Fax	416-597-3892
Email	hr@canadalife.com
Website	www.canadalife.com

The Canada Life Assurance Company, with assets of over $23 Billion, is ranked among the top four insurance companies in Canada. The company has operations in the United States, Ireland, Great Britain and Canada. Canada Life also has a number of subsidiaries that specialize in specific product lines, such as INDAGO Investments, Canada Life Casualty Insurance Company, Canada Life Mortgage Services and Adason Properties. Leadership and people are the foundation of Canada Life's strategic plan of bold growth and expansion. The corporate culture is characterized by the fact that Canada Life is a learning organization and a performance driven organization. There are 1,700 employees at this location, 2,300 employees in Canada and a total of 5,000 employees worldwide. Graduates most likely to be hired come from the following academic areas: Bachelor of Arts (General), Bachelor of Science (General, Actuarial, Computer Science, Nursing, Occupational Therapy), Bachelor of Engineering (Computer Science), Bachelor of Commerce/Business Administration (General), Chartered Accountant, Master of Business Administration (Accounting, Finance, Investments) and Community College Diploma (Accounting, Administration, Business, Human Resources, Information Systems, Insurance, Secretarial, Legal Assistant, Computer Science, Dental Assistant, Dental Hygiene, Nursing RN/RNA). Graduates would occupy Actuarial Student, Portfolio Management Trainee, Health/Dental Claims Analyst, Pension Administration Clerk, Business Analyst, Underwriter, Programmer/Analyst and Auditor positions. Integrity, partnership, customer commitment, leadership skills, continuous learning, entrepreneurial and community involvement are all listed as desirable non-academic qualifications. Company benefits and the potential for advancement are both rated as excellent. The most suitable method for initial contact by those seeking employment is to mail a resume with a covering letter. The Canada Life Assurance Company does hire summer and co-op work term students. *Contact:* Human Resources Department.

CANADA MARKET RESEARCH LIMITED
1255 Bay Street, Suite 600
Toronto, ON M5R 2A9

Tel. 416-964-9222
Fax 416-964-3937

Canada Market Research Limited provides social research, marketing and advertising services to both the private and public sector. There are over 25 employees at this location. Post-secondary graduates are hired, but they are hired only on a part-time basis as Market Research Interviewers. As Market Research Interviewers graduates work by telephone, door-to-door or through scheduled interviews with business executives. Applicants should possess a strong command of the English language, pleasant voice and an outgoing personality. All work is hourly paid, with rates varying. The majority of the work is in the evenings and on weekends. The most suitable method for initial contact by those seeking employment is to mail a resume with a covering letter. *Contact:* Fieldwork Director.

CANADA POST CORPORATION
1 Dundas Street West, Suite 700
Toronto, ON M5G 2L5

Tel. 416-204-4441
Fax 416-204-4115
Website .... www.canadapost.ca

Canada Post Corporation is a crown corporation in business to serve all Canadians, businesses and organizations through the secure delivery of letters and parcels to all addresses in Canada and around the world. In meeting this need, 30 million Canadians and more than 900,000 businesses and public institutions are served through one of the most sophisticated mail processing and distribution systems in the world. Each year, Canada Post and its subsidiary Purolator Courier Limited are entrusted with 9 billion messages and parcels. These materials are processed through 22 major plants and many other facilities for delivery to over 12.7 million addresses in Canada. There are more than 20,000 retail points of purchase where customers can access postal services. In addition to being a key player in Canada's vital communications market, Canada Post is a major contributor to the national economy. It is ranked 32nd among Canadian businesses in terms of consolidated revenue and is the fifth largest employer in the country employing more than 63,000 people on a full and part-time basis. Graduates most likely to be hired come from the following academic areas: Bachelor of Engineering (Industrial), Bachelor of Commerce/Business Administration (Accounting, Finance, Human Resources, Marketing), Chartered Accountant, Certified Management Accountant, Certified General Accountant, Master of Business Administration (Accounting, Finance, Human Resources, Marketing), Community College Diploma (Administration, Business, Human Resources, Marketing/Sales, Secretarial, Legal Assistant) and High School Diploma. Graduates would occupy Engineer, Technician, Mechanic, Human Resource, Finance etc. positions. Company benefits are rated above average. The potential for advancement is listed as being good. The average annual starting salary falls within the $25,000 to $30,000 range. The most suitable method for initial contact by graduates seeking employment is to mail a resume with a covering letter. Canada Post Corporation does hire summer students. *Contact:* Staffing Officer, Employee Relations.

CANADA TRUST
275 Dundas Street, 17th Floor
London, ON N6A 4S4

Tel. 519-663-1977
Fax 519-667-3581
Website .... www.canadatrust.com

Canada Trust is one of the nation's largest financial institutions providing a broad range of personal and independent business financial solutions in Canada. Canada Trust's comprehensive services include deposit-taking, lending, mutual funds, financial planning, investment management and counsel, brokerage and insurance. With its head office in London, Ontario and executive offices and corporate operations in both London and Toronto, Canada Trust employs more than 14,000 people serving millions of Canadians through a coast-to-coast branch network. Graduates most likely to be hired come from the following academic areas: Bachelor of Arts (Journalism), Bachelor of Science (Computer Science, Mathematics), Bachelor of Commerce/Business Administration (Accounting, Finance), Chartered Accountant, Certified Management Accountant, Certified General Accountant and Community College Diploma (Accounting, Business, Data Processing, Computer Science). Commitment, teamwork, service orientation, and strong communication and interpersonal skills are all listed as desirable non-academic qualifications. Company benefits and the potential for advancement are both rated as excellent. The average annual starting salary is dependent upon the position being considered. The most suitable method for initial contact by graduates seeking employment is to mail a resume with a covering letter. *Contacts:* Personnel (Head Office Positions - Fax & Phone Above) or Southwestern Ontario Region Office (Branch Positions).

CANADIAN AIRLINES

6001 Grant McConachie Way, Maildrop YVR0284
Richmond, BC V7B 1K3

Tel.	416-207-0247
Fax	604-270-5848
Email	employment@cdnair.ca
Website	www.cdnair.ca

Canadian Airlines is Canada's second largest airline, serving five continents. Together with their "Oneworld Alliance Partners", Canadian Airlines provides business and pleasure travel, airfreight shipments and cargo services to over 600 destinations. Over 16,000 people are employed at locations in Vancouver, Toronto and Calgary (head office), with support offices in most Canadian cities. Graduates most likely to be hired come from the following academic areas: Bachelor of Commerce/Business Administration, Master of Business Administration (General, Finance, Marketing) and Community College Diploma (Accounting, Secretarial, Travel/Tourism, Marketing/Sales, Aircraft/Vehicle Mechanic). Graduates would occupy Customer Service Agent, Sales and Marketing Representative, Engineer, Technician (Avionics), Clerical and Secretarial positions and a wide spectrum of Supervisory and Management positions. Flexible, dependable and excellent interpersonal skills are listed as desirable non-academic qualifications. Company benefits are rated as excellent. The potential for advancement is listed as being good. The average annual starting salary for unionized part time positions falls within the $15,000 to $25,000 range. Management starting salaries fall within the $30,000 to $37,000 range. The most suitable method for initial contact by graduates seeking employment is to contact the company's automated Employment Information Line at (416) 207-0247, or mail a resume with a covering letter to the Vancouver Office, quoting the competition of interest. Please note that Canadian Airlines uses an automated resume tracking system, and for this reason the resume format used should be simple and content specific. *Contact:* Employment Services.

CANADIAN ARMED FORCES

National Defence Headquarters
Ottawa, ON K1A 0K2

Tel.	613-992-6259
Fax	613-995-0786
Website	www.dnd.ca

The Canadian Armed Forces is Canada's military service. The forces employ a total of 76,000 people. The Canadian Armed Forces employs University and Community College graduates from the complete academic spectrum, as well as employing those with a High School Diploma. Specific employment will depend on educational qualifications and other factors as determined during recruitment processing. Applicants may discuss, without obligation, individual particulars with staff at the nearest recruiting centre. Employment opportunities include the following: uniformed personnel of the Canadian Armed Forces, entry level and skilled entry level positions, and part-time employment with the Reserve Force. Employee benefits are rated above average. The potential for advancement is listed as being good. The most suitable methods for initial contact by those interested in a career with The Canadian Armed Forces are to visit, call, write or e-mail the local Canadian Forces Recruiting Centre (listed in the Yellow Pages under recruiting or through the website). *Contact:* Canadian Forces Recruiting Centre.

CANADIAN CENTRE FOR OCCUPATIONAL HEALTH & SAFETY, THE

250 Main Street East
Hamilton, ON L8N 1H6

Tel.	905-572-2981
Fax	905-572-4419
Email	custserv@ccohs.ca
Website	www.ccohs.ca

The Canadian Centre for Occupational Health & Safety is the national resource for occupational health and safety information. The centre operates a worldwide electronic service as well as an inquiries service. There are 72 full time staff and three term staff. Graduates most likely to be hired come from the following academic areas: Bachelor of Science (Biology, Chemistry, Computer Science, Ergonomics, Toxicology), Bachelor of Engineering (Computer Systems, Industrial Chemistry), Certified Management Accountant, Certified General Accountant, Master of Business Administration (Accounting, Information Systems, Marketing), Master of Science, Master of Engineering, Community College Diploma (Accounting, Marketing/Sales, Office Administration, Secretarial, Graphic Arts, Computer Science, Information Systems) and High School Diploma. Graduates would occupy Programmer, Analyst, System Analyst, Technical Illustrator, Scientist/Subject Specialist, Marketing Officer, Technical Specialist, Information Specialist, Data Entry Technician, Clerk and Secretarial positions. Work experience, project management experience, attentive to details, team player, flexible, and excellent interpersonal, communication and organizational skills are all listed as desirable non-academic qualifications. Company benefits are rated above average. The potential for advancement is listed as average. The average annual starting salary falls within the $30,000 to $35,000 range. The most suitable methods for initial contact by those seeking employment are to mail, fax or e-mail a resume with a covering letter. The Canadian Centre for Occupational Health & Safety hires summer students on a limited basis. *Contacts:* Louise Henderson, Manager, Human Resources or Lynn Walker, Human Resources Officer.

CANADIAN DEPOSITORY FOR SECURITIES LIMITED / CDS

85 Richmond Street West
Toronto, ON M5H 2C9

Tel.	416-365-8400
Fax	416-365-0758
Email	ashields@cds.ca
Website	www.cds.ca

Canadian Depository for Securities Limited / CDS provides securities clearing and depository services for domestic and international financial markets. The services provided include, clearing, custody and settlement of transactions. There are over 300 employees at this location and a total of 500 employees in Canada. Graduates most likely to be hired come from the following areas: Bachelor of Arts (Economics), Bachelor of Science (Computer Science), Bachelor of Commerce/Business Administration (Finance), Chartered Accountant, Certified Management Accountant and Community College Diploma (Finance, Business, Secretarial). The types of positions vary, most are clerical and analytical in nature. Outgoing, self motivated, able to work effectively within a team or project environment and knowledge of spreadsheet, word processing and database applications are all listed as desirable non-academic qualifications. Company benefits are rated as excellent. The potential for advancement is listed as being good. The average annual starting salary falls within the $25,000 to $30,000 range. The most suitable methods for initial contact by graduates seeking employment are to mail, fax or e-mail a resume with a covering letter. The Canadian Depository For Securities Ltd. does hire summer and co-op work term students. *Contact:* Anne Shields, Manager, Human Resources Development.

CANADIAN FREIGHTWAYS LIMITED
4041A - 6th Street, PO Box 1108, Station T
Calgary, AB T2H 2J1

Tel. 403-287-1090
Fax 403-287-4343

Canadian Freightways Limited is a federally regulated freight transportation company, normally a less than truckload (LTL) carrier. In addition, the company provides logistic solutions for cross border transportation and customs clearance. There are 90 employees at the head office location in Calgary and a total of 900 employees across western Canada. Graduates most likely to be hired come from the following academic areas: Bachelor of Arts (General), Bachelor of Science (Computer Science), Bachelor of Commerce/Business Administration (Accounting, Human Resources, Marketing, Operations Management, Transportation and Logistics), Certified Management Accountant, Certified General Accountant, Community College Diploma (Accounting, Administration, Business, Human Resources, Marketing/Sales, Purchasing/Logistics, Secretarial) and High School Diploma. Graduates would occupy Technician, Computer Operator, Management/Information Systems Trainee, Sales/Marketing and Operations Trainee positions. Previous summer work experience, good organizational and planning skills, time management skills, team player and good communication skills are all listed as desirable non-academic qualifications. Company benefits are rated above average. The potential for advancement is listed as excellent. The average annual starting salary falls within the $35,000 to $38,000 range, depending upon the position being considered. The most suitable method for initial contact by those seeking employment is to mail a resume with a covering letter. Canadian Freightways Limited does hire co-op and summer students. Summer students are hired primarily for unionized dock operation positions. *Contacts:* Bruce Ogilvie, Manager, Human Resource Services; Ken Czech, Director, Human Resource Services or Gerry Paik, Service Centre Manager.

CANADIAN HEARING SOCIETY, THE
271 Spadina Road
Toronto, ON M5R 2V3

Tel. 416-928-2515
Fax 416-928-2517
Email .... jobs@chs.ca
Website .... www.chs.ca

The Canadian Hearing Society is a non-profit organization providing services and counselling for deaf, deafened and hard of hearing individuals and their families. The society also provides products and support services to these individuals. There are approximately 100 employees at this location and a total of 300 employees in Ontario. Graduates most likely to be hired come from the following academic areas: Bachelor of Arts (Psychology, Social Work), Bachelor of Science (Audiology, Psychology, Speech Pathology), Bachelor of Commerce/

Business Administration (Human Resources, Information Systems, Marketing), Community College Diploma (Office Administration, Secretarial, Social Work, Information Systems, Hearing Instrument Dispenser) and High School Diploma. Graduates would occupy General Social Services Counsellor, Employment Counsellor, Sign Language Interpreter, Audiologist, Speech Therapist and Hearing Instrument Dispenser positions. Fluency in American Sign Language (ASL), or a willingness to learn is required. In addition, computer skills, team player and an awareness of deaf culture are all listed as desirable non-academic qualifications. Company benefits are rated as industry standard. The potential for advancement is listed as average. The average annual starting salary falls within the $25,000 to $35,000 range, depending upon the position being considered. The most suitable methods for initial contact by those seeking employment are to mail, fax or e-mail a resume with a covering letter, stating the area of employment or the position being sought. Applicants may also view current vacancies online on the society's website. The Canadian Hearing Society does hire summer and co-op work term students, as government funding permits. *Contact:* Human Resources.

CANADIAN MEDICAL LABORATORIES LTD.
1644 Aimco Boulevard
Mississauga, ON L4W 1V1

Tel. 905-624-0440
Fax 905-629-1831
Website .... www.canmedlab.com

Canadian Medical Laboratories Ltd. provides physicians, hospitals, and long-term care facilities with diagnostic laboratory capabilities. The company consists of a network of laboratories serving the city of Toronto and the Golden Horseshoe area of Ontario. Since its beginning in 1976, Canadian Medical Laboratories has expanded to offer a wide range of specialized services for the medical professions. Today, the company offers diverse consulting capabilities in such areas as diagnostics, medical computer systems, and medical building development. Graduates most likely to be hired come from the following academic areas: Bachelor of Science (Chemistry, Microbiology) and Community College Diploma (Laboratory Technician). Graduates would occupy Registered Technologist, Laboratory Technician and Laboratory Assistant positions. Good communication skills, a sense of business maturity, an ability to take on responsibility, and a familiarity with mainframe terminals and personal computers are all listed as desirable non-academic qualifications. Company benefits are rated above average. The potential for advancement is listed as average. The average annual starting salary at the new graduate level for a Laboratory Assistant or Technician falls within the $20,000 to $25,000 range. The most suitable method for initial contact by those seeking employment is to mail a resume with a covering letter. Canadian Medical Laboratories does hire summer students (typically these are required "work assignments" necessary to graduate, 5 to 10 work days). *Contact:* Human Resources.

CANADIAN MEMORIAL CHIROPRACTIC COLLEGE
1900 Bayview Avenue
Toronto, ON M4G 3E6

Tel. 416-482-2340
Fax 416-482-9745
Email .... tgeorgas@cmcc.ca
Website .... www.cmcc.ca

Canadian Memorial Chiropractic College is a charitable, not-for-profit educational institution. Their mission is to advance the art, science and philosophy of chiropractic medicine. The college educates chiropractors to further the development of the chiropractic profession, and to improve the health of the society as a whole. The college employs approximately 180 employees, both full and part-time faculty and administrative staff. Faculty most likely to be hired will have a related health sciences background and are a Doctor of Chiropractic, with a minimum of five years experience. Applicants applying for positions in the areas of accounting and administration must have related experience, and strong interpersonal and communication skills. Benefits and the potential for advancement are both rated as excellent. The average annual starting salary varies depending upon the position being considered. The most suitable method for initial contact by those seeking employment is to mail a resume with a covering letter. Students enrolled at Canadian Memorial Chiropractic College are selected for summer job opportunities when available. *Contact:* Susan Sanderson, Director, Human Resources.

CANADIAN NATIONAL INSTITUTE FOR THE BLIND / CNIB

1929 Bayview Avenue
Toronto, ON M4G 3E8

Tel. 416-486-2500
Fax 416-480-7699
Website .... www.cnib.org

The Canadian National Institute for the Blind / CNIB is a non-profit organization providing services to blind, visually impaired and deaf / blind individuals. This includes low vision assessment, rehabilitation teaching, mobility training, and vocational assessment and teaching. There are approximately 200 employees at this location and over 1,200 employees across Canada. Graduates most likely to be hired come from the following academic areas: Bachelor of Arts (General, Gerontology, Psychology), Bachelor of Science (Nursing RN), Bachelor of Education (Special Needs Education), Bachelor of Commerce/Business Administration (Accounting, Human Resources), Community College Diploma (Accounting, Human Resources, Secretarial, Nursing, Orientation and Mobility Rehabilitation) and High School Diploma. Graduates would occupy Rehabilitation Teacher, Low Vision Nurse, Orientation and Mobility Instructor, Deaf-Blind Intervener, Clerical, Secretarial, Accounting and Management positions. Two to five years work experience (preferably in the not-for-profit sector), team player, detail oriented and empathetic to disabled individuals are all listed as desirable non-academic qualifications. Company benefits are rated above average. The potential for advancement is listed as being good. The average annual starting salary falls within the $25,000 to $30,000 range. The most suitable method for initial contact by those seeking employment is to mail a resume with a covering letter. The CNIB does hire summer students. *Contact:* Fran Gard, Human Resources.

CANADIAN OCCIDENTAL PETROLEUM LTD.

635 - 8th Avenue SW, Suite 1500
Calgary, AB T2P 3Z1

Tel. 403-234-6700
Fax 403-234-1050
Email .... hr_staffing@cdnoxy.com
Website .... www.cdnoxy.com

Canadian Occidental Petroleum Ltd. (COPL/

CanadianOxy) is a global oil and gas exploration and production company. The company is also a low cost producer and marketer of industrial bleaching chemical products in North America. CanadianOxy's diversified business interests are managed through a number of wholly owned subsidiaries. These are as follows: Wascana Energy (manages Canadian oil and gas assets and operations), Canadian Petroleum Ltd. (manages international oil and gas assets and activities), CXY Chemical (manufactures and markets chemical products in Canada and the United States), CXY Energy (manages U.S. oil and gas assets and operations), CXY Energy Marketing (Canadian, U.S., and international marketing activities of oil and gas products). The corporate functions that support CanadianOxy as a whole are based in Calgary, Alberta. These include Human Resources, Procurement, Security, Legal, Corporate Affairs, Environment, Health and Safety, Investor Relations, and Finance and Treasury. There is often operational representation of these functions within the subsidiaries with policies and procedures established corporately. CanadianOxy employs 745 people at this location, a total of 1,532 in Canada, and a total of 1,710 employees worldwide. Graduates most likely to be hired come from the following academic areas: Bachelor of Arts (Economics), Bachelor of Science (Computer Science, Geology), Bachelor of Engineering (General, Civil, Mechanical, Computer Systems, Geological Engineering), Bachelor of Commerce/Business Administration (General, Accounting, Finance, Human Resources), Chartered Accountant, Certified Management Accountant, Certified General Accountant, Master of Business Administration (General, Accounting, Finance, Human Resources) and Community College Diploma (Accounting, Administration, Business, Human Resources, Information Systems, Legal Assistant, Computer Science). Graduates would occupy Analyst, Clerk, Junior Accountant, Engineer, Geologist, Geophysicist, Legal Administrator Assistant, Administrative Assistant and Computer Operator positions. Adaptable to change, excellent interpersonal and communication skills, team player, culturally sensitive, and an understanding of the oil and gas business are all listed as desirable non-academic qualifications. Company benefits are rated as excellent. The potential for advancement is listed as being good. The average annual starting salary falls within the $35,000 to $40,000 range, and varies depending on discipline. Initial contact is best made by mailing, faxing or e-mailing a resume with a cover letter, or via the company's website. CanadianOxy does hire summer and co-op students. *Contacts:* Staffing & Corporate Resources (Domestic) or International Human Resources (International).

CANADIAN PACIFIC HOTELS

1 University Avenue, Suite 1400
Toronto, ON M5J 2P1

Tel. 416-367-7111
Fax 416-367-8226
Email .... pciccia@cor.cphotels.ca
Website .... www.cphotels.com

Canadian Pacific Hotels is the largest owner-operated hotel company in Canada and one of the leading hotel companies in the world. Founded in 1886, the company operates full service hotels, offering accommodation, food and beverage, banquet and conference facilities, and recreational facilities in the company's resort properties. Canadian Pacific operates 27 distinctive hotels and resorts from coast to coast in Canada, from Victoria to St John's and 7 luxury resorts in the United States, Mexico, Bermuda and Barbados. In addition, the company is the largest single owner-operator of golf resorts in Canada and one of the leading owners of golf resorts in the world with 16 golf courses in 5 countries. Canadian Pacific Hotels employs a total of 15,000 people. Graduates most likely to be hired come from the following academic areas: Bachelor of Arts (English), Bachelor of Science (Forestry), Bachelor of Commerce/Business Administration (Accounting, Finance, Human Resources, Information Systems, Marketing, Public Administration), Chartered Accountant, Certified Management Accountant, Certified General Accountant, Master of Business Administration (Accounting, Finance, Human Resources, Information Systems, Marketing, Public Administration), Community College Diploma (Accounting, Administration, Business, Communications, Human Resources, Marketing/Sales, Purchasing/Logistics, Secretarial, Cooking, Hospitality, Security/Enforcement, Travel/Tourism, HVAC Systems, Massage Therapy) and High School Diploma. Graduates would occupy Front Office Clerk, Accounting Clerk, Cook, Server, Massage Therapist, Room Attendant and Concierge positions. Strong interpersonal and problem solving skills, empathy, intuition, and good verbal and written communication skills are all listed as desirable non-academic qualifications. Company benefits are rated as excellent. The potential for advancement is listed as being good. The average annual starting salary falls within the $20,000 to $25,000 range. The most suitable method for initial contact by those seeking employment is to mail a resume with a covering letter. Canadian Pacific Hotels does hire summer students. *Contacts:* Supervisor, Human Resources (Corporate Office) or Human Resources Department (Individual Property Locations).

CANADIAN THERMOS PRODUCTS INC.
2040 Eglinton Avenue East
Toronto, ON M1L 2M8

Tel. 416-757-6231
Fax 416-757-6230
Website .... www.thermos.com

Canadian Thermos Products Inc. manufactures and distributes miscellaneous plastic food storage products. Canadian Thermos Products Inc. is a subsidiary of the Thermos Group headquartered in Schaumburg, Illinois. Established in 1904, the Thermos Group is the world's leading manufacturer of portable insulated food and beverage containers. Product lines include Thermos brand and Thermos Nissan brand steel vacuumware, glass vacuumware, foam insulated travel tumblers, foam insulated hard and soft coolers and jugs and licensed children's lunch kits. Activities at Canadian Thermos Products Inc. include accounting, maintenance, marketing and sales, data processing, and shipping and receiving. There are more than 100 employees at this location. Graduates most likely to be hired come from the following academic areas: Bachelor of Science (Chemistry, Computer Science), Bachelor of Engineering (Chemical, Robotics), Bachelor of Commerce/Business Administration (Accounting, Finance, Human Resources, Marketing), Chartered Accountant and Community College Diploma (Accounting, Business, Marketing/Sales, CAD/CAM/Autocad, Computer Science). Initiative, excellent communication skills, team player and team building skills are all listed as desirable non-academic qualifications. Company benefits are rated above average. The potential for advancement is listed as average. The average annual starting salary falls within the $25,000 to $30,000 range. The most suitable method for initial contact by graduates seeking employment is to mail a resume with a covering letter. Canadian Thermos Products Inc. does hire summer students. *Contact:* Janice Cameron, Human Resources Manager.

CANBRA FOODS LTD.
2415 - 2nd A Avenue N, PO Box 99
Lethbridge, AB T1J 3Y4

Tel. 403-329-5573
Fax 403-328-7933
Email .... canbra@canola.com
Website .... www.canola.com

Canbra Foods Ltd. is a fully integrated canola processing plant. Activities range from seed procurement, to refining, to packaging of both edible and non-edible products. There are more than 300 employees at this location. Graduates most likely to be hired come from the following academic areas: Bachelor of Science (Chemistry), Bachelor of Engineering (Industrial, Mechanical), Bachelor of Commerce/Business Administration (Finance), Certified Management Accountant, Certified General Accountant and Community College Diploma (Accounting, Human Resources, Architecture/Drafting, Engineering, Industrial Design, Mechanic). Graduates would occupy Engineering Manager, Q.C. Manager, Operations Manager, Package Products Manager, Draftsperson, Maintenance Supervisor, Human Resources Assistant, Accounts Payable Manager and Accounts Receivable Manager positions. Company benefits are rated above average. The potential for advancement is listed as being good. The average annual starting salary falls within the $35,000 to $40,000 range. The most suitable method for initial contact by those seeking employment is to mail a resume with a covering letter. *Contacts:* Keith L. Beerling, Vice President, Human Resources & Corporate Secretary or Jason T. Elliott, Supervisor, Human Resources.

CANGENE CORPORATION
104 Chancellor Matheson Road
Winnipeg, MB R3T 5Y3

Tel. 204-989-6895
Fax 204-269-7003
Website .... www.cangene.ca

Cangene Corporation is a world leader in the development, manufacture and distribution of specialty hyperimmune plasma and biotechnology products. Cangene's research collaborations and marketing efforts span the globe. The company has over 160 employees, with manufacturing and research facilities across Canada. Graduates most likely to be hired come from the following academic areas: Bachelor of Science (Biology, Chemistry, Computer Science, Microbiology, Immunology, Nursing, Pharmacy), Bachelor of Engineering (Chemical, Biotechnology, Industrial Chemistry, Biomedical Electronics, Computer Systems), Bachelor of Commerce/Business Administration (Accounting, Finance, Human Resources, Information Systems, Marketing), Certified Management Accountant, Certified General Accountant, Master of Business Administration (Accounting, Finance, Human Resources, Information Systems, Marketing), Master/Doctorate of Science, Community College Diploma (Accounting, Human Resources, Marketing/Sales, Computer Science, Electronics Technician, Engineering Technician, Laboratory Technician) and High School Diploma. Graduates would occupy Clerk, Laboratory Technician, Associate, Administrator, Assistant, and Co-ordinator, etc. positions. Good verbal and written communication skills, manual dexterity and team player are listed as desirable non-academic qualifications. Company benefits are rated as excellent. The potential for advancement is listed as being good. The average annual starting salary falls within the $25,000 to $35,000 range. The most suitable method for initial contact by those seeking employment is to mail a resume with a covering letter. Cangene Corporation does hire summer students. *Contact:* Gisèle Marks, Human Resources.

Canon

hr.markham @ canade

CANON CANADA INC.
6390 Dixie Road
Mississauga, ON L5T 1P7

Tel.	905-795-2107
Fax	905-795-2046
Email	hrmississauga@canada.canon.com
Website	www.canon.ca

Canon Canada Inc., headquartered in Mississauga with branch offices across Canada, is an industry leader in professional and consumer imaging equipment and information systems. Canon's extensive product line enables businesses and consumers worldwide to capture, store and distribute visual information. Canon products include digital, analogue and full-color copiers, laser printers, color Bubble Jet printers, digital imaging systems, facsimile machines, calculators, video camcorders, cameras and lenses, semiconductors, broadcast and optical equipment and other specialized industrial products. Canon Canada Inc. offers many challenging and rewarding career opportunities for graduates. Graduates most likely to be hired come from the following academic areas: Bachelor of Arts (General, Economics), Bachelor of Science (General, Computer Science), Bachelor of Commerce/Business Administration (General, Accounting, Marketing), Chartered Accountant, Certified General Accountant, Master of Business Administration (General, Marketing) and Community College Diploma (Advertising, Communications/Public Relations, Marketing/Sales, Computer Science, Electronics Technician, Information Systems). Graduates are hired to join one of Canon's professional teams in sales, sales support, marketing, service technology, accounting, advertising, computer networking, administration and operations. Canon, including its direct sales division, offers excellent career growth potential and mobility, supported by the stability of a globally successful company. Canon offers comprehensive rewards designed to meet the needs of their employees today and throughout their careers. The most suitable methods for initial contact by graduates seeking employment are to mail, fax or e-mail a resume with covering letter, or to inquire about available job opportunities contact the Job Line at (905) 795-2107. *Contact:* Human Resources.

CAPITAL HEALTH REGION
2101 Richmond Avenue
Victoria, BC V8R 4R7

Tel.	250-370-8522
Fax	250-370-8570
Email	jobs@caphealth.org
Website	www.caphealth.org

Capital Health Region (CHR) provides a full range of health services to the 340,000 people of southern Vancouver Island and the Southern Gulf Islands and serves as the major referral centre for Vancouver Island's 650,000 people. With 9,000 employees, the CHR oversees, manages and coordinates a comprehensive range of health care services, including: the region's four acute care hospitals, long term and residential care facilities, rehabilitation, acute and community based mental health services, community based programs such as in schools, environmental and public health, home support and home care. Graduates most likely to be hired at this site come from the following academic areas: Bachelor of Arts (Criminology, Recreation Studies, Social Work), Bachelor of Science (Biology, Chemistry, Microbiology, Nursing, Nutritional Sciences, Occupational Therapy, Pharmacy, Physical Therapy, Psychology, Speech Pathology), Chartered Accountant, Certified Management Accountant, Certified General Accountant, Master of Business Administration (Accounting, Finance, Human Resources, Information Systems, Public Administration) and Community College Diploma (Human Resources, Recreation Studies, Laboratory Technician, Nuclear Medicine Technician, Radiology Technician, Respiratory Therapy, Ultrasound Technician). One or two years previous work experience is listed as a definite asset. The most suitable method for initial contact by those seeking employment is to mail a resume with a covering letter. *Contacts:* Donna Scott, Manager, Employment Services, Human Resources or Marlane Worthington, Employment Services Representative, Human Resources.

CARBONE OF AMERICA (LCL) LTD.
496 Evans Avenue
Toronto, ON M8W 2T7

Tel.	416-251-2334
Fax	416-252-1742

Carbone of America (LCL) Ltd. manufactures carbon brushes for electric motors. The company employs a total of 115 people. Graduates most likely to be hired come from the following academic areas: Bachelor of Arts (General), Bachelor of Engineering (Electrical, Mechanical), Bachelor of Commerce/Business Administration (General, Accounting, Finance, Human Resources, Marketing), Master of Business Administration (Finance), Community College Diploma (Accounting, Administration, Business, Human Resources, Marketing/Sales, Purchasing/Logistics, Engineering Technician) and High School Diploma. Team player, a good attitude and previous work experience are all listed as desirable non-academic qualifications. Company benefits and the potential for advancement are both rated as excellent. The most suitable method for initial contact by those seeking employment is to mail a resume with a covering letter. Carbone of America (LCL) Ltd. does hire summer students. *Contact:* Nancy DiBernardo, Human Resources.

CARGILL LIMITED
240 Graham Avenue, Suite 300, PO Box 5900
Winnipeg, MB R3C 4C5

Tel.	204-947-6251
Fax	204-947-6222
Website	www.cargill.com

Cargill Limited is involved in grain merchandising, grain handling, crop inputs, feed manufacturing, meat processing, fertilizer manufacturing, oilseed crushing, salt and flax fibre processing. A diversified operation with an enviable record of growth, Cargill Limited is the Canadian subsidiary of US based Cargill Incorporated, an international marketer, processor and distributor of agricultural, food, financial and industrial products with some 80,000 employees in 65 countries. Operating in Canada for over 60 years, Cargill employs 220 people in its Winnipeg head office and approximately 4,000 people across Canada. Graduates most likely to be hired come from the following academic areas: Bachelor of Science (Agriculture, Computer Science), Bachelor of Engineering (Civil), Bachelor of Commerce/Business Administration (Accounting), Certified Management Accountant, Certified General Accountant, Master of Science (Agriculture) and Community College Diploma (Accounting, Marketing/Sales, Agriculture/Horticulture). Most positions start at the trainee level and within the Grain/Crops Inputs Division, transferability is required with initial assignments usually being located in farm communities. Positions occupied by graduates include Farm Service Centre Assistant, IT Associate, Accounting Trainee, Production Management Trainee, Plant Manager Trainee, Territory Manager and Marketing Manager. Highly motivated, good communication skills, team player, integrity, strong customer service skills and related work experience are all listed as desirable non-academic qualifications. Company benefits are rated above average. The potential for advancement is listed as excellent. The average annual starting salary falls within the $25,000 to $35,000 range. The most suitable methods for initial contact by graduates seeking employment are to mail, fax or e-mail a resume with a covering letter. E-mail applications can also be made through the company's website (no attachments please). Cargill Limited does hire summer and co-op work term students in Accounting, Information Technology and Agriculture. *Contact:* Bob Johnson, Director, Human Resources.

CARLINGVIEW AIRPORT INN
221 Carlingview Drive
Rexdale, ON M9W 5E8

Tel. 416-675-3303

Carlingview Airport Inn in full service hotel with restaurant. The hotel employs approximately 50 people. Postsecondary education is not listed as a prerequisite for employment application. Graduates would occupy entry-level Front Desk Clerk, Night Audit Clerk and Housekeeping positions. Previous hotel work experience is listed as a desirable non-academic qualifications. Company benefits are rated above average. The potential for advancement is listed as being good. The average annual starting salary falls in the $15,000 plus range. The most suitable method for initial contact regarding employment opportunities is to mail a resume with a covering letter. The Carlingview Airport Inn does hire summer students. *Contacts:* Paul Lira, Controller/Manager or Verge Jacobelli, Managing Director.

CARLSON MARKETING GROUP CANADA LTD. / CMG
3300 Bloor Street West, Centre Tower, 15th Floor
Toronto, ON M8X 2Y2

Tel. 416-236-1991
Fax 416-236-9915
Email .... hr@carlsoncanada.com
Website .... www.cmg.carlson.com

Carlson Marketing Group Canada Ltd. / CMG is a leading provider of relationship marketing solutions. CMG helps clients improve their sales and profits by designing marketing strategies that create and strengthen relationships with the audiences that CMG's clients depend on for their success: employees, channel partners and customers. In order to achieve measurable results, CMG uses five proven disciplines which include Direct Marketing, Event Marketing, Loyalty Marketing, Performance Improvement and Sales Promotion. CMG's sales

professionals are strategic marketing experts backed by an extensive array of marketing services, utilizing the latest technological advances in electronic marketing. CMG is able to act locally or globally by tapping into a worldwide network to deliver a single service or to integrate a wide spectrum of marketing services for any business. CMG employs nearly 400 people at the Canadian head office in Toronto. The company is always seeking talented individuals interested in the areas of customer service, travel, event coordination and marketing. Graduates most likely to be hired come from the following academic areas: Bachelor of Arts (General, French), Bachelor of Science (Computer Science), Bachelor of Commerce/Business Administration (Marketing, Public Administration) and Community College Diploma (Communications/Public Relations, Marketing/Sales, Hospitality, Travel/Tourism). Graduates would occupy Customer Service Representative, Travel Service Representative and Marketing Coordinator positions. Good communication skills, computer literacy, bilingual (French/English) and an eagerness to help out where required are all listed as desirable non-academic qualifications. Company benefits are rated as industry standard. The potential for advancement is listed as being good. The most suitable methods for initial contact by those seeking employment are to fax or e-mail a resume with a covering letter. Carlson Marketing Group Canada Ltd. does hire summer and co-op work term students. *Contact:* Human Resources Department.

CARRIER CANADA LIMITED
1515 Drew Road
Mississauga, ON L5S 1Y8

Tel. 905-672-0606
Fax 905-405-4003
Email .... cathy.sciberras@carrier.utc.com
Website .... www.carrier.com

Carrier Canada Limited sells, distributes and services heating ventilation and air conditioning (HVAC) equipment across Canada. The company employs approximately 140 people at this location and a total of 475 people across Canada. Graduates most likely to be hired come from the following academic areas: Bachelor of Arts (General), Bachelor of Engineering (Mechanical), Bachelor of Commerce/Business Administration (Accounting, Finance), Certified Management Accountant, Certified General Accountant, Master of Business Administration (Finance) and Community College Diploma (Accounting, Engineering Technician, HVAC Systems). Graduates would occupy Accountant, Accounting Clerk, Customer Service Representative, Finance and Budget Managers, Counter Sales Representative, Inside Sales Representative and Technical Representative positions. Team player, bilingual (French/English), computer literacy, excellent communication and interpersonal skills and a working knowledge of the HVAC industry are all listed as desirable non-academic qualifications. Company benefits are rated as excellent. The potential for advancement is listed as being good. The average annual starting salary depends upon the position being considered, the previous work experience and educational background of the applicant. The most suitable methods for initial contact by those seeking employment are to mail or fax a resume with a covering letter. Carrier Canada Limited hires summer students for junior positions and some warehouse/shipping positions in other branches. Co-op work term students are also hired. Carrier Canada Limited is dedicated to employment equity. *Contact:* Cathy Sciberras, Human Resources.

CARSEN GROUP INC.
151 Telson Road
Markham, ON L3R 1E7

Tel. 905-479-4100
Fax 905-479-2595
Website .... www.carsengroup.com

Carsen Group Inc. is a national distributor of medical instruments, precision instruments, industrial technology, and related consumer products. The company employs approximately 120 people. Graduates most likely to be hired come from the following academic areas: Bachelor of Arts (General), Bachelor of Science (General) and Bachelor of Commerce/Business Administration (General, Information Systems). Graduates would occupy Customer Service Representative, Sales Representative, Technical Service Representative, Sales Coordinator and Product Manager positions. Excellent communication and interpersonal skills, team player and computer literacy are all listed as desirable non-academic qualifications. Company benefits are rated as excellent. The potential for advancement is listed as being good. The average annual starting salary depends upon the position being considered, and the previous work experience of the applicant. The most suitable methods for initial contact by those seeking employment are to mail or fax a resume with a covering letter. Carsen Group Inc. does hire summer students. Carsen Group Inc. supports employment equity. Contact: Gladys Soer, Human Resources Manager.

CAUGHT IN THE WEB, INC.
36 Lombard Street, 5th Floor
Toronto, ON M5C 2X3

Tel. 416-941-9340
Fax 416-941-9183
Email .... careers@citw.com
Website .... www.citw.com

Caught in the Web, Inc. is one of Canada's leading full-service Internet commerce companies. The company identifies ground-breaking opportunities and develops innovative business solutions for its world class clientele. Caught in the Web's proven approach delivers innovative marketing, technical and creative solutions for many of North America's leading companies. Graduates most likely to be hired come from the following academic areas: Bachelor of Science (Computer Science), Bachelor of Engineering (Computer Systems) and Bachelor of Commerce/Business Administration (Accounting, Finance). Graduates would occupy Computer Technical Development, Computer/Graphic Designer, Marketing/Sales Trainee, Accounting Assistant and Public Relations positions. Team player, enthusiastic, friendly, good communication skills, previous work experience and creativity are all listed as desirable non-academic qualifications. The company seeks committed professionals with an emphasis on excellence as a performance standard. Caught in the Web offers a competitive salary, an outstanding benefits package and an innovative working environment. The most suitable methods for initial contact by those seeking employment are to fax or e-mail a resume with a covering letter. Caught in the Web, Inc. does hire summer and co-op work term students. Contact: Human Resources.

CAVENDISH FARMS
PO Box 3500
Summerside, PE C1N 5J5

Tel. 902-836-5555
Fax 902-836-3299

Cavendish Farms is involved in the production of frozen potato food products. The company employs approximately 900 people. Graduates most likely to be hired come from the following academic areas: Bachelor of Science (Agriculture, Biology, Chemistry, Computer Science, Environmental), Bachelor of Engineering (Food Processing, Pollution Treatment, Electrical, Instrumentation, Mechanical, Industrial Production), Bachelor of Architecture, Bachelor of Commerce/Business Administration (General, Accounting, Finance, Human Resources, Information Systems, Marketing), Community College Diploma (Accounting, Administration, Business, Financial Planning, Human Resources, Computer Science, Electronics Technician, Engineering Technician) and High School Diploma. Graduates would occupy Clerk, Maintenance, Managerial and Supervisory positions. Previous work experience, leadership skills, facilitator, team player, adaptability and good communication skills are all listed as desirable non-academic qualifications. The most suitable method for initial contact by those seeking employment is to mail a resume with a covering letter. Cavendish Farms does hire summer students. Contact: Daniel Hughes, Human Resource Manager.

CBC / RADIO CANADA
PO Box 500, Station A
Toronto, ON M5W 1E6

Tel. 416-205-3311
Fax 416-205-5622
Website .... www.cbc.ca

The CBC / Radio Canada operates Canada's national and international public television and radio networks. The CBC / Radio Canada is a crown corporation governed by the 1991 Broadcasting Act and subject to regulations of the Canadian Radio-television and Telecommunications Commission (CRTC). The corporation employs over 7,000 permanent staff and over 600 temporary staff across Canada. In Toronto this involves the operation of television stations and radio stations, as well as the production of national programs including Midday and The National. For other facility locations across the country check your local telephone white pages or visit the CBC's website. Graduates most likely to be hired at the Toronto location come from the following academic areas: Bachelor of Arts, Bachelor of Science, Bachelor of Engineering, Bachelor of Laws, Bachelor of Commerce/Business Administration, Master of Business Administration, Master of Arts (Political Science) and Community College Diploma (General/Related). Graduates would occupy a wide variety of positions in Sales, Broadcasting, Technical and Production. Company benefits and the potential for advancement are both rated as excellent. The average annual starting salary varies widely with the position and experience of the applicant. The most suitable method for initial contact by those seeking employment is to visit the Job Shop at 25 John Street, between 10:30 to 1:30 weekdays only. Applicants are invited to apply for available positions that are a match to their qualifications (please, no unsolicited resumes). The CBC / Radio Canada does hire summer students for short term positions. Contact: Human Resources - The Job Shop.

CELESTICA INTERNATIONAL INC.
146 Adesso Drive
Concord, ON L4K 3C3

Tel. 905-660-9819
Fax 905-660-9567

Email .... kenl@celestica.com
Website .... www.celestica.com

Celestica International Inc. provides a broad range of services including design, prototyping, assembly, testing, product assurance, supply chain management, worldwide distribution and after-sales service. Celestica power systems is a leading supplier of power solutions for Tier 1 OEMs in the data processing, communications and office product markets. The company focuses on the development and manufacture of complete system solutions utilizing DC/DC, AC/DC, High Voltage and Power-ASIC technologies. Celestica has 400 employees at this location, a total of 4,000 in Canada, and 15,000 employees worldwide. Graduates most likely to be hired come from the following academic areas: Bachelor of Science (Computer Science), Bachelor of Engineering (Electrical, Mechanical, Industrial Engineering, Industrial Production/Manufacturing), Bachelor of Commerce/Business Administration (General, Information Systems, Marketing), Master of Business Administration (General, Marketing) and Community College Diploma (Business, CAD/CAM Autocad, Computer Science, Electronics Technician, Engineering Technician). Team player and good problem skills are both listed as desirable non-academic qualifications. Company benefits are rated above average. The potential for advancement is listed as being good. The most suitable methods for initial contact by those seeking employment are to mail, fax or e-mail a resume with a covering letter, or by applying through the company's website. Celestica International Inc. does hire summer and co-op work term students. *Contacts:* Dora Malizia, Human Resources Assistant or Ken Lawrence, Human Resources Manager.

CENTRAL PARK LODGES LTD.
175 Bloor Street East, Suite 601, South Tower
Toronto, ON M4W 3R8

Tel. 416-929-5450
Fax 416-929-1339

Central Park Lodges Ltd., established in 1961, founded the first chain of retirement lodges and nursing homes in Canada. Today, the company has expanded its operations to 27 facilities covering a geographic base which includes the provinces of British Columbia, Alberta, Manitoba, Ontario, and Quebec. There are approximately 50 employees at this location and more than 2,500 employees in Canada. Graduates most likely to be hired come from the following academic areas: Bachelor of Arts (General, Economics, Psychology, Recreation, Social Work), Bachelor of Science (Nursing), Bachelor of Commerce/Business Administration (Accounting, Finance, Human Resources, Information Systems, Marketing), Chartered Accountant (Finance), Certified Management Accountant (Finance), Certified General Accountant (Finance) and Community College Diploma (Accounting, Administration, Business, Facility Management, Human Resources, Marketing, Secretarial, HVAC Systems, Dietician/Nutrition, Nursing RN/RNA). Graduates would occupy RN, RNA, Health Care Aide, Dietary Aide, Cook, Janitor, Activity Aide, Food Service Supervisor, Maintenance Supervisor, Activity Director and Accounting positions. Good communication, organization, marketing, critical thinking skills, patience, flexibility and comfort with seniors are all listed as desirable non-academic qualifications. Company benefits are rated as industry standard. The potential for advancement is listed as being good. The most suitable method for initial contact by those seeking employment is to mail a resume with a covering letter. Central Park Lodges Ltd. does hire summer students. *Contacts:* Human Resources, Retirement Division or Human Resources Officer.

CENTRAL PROJECTS GROUP INC.
250 Shields Court, Unit #15
Markham, ON L3R 9W7

Tel. 905-470-6570
Fax 905-470-0958
Email .... rdevries@ibm.net
Website .... www.cpg.ca

Central Projects Group Inc. is an engineering firm. The firm provides environmental audits and assessments, emergency response, project management, environmental remediation and engineering design services. There are 20 employees at this location and a total of 25 employees in Canada. Graduates most likely to be hired come from the following academic areas: Bachelor of Science (Environmental), Bachelor of Engineering (Pollution Treatment, Civil, Resources/Environmental), Master of Science (Environmental), Master of Engineering (Environmental) and Community College Diploma (Engineering Technician). Graduates would occupy Technician and Project Manager positions. Excellent verbal and written communication skills and work experience in site assessment/remediation are listed as desirable non-academic qualifications. Company benefits and the potential for advancement are both rated as excellent. The average annual starting salary falls within the $25,000 to $30,000 range. The most suitable method for initial contact by those seeking employment is to mail a resume with a covering letter. Central Projects Group Inc. does hire summer students. *Contacts:* Mr. Harry Kim or Mr. René De Vries.

CENTRES JEUNESSE DE MONTRÉAL, LES
9335, rue St-Hubert
Montreal, QC H2M 1Y7

Tel. 514-858-3903
Fax 514-858-3914
Website .... www.mtl.centresjeunesse.qc.ca

Les Centres Jeunesse de Montréal provides social services and rehabilitation counselling in a youth protection centre. There are approximately 4,000 employees throughout the organization. Graduates most likely to be hired come from the following academic areas: Bachelor of Arts (Criminology, Psychology, Social Work), Bachelor of Science (Computer Science, Nursing), Bachelor of Engineering (Civil), Bachelor of Education (Special Needs), Bachelor of Laws (Rehabilitation Law), Bachelor of Commerce/Business Administration (General, Accounting, Finance, Human Resources, Information Systems, Public Administration), Chartered Accountant, Certified General Accountant, Master of Business Administration (General, Public Administration) and Community College Diploma (Accounting, Administration, Human Resources, Secretarial, Recreation Studies, Social Work, Rehabilitation Therapy). The average annual starting salary falls within the $20,000 to $25,000 range. The most suitable method for initial contact by those seeking employment is to mail a resume with a covering letter. Les Centres Jeunesse de Montréal does hire summer students. *Contact:* Nicole Godfroy, technicienne en administration, Direction des ressources humaines.

CENTRIFUGAL COATERS INC.
1317 Speers Road
Oakville, ON L6L 2X5

Tel.	905-827-1156
Fax	905-827-0868

Centrifugal Coaters Inc. is a tier two supplier and custom coater (paint) of decorative trim parts supplied to the automotive industry. The company employs a total of 130 people. Graduates most likely to be hired come from the following academic areas: Bachelor of Arts (General), Bachelor of Engineering (Chemical, Automation/Robotics), Doctorate (Engineering) and Community College Diploma (Engineering Technician, Quality Management). Graduates would occupy Process Engineer/Technician, Quality Auditor, Scheduler/Purchaser and Data Entry Clerk positions. Team player, good interpersonal skills, ability to self-motivate and take initiative and good organization skills are all listed as desirable non-academic qualifications. Company benefits are rated above average. The potential for advancement is listed as average. The average annual starting salary falls within the $25,000 to $30,000 range. The most suitable method for initial contact by those seeking employment is to mail a resume with a covering letter. *Contact:* Human Resources.

CFMT-TV / ROGERS BROADCASTING LTD.
545 Lakeshore Boulevard West
Toronto, ON M5V 1A3

Tel.	416-260-0047
Fax	416-260-3615
Website	www.rogers.com

CFMT-TV is a television broadcasting station owned by Rogers Broadcasting Limited. Programming activities involve purchased programming and in-house production. The station employs between 180 and 200 people. Graduates most likely to be hired come from the following academic areas: Bachelor of Arts (General, Journalism, Languages), Bachelor of Engineering (Electrical, Mechanical, Telecommunications), Bachelor of Commerce/Business Administration (General, Accounting, Finance, Human Resources, Information Systems, Marketing), Chartered Accountant, Certified General Accountant, Master of Business Administration (Marketing), Community College Diploma (Accounting, Administration, Business, Communications/Public Relations, Human Resources, Information Systems, Marketing/Sales, Secretarial, Graphic Arts, Journalism, Television/Radio Arts, Broadcasting, Electronics Technician, Engineering Technician) and High School Diploma. Graduates would occupy Production Assistant, Junior Writer, Clerk, Accountant and Sales Representative positions. Possessing a high level of maturity, good judgment, a positive attitude and related work experience are all listed as desirable non-academic qualifications. Company benefits and the potential for advancement are both rated as excellent. The average annual starting salary falls within the $25,000 to $30,000 range, and for certain positions it is commission based. The most suitable methods for initial contact by graduates seeking employment are to mail or fax a resume with a covering letter. CFMT-TV does hire summer students on a volunteer basis, as well as hiring co-op work term students. *Contact:* Marisa Tenuta, Human Resource Manager.

CGI GROUP INC.
275 Slater Street, 14th Floor
Ottawa, ON K1P 5H9

Tel.	613-234-2155
Fax	613-234-6934
Email	karen.savoy@cgi.ca
Website	www.cgi.ca

CGI Group Inc. provides end-to-end information technology (IT) services and business solutions to some 2,000 clients in Canada, the United States and in 20 countries around the world. The company employs 315 people at this location and over 9,000 people worldwide. Graduates most likely to be hired come from the following academic areas: Bachelor of Science (Computer Science), Bachelor of Engineering (Electrical, Telecommunications), Bachelor of Commerce/Business Administration (Information Systems), Master of Business Administration (Information Systems) and Community College Diploma (Facility Management, Financial Planning, Computer Science). Graduates would be hired to occupy Programmer and Systems Analyst positions. Company benefits are rated above average. The potential for advancement is listed as excellent. The most suitable methods for initial contact by those seeking employment are to mail or e-mail a resume. CGI Group Inc. does hire summer students, depending upon the contracts the company has at that particular time. *Contact:* Kathy St. Pierre, Manager Human Resources.

CGU GROUP CANADA LTD.
2206 Eglinton Avenue East
Toronto, ON M1L 4S8

Tel.	416-288-1800
Fax	416-288-9106
Website	www.cgu.ca

CGU Group Canada Ltd. is the largest property and casualty insurer in Canada with annual premiums in excess of $1.6 billion. The company is the result of the the recent integration of Canadian General Insurance, General Accident Group (Canada) and Commercial Union Assurance. CGU Group Canada Ltd. is a wholly owned subsidiary of London, United Kingdom based CGU plc. CGU Group Canada Ltd. partners with a national network of more than 3,000 independent insurance brokers and conducts business through the the following wholly owned subsidiaries: CGU Insurance Company of Canada, Traders General Insurance Company, Scottish & York Insurance Co. Limited and Elite Insurance Company. CGU Group Canada offers traditional home, automobile and commercial insurance as well as group home, group automobile and specialty personal lines niche products. The company is a dominant insurer of such products as mobile homes and recreational vehicles. It's also a leading provider of specialty commercial products and construction surety bonding. CGU Group Canada Ltd. employs approximately 500 people at this location and a total of 2,300 people across Canada. Graduates most likely to be hired come from the following academic areas: Bachelor of Arts (General, Criminology, Economics), Bachelor of Science (General, Actuarial, Computer Science), Bachelor of Engineering (Computer Systems, Telecommunications), Bachelor of Commerce/Business Administration (General, Accounting, Finance), Master of Business Administration (General, Accounting, Finance) and Community College Diploma (Accounting, Computer Science). Graduates would occupy Claims Adjuster Trainee, Junior Underwriter Trainee, Reinsurance Analyst Trainee, Junior Accountant, Actuarial Analyst Trainee and various Administrative positions. Good communication and customer relations skills, self-starter, reliable, initiative, performance and results oriented, team player and excellent time management skills are all listed as desirable non-academic qualifications. Company benefits are rated above average. The potential for advancement is listed as being good. The most suitable methods for initial contact by those seeking employment are to fax or e-mail a resume with a covering letter, or via the company's website (visit the website for appropriate e-mail addresses). CGU Group Canada Ltd. does hire summer and co-op work term students. *Contact:* Human Resources.

CH2M GORE & STORRIE LTD.
255 Consumers Road
Toronto, ON M2J 5B6

Tel. 416-499-9000
Fax 416-499-4687

CH2M Gore & Storrie Ltd. is a leading Canadian consulting engineering company. The company provides environmental engineering and scientific services for industries and municipalities in Canada and abroad. There are approximately 350 employees in five Ontario locations, Calgary and Vancouver. Graduates most likely to be hired come from the following academic areas: Bachelor of Arts (Urban Geography), Bachelor of Science (Biology, Computer Science, Environmental), Bachelor of Engineering (Chemical, Metallurgy, Architectural/ Building, Surveying, Electrical, Instrumentation, Mechanical, Aerospace), Bachelor of Commerce/Administration (Accounting, Finance, Human Resources, Information, Systems), Master of Business Administration (Accounting, Finance, Human Resources) and Community College Diploma (Accounting, Architecture/Drafting, CAD/CAM/Autocad, HVAC Systems). Graduates would occupy Engineering, Process, Building Services, Environmental Planning, Contaminant Sciences and Administration positions. Quality conscious, flexible, technically sound, team players, maintain a professional approach and presentation, and excellent verbal and written communication skills are all listed as desirable non-academic qualifications. Company benefits are rated above average. The average annual starting salary falls within the $20,000 to $45,000 range, depending upon the position and the applicant's qualifications. The most suitable method for initial contact by those seeking employment is to mail a resume with a covering letter. *Contact:* Human Resources.

CHAMPION ROAD MACHINERY LIMITED
PO Box 10, Maitland Road
Goderich, ON N7A 3Y6

Tel. 519-524-2601
Fax 519-524-3013

Champion Road Machinery Limited is one of the world's leading manufacturers of graders and related equipment used in the construction and maintenance of roads. Champion's products are sold primarily through 170 independent dealers who operate approximately 300 sales and service outlets throughout the United States, Canada, and 96 other countries, and through four company-owned retail outlets in Ontario. There are approximately 590 employees at this location and a total of 700 employees in Canada. Graduates most likely to be hired come from the following academic areas: Bachelor of Arts (Economics), Bachelor of Science (Computer Science, Mathematics), Bachelor of Engineering (General, Electrical, Mechanical, Industrial Design, Industrial Production, Welding), Bachelor of Commerce/Business Administration (Accounting, Finance, Human Resources, Information Systems, Marketing), Chartered Accountant, Certified Management Accountant, Certified General Accountant, Master of Business Administration (Accounting, Finance, Information Systems, Marketing) and Community College Di-

ploma (Accounting, Business, Human Resources, Purchasing/Logistics, CAD/CAM/Autocad, Computer Science, Engineering Technician, Welding). Graduates would occupy Junior Engineer, Marketing Management Trainee, Systems Analyst, Financial Analyst, Draftsperson, Welding Technician and Planner positions. Company benefits are rated as excellent. The potential for advancement is listed as being good. The average annual starting salary falls within the $30,000 to $35,000 range. The most suitable method for initial contact by those seeking employment is to mail a resume with a covering letter. Engineering, Finance, Information Systems, Industrial Engineering and Marketing students are hired for summer positions. *Contact:* Human Resources Manager.

Great Books Are Just The Beginning

CHAPTERS INC.
90 Ronson Drive
Toronto, ON M9W 1C1

Tel. 416-243-3138
Fax 416-243-5420
Website .... www.chapters.ca

Chapters Inc. was created in 1995 from the merger of Canada's two leading book retailers, Coles and SmithBooks. Chapters Inc. (Toronto Stock Exchange - CHP) has more than 250 mall-based and main-street bookstores with representation in every province. Launched in the fall of 1995, the Chapters' superstores carry more than 100,000 titles and offer learning and play areas for children, comfortable armchairs for curling up with a favourite selection and a coffee bar for customers. In addition to books and magazines, SmithBooks, Coles and Chapters' superstores stores carry related multimedia products such as audio tapes, books on CD-ROM and music CDs. Chapters Internet (www.chapters.ca), a Canadian e-commerce company, was launched in October 1998 and has become a major player in Canada's e-commerce marketplace. At Chapters.ca, customers have access to millions of book titles as well as a wide selection of videos and DVDs, music CDs and software. In 1999, the company received Internet World Canada's Site of the Year Award for its impact on the lives of Canadians. Chapters Inc. has 180 employees at its head office and more than 5,600 employees across Canada. Graduates most likely to be hired come from the following academic areas: Bachelor of Arts (General), Bachelor of Commerce/ Business Administration and Community College Diploma (Business). Graduates are hired to occupy Retail Management, and Sales and Merchandising positions. Entrepreneurial spirit, sales building, strong work ethic, persuasiveness, dependability, a passion for retail and a love of books are all listed as desirable non-academic qualifications. Company benefits are rated above average. The potential for advancement is listed as excellent. The average annual starting salary falls within the $25,000 to $30,000 range. The most suitable methods for initial contact by those seeking employment are to mail of fax a resume with a covering letter. Summer students are hired at retail store locations (check white/yellow pages for the nearest location). *Contact:* Human Resources Department.

CHARTERWAYS TRANSPORTATION LIMITED
35 Crockford Boulevard
Toronto, ON M1R 3B7

Tel.	416-752-6120
Fax	416-752-4641

Charterways Transportation Limited operates school bus services for a number of individual school boards. This also involves transporting physically disabled children and children requiring special education services. Graduates most likely to be hired come from the following academic areas: Bachelor of Commerce/Business Administration and Community College Diploma (General). Graduates would occupy Management, Accounting, Secretarial and Clerical positions. Possessing a positive attitude and previous work experience are both listed as desirable non-academic qualifications. Company benefits are rated above average. The potential for advancement is listed as being good. The average annual starting salary falls within the $20,000 to $25,000 range. The most suitable method for initial contact by those seeking employment is to mail a resume with a covering letter. Charterways Transportation Limited does hire summer students on a regular basis. *Contact:* Recruiting Department.

CHEVRON CANADA RESOURCES
500 - 5th Avenue SW
Calgary, AB T2P 0L7

Tel.	403-234-5000
Fax	403-234-5837
Email	hiar@chevron.com
Website	www.chevron.com

Chevron Canada Resources is involved in the exploration, production and marketing of oil and gas. Chevron Canada Resources is a subsidiary of Chevron Corporation based in San Francisco, California. Chevron Corporation is one of the world's largest integrated petroleum companies involved in every aspect of the industry, from exploration and production to transportation, refining and retail marketing, as well as chemicals manufacturing and sales. The company is active in more than 90 countries and employs about 33,000 people worldwide. Chevron Canada Resources employs 500 people at this location and a total of 800 people across Canada. Graduates most likely to be hired come from the following academic areas: Bachelor of Science (Computer Science, Geology) and Bachelor of Engineering (General, Chemical, Industrial Chemistry, Civil, Electrical, Instrumentation, Mechanical, Resources/Environmental, Petroleum). Graduates would begin as a trainee in their chosen field and progress to a fully trained professional in their field of specialization. Good communication skills and being a demonstrated team player are both listed as desirable non-academic qualifications. Company benefits and the potential for advancement are both rated as excellent. The average annual starting salary falls within the $30,000 to $35,000 range, and is dependent upon the position being filled and the qualifications of the individual applicant. The most suitable method for initial contact by those seeking employment is to mail a resume with a covering letter. Chevron Canada Resources does hire summer stu-

dents. *Contact:* Jim Causgrove, Manager, Strategy, People and Technology Development.

CHILDREN'S AID SOCIETY OF TORONTO
4211 Yonge Street, Suite 400
Toronto, ON M2P 2A9

Tel.	416-924-4646
Fax	416-324 2375
Email	ebodie@casmt.on.ca
Website	www.casmt.on.ca

Children's Aid Society of Toronto is the largest board operated child welfare agency in North America. There are 650 full-time staff in six branches, and in partnership with foster parents and volunteers, a range of protection and prevention services are provided. Graduates most likely to be hired come from the following academic areas: Bachelor of Social Work, Master of Social Work and Community College Diploma (Child and Youth Worker). Graduates would occupy Social Worker, and Residential Child and Youth Care Worker. Applicants should have related experience with children and families, a driver's license and access to an automobile. Employee benefits are rated above average. The potential for advancement is listed as being good. The average annual starting salary for a Child and Youth Worker is $33,349 and for a Social Worker it is $38,493. The most suitable method for initial contact by those seeking employment is to mail a resume with a covering letter. Children's Aid Society of Toronto does hire summer and co-op work term students. *Contact:* Human Resources.

CHILDREN'S AND WOMEN'S HEALTH CENTRE OF BRITISH COLUMBIA
4480 Oak Street, Suite A119
Vancouver, BC V6H 4C9

Tel.	604-875-2570
Fax	604-875-2599
Website	www.cw.bc.ca

The Children's and Women's Health Centre of British Columbia provides health and medical services to the women and children of the community. Programs include sexual assault, PMS, osteoporosis, HIV program, and menopause. The hospital and health centre employ a total of 975 people. Graduates most likely to be hired come from the following academic areas: Bachelor of Arts (General), Bachelor of Science (General, Health Sciences), Bachelor of Commerce/Business Administration (Accounting, Finance, Human Resources, Information Systems, Marketing, Public Administration), Certified Management Accountant, Certified General Accountant, Master of Business Administration (Accounting, Finance, Information Systems, Marketing, Public Administration), Master of Arts (Social Work), Community College Diploma (Accounting, Administration, Advertising, Business, Communications, Financial Planning, Human Resources, Purchasing/Logistics, Secretarial, Social Work, Laboratory Technician, Nursing RN) and High School Diploma. Graduates would occupy RN, Clerical, Social Worker, Physiotherapist, Accounting, Counsellor, and Housekeeping, etc. positions. Previous work experience, good work ethic, team player, good attendance record and a high level of motivation are all listed as desirable non-academic qualifications. The potential for advancement is rated as being good. The average annual starting salary falls within the $25,000 to $40,000 range, varying with the position being considered. The most suitable method for initial contact by those seeking employment is to mail a resume with a covering letter. Children's and Women's Health

Centre of British Columbia does hire summer students in some departments (eg. housekeeping, clerical, etc.). *Contact:* Human Resource Consultant.

CHILDREN'S HOSPITAL OF EASTERN ONTARIO / CHEO
401 Smyth Road
Ottawa, ON K1H 8L1

Tel. 613-737-7600
Fax 613-738-4233
Email .... personnel@cheo.on.ca
Website .... www.cheo.on.ca

Children's Hospital of Eastern Ontario / CHEO is an acute care, teaching hospital affiliated with the University of Ottawa. The hospital employs approximately 2,000 people. Graduates most likely to be hired come from the following academic areas: Bachelor of Science (Nursing, Occupational Therapy, Pharmacy), Bachelor of Engineering (Computer Systems), Bachelor of Commerce/Business Administration (Information Systems), Master of Science (Social Work, Audiology, Speech Pathology) and Community College Diploma (Dental Assistant, Dental Hygiene, Laboratory Technician, Nuclear Medicine, Nursing RN/RPN, Radiology, Respiratory Therapy, Ultra-Sound Technician). Graduates would occupy Registered Nurse, Registered Practical Nurse, Speech/Language Pathologist, Audiologist, Pharmacist, Occupational Therapist, Social Worker, Information Systems, Network/System Analyst and Technical support positions. Team player, bilingual (French/English) and excellent communication skills are all listed as desirable non-academic qualifications. Company benefits are rated above average. The potential for advancement is listed as average. The average annual starting salary falls within the $30,000 to $35,000 range. The most suitable method for initial contact by those seeking employment is to mail a resume with a covering letter. Children's Hospital of Eastern Ontario does hire a limited number of summer and co-op work term students annually. *Contact:* Human Resources.

CHOREO SYSTEMS INC.
112 Kent Street, Suite 1300
Ottawa, ON K1P 5P2

Tel. 613-238-1050
Fax 613-238-4453
Email .... info@choreosystems.com
Website .... www.choreosystems.com

Choreo Systems Inc. is a leader in systems integration providing business and technology solutions in three highly specialized areas of information management, including: security, directory services and messaging infrastructure. Choreo Systems Inc. is a division of Vancouver based Burnt Sand Solutions Inc. In addition to the Ottawa location, Choreo has locations in St.-Laurent, Toronto, Calgary and Vancouver. Choreo Systems Inc. employs 33 people at this location and a total of 41 people in Canada. Graduates most likely to be hired come from the following academic areas: Bachelor of Science (Computer Science), Master of Science (Computer Science) and Community College Diploma (Computer Science, Engineering Technician). Graduates would occupy Product Support Specialist in response services, Project Specialist in engineering services, Inside Sales Representative, and Account Executive positions. Team player, good interpersonal skills, ambitious, driven, organized and good communication skills are all listed as desirable non-academic qualifications. Company benefits are rated above average. The potential for advancement is listed

as being good. The most suitable method for initial contact by those seeking employment is to mail a resume with a covering letter. *Contact:* Human Resources.

CHRISTIAN HORIZONS
384 Arthur Street South
Elmira, ON N3B 2P4

Tel. 519-669-1571
Fax 519-669-1574
Website .... www.domino.christian-horizons.org

Christian Horizons supports individuals with developmental disabilities through the provision of residential and other support services across Ontario. Christian Horizons is a non-denominational, evangelical, not-for-profit organization employing approximately 1,600 people throughout Ontario. This includes full-time, part-time, and relief staff. Graduates most likely to be hired come from the following academic areas: Bachelor of Arts (General, Psychology, Recreation Studies, Social Work), Bachelor of Science (Computer Science), Bachelor of Education (Special Needs), Community College Diploma (Accounting, Business, Social Work/DSW, Health/Home Care Aide, Nursing RN) and High School Diploma. Graduates would occupy Support Worker, Relief Support Worker, Program Manager and Administrative Support positions in Accounting, Human Resources and Administration. Leadership skills, patient, dependable, responsible, professional, organized, diligent, flexible, adaptable, confident and good oral and written communication skills are all listed as desirable non-academic qualifications. Company benefits are rated as industry standard. The potential for advancement is listed as being good. The average annual starting salary falls within the $20,000 to $25,000 range. The most suitable method for initial contact by those seeking employment is to mail a resume with a covering letter. Christian Horizons does hire summer students. *Contacts:* Coordinator of Services and Supports, Human Resources or Human Resources Generalist.

CHRISTIE BROWN & CO. / NABISCO LTD.
2150 Lakeshore Blvd. West
Toronto, ON M8V 1A3

Tel. 416-503-6000
Fax 416-503-6022
Website .... www.nabisco.ca

Christie Brown & Co., a division of Nabisco Ltd., is an industry leader in the manufacture of premium products such as Chips Ahoy, Ritz and Oreo. There are 1,200 employees at this location and approximately 3,500 employees across Canada. Graduates most likely to be hired come from the following academic areas: Bachelor of Arts (General), Bachelor of Science (Microbiology, Nutritional Sciences), Bachelor of Engineering (General, Chemical, Food Processing, Industrial Chemistry, Materials Science, Electrical, Mechanical), Bachelor of Commerce/Business Administration (Accounting, Finance, Information Systems, Marketing), Chartered Accountant, Certified Management Accountant, Certified General Accountant, Master of Business Administration (Accounting, Finance, Information Systems) and High School graduates for bakery positions. Post-secondary graduates would occupy Financial Analyst, Production Supervisor, Assistant Product Manager, P.C. Coordinator and Sales Representative positions. Outgoing, flexible, adaptable, results oriented, team player, excellent analytical skills, previous work experience, and good written and verbal communication skills are all listed as desirable non-academic qualifications. Company benefits are rated above average. The potential for advancement is listed as being good. The average annual starting salary falls within the $30,000 to $35,000 range. The most suitable method for initial contact by graduates seeking employment is to mail a resume with a covering letter. *Contacts:* Susie Baggio, Human Resources Representative or Kelly Sheehan, Human Resources Representative.

CHROMATOGRAPHIC SPECIALTIES INC.
300 Laurier Boulevard, PO Bag 1150
Brockville, ON K6V 5W1

Tel. 613-342-4678
Fax 613-342-1144
Email .... sales@chromspec.com
Website .... www.chromspec.com

Chromatographic Specialties Inc. is a leading supplier of chromatographic products to the Canadian laboratory marketplace. Founded in 1964, the company employs a total of 35 people, offering premium products and backing them with superior customer service and technical support. Recently, Chromatographic Specialties Inc. founded a sister company, MJS BioLynx, to provide the same services to the Canadian life sciences market. Both companies maintain their head offices in Brockville. Graduates most likely to be hired come from the following academic areas: Bachelor of Science (Biology, Chemistry, Environment/Ecology, Microbiology), Bachelor of Engineering (Chemical) and Community College Diploma (Laboratory Technician). Graduates would occupy Product Support Specialist positions, based at the head office locations, and Technical Sales Representative positions, strategically located across the country covering specific geographic territories. These two positions work closely as a team and are required to provide input into the technical marketing of the company's products. Previous hands-on chromatographic work experience (GC and/or HPLC), team player, and strong organizational, time management and communication skills are all listed as desirable non-academic qualifications. Company benefits are rated as industry standard. The potential for advancement is listed as being good. The average annual starting salary falls within the $30,000 to $35,000 range. The most suitable method for initial contact by those seeking employment is to fax a resume with a covering letter. *Contact:* Ken Jordan, Sales and Product Support Manager.

CHRYSLER CANADA LTD. / ETOBICOKE CASTING PLANT
15 Browns Line
Toronto, ON M8W 3S3

Tel. 416-253-2300
Fax 416-253-2317
Website www3.daimlerchrysler.com

The Chrysler Canada Ltd. / Etobicoke Casting Plant is an aluminum casting plant for automotive castings. There are approximately 500 employees at this location. Graduates most likely to be hired come from the following academic areas: Bachelor of Science (Chemistry, Metallurgy), Bachelor of Engineering (Mechanical, Electrical), Bachelor of Commerce/Business Administration (Accounting), Certified Management Accountant and Master of Business Administration (Information Systems). Graduates would occupy supervisory production and maintenance positions for engineering projects, and a variety of staff positions. Applicants should not mind working on the production floor. Company benefits and the potential for advancement are both rated as excellent.

The average annual starting salary falls within the $25,000 to $30,000 range. The most suitable method for initial contact by graduates seeking employment is to mail a resume with a covering letter. Chrysler Canada Ltd. / Etobicoke Casting Plant does hire summer students on a limited basis. *Contact:* Personnel Manager.

CHUBB SECURITY CANADA INC.
5201 Explorer Drive
Mississauga, ON L4W 4H1

Tel. 905-629-2600
Fax 905-206-8447
Website .... www.chubbsecurity.com

Chubb Security Canada Inc. designs, develops and manufactures security related products. Products include alarm, access control, and software security systems. There are more than 250 employees at this location. Graduates most likely to be hired come from the following academic areas: Bachelor of Arts (General), Bachelor of Science (Computer Science), Bachelor of Engineering (Computer Systems), Bachelor of Commerce/Business Administration (Accounting, Marketing, Finance), Certified Management Accountant (Finance), Certified General Accountant (Finance), Master of Business Administration and Community College Diploma (Marketing/Sales, Secretarial, Security/Enforcement, Computer Science, Electronics). Graduates would occupy Accounting/Finance, Sales, Marketing and Research and Development positions. A high level of initiative, self-motivated and strong leadership skills are all listed as desirable non-academic qualifications. Company benefits are rated above average. The potential for advancement is listed as being good. The average annual starting salary falls within the $25,000 to $40,000 range. The most suitable method for initial contact by those seeking employment is to mail a resume with a covering letter. Chubb Security Canada Inc. does hire summer and co-op work term students. *Contact:* Human Resources Group - Recruitment.

CIBC WORLD MARKETS
181 Bay Street, Suite 3800, PO Box 859
Toronto, ON M5J 2T3

Fax 416-368-0859
Website .... www.cibcwm.com

CIBC World Markets is the global investment banking arm of the Canadian Imperial Bank of Commerce (CIBC). CIBC World Markets provides clients with advice and capital from an integrated platform of product and industry groups. In recent years, the company has dramatically enhanced its capabilities through the strategic acquisition of companies and talent. CIBC World Markets employs 8,700 people worldwide through a network of offices in 67 cities. Graduates most likely to be hired come from the following academic areas: Bachelor of Commerce/Business Administration (Accounting, Finance, Marketing), Master of Business Administration (Finance), Bachelor of Arts (Economics), Bachelor of Science (Computer Science, Mathematics), Bachelor of Engineering (Computer Systems, Telecommunications, Forest Resources, Mining, Petroleum), Bachelor of Laws (Corporate), Chartered Accountant, Certified Management Accountant, Certified General Accountant, CSC and CPH designations. Strong analytical and effective interpersonal skills are listed as desirable non-academic qualifications. Company benefits are rated above average. The potential for advancement is listed as being good. The most suitable method for initial contact by graduates seeking employment is to mail a resume with a covering letter. CIBC Wood Gundy does hire summer students. Resumes for summer positions are accepted beginning in February. *Contact:* Resourcing.

CIGNA INSURANCE COMPANY OF CANADA

2 First Canadian Place
Exchange Tower, 12th Floor, PO Box 18
Toronto, ON M5X 1A8

Tel. 416-368-2911
Fax 416-368-9825

CIGNA Insurance Company of Canada is a commercial insurance company. CIGNA Insurance Company of Canada is a member of CIGNA Corporation, headquartered in both Philadelphia, Pennsylvania and Bloomfield, Connecticut. CIGNA is a leading provider of health care, employee benefits, insurance, and financial services throughout the United States and around the world. CIGNA Insurance Company of Canada employs more than 115 staff at this location and a total of 145 in Canada. Graduates most likely to be hired come from the following academic areas: Bachelor of Arts (General, Economics, Languages, Urban Geography), Bachelor of Science (General, Computer Science, Environment/Ecology, Forestry, Mathematics, Metallurgy), Bachelor of Engineering (General, Civil, Electrical, Mechanical, Computer Systems, Engineering Physics, Environmental/Resources, Forest Resources, Industrial Design, Industrial Engineering, Marine, Metallurgy, Mining, Petroleum/Fuels, Pollution Treatment, Power/Hydro, Pulp and Paper, Surveying, Telecommunications, Transportation), Bachelor of Commerce/Business Administration (General, Accounting, Finance, Human Resources, Information Systems, Marketing, Public Administration, Chartered Accountant, Certified Management Accountant, Certified General Accountant, Master of Business Administration (General, Accounting, Finance, Human Resources, Information Systems) and Community College Diploma (Accounting, Business, Facility Management, Human Resources, Insurance, Marketing/Sales, Office Administration, Secretarial). Graduates would occupy Underwriting Assistant, Executive Assistant, Junior Claims Representative and Accounting Clerk positions. Good communication and customer service skills and previous insurance experience/knowledge are all listed as desirable non-academic qualifications. Company benefits are rated as excellent. The potential for advancement is listed as being good. The average annual starting salary falls within the $28,000 to $35,000 range and is dependent upon the position being considered. The most suitable methods for initial contact by those seeking employment are to mail, fax or e-mail a resume with a covering letter. CIGNA Insurance Company of Canada does hire summer and co-op work term students. *Contacts:* Norma Ross, Director, Human Resources or Nadia Ranieri, Human Resources Representative.

CIMMETRY SYSTEMS, INC. / CSI

6700 Cote-de-Liesse, Suite 206
St-Laurent, QC H4T 2B5

Tel. 514-735-3219
Fax 514-735-6440
Email .... resumes@cimmetry.com
Website .... www.cimmetry.com

Cimmetry Systems, Inc. / CSI is a world leader in the development of viewing and mark-up software. CSI targets worldwide markets in CAD, document management, engineering, imaging, and workflow. Products are available in several languages to corporate customers in over fifty countries. Graduates most likely to be hired come from the following academic areas: Bachelor of Arts (General), Bachelor of Engineering (General, Electrical, Computer Systems), Bachelor of Commerce/Business Administration (Marketing), Master of Business Administration (Marketing), Community College Diploma (Administration, Business, Marketing/Sales, Secretarial, Computer Science) and High School Diploma. Graduates would occupy Software Developer, Technical Support, Inside Sales, Marketing and General Office Clerk positions. Autonomous, organized, proficiency in English, previous work experience in the computer/software industry, and interested in a dynamic, challenging and fast paced career are all listed as desirable non-academic qualifications. Company benefits are rated as industry standard. The potential for advancement is listed as average. The average annual starting salary falls within the $20,000 to $45,000 range, depending on the position being considered. The most suitable methods for initial contact by those seeking employment are to mail or fax a resume with a covering letter. Cimmetry Systems, Inc. does hire summer students. *Contact:* Gabriel Takacs, Personnel Manager.

CINRAM INTERNATIONAL INC.

2255 Markham Road
Toronto, ON M1B 2W3

Tel. 416-298-8190
Fax 416-298-0627
Website .... www.cinram.ca

Cinram International Inc. is a custom manufacturer of various media including DVD, audio compact disc, CD-ROM, pre-recorded audio cassette tapes, and pre-recorded video cassette tapes. The company supplies its products to many of the major recording companies, movie studios, publishing and software companies in North America and Europe. The company has locations in the United States, Europe and Latin America. In Canada, Cinram has two manufacturing facilities located in Toronto with sales offices in Ontario, Quebec and Western Canada. In addition, Cinram's Canadian operations includes The Amazing Video Network, a distributor of pre-recorded videos. This location is involved in the manufacture of audio compact discs. Graduates most likely to be hired come from the following academic areas: Bachelor of Engineering (Electrical, Mechanical, Industrial Production/Manufacturing), Bachelor of Commerce/Business Administration (Accounting, Finance, Information Systems), Certified General Accountant, Community College Diploma (Accounting) and High School Diploma. Company benefits are rated as above average. The potential for advancement is listed as being good. The average annual starting salary falls within the $30,000 to $35,000 range. The most suitable methods for initial contact by those seeking employment are to mail or fax a resume with a covering letter, or via the company's website. Cinram International Inc. does hire summer students. *Contact:* Cheryl Givelas, Manager, Human Resources.

CINRAM VIDEO CENTRE

5590 Finch Avenue East
Toronto, ON M1B 1T1

Tel. 416-332-9000
Fax 416-332-9018
Website .... www.cinram.ca

Cinram Video Centre, a manufacturing location of Cinram International Inc., is a high tech manufacturer of video tapes. Cinram Video Centre employs 400 people. Graduates most likely to be hired at this location come from the following academic areas: Bachelor of Engineering (Electrical, Mechanical, Industrial Engineering), Bachelor of Commerce/Business Administration (Accounting, Information Systems), Certified General Accountant and Community College Diploma (Accounting, Marketing/Sales). Dedication and stability are both listed as desirable non-academic qualifications. Company benefits are rated above average. The potential for advancement is listed as being good. The average annual starting salary falls within the $25,000 to $35,000 range. The most suitable methods for initial contact by those seeking employment are to mail or fax a resume with a covering letter, or via the company's website. Cinram Video Centre does hire summer students. *Contact:* Dina Plahouras, Manager, Human Resources.

CIRCON TECHNOLOGY CORPORATION
1503 Cliveden Avenue
Delta, BC V3M 6P7

Tel. 604-521-9162
Fax 604-521-9168
Email .... jobs@circon.com
Website .... www.circon.com

Circon Technology Corporation designs and manufactures open protocol building automation systems that integrate control of security, access, lighting, heating, energy management, ventilation, air conditioning and other building functions. The company's mission is to apply the latest technologies to help building owners, managers and systems integrators cost-effectively meet the demands of modern building automation. Circon employs approximately 20 people. Graduates most likely to be hired come from the following academic areas: Bachelor of Science (Computer Science), Bachelor of Engineering (Architectural/Building, Computer Systems, Telecommunications, Industrial Design, Industrial Production), Master of Engineering (Building Automation) and Community College Diploma (Facility Management, CAD/CAM/Autocad, Computer Science, Engineering Technician, HVAC Systems). Work experience with a start-up company, dynamic, multi-tasking capabilities and able to work well in a team environment are listed as desirable non-academic qualifications. Company benefits are rated as excellent. The potential for advancement is listed as being good. The most suitable method for initial contact by those seeking employment is to mail a resume with a covering letter. Circon Technology Corporation does hire summer students. *Contact:* Human Resources Manager.

the citadel

CITADEL GENERAL ASSURANCE COMPANY, THE
1075 Bay Street
Toronto, ON M5S 2W5

Tel. 416-928-5580
Fax 416-928-5556

The Citadel General Assurance Company provides commercial and personal automobile insurance, property insurance, and special risk insurance. The company employs more than 250 people. Graduates most likely to be hired come from the following academic areas: Bachelor of Arts (General), Bachelor of Commerce/Business Administration and Community College Diploma (Accounting, Administration, Business, Insurance, Secretarial, Human Resources). Preference is given to graduates who possess or are working toward the AIIC designation. Graduates would occupy Claims Adjuster Trainee, Underwriter Trainee and Accounting Clerk positions. Good organizational skills, flexible, team player, an ability to think independently, good problem solving and communication skills, able to work well with others and committed to life long learning are all listed as desirable non-academic qualifications. Company benefits are rated above average. The potential for advancement is listed as being good. The average annual starting salary falls within the $20,000 to $25,000 range. The most suitable methods for initial contact by those seeking employment are to mail or fax a resume with a covering letter. The Citadel General Assurance Company does hire summer students. *Contact:* Human Resources Representative.

CIVIL SERVICE CO-OPERATIVE CREDIT SOCIETY / CS CO-OP
400 Albert Street
Ottawa, ON K1R 5B2

Tel. 613-560-0100
Fax 613-560-6385
Website .... www.cscoop.ca

The Civil Service Co-operative Credit Society / CS CO-OP is Ontario's first credit union with over 143,000 members. Founded in 1908, The CS CO-OP provides innovative financial services, striving to set itself apart from the competition by working to anticipate and meet its members' financial needs. In doing so, the cooperative's ultimate goal is to build a lifetime partnership with each of its members. Originally open only to federal government employees and their families, the membership has recently been expanded to include virtually all Ontario residents. Today the CS CO-OP employs over 200 employees at the head office location and more than 150 employees at its branch locations. Graduates most likely to be hired come from the following academic areas: Bachelor of Arts (Economics), Bachelor of Science (Computer Science), Bachelor of Engineering (Computer Systems), Bachelor of Commerce/Business Administration (General, Accounting, Finance, Human Resources, Information Systems, Marketing, Public Administration), Chartered Accountant, Certified Management Accountant, Certified General Accountant, Master of Business Administration (General, Accounting, Finance, Human Resources, Information Systems, Marketing, Public Administration), Community College Diploma (Accounting, Advertising, Business, Communications/Public Relations, Financial Planning, Human Resources, Insurance, Marketing/Sales, Office Administration, Computer Science, Information Systems) and I.F.I.C., C.S.C, Institute of Canadian Bankers and C.F.P. designations. The CS CO-OP offers opportunities for permanent and temporary, part-time and full-time work in its branches and various supporting departments, such as Administration, Human Resources, Accounting, Marketing and Information Technology. The ability to work well under pressure, great communication skills, team worker and good problem solving skills are all listed as desirable non-academic qualifications. Company benefits are rated as industry standard. The potential for advancement is listed as being good. The average annual starting salary falls within the $30,000 to $35,000 range. The most suitable methods for initial contact by those seeking employment are to mail or fax a resume with a covering letter, or via the company's website. The CS CO-OP does hire summer students and students enrolled in cooperative work programs. *Contact:* Human Resources Department.

CLARICA™

CLARICA / IT PROFESSIONALS
227 King Street South
Waterloo, ON N2J 4C5

Fax	519-888-2727
Email	itjobs@clarica.com
Website	www.clarica.com

Clarica is one of Canada's fastest growing financial organizations, specializing in investments, insurance and employee benefits. Clarica (formerly The Mutual Group) has been helping people make clear financial choices for over 129 years. The company has taken a leadership role within the industry by being the first Canadian insurance company to demutualize and be traded on the Toronto Stock Exchange. The innovative use of technology is key to maintaining Clarica's competitive advantage in the financial services industry. As a proven industry leader in the development and use of state-of-the-art technologies, the company's information services team provides technology solutions that are fundamental to Clarica's growth and commitment to its customers. Clarica's Information Services team primarily seeks out graduates in the following specialized programs: Computer Science, Mathematics, Business and Computer Engineering. Opportunities are also open to students from other faculties who have a passion for technology and experience in the IT industry. In addition, Clarica's information Services team looks for innovative people with an aptitude for technology, a desire for lifelong learning, are results oriented, excellent communicators, team players, proven leaders and are able to manage change well. The most suitable method for initial contact by those seeking employment is to fax or e-mail your resume with a covering letter. In order to learn more about career opportunities and the Clarica story please visit the company's website. *Contact:* IT Resourcing Consultant.

CLARICA™

CLARICA / SALES PROFESSIONALS
227 King Street South
Waterloo, ON N2J 4C5

Tel.	888-882-4268
Fax	519-888-2107
Email	Rosemarie.Mask@Clarica.com
Website	www.clarica.com

Clarica is one of Canada's fastest growing financial organizations, specializing in investments, insurance and employee benefits. The company's mission is to thoroughly understand a customer's needs and goals before they discuss any financial products or options. Clarica (formerly The Mutual Group) has been providing solutions this way since 1870. The company has taken a leadership role within the industry by being the first Canadian insurance company to demutualize and be traded on the Toronto Stock Exchange. Clarica will continue to be innovators and lead the competition. Clarica hires individuals from all kinds of academic backgrounds, but a university degree or college diploma is required. The company seeks individuals who are interested in building their own financial services practice and who are passionate about helping people. For these people, Clarica provides the opportunity to work one-on-one with customers, to understand their hopes and needs and to provide a solution that best suits them. In the process of helping people, graduates will satisfy their entrepreneurial side by building their own customer base. As an agent, graduates receive commissions and bonuses, with compensation directly tied to each individual's efforts. Clarica rewards agents for creating and maintaining trusting relationships that stand the test of time. The most suitable method for initial contact by those seeking employment is to mail a resume with a covering letter. In order to learn more about career opportunities and the Clarica story please visit the company's website. *Contact:* Rosemarie Mask, Agent Recruiting and Selection.

CLEARNET COMMUNICATIONS INC.
300 Consilium Place, 9th Floor
Toronto, ON M1H 3G2

Tel.	416-296-7836
Fax	416-296-7835
Website	www.clearnet.com

Clearnet Communications Inc. is a leading Canadian wireless communications company. Clearnet is unique in offering two state-of-the-art digital wireless communications services, Mike for business people, and Clearnet PCS for consumers. Mike is a fully digital service that offers business workgroups the ability to save time and money by integrating Mike's direct connect, two-way radio mobile digital phone, text messaging with acknowledgment (paging) and internet communications, all in a single handset operating on a single wireless network. Clearnet PCS offers individual consumers an easy-to-use and easy-to-purchase digital wireless communications product. Utilizing a dual-mode, dual-band digital PCS/analogue cellular phone that works everywhere in Canada that cellular does, Clearnet PCS offers affordable talktime plans, fair per second billing and extra calling features included without additional charges. Clearnet employs 1,120 people at this location and more than 2,000 people in Canada. Graduates most likely to be hired come from the following academic areas: Bachelor of Arts (French, Languages), Bachelor of Science (Computer Science), Bachelor of Engineering (General, Electrical, Computer Systems, Engineering Physics, Industrial Engineering, Telecommunications), Bachelor of Education (Adult), Bachelor of Laws, Bachelor of Commerce/Business Administration (General, Accounting, Finance, Human Resources, Information Systems, Marketing), Chartered Accountant, Certified Management Accountant, Certified General Accountant, Master of Business Administration (General, Accounting, Finance, Human Resources, Information Systems, Marketing) and Community College Diploma (Accounting, Administration, Advertising, Business, Communications/Public Relations, Facility Management, Financial Planning, Human Resources, Information Systems, Marketing/Sales, Purchasing/Logistics, Secretarial, Electronics Technician, Engineering Technician). Graduates would occupy SAP Analyst, Accounts Receivable, Computing Support Team Leader, Information Resources Manager, Account Executive, Channel Business Analyst, Client Business Analyst, Bilingual Internet Communications Specialist and Network Engineer positions. Strong communication skills, team player, bilingual (French, Mandarin, Cantonese), computer literacy (eg. Windows environment, Word, Excel, PowerPoint), organized and strong interpersonal skills are all listed as desirable non-academic qualifications. Company benefits are rated as excellent. The potential for advancement is listed as being good. The most suitable method for initial contact by those seeking employment is through the company's website at www.clearnet.com. Clearnet Communications Inc. does hire students for summer and co-op work terms. *Contact:* Human Resources.

CLOSER TO HOME COMMUNITY SERVICES
1610 - 37th Street SW, Suite 206
Calgary, AB T3C 3P1

Tel. 403-543-0550
Fax 403-246-6406

Closer To Home Community Services is a non-profit organization providing counselling, training and placement services for children with behavioral and emotional problems. The service employs 70 people in the operation of family support programs, family resource centres, group homes, foster care and a semi-independent living program. Graduates most likely to be hired come from the following academic areas: Bachelor of Arts (Psychology, Social Work), Bachelor of Science (Psychology), Bachelor of Education (Special Needs), Master of Arts (Psychology, Social Work), Master of Science (Psychology) and Community College Diploma (Social Work/DSW). Graduates would occupy Counsellor, Family Counsellor, Social Worker and Case worker positions. A good attitude towards learning and performance evaluations, optimistic and flexible are all listed as desirable non-academic qualifications. Company benefits are rated above average. The potential for advancement is listed as excellent. The average annual starting salary falls within the $25,000 to $30,000 range. The most suitable method for initial contact by those seeking employment is to mail a resume with a covering letter. Closer To Home Community Services does hire summer students. *Contact:* Larry Mathieson, MBA, Operations Director.

CLUB MONACO INTERNATIONAL
430 King Street West
Toronto, ON M5V 1L5

Tel. 416-585-4896
Fax 416-585-4176
Email .... recruitment@clubmonaco.com
Website .... www.clubmonaco.com

Club Monaco International is a brand of fresh, modern products for men, women, boys and girls, sold exclusively in 115 Club Monaco stores worldwide. The Club Monaco brand encompasses products ranging from clothing and accessories to eyewear, watches, cosmetics, silver jewellry and items for the home. Based in Toronto, the Club Monaco World Headquarters employs more than 100 people in the design, development and marketing of the Club Monaco brand internationally. Graduates most likely to be hired come from the following academic areas: Bachelor of Arts (Journalism), Bachelor of Commerce/Business Administration (Accounting, Finance, Human Resources, Information Systems, Marketing) and Community College Diploma (Accounting, Administration, Communications/Public Relations, Human Resources, Information Systems, Marketing/Sales, Real Estate Sales, Secretarial, Fashion Arts, Graphic Arts, Journalism). At the World Headquarters, graduates would occupy Accounting and Finance, Advertising and Marketing, Buying and Product Development, Communications, Design Team, Distribution and Traffic, Franchise, Human Resources, Information Technology, Loss Prevention, Merchandise Planning and Analysis, Real Estate and Leasing, Technical and Quality Control, and Visual Merchandising and Presentation positions. At Store locations, graduates would occupy Sales Associate, Stock Person, Cashier, In-Store Visual Presentation Technician, Makeup Specialist, Assistant Store Manager, Store Manager, Product Manager, Sales and Resource Manager, General Manager, District Manager and Regional Manager positions. Company benefits are rated as industry standard and include a discount on Club Monaco merchandise, bonuses that reward outstanding performance, employee referral bonuses, group insurance benefits and more. The potential for advancement is listed as excellent. The average annual starting salary varies according to the position being considered. For opportunities at the Club Monaco Headquarters, the most suitable methods for initial contact by those seeking employment are to mail or fax a resume with a covering letter. For a list of current job opportunities at the Toronto Headquarters, applicants should visit the company's website. For Store opportunities candidates should apply directly to the store of their choice, see website for the nearest location. Club Monaco International does hire students for summer and co-op work terms. *Contact:* The Recruitment Team.

CML TECHNOLOGIES
75, boul. de la Technologie
Hull, QC J8Z 3G4

Tel. 819-778-2053
Fax 819-778-3408

Email .... cmlhr@cmltech.com
Website .... www.cmltech.com

CML Technologies is a leader in specialized areas of the international telecommunications industry. Since 1979, CML has steadily grown into a multi-million dollar enterprise, and currently employs over 150 people. Headquarters within North America are found in Hull, Quebec and Atlanta, Georgia. Numerous branch office locations are found throughout the United States. CML's product lines include mobile radio consoles, enhanced 911 emergency calling systems, and other specialized switching systems for customized computer telephony applications. Products and services are sold through major organizations in the telecommunications industry, as well as directly through CML's own sales network. Graduates most likely to be hired come from the following academic areas: Bachelor of Science (Computer Science), Bachelor of Engineering (Electrical), Bachelor of Commerce/Business Administration (Finance, Marketing), Master of Business Administration (Finance, Marketing), Bachelor of Arts (Technical Writing) and Community College Diploma (Accounting, Administration, Computer Science, Electronics Technician, Engineering Technician, Technical Writing). Graduates would occupy software Designer, Hardware Designer, Technician, Market Specialist, Project Coordinator (Technical) and Technical Writer positions. Team player, good work ethic, and initiative are listed as desirable non-academic qualifications. Company benefits are rated as industry standard. The potential for advancement is listed as excellent. The average annual starting salary falls within the $35,000 to $40,000 range. The most suitable methods for initial contact by those seeking employment are to mail, fax, or e-mail a resume with a covering letter, or by applying through the company's website at www.cmltech.com. CML Technologies does hire summer and co-op work term students. *Contact:* Human Resources Department.

CO-OP ATLANTIC
123 Halifax Street, PO Box 750
Moncton, NB E1C 8N5

Tel. 506-858-6028
Fax 506-858-6473

Co-op Atlantic is a regional co-operative wholesaler and supplier of farm inputs. The co-op provides services and products to 160 retail and agricultural co-ops, buying clubs, and agricultural societies. In addition, 25 other associated co-operatives are also members of Co-op Atlantic. Co-op Atlantic employs approximately 700 people in the Atlantic provinces and the Magdalen Islands. Graduates most likely to be hired come from the following academic areas: Bachelor of Arts (Graphic Arts, Journalism, Languages), Bachelor of Science (Computer Science), Bachelor of Engineering (Environmental), Bachelor of Commerce/Business Administration (General, Accounting, Finance, Human Resources, Information Systems, Marketing), Chartered Accountant, Certified Management Accountant, Certified General Accountant, Master of Business Administration (Accounting, Finance, Human Resources, Information Systems, Marketing), Community College Diploma (Accounting, Administration, Advertising, Business, Communications, Facility Management, Financial Planning, Human Resources, Marketing, Purchasing/Logistics, Secretarial, Graphic Arts, Journalism, Computer Science) and High School Diploma. Graduates would occupy Communications Officer, Typesetter, Member Relations Officer, Analyst Programmer, Engineering Technologist, Accountant, Mechanic, Distribution, Administration and various Retail positions. Good communication and interpersonal skills, team player, analytical, organized and supervisory skills are all listed as desirable non-academic skills. Company benefits are rated as excellent. The potential for advancement is listed as being good. The average annual starting salary falls within the $25,000 to $35,000 range, depending on the position being considered. The most suitable method for initial contact by those seeking employment is to mail a resume with a covering letter. Co-op Atlantic does hire summer students. *Contact:* Angela Vautour, Human Resources Area Manager.

CO-OPERATIVE TRUST CO. OF CANADA
333 - 3rd Avenue North
Saskatoon, SK S7K 2M2

Tel. 306-956-5100
Fax 306-244-1176
Email .... mdeutscher@co-operativetrust.ca
Website .... www.co-operativetrust.ca

Co-operative Trust Co. of Canada provides a full range of financial services and products. The company strives to be a dynamic industry leader through the design and delivery of innovative financial products and the development of strategic partnerships with co-operative and other like-minded organizations that value both the individuals and the communities they serve. Headquartered in Saskatoon, Co-operative Trust operates nationally with a branch network that extends from Vancouver to Halifax. The company manages assets of over $800 million and trustees assets in excess of $8 billion. Co-operative Trust's primary products are deposits, mortgages and personal and corporate trust services. Co-operative Trust employs 125 people at this location and a total of 200 people in Canada. Graduates most likely to be hired come from the following academic areas: Bachelor of Commerce/Business Administration (Accounting, Finance, Human Resources, Information Systems, Marketing, Public Administration), Chartered Accountant, Certified Management Accountant, Certified General Accountant, Master of Business Administration and Community College Diploma (Accounting, Administration, Advertising, Business, Communications, Financial Planning, Human Resources, Marketing/Sales, Secretarial). Initiative and strong interpersonal skills are both listed as desirable non-academic qualifications. Company benefits are rated as excellent. The potential for advancement is listed as being good. The average annual starting salary falls within the $20,000 to $25,000 range. The most suitable method for initial contact by those seeking employment is to mail a resume with a covering letter. Co-operative Trust Co. of Canada does hire summer students. *Contact:* Manager, Human Resources.

COAST MOUNTAIN BUSLINK COMPANY LTD.
13401 - 108th Avenue, Suite C650
Surrey, BC V3T 5T4

Tel. 604-540-3000
Fax 604-540-3005
Website .... www.translink.bc.ca

Coast Mountain BusLink Company Ltd., an operating subsidiary of TransLink, is responsible for bus public transit services in the Greater Vancouver region. The company's services encompass all bus, trolley bus and SeaBus services in the Vancouver region (excluding the West Vancouver "Blue Bus" system). Coast Mountain BusLink employs 368 people at this location and a total of 4,017 people in the Greater Vancouver region. The company reviews applications from individuals from all degree and diploma areas, depending upon the position under consideration. There is a general equivalency for all positions. Applications for the position of Transit Operator and general positions such as Customer Information Clerk, Farebox Attendant, Farebox Receipts Attendant and Traffic Checker can be downloaded directly from the website. Company benefits are rated as excellent. The average annual starting salary falls within the $25,000 to $30,000 range. Coast Mountain BusLink does hire summer students, with applications accepted starting in January and most summer positions filled by April. Coast Mountain BusLink Company Ltd. is committed to employment equity. *Contact:* Employment Services.

COATS CANADA INC.
1001 Roselawn Avenue
Toronto, ON M6B 1B8

Tel.	416-782-4481
Fax	416-782-8982
Website	www.coats.com

Coats Canada Inc. is a manufacturer and distributor of hand knitting yarns and sewing aids. Coats Canada Inc. is part of Coats Viyella, a 200-year old United Kingdom based textile business and the world's largest manufacturer of sewing thread and accessories for industrial and home sewing, and a wide variety of craft products for consumers. With locations around the globe, Coats Viyella employs over 60,000 people worldwide. Coats Canada Inc. employs 240 people at this location and a total of 300 people in Canada. Graduates most likely to be hired come from the following academic areas: Bachelor of Engineering (Electrical, Computer Systems, Mechanical, Industrial), Bachelor of Commerce/Business Administration (Finance, Marketing) and Community College Diploma (Marketing/Sales, Purchasing/Logistics, Welding). Graduates would occupy Management Trainee positions. Excellent communication skills, motivation, drive, team player and the flexibility to fit into a multicultural work environment are all listed as desirable non-academic qualifications. Company benefits are rated above average. The potential for advancement is listed as being good. The average annual starting salary falls within the $25,000 to $30,000 range. The most suitable method for initial contact by those seeking employment is to mail a resume with a covering letter. Coats Canada Inc. does hire summer students, usually Industrial Engineering and third year Electrical and Mechanical Engineering students. *Contact:* Human Resources Department.

COCHRANE ENGINEERING LTD.
1230 Blackfoot Drive, Suite 200
Regina, SK S4S 7G4

Tel.	306-585-1990
Fax	306-586-1560
Email	cstouffer@cochrane-group.ca
Website	www.cochrane-group.ca

Cochrane Engineering Ltd. is the subsidiary of the Cochrane Group which provides integrated, multi-discipline engineering and project management services across Canada. With additional offices in Vancouver, Calgary, Edmonton, Saskatoon, Winnipeg, Burlington and Toronto the company offers a full range of consulting engineering services for development and infrastructure, water resources and environment, industrial and agri-food, buildings and building science. Cochrane employs 70 people at this location, 104 in Canada and a total of 156

employees worldwide. Graduates most likely to be hired come from the following academic areas: Bachelor of Science (Agriculture, Computer Science), Bachelor of Engineering (Architectural/Building, Surveying, Electrical, Instrumentation, Power, Mechanical, Industrial Design, Environmental, Water Resources) and Community College Diploma (Accounting, Secretarial, Architecture/Drafting, CAD/CAM/Autocad, Computer Science, HVAC Systems). Graduates would occupy Engineer and Technologist positions. An entrepreneurial spirit, a high level of initiative and previous work experience are all listed as desirable non-academic qualifications. Company benefits are rated as excellent. The potential for advancement is listed as being good. The average annual starting salary is dependent upon the position being considered and the applicants qualifications. The most suitable method for initial contact by those seeking employment is to mail a resume with a covering letter. Cochrane Engineering Ltd. does hire a limited number of summer students annually. *Contact:* Human Resources Manager.

COGNICASE
1080 Beaver Hall Hill, Suite 2000
Montreal, QC H2Z 1S8

Tel.	514-866-6161
Fax	514-866-6260
Email	cv@cognicase.ca
Website	www.cognicase.ca

COGNICASE provides Fortune 1000 companies with innovative solutions, added-value consulting services in the area of information technology and business partnerships. Founded in 1991, the company has more than 2,300 employees who serve customers from business offices in fifteen cities in Canada, the United States, Europe and Australia. In addition to the Montreal headquarters, COGNICASE has Canadian office locations in Quebec, Ottawa, Toronto and Calgary. There are 300 employees at this location and a total of 1,800 employees in Canada. Graduates most likely to be hired come from the following academic areas: Bachelor of Science (Computer Science), Bachelor of Engineering (Computer Systems, Telecommunications), Bachelor of Commerce/Business Administration (Information Systems), Master of Business Administration (Information Systems) and Community College Diploma (Computer Science, Information Systems). Graduates would occupy Project Manager, Project Leader, System Analyst, Analyst/Programmer, Programmer, and Technician positions. Team work skills and autonomy are listed as desirable non-academic qualifications. Company benefits and the potential for advancement are both rated as excellent. The average annual starting salary falls within the $25,000 to $30,000 range. The most suitable method for initial contact by those seeking employment is to e-mail a resume with a covering letter. COGNICASE does hire summer and co-op work term students. *Contact:* Recruiting Services.

COGNOS INCORPORATED
3755 Riverside Drive, PO Box 9707
Ottawa, ON K1G 4K9

Tel.	613-738-1440
Fax	613-738-8882
Email	jobs@cognos.com
Website	www.cognos.com

Cognos Incorporated is a leading strategic supplier of enterprise business intelligence solutions and software that allow users to easily extract critical information through data access, reporting, analysis and forecasting. The company's products are designed to consistently deliver the highest productivity gains to the user, the most manageable solution to the administrator and the fastest return on investment to the enterprise. Founded in 1969, Cognos is an international corporation with corporate headquarters in Ottawa and U.S. sales headquarters in Burlington, Massachusetts. Cognos also operates in offices in Australia, Austria, Belgium, France, Germany, Hong Kong, Italy, Japan, The Netherlands, Norway, Singapore, South Africa, Sweden and the United Kingdom. Cognos is a publicly held company traded on NASDAQ as COGN and on the Toronto Stock Exchange as CSN. The company's products are sold through its direct sales force and an extensive network of resellers and distributors. Cognos employs more than 1,700 people worldwide. Graduates most likely to be hired come from the following academic areas: Bachelor of Arts (Graphic Arts), Bachelor of Science (Computer Science, Mathematics), Bachelor of Engineering (Electrical, Computer Systems), Bachelor of Commerce/Business Administration (Accounting, Finance, Human Resources, Information Systems, Marketing), Chartered Accountant, Certified Management Accountant, Certified General Accountant, Master of Business Administration (Finance, Information Systems, Marketing), Master of Science (Computer Science) and Community College Diploma (Accounting, Financial Planning, Human Resources, Marketing/Sales, Computer Science, Engineering Technician). Graduates would occupy Software Engineer, Technical Analyst, Programmer Analyst, Software Architect, Computer Operator, Quality Control Analyst, Marketing Specialist, Accountant, Writer, Editor, Customer Support, Education Specialist, Marketing Specialist, Sales Representative, Public Relations Specialist and Translator positions. An ability to work in a team environment, positive attitude, good verbal and written communication skills, love of learning and demonstrated prior success are all listed as desirable non-academic qualifications. Company benefits and the potential for advancement are both rated as excellent. The average annual starting salary falls within the $25,000 to $35,000 range. The most suitable methods for initial contact by those seeking employment are to mail or e-mail a resume with a covering letter. Cognos Incorporated does hire summer students, primarily those who are enrolled in university or college. *Contact:* Human Resoucers (Corporate).

COLE, SHERMAN & ASSOCIATES LTD.
75 Commerce Valley Drive East
Thornhill, ON L3T 7N9

Tel. 905-882-4401
Fax 905-882-4399
Email .... colesherman@urscorp.com
Website .... www.colesherman.com

Cole, Sherman & Associates Ltd. has been providing a full range of consulting engineering, architectural and planning services to government and private-sector clients since 1954. In 1997, Cole, Sherman joined with San Francisco, California based URS Greiner Woodward-Clyde (URSWC), giving Canadian clients access to worldwide technical expertise. Cole, Sherman now participates in international projects and brings to Canadian clients URSWC's proven excellence in the areas of air transportation, commercial/industrial, facilities, railroads/transit, surface transportation and water/wastewater. Cole, Sherman & Associates Ltd. employs a total of 125 people in Canada. Graduates most likely to be hired come from the following academic areas: Bachelor of Arts (Graphic Arts), Bachelor of Science (Computer Science), Bachelor of Engineering (Civil, Architectural/Building),

Bachelor of Architecture, Bachelor of Landscape Architecture, Master of Engineering (Structural, Transportation), Doctorate (Structural Engineering) and Community College Diploma (Computer Science, HVAC Systems). Company benefits and the potential for advancement are both rated as excellent. The average annual starting salary falls within the $25,000 to $35,000 range. The most suitable method for initial contact by graduates seeking employment is to mail a resume with a covering letter. Cole, Sherman & Associates Ltd. does hire a limited number of summer students annually. *Contact:* Personnel Manager.

COLGATE-PALMOLIVE CANADA INC.
99 Vanderhoof Avenue
Toronto, ON M4G 2H6

Tel. 416-421-6000
Fax 416-421-0286
Website .... www.colgate.ca

Colgate-Palmolive Canada Inc. is a major manufacturer of household goods such as soaps, cleaners, detergents and toiletries. Colgate-Palmolive Canada Inc. is a subsidiary of Colgate-Palmolive Company based in New York, New York. The company employs 150 people at this location and a total of 500 people in Canada. Graduates most likely to be hired come from the following academic areas: Bachelor of Science (Chemistry), Bachelor of Engineering (Chemical), Bachelor of Commerce/Business Administration (Accounting, Information Systems), Chartered Accountant, Certified Management Accountant, Certified General Accountant, Master of Business Administration (Finance, Marketing) and Community College Diploma (Human Resources, Secretarial, Laboratory Technician). Graduates would occupy Product Assistant (Marketing), Laboratory Technician and Clerical (Finance) positions. Previous work experience, team player and leadership skills are all listed as desirable non-academic qualifications. The most suitable method for initial contact by those seeking employment is to mail a resume with a covering letter. *Contact:* Rob Madeley, Manager Human Resources.

COLLINS BARROW, CALGARY
777 - 8th Avenue SW, Suite 1400
Calgary, AB T2P 3R5

Tel. 403-298-1500
Fax 403-298-5814
Email .... calgary@collinsbarrow.com
Website .... www.collinsbarrow.com

Collins Barrow, Calgary is a chartered accounting firm providing a comprehensive range of accounting and business services. Collins Barrow has 26 office locations across Canada. In addition, Collins Barrow is a founding member of Moores Rowland International, an international association of leading independent accounting firms. Collins Barrow employs 110 people at its Calgary office. Graduates most likely to be hired at the Calgary location come from the following academic areas: Bachelor of Commerce/Business Administration (Accounting), Chartered Accountant and Certified General Accountant. Company benefits are rated as industry standard. The potential for advancement is listed as being excellent. The most suitable methods for initial contact by those seeking employment are to mail or fax a resume with a covering letter. Collins Barrow, Calgary does hire summer and co-op work term students. *Contact:* Human Resources Coordinator.

COLUMBIA HOUSE COMPANY, THE
5900 Finch Avenue East
Toronto, ON M1B 5X7

Tel. 416-299-9400
Fax 416-299-7491
Website .... www.columbiahouse.com

The Columbia House Company is involved in direct mail order marketing of music and video entertainment products. The company employs approximately 420 people at this location, and a total of 5,000 employees worldwide. Operational activities include repertoire selection for new releases, marketing, and distribution. Graduates most likely to be hired come from the following academic areas: Bachelor of Arts (Journalism, Music), Bachelor of Commerce/Business Administration (Accounting, Marketing), Chartered Accountant (Finance), Certified General Accountant, Community College Diploma (Accounting, Business, Marketing/Sales, Purchasing/Logistics, Secretarial, Graphic Design) and High School Diploma. Graduates would occupy positions in Customer Service, Purchasing/Order Inventory, Graphic Arts, Desk-Top Publishing, Marketing and Distribution. Strong verbal and written communication skills, familiarity with Lotus 123, music background and musical interests are all listed as desirable non-academic qualifications. Company benefits are rated above average. The potential for advancement is listed as average. The average annual starting salary falls within the $22,000 to $25,000 range. The most suitable method for initial contact by those seeking employment is to mail a resume with a covering letter. Contacts: Jan Thompson, CHRP, Director of Personnel or Michelle Lopez, Recruitment Manager.

COM DEV INTERNATIONAL
155 Sheldon Drive
Cambridge, ON N1R 7H6

Tel. 519-622-2300
Fax 519-622-5543
Email .... spacetech.resumes@comdev.ca
Website .... www.comdev.ca

COM DEV International is one of the world's leading developers and manufacturers of products for communications satellites, as well as a rapidly-growing producer of ground-based wireless communications products. Canadian based, COM DEV employs more than 1,200 people in facilities in Ontario, New Brunswick, the United Kingdom, the United States and China. There are more than 400 employees at this location. Graduates most likely to be hired come from the following academic areas: Bachelor of Science (Computer Science, Mathematics, Metallurgy, Ergonomics), Bachelor of Engineering (Electrical, Mechanical, Aerospace, Engineering Physics, Industrial Production/Manufacturing, Metallurgy, Telecommunications), Bachelor of Commerce/Business Administration (Accounting, Finance), Community College Diploma (Human Resources, Office Administration, Purchasing/Logistics, Electronics Technician, Engineering Technician, Information Systems, Tool and Die/Machinist) and High School Diploma. Graduates would occupy Engineer, Technologist, Administrative, Network Administration, Programmer and Systems Analyst positions. Team player, a positive attitude, good work record and relevant work experience are listed as desirable non-academic qualifications. Company benefits are rated above average. The potential for advancement is listed as being good. The most suitable method for initial contact by those seeking employment is to mail a resume with a covering letter. COM DEV International does hire a few summer students annually. Contact: Recruitment Specialist.

COMCARE HEALTH SERVICES
2300 Yonge Street, Suite 904, PO Box 2341
Toronto, ON M4P 1E4

Tel. 416-484-4433
Fax 416-484-4636

Comcare Health Services is a Canadian leader in delivering innovative health care services. The company offers a comprehensive range of services provided twenty-four hours a day, seven days a week including nursing visits, foot care services, occupational nursing, palliative care, home support services, occupational and physiotherapy services. There are approximately 250 employees at this location and 1,500 employees across Canada. Graduates most likely to be hired come from the following academic areas: Bachelor of Arts (General), Bachelor of Science (Nursing, Occupational Therapy, Physical Therapy), Bachelor of Education (Special Needs) and Community College Diploma (Business, Nursing RN, Nursing RNA). Graduates would occupy supervisor, field staff, and marketing positions. Team player, highly motivated, creative and excellent organizational skills are all listed as desirable non-academic qualifications. Company benefits are rated as industry standard. The potential for advancement is listed as average. The most suitable methods for initial contact by those seeking employment are to mail or fax a resume with a covering letter. Comcare Health Services does hire summer students. (Other Locations: Comcare Health Services, 2130 Lawrence Avenue East, Suite 404, Scarborough, ON, M1R 3A6, Phone 416-759-8242, Fax 416-759-9677; Comcare Health Services, 720 Spadina Avenue, Suite 409, Toronto, ON, M5S 2T9, Phone 416-929-3364, Fax 416-929-1738). Contact: Human Resources.

COMINCO LTD.
200 Burrard Street, Suite 500
Vancouver, BC V6C 3L7

Tel. 604-682-0611
Fax 604-685-3019
Website .... www.cominco.com

Cominco Ltd. is an international integrated mining & metals company whose principal activities are mineral exploration, mining, smelting and refining. Cominco employs approximately 100 employees at this location, a total of 4,000 across Canada and 5,500 employees worldwide. Graduates most likely to be hired come from the following academic areas: Bachelor of Science (Geology) and Bachelor of Engineering (Chemical, Materials Science, Metallurgy, Mining). Graduates are hired for Geologist and Engineer-in-training positions. Enthusiasm, flexibility, a strong work ethic and related work experience are all listed as desirable non-academic qualifications. Company benefits and the potential for advancement are both listed as excellent. The average annual starting salary falls within the $35,000 to $40,000 range. The most suitable method for initial contact by those seeking employment is to mail a resume with a covering letter. Cominco Ltd. does hire summer students. Contact: Human Resources.

COMMUNITY CARE ACCESS CENTRE NIAGARA
PO Box 215
St. Catharines, ON L2R 6S4

Tel. 905-684-9441
Fax 905-684-2297

The Community Care Access Centre Niagara offers information, referral and access to services to help individuals maintain health, independence and quality of life. Services are available for all age groups and include help for clients with acute illness, disabilities and those requiring placement to a long-term care facility. Services are available in the home, school, workplace or long-term care facility. Graduates most likely to be hired come from the following academic areas: Bachelor of Science (Nursing, Occupational Therapy, Physical Therapy). Graduates would occupy Case Manager and Coordinator positions that work with individuals and their caregivers to access professional and support services. Excellent assessment skills, team player, two years case management experience and good organizational and time management skills are all listed as desirable non-academic qualifications. Company benefits are rated as industry standard. The potential for advancement is listed as being average. The average annual starting salary falls within the $40,000 to $45,000 range. The most suitable method for initial contact by those seeking employment is to mail a resume with a covering letter. The Community Care Access Centre Niagara does hire co-op work term students. *Contact:* Joanne MacLeod, Manager of Human Resources.

COMMUNITY CARE ACCESS CENTRE OF PEEL
199 County Court Boulevard
Brampton, ON L6W 4P3

Tel. 905-796-0040
Fax 905-796-7057
Website .... www.ccacpeel.org

Community Care Access Centre of Peel plays a leading role in managing and providing community based healthcare and long term care services in the Region of Peel. Operating as a not-for-profit organization, the centre employs a total of 200 people. Graduates most likely to be hired come from the following academic areas: Bachelor of Arts (Communications, Journalism), Bachelor of Science (Nursing), Bachelor of Commerce/Business Administration (Human Resources, Information Systems), Certified Management Accountant, Certified General Accountant and Community College Diploma (Accounting, Human Resources, Information Systems, Secretarial, Public Health Nurse). Graduates would occupy Case Manager, Accounting, Communications, and Administrative Support positions. Team player, community nursing experience, an ability to manage multiple priorities and good communication skills are all listed as desirable non-academic qualifications. Company benefits are rated above average. The potential for advancement is listed as average. The average annual starting salary falls within the $30,000 to $35,000 range. The most suitable method for initial contact by those seeking employment is to mail a resume with a covering letter. *Contact:* Human Resources Associate.

COMMUNITY CARE ACCESS CENTRE OF YORK REGION
1100 Gorham Street, Unit 1
Newmarket, ON L3Y 7V1

Tel. 905-895-1240
Fax 905-895-7205
Email .... hr@ccacyorkregion.on.ca
Website .... www.ccacyorkregion.on.ca

The Community Care Access Centre of York Region provides community care, placement, information and referral services for people of all ages through a visible, single point of access. The centre is a not-for-profit organization working in partnership with clients and their families, community agencies, schools and hospitals. The

centre enables children, adults and seniors to access health care and personal support services to help them live independently. The centre employs a total of 244 people. Graduates most likely to be hired come from the following academic areas: Bachelor of Social Work, Bachelor of Science (Nursing, Occupational Therapy, Physiotherapy, Speech Pathology), Bachelor of Commerce/Business Administration (Accounting, Finance, Human Resources, Information Systems) and Community College Diploma (Accounting, Business, Human Resources, Office Administration, Secretarial, Nursing RN). Graduates would occupy Case Manager, Accounting, Secretarial, Clerical and Administration positions. Excellent communication skills, related community-based healthcare experience and the ability to work evenings and weekends are all listed as desirable non-academic qualifications. Company benefits are rated as excellent. The potential for advancement is listed as being average. The most suitable methods for initial contact by those seeking employment are to mail or fax a resume with a covering letter. The Community Care Access Centre of York Region does hire summer students. *Contacts:* Susan Richards, Recruiting Coordinator or Sylvia Fader, Secretary, Human Resources.

COMMUNITY CARE ACCESS CENTRE, SCARBOROUGH
1940 Eglinton Avenue East, 3rd Floor
Toronto, ON M1L 4R1

Tel. 416-750-2444
Fax 416-750-4116
Email .... info@scarbccac.org
Website .... www.scarbccac.org

The Community Care Access Centre of Scarborough is a community based, not-for-profit, client focused organization providing placement services into long term care facilities as well as health, social and support services in the home and community. Graduates most likely to be hired come from the following academic areas: Bachelor of Arts (Social Work) and Bachelor of Science (Nursing, Occupational Therapy, Physiotherapy). Graduates would occupy Co-ordinator positions. The ability to work on multi-disciplinary teams, flexible and a working knowledge of a second language are all listed as desirable non-academic qualifications. Company benefits are rated as industry standard. The potential for advancement is listed as being average. The average annual starting salary falls within the $45,000 to $50,000 range. The most suitable methods for initial contact by those seeking employment are to mail or fax a resume with a covering letter. The Scarborough Community Care Access Centre does hire summer students. *Contact:* Gregory Kolesar.

COMMUNITY LIVING LONDON
190 Adelaide Street South
London, ON N5Z 3L1

Tel. 519-686-3000
Fax 519-686-5490
Website .... www.communitylivinginc.org

Community Living London is active in supporting persons with developmental challenges within the community. Support services include accommodations, vocational, employment, leisure, and senior's support services. Community Living London employs 380 people. Graduates most likely to be hired come from the following academic areas: Bachelor of Arts (General, Psychology, Social Work), Bachelor of Science (Psychology) and Developmental Service Worker. Graduates would occupy the following positions: Support Worker (to work with developmentally challenged children and adults) and Family Support Worker (to work with families). Previous experience with developmentally challenged individuals, team player and excellent communication skills are listed as desirable non-academic qualifications. Company benefits are rated above average. The potential for advancement is listed as average. The average annual starting salary for full time staff falls in the $30,000 range (staff generally must work part time initially). The most suitable method for initial contact by those seeking employment is to mail a resume with a covering letter. *Contact:* Human Resources.

COMMUNITY LIVING MISSISSAUGA

755 The Queensway East
Mississauga, ON L4Y 4C5

Tel.	905-275-4705
Fax	905-566-1365

Community Living Mississauga is a non profit organization providing services and support to people who have an intellectual handicap, assisting them to live and participate in community life. Support services include, group homes, supported employment, preschool, independent living, sheltered work shops, associate families, respite, and leisure. Community Living employs approximately 300 people in Mississauga. Graduates most likely to be hired come from the following academic areas: Bachelor of Arts (General, Psychology, Social Work), Bachelor of Science (Nursing, Occupational Therapy, Physical Therapy, Psychology), Bachelor of Education (Early Childhood, Adult, Physical and Health, Special Needs), Bachelor of Commerce/Business Administration (General, Accounting, Human Resources, Information Systems), Certified Management Accountant (Non-Profit), Certified General Accountant (Non-Profit) and Community College Diploma (Accounting, Business, Human Resources, Recreation Studies, Social Work, Developmental Service Worker, Nursing RN/RNA). Graduates would occupy Support Worker (assisting those who have an intellectual handicap), Management (most positions are often filled from within) and Administrative support positions. An ability to communicate with ease, empathetic, caring, considerate to people's needs, team player, enthusiastic, organized, leadership skills, flexible and strong communication skills are all listed as desirable non-academic qualifications. Company benefits are rated as excellent. The potential for advancement is listed as average. The average annual starting salary falls within the $25,000 to $30,000 range. The most suitable method for initial contact by those seeking employment is to mail a resume with a covering letter. Summer students are hired for leisure activities. This is usually done through Support Services (905) 615-1630 and is usually completed by the end of May. *Contact:* Human Resources.

COMMUNITY RESOURCE SERVICES

3365 Harvester Road
Burlington, ON L7N 3N2

Tel.	905-632-6531
Fax	905-632-6560

Community Resource Services serves the wider community by helping at risk youth and young adults to improve relationships with others, identify and work toward reaching their full potential and interact with their community in a positive way. Community Resource Services was established as a community development project of the Burlington Social Planning Council in 1981 to meet the identified needs of Burlington youth involved with, or at risk of becoming involved with, the criminal justice system. Today, the service has residential facilities in Burlington, Milton and Acton. Graduates most likely to be hired come from the following academic areas: Bachelor of Arts (Psychology, Recreation Studies, Social Worker), Bachelor of Science (Psychology) and Community College Diploma (Recreation Studies, Security/Enforcement, Social Worker, Child and Youth Worker). Graduates would occupy Residential Counsellor and Community Worker positions. Previous experience working with youth, excellent communication skills, team skills and the ability to work under pressure are all listed as desirable non-academic qualifications. The average annual starting salary falls within the $25,000 to $30,000 range. The most suitable methods for initial contact by those seeking employment are to mail or fax a resume with a covering letter. Community Resource Services does hire summer students with support from Human Resources Development Canada. *Contact:* Karen Howden, Human Resources Department.

COMPAGNIE MINIERE QUÉBEC CARTIER

Route 138
Port Cartier, QC G5B 2H3

Tel.	418-768-2269
Fax	418-768-2105

Compagnie Miniere Québec Cartier operates the iron ore mine and the associated pellet plant in Port Cartier. In addition, the company is responsible for the management of the town, railway, port, etc. The company employs approximately 2,000 people. Graduates most likely to be hired come from the following academic areas: Bachelor of Science (Computer Science, Metallurgy), Bachelor of Engineering (Industrial Chemistry, Metallurgy, Electrical, Computer Systems, Instrumentation, Power, Industrial Design, Industrial Production, Marine, Welding, Mining), Bachelor of Commerce/Business Administration (Accounting, Finance, Human Resources), Master of Business Administration (Accounting, Finance) and Community College Diploma (Business, Financial Planning, Human Resources, Aircraft Maintenance, Auto Mechanic, Computer Science, Electronics Technician, Marine Engineering Technician). Previous related work experience, team player and able to live and work in an isolated area are listed as desirable non-academic qualifications. Company benefits are rated as excellent. The potential for advancement is listed as average. The average annual starting salary falls within the $45,000 to $50,000 range. The most suitable method for initial contact by those seeking employment is via telephone. Compagnie Miniere Québec Cartier does hire summer students. *Contact:* Director of Employment.

COMPUSEARCH MICROMARKETING DATA AND SYSTEMS

330 Front Street West, Suite 1100
Toronto, ON M5V 3B7

Tel.	416-348-9180
Fax	416-581-1526
Email	info@polk.ca
Website	www.polk.ca

Compusearch Micromarketing Data and Systems conducts research and analytical studies, sells and markets demographic information and develops software packages. Compusearch is a Polk Canada Marketing Services company. Graduates most likely to be hired come from the following academic areas: Bachelor of Arts (Geography, Psychology), Bachelor of Science (Computer Science), Bachelor of Commerce/Business Administration (Marketing), Master of Business Administration, Masters (Geography, Statistics), Doctorate (Geography, Statistics) and Community College Diploma (Statistics/Research). Graduates would occupy Researcher, Marketing Representative, Programmer/Analyst, Product Manager and Administrative positions. Sales ability, self-starting, management experience, analytical skills, good organizational and communication skills are all listed as desirable qualifications. Company benefits are rated above average. The potential for advancement is listed as average. The average annual starting salary falls within the $20,000 to $30,000 range. The most suitable method for initial contact by those seeking employment is to mail a resume with a covering letter. Compusearch Micromarketing Data and Systems does hire summer students. *Contact:* Human Resources.

COMPUTER TASK GROUP / CTG
1 Yonge Street, Suite 1902
Toronto, ON M5E 1E5

Tel. 416-868-1212
Fax 416-868-9449
Email .... toronto@ctg.com
Website .... www.ctg.com

Computer Task Group / CTG is an information technology consulting firm providing variable workforce solutions to business clients. Services provided range from high level consulting to providing technical resources with skills in both the mainframe and client server area. CTG's head office is located in Buffalo, New York. The company employs 60 people across Canada and a total of 6,000 people worldwide. Graduates most likely to be hired come from the following academic areas: Bachelor of Science (Computer Science) and Community College Diploma (Computer Science). Graduates would occupy Junior Software Engineer positions. Team player, willing to learn, and an ability to feel comfortable meeting new people and entering into new situations are all listed as desirable non-academic qualifications. Company benefits are rated above average. The potential for advancement is listed as being good. The average annual starting salary falls within the $50,000 to $55,000 range. The most suitable method for initial contact by those seeking employment is to mail a resume with a covering letter. *Contact:* Recruiters.

COMPUTING DEVICES CANADA LTD. / CDC
3785 Richmond Road
Nepean, ON K2H 5B7

Tel. 613-596-7194
Fax 613-596-7637
Website .... www.computingdevices.com

Computing Devices Canada Ltd. / CDC is a defence electronics contractor. CDC employs expertise in the areas of electrical, mechanical, and software engineering, and has become one of the country's largest hi-tech employers, with 800 employees at this location and a total of 1,500 employees in Canada. Graduates most likely to be hired come from the following academic areas: Bachelor of Science (Computer Science), Bachelor of Engineering (Electrical, Mechanical, Computer Systems, Industrial Engineering) and Community College Diploma (Information Systems, Electronics Technician, Engineering Technician, Nursing RN). Graduates would occupy Junior Software Engineer, Junior Hardware Engineer, Manufacturing Engineer and Technician positions. Team Player,

and excellent interpersonal and communication skills are all listed as desirable non-academic qualifications. Company benefits are rated as industry standard. The potential for advancement is listed as being good. The average annual starting salary falls within the $40,000 to $45,000 range. The most suitable method for initial contact by those seeking employment is through the company's website. Computing Devices Canada Ltd. does hire students for summer and co-op work terms. *Contact:* Doreen Pasternack, Human Resources Advisor.

COMSTOCK CANADA LTD.
3455 Landmark Road
Burlington, ON L7M 1T4

Tel. 905-335-3333
Fax 905-335-4265
Email .... dflynn@comstockcanada.com
Website .... www.comstockcanada.com

Comstock Canada Ltd. provides a wide range of engineering services, including mechanical and electrical construction, building maintenance, power production and electrical transmission. There are approximately 950 employees at this location, a total of 1,600 in Canada, and 20,000 employees worldwide. Graduates most likely to be hired come from the following academic areas: Bachelor of Engineering (General, Chemical, Pollution Treatment, Pulp and Paper, Electrical, Automation/Robotics, Power, Mechanical, Industrial Design, Industrial Production, Welding), Bachelor of Commerce/Business Administration (General, Marketing), Master of Engineering (Electrical, Mechanical), Community College Diploma (Accounting, Administration, Business, Secretarial, Architecture/Drafting, CAD/CAM/Autocad, Engineering Technician, Welding) and High School Diploma. Graduates would occupy Estimator, Project Engineer, Project Manager, Technician, Trainee, Clerk, Accounting and Administration positions. An insistence on quality, devotion to work and an interest in advancement are all listed as desirable non-academic qualifications. Company benefits and the potential for advancement are both rated as excellent. The average annual starting salary falls within the $30,000 to $35,000 range, depending upon the applicants experience and ability. The most suitable method for initial contact by those seeking employment is to mail a resume with a covering letter. Comstock Canada Ltd. does hire co-op work term students. *Contact:* Vice President.

CON-DRAIN COMPANY (1983) LTD.
30 Floral Parkway
Concord, ON L4K 4R1

Tel. 905-669-5400
Fax 905-669-2296

Con-Drain Company (1983) Ltd. is a sewer and water main general contractor. The company employs more than 250 people. Graduates most likely to be hired come from the following academic areas: Bachelor of Engineering (Civil), Bachelor of Commerce/Business Administration (Finance, Accounting), Certified Management Accountant and Community College Diploma (Civil Engineering). Graduates would be hired to occupy Supervisor, Project Manager, Estimator, Foreman, Controller and Purchasing Agent positions. Company benefits are rated as excellent. The potential for advancement is listed as being good. The average annual starting salary falls within the $25,000 to $30,000 range. The most suitable method for initial contact by graduates seeking employment is to mail a resume with a covering letter. Con-

Drain Company (1983) Ltd. does hire summer students. *Contact:* Nunzio Bitondi, CMA, Controller.

CONAIR AVIATION LTD.
PO Box 220
Abbotsford, BC V2S 4N9

Tel.	604-855-1171
Fax	604-855-1017
Email	work@conair.ca
Website	www.conair.ca

Conair Aviation Ltd. has two key areas of business, aircraft maintenance and aircraft operations. The first business area, aircraft maintenance, involves repair and overhaul services for commuter aircraft and narrow body jets. In addition, the company also provides aeronautical engineering services (design, analysis, certification) and services for corporate aircraft refurbishment (paint, interiors, avionics). The second business area, aircraft operations, involves the operation of a large fleet of airplanes and helicopters, providing specialty services such as aerial fire control, forest fertilization, oil and gas seismic exploration. In operation for 30 years, Conair is privately owned, headquartered in Abbotsford, and employs approximately 330 people. Graduates most likely to be hired come from the following academic areas: Bachelor of Engineering (Aerospace) and Community College Diploma (Aircraft Maintenance). Graduates would occupy Aircraft Maintenance Engineer positions. Team player and previous work experience are both listed as desirable non-academic qualifications. Conair is a dynamic, flexible workplace, with competitive starting salaries ($40,000 to $45,000 range) and a full benefits package. The company offers a challenging and interesting work environment, and a corporate commitment to employee training and development. Accordingly, company benefits are rated as industry standard and the potential for advancement is listed as being good. The most suitable method for initial contact by those seeking employment is to mail a resume with a covering letter. Conair Aviation Ltd. occasionally hires co-op work term students. *Contact:* Human Resources Department.

CONCORD ELEVATOR INC.
107 Alfred Kuchne Blvd.
Brampton, ON L6T 4K3

Tel.	905-791-5555
Fax	905-791-2222
Email	info@concordelevator.com
Website	www.concordelevator.com

Concord Elevator Inc. is a leading designer and manufacturer of a complete line of public and residential elevators, incline wheelchair platform lifts, vertical accessibility lifts and stair lifts. Concord maintains the largest in-house engineering department in the industry, and many of the innovative ideas developed by the department have become recognized standards by which all accessibility lifts are judged. Over the past two decades, the company has grown internationally and is increasingly recognized and respected for its leadership in lift research and development. Headquartered in Brampton, the company's largest plant is over 140,000 square feet with manufacturing also performed in several other locations. Concord employs approximately 180 people at this location and a to-

tal of 220 people in Canada. Graduates most likely to be hired come from the following academic areas: Bachelor of Engineering (Civil, Architectural/Building, Electrical, Mechanical, Industrial Design, Industrial Production), Bachelor of Commerce/Business Administration (General, Accounting, Finance, Marketing), Master of Business Administration (General, Accounting, Finance, Marketing) and Community College Diploma (Accounting, Administration, Advertising, Business, Marketing/Sales, Purchasing/Logistics). Graduates would occupy Production Engineer, R & D Engineer, Sales and Marketing, Personnel and Purchasing positions. Personable, ambitious, confident, team player and good communication skills are all listed as desirable non-academic qualifications. Company benefits are rated as industry standard. The potential for advancement is listed as being good. The average annual starting salary falls within the $25,000 to $30,000 range. The most suitable method for initial contact by those seeking employment is to mail a resume with a covering letter. Concord Elevator Inc. does hire summer students for Junior Engineering positions and special projects. *Contact:* Human Resources Manager.

CONCORDIA LIFE INSURANCE COMPANY
2 St. Clair Avenue East, 6th Floor
Toronto, ON M4T 2V6

Tel.	416-960-3601
Fax	416-950-5291

Concordia Life Insurance Company provides individual life insurance, annuities and segregated funds through brokers and independent agents from coast to coast. Graduates most likely to be hired come from the following academic areas: Bachelor of Science (Actuarial, Computer Science, Mathematics), Bachelor of Commerce/Business Administration (Accounting, Finance, Information Systems, Marketing), Master of Business Administration (Marketing), Community College Diploma (Administration, Business, Secretarial) and High School Diploma. Graduates would occupy Technician, Administrator, Analyst, Coordinator and Assistant positions. Previous work experience, self-starters, good oral and written communication skills, excellent interpersonal skills, working knowledge of the French language and life insurance experience are all listed as desirable non-academic qualifications. Company benefits are rated above average. The potential for advancement is listed as average. The average annual starting salary depends on the qualifications of the applicant. The most suitable method for initial contact by those seeking employment is to mail a resume with a covering letter. Concordia Life Insurance Company does hire a limited number of summer students annually. *Contact:* Susan Fors, Human Resources Manager.

CONESTOGA-ROVERS & ASSOCIATES LIMITED
651 Colby Drive
Waterloo, ON N2V 1C2

Tel.	519-884-0510
Fax	519-725-5240
Email	hr@rovers.com
Website	www.rovers.com

Conestoga-Rovers & Associates Limited is an international environmental consulting firm providing a wide range of comprehensive consulting services. The firm specializes in hazardous waste remediation, environmental assessment, hydrogeology, municipal infrastructure, water supply and treatment, waste water treatment, water resources, site remediation, sold waste management, air quality, and design and construction. There are approximately 280 employees at this location, a total of 300 in Canada, and a total of 880 employees worldwide. Graduates most likely to be hired come from the following academic areas: Bachelor of Science (Computer Science, Geology, Mathematic), Bachelor of Engineering (General, Chemical, Civil, Electrical, Mechanical, Environmental/Resources, Geological Engineering, Industrial Chemistry, Pollution Treatment, Water Resources) and Community College Diploma (Information Systems, CAD-CAM/Autocad, Engineering Technician). Graduates would occupy Professional Engineer, Analytical Chemist, Environmental Scientist, Environmental Planner, Geologist, Hydrogeologist, Industrial/Occupational Hygienist, Technician and Technologist positions. Previous work experience, leadership skills, initiative, growth potential, strong interpersonal skills and good work habits are all listed as desirable non-academic qualifications. Company benefits and the potential for advancement are both rated as excellent. The starting annual salary for a new engineering graduate is $33,500. The most suitable methods for initial contact by those seeking employment are to mail, fax or e-mail a resume with a covering letter. Conestoga Rovers & Associates uses the University of Waterloo's Co-op Program for student and part-time needs throughout the year. *Contact:* Paul Hutcheson, Human Resources Manager.

CONFERENCE BOARD OF CANADA, THE
255 Smyth Road
Ottawa, ON K1H 8M7

Tel. 613-526-3280
Fax 613-526-4857
Email .... recruit@conferenceboard.ca
Website .... www.conferenceboard.ca

The Conference Board of Canada is the country's leading private independent applied research institution delivering objective public policy and decision-making information to 500 member organizations. The board's mission is to help its members anticipate and respond to the increasingly changing global economy. The board does this through the development and exchange of knowledge about organizational strategies and practices, emerging economic and social trends and key public policy issues. The Conference Board of Canada's members are Canadian business, government and public-sector organizations, and its partners include organizations with an interest in the Canadian economy, public policies and organizational practices. The board employs a total of 195 people. Graduates most likely to be hired come from the following academic areas: Bachelor of Arts (Economics, Political Science), Bachelor of Science (Environment/Ecology), Bachelor of Engineering (Environmental/Resources), Bachelor of Commerce/Business Administration (Human Resources), Master of Business Administration (General, Human Resources, Public Administration), Master of Arts and Community College Diploma (Business, Communications/Public Relations, Human Resources, Information Systems). Company benefits are rated above average. The potential for advancement is listed as being good. The most suitable methods for initial contact by those seeking employment are to mail, fax or e-mail a resume with a covering letter, or via the board's website. The Conference Board of Canada does hire summer and co-op work term students. *Contact:* Recruiter, Human Resources.

COOPÉRATIVE FÉDÉRÉE DE QUÉBEC, LA
9001, boul l'Acadie, bureau 200
Montreal, QC H4N 3H7

Tel. 514-858-2013
Fax 514-385-1041

La Coopérative Fédérée de Québec is an agriculture cooperative. There are 300 employees at this location, and a total of 5,000 employees in the cooperative. Graduates most likely to be hired come from the following academic areas: Bachelor of Science (Agriculture), Bachelor of Commerce/Business Administration (Accounting, Human Resources), Chartered Accountant, Certified Management Accountant, Certified General Accountant and Community College Diploma (Accounting, Human Resources, Information Systems, Agriculture/Horticulture, Animal Health). Graduates would occupy Secretarial, Clerk, Technician, Representative and Management positions. Team player, autonomy, initiative, and previous work experience are all listed as desirable non-academic qualifications. Company benefits are rated above average. The potential for advancement is listed as being good. The average annual starting salary falls within the $20,000 to $25,000 range. The most suitable method for initial contact by those seeking employment is to mail a resume with a covering letter. La Coopérative Fédérée de Québec does hire summer and co-op work term students. *Contacts:* Lise Arsenault or Yuan de La Cheurotière.

CORADIX TECHNOLOGY CONSULTING LTD.
2500 Don Reid Drive
Ottawa, ON K1H 1E1

Tel. 613-737-9800
Fax 613-737-9721
Email .... hr@coradix.com
Website .... www.coradix.com

Coradix Technology Consulting Ltd. provides informatics consulting services in three strategic areas. These include application development, network services, and management consulting. Coradix employs a total of 80 people. Graduates most likely to be hired come from the following academic areas: Bachelor of Science (Computer Science) and Bachelor of Commerce/Business Administration (Information Systems). Graduates would occupy Programmer Analyst and Network Administrator positions. Good communication skills, professional appearance and presentation, a positive attitude and a focus on quality are all listed as desirable non-academic qualifications. The average annual starting salary falls within the $35,000 to $40,000 range. The most suitable methods for initial contact by those seeking employment are to mail or e-mail a resume with a covering letter. *Contacts:* Tony Carmanico, Director of Professional Services or Jean Beaulieu, Director of Business Development.

CORECO INC.
6969, route Transcanadienne, Suite 142
St-Laurent, QC H4T 1V8

Tel. 514-333-1301
Fax 514-333-1388
Email .... info@coreco.com
Website .... www.coreco.com

Coreco Inc. is a high-technology company that develops and markets image processors, DSP engines, and software to OEMs and developers serving the machine vision, medical and scientific imaging markets. Established in 1979, the company is committed to developing imaging and DSP products to advance computer vision technology. Publicly-traded, Coreco is listed on the Toronto and Montreal Stock Exchanges under the symbol CRC. There are 95 employees at this location and a total of 101 employees in Canada. Graduates most likely to be hired come from the following academic areas: Bachelor of Engineering (Electrical, Automation/Robotics). Graduates would occupy Research and Development, Hardware Engineer and Test Technician positions. Enthusiasm, a willingness to learn, motivated, team player, self-starter and interested in taking on challenges are all listed as desirable non-academic qualifications. Company benefits are rated above average. The potential for advancement is listed as being good. The average annual starting salary falls within the $35,000 to $40,000 range. The most suitable method for initial contact by those seeking employment is to mail a resume with a covering letter. Coreco Inc. does hire summer and co-op work term students. *Contact:* Suzanne Morin.

COREL CORPORATION
1600 Carling Avenue, 5th Floor
Ottawa, ON K1Z 8R7

Tel.	613-728-8200
Fax	613-761-1146
Email	hr@corel.ca
Website	www.corel.com

Corel Corporation is a major Canadian computer software development company and an internationally recognized developer of award-winning graphics and business productivity applications. The company employs approximately 950 people at this location and a total of 1,500 worldwide. Graduates most likely to be hired come from the following academic areas: Bachelor of Arts (General, Economics, Graphic Arts, Journalism), Bachelor of Science (Computer Science, Mathematics), Bachelor of Engineering (Computer Systems), Bachelor of Laws, Bachelor of Commerce/Business Administration (General, Accounting, Information Systems, Marketing), Chartered Accountant, Master of Business Administration (Marketing), Master of Science (Computer Science), Doctorate (Computer Science) and Community College Diploma (Accounting, Administration, Advertising, Business, Communications, Marketing/Sales, Journalism, Legal Assistant, Computer Science). Graduates would occupy Software Developer, Quality Assurance Specialist, Technical Support, Inside Sales, Project Manager, Advertising, Graphic Designer, Technical Writer and MIS positions. Organized, team player, open minded, enthusiastic, and a willingness to learn are all listed as desirable non-academic qualifications. Company benefits and the potential for advancement are both rated as excellent. The average annual starting salary falls within the $35,000 to $40,000 range. The most suitable methods for initial contact by those seeking employment are to mail or e-mail your resume with a covering letter. Corel Corporation does hire summer and co-op work term students. *Contact:* Human Resources.

CORRECTIONAL SERVICE OF CANADA
3, Place Laval, Suite 200
Laval, QC H7N 1A2

Tel.	450-967-3333
Fax	450-967-3468
Website	www.csc-scc.gc.ca

The Correctional Service of Canada, as part of the criminal justice system helps offenders become law-abiding citizens, while exercising reasonable, safe, secure and humane control. The service seeks to integrate those individuals into the community as law abiding citizens, while exercising reasonable supervision and control to ensure public safety. The Correctional Service of Canada employs approximately 3,140 people in the Quebec region and a total of 11,300 people across Canada. Graduates most likely to be hired come from the following academic areas: Bachelor of Arts (Criminology, Psychology, Social Work, Sociology), Bachelor of Science (Nursing, Psychology), Bachelor of Engineering (Computer Systems), Bachelor of Commerce/Business Administration (Human Resources), Master of Business Administration (Finance), Master of Arts (Psychology), Community College Diploma (Accounting, Cooking, Security/Police/Enforcement, Social Worker, Corrections Worker, Computer Science, Nursing RN) and High School Diploma. Graduates would occupy Corrections Officer, Case Administrator, Psychologist, Nurse, Human Resources Counsellor, Financial Controller, Financial Services Manager, Cook, Information Services Analyst, Administration, Secretarial and Warehouse positions. Employee benefits are rated as excellent. The potential for advancement is rated as being good. The most suitable method for initial contact by those seeking employment is to mail a resume with a covering letter. The Correctional Service of Canada does hire summer students. *Contacts:* Human Resources Division or Regional Manager, Human Resources.

COSYN TECHNOLOGY
9405 - 50 Street, Suite 101
Edmonton, AB T6B 2T4

Tel.	780-440-7000
Fax	780-462-3897
Email	tanghe.susan@syncrude.com

CoSyn Technology provides engineering, procurement and construction management services to Syncrude through an alliance partnering relationship. The alliance is a long term commitment to achieve specific business objectives. The resources of both alliance partners are focused on improving the core business. The scope of the work includes preliminary engineering work, preparation of basic engineering packages, the preparation of cost estimates, planning and scheduling, and project management for large and small projects. Staff are employed in a multidisciplinary environment including mechanical, process, electrical, civil/structural, piping, instrumentation controls, extraction, project services, office services and financial services. CoSyn has a structured quality system that is registered to the ISO 9000 Standard. CoSyn does high quality work for Syncrude and is committed to continuous improvement. Established in 1991, CoSyn is a division of Colt Engineering Corporation. CoSyn employs 160 people at this location and a total of 187 in Canada. Graduates most likely to be hired come from the following academic areas: Bachelor of Science (Computer Science), Bachelor of Engineering (General, Chemical, Civil, Electrical, Mechanical, Computer Systems, Environmental Resources, Instrumentation, Mining, Petroleum/Fuels), Bachelor of Commerce/Business Administration (Human Resources), Master of Business Administration, Master of Engineering, Community College Diploma (Purchasing/Logistics, Secretarial, Architectural Technician, CAD/CAM/Autocad, Computer Science, Electronics Technician, Engineering Technician) and High School Diploma. Graduates would occupy Engineering Technologist, Engineer, Department Head, Project Coordinator, Project Engineer, Estimator, Expediter, Buyer, Cost Controller/Scheduler, Draftsperson, CAD Operator and Designer positions. Excellent communication, interpersonal, judgement, decision making and project management skills are all listed as desirable non-academic qualifications. Company benefits are rated above average. The potential for advancement is listed as being good. The most suitable methods for initial contact by those seeking employment are to mail, fax or e-mail a resume with a covering letter. CoSyn Technology does hire summer and co-op work term students. *Contact:* Susan Tanghe, Human Resources Leader.

COUGAR AUTOMATION TECHNOLOGIES INC.
45 Sheppard Avenue East, Suite 307, Sheppard Centre
Toronto, ON M2N 5W9

Tel.	416-221-6076
Fax	416-221-6498
Email	currie_g@cougar-at.com
Website	www.cougar-at.com

Cougar Automation Technologies Inc., with offices in Toronto and Calgary, is a partnership of electrical engineering professionals offering services to end users and other engineering firms in all areas of automation technology. Cougar works in the manufacturing and process industries, including: oil and gas, food and beverage, and specialized machinery and material handling industries. The company provides management & engineering expertise on PLC/DCS, Device Networks, Human Machine Interfaces, SCADA, Manufacturing Execution Systems(MES) and Management Information Systems (MIS). Cougar employs a total of 25 people in Canada. Graduates most likely to be hired are Bachelor of Engineering graduates specializing in Electrical and Instrumentation engineering. Graduates would occupy the position of Electrical Control Systems Designer. Previous work experience (ACAD, PLC, HMI, SCADA), team player, driven, able to work alongside others, an interest in learning and a high level of initiative are all listed as desirable non-academic qualifications. Company benefits are rated as industry standard. The potential for advancement is listed as being good. The average annual starting salary falls within the $35,000 to $40,000 range. The most suitable methods for initial contact by those seeking employment are to fax or e-mail a resume with a covering letter. Cougar Automation Technologies Inc. occasionally hires summer students. *Contacts:* Currie Gardner or Andrew Kooiman.

CPI PLASTICS GROUP LTD.
979 Gana Court
Mississauga, ON L5S 1N9

Tel.	416-798-9333
Fax	416-798-9229
Website	www.cpiplastics.com

CPI Plastics Group Ltd. is a leading North American supplier of extruded thermoplastic systems, functional components and decorative trims. The company is one of the most diversified extruders in North America and is recognized by its customers for the innovative design, engineering and manufacturing of extruded profiles. CPI has evolved from a producer of generic products to a sophisticated custom extrusion company offering highly engineered plastic profiles and post extrusion fabrication. Headquartered in Mississauga, with additional manufacturing in Bolton, Ontario and a distribution facility in Elkhart, Indiana, CPI has 275,000 square feet of manufacturing space and employs more than 500 people. Graduates most likely to be hired come from the following academic areas: Bachelor of Arts (General), Bachelor of Science (General), Bachelor of Engineering (General, Mechanical, Industrial Design, Industrial Production), Bachelor of Commerce/Business Administration (General, Accounting, Finance, Human Resources), Community College Diploma (Accounting, Administration, Business, Human Resources, Marketing/Sales, CAD/CAM/Autocad) and High School Diploma. Graduates would occupy Engineer (Cost Estimator, CAD Designer), Quality Control Inspector, Accounts Payable Clerk, Accounts Receivable Clerk, Inside Sales/Customer Service Representative, Secretary, Receptionist, Data Entry Clerk and Marketing Assistant positions. Previous work experience, a positive attitude, team player, developed skill sets, ambition and enthusiasm are all listed as desirable non-academic qualifications. The most suitable methods for initial contact by those seeking employment are to mail or fax a resume with a covering letter. CPI Plastics Group Ltd. does hire summer students. *Contact:* Leonard Starrett, Human Resources Manager.

CRAMER NURSERY INC.
1002 St-Dominique Road
Les Cedres, QC J7T 3A1

Tel.	450-452-2121
Fax	450-452-4053

Cramer Nursery Inc. is a production nursery operating 1,500 acres of ornamental nursery stock. In addition, the company operates three garden centres in the Montreal region. Graduates most likely to be hired come from the following academic areas: Bachelor of Science (Agriculture, Biology, Forestry, Horticulture), Bachelor of Engineering (Forest Resources), Bachelor of Landscape Architecture, Bachelor of Commerce/Business Administration and Community College Diploma (Accounting, Administration, Business, Marketing/Sales, Secretarial, Agriculture, Forestry, Horticulture). In horticultural activities, graduates would occupy Propagation, Pruning, Harvesting and Maintenance positions. In administration, graduates would occupy Sales, Office and Clerical positions. Company benefits are rated above average. The potential for advancement is listed as excellent. The average annual starting salary is dependent upon the position being considered. The most suitable methods for initial contact by those seeking employment are to mail or fax a resume with a covering letter. Cramer Nursery Inc. does hire co-op work term students, and summer students to work in the garden centres and at the production nursery, where on-site lodging is available (Toll Free Number 1-888-8CRAMER). *Contacts:* Walter Cramerstetter, Sales, Administration & Research or Mario Cramerstetter, Production, General Labour.

CRAWFORD ADJUSTERS CANADA INC.
185 The West Mall, Suite 1200
Toronto, ON M9C 5L5

Tel.	416-620-7248 x 302
Fax	416-620-7046

Crawford Adjusters Canada Inc. provides insurance adjusting services, health and risk management services. There are more than 25 employees at this location and more than 250 employees across Canada. Graduates most likely to be hired come from the following academic areas: Bachelor of Arts (General), Bachelor of Science (General, Computer Science, Forestry, Geography, Geology, Health Sciences, Nursing, Psychology), Bachelor of Engineering (General, Environmental, Materials Science), Bachelor of Commerce/Business Administration (Marketing) and Community College Diploma (Accounting, Administration, Business, Communications, Insurance,

Marketing/Sales, Secretarial, Human Resources, Computer Science, Nursing RN). Graduates would occupy Insurance Adjuster, Secretary, Administrative Assistant, Data Entry Clerk, Receptionist, Computer System Coordinator, Medical/Vocational and Employment Consultant positions. Previous work experience in adjusting (claims) and appraising are both listed as desirable non-academic qualifications. Company benefits and the potential for advancement are both rated as excellent. The average annual starting salary falls within the $15,000 to $20,000 range. The most suitable method for initial contact by those seeking employment is to mail a resume with a covering letter. Crawford Adjusters Canada Inc. does hire summer students. *Contact:* Human Resources Advisor.

CRESTAR ENERGY INC.
333 - 7th Avenue SW, PO Box 888
Calgary, AB T2P 4M8

Tel. 403-231-6700
Fax 403-231-6811
Email .... hr@crestarenergy.com
Website .... www.crestarenergy.com

Crestar Energy Inc. is a senior Canadian oil and gas producer, operating in western Canada. The company's growth is fueled by a three-tiered strategy comprised of a blend of development, acquisition and exploration activities. Crestar Energy Inc. is publicly traded on the Toronto and Montreal stock exchanges and is included in the TSE 300 Composite Index. The company employs approximately 270 employees at this location and a total of 450 employees in Canada. Graduates most likely to be hired come from the following academic areas: Bachelor of Science (Chemistry, Computer Science, Geology), Bachelor of Engineering (Chemical, Civil, Electrical, Instrumentation, Resources/Environmental, Petroleum), Bachelor of Commerce/Business Administration (Accounting, Finance, Marketing), Certified Management Accountant and Community College Diploma (Accounting, Administration, Human Resources). Graduates would occupy Engineer, Geologist, Geophysicist, Accountant and Marketing positions. Team player, innovative and risk taker are listed as desirable non-academic qualifications. Company benefits are rated as excellent. The potential for advancement is listed as average. The most suitable method for initial contact by those seeking employment is to mail a resume with a covering letter. Crestar Energy Inc. does hire summer students. *Contact:* Human Resources Advisor.

CROSSKEYS SYSTEMS CORPORATION
350 Terry Fox Drive
Kanata, ON K2K 2W5

Tel. 613-591-1600
Fax 613-599-2310
Email .... careers@crosskeys.com
Website .... www.crosskeys.com

CrossKeys Systems Corporation is an independent software vendor. The company develops, markets and supports telecommunications-management software products and services for telecommunications service providers around the world. Founded in 1992, CrossKeys' software products and associated services meet the needs of service providers who require open, scaleable products that operate on multiple software platforms and integrate equipment from multiple vendors. The company's core competency is delivering element, network and service management applications, primarily in the areas of performance, accounting and configuration management.

CrossKeys also offers professional services and customer support, including customization, project management, training, installation and post-warranty support. Graduates most likely to be hired come from the following academic areas: Bachelor of Science (Computer Science) and Bachelor of Engineering (Computer Systems). Graduates would occupy Software Developer and Product Verification Engineer positions. Previous telecommunications experience, self-motivated, team player and strong communication skills are all listed as desirable non-academic qualifications. Company benefits and the potential for advancement are both rated as excellent. The average annual starting salary is dependent upon the position being considered. The most suitable methods for initial contact by those seeking employment are to fax a resume with a covering letter, or via the company's website. CrossKeys Systems Corporation does hire summer and co-op work term students. *Contact:* Human Resources.

CROWNE PLAZA CHATEAU LACOMBE
10111 Belamy Hill
Edmonton, AB T5J 1N7

Tel. 780-428-6611
Fax 780-420-8378
Website .... www.chateaulacombe.com

Crowne Plaza Chateau Lacombe is a beautifully renovated 24 floor, luxury hotel overlooking Edmonton's river valley. For over 30 years the hotel has distinguished itself by offering hospitality that is highly competent, yet genuine and warm. The hotel currently employs 240 people. Graduates most likely to be hired come from Community College Diploma Programs in Accounting, Administration, Business, Marketing/Sales, Cook/Chef Training, Hospitality, and Travel/Tourism. Graduates would occupy Administrative Assistant, Front Desk Agent, Reservations Agent, Sous Chefs, Apprentice Cooks, Sales Management, Catering Coordinator, Night Audit, Food and Beverage Servers and Management positions. The Crowne Plaza Chateau Lacombe is always on the look out for enthusiastic, friendly, high-energy people with a desire to exceed guest expectations. Accordingly, customer service oriented, team player, strong interpersonal and communication skills, enthusiasm, excellent organizational abilities, a high energy level, and good verbal and written communication skills are all listed as desirable non-academic qualifications. The hotel provides competitive starting salaries ($20,00 to $30,000 range), great employee benefits, advancement opportunities, and a team oriented fun atmosphere. The most suitable methods for initial contact by those seeking employment are to mail or fax a resume with a covering letter, or by applying in person at the hotel. Crowne Plaza Chateau Lacombe does hire a limited number of summer students and co-op work term students. *Contact:* Sherry Mattson, Human Resources.

CROWNE PLAZA TORONTO CENTRE
225 Front Street West
Toronto, ON M5V 2X3

Tel. 416-597-1400
Fax 416-597-8164
Email .... bosborne@crowneplazatoronto.com
Website .... www.crowneplazatoronto.com

Crowne Plaza Toronto Centre is a busy 587 guest room hotel located in downtown Toronto. There are 15 meeting rooms, 4 food and beverage outlets and 2 levels of service. The hotel employs more than 250 people. Graduates most likely to be hired come from the following academic areas: Community College Diploma (Marketing/ Sales, Cooking, Hospitality, Recreation, Security/Enforcement, Travel/Tourism). Graduates would occupy Front Desk Receptionist, Console Operator, Reservation Clerk, Waitress, 1st - 2nd - 3rd Cook, Recreation Club Attendant, Housekeeper and Busperson positions. Outgoing, organized, honest, reliable, dependable and people oriented are all listed as desirable non-academic qualifications. Company benefits are listed as excellent. The average annual starting salary falls within the $15,000 to $25,000 range. The most suitable method for initial contact by those seeking employment is to mail a resume with a covering letter. *Contact:* Human Resources.

CRYOVAC CANADA INC.
2365 Dixie Road
Mississauga, ON L4Y 2A2

Tel. 905-273-5656
Fax 905-273-3572
Website .... www.cryovac.com

Cryovac Canada Inc. is a Fortune 100 manufacturer of flexible plastic packaging products, packaging machines and art services. The company employs more than 250 people. Graduates most likely to be hired come from the following academic areas: Bachelor of Arts (General, Economics, Fine Arts, Psychology, Sociology), Bachelor of Science (Biology, Chemistry, Computer Science, Mathematics, Physics, Psychology), Bachelor of Engineering (General, Chemical, Environmental, Electrical, Industrial, Mechanical), Bachelor of Commerce/Business Administration (Accounting), Master of Business Administration (General), Master of Science (Chemistry), Master of Engineering (Chemical, Electrical, Mechanical) and Community College Diploma (Accounting, Administration, Business, Purchasing/Logistics, Graphic Arts, Human Resources, Computer Science, Electronics Technician, Engineering Technician, Mechanic, Laboratory Technician). Graduates would occupy Technician, Technologist, Junior Engineer, Production Planner, Junior Buyer, Customer Service Representative, Credit Analyst and Office Clerk positions. Enthusiasm, creativity, a positive attitude, flexibility, patience and persistence are all listed as desirable non-academic qualifications. Company benefits are rated as excellent. The potential for advancement is listed as being good. The average annual starting salary falls within the $25,000 to $35,000 range. The most suitable method for initial contact by graduates seeking employment is to mail a resume with a covering letter. Cryovac Canada Inc. does hire a limited number of summer students. *Contact:* Dick Irvine, Employee Development Manager.

CSA INTERNATIONAL
178 Rexdale Boulevard
Toronto, ON M9W 1R3

Tel. 416-747-4365
Fax 416-401-6729

Email .... reaj@csa.ca
Website .... www.csa-international.org

CSA International is a leader in the field of standards development and their application through certification and testing programs and quality management systems. CSA International is an independent, private sector, not-for-profit organization supported by its members and employees in a network of offices across Canada, the USA and around the world. The organization employs 1,100 people worldwide. Graduates most likely to be hired come from the following academic areas: Bachelor of Arts (General), Bachelor of Science (Biology, Chemistry, Computer Science, Environment/Ecology, Forestry, Geography, Geology, Metallurgy, Meteorology), Bachelor of Engineering (General, Chemical, Civil, Electrical, Mechanical, Biomedical Electronics, Computer Systems, Environmental, Forest Resources, Geological Engineering, Industrial Chemistry, Instrumentation, Metallurgy, Microelectronics, Telecommunications, Transportation, Water Resources), Bachelor of Commerce/Business Administration (Accounting, Finance, Human Resources, Information Systems, Marketing), Certified Management Accountant, Certified General Accountant and Community College Diploma (Business, Communications, Human Resources, Office Administration, Secretarial, Legal Assistant, Computer Science, Electronics Technician, Engineering Technician, HVAC, Information Systems). Graduates would occupy Engineer, Technician and Technologist positions. Strong interpersonal skills, team player, good communication skills and the ability to handle multiple projects are all listed as desirable non-academic qualifications. Company benefits and the potential for advancement are both rated as excellent. The average annual starting salary falls within the $35,000 to $40,000 range, depending on the position being considered. Initial contact by those seeking employment is best made via the company's website. CSA International does hire summer and co-op work term students. *Contact:* Human Resources.

CTV TELEVISION INC.
PO Box 9, Station O
Toronto, ON M4A 2M9

Tel. 416-332-5000
Fax 416-332-6491
Website .... www.ctv.ca

CTV Television Inc. is a national television broadcaster. The network is wholly owned by Baton Broadcasting Incorporated and employs 2,400 people across Canada. Baton's other holdings include: CTV News 1; Talk TV and interests in The Comedy Network; CTV Sports Net; Outdoor Life Network; CTV Pay-Per-View Sports and History Television. Graduates most likely to be hired come from the following academic areas: Bachelor of Arts (Economics, English, Journalism, Political Science), Bachelor of Science (General, Computer Science), Bachelor of Engineering (General, Electrical, Mechanical, Automation/ Robotics, Computer Systems, Telecommunications), Bachelor of Laws, Bachelor of Commerce/Business Administration (General, Accounting, Finance, Human Resources, Information Systems, Marketing), Chartered Accountant, Certified Management Accountant, Certified General Accountant, Master of Business Administration (Finance, Information Systems, Marketing) and Community College Diploma (Accounting, Advertising, Business, Communications/Public Relations, Human Resources, Marketing/Sales, Graphic Arts, Journalism, Legal Assistant, Television/Radio Arts, Broadcasting, CAD/CAM/ AutoCAD, Computer Science, Electronics Technician,

Engineering Technician, Information Systems). Company benefits are rated as industry standard. The potential for advancement is listed as being average. The average annual starting salary falls within the $25,000 to $30,000 range. The most suitable method for initial contact by those seeking employment is to call the CTV Job Opportunity Line at 1-888-398-JOBS (5627) or to mail or fax a resume with a covering letter. CTV Television Inc. does hire a limited number of summer students, as well as co-op/work term students. *Contact:* Human Resources Department.

CUSTOMER CARE INSURANCE AGENCY LTD. / CCIA
3 Robert Speck Parkway, 4th Floor
Mississauga, ON L4Z 3Z9

Tel. 905-306-3900
Fax 905-306-3148

Customer Care Insurance Agency Ltd. / CCIA is a leading provider of customer care solutions, offering proactive telephone based assistance to clients of CIBC Insurance. Customer Care is a wholly owned subsidiary of TeleTech Holdings Incorporated, a leading global provider of customer care solutions to Fortune 500 and international business. Through the integration of talented people, ISO processes, and leading technology, TeleTech handles over 400,000 interactions for clients every day. There are 400 employees at this location, and a total of 10,000 employees worldwide. Graduates most likely to be hired come from the following academic areas: Bachelor of Arts (General), Bachelor of Science (General, Actuarial, Computer Science), Bachelor of Education (General, Adult), Bachelor of Commerce/Business Administration (General, Human Resources), Master of Business Administration (General, Human Resources) and Community College Diploma (Administration, Business, Facility Management, Human Resources, Information Systems, Insurance, Marketing/Sales, Secretarial). Qualified applicants are hired for positions in Customer Service, Sales, Quality Assurance, Operations, Technology, Human Resources, Training and Administration. Creativity, initiative, team player and customer sensitive are listed as desirable non-academic qualifications. Customer Care offers employees viable career opportunities, an exciting environment, generous benefits and extensive training. The average annual starting salary falls within the $30,000 to $35,000 range. The most suitable method for initial contact by those seeking employment is to fax a resume with a covering letter. *Contacts:* Stan Arnold, Human Resources Manager or Sandra Melanson, Human Resources Generalist.

DAEDALIAN SYSTEMS GROUP INC.
34 King Street East, 8th Floor
Toronto, ON M5C 1E5

Tel. 416-862-1401
Fax 416-862-2656
Email .... careers@daedalian.com
Website .... www.daedalian.com

Daedalian Systems Group Inc. is a rapidly expanding systems development and integration firm specializing in client server and internet projects. Daedalian's technological expertise and superior client relations have earned it a reputation for outstanding service. The company offers extensive training in software applications, and seeks candidates with Bachelor, Master, or Doctorate degrees in Engineering, Science, or Mathematics. Graduates would

occupy the full-time positions of Programmer/Analyst and Systems Integrator. Team player, good communication skills, and strong analytical and problem solving skills are all listed as desirable non-academic qualifications. Company benefits and the potential for advancement are both rated as excellent. The average annual entry-level salary falls within the $35,000 to $40,000 range. The most suitable method for initial contact by those seeking employment is to fax a resume with a covering letter. Daedalian Systems Group Inc. does hire summer and co-op students. *Contact:* Miriam Rubin.

DANFOSS MANUFACTURING COMPANY LIMITED
7880 Tranmere Drive
Mississauga, ON L5S 1L9

Tel. 905-676-6000
Fax 905-676-0279
Email .... delean@e-mail.com
Website .... www.danfoss.com

Danfoss Manufacturing Company Limited is a leading producer of precision mechanical and electronic components and controls designed for residential, commercial, and industrial applications. The company boasts modern factories located on four continents, sales companies and agents in more than 100 countries. Danfoss has pioneered technical innovations in areas as diverse as load sensing hydraulics, intelligent refrigeration controls, CFC free compressors and water hydraulics. There are 45 employees at this location, a total of 60 in Canada and 20,000 employees worldwide. Graduates most likely to be hired come from the following academic areas: Bachelor of Arts (General), Bachelor of Engineering (Electrical, Mechanical), Bachelor of Commerce/Business Administration (Accounting, Finance, Human Resources, Information Systems, Marketing), Master of Business Administration (Finance) and Community College Diploma (Accounting, Human Resources, Marketing/Sales, Office Administration, Purchasing/Logistics, CAD/CAM/Autocad, Electronics Technician, HVAC Systems, Information Systems). Graduates would occupy Trainee, Electrical Engineer, Design/Application Engineer, Sales, Distribution, Assembly, Administration (e.g. Credit, A/P) and Market Development positions. Strong leadership skills, self-directed, team oriented and excellent communication skills are all listed as desirable non-academic qualifications. Company benefits are rated above average. The potential for advancement is listed as being good. The average annual starting salary falls within the $30,000 to $35,000 range. The most suitable method for initial contact by those seeking employment is to mail a resume with a covering letter. Danfoss Manufacturing Company Limited does hire summer and co-op work term students. *Contact:* Sandra deLean, Human Resource Development Manager.

DANKA CANADA
13351 Commerce Parkway, Suite 1163
Richmond, BC V6V 2X7

Tel. 604-273-3224
Fax 604-273-3839
Website .... www.danka.com

Danka is one of the world's largest independent suppliers of office imaging equipment and related services, parts, and supplies. Danka's strategy is to become the preferred source for document solutions by acting as an advocate for its customers. The company's vision extends beyond copiers and network printers. In order to deliver value to its customers, Danka considers their organizational culture, that being the people, processes and technologies involved in how they use information. Danka is a worldwide corporation with over 20,000 employees in 700 office locations in 30 countries. There are 70 employees at this location. Graduates most likely to be hired come from the following academic areas: Bachelor of Arts (General, Economics), Bachelor of Engineering (Electrical, Mechanical, Computer Systems), Bachelor of Commerce/Business Administration (General, Marketing) and Community College Diploma (Marketing/Sales, Secretarial). Graduates would occupy Field Technician, Systems Engineer, Clerk, Receptionist and Sales Representative positions. Self-starter and team player are both listed as desirable non-academic qualifications. Company benefits are rated above average. The potential for advancement is listed as being good. The average annual starting salary falls within the $25,000 to $30,000 range, and is salary plus commission based for marketing positions. The most suitable methods for initial contact by those seeking employment are to mail or fax a resume with a covering letter. *Contacts:* Cliff Leduc, Service Department; John Saleski, Sales Department or Mollie Joestl, Administration Department.

DATALINK SYSTEMS CORPORATION
1500 West Georgia Street, Suite 1590
Vancouver, BC V6G 2Z6

Tel. 604-257-2700
Fax 604-602-0817
Email .... hresources@datalink.net
Website .... www.datalink.net

DataLink Systems Corporation provides powerful, ubiquitous information services geared to the needs of people on-the-go. Those enabled with wireless (PCS phones and pagers) and internet technology (PC's with browsers and e-mail) would benefit most directly from DataLink's innovative services. At the confluence of the internet and wireless worlds, Datalink's "MessageX" site is a universal portal that provides both messaging services and information services to its users. Via the internet, messages (pages) can be sent from virtually any location in the world to any user with a PCS phone or pager. At the same time, financial, news, sports and other lifestyle information services are provided at the user's fingertips wherever and whenever required. Datalink's information services are provided on both a "push" and "pull" basis. Users specify their information needs and preferences on DataLink's website. DataLink's information system, drawing on a wide variety of information feeds, delivers relevant messages (even e-mail) in real time directly to the users' wireless devices. This information may also be accessed on demand with a two-way pager or a smart phone. Using the home or office PC and its browser, this information can be retrieved from DataLink's website. The user can even dial a telephone number and listen to e-mail or other text messages converted to speech or can have these messages sent to a fax machine close at hand. Graduates most likely to be hired at DataLink come from the following academic areas: Bachelor of Science (Computer Science) and Bachelor of Engineering (Electrical). Graduates would occupy Software Engineer and Software Developer positions. Company benefits are rated above average. The potential for advancement is listed as excellent. The average annual starting salary falls within the $40,000 to $45,000 range. The most suitable method for initial contact by those seeking employment is to e-mail a resume with a covering letter. DataLink Systems Corporation does hire co-op work term students. *Contact:* Cormez Fota, Vice President, Engineering.

DDM PLASTICS INC.
50 Clearview Drive, PO Box 574
Tillsonburg, ON N4G 4J1

Tel. 519-668-1060
Fax 519-688-0970

DDM Plastics Inc. is involved in plastic injection moulding, painting and light assembly work. The company operates large tonnage (1300 - 3000 ton) mould machines and 2K paint systems using robotics. The company employs a total of 700 people. Graduates most likely to be hired come from the following academic areas: Bachelor of Science (General, Computer Science, Mathematics), Bachelor of Engineering (General, Chemical, Industrial Chemistry, Electrical, Automation/Robotics, Instrumentation, Mechanical, Industrial Design, Industrial Production), Bachelor of Commerce/Business Administration (Accounting, Finance, Human Resources, Information Systems, Marketing), Certified General Accountant, Master of Business Administration (Accounting, Finance, Human Resources) and Community College Diploma (Business, Facility Management, Financial Planning, Human Resources, Marketing/Sales, Purchasing/Logistics, CAD/CAM/Autocad, Computer Science, Electronics Technician, Engineering Technician, Nursing RNA). Graduates would occupy Production Supervisor, Production Engineer, Process Engineer, Chemical Engineer, Cost Accountant, Controller and Sales Representative positions. Good organizational, leadership and problem solving skills and two to four years manufacturing experience are all listed as desirable non-academic qualifications. Company benefits are rated above average. The potential for advancement is listed as excellent. The most suitable method for initial contact by those seeking employment is to mail a resume with a covering letter. DDM Plastics Inc. does hire summer students. *Contacts:* Rita Scott, Manager, Human Resources or General Affairs Department.

DELCAN CORPORATION
133 Wynford Drive
Toronto, ON M3C 1K1

Tel. 416-441-4111
Fax 416-447-6497
Email .... hr@delcan.com
Website .... www.delcan.com

Delcan Corporation is a leading international engineering, planning and project management firm whose record of success spans more than 45 years and encompasses major international projects in over 70 countries. Headquartered in Toronto, the company engages in consulting, contracting (negotiated/non-competitive), design/build, equity investments in projects, privatization (BOT etc.), procurement and project management. Delcan provides these services in North America through a network of ten regional and local offices in Canada and the United States and from international offices in Hong Kong, Taiwan, Venezuela, Barbados, Malawi, Ethiopia and Turkey. The company employs more than 500 people including engineers, architects, planners, computer scientists, economists and environmental scientists, as well as experts in project management and procurement. Graduates most likely to be hired come from the following academic areas: Bachelor of Arts (Economics, Urban Geography/Planning), Bachelor of Science (Biology, Computer Science, Environment/Ecology) and Bachelor of Engineering (Civil). Graduates would occupy Junior Engineer, Junior Planner, Junior Architect and Project Engineer positions. Team player and flexibility are listed as desirable non-academic qualifications. Company benefits are rated above average. The potential for advancement is listed as being good. The average annual starting salary falls within the $35,000 to $40,000 range. The most suitable method for initial contact by those seeking employment is to e-mail a resume with a covering letter. Delcan Corporation does hire summer and co-op work term students. *Contacts:* Caryl Cuizon, Human Resources Consultant or Greg Scian, Human Resources Consultant.

DELFOUR CORPORATION
140 Renfrew Drive, Suite 101
Markham, ON L3R 6B3

Tel.	905-415-9779
Fax	905-415-9778
Email	info@delfour.com
Website	www.delfour.com

Delfour Corporation is a global company offering a complete solution of advanced software products, consulting services, education, support and data services designed specifically for the warehousing logistics industry. The company has been a pioneer in using relational database management systems (RDBMS) for the warehousing industry, developing unique features which are now commonly used by other software companies. Founded in 1988, Delfour is a privately held corporation that was established by four partners who had a vision of creating a software system that would be leading edge in warehouse management systems. Today, the company has 89 employees at this location and a total of 110 employees worldwide. Headquartered in Markham, Delfour is also incorporated in England, Australia, Argentina, Chile, Brazil and Atlanta, Georgia. Graduates most likely to be hired come from the following academic areas: Bachelor of Science (Computer Science), Bachelor of Engineering (Computer Systems, Industrial Engineering, Industrial Production/Manufacturing), Bachelor of Commerce/Business Administration (Information Systems), Master of Business Administration (Information Systems) and Community College Diploma (Purchasing/Logistics, Computer Science, Information Systems). Graduates would occupy Programming, Application Design, Architectural Design, Testing, Implementation and Support positions. Leadership skills, self-motivated, team player, strategic thinking skills and dynamic software skills are all listed as desirable non-academic qualifications. Company benefits and the potential for advancement are both rated as excellent. The average annual starting salary falls within the $45,000 to $50,000 range. The most suitable methods for initial contact by those seeking employment are to fax or e-mail a resume with a covering letter, or by applying through the company's website. Delfour Corporation does hire summer and co-op work term students. *Contact:* Human Resources.

DELOITTE & TOUCHE
181 Bay Street, BCE Place
Suite 1400, Bay Wellington Tower
Toronto, ON M5J 2V1

Tel.	416-601-6150
Fax	416-601-6151
Email	tmacaulay@deloitte.ca
Website	www.deloitte.ca

Deloitte & Touche is one of Canada's leading professional services firms, providing accounting and auditing, tax, and management consulting services throughout the country. The firm employs approximately 4,000 people in over fifty offices across Canada. Deloitte & Touche Canada is part of Deloitte Touche Tohmatsu, a global leader in professional services with more than 82,000 employees in over 130 countries. Graduates most likely to be hired come from the following academic areas: Bachelor of Arts (Economics), Bachelor of Commerce/Business Administration (General, Accounting, Finance), Master of Business Administration (General, Accounting, Finance, Information Systems) and Community College Diploma (Computer Science). Graduates would occupy the position of Staff Accountant. Leadership, team building and entrepreneurial skills combined with a strong academic standing are listed as desirable qualifications. The potential for advancement is listed as being excellent. The most suitable method for initial contact by graduates seeking employment is through on-campus recruitment programs (see your campus career centre for details). Deloitte & Touche does hire summer students on a regular basis. *Contact:* Human Resources Department.

DELTA HOTELS & RESORTS
350 Bloor Street East, Suite 300
Toronto, ON M4W 1H4

Tel.	416-926-7800
Fax	416-926-7809
Website	www.deltahotels.com

Delta Hotels and Resorts is a management company providing hotel management services. The company operates hotels and resorts across Canada, Florida, the Caribbean, Thailand, Philippines, Vietnam, and Malaysia. Delta employs 60 people at the corporate office, a total of 4,500 across Canada and 7,000 people worldwide. Graduates most likely to be hired come from the following academic areas: Bachelor of Commerce/Business Administration (Accounting, Human Resources, Information Systems), Community College Diploma (Accounting, Administration, Human Resources, Secretarial, Hospitality, Travel and Tourism) and High School Diploma. Graduates would occupy Hospitality positions within the Hotels, including Food and Beverage, Front Office, and Housekeeping positions, as well as Engineering, Human Resources and Finance positions. Initiative, team oriented, very personable and approachable and a willingness to do that "extra-mile" for the customer are all listed as desirable non-academic qualifications. Company benefits and the potential for advancement are both listed as excellent. The average annual starting salary falls within the $20,000 to $25,000 range for entry level positions. The most suitable method for initial contact by those seeking employment is to mail a resume with a covering letter to the hotel of their choice. Delta Hotels and Resorts does hire summer students at the hotel level but not at the corporate office. *Contacts:* Human Resources Director (at each Hotel location) or Human Resources Coordinator (Corporate Office).

DELTA HUDSON ENGINEERING LTD.
8500 Macleod Trail South
Suite 400, PO Box 5244, Station A
Calgary, AB T2H 2N7

Tel.	403-258-6411
Fax	403-258-6614
Email	resume.hr@mcdermott.com
Website	www.deltahudson.com

Delta Hudson Engineering Ltd. provides engineering, procurement, construction, construction management, and contract maintenance services. There are 230 employees at this location, and a total of 430 employees across Canada. Graduates most likely to be hired come from the following academic areas: Bachelor of Science (General, Chemistry, Computer Science), Bachelor of Engineering (General, Chemical, Pollution Treatment, Pulp and Paper, Civil, Electrical, Instrumentation, Power, Mechanical, Industrial Design), Bachelor of Commerce/ Business Administration (Accounting, Information Systems), Master of Business Administration (Accounting, Information Systems), Community College Diploma (Accounting, Human Resources, Secretarial, Architecture/ Drafting, CAD/CAM/Autocad, Computer Science, Engineering Technician) and High School Diploma. Graduates would occupy Clerk, Secretary, Document Control, Data Entry, Administrative Assistant, Drafter, Designer/ Checkers, Design Specialist, Sub-Contract Specialist, Technician/Specialist, Engineer, Buyer, Expeditor, Project Control (Planner/Scheduler), Programmer/Analyst, Hardware/Software Support Technician and QA/QC Inspector positions. Previous work experience, strong communication skills, self starter, results oriented and an ability to work effectively with others and independently are all listed as desirable non-academic qualifications. Company benefits are rated above average. The potential for advancement is listed as being good. The average annual starting salary falls within the $30,000 to $35,000 range. The most suitable method for initial contact by those seeking employment is to apply through the company's website at www.deltahudson.com. Delta Hudson Engineering Ltd. does hire co-op work term students. *Contacts:* S. Boland, Manager, Staff Human Resources or J. Cox, Principal Human Resources Representative, Human Resources.

DELTA MEADOWVALE RESORT & CONFERENCE CENTRE
6750 Mississauga Road
Mississauga, ON L5N 2L3

Tel.	905-542-6726
Fax	905-542-6757
Website	www.hostmarriott.com

The Delta Meadowvale Resort & Conference Centre of Mississauga is a full service hotel providing accommodation, restaurant, conference and resort facilities. The hotel employs more than 350 people. Graduates most likely to be hired come from the following academic areas: Bachelor of Arts, Bachelor of Commerce/Business Administration and Community College Diploma (Hospitality, Hotel/Restaurant Management). Graduates would occupy Entry-Level Supervisory positions. The exact type and level of position is determined upon the experience of the applicant. Initiative, team player, self-motivated and strong customer service skills are all listed as desirable non-academic qualifications. Company benefits and the potential for advancement are both rated as excellent. The average annual starting salary falls within the $20,000 to $25,000 range. The most suitable method for initial contact by those seeking employment is to fax a resume with a covering letter. The Delta Meadowvale Resort & Conference Centre does offer co-op work term placements in the majority of its departments. *Contacts:* Nancy McTeague, Director of Human Resources or Reni Kalirai-Chakal, Human Resources Coordinator.

DEPARTMENT OF THE SOLICITOR GENERAL, NEW BRUNSWICK
PO Box 6000
Fredericton, NB E3B 5H1

Tel.	506-453-3992
Fax	506-453-7481
Website	www.gov.nb.ca

New Brunswick's Department of the Solicitor General is the province's principal agency responsible for and providing leadership in the areas of public order and community safety. As part of the Justice System, the department works in partnership with the community to prevent crime, to create opportunities for offenders to change, to deliver services to assist the victims of crime, and the delivery of Sheriff/Coroner services, all of which contribute to the well being and quality of life for the people of New Brunswick. The department employs approximately 700 people. Graduates most likely to be hired come from the following academic areas: Bachelor of Arts (Criminology, Political Science, Psychology, Social Work, Sociology), Bachelor of Science (Computer Science), Bachelor of Education (Intermediate Senior, Adult, Special Needs), Bachelor of Laws, Bachelor of Commerce/ Business Administration (Accounting, Finance, Human Resources, Information Systems, Public Administration), Master of Business Administration (Finance, Public Administration), Master of Arts (Criminology), Master of Science (Clinical Psychology) and Community College Diploma (Secretarial, Cooking, Security/Law Enforcement, Computer Science). Graduates would occupy Accounting Officer, Human Resources Officer, Information Systems, Research and Planning Officer, Correctional Services Supervisor, Correctional Institutions Superintendent, Nurse, Social Worker, Correctional Officer, Youth Counsellor, Probation Officer, Parole Officer, Clinical Psychologist, Victim Services Coordinator, Inspector, Sheriff/Coroner and Commercial Vehicle Enforcement positions. The most suitable methods for initial contact by those seeking employment are to mail a resume with a covering letter, or through job fair competitions (visit your campus career centre for details). The Department of the Solicitor General hires summer students through Job Creation Programs. *Contacts:* John Oxner, Corrections / Ed Peterson, Law Enforcement or Sandra Cameron/Jerry Fife, Sheriff/Coroner Policing.

DEPARTMENT OF TRANSPORTATION, NORTHWEST TERRITORIES
PO Box 1320
Yellowknife, NT X1A 2L9

Tel.	867-920-3459
Fax	867-873-0283
Email	shupen@internorth.com
Website	www.gov.nt.ca

The Department of Transportation is responsible for planning, designing, constructing, reconstructing, acquiring, operating and maintaining the public transportation infrastructure in Northwest Territories. This includes community airports, docks and the highway system. The department also regulates and licences individuals and vehicles. The department employs 315 people throughout NWT. Graduates most likely to be hired come from the following academic areas: Bachelor of Engineering (Civil), Bachelor of Commerce/Business Administration (Accounting, Finance, Human Resources, Information Systems, Public Administration), Chartered Accountant, Certified Management Accountant, Certified General Accountant, Master of Business Administration (Accounting, Finance, Human Resources, Information Systems, Public Administration), Master of Engineering, Community College Diploma (Accounting, Administration, Engineering Technician) and High School Diploma. Graduates would occupy Project Technician, Highway Technician, Design Engineer, Structural Technician, Soils Technician and Drafting Technician positions. A willingness to work in remote and isolated areas, team player and able to work in cross-cultural settings are all listed as desirable non-academic qualifications. The most suitable methods for initial contact by those seeking employment are to mail, fax or e-mail a resume with a covering letter. The Department of Transportation does hire summer students, primarily NWT students. *Contacts:* Colleen Kilty, Manager, Human Resources or Neal Shupe, Human Resources Specialist; Dale Dean, Human Resources Specialist.

DERIVION CORPORATION
3950 Fourteenth Avenue, Suite 405
Markham, ON L3R 0A9

Tel. 905-947-9730
Fax 905-947-9744
Email .... careers@derivion.com
Website .... www.derivion.com

Derivion Corporation provides internet-based software solutions that work to help businesses maximize their markets around the globe. Founded in 1998, Derivion's four main principles are to provide best in class products, world-class services, high return to its shareholders and a great work environment for its employees. Based in Atlanta, Georgia, the company employs 22 people at this location and a total of 33 people worldwide. Graduates most likely to be hired come from the following academic areas: Bachelor of Science (Computer Science), Bachelor of Engineering (Computer Systems), Master of Business Administration (Information Systems) and Community College Diploma (Computer Science, Information Systems). Graduates would occupy Programmer positions. Hard working, team player and flexible are all listed as desirable non-academic qualifications. Company benefits and the potential for advancement are both rated as excellent. The average annual starting salary falls within the $60,000 plus range. The most suitable method for initial contact by those seeking employment is to e-mail a resume with a covering letter. *Contact:* Helen Kozovski, Office Manager.

DH HOWDEN DIVISION
3232 White Oak Road, PO Box 5485
London, ON N6A 4G8

Tel. 519-686-2200
Fax 519-686-2333

DH Howden Division is a wholesaler of hardware and renovation products. The company employs approximately 275 people at this location, and a total of 300 people. Graduates most likely to be hired come from the following academic areas: Bachelor of Arts (General), Bachelor of Commerce/Business Administration (General), Community College Diploma (Advertising, Business, Marketing/Sales, CAD/CAM/Autocad) and High School Diploma. Graduates would occupy Clerk, Coordinator and Analyst positions. Flexibility and the ability to react quickly to changing market conditions are both listed as desirable non-academic qualifications. Company benefits are rated as industry standard. The potential for advancement is listed as average. The average annual starting salary falls within the $20,000 to $25,000 range. The most suitable method for initial contact by those seeking employment is to mail a resume with a covering letter. DH Howden Division does hire summer and co-op work term students. *Contact:* Marc Fraser, Manager, Human Resources.

DIANA SWEETS LTD.
75 The Donway West
Toronto, ON M3C 2E9

Tel. 416-441-6380
Fax 416-441-6376

Diana Sweets Ltd. is a licensed, full-service restaurant chain with three locations in Greater Toronto. The company has been in operation since 1912 and is the longest established restaurant chain that is still under the ownership of the original operating family. Each location employs more than 25 people. Graduates most likely to be hired come from Community College programs in Hotel and Restaurant Management. Graduates are hired as Junior/Assistant Managers or for Kitchen Staff positions. Good communication and interpersonal skills, flexible, sound judgment, common sense, a good work ethic, team player, initiative and an eagerness and ability to learn quickly are all listed as desirable non-academic qualifications. Company benefits are rated above average. The potential for advancement is listed as being good. The most suitable method for initial contact by graduates seeking employment is to mail a resume with a covering letter. Diana Sweets Ltd. does hire summer students when positions are available. *Contact:* Diane Bolgyesi, Vice President Personnel.

DIMPLEX NORTH AMERICA LIMITED
1367 Industrial Road, P.O. Box 1726
Cambridge, ON N1R 7G8

Tel. 519-650-3630
Website .... www.dimplex.com

Dimplex North America Limited is a leading manufacturer of electric heating products. The company was formed in 1991 through the acquisitions by The Glen Dimplex Group of Dublin, Ireland of two of Canada's leading electric heating manufacturers; Westcan Electric Heating Inc. and Chromalox Canada Inc. Dimplex currently employs more than 300 people in Canada, manufacturing and marketing a full range of residential, commercial and industrial electric heating products. The company operates as a fully autonomous business with its own research, development and design capabilities. Graduates most likely to be hired come from the following academic areas: Bachelor of Arts (Social Sciences), Bachelor of Engineering (Mechanical, Electrical), Bachelor of Commerce/Business Administration, Certified Management Accountant and Community College Diploma (Accounting, Electrical Technician, Computer Science). Graduates would occupy Human Resources, Engineering, Accounting, Information Systems, and Technical Sales positions. Good problem solving and decision making abilities, computer literacy and strong verbal and written communication skills are all listed as desirable non-academic qualifications. Company benefits are rated as excellent. The potential for advancement is listed as average. The average annual starting salary falls within the $30,000 to $35,000 range. The most suitable method for initial contact by those seeking employment is to mail a resume with a covering letter. *Contact:* Human Resources.

DINECORP HOSPITALITY INC.
230 Bloor Street West, 2nd Floor
Toronto, ON M5S 1T8

Tel. 416-324-9770
Fax 416-324-9774

Dinecorp Hospitality Inc. (founded 1981), is a dynamic Canadian company with restaurant complexes in seven Canadian provinces. Dinecorp is the largest holder of Swiss Chalet and Harvey's franchises, operating 27 Swiss Chalet and 16 Harvey's restaurants which generate annual sales of $75 million and employ more than 2,000 team members in total. Dinecorp is committed to professional management in the food service industry. Graduates most likely to be hired in restaurant operations come from the following academic areas: Bachelor of Arts (General, Economics, English), Bachelor of Commerce/Business Administration (Commerce, Accounting, Finance, Marketing), Certified Management Accountant, Certified General Accountant, Community College Diploma (Accounting, Administration, Business, Cooking, Hospitality) and High School Diploma. Personable, sales oriented and good communication skills are listed as desirable non-academic qualifications. Company benefits and the potential for advancement are both rated as excellent, since Dinecorp strongly believes in promotion from within and in people development. The average starting salary falls within the $24,000 to $34,000 range. The most suitable method for initial contact by those seeking employment is to mail a resume with a covering letter. Summer students are hired at the restaurant level for entry level positions. *Contact:* Mr. P. Metelski.

DirectProtect®

Fast, easy insurance from The Co-operators Group

DIRECTPROTECT
5600 Cancross Court
Mississauga, ON L5R 3E9

Tel.	800-810-4990
Fax	905-507-8661
Email	hbhr@istar.ca
Website	www.directprotect.com

DirectProtect is a direct insurance service offered by HB Group Insurance Management Ltd. DirectProtect provides Canadian consumers with the ability to request no-obligation auto and home insurance quotes over the telephone and the internet. DirectProtect operates call centres in Mississauga, Calgary, and Laval. There are 450 employees at this location and a total of 650 employees across Canada. Graduates most likely to be hired come from the following academic areas: Bachelor of Arts (General), Bachelor of Commerce/Business Administration (General, Finance) and Community College Diploma (Business, Insurance). Graduates would occupy Licensed Insurance Representative (Home and Automobile), Claim Service Advisor, Administration and Accounting positions. Organized, a team player, excellent customer service skills, multi-tasking abilities, computer literacy and strong time-management skills are all listed as desirable non-academic qualifications. Company benefits are rated above average. The potential for advancement is listed as being good. The average annual starting salary falls within the $25,000 to $30,000 range. The most suitable methods for initial contact by those seeking employment are to mail, fax or e-mail a resume with a covering letter, or via the company's website. DirectProtect does hire summer and co-op work term students. *Contact:* Human Resources Department.

DISCOUNT CAR AND TRUCK RENTALS
720 Arrow Road
Toronto, ON M9M 2M1

Tel.	416-744-0123
Fax	416-744-9829
Email	hr@discountcar.com
Website	www.discountcar.com

Discount Car and Truck Rentals is at the forefront of the automobile rental industry. The company maintains locations across Canada with many more opening in the United States and around the world. Discount's spectacular growth has created many opportunities for ambitious and hard-working individuals who are interested in long-term growth and a dynamic work environment. Graduates most likely to be hired come from the following academic areas: Bachelor of Arts (General), Bachelor of Science (General), Bachelor of Commerce/Business Administration (General, Marketing) and Community College Diploma (Business). Graduates would occupy Management Trainee positions. Team player, outgoing, a strong desire to rise to the top and previous sales experience are all listed as desirable non-academic qualifications. Company benefits are rated above average. The potential for advancement is listed as excellent. The average annual starting salary falls within the $20,000 to $25,000 range. The most suitable methods for initial contact by those seeking employment are to mail, fax or e-mail a resume with a covering letter. Discount Car and Truck Rentals does hire summer students. *Contacts:* Joanne Fessenden, Recruiter or Monica Nagasuye, Human Resources Coordinator.

DIVERSEYLEVER
2401 Bristol Circle
Oakville, ON L6H 6P1

Tel.	905-829-1200
Fax	905-829-4908
Website	www.diverseylever.com

DiverseyLever is involved in the manufacturing, marketing and selling of specialized chemicals used for cleaning and sanitation purposes. Headquartered in Amsterdam, The Netherlands, DiverseyLever works in more than 60 countries across Europe, North America, Asia Pacific, Latin America, Africa and the Middle East. DiverseyLever is part of the Unilever Group, an Anglo-Dutch company, with a corporate centre that has offices in London, United Kingdom and Rotterdam, The Netherlands. The group employs nearly 270,000 people, working in more than 90 countries, with brands on sale in an additional 70 countries. DiverseyLever (Canada) employs approximately 725 people. Graduates most likely to be hired come from the following academic areas: Bachelor of Science (Chemistry, Microbiology), Bachelor of Engineering (Chemical, Environmental, Mechanical), Master of Science (Chemistry), Doctorate of Science (Chemistry) and Community College Diploma (Accounting, Administration, Marketing/Sales, Computer Science, Engineering, Industrial Design). Computer skills, related work experience and good communication skills are listed as desirable non-academic qualifications. Company benefits are rated above average. The potential for advancement is listed as being good. The average annual starting salary falls within the $30,000 to $35,000 range. The most suitable method for initial contact by those seeking employment is to mail a resume with a covering letter. DiverseyLever Canada does hire summer students. *Contact:* Human Resources.

DIVERSINET CORPORATION

200 Yorkland Boulevard, Suite 605
Toronto, ON M2J 5C1

Tel.	416-756-2324
Fax	416-756-7346
Email	humanresources@dvnet.com
Website	www.dvnet.com

Diversinet Corporation, using enhanced public-key technology, offers end to end security solutions for wireless e-commerce applications. The company has created the next generation of technologies for identification, authentication and authorization for digital communications and electronic commerce over corporate networks, the Internet, or telecommunication systems. Based in Toronto, Diversinet is a public corporation traded on NASDAQ (DVNT) and under the Canadian Dealing Network (DVNT). The company employs a total of 30 people. Graduates most likely to be hired come from the following academic areas: Bachelor of Engineering (Computer Systems), Bachelor of Commerce/Business Administration (Accounting, Finance, Human Resources, Information Systems, Marketing), Chartered Accountant, Certified Management Accountant, Certified General Accountant and Community College Diploma (Information Systems). Company benefits are rated as excellent. The average annual starting salary falls within the $35,000 to $40,000 range. The most suitable methods for initial contact by those seeking employment are to e-mail a resume with a covering letter, or via the company's website. *Contact:* Human Resources.

DMR CONSULTING GROUP INC.

252 Adelaide Street East
Toronto, ON M5A 1N1

Tel.	416-363-8661
Fax	416-363-4739
Email	dmr_recruiting@dmr.ca
Website	www.dmr.com

DMR Consulting Group Inc., Amdahl's professional services company, is a leading international provider of management consulting and information technology (IT) services to businesses and public enterprises. Founded in Montreal in 1973, the group has a reputation for providing integrated business and IT solutions that enable clients to increase their competitive position, market share and productivity. The company has served thousands of businesses and public enterprises internationally, accumulating experience in managing large-scale systems development and integration projects, combined with expertise in management consulting, a unique ability to engineer solutions and a suite of proven methods. DMR employs 2,000 professionals in Canada and has more than 60 offices in the United States, Canada, Asia-Pacific and Europe employing approximately 10,000 professionals worldwide. Graduates most likely to be hired come from the following academic areas: Bachelor of Science (Computer Science, Mathematics), Bachelor of Engineering (Computer Systems), Bachelor of Commerce/Business Administration (Information Systems), Master of Business Administration (Accounting, Finance, Human Resources, Information Systems, Marketing), Master of Science (Computer Science) and Community College Diploma (Computer Science). Graduates would occupy Programmer/Analyst and Consultant positions. Team player and mobility are both listed as desirable non-academic qualifications. Company benefits are rated above average. The potential for advancement is listed as excellent. The average annual starting salary falls within the $40,000 to $45,000 range, depending upon location

of employment. The most suitable methods for initial contact by those seeking employment are to mail or e-mail a resume with a covering letter. DMR Consulting Group Inc. hires co-op students from Computer Science programs. *Contact:* Recruiting Coordinator.

DOMINION COMPANY, THE

555 Burrard Street, Suite 300, Two Bentall Centre
Vancouver, BC V7X 1S9

Tel.	604-631-1000
Fax	604-631-1100

The Dominion Company is one of western Canada's leading development, design and construction companies. The company maintains offices in Vancouver, Calgary, Edmonton, Regina, Winnipeg, and Santa Ana, California. Over the past 84 years, The Dominion Company has established itself as a design-builder of some of the most prominent commercial, industrial, and retail properties in western Canada. The company employs 100 people at this location, an additional 50 people in Canada, and 21 employees in the United States. Graduates most likely to be hired come from the following academic areas: Bachelor of Engineering (Civil, Architectural/Building, Surveying, Electrical, Mechanical, Industrial Design), Bachelor of Architecture, Bachelor of Commerce/Business Administration (Accounting, Information Systems), Certified Management Accountant, Certified General Accountant and Community College Diploma (Accounting, CAD/CAM/Autocad, Engineering Technician). Graduates would occupy Junior Mechanical Engineer, Junior Structural Engineer, Junior Electrical Engineer, Architectural Technologist, Project Assistant and Accounting Clerk positions. A commitment to leaning, resource management, innovative, achievement oriented, teamwork, customer focus, leadership and problem solving skills are all listed as desirable non-academic qualifications. Company benefits are rated above average. The potential for advancement is listed as being good. The most suitable methods for initial contact by those seeking employment are to mail or fax a resume with a covering letter. The Dominion Company does hire summer students. *Contact:* Human Resources.

DOMINION OF CANADA GENERAL INSURANCE COMPANY, THE

165 University Avenue
Toronto, ON M5H 3B9

Tel.	416-350-3740
Fax	416-362-1602
Email	careers@thedominion.ca
Website	www.thedominion.ca

The Dominion of Canada General Insurance Company provides a full range of insurance products and services. In business since 1887, the company is one of Canada's largest property and casualty insurance companies, providing high quality home, automobile and business insurance products through the independent broker system. Offices are located in Halifax, Ottawa, Scarborough, Toronto, Oakville, London, Calgary, Edmonton, and Vancouver. There are 250 employees at the Toronto location and a total of 900 employees across Canada. Graduates most likely to be hired come from the following academic areas: Bachelor of Arts (General, Economics, Political Science, Psychology), Bachelor of Science (General, Actuarial, Computer Science, Mathematics), Bachelor of Engineering (Electrical, Computer Systems), Bachelor of Commerce/Business Administration (General, Accounting, Finance, Human Resources, Information Systems,

Marketing), Chartered Accountant, Master of Business Administration (General, Accounting, Finance) and Community College Diploma (Accounting, Business, Insurance, Office Administration, Secretarial, Computer Science, Information Systems). Graduates would occupy Commercial Lines Underwriter Trainee, Personal Lines Underwriter Trainee, Claims Service Representative Trainee, Actuarial Analyst, Programmer/Analyst, Financial Analyst, Accounting Clerk, and Customer Service Representative positions. Good customer service skills, team player, results oriented, initiative, excellent problem solving and decision making skills, good communication skills, and an ability to learn are all listed as desirable non-academic qualifications. Company benefits are rated above average. The potential for advancement is listed as being good. The average annual starting salary is dependent upon the position. The most suitable methods for initial contact by those seeking employment are to mail, fax or e-mail a resume with a covering letter. The Dominion does hire summer and co-op work term students. *Contact:* Employee Services Coordinator, Human Resources.

DOMTAR PAPERS, CORNWALL PLANT
800 Second Street West
PO Box 40, Cornwall Business Centre
Cornwall, ON K6H 5S3

Tel.	613-932-6620
Fax	613-938-4567
Website	www.domtar.com

Domtar Papers, Cornwall Plant is an integrated pulp mill with four paper machines and a finishing department producing fine grade paper. There are 1,100 employees at this location, while Domtar employs a total of 9,000 people in Canada and a total of 9,200 people worldwide. Graduates most likely to be hired come from the following academic areas: Bachelor of Science (Chemistry, Computer Science, Environmental), Bachelor of Engineering (Chemical, Industrial Chemistry, Pollution Treatment, Pulp and Paper, Architectural/Building, Instrumentation, Industrial Design, Industrial Production, Water Resources), Bachelor of Commerce/Business Administration (Finance, Human Resources, Information Systems), Chartered Accountant, Certified Management Accountant, Certified General Accountant, Master of Business Administration (Accounting, Finance, Human Resources, Information Systems), Master of Engineering (Mechanical, Electrical, Pulp and Paper) and Community College Diploma (Accounting, Administration, Business, Purchasing/Logistics, Secretarial, Security/Enforcement, Computer Science, Welding). Graduates would occupy a variety of entry level jobs based upon each candidate's education and experience. Customer oriented, team player, follow-up skills, flexibility and computer skills are all listed as desirable non-academic qualifications. Company benefits and the potential for advancement are both rated as excellent. The average annual starting salary is dependent upon the position being considered. The most suitable method for initial contact by those seeking employment is to mail a resume with a covering letter. Domtar Papers does hire summer students. *Contact:* Human Resources Department.

DRS FLIGHT SAFETY AND COMMUNICATIONS
115 Emily Street
Carleton Place, ON K7C 4J5

Tel.	613-253-3020
Fax	613-253-7218
Email	hr@drs.ca
Website	www.drs.com

DRS Flight Safety and Communications is involved in the design, development and manufacture of advanced systems for aerospace and defence electronic applications. The company works closely with its partners and customers to provide reliable transportation by developing flight safety systems solutions and aircraft health and usage monitoring systems that meet the needs of the aviation industry. In addition, DRS develops innovative communications systems solutions for the naval environment and has established a worldwide reputation for competitive manufacturing, integration and testing of complex assemblies and systems requiring the highest quality standards. DRS Flight Safety and Communications is a division of DRS Technologies Inc. headquartered in Parsippany, New Jersey. In addition to the Nepean and Carlton Place locations, DRS has locations in Maryland, Pennsylvania, California, Florida, Minnesota, Illinois in the United States and locations in the United Kingdom and Bulgaria. DRS Technologies employs 1,470 people worldwide. Graduates most likely to be hired at DRS Flight Safety and Communications come from the following academic areas: Bachelor of Science (Computer Science), Bachelor of Engineering (Electrical, Aerospace, Computer Systems, Engineering Physics, Industrial Engineering, Industrial Production/Manufacturing, Telecommunications), Master of Science (Computer Science, Physics), Master of Engineering (Computer Hardware/ Software, Aerospace, Telecommunications) and Doctorate (Computer Science, Engineering, Physics). Graduates would occupy Hardware Engineer, Software Engineer/Developer, Hardware/Software Technologist and Hardware Technician. Strong interpersonal skills, team work experience and excellent verbal and written communication skills are all listed as desirable non-academic qualifications. Company benefits and the potential for advancement are both rated as excellent. The most suitable methods for initial contact by those seeking employment are to mail, fax or e-mail a resume with a covering letter. DRS Flight Safety and Communications does hire summer and co-op work term students. *Contact:* Human Resources.

DRUMMOND WELDING AND STEEL WORKS INC.
700 Talon
Longueuil, QC J4G 1P7

Tel.	450-526-4411
Fax	450-679-1686

Drummond Welding and Steel Works Inc. is involved in the manufacturing of steel tanks and pressure vessels. There are 95 employees at this location and a total of 100 employees in the company. Graduates most likely to be hired come from the following academic areas: Bachelor of Science (Computer Science, Metallurgy), Bachelor of Engineering (Civil, Architectural/Building, Industrial Design, Industrial Production, Mechanical, Metallurgy, Welding, Petroleum), Bachelor of Commerce/Business Administration (Accounting, Human Resources, Marketing), Community College Diploma (Accounting, Marketing/Sales, Purchasing/Logistics, Secretarial, CAD/CAM/ Autocad, Engineering Technician, Welding) and High School Diploma. Graduates would occupy Draftsperson, Inside Sales Representative, Design Engineer, Production Planner, Estimator, Buyer, Inspector and Accountant positions. Initiative, dynamic, and a working knowledge of French and English are all listed as desirable non-academic qualifications. Company benefits are rated as industry standard. The potential for advancement is listed as being good. The average annual starting salary falls within the $20,000 to $25,000 range. The most suitable method for initial contact by those seeking employment is to mail a resume with a covering letter. *Contacts:* Christine Bellefeuille, Human Resources Manager or Louis Caissie, Human Resources Manager.

DUCKS UNLIMITED CANADA
PO Box 1160, Oak Hammock Marsh
Stonewall, MB R0C 2Z0

Tel.	204-467-3000
Fax	204-467-9028
Email	c_barber@ducks.ca
Website	www.ducks.ca

Ducks Unlimited Canada is a non-profit, private company dedicated to the preservation of breeding habitat in Canada for waterfowl. The company provides assistance to farmers in land use which benefits the environment and provides water for agriculture, domestic and recreational uses. There are approximately 120 employees at this location and a total of 500 employees across Canada. Graduates most likely to be hired come from the following academic areas: Bachelor of Arts (History), Bachelor of Science (Agriculture, Biology, Computer Science, Wetland and Marsh Management), Bachelor of Engineering (Environmental/Resources, Water Resources), Bachelor of Commerce/Business Administration (Accounting, Finance, Information Systems, Marketing), Chartered Accountant (Finance), Certified Management Accountant (Finance), Certified General Accountant (Finance), Master of Business Administration (Accounting, Finance, Information Systems, Marketing), Master of Science (Wetland and Marsh Management) and Community College Diploma (Accounting, Communications/Public Relations, Human Resources, Information Systems, Secretarial, Audio/Visual Technician, Journalism, Recreation Studies, Travel/Tourism, Agriculture/Horticulture, CAD-CAM/Autocad, Computer Science). Graduates would occupy Biologist, Agrologist, Research Biologist, Interpreter, Fund Raiser, Administrative Assistant, Writer, GIS Specialist, IS Developer, IS Analyst, Engineer, Computer Technician and Computer Operator positions. Initiative, team player, risk taker, quality and goal oriented are all listed as desirable nonacademic qualifications. In addition, most positions call for two to five years related work experience. Company benefits are rated above average. The potential for advancement is listed as average. The most suitable method for initial contact by those seeking employment is to mail a resume with a covering letter. Ducks Unlimited Canada does hire local summer students for the interpretive program, from history (history of Oak Hammond Marsh) and biology (waterfowl and plants) programs. *Contacts:* Ms. C. Barber, Personnel or for other Provinces contact the Manager of Field Operations.

DUN & BRADSTREET CANADA
5770 Hurontario Avenue
Mississauga, ON L5R 3G5

Tel.	905-568-6350
Fax	905-568-6360
Website	www.dnb.ca

Dun & Bradstreet Canada provides a host of business information services to support companies in making business to business decisions. In addition to credit reports, marketing services and collection services, Dun & Bradstreet conducts education seminars. The company employs 300 people at this location, a total of 560 in Canada, and 16,000 people worldwide. Graduates most likely to be hired come from the following academic areas: Bachelor of Arts (General), Bachelor of Commerce/ Business Administration (General, Accounting, Finance, Human Resources, information Systems, Marketing), Master of Business Administration (General) and Community College Diploma (Accounting, Administration, Advertising, Human Resources, Information Systems, Insurance, Marketing/Sales, Secretarial, Graphic Arts). Graduates would occupy Business Analyst, Accountant, Programmer and Collections Officer positions. Self-starter, a high level of initiative, drive and creativity are all listed as desirable non-academic qualifications. The most suitable methods for initial contact by those seeking employment are to mail or fax a resume with a covering letter. Dun & Bradstreet Canada does hire summer and co-op work term students. *Contact:* Cathy Partridge, Human Resources.

DuPont Canada

DUPONT CANADA INC.
PO Box 2200, Streetsville
Mississauga, ON L5M 2H3

Tel.	905-821-3300
Fax	905-821-5592
Email	hr.recruiting@can.dupont.com
Website	www.dupont.ca

DuPont Canada Inc. is a diversified chemical company that manufactures specialty chemicals and fibres, plastics and polymer films. The wide range of DuPont products sold include synthetic fibres, polymer resins, packaging films, automotive finishes, agricultural and industrial chemicals. There are 350 employees at the head office in Mississauga and a total of 3,200 employees in five manufacturing facilities located in Ontario. These include, Ajax, Corunna, Kingston, Maitland and Whitby. Graduates most likely to be hired come from the following academic areas: Bachelor Science (Chemistry, Computer Science), Bachelor of Engineering (Chemical, Mechanical, Electrical), Bachelor of Commerce/Business Administration, Master/Doctorate of Science (Chemistry, Computer Science), and Master/Doctorate of Engineering (Chemical, Mechanical, Electrical). Company benefits are rated above average. The potential for advancement is listed as being good. DuPont Canada is committed to setting and meeting high safety, health and environmental standards. The most suitable methods for initial contact by those seeking employment are to mail a resume with a covering letter, indicating the preferred field of work (eg. accounting, chemical engineering, administration, etc.), or via your campus career centre. *Contact:* The Staffing Team, Human Resources & Communications.

DURA AUTOMOTIVE
617 Douro Street
Stratford, ON N5A 6V5

Tel.	519-273-0840
Fax	519-273-4045
Email	Human_Resources@duraauto.com

Dura Automotive is a leading original equipment manufacturer (OEM) parts supplier. The company manufactures and designs cables for parking brake systems. Dura Automotive employs 500 people at this location, a total of 750 in Canada and a total of 20,000 employees worldwide. Graduates most likely to be hired come from the following academic areas: Bachelor of Engineering (Mechanical, Industrial Engineering, Industrial Production/Manufacturing), Bachelor of Commerce/Business Administration (Accounting) and Community College Diploma (Business, CAD/CAM/Autocad). Company benefits are rated as industry standard. The potential for advancement is listed as being good. The average annual starting salary falls within the $35,000 to $40,000 range. The most suitable method for initial contact by those seeking employment is e-mail a resume with a covering letter. Dura Automotive does hire co-op work term students. *Contact:* Christa Pynenburg, Manager, Human Resources.

DYNAPRO
800 Carleton Court, Annacis Island
New Westminster, BC V3M 6L3

Tel. 604-521-3962
Fax 604-521-8474
Email .... debbie_paulsen@dynapro.com
Website .... www.dynapro.com

Dynapro simplifies interaction between people and technology by designing and manufacturing touch products from touch screen components to touch computers, terminals and monitors. Dr. Karl Brackhaus founded Dynapro in 1976 and today the company employs 320 people in two facilities in Vancouver and Milwaukee, Wisconsin. Graduates most likely to be hired come from the following academic areas: Bachelor of Arts (General), Bachelor of Science (Chemistry, Physics), Bachelor of Engineering (Chemical, Electrical, Mechanical, Computer Systems, Engineering Physics, Industrial Chemistry, Materials Science), Bachelor of Commerce/Business Administration (General), Certified Management Accountant, Master of Business Administration and Community College Diploma (Accounting, Facility Management, Human Resources, Office Administration, Electronics Technician, Engineering Technician, Information Systems). Graduates would occupy Engineer, Technologist, Technician, Management, Support and Accounting positions. Good verbal and written communication skills, previous work experience, team player and PC skills are all listed as desirable non-academic qualifications. Company benefits are rated as excellent. The potential for advancement is listed as average. The average annual starting salary falls within the $40,000 to $45,000 range. The most suitable methods for initial contact by those seeking employment are to e-mail a resume with a covering letter, or via the company's website. Dynapro does hire summer and co-op work term students. *Contacts:* Debbie Paulsen, Human Resources Director or Paula Thompson, Human Resources Administrator.

EBCO INDUSTRIES LTD.
7851 Alderbridge Way
Richmond, BC V6X 2A4

Tel. 604-278-5578
Fax 604-276-1502
Email .... jpeters@ebco.com
Website .... www.ebco.com

Ebco Industries Ltd. is a large custom manufacturer specializing in the machining, fabricating, and assembly of large and small components and equipment.

Headquartered in Richmond, Ebco's facilities include 300,000 square feet of manufacturing space including advanced CNC machines, large steel and alloy fabrication and welding equipment and lifting capabilities to 180 tons. The company serves a wide range of corporations in North America and around the world including pulp and paper and mining companies and the power generation, offshore oil production, aerospace, defence and medical industries. Graduates most likely to be hired come from the following academic areas: Bachelor of Engineering (Mechanical) and Community College Diploma (Tool & Die/Machinist, Welding, Steel Fabricator). Graduates would occupy Machinist, CNC Machinist, Welder, Fabricator, Tool and Die Maker and Millwright positions. A positive attitude, team player, healthy lifestyle and a willingness to work shifts and overtime are all listed as desirable non-academic qualifications. Company benefits are rated as industry standard. The potential for advancement is listed as being good. The average annual starting salary falls within the $50,000 to $55,000. The most suitable methods for initial contact by those seeking employment are to mail, fax or e-mail a resume with a covering letter, or via the company's website. Ebco Industries Ltd. also maintains a comprehensive apprenticeship and training program. *Contact:* Janice Peters, Human Resources Coordinator.

ECE GROUP LTD., THE
205 Lesmill Road
Don Mills, ON M3B 2V1

Tel. 416-449-1030
Fax 416-449-2876

The ECE Group Ltd., founded in 1955, provides consulting and engineering services in electrical and mechanical engineering. In addition, the company provides services in specialty disciplines of communication, security and associated environmental engineering needs. ECE's experience has been gathered in the design of a wide range of commercial, institutional, public and special-purpose buildings. The company's range of services includes investigations, reports, research, design and inspection. Through a wholly owned subsidiary, the company also provides facility management services. ECE employs 64 people at this location. Graduates most likely to be hired come from the following academic areas: Bachelor of Engineering (Electrical, Mechanical, Computer Systems, Industrial Design) and Community College Diploma (Architectural Technician, CAD/CAM/Autocad, Engineering Technician, HVAC Systems). Graduates would occupy Mechanical and Electrical CAD Designer, Technician and Engineering positions. Energetic, hardworking, self-directed, able to work well with others, and good oral and verbal communication skills are all listed as desirable non-academic qualifications. Company benefits and the potential for advancement are both rated as excellent. The average annual starting salary falls within the $32,000 to $38,000 range. The most suitable method for initial contact by graduates seeking employment is to mail a resume with a covering letter. The ECE Group Ltd. does hire summer and co-op work term students. *Contact:* Marianne Villa, Manager, Human Resources.

ECOLAB LTD.
5105 Tomken Road
Mississauga, ON L4W 2X5

Tel. 905-238-0171
Fax 905-238-2006
Website .... www.ecolab.com

Ecolab Ltd. provides sanitation solutions and services to the hospitality, health care and foodservices markets. The company's products are sold worldwide via a direct sales force. Ecolab employs a total of 400 people and maintains one manufacturing facility in Canada. Graduates most likely to be hired come from the following academic areas: Bachelor of Science (General, Biology, Chemistry, Microbiology), Bachelor of Engineering (General, Environmental, Chemical), Bachelor of Commerce/Business Administration and Community College Diploma (Accounting, Administration, Secretarial, Engineering, Mechanic). Graduates would to occupy Territory Manager Trainee, Engineer and Production Supervisor positions. Sales ability, good organizational skills and a strong sense of urgency are listed as desirable non-academic qualifications. Company benefits are rated as industry standard. The potential for advancement is listed as excellent. The average annual starting salary falls within the $30,000 to $35,000 range, and is commission based for some positions. The most suitable method for initial contact by those seeking employment is to mail a resume with a covering letter. Ecolab Ltd. does hire summer students. *Contact:* Jan Moody, Human Resources Coordinator.

ECONOMICAL INSURANCE GROUP, THE

111 Westmount Road South, PO Box 2000
Waterloo, ON N2J 4S4

Tel.	519-570-8200
Fax	519-570-8239
Email	hrd@economicalinsurance.com
Website	www.economicalinsurance.com

The Economical Insurance Group is a leading, Canadian owned, property and casualty insurance company. The company's track record of success spans over 125 years. Today, The Economical is expanding its products, services and technology to meet the challenges of the new millennium, and is committed to working with its business partners to meet these goals. The company is a recognized market leader in interface technology and in its ability to succeed in new product markets. Presently, there are 420 employees at this location and a total of 1,300 employees in Canada. Economical believes in recruiting, training and rewarding dedicated people who believe in their ability to achieve. Graduates most likely to be hired come from the following academic areas: Bachelor of Arts (General, Economics, English, Geography), Bachelor of Science (General, Actuarial, Computer Science, Mathematics), Bachelor of Commerce (General, Accounting, Finance, Human Resources, Information Systems), Chartered Accountant, Certified Management Accountant, Certified General Accountant, Master of Business Administration (General) and Community College Diploma (Accounting, Administration, Business, Human Resources, Information Systems, Insurance, Secretarial). Graduates would occupy Administrative Assistant, Accounting Clerk, Computer Programmer/Analyst, Financial Analyst, Claims Trainee and Underwriter Trainee positions. Excellent written and oral communication skills, team player, good organizational skills, flexible, a demonstrated ability to rise above and beyond the expected and a willingness to seek skills and knowledge through the challenge of continuous learning are all listed as desirable non-academic qualifications. Company benefits are rated above average. The potential for advancement is listed as being good. The average annual starting salary falls within the $20,000 to $25,000 range. The most suitable methods for initial contact by those seeking employment are to mail, fax or e-mail a resume with a covering letter. The Economical Insurance Group does

hire summer and co-op work term students. *Contact:* Carol Boss, Specialist - Staffing, Human Resources.

EDELSTEIN DIVERSIFIED COMPANY LIMITED

21 Mount Vernon
Montreal, QC H8R 1J9

Tel.	514-489-8689
Fax	514-489-9707
Email	info@edelstein.com
Website	www.edelstein.com

Edelstein Diversified Company Limited, established in 1973, is a leading supplier of specialty pressure sensitive tapes. The corporate headquarters is located in Montreal, with sales and warehousing facilities maintained and operated in Chicago, Los Angeles, Norfolk, Toronto and Vancouver. The company employs approximately 60 people at this location, a total of 75 in Canada, and a total of 90 people worldwide. Edelstein supplies pressure sensitive tapes to every segment of industry including the leading paper, food, tobacco, metal and plastic manufacturers. The company's research and development facilities work to provide the most technically advanced products at competitive pricing. Graduates most likely to be hired come from the following academic areas: Bachelor of Arts (Economics, Psychology), Bachelor of Engineering (General, Forest Resources, Industrial Engineering, Industrial Production/Manufacturing, Materials Science, Pulp and Paper), Bachelor of Commerce/Business Administration (General, Finance, Marketing), Master of Business Administration (Marketing) and Community College Diploma (Business, Marketing/Sales). Edelstein continually seeks graduates for Sales positions. Team player, initiative, drive, enthusiasm, problem solving skills, computer literacy and sales experience are all listed as desirable non-academic qualifications. Company benefits are rated above average. The most suitable methods for initial contact by those seeking employment are to mail or fax a resume with a covering letter. Edelstein Diversified Company Limited does hire summer students. *Contact:* Human Resource Department.

EDS CANADA

33 Yonge Street, Suite 500
Toronto, ON M5E 1G4

Tel.	416-814-4500
Fax	416-814-4856
Email	canada-staffing@eds.com
Website	www.eds.ca

EDS Canada has been active in the Canadian marketplace since 1985 and has quickly evolved into a leading provider of information technology services. From offices in 21 Canadian cities, more than 2,000 highly skilled employees provide a broad range of professional services that are used to enhance business systems and processes for more than 50 private and public sector client organizations. Graduates are hired from the following academic areas: Bachelor of Science (General, Computer Science, Mathematics), Bachelor of Engineering (General, Systems, Electrical, Mechanical), Bachelor of Commerce/Business Administration (Information Systems) and Community College Diploma (Business Administration, Information Systems, Computer Programming, Electronics Technology). EDS is interested in well rounded individuals who possess a variety of skills such as leadership ability, a high level of professionalism and technical aptitude. Good communication and customer relation skills are also requirements. Rewards are based on performance, creativity, and contribution to the organization. Promotions at EDS occur from within, allowing the best qualified and available employees the opportunities for advancement. EDS is committed to an equal employment opportunity policy in all its operations and in all employment practices. Interested applicants should mail a resume and covering letter to Staffing Services. Summer students are encouraged to apply by January 15th. *Contact:* Staffing Services.

EDS SYSTEMHOUSE INC.
50 O'Connor Street, Suite 501
Ottawa, ON K1P 6L2

Tel.	613-236-9734
Fax	613-236-2043
Website	www.eds.ca

EDS Systemhouse Inc. is the predominant Information Technology (IT) services provider in Canada. The company provides IT consulting, systems integration, networking, systems management, network solutions, outsourcing expertise and electronic commerce in the financial services, government services, health, manufacturing, energy, and communications industries. Headquartered in Toronto, EDS Systemhouse employs just under 10,000 people and has 80 office locations in every major city and every province. EDS Systemhouse Inc. is a subsidiary of EDS Corporation, based in Plano, Texas. Graduates most likely to be hired at the Ottawa location come from the following academic areas: Bachelor of Science (Computer Science), Bachelor of Engineering (Electrical, Computer Systems), Bachelor of Commerce/Business Administration (Information Systems), Master of Business Administration (Information Systems) and Community College Diploma (Information Systems, Computer Science). Graduates would occupy Programmer Analyst, Associate Network Analyst, Associate Help Desk Analyst and Business Analyst positions. Team player, a high level of initiative, strong communication skills and customer service experience are all listed as desirable non-academic qualifications. Company benefits are rated as excellent. The potential for advancement is listed as being good. The average annual starting salary falls within the $30,000 to $35,000 range. The most suitable methods for initial contact by those seeking employment are to mail, fax, or e-mail a resume with covering letter, or by applying through the company's website. EDS Systemhouse Inc. does hire summer and co-op work term students, with postings made at campus career centres. *Contact:* Local Human Resource Departments for Specific Opportunities.

EDS SYSTEMHOUSE INC.
1881 Scarth Street, Suite 1800
Regina, SK S4P 4K9

Tel.	306-525-7100
Fax	306-352-8001
Website	www.eds.ca

EDS Systemhouse Inc. is the predominant Information Technology (IT) services provider in Canada. The company provides IT consulting, systems integration, networking, systems management, network solutions, outsourcing expertise and electronic commerce in the financial services, government services, health, manufacturing, energy, and communications industries. Headquartered in Toronto, EDS Systemhouse employs just under 10,000 people and has 80 office locations in every major city and every province. EDS Systemhouse Inc. is a subsidiary of EDS Corporation, based in Plano, Texas. Graduates most likely to be hired at the Regina location come from the following academic areas: Bachelor of Science (Computer Science), Bachelor of Engineering (Computer Systems) and Community College Diploma (Computer Science, Information Systems). Team player, professionalism and a positive attitude all listed as desirable non-academic qualifications. Company benefits are rated above average. The potential for advancement is listed as being excellent. The average annual starting salary falls within the $35,000 to $40,000 range. The most suitable methods for initial contact by those seeking employment are to mail, fax or e-mail a resume with a covering letter. EDS Systemhouse Inc. does hire summer and co-op work term students at the Regina location. *Contact:* Recruiting.

EDS SYSTEMHOUSE INC.
112 - 4th Avenue SW, 4th Floor
Calgary, AB T2P 0H3

Tel.	403-233-6627
Fax	403-233-5860
Website	www.eds.ca

EDS Systemhouse Inc. is the predominant Information Technology (IT) services provider in Canada. The company provides IT consulting, systems integration, networking, systems management, network solutions, outsourcing expertise and electronic commerce in the financial services, government services, health, manufacturing, energy, and communications industries. Headquartered in Toronto, EDS Systemhouse employs just under 10,000 people and has 80 office locations in every major city and every province. EDS Systemhouse Inc. is a subsidiary of EDS Corporation, based in Plano, Texas. Graduates most likely to be hired at the Calgary location come from the following academic areas: Bachelor of Science (Computer Science), Bachelor of Engineering (Computer Systems), Bachelor of Commerce/Business Administration (Information Systems) and Community College Diploma (Information Systems, Computer Science). Graduates would occupy Associate Help Desk Analyst, Programmer and Associate Technical Service Representative positions. An interest in continual learning and previous related work experience are both listed as desirable non-academic qualifications. Company benefits are rated above average. The potential for advancement is listed as being excellent. The average annual starting salary falls within the $30,000 to $35,000 range. The most suitable methods for initial contact by those seeking employment is to mail or e-mail a resume with a covering letter, or via the company's website. EDS Systemhouse Inc. does hire summer and co-op work term students at the Calgary location. *Contact:* Recruiting Department.

EDSCHA OF CANADA
PO Box 660
Niagara Falls, ON L2E 6V5

Tel.	905-374-3400
Fax	905-374-3614

Edscha of Canada is involved in the manufacturing of auto parts, primarily door hinges and checks. There are approximately 230 employees at this location. Graduates most likely to be hired come from the following academic areas: Bachelor of Engineering (General, Electrical, Automation/Robotics, Computer Systems, Mechanical, Industrial Design, Industrial Production), Bachelor of Commerce/Business Administration (General, Accounting, Finance, Human Resources, Information Systems, Marketing), Chartered Accountant (Auto Manufacturing), Certified Management Accountant (Auto Manufacturing), Certified General Accountant (Auto Manufacturing), Master of Business Administration (Accounting, Finance, Human Resources, Information Systems, Marketing), Community College Diploma (Accounting, Administration, Business, Financial Planning, Human Resources, Marketing/Sales, Purchasing/Logistics, Secretarial, CAD/CAM/Autocad Computer Science, Engineering Technician) and High School Diploma. Graduates would occupy Accounting Clerk, Engineer and Trainee positions. Previous work experience, team player, and good communication skills are listed as desirable non-academic qualifications. Company benefits are rated above average. The potential for advancement is listed as average. The average annual starting salary depends upon the position being considered, ranging from $30,000 to $35,000 for administrative positions, and $40,000 to $45,000 for technical positions. The most suitable methods for initial contact by those seeking employment are to mail a resume with a covering letter, or through job placement agencies. Edscha of Canada does hire summer students, although not every summer. *Contact:* Payroll and Benefits Administration.

Edward Jones®

Serving Individual Investors

EDWARD JONES
90 Burnhamthorpe Road West, Suite 902
Sussex Centre
Mississauga, ON L5B 3C3

Tel. 800-380-4517
Fax 905-306-8528
Email .... careeropcan@edwardjones.com
Website .... www.jonesopportunity.com

Edward Jones is a full-service financial services firm that serves the long-term investment needs of individuals. Edward Jones pioneered the concept of single-broker, community-oriented branch offices, and has built the largest brokerage office network throughout the United States, Canada and the United Kingdom. The cornerstone of Edward Jones' heritage is its face-to-face investment approach that serves the individual conservative investor. This approach is essential to the company's ongoing success and plans. Presently, Edward Jones employs 700 people in Canada, and a total of 12,000 people worldwide. Graduates most likely to be hired come from the following academic areas: Bachelor of Arts (Economics), Bachelor of Commerce/Business Administration (General, Accounting, Finance, Marketing), Chartered Accountant, Certified Management Accountant, Certified General Accountant, Master of Business Administration (General, Accounting, Finance, Marketing) and Community College Diploma (Accounting, Business, Financial Planning, Insurance, Marketing/Sales, Real Estate Sales). Graduates are hired as Investment Representatives. As an Investment Representative, graduates start at the top, getting right to work building a business and running their own Edward Jones branch office. Edward Jones provides training and a fully equipped and furnished office, which includes a full-time assistant, advanced computer and satellite video technology, and much more. The com-

pany seeks self-reliant, highly ambitious, energetic, committed, hard working, and highly successful people who are determined to build and manage their own profitable business without the cash investment that usually accompanies a startup. Applicants should be acutely aware of the entrepreneurial opportunities that exist in the growth environment of Edward Jones. The company is an equal opportunity employer and offers a competitive salary and benefits package. Accordingly, company benefits and the potential for advancement are both rated as excellent. The average annual starting salary falls within the $50,000 to $55,000 range. The most suitable methods for initial contact by those seeking employment with Edward Jones, are to call 1-800-380-4517 or through the company's website. *Contact:* Mina Modarelli, Recruiting Coordinator.

EFA SOFTWARE SERVICES LTD.
605 - 5th Avenue SW, Suite 800
Calgary, AB T2P 3H5

Tel. 403-265-6131
Fax 403-265-2893
Email .... efa@efasoftware.com
Website .... www.efasoftware.ab.ca

EFA Software Services Ltd. develops leading edge applications for securities trading, production revenue accounting systems as well as providing expert consulting services. Founded in 1985, EFA has grown into a diverse business employing more than 110 professionals servicing more than 100 customers around the world. Graduates most likely to be hired come from the following academic areas: Bachelor of Science (Computer Science), Bachelor of Commerce/Business Administration (Information Systems) and Community College Diploma (Journalism, Computer Science). The average annual starting salary is currently being reviewed. The most suitable method for initial contact by those seeking employment is to mail a resume with a covering letter. *Contacts:* Geoff Thompson, Vice President or Jim Bird, Manager.

EG&G OPTOELECTRONICS CANADA
22001 Dumberry Road
Vaudreuil, QC J7V 8P7

Tel. 450-424-3300
Fax 450-424-3413

EG & G Optoelectronics Canada's principle focus is on optoelectronic products and applications such as emitters, photocells, lasers, detectors and electronic imaging devices. EG & G Inc. was founded over 45 years ago by H. Edgerton, K. F. Germeshausen and H. E. Grier, whose initials form the company name. Today, EG & G Inc., headquartered in Wellesley, Massachusetts, is a diversified high-tech company with over 14,000 employees. The company's customer base includes companies who manufacture fibre optics and communication systems, medical and analytical instruments, automobiles, smoke alarms, etc. There are approximately 213 employees at this location. Graduates most likely to be hired come from the following academic areas: Bachelor of Science (Chemistry, Physics), Bachelor of Engineering (Chemical, Industrial Chemistry, Electrical, Microelectronics, Telecommunications), Bachelor of Commerce/Business Administration (Accounting, Finance, Human Resources, Information Systems, Marketing), Certified Management Accountant, Master of Science (Chemistry, Physics), Master of Engineering (Chemistry, Electrical) and Community College Diploma (Accounting, Administration, Business, Marketing/Sales, Purchasing/Logistics, Secretarial, Electronics Technician, Engineering Technician, HVAC Systems). Graduates would occupy Engineer, member of Technical Staff, Technician, Technician Assistant, Clerk, Secretary and Administrator positions. Bilingualism, mobility, available to work on shifts (Technicians) and previous experience in a manufacturing environment are all listed as desirable non-academic qualifications. The average annual starting salary falls within the $30,000 to $35,000 range. The most suitable method for initial contact by those seeking employment is to mail a resume with a covering letter. *Contacts:* Barbara Blair or Lucie Giguère.

EHVERT ENGINEERING
Professional Technology Services

EHVERT ENGINEERING
1 University Avenue, Suite 604
Toronto, ON M5J 2P1

Tel. 416-868-1933
Fax 416-868-6229
Email .... recruiting@ehvert.com
Website .... www.ehvert.com

Ehvert Engineering is a multi-faceted technology services firm and Microsoft certified solution provider. The company's specialized team offers superior professional technical services and expertise in several diverse fields to large organizations. Ehvert is vendor independent, and therefore can work objectively in a multi-vendor environment to design and implement technology solutions that best meet the needs of its clients. Whether it is network and systems integration services, software development, resource and project management or technical support, Ehvert Engineering is able to provide professional services that complement an organization's own technical resources. The company strives to provide the highest quality of service and support for corporations that are implementing or supporting technology infrastructures. Ehvert Engineering's specialized engineers and technicians form a team that can provide a complete technology solution, and are certified by a broad range of vendors. Graduates most likely to be hired come from the following academic areas: Bachelor of Science (Computer Science), Bachelor of Engineering (General, Civil, Electrical, Mechanical, Architectural/Building, Computer Systems, Engineering Physics, Telecommunications), Bachelor of Commerce/Business Administration (Accounting, Finance, Human Resources, Information Systems, Marketing), Chartered Accountant, Master of Business Administration (Accounting, Finance, Information Systems, Marketing) and Community College Diploma (Accounting, Human Resources, Information Systems, CAD/CAM/Autocad, Computer Science, Engineering Technician). Graduates would occupy Technical Support Specialist, Network & Systems Engineer, Software Developer, Infrastructure/Site Engineering Specialist, Consultant, Project Manager, Accounting Clerk, Marketing/Sales Representative. Good interpersonal and communication skills, self-starter, team player, strong technical abilities, good presentation skills and previous work experience are all listed as desirable non-academic qualifications. The most suitable methods for initial contact by those seeking employment are to fax or e-mail a resume with a covering letter, or by applying through the company's website at www.ehvert.com. Ehvert Engineering does hire co-op work term students. *Contact:* Debra Zanon, Human Resources.

ELECTRO SONIC INC.
1100 Gordon Baker Road
Toronto, ON M2H 3B3

Tel. 416-494-1666
Fax 416-496-3030
Website .... www.e-sonic.com

Electro Sonic Inc. is one of Canada's largest distributors of electronic components and parts. Electro Sonic is a supplier of both the repair and maintenance, as well as the original equipment manufacturers' markets. An ISO 9002 registered company, ElectroSonic employs a total of 373 people in Canada. Graduates most likely to be hired come from the following academic areas: Bachelor of Arts (General, Economics, Philosophy, Political Science, Psychology), Bachelor of Science (Computer Science, Mathematics, Psychology), Bachelor of Engineering (Electrical, Computer Systems, Environmental/Resources, Industrial Design, Industrial Engineering, Microelectronics, Telecommunications), Bachelor of Commerce/Business Administration (General, Accounting, Finance, Human Resources, Information Systems, Marketing), Chartered Accountant, Certified Management Accountant, Certified General Accountant, Master of Business Administration (Finance, Human Resources, Marketing), Master of Engineering (Industrial Design), Community College Diploma (Accounting, Administration, Advertising, Business, Communications/Public Relations, Human Resources, Information Systems, Marketing/Sales, Purchasing/Logistics, Secretarial, Computer Science, Electronics Technician, Engineering Technician), High School Diploma, those with CMP, APRC, PMAC, CHRP, CHRY designations and graduates from the Canadian Securities Course. Graduates would occupy Trainee, Technician, Product Manager, Account Manager, Inside Sales Representative, A/P Coordinator, Financial Analyst and Customer Service Representative. Strong interpersonal skills, detail oriented, good organizational skills, technical, results oriented, and the ability to deal and work with tight deadlines are all listed as desirable non-academic qualifications. Company benefits are rated above average. The potential for advancement is listed as being good. The average annual starting salary falls within the $30,000 to $35,000 range. The most suitable method for initial contact by those seeking employment is to mail a resume with a covering letter. Electro Sonic does hire summer and co-op students. *Contact:* Human Resources.

ELECTRONIC DIRECT MARKETING LTD. / EDM
39 Casebridge Court
Toronto, ON M1B 5N4

Tel. 416-282-1201
Fax 416-282-1897
Website .... www.edm-ltd.com

Electronic Direct Marketing Ltd. / EDM is a state-of-the-art call centre and fulfillment company. The company provides all levels of inbound and outbound services including customer/technical support, order taking and telesales. EDM's clients include various Fortune 500 companies. The company employs over 800 people in Canada. Graduates most likely to be hired come from the following academic areas: Bachelor of Arts (General, English, French, Languages), Bachelor of Commerce/Business Administration (General, Human Resources,

Information Systems, Marketing), Master of Business Administration (General, Accounting, Information Systems) and Community College Diploma (Administration, Business, Communications/Public Relations, Human Resources, Information Systems, Marketing/Sales). Graduates would occupy Call Centre Associate, Programmer, Systems Administrator, Billing Clerk, Recruiter and Trainer positions. Team player, excellent communication skills, drive to succeed and adaptability are all listed as desirable non-academic qualifications. Company benefits are rated as industry standard. The potential for advancement is listed as excellent. The average annual starting salary falls within the $20,000 to $25,000 range. The most suitable method for initial contact by those seeking employment is to fax a resume with a covering letter. EDM does hire summer students. (Other Toronto Location: Electronic Direct Marketing Ltd., 100 Sheppard Avenue East, Toronto, ON, M2N 6N5, Phone 416-226-1076.) *Contact:* Mr. Jamie Allison, Manager, Human Resources.

ELECTROPHOTONICS CORPORATION
7941 Jane Street, Unit 200
Concord, ON L4K 4L6

Tel. 905-669-4660
Fax 905-669-3722
Email .... careers@electrophotonics.com
Website .... www.electrophotonics.com

ElectroPhotonics Corporation is involved in the development of products in fiber optic sensing systems and fiber optic telecommunication devices. The company was formed in 1993 as a spin-off from the University of Toronto Fiber Optic Smart Structures Laboratory. Innovation is the key to ElectroPhotonics' success, demonstrating a strong ability to take novel technological concepts through to product development and commercial reality, both in the telecommunication and sensing arenas. A critical factor in this regard is the ability to attract and motivate a highly skilled group of individuals. The company's early success has been in pioneering the development of fiber optic Bragg grating sensing technology and a line of commercial sensing systems. The engineering team's knowledge and experience have been essential to the development of the novel concepts and devices integral to the ElectroPhotonics' novel telecom products. ElectroPhotonics' proprietary technology is poised to provide solutions to significant needs in the burgeoning market for high capacity fiber transmission systems. The company was formed by professionals with a strong and unique blend of backgrounds in research and product development. The company's staff consists of highly skilled individuals with complimentary background and experience. The disciplines represented include electronics, fiber optics, mechanics and materials, and physics. The staff make-up provides ElectroPhotonics with a unique spectrum of knowledge and skill with which to pursue its highly interdisciplinary product development program. Graduates most likely to be hired come from the following academic areas: Bachelor of Science (Physics), Bachelor of Engineering (General, Electrical, Mechanical, Computer Systems, Engineering Physics, Instrumentation, Microelectronics, Telecommunications), Bachelor of Commerce/Business Administration (General), Master of Science, Master of Engineering and Community College Diploma (CAD/CAM/Autocad, Electronics Technician, Engineering Technician). Innovative, team player, expertise, initiative, self-motivated and flexibility are all listed as desirable non-academic qualifications. Company benefits are rated above average. The potential for advancement is listed as excellent. The average annual starting salary falls within the $35,000 to $40,000 range. The most suitable methods for initial contact by those seeking employment are to mail a resume with a covering letter, or by applying through the company's website at www.electrophotonics.com. ElectroPhotonics Corporation does hire summer and co-op work term students. *Contact:* Human Resources.

ELI LILLY CANADA INC.
3650 Danforth Avenue
Toronto, ON M1N 2E8

Tel. 416-694-3221
Fax 416-699-7241
Website .... www.lilly.com

Eli Lilly Canada Inc. is involved in the research and development, sales and marketing, and related corporate services that are focused towards the promotion of ethical pharmaceutical products. The company employs more than 400 people in Canada. Graduates most likely to be hired come from the following academic areas: Bachelor of Science, Bachelor of Engineering, Bachelor of Commerce/Business Administration, Chartered Accountant, Certified Management Accountant, Master of Business Administration, Masters (Science/General) and Community College Diploma (Business, Operations Management). Graduates would occupy Sales Representative, Financial Analyst and Clinical Research Associate position. Company benefits are rated above average. The potential for advancement is listed as being good. The average annual starting salary is dependent upon the level of the position. The most suitable method for initial contact by graduates seeking employment is to mail a resume with a covering letter. Eli Lilly Canada Inc. does hire summer and co-op work term students. *Contacts:* Marie Walton, Recruitment & Relocation Co-ordinator or Human Resources.

EMERALD GATEWAY INTERNATIONAL
7895 Tranmere Drive, Suite 201
Mississauga, ON L5S 1V9

Tel. 905-678-2961
Fax 905-678-5181
Email .... cullena@dscltd.com
Website .... www.emeraldgateway.com

Emerald Gateway International, a member of the DSC Group of companies, engineers and manufactures consumer electronics for energy management and home automation. Emerald Gateway employs approximately 15 people. Graduates most likely to be hired come from the following academic areas: Bachelor of Science (Computer Science), Bachelor of Engineering (Electrical, Power/Hydro), Master of Science (Computer Science), Master of Engineering (Electrical), Doctorate (Computer Science, Engineering) and Community College Diploma (CAD/CAM/Autocad, Electronics Technician, Engineering Technician). Graduates would occupy Programmer, Engineer (only if licensed), Technician and Technologist positions. Company benefits are rated as industry standard. The potential for advancement is listed as being excellent. The average annual starting salary falls within the $40,000 to $45,000 range. The most suitable method for initial contact by those seeking employment is to e-mail a resume with a covering letter. *Contacts:* Andrew M. Cullen, P. Eng. / Manager, R & D or Richard Worrall, P. Eng / Manager, Operations.

ENBRIDGE CONSUMERS GAS
PO Box 650
Toronto, ON M1K 5E3

Tel. 416-495-5459
Fax 416-495-5739
Email .... recruiting@cgc.enbridge.com
Website .... www.cgc.enbridge.com

Enbridge Consumers Gas distributes natural gas throughout specific geographic areas. There are more than 1,000 people employed at this location. Graduates most likely to be hired come from the following academic areas: Bachelor of Arts (General), Bachelor of Engineering (Civil, Electrical, Mechanical), Bachelor of Laws and Master of Business Administration (Finance). Graduates would occupy entry-level Clerical, Operations Engineer, Associate Corporate Solicitor and Financial Analyst positions. Customer service and computer skills are both listed as desirable non-academic qualifications. Company benefits are rated as industry standard. The potential for advancement is listed as being good. The average annual starting salary falls within the $30,000 to $35,000 range. The most suitable method for initial contact by those seeking employment is to mail a resume with a covering letter. Enbridge Consumers Gas does hire summer students. *Contact:* Human Resources Recruiting.

ENERTEC GEOPHYSICAL SERVICES LIMITED
615 Macleod Trail SE, Suite 900
Calgary, AB T2G 4T8

Tel. 403-233-7830
Fax 403-233-9368

Enertec Geophysical Services Limited provides land and marine geophysical seismic survey and processing services to the oil and gas industry. The company currently operates out of Calgary, Houston and Baton Rouge. Enertec is a public company, traded on the Toronto Stock Exchange as ERS. There are 50 employees at the Calgary head office, a total of 400 employees in Canada, and a total of 500 employees worldwide. Graduates most likely to be hired come from the following academic areas: Bachelor of Science (Computer Science) and Bachelor of Engineering (Computer Systems, Engineering Physics, Geological Engineering). Graduates would occupy Junior Processing Geophysicist, Junior Systems/Applications Programmer and Junior Sales Representative positions. Dedicated, solid work ethic, team player, active and healthy lifestyle and a positive attitude are all listed as desirable non-academic qualifications. Company benefits are rated as excellent. The potential for advancement is listed as being good. The average annual starting salary falls within the $30,000 to $35,000 range, with a performance bonus for experienced employees in most departments. The most suitable method for initial contact by those seeking employment is to mail a resume with a covering letter. Enertec Geophysical Services Limited does hire summer students, occasionally. *Contact:* Dave Martin, General Manager.

ENGINEERED FOAM PRODUCTS CANADA LTD.
12 Kenhar Drive
Toronto, ON M9L 1N1

Tel. 416-746-7334

Engineered Foam Products Canada Ltd. is involved in the manufacture of flexible foam products. The company employs more than 25 people. Post-secondary graduates are hired. The specific academic areas recruited from is dependent upon the position to be filled. To inquire about employment opportunities and the qualifications required for available positions, please telephone the company directly at 416-746-7334. *Contact:* Human Resources.

EntreVision

Strategy   Design   Technology

ENTREVISION INC.
210 Dundas Street West
Toronto, ON M5G 2E8

Tel. 416- 364-3590
Fax 416-364-3526
Email .... humanresources@entrevision.com
Website .... www.entrevision.com

EntreVision Inc. is a world leader in the development of leading edge e-business solutions using Lotus, Microsoft and IBM e-business technology. The company provides industry leaders such as General Motors, Gillette, IBM and Prudential with best web-enabled self-service applications, e-commerce solutions, corporate intranets and extranets. Founded in 1994, EntreVision Inc. employs a total of 90 people in offices located in Toronto and Boston, Massachusetts. Graduates most likely to be hired come from the following academic areas: Bachelor of Science (Computer Science), Bachelor of Engineering (General, Computer Systems), Bachelor of Commerce/Business Administration (Information Systems), Master of Business Administration (Information Systems), Master of Science (Computer Science), Community College Diploma (Marketing/Sales, Graphic Arts, Computer Science) and High School Diploma. Graduates would occupy Junior Consultant, Intermediate Consultant, Senior Consultant, Project Manager, System Administrator, Developer and Business Analyst positions. Team player, enthusiastic, entrepreneurial spirit, dependable and "like to have fun" are all listed as desirable non-academic qualifications. EntreVision has developed an unique corporate culture, with a relaxed office environment combined with a strong "family" atmosphere. The company encourages and supports this environment by sponsoring continued training and education, family events and social activities. EntreVision's culture, combined with interesting and high profile projects enable it to enjoy one of the highest employee retention rates in the industry. Accordingly, company benefits are rated above average and the potential for advancement is listed as excellent. The average annual starting salary falls within the $30,000 to $35,000 range. The most suitable method for initial contact by those seeking employment is to apply through the company's website. EntreVision Inc. does hire summer and co-op work term students. *Contact:* Human Resources Department.

EQUINOX ENGINEERING LTD.
640 - 12 Avenue SW, Suite 472
Calgary, AB T2R 0H5

Tel. 403-205-3833
Fax 403-205-3818
Email .... equinox@cadvision.com

Equinox Engineering Ltd. is a dynamic engineering consulting firm specializing in facilities design, implementation, and operation assistance for the oil and gas industry. The company has in-depth knowledge of oil and gas production and processing, oil and gas pipelines, oil refining and chemical industry projects. Equinox provides over 80 years of expertise in preliminary and detailed engineering services in natural gas gathering systems and pipelines, compressor stations, natural gas treatment, LPG separation, underground storage of hydrocarbons and oil battery design. The company provides ongoing involvement with its clients' facilities in the areas of troubleshooting, facility operations assistance and upgrading for revised feedstock and market conditions. Equinox employs 21 people at this location. Graduates most likely to be hired come from the following academic areas: Bachelor of Engineering (General, Chemical, Electrical, Mechanical, Instrumentation, Petroleum/Fuels). Graduates would occupy EIT's and Technologist positions. Team player (very important), innovative, organized and motivated are all listed as desirable non-academic qualifications. Company benefits are rated as industry standard. The potential for advancement is listed as being good. The average annual starting salary falls within the $35,000 to $40,000 range. The most suitable method for initial contact by those seeking employment is to mail a resume with a covering letter. *Contact:* Carey Haarmann.

EQUION SECURITIES CANADA LIMITED
320 Bay Street, Suite 1100, PO Box 15
Toronto, ON M5H 4A6

Tel.	416-216-6500
Fax	416-216-6510
Website	www.equion.com

Equion Securities Canada Limited is a partnership of financial service professionals who have become one of Canada's premier financial planning and money management organizations. Equion specializes in helping clients identify and achieve their financial goals in a manner which is consistent with their personal lifestyle and level of comfort. The goal of the company is to help clients achieve and maintain financial independence and the peace of mind that comes from knowing that they have an effective long-term plan in place. Equion is committed to providing clients with the best in financial advice, products and service. There are 85 employees at this location and a total of 270 employees in Canada. Graduates most likely to be hired come from the following academic areas: Bachelor of Arts (General, Economics, English, Psychology), Bachelor of Commerce/Business Administration (Accounting, Finance, Information Systems), Chartered Accountant, Certified Management Accountant, Master of Business Administration (Accounting, Finance) and Community College Diploma (Business). Graduates would occupy Sales Assistant, Marketing Assistant, Administrative Assistant, Client Service Representative and Administrator positions. Excellent verbal and written communication skills, professional, minimum six months work experience - preferably in financial services and strong computer software skills are all listed as desirable non-academic qualifications. Company benefits are rated above average. The potential for advancement is listed as being good. The average annual starting salary falls within the $25,000 to $30,000 range, depending upon experience. The most suitable method for initial contact by those seeking employment is to mail a resume with a covering letter. Equion Securities Canada Limited does hire summer students. *Contact:* Cindy Grant, Manager, Equion University.

EQUIPEMENT LABRIE LTÉE
175, route Du Pont, CP 37
St-Nicolas, QC G7A 2T3

Tel.	418-831-8250
Fax	418-831-4052
Website	www.labrie.qc.ca

Equipement Labrie Ltée manufactures garbage and recycling trucks. The company employs approximately 230 people. Graduates most likely to be hired come from the following academic areas: Bachelor of Science (Mathematics, Metallurgy), Bachelor of Engineering (Metallurgy, Mechanical, Industrial Production, Welding), Bachelor of Commerce/Business Administration (Accounting, Human Resources, Marketing), Master of Business Administration (Finance) and Community College Diploma (Accounting, Administration, Purchasing/Logistics, Secretarial, Welding, Mechanic). Company benefits are rated as industry standard. The potential for advancement is listed as being good. The average annual starting salary falls within the $25,000 to $30,000 range, depending upon the position being considered. The most suitable method for initial contact by those seeking employment is to mail a resume with a covering letter. Equipement Labrie Ltée does hire summer students. *Contact:* Joseé Morin, Human Resources Manager.

ERNST & YOUNG
90 Burnhamthorpe Road West
Ernst & Young Tower, Suite 1100
Mississauga, ON L5B 3C3

Tel.	905-270-2121
Fax	905-270-9984
Website	www.eycan.com

Ernst & Young is one of the world's leading professional services organizations, offering a broad range of careers in assurance and advisory business services, financial advisory services, consulting and tax. The practice areas in the Mississauga and Brampton office include audit, entrepreneurial services, tax (corporate and personal), insolvency, actuarial benefits consulting, compensation and pay equity consulting, executive search and general management consulting. There are more than 100 employees at this location. Graduates most likely to be hired come from the following academic areas: Bachelor of Arts (General, Economics), Bachelor of Science (General), Bachelor of Engineering (General), Bachelor of Commerce/Business Administration (Accounting, Finance), Chartered Accountant (Finance) and Master of Business Administration (Accounting, Finance). Graduates would start as CA students in the audit and entrepreneurial services practice area. Having obtained leadership positions in extracurricular activities, and possessing excellent interpersonal and communications skills are listed as desirable non-academic qualifications. Company benefits are rated as industry standard. The potential for advancement is listed as being good. The average annual starting salary falls within the $25,000 to $30,000 range. The most suitable method for initial contact by graduates seeking employment is to mail a resume, cover letter, and a copy of a university transcript. This Ernst & Young location does hire summer students occasionally. *Contact:* Office Managing Partner.

ERNST & YOUNG
222 Bay Street
Ernst & Young Tower, PO Box 251, TD Centre
Toronto, ON M5K 1J7

Tel.	416-864-1234

Fax 416-864-1174
Website .... www.eycan.com

Ernst & Young is one of the world's leading professional services organizations, offering a broad range of careers in assurance and advisory business services, financial advisory services, consulting and tax. Ernst & Young employs more than 3,000 people across Canada, with a total network of over 85,000 people. Graduates most likely to be hired at Ernst & Young's Toronto office come from the following academic areas: Bachelor of Science (Actuarial), Bachelor of Engineering (General), Bachelor of Commerce/Business Administration (Accounting, Finance, Information Systems), Chartered Accountant, Certified Management Accountant, Certified General Accountant, Master of Business Administration (Accounting, Finance, Marketing), Master of Science and Master of Engineering. Company benefits are rated above average. The potential for advancement is listed as good. The most suitable method for initial contact by those seeking employment is to mail a resume with a covering letter. For further information about career paths and opportunities, visit the company's website or visit your campus career centre for scheduled career fair dates. Ernst & Young / Toronto does hire summer students. *Contact:* Human Resources Department.

EUCLID-HITACHI HEAVY EQUIPMENT LTD.
200 Woodlawn Road West
Guelph, ON N1H 1B6

Tel. 519-823-2000
Fax 519-837-4220
Website .... www.euclid-hitachi.com

Euclid-Hitachi Heavy Equipment Ltd. manufactures off-highway and mining rigid hauler trucks. There are approximately 300 employees at this location and a total of 500 employees worldwide. Graduates most likely to be hired come from the following academic areas: Bachelor of Engineering (Industrial Design, Industrial Production, Welding), Bachelor of Commerce/Business Administration (Accounting, Finance, Human Resources, Information Systems, Marketing) and Community College Diploma (Engineering Technician, Welding). Able to accomplish goals on a timely basis and a high energy level are both listed as desirable non-academic qualifications. Company benefits are rated above average. The potential for advancement is listed as being good. The most suitable method for initial contact by those seeking employment is to mail a resume with a covering letter. *Contact:* Manager Human Resources.

EVEREST & JENNINGS CANADIAN LIMITED
111 Snidercroft Road
Concord, ON L4K 2J8

Tel. 905-669-2381
Fax 905-660-7875
Email .... percept@interlog.com
Website . www.coast-resources.com/everestandjennings

Everest & Jennings Canadian Limited manufactures of metal folding wheelchairs, hospital and sick room equipment, and other invalid aids. Production facilities were first established in 1962 in Don Mills, Ontario. Since 1970, Everest & Jennings has been involved with products that include folding, non-folding, manual and battery powered wheelchairs; distributors of patient lifters, institutional beds, commodes, cushions and seating systems. The company employs a total of 165 people. Graduates most likely to be hired come from the following academic areas: Bachelor of Engineering (Mechanical, Industrial Design), Bachelor of Commerce/Business Administration (Accounting, Human Resources, Marketing), Certified Management Accountant, Certified General Accountant, Master of Science, Community College Diploma (Accounting, Administration, Business, Marketing, Purchasing/Logistics, Secretarial, CAD/CAM/Autocad, Computer Science, Electronics Technician, Engineering Technician), CHRM, PAAC, CEBS and High School Diploma. Graduates would occupy Accounting, Accounting Clerk, Accounts Receivable/Payable Clerk, CAD Operator, Customer Service Representative, General Labourer, Marketing Manager, Mechanical Design Engineer, Engineering Technologist, Programmer, Sales Representative, Purchasing/Logistics Administrator, Secretary and Skilled Trades positions. Results oriented, excellent interpersonal and communications skills, customer focussed, innovative, self-directed, continuous learner, excellent computer skills and good organizational and analytical skills are all listed as desirable non-academic qualifications. Company benefits are rated as industry standard. The potential for advancement is listed as excellent. The average starting salary falls within the $30,000 to $35,000 range. The most suitable method for initial contact by those seeking employment is to mail a resume with a covering letter. Everest & Jennings Canadian Limited does hire summer students for general office help and general labourer positions. *Contacts:* Manager, Manufacturing or Manager, Engineering & Product Development.

EXCEL TECH LTD. / XLTEK
2568 Bristol Circle
Oakville, ON L6H 8S1

Tel. 905-829-5300
Fax 905-829-5304
Email .... tcrellin@xltek.com
Website .... www.xltek.com

Excel Tech Ltd. / XLTEK is a well established major provider of advanced electrodiagnostic and therapy equipment. The company manufactures technologically advanced neuromuscular and neurophysiological instruments for the complete spectrum of diagnostics through monitoring and therapeutic applications. XLTEK is a vertically integrated company that designs, builds and manufactures all of its own products. XLTEK has been manufacturing and selling medical instrumentation for over 15 years and produces over 500 instruments per month for medical communities in North America and around the world. Through a history of advancements in multiple areas of research and development, such as electronic layout and design, fully robotic surface mount technology assembly, 3D mechanical design, fully robotic mechanical manufacturing and advanced process control, XLTEK has earned the expertise to provide the most reliable, technologically advanced, high performance systems available today. The company employs a total of 105 people. Graduates most likely to be hired come from the following academic areas: Bachelor of Arts (General), Bachelor of Engineering (Electrical, Mechanical, Biomedical Electronics, Biotechnology, Bioengineering), Bachelor of Commerce/Business Administration (Accounting) and Community College Diploma (Accounting, Engineering Technician, Tool and Die/Machinist). Bachelor of Arts graduates would occupy Administration and Customer Service positions. Bachelor of Engineering graduates would occupy Software Design, Hardware Technician, and Biomedical Technical Support and Service positions. Community College Diploma graduates would occupy Technician positions. Team player, trustworthy, goal oriented, pro-active and creative are all listed as desirable non-academic qualifications. Company benefits are rated above average. The potential for advancement is listed as being excellent. The average annual starting salary depends on the position being considered. The most suitable method for initial contact by those seeking employment is to e-mail a resume with a covering letter. Excel Tech Ltd. / XLTEK hires co-op work term students for long term internships (16 months) and occasionally hires summer students. *Contact:* Tracy Crellin.

EXECUTRAIN OF TORONTO
5140 Yonge Street, Suite 800
Toronto, ON M2N 6L7

Tel.	416-221-5353
Fax	416-221-5352
Email	hr@executrain.ca
Website	www.executrain.ca

ExecuTrain is a global training organization offering training in computer applications as well as certification programs for Microsoft, Novell, and Lotus. The company employs 22 people at this location, 75 people in Canada and a total of 1,235 people worldwide. Graduates most likely to be hired come from the following academic areas: Bachelor of Arts (General), Bachelor of Science (Computer Science), Bachelor of Education (Adult), Bachelor of Commerce (General, Information Systems) and Community College Diploma (Information Systems, Marketing/Sales, Computer Science). Graduates would occupy Sales and Marketing, Instructor and Operational positions. Team player, motivated, positive attitude, willing to learn and flexible are all listed as desirable non-academic qualifications. Company benefits are rated above average. The potential for advancement is listed as excellent. The average annual starting salary falls within the $30,000 to $35,000 range. The most suitable methods for initial contact by those seeking employment are to fax or e-mail a resume with a covering letter. ExecuTrain of Toronto does hire summer and co-op work term students. *Contacts:* Bruce Saumure, Manager of Technology & Training or Pam White, Manager of Operations.

EXEL LOGISTICS AMERICAS
100 Sandalwood Parkway West
Brampton, ON L7A 1A8

Tel.	905-840-7540
Fax	905-840-4319
Email	ahellemans@exelna.com
Website	www.exel.com

Exel Logistics Americas is a leading third-party provider of worldwide supply chain management solutions. The company provides warehousing, transportation, information systems, packaging and logistics planning services to the automotive, chemical, consumer and electronics markets. Exel Logistics Americas has worked with leading corporations such as Kellogg Canada, Lever Brothers, Eveready Battery Co., PPG Industries Inc., DuPont, Nabisco, Shell Chemical, Proctor & Gamble Co., General Mills Inc. and Becton Dickinson & Company. The company is the supply chain specialist within London, UK based, NFC plc, a $4 billion leading international logistics and moving services company. Headquartered in Columbus, Ohio Exel Logistics Americas entered the North American Market in 1987, and today employs 200 people in Canada and a more than 10,000 people worldwide. Graduates most likely to be hired come from the following academic areas: Bachelor of Arts, Bachelor of Science, Bachelor of Engineering, Bachelor of Com-

merce/Business Administration (General, Logistics) and Community College Diploma (Business, Human Resources, Purchasing/Logistics). Graduates would occupy Operations Supervisor, Customer Service Representative, various Warehouse positions and enter the Management Trainee Program. Flexible, a willingness to travel, and consumer industry and supervisory experience are all listed as desirable non-academic qualifications. Company benefits are rated as industry standard. The potential for advancement is listed as being excellent. The average annual starting salary falls within the $30,000 to $35,000 range. The most suitable methods for initial contact by those seeking employment are to fax or e-mail a resume with a covering letter. *Contacts:* Regional Human Resources Manager or Human Resources Assistant.

EXETER MACHINE PRODUCTS (1995) LTD.
87 Canada Avenue, PO Box 541
Huron Park, ON N0M 1Y0

Tel.	519-228-6685
Fax	519-228-6147

Exeter Machine Products (1995) Ltd. is a production machining facility of certified diesel engine components. The company employs over 160 personnel. Graduates most likely to be hired come from the following academic areas: Bachelor of Science (Metallurgy), Bachelor of Engineering (Mechanical, Industrial Engineering) and Community College Diploma (Purchasing/Logistics, Engineering Technician, Tool and Die/Machinist). Graduates would occupy Manufacturing Engineer, Junior Manufacturing Engineer, Senior Inspector (Q.A.), Materials Manager and Industrial Mechanic positions. Hands on experience, team player, good communication skills and knowledge of QS9000 standards are all listed as desirable non-academic qualifications. Company benefits are rated as industry standard. The potential for advancement is listed as being good. The average annual starting salary falls within the $35,000 to $40,000 range. The most suitable methods for initial contact by those seeking employment are to mail or fax a resume with a covering letter. *Contact:* Cathy Day-McQuarrie, Human Resources.

EXFO ELECTRO-OPTICAL ENGINEERING INC.
465 Godin Avenue
Vanier, QC G1M 3G7

Tel.	418-683-0211
Fax	418-683-2170
Email	resume@exfo.com
Website	www.exfo.com

EXFO Electro-Optical Engineering Inc. designs and manufactures fiber-optic test and measurement equipment. Fiber optics is a high technology field that is rapidly growing due to the importance of information technologies and the undeniable advantages of fiber-optic networks over traditional communication networks. With 350 employees in Canada and a total of 400 employees worldwide, EXFO ranks fourth in its category on a worldwide scale. The company exports over 95% of its products to more than 100 countries throughout the world. Its main customers are telephone and cable service providers, as well as research and development laboratories. EXFO Europe in Versailles, France, EXFO America in Dallas, Texas, and sales offices in Montreal, Toronto, Vancouver, Chicago, Atlanta, Denver, Harrisburg, San Jose, and Hungary constitute the EXFO sales network around the globe. EXFO has set out to become the world's number one fiber-optic test equipment manufacturer, and has recently bought a Swiss firm (GAP Optique), and the optoelectronics division of a French company (Froilabo). Graduates most likely to be hired come from the following academic areas: Bachelor of Engineering (Electrical, Mechanical, Engineering Physics, Microelectronics, Telecommunications), Master of Engineering and Community College Diploma (Electronics Technician). Graduates would occupy Researcher, Engineer and Technician positions. Team player, dynamism, bilingual (French/English) and good communication skills are all listed as desirable non-academic qualifications. Company benefits are rated above average. The potential for advancement is listed as being good. The average annual starting salary falls within the $35,000 to $40,000 range. The most suitable method for initial contact by those seeking employment is through the company's website at www.efco.com/carrieres. EXFO does hire summer and co-op work term students. *Contact:* Human Resources Depatment.

EXOCOM GROUP, THE

45 O'Connor Street, Suite 1400, World Exchange Plaza
Ottawa, ON K1P 1A4

Tel. 613-237-0257
Fax 613-237-0314
Email .... hr@ottawa.exocom.com
Website .... www.exocom.com

EXOCOM is a leading provider of innovative, business driven, strategic information technology (IT) solutions. For over 15 years the company has achieved a cumulative growth rate in excess of 30 per cent per year and employs over 160 of the highest calibre IT professionals in the industry. Canadian owned, EXOCOM maintains offices in Ottawa (Head Office), Toronto, Calgary and Halifax. The company's clients are comprised of both federal and provincial government clients, and a solid corporate client base including prominent corporations such as Sprint Canada, NBTel, the Bank of Nova Scotia and Mackenzie Financial. EXOCOM's fully integrated suite of IT offerings include strategic information management and planning, business process design, change and performance management, enterprise networking, secure Internet and e-Commerce applications, client/server applications development, IT Security solutions and document management solutions. Current IT business partners include Microsoft, Cognos, Entrust, Mobius, TimeStep, Nortel and the Gartner Group. Graduates most likely to be hired come from the following academic areas: Bachelor of Science (Computer Science, Mathematics), Bachelor of Engineering (Electrical, Computer Systems), Bachelor of Commerce/Business Administration, Master of Business Administration and Community College Diploma (Computer Science, Marketing/Sales). Graduates would occupy Application Developer and Network Engineer positions. Other positions include Technical Analyst, Technical Architect and Project Leader/Manager. Career oriented, solid interpersonal skills, strong initiative, a good team player and a high level of professionalism, enthusiasm and commitment are all listed as desirable non-academic qualifications. Company benefits and the potential for advancement are both rated as excellent. The average annual starting salary falls within the $35,000 to $45,000 range. The most suitable methods for initial contact by those seeking employment are to e-mail a resume with a covering letter, or by applying through the company's website. EXOCOM does hire co-op work term students. *Contacts:* Pierre Côté, IT Recruiter - HR Division or Jennifer Beaudoin-Brandt, IT Recruiter - HR Division.

EXPLORER HOTEL, THE

Postal Service 7000
Yellowknife, NT X1A 2R3

Tel. 867-873-3531
Fax 867-873-2789
Email .... explorer@internorth.com
Website .... www.explorerhotel.nt.ca

The Explorer Hotel is a 128 bedroom, full service luxury hotel, located just steps away from the commercial and government centre of Yellowknife. In addition to a warm welcome, the hotel provides facilities for pleasure and business travellers alike. The Explorer Hotel employs approximately 100 people. Graduates most likely to be hired come from the following academic areas: Bachelor of Arts (General), Bachelor of Engineering (General, Electrical, Mechanical), Bachelor of Commerce/Business Administration (General, Accounting, Finance, Human Resources, Marketing) and Community College Diploma (Accounting, Administration, Business, Communications/Public Relations, Facility Management, Human Resources, Marketing/Sales, Secretarial, Cook/Chef Training, Hospitality, Travel/Tourism, Carpentry, Plumber). Graduates would occupy Cook, Waitperson, Maintenance, Front Desk, Housekeeper and Junior Manager positions. Adaptable, efficient, leadership skills, personable, responsible, decisive, organized, flexible, productive, confident and professional are all listed as desirable non-academic qualifications. Company benefits and the potential for advancement are both rated as excellent. The average annual starting salary falls within the $15,000 to $25,000 range. The most suitable methods for initial contact by those seeking employment are to mail or fax a resume with a covering letter, or by applying in person at the hotel. The Explorer Hotel does hire summer and co-op work term students. *Contact:* General Manager, Regency International Hotels.

EXPRESS INFORMATION TECHNOLOGY CORPORATION

101 - 6 Avenue SW, Suite 1220
Calgary, AB T2P 0R2

Tel. 403-265-8666
Fax 403-215-3803
Email .... corporate@eitc.net
Website .... www.eitc.net

Express Information Technology Corporation is a total information technology solution provider and a Top 100 Value Added reseller of hardware and software in Canada. The company employs approximately 30 people in the provision of both quality products and services to corporations, ranging from home based businesses to Fortune 100 companies. Its group of companies provide Microsoft certified professional services, Novell services and supports, as well as HP Unix systems support and outsourcing functions of IT departments. The company is also a ValueNet Partner of FileNet Corporation, the largest integrated document management corporation in the world. Express Information Technology Corporation is a fast growing technology company that strives for excellence and complete customer satisfaction as its top priority. Graduates most likely to be hired come from the following academic areas: Bachelor of Science (Computer Science), Bachelor of Engineering (Electrical, Computer Systems, Telecommunications), Bachelor of Commerce/Business Administration (Accounting, Human Resources, Information Systems, Marketing), Certified Management Accountant, Master of Business Administration (Human Resources, Information Systems, Marketing), and Community College Diploma (Administration, Communications/Public Relations, Information Systems, Marketing/ Sales, Purchasing/Logistics, CAD/CAM/Autocad, Computer Science, Electronics Technician). Graduates would occupy Computer Systems Engineer, Computer Systems Consultant, Marketing and Promotions Manager, Office Administrator, and Financial Controller positions. Excellent communication and organization skills, strong work ethic, team player and strong leadership skills are all listed as desirable non-academic qualifications. Company benefits are rated above average. The potential for advancement is listed as excellent. The average annual starting salary falls within the $25,000 to $30,000 range. The most suitable method for initial contact by those seeking employment is to e-mail a resume with a covering letter. Express Information Technology Corporation does hire summer and co-op work term students. *Contacts:* Winston Chow, General Manager or Polinda So, IT Administrator.

EXTENDICARE (CANADA) INC. / PARAMED
3000 Steeles Avenue East, Suite 700
Markham, ON L3R 9W2

Tel. 905-470-4000
Fax 905-470-5588
Website .... www.extendicare.com

Extendi care (Canada) Inc. / ParaMed owns and operates approximately 50 nursing homes across Canada, and provides home-care, hospital management and rehabilitative therapy services. Graduates most likely to be hired come from the following academic areas: Bachelor of Arts (General, Recreation), Bachelor of Science (Mathematics, Nursing), Bachelor of Commerce/Business Administration (Accounting, Finance, Marketing), Chartered Accountant (Finance), Certified Management Accountant (Finance), Certified General Accountant (Finance), Master of Business Administration (Accounting, Finance, Marketing) and Community College Diploma (Accounting, Administration, Advertising, Business, Communications, Purchasing/Logistics, Secretarial, Human Resources, Journalism, Recreation, Computer Science, Food/ Nutrition, Nursing RN/RNA). This is the head office location, employing more than 100 people in largely accounting and administrative functions. Graduates would occupy Senior Analyst, Accounts Receivable Clerk, Accounts Payable Clerk, General Accounting Clerk, Secretarial and Office Clerk positions. Good communication, organization and analytical skills are all listed as desirable non-academic qualifications. Company benefits and the potential for advancement are both rated as excellent. The most suitable method for initial contact by graduates seeking employment is to mail a resume with a covering letter. Extendicare (Canada) Inc. / ParaMed does hire summer students. *Contact:* Director, Employment Services, Human Resources Department.

FAIRVIEW COLLEGE
PO Box 3000
Fairview, AB T0H 1L0

Tel. 780-835-6658
Fax 780-835-6790
Email .... carkinstall@fairviewc.ab.ca
Website .... www.fairviewc.ab.ca

Fairview College serves 15 communities, with three main campuses in Fairview, Peace River and High Level. The college offers quality career programs in agriculture, business and trade technologies designed to prepare students for a wide range of challenging careers. Opened in 1951,

Fairview College's primary service area is within a territory of approximately 102,000 square kilometers or approximately 16% of Alberta. The college employs 300 full and part-time staff serving more that 3,000 students annually, and has developed a reputation for friendliness, innovation and quality that draws students from across Canada and around the world. Graduates most likely to be hired come from the following academic areas: Bachelor of Arts (General), Bachelor of Science (Agriculture, Computer Science), Bachelor of Education, Bachelor of Commerce/Business Administration, Certified General Accountant, Master of Business Administration, Doctor of Veterinary Medicine, Community College Diploma (Accounting, Business, Office Administration, Agriculture/Horticulture, Automotive Mechanic, Carpentry, Computer Science, Plumber, Welding, Animal Health) and High School Diploma. Graduates would occupy Instructor, Manager, Computer Centre/Information Technology, Accountant, Tradesman, Recreation Coordinator and Administrative positions. Enthusiasm, self-motivation, team player and a commitment to the value of applied education are all listed as desirable non-academic qualifications. Company benefits are rated as industry standard. The potential for advancement is listed as being average. The average annual starting salary falls within the $30,000 to $35,000 range. The most suitable methods for initial contact by those seeking employment are to fax a resume with a covering letter. Fairview College does hire summer and co-op work term students. *Contact:* Carole Arkinstall, Human Resources Assistant.

FALCONBRIDGE

FALCONBRIDGE LIMITED
95 Wellington Street West, Suite 1200
Toronto, ON M5J 2V4

Tel. 416-956-5700
Fax 416-956-5869
Email .... jobs@falconbridge.com
Website .... www.falconbridge.com

Falconbridge Limited is an international resource company engaged in the exploration, development, mining, processing and marketing of metals and minerals. Falconbridge employs approximately 6,800 people in locations across Canada and around the globe. There are approximately 100 employees at this location, which is the corporate office, and includes the administration, finance, sales, and marketing departments. Graduates most likely to be hired come from the following academic areas: Bachelor of Arts (General), Bachelor of Science (Computer Science, Geology, Mathematics, Metallurgy), Bachelor of Engineering (Chemical, Civil, Environmental, Materials Science, Metallurgy, Mining), Bachelor of Commerce/Business Administration (Accounting, Finance, Marketing), Chartered Accountant, Certified Management Accountant, Certified General Accountant, Master of Business Administration (Finance, Marketing),

Master of Engineering (Chemical, Mining, Metallurgy), Doctorate of Engineering and Community College Diploma (Business, Marketing/Sales, Secretarial, Human Resources, Journalism, Engineering). Team player, and excellent interpersonal and communication skills are listed as desirable non-academic qualifications. The most suitable methods for initial contact by those seeking employment are to mail or fax a resume with a covering letter. *Contact:* Paula Petrie, Manager, Recruiting.

FAMILY AND CHILDREN'S SERVICES OF WATERLOO

200 Ardelt Avenue
Kitchener, ON N2C 2L9

Tel.	519-576-0540
Fax	519-570-0160

Family and Children's Services is the children's aid society for the Region of Waterloo. It is incorporated as a charitable, non-profit social service agency working under the authority of Ontario child welfare legislation. Family and Children's Services provides protection and preventative service as mandated under the Child and Family Services Act to families and children. The service employs a total of 250 people in the Region of Waterloo. In addition, Family and Children's Services is located within a region of abundant affordable housing and both Wilfrid Laurier and the University of Waterloo offer social work programs. Graduates most likely to be hired come from the following academic areas: Bachelor of Arts (Social Work), Master of Arts (Social Work) and Community College Diploma (Social Work/DSW). Bachelor and Master of Social Work graduates would occupy Family Service Worker and Intake Worker positions. Proven oral and written communication skills, willing to work as an integral member of a team and strong time management skills are all listed as desirable non-academic qualifications. Company benefits are rated above average. The potential for advancement is listed as being good. The average annual starting salary falls within the $40,000 to $45,000 range. The most suitable method for initial contact by those seeking employment is to mail or fax a resume with a covering letter. Family and Children's Services does hire summer students. *Contact:* Lynn Taylor Miceli, Supervisor, Human Resource Administration.

FAMILY SERVICE ASSOCIATION OF TORONTO

355 Church Street
Toronto, ON M5B 1Z8

Tel.	416-595-9230
Fax	416-595-2895
Email	hrdep@fsamt.on.ca
Website	www.fsamt.on.ca

The Family Service Association of Toronto is a non-profit social service agency providing a range of services to individuals and families who are vulnerable and/or in distress. Services offered include counselling, family life education, community development, etc. The association employs approximately 160 people across Toronto. Graduates most likely to be hired are Master of Social Work graduates. These graduates would occupy Social Worker positions. Relevant work experience, and experience in cross-cultural counselling are both listed as desirable non-academic qualifications. The average annual starting salary falls within the $35,000 to $40,000 range. The most suitable method for initial contact by those seeking employment is to mail a resume with a covering let-

ter. The Family Service Association of Toronto does hire a number of summer students to work in their Residential Children's Summer Camp which is located in Bolton, Ontario. *Contact:* Human Resource Services.

FARM BOY INC.

2255 St. Laurent Boulevard, Suite 300
Ottawa, ON K1G 4K3

Tel.	613-247-1007
Fax	613-247-8731
Email	fbmail@farmboy.on.ca
Website	www.farmboy.on.ca

Farm Boy Inc. is a family run retail business specializing in fresh food (especially produce), with five stores in eastern Ontario located in Cornwall and Ottawa. The company employs a total of 600 people. Graduates most likely to be hired come from the following academic areas: Bachelor of Arts (Economics), Bachelor of Commerce/Business Administration (General, Accounting, Finance, Human Resources, Information Systems, Marketing), Chartered Accountant, Master of Business Administration (General, Accounting, Finance, Human Resources, Information Systems, Marketing), Community College Diploma (Accounting, Administration, Advertising, Business, Communications, Human Resources, Marketing/Sales, Secretarial, Computer Science) and High School Diploma. Graduates would occupy Financial Manager/Analyst, Controller, Human Resources Coordinator, Payroll Clerk, Accountant, Store Manager, Department Manager, Computer Technician, Executive Secretary, Executive Assistant, Administrative Assistant and Retail Operations Analyst positions. Food retail experience, good communication and entrepreneurial skills, people oriented, team builder and an ability to delegate are all listed as desirable non-academic qualifications. Company benefits are rated as industry standard. The potential for advancement is listed as being excellent. The average annual starting salary falls within the $35,000 to $40,000 range. The most suitable method for initial contact by those seeking employment is to mail a resume with a covering letter. *Contact:* Daniel Bellemare, Director of Human Resources.

FARM CREDIT CORPORATION

1800 Hamilton Street, 9th Floor, PO Box 4320
Regina, SK S4P 3L3

Tel.	306-780-8100
Fax	306-780-5508
Email	hrfcc@sk.sympatico.ca
Website	www.fcc-sca.ca

Farm Credit Corporation is a federal Crown corporation which provides financial services to the agricultural and agribusiness community on a Canada wide basis. The corporation employs 250 people at this location and a total of 800 people in Canada. Graduates most likely to be hired come from the following academic areas: Bachelor of Arts (Journalism), Bachelor of Science (Agriculture/Horticulture, Computer Science), Bachelor of Engineering (Agricultural Engineering), Bachelor of Education (Adult), Bachelor of Commerce/Business Administration (General, Accounting, Finance, Human Resources, Information Systems, Marketing), Chartered Accountant, Certified Management Accountant and Community College Diploma (Accounting, Agriculture/Horticulture, Computer Science). Graduates would occupy Agriculture Credit Advisor, Accounting Technician, Accounting Manager, Communications Officer, Marketing Analyst,

Human Resources Consultant and Information Technology positions. A high level of initiative, attention to detail, analytical, flexible, innovative, creative, and excellent teamwork and project management skills are all listed as desirable non-academic qualifications. Company benefits are rated above average. The potential for advancement is listed as being good. The average annual starting salary falls within the $35,000 to $40,000 range. The most suitable method for initial contact by those seeking employment is to mail a resume with a covering letter. Farm Credit Corporation does hire summer and co-op work term students at this location and at the individual regional offices (check website/white/yellow pages for the nearest location). *Contact:* Manager, Staffing & Employee Relations.

FARMERS CO-OP SEEDS LTD.
PO Box 579
Rivers, MB R0K 1X0

Tel.	204-328-5346
Fax	204-328-7400

Farmers Co-Op Seeds Ltd. is a dynamic, growth oriented agricultural seed company. The company is involved in all areas of seed production, processing, conditioning, warehousing, and distribution at retail and wholesale levels. Farmers Co-Op Seeds is also involved in field production of pedigree seeds, performs seed quality testing, and seed coatings of fungicides and insecticides. There are approximately 22 employees in the company. Graduates most likely to be hired come from the following academic areas: Bachelor of Science (Agriculture, Computer Science), Bachelor of Commerce/Business Administration (Accounting, Human Resources, Marketing), Master of Business Administration (Accounting, Human Resources, Marketing) and Community College Diploma (Accounting, Administration, Advertising, Human Resources, Marketing/Sales, Secretarial). Graduates would occupy Clerical, Management, Production and Technical positions. Quality oriented, self motivated, above average abilities within specific field of expertise, and driven and aggressive team player are all listed as desirable non-academic qualifications. Company benefits and the potential for advancement are both rated as excellent. The average annual starting salary falls within the $20,000 to $25,000 range. The most suitable method for initial contact by those seeking employment is to mail a resume with a covering letter. Farmers Co-Op Seeds Ltd. hires summer students occasionally, on a part-time basis. *Contact:* Glen Jardine, Sales Manager.

FARMERS CO-OPERATIVE DAIRY
PO Box 8118, Station A
Halifax, NS B3K 5Y6

Tel.	902-835-4005
Fax	902-835-4015
Email	resume@farmersdairy.ns.ca

Farmers Cooperative Dairy Ltd. manufactures and distributes dairy and related products across Atlantic Canada. Production facilities are located in Bedford and Truro, Nova Scotia, St. Johns and Deerlake, Newfoundland, and Hunter River, Prince Edward Island. There are 400 employees at this location, and a total of 500 employees in Atlantic Canada. Graduates most likely to be hired come from the following academic areas: Bachelor of Science (Agriculture, Biology, Computer Science), Bachelor of Engineering (General, Chemical, Mechanical, Agricultural, Food Processing, Industrial Engineering, Industrial Production/Manufacturing), Bachelor of Commerce/Business Administration (General, Accounting, Finance, Human Resources, Information Systems, Marketing), Chartered Accountant, Certified Management Accountant, Master of Business Administration and Community College Diploma (Accounting, Human Resources, Information Systems, Marketing/Sales, Purchasing/Logistics, Industrial Mechanic, Computer Science, Welding). Graduates would occupy Sales Representative, Accounting Clerk, Computer Programmer, Industrial Mechanic, Electrician, Operations Management (eg. Plant or Distribution Supervisor), Purchasing (Buyer or Releaser), and Human Resource Administrator positions. Team player, initiative, problem solving skills, specialized knowledge and good interpersonal skills are all listed as desirable non-academic qualifications. Company benefits are rated above average. The potential for advancement is listed as being good. The average annual starting salary falls within the $30,000 to $35,000 range. The most suitable method for initial contact by those seeking employment is to mail a resume with a covering letter. Farmers Cooperative Dairy Ltd. hires summer and co-op work term students for a variety of positions, including Accounting, Human Resources, Sales, and Plant positions. *Contacts:* Joanne Brown, Human Resources Manager, Human Resources Department or Kellie Hogan, Human Resources Administrator, Human Resources Department.

FEDERAL MOGUL CANADA LIMITED
336 Courtland Avenue
Vaughan, ON L4K 4Y1

Tel.	905-761-5400
Fax	905-761-2709

Federal Mogul Canada Limited is a manufacturer providing innovative solutions and systems to customers in the automotive, light truck, heavy-duty, railroad, farm and industrial markets. The company employs approximately 120 people at this location. Graduates most likely to be hired come from the following academic areas: Bachelor of Arts (Economics), Bachelor of Commerce/Business Administration (General, Accounting, Finance, Information Systems, Marketing), Certified Management Accountant, Certified General Accountant and Community College Diploma (Accounting, Advertising, Business, Marketing/Sales). Graduates would occupy Marketing Co-ordinator, Product Manager and Customer Service Representative positions. Computer skills, and excellent communication skills are both listed as desirable non-academic qualifications. Company benefits are rated as excellent. The potential for advancement is listed as being good. The average annual starting salary falls within the $25,000 to $30,000 range. The most suitable method for initial contact by those seeking employment is to mail a resume with a covering letter. Federal Mogul Canada Limited does hire summer students. *Contact:* Director of Human Resources.

FERGUSON SIMEK CLARK / FSC GROUP
4910 - 53rd Street, PO Box 1777
Yellowknife, NT X1A 2P4

Tel.	867-920-2882
Fax	867-920-4319
Email	louise@fsc.ca
Website	www.fsc.ca

Ferguson Simek Clark / FSC Group is a Yellowknife based firm of consulting engineers and architects specializing in remote, cold regions technology. The company, which has operated continuously in Canada's north since 1976, employs approximately 60 people in offices in

Yellowknife and Iqaluit, Northwest Territories and most recently in Whitehorse. FSC is the only integrated architectural/engineering firm in northern Canada with resident staff covering the full spectrum of architectural and engineering services including civil, structural, mechanical, electrical, environmental and project management. The firm has worked in every community in the Northwest Territories. Graduates most likely to be hired come from the following academic areas: Bachelor of Engineering (Civil, Electrical, Mechanical, Environmental) and Bachelor of Architecture. Graduates would occupy Engineer In Training and Intern Architect positions. Computer and independent work skills are listed as desirable non-academic qualifications. Company benefits are rated as industry standard. The potential for advancement is listed as being good. The average annual starting salary falls within the $35,000 to $40,000 range. The most suitable methods for initial contact by those seeking employment are to mail, fax or e-mail a resume with a covering letter. Ferguson Simek Clark does hire summer and co-op work term students. *Contacts:* Louise Nielsen or Jerry Jaud.

FGI
10 Commerce Valley Drive E., Suite 200
Thornhill, ON L3T 7N7

Tel.	905-886-2157
Fax	905-886-4337
Website	www.fgiworld.com

FGI offers professional services in the areas of employee assistance programs, global relocation support programs, work ability (psychological counselling service for disability management) and community based services. FGI employs 75 people at this location, a total of 170 people in Canada, and an additional 10 people outside of Canada. Graduates most likely to be hired come from the following academic areas: Bachelor of Arts (Psychology, Social Work), Bachelor of Science (Psychology) and Master of Arts (Psychology, Social Work). Graduates would occupy EAP and International Service Co-ordinator positions. Previous crises counselling experience and bilingualism (French/English) are both listed as desirable non-academic qualifications. Company benefits are rated above average. The potential for advancement is listed as average. The average annual starting salary falls within the $30,000 to $35,000 range. The most suitable methods for initial contact by those seeking employment are to mail a resume with a covering letter, or by applying through the company's website www.fgiworld.com. FGI does hire summer and co-op work term students. *Contact:* Supervisor of Service Co-ordinators.

FIDELITY INVESTMENTS CANADA LIMITED
483 Bay Street, Suite 200
Toronto, ON M5G 2N7

Tel.	416-307-5300
Fax	416-307-5520
Email	resumes@fidelity.com
Website	www.fidelity.ca

Fidelity Investments Canada Limited is a member of Fidelity Investments, the world's largest mutual fund company with more than $648 billion under management on behalf of over 11 million investors. Fidelity serves Canadians through Fidelity Investments Canada Limited and Fidelity Group Pensions Canada in managing over 25 mutual funds and more than $10.5 billion. Fidelity mutual funds are sold by independent investment professionals. There are 425 employees at this location and a total of 450 employees in Canada. Fidelity considers graduates whose academic credentials include: Bachelor of Arts (General, Economics, English, French, Political Science, Psychology), Bachelor of Education (Adult), Bachelor of Commerce/Business Administration (General, Accounting), Chartered Accountant, Certified Management Accountant, Certified General Accountant, Master of Business Administration (General, Accounting), Community College Diploma (Accounting, Administration, Business, Secretarial, Graphic Arts, Computer Science), High School Diploma and CSC and IFIC designations. Graduates would occupy positions in Sales and Marketing, Client Services, Corporate Services, Fund Operations, Transfer Agency, Information Systems and other Fidelity business units. Applicants should posses a strong customer service orientation. Fidelity offers substantial company benefits and the "Position Yourself Program" to promote employee advancement. Both full time and contract work are offered. The most suitable methods for initial contact by those seeking employment are to mail or fax a resume with a covering letter. Fidelity Investments hires college and university students for summer positions. *Contact:* Human Resources.

FIESTA BARBEQUES LIMITED
2 Walker Drive
Brampton, ON L6T 5E1

Tel.	905-791-3200
Fax	905-791-0781

Fiesta Barbeques Limited is one of Canada's leading consumer products companies and one of North America's fastest growing gas barbeque manufacturers. The company employs a total of 300 people. Graduates most likely to be hired come from the following academic areas: Bachelor of Engineering (Mechanical, Industrial Engineering, Industrial Production/Manufacturing), Bachelor of Commerce/Business Administration (Accounting, Finance, Human Resources, Information Systems, Marketing), Certified Management Accountant, Certified General Accountant, Community College Diploma (Accounting, Human Resources, Marketing/Sales, CAD/CAM/Autocad, Engineering Technician) and High School Diploma. Graduates would occupy Clerk, Technician, Engineer, Generalist, Manager and Supervisor positions. A high level of initiative, team player, integrity, flexibility and previous work experience are all listed as desirable non-academic qualifications. Company benefits are rated as industry standard. The potential for advancement is listed as being good. The most suitable method for initial contact by those seeking employment is to fax a resume with a covering letter. Fiesta Barbeques Limited does hire co-op work term students. *Contact:* Shellie Robinson, Human Resources Manager.

FINANCIAL MODELS COMPANY INC. / FMC
5255 Orbitor Drive
Mississauga, ON L4W 4Y8

Tel.	905-629-8000
Fax	905-629-0022
Email	careers@fmco.com
Website	www.fmco.com

Financial Models Company Inc. / FMC is a leading provider to financial institutions of a comprehensive suite of mission-critical and decision support products, securities data, and related services to automate, integrate and support the front, middle and back office needs of its customers. FMC's philosophy of providing "solutions and not just software" has helped to make it the leading supplier of investment management software to large investment management institutions in Canada, with a significant and growing base of clients in the United States, the United Kingdom and Europe. Currently, FMC's products and services are used by more than 300 clients worldwide with total assets under management in excess of $3 trillion. True straight-through processing, the focus of FMC's mission, guides the development of all of FMC's core products and decision support tools. After 23 years of award winning achievement producing an impressive tradition of growth, the company enjoys a solid reputation as a proven corporate leader, and along with its commitment to client service FMC attracts the loyalty of many of the most sophisticated organizations in the world. Publicly traded on the Toronto Stock Exchange and headquartered in Mississauga, the company maintains offices in Montreal, New York, London, Chicago and San Diego. There are 290 employees at this location, a total of 310 in Canada and a total of 460 employees worldwide. Graduates most likely to be hired come from the following academic areas: Bachelor of Arts (Economics), Bachelor of Science (Computer Science, Mathematics), Bachelor of Engineering (Computer Systems), Bachelor of Commerce/Business Administration (Finance, Information Systems), Master of Business Administration (General, Finance, Information Systems), Master of Science (Computer Science) and Master of Engineering (Computer Science). Graduates would occupy Software Developer, Systems Implementation, Object Oriented Modeler, Data Modeler, DBA, Systems Services, LAN/WAN Specialist, PC Support, Client Services, Business Analyst, Quality Assurance and Documentation positions. Adaptable, team player, a desire to learn, initiative and excellent communication and interpersonal skills are all listed as desirable non-academic qualifications. FMC offers a comprehensive incentive package for computer science, or equivalent recent graduates including a student loan repayment program. The company also offers an excellent health benefits package, yearly bonus and training allowance program. Accordingly, company benefits and the potential for advancement are both rated as excellent. The most suitable methods for initial contact by those seeking employment are to fax or e-mail a resume with a covering letter. Financial Models Company Inc. / FMC does hire co-op work term students. *Contact:* Human Resources.

FISHERY PRODUCTS INTERNATIONAL LTD. / FPI
70 O'Leary Avenue, PO Box 550
St. John's, NF A1C 5L1

Tel.	709-570-0000
Fax	709-570-0209
Website	www.fpil.com

Fishery Products International Ltd. / FPI is a global seafood enterprise which produces and markets a full range of seafood products. Through the company's seafood sourcing network, FPI provides its customers with a variety of seafood items from throughout North America, Southeast Asia, South America, and Europe. The company's harvesting and processing operations include eight deep-sea trawlers, five scallop draggers, a shrimp freezer trawler, three value-added processing plants, four primary groundfish processing plants, a shrimp processing plant,

and a crab processing plant. Canadian sales offices are located in St. John's, Montreal, Toronto, and Vancouver. United States sales offices are located in Danvers, Massachusetts and Seattle, Washington, and European sales offices are located in Reading, England and Cuxhaven, Germany. There are 90 employees at this location, approximately 2,600 across Canada, and a total of 3,000 employees worldwide. Graduates most likely to be hired come from the following academic areas: Bachelor of Arts (Economics), Bachelor of Science (Chemistry, Computer Science, Nursing), Bachelor of Engineering (Computer Systems, Mechanical), Bachelor of Commerce/Business Administration (Accounting, Finance, Human Resources, Information Systems, Marketing), Master of Business Administration (Accounting, Finance, Human Resources, Information Systems, Marketing), Master of Science (Biochemistry, Biology), Community College Diploma (Accounting, Administration, Human Resources, Insurance, Marketing/Sales, Purchasing/Logistics, Secretarial, Cooking, Computer Science, Electronics Technician, Marine Engineering, Nursing RN) and High School Diploma. Team player, initiative, analytical, good communication and interpersonal skills and adaptive to change are all listed as desirable non-academic qualifications. Company benefits are rated above average. The potential for advancement is listed as being good. The average annual starting salary falls within the $25,000 to $30,000 range. The most suitable methods for initial contact by those seeking employment are to mail a resume with a covering letter, or via telephone. Fishery Products International Ltd. does hire summer students. *Contact:* Donna M. Crockwell, Personnel Supervisor.

FLOW AUTOMATION
970 Syscon Road
Burlington, ON L7L 5C2

Tel.	905-681-8575
Fax	905-681-8580
Email	lgibson@flowcorp.com
Website	www.flowautomationcorp.com

Flow Automation is a leader in the design and manufacture of specialized automation equipment, robotic work cells, and vibratory feeder systems. Flow International, the parent company, operates out of Kent, Washington, and designs, develops, manufactures, markets and services ultra high pressure water-jet cutting and cleaning systems. The company employs 130 people at this location and a total of 1,000 people worldwide. Graduates most likely to be hired come from the following academic areas: Bachelor of Engineering (Electrical, Mechanical, Automation/Robotics, Industrial, Welding), Bachelor of Commerce/Business Administration (Accounting, Human Resources, Information Systems, Marketing), Chartered Accountant, Certified Management Accountant, Certified General Accountant, Master of Business Administration, Master of Engineering and Community College Diploma (Accounting, Business, Human Resources, Marketing/Sales, Purchasing/Logistics, Secretarial, CAD/CAM/Autocad, Tool and Die/Machinist, Welding). Graduates would occupy Electrical Designer, Mechanical Designer, Machinist, Junior Machine Builder, Purchasing Clerk, Receptionist and Sales Assistant positions. A willingness to travel, flexible, team player and able to work flexible hours are all listed as desirable non-academic qualifications. Company benefits are rated above average. The potential for advancement is listed as being good. The average annual starting salary falls within the $35,000 to $40,000 range. The most suitable methods for initial contact by those seeking employment are to mail or fax a resume with a covering letter. Flow Automation does hire summer and co-op work term students. *Contacts:* Laura Gibson, Human Resources Manager or Sara Birdsell, Human Resources Assistant.

FLUOR DANIEL CANADA INC.
10101 Southport Road SW
Calgary, AB T2W 3N2

Tel. 403-259-1110
Fax 800-982-4850
Email .... resumes@fluordaniel.com
Website .... www.fluordanielcanada.com

Fluor Daniel Canada Inc. is a fully integrated company providing total responsibility engineering, procurement, construction management and maintenance services. Fluor Daniel Canada Inc. is the Canadian head office of Irvine, California based Fluor Daniel Inc., which in turn is the principal subsidiary of Fluor Corporation. The company is ranked as the best of Fortune's 500 Service companies, maintaining more than 50 offices and locations on six continents and employing more than 40,000 people worldwide. Fluor Daniel Canada Inc. employs 1,100 people at its Calgary head office location. Graduates most likely to be hired come from the following academic areas: Bachelor of Engineering (Chemical, Civil, Electrical, Mechanical, Metallurgy). Graduates would occupy New Graduate Engineer positions. Previous work experience and good communication and team skills are all listed as desirable non-academic qualifications. Company benefits are rated above average. The potential for advancement is listed as being good. The average annual starting salary falls within the $40,000 to $45,000 range. The most suitable method for initial contact by those seeking employment is to apply through campus career centres. Fluor Daniel Canada Inc. does hire summer and co-op work term students. *Contact:* Ryan Jones.

FOCUS CORPORATION LTD., THE
7605 - 50 Street
Edmonton, AB T6B 2W9

Tel. 780-466-6555
Fax 780-468-6175
Email .... bmoren@focus.ca
Website .... www.focus.ca

The Focus Corporation Ltd. provides quality geomatics and engineering services to clients throughout Canada and around the world. Focus and its group of companies have nearly fifty years of geomatics experience and currently offer surveying, engineering, mapping, geographic information systems (GIS), global positioning systems (GPS), land administration, consulting and project management services to the resource, infrastructure and land development sectors worldwide. Services are offered to private industry, First Nations and all levels of government in Canada. Focus is an employee-owned organization with offices in major centres throughout British Columbia, Alberta, Saskatchewan and Ontario. The company is one of Canada's largest geomatics companies, employing 55 people at this location, a total of 225 in Canada and a total of 230 people worldwide. Graduates most likely to be hired come from the following academic areas: Bachelor of Arts (Geography, Urban Geography), Bachelor of Science (Computer Science, Environment/Ecology, Geography), Bachelor of Engineering (Civil, Computer Systems, Environmental/Resources, Geomatics, Microelectronics, Surveying, Water Resources), Bachelor of Landscape Architecture, Bachelor of Commerce/Business Administration (Accounting, Finance, Human Resources, Information Systems, Marketing), Chartered Accountant, Certified Management Accountant, Certified General Accountant, Master of Business Administration (Accounting, Finance, Human Resources, Information Systems, Marketing), Community College Diploma (Accounting, Business, Communications/Public Relations, Financial Planning, Human Resources, Marketing/Sales, Office Administration, Secretarial, Graphic Arts, Legal Assistant, Urban Planning, Architectural Technician, CAD/CAM/Autocad, Computer Science, Electronics Technician, Engineering Technician, Information Systems) and High School Diploma. Graduates would occupy Technician, Engineer-in-Training and Articling Land Surveyor positions. Team player, a positive attitude, strong interpersonal skills and the ability to take ownership of assignments are all listed as desirable non-academic qualifications. Company benefits are rated as excellent. The potential for advancement is listed as being good. The average annual starting salary falls within the $25,000 to $30,000 range. The most suitable methods for initial contact by those seeking employment are to mail, fax or e-mail a resume with a covering letter, or via the company's website at www.focus.ca. The Focus Corporation Ltd. does hire summer and co-op work term students. *Contact:* Brenda Moren, Manager, Human Resources.

FORT JAMES CANADA INC.
137 Bentworth Avenue
Toronto, ON M6A 1P6

Tel. 416-789-5151
Fax 416-789-2271

Fort James Canada Inc. is involved in the manufacturing and distribution of paper and plastic cups, plates and cutlery. The company employs approximately 450 people. Graduates most likely to be hired come from the following academic areas: Bachelor of Engineering (Mechanical, Chemical, Electrical), Bachelor of Commerce/Business Administration, Chartered Accountant and Community College Diploma (Purchasing/Logistics, Mechanic, Engineering Technician). Self-starter, upwardly mobile and a strong team player are all listed as desirable non-academic qualifications. Graduates would occupy Purchasing, Scheduling, Finance, Maintenance, Traffic and Engineering positions. Company benefits are rated above average. The potential for advancement is listed as being good. The most suitable method for initial contact by graduates seeking employment is to mail a resume with a covering letter. *Contact:* Fay Lue Kim, Employee Relations Coordinator.

FORVEST BROADCASTING CORPORATION
345 - 4th Avenue South
Saskatoon, SK S7K 5S5

Tel. 306-244-1975
Fax 306-665-8484
Email .... cjwwradio@sk.sympatico.ca
Website .... www.cjwwradio.com

Forvest Broadcasting Corporation is a privately owned operator of country music radio stations, CJWW 600 AM and Hot 93 FM (http://www.hot93.com). CJWW has been Saskatchewan's country music station of the year for the past five consecutive years, maintaining a high profile community involvement. Forvest Broadcasting employs approximately 50 people. Graduates most likely to be hired come from the following academic areas: Bachelor of Arts (Journalism), Bachelor of Engineering (General, Electrical, Computer Systems), Bachelor of Commerce/Business Administration (General, Accounting, Finance, Human Resources, Information Systems, Public Administration, Marketing), Certified Management Accountant, Certified General Accountant, Master of Business Administration, Community College Diploma (Accounting, Administration, Advertising, Communications, Human Resources, Marketing/Sales, Secretarial, Journalism, Television/Radio Arts, Electronics Technician, Engineering Technician, Broadcasting) and High School Diploma. Graduates would occupy Accounting, Secretarial, Creative Writing, Production, On-Air Staff/Announcing, News, Sales and Marketing and Promotion positions. A willingness to learn and take on new tasks, team player, good attitude and flexibility are all listed as desirable non-academic qualifications. For certain positions, applicants should possess related work experience. Company benefits are rated as excellent. The potential for advancement is listed as being good. The average annual starting salary falls within the $15,000 to $20,000 range. The most suitable method for initial contact by those seeking employment is to mail a resume with a covering letter. *Contacts:* Vic Dubois, Senior V.P. and G.M. (Technical/On Air Positions) or Irene Osborn, Chief Accountant (Administrative Positions).

FORZANI GROUP LTD., THE
824 - 41st Avenue NE
Calgary, AB T2E 3R3

Tel.	403-717-1400
Fax	403-717-1491
Website	www.forzanigroup.com

The Forzani Group Ltd. is a leading national sporting goods retailer, providing customers with a wide selection of merchandise, ranging from clothing to sporting equipment. The company operates under the banners of Sport Chek, Forzani's and Sports Experts. The company employs a total of 4,200 employees in its corporate stores and at the Calgary corporate office location. The company has a separate office in Laval, to oversee its 140 franchise stores across Canada, operating under the banners of RnR Outdoors, Podium, Zone Athletik, Jersey City and Sports Experts. Graduates most likely to be hired come from the following academic areas: Bachelor of Commerce/Business Administration (Accounting, Finance, Human Resources, Information Technology, Marketing), Certified General Accountant, and Community College Diploma (Accounting, Advertising, Human Resources, Information Technology, Purchasing/Logistics, Secretarial). Graduates would occupy IT Support, General Accounting, Graphic Design, Desktop Publishing, Financial Analyst and Administrative Assistant positions. Good communication skills, initiative, team player, self-motivated and strong interpersonal skills are all listed as desirable non-academic qualifications. Company benefits are rated above average. The potential for advancement is listed as being good. The average annual starting salary falls within the $20,000 to $25,000 range. The most suitable method for initial contact by those seeking employment is to mail a resume with a covering letter. The Forzani Group Ltd. does hire summer and co-op work term students. *Contact:* Human Resources Department.

FOUR SEASONS HOTEL, TORONTO
21 Avenue Road
Toronto, ON M5R 2G1

Tel.	416-964-0411
Fax	416-964-6152
Website	www.fourseasons.com

The Four Seasons Hotel in Toronto is a full-service 380 guestroom hotel, located in the heart of the city's fashionable Yorkville district. The hotel employs approximately 500 people. Graduates most likely to be hired come from the following academic areas: Bachelor of Arts, Bachelor of Commerce/Business Administration, Chartered Accountant, Certified Management Accountant, Certified General Accountant, Master of Business Administration and Community College Diploma (Hospitality, Travel/Tourism). The types of positions occupied by graduates varies with academic qualifications accordingly. They may be service oriented, administrative or junior management positions. An excellent attitude and directly or indirectly related work experiences are listed as desirable non-academic qualifications. Company benefits and the potential for advancement are both rated as excellent. The most suitable methods for initial contact by those seeking employment are to visit the Human Resources Department from Monday to Friday, 9:00am to 5:00pm, telephone call, or mail a resume with covering letter. The Four Seasons Hotel does hire summer students when suitable positions are available. *Contact:* Human Resources.

FRAMATOME CONNECTORS CANADA INC. / FCI
2233 de L'aviation
Dorval, QC H9P 2X6

Tel.	514-822-2762
Fax	514-822-2845
Email	scollard@fciconnect.com
Website	www.fciconnect.com

Framatome Connectors Canada Inc. / FCI, a division of Framatome Connectors International, is a supplier of electronic and electrical interconnection systems. Created in 1989, FCI has grown into the world's second largest connector manufacturer, helping to set the pace in various high technology activities. FCI is part of Framatome, a leading European industrial group with over 17,000 employees and more than 60 production facilities worldwide. Framatome is headquartered in Paris, France. Graduates most likely to be hired come from the following academic areas: Bachelor of Science (Computer Science), Bachelor of Engineering (Chemical, Electrical, Mechanical), Bachelor of Commerce/Business Administration (Accounting, Information Systems) and Community College Diploma (Accounting, Purchasing/Logistics, CAD/CAM/Autocad, Computer Science, Electronics Technician, Engineering Technician, Information Systems, Plumber, Tool & Die, Machinist, Welding). Graduates would occupy Technician and Engineer positions. Team player, autonomous, good organizational skills, a high level of initiative and good decision making abilities are all listed as desirable non-academic qualifications. Company benefits are rated above average. The potential for advancement is listed as being average. The average annual starting salary falls within the $35,000 to $40,000 range. The most suitable methods for initial contact by those seeking employment are to fax or e-mail a resume with a covering letter. Framatome Connectors Canada Inc. / FCI does hire summer and co-op work term students. *Contacts:* Sophie Collard, Human Resources or Laure Tastayre, Human Resources.

FREDERICTON, CITY OF
PO Box 130, Station A
Fredericton, NB E3B 4Y7

Tel. 506-460-2148
Fax 506-460-2074
Website .... www.city.fredericton.nb.ca

The City of Fredericton provides municipal government services. Services include planning and development, public works, recreation, police, fire, transit, human resources, treasury, purchasing, and legal services. The city employs 560 people. Graduates most likely to be hired come from the following academic areas: Bachelor of Arts (English, Psychology, Recreation Studies, Urban Geography), Bachelor of Science (Computer Science, Environmental, Forestry, Geology, Geography, Psychology), Bachelor of Engineering (Architectural/Building, Surveying, Computer Systems, Environmental, Water Resources), Bachelor of Laws, Bachelor of Commerce/Business Administration (Accounting, Finance, Human Resources, Information Systems, Marketing, Public Administration), Chartered Accountant, Certified Management Accountant, Certified General Accountant, Master of Business Administration (General, Human Resources), Master of Health Sciences, Community College Diploma (Accounting, Administration, Facility Management, Financial Planning, Human Resources, Secretarial, Hospitality, Journalism, Legal Assistant, Recreation Studies, Security/Enforcement, Urban Planning, Auto Mechanic, CAD/CAM/Autocad, Computer Science, Electronics Technician, Engineering Technician, Forestry, HVAC Systems, Welding) and High School Diploma. Graduates would occupy a wide variety of positions in all city departments. Previous related work experience, computer skills, management or supervisory skills (where applicable), team player, good attitude, initiative, motivated, and good interpersonal and communication skills are all listed as desirable non-academic qualifications. Company benefits and the potential for advancement are both rated as excellent. The average annual starting salary falls within the $25,000 to $30,000 range. The most suitable methods for initial contact by those seeking employment are to mail a resume with a covering letter, apply in person, or via telephone. The City of Fredericton does hire summer students. Contact: Human Resources.

FRIESENS CORPORATION
1 Printers Way, PO Box 720
Altona, MB R0G 0B0

Tel. 204-324-6401
Fax 204-324-1333
Email .... riak@friesens.com
Website .... www.friesens.com

Friesens Corporation is a full service printing and book binding company, including desktop publishing. There are 350 employees at this location and a total of 500 employees across Canada. Graduates most likely to be hired come from the following academic areas: Bachelor of Arts (Graphic Arts), Bachelor of Engineering (Telecommunications, Electrical) and Community College Diploma (Business, Graphic Arts, Electronics Technician). Graduates would occupy Technician and Trainee positions. A positive attitude, team player and a willingness to work shift work are listed as desirable non-academic qualifications. Company benefits are rated as excellent. The potential for advancement is listed as being good. The most suitable method for initial contact by those seeking employment is to mail a resume with a covering letter. Friesens Corporation does hire summer students. Contacts: Tina Barkman, Human Resources Manager or Ike Braun, Production Manager.

FULLER LANDAU
1010 rue de la Gauchetiere Ouest, Suite 200
Montreal, QC H3B 2N2

Tel. 514-875-2865
Fax 514-866-0247
Email .... HR@fuller-landau.ca
Website .... www.fuller-landau.ca

Fuller Landau, Chartered Accountants is a chartered accountancy firm. Graduates most likely to be hired come from the following academic areas: Bachelor of Commerce/Business Administration (General, Accounting), Chartered Accountant, Certified Management Accountant and Certified General Accountant. Graduates would occupy accounting Trainee positions. Bilingualism and self-starter are both listed as desirable non-academic qualifications. Company benefits are rated above average. The potential for advancement is listed as being excellent. The most suitable methods for initial contact by those seeking employment are to fax or e-mail a resume with a covering letter, or via the company's website. Fuller Landau hires summer and co-op work term students for accounting positions. Contact: Dyane Richer, HR Director.

FUTURE STRATEGY, INC.
1635 Sherbrooke West, Suite 405
Montreal, QC H3H 1E2

Tel. 514-932-3295
Fax 514-932-4639
Email .... jobs@futurestrategy.com
Website .... www.futurestrategy.com

Future Strategy, Inc. is a strategic management consultancy specializing in business consulting, management development and software development. Founded in 1981, Future Strategy provides managers with the processes and strategic tools critical to corporate competitiveness. The company's client base is comprised of global organizations in consumer packaged-goods, telecommunications, pharmaceuticals, health and beauty aids, food, and services. Future Strategy is a pioneer in the development and marketing of strategic enterprise-wide decision support and planning solutions for marketing, sales, new business development and corporate management. At the leading edge of technology, these solutions are currently in use in Fortune 500 companies in 52 countries around the world. The company employs a total of 35 people in Canada and an additional 12 partners worldwide. Graduates most likely to be hired come from the following academic areas: Bachelor of Science (Computer Science), Bachelor of Engineering (General, Computer Systems), Bachelor of Commerce/Business Administration (Information Systems), Master of Business Administration (Information Systems, Marketing, Strategy) and Community College Diploma (Computer Science, Information Systems). Graduates would occupy Programmer, Programmer/Analyst, Software Engineer, Associate Manager (Trainer, Copywriter), Consultant and Information Analyst positions. Team player, well developed interpersonal skills, strong communication abilities, analytical, good time and management skills, able to handle pressure, disciplined and a high level of maturity are all listed as desirable non-academic qualifications. Company benefits are rated as industry standard. The potential for advancement is listed as being excellent. The average annual starting salary falls within the $35,000 to $40,000 range. The most suitable method for initial contact by those seeking employment is to apply through the company's website. Future Strategy, Inc. does hire summer and co-op work term students. Contact: Nanette Hansen, Human Resources Manager.

G.F.I. CONTROL SYSTEMS INC.
100 Hollinger Crescent
Kitchener, ON N2K 2Z3

Tel.	519-576-4270
Fax	519-576-7045
Email	sheldman@wchat.on.ca

G.F.I. Control Systems Inc. develops natural gas and propane fuel delivery systems for the Ford Engineering, Development and Production Company. The company employs 110 people at this location and a total of 130 people worldwide. G.F.I. is a division of Devtek, a $400 million Canadian company involved in the development of new fuel injection technology, software (Intel and Motorola) development and computer hardware engineering. Devtek is part of a 50% joint venture with Stuart Stevenson USA, involving international sales and marketing, research and development and production activities. Graduates most likely to be hired at G.F.I. Control Systems come from the following academic areas: Bachelor of Science (Computer Science), Bachelor of Engineering (Chemical, Electrical, Mechanical, Automation/Robotics, Computer Systems, Industrial Engineering, Industrial Production/Manufacturing, Microelectronics, Petroleum/Fuels), Chartered Accountant, Master of Business Administration (Marketing) and Community College Diploma (Accounting, Facility Management, Information Systems, Purchasing/Logistics, Automotive Mechanic, CAD/CAM/Autocad, Computer Science, Electronics Technician, Engineering Technician, Tool and Die, Machinist). Graduates would occupy Junior Chemical Engineer, Junior Mechanical Engineer, Electronics Technician, Mechanical Technician, Electrical Technician, Software Developer, Buyer, Industrial Engineer, Process Planner and Master Scheduler positions. Flexibility, team skills, personality and good problem solving skills are all listed as desirable non-academic qualifications. Company benefits are rated as industry standard. The potential for advancement is listed as excellent. The average annual starting salary falls within the $30,000 to $35,000 range. The most suitable methods for initial contact by those seeking employment are to mail, fax or e-mail a resume with a covering letter. G.F.I. Control Systems Inc. does hire summer and co-op work term students. *Contact:* Marg Gallinger.

G. F. STRONG REHABILITATION CENTRE
4255 Laurel Street
Vancouver, BC V5Z 2G9

Tel.	604-737-6350
Fax	604-737-6494

The G. F. Strong Rehabilitation Centre is a tertiary rehabilitation centre for severely physically disabled adults. The centre employs approximately 1,050 people, and also maintains an on-site integrated daycare facility. The G. F. Strong Rehabilitation Centre is part of the Vancouver Hospital and Health Sciences Centre. The centre is one of North America's leading health care centres and Canada's second largest hospital with 1,900 beds and treating nearly 116,000 patients every year. Graduates most likely to be hired come from the following academic areas: Bachelor of Arts (Recreation Studies), Bachelor of Science (Audiology, Nursing, Nutritional Sciences, Occupational Therapy, Pharmacy, Physical Therapy, Psychology, Speech Pathology), Bachelor of Education (Early Childhood, Special Needs), Bachelor of Commerce/Business Administration (Accounting, Finance, Human Resources, Information Systems, Public Administration), Master of Business Administration (Accounting, Finance, Human Resources, Information Systems, Public Admin-

istration), Master of Arts (Social Work), Master of Science (Nursing, Counselling Psychology, Speech Pathology, Physical Therapy), Master of Education (Adult, Special Needs), Medical Doctor (Psychologist, Physical/Rehabilitative Medicine) and Community College Diploma (Accounting, Administration, Business, Communications, Facility Management, Human Resources, Purchasing/Logistics, Secretarial, Recreation Studies, Computer Science, Electronics Technician, Dietician, Emergency Technician, Nursing RN/RNA, Radiology Technician, Respiratory Therapy, Social Work, Rehabilitation Assistant, Orthotics, Prosthetics). Graduates would occupy positions directly related to their academic backgrounds. Recent, related experience in discipline, experience working in a multidisciplinary team and effective communication skills are all listed as desirable non-academic qualifications. Company benefits are rated above average. The potential for advancement is listed as average. The average annual starting salary falls within the $30,000 to $35,000 range. The most suitable method for initial contact by those seeking employment is to mail a resume with a covering letter. The G. F. Strong Rehabilitation Centre does support numerous academic practicums and internship programs. *Contact:* Human Resources.

G. N. JOHNSTON EQUIPMENT CO. LTD.
1400 Courtney Park Drive
Mississauga, ON L5T 1H1

Tel.	416-675-6460
Fax	905-564-1698
Website	www.gnjohnston.com

G. N. Johnston Equipment Co. Ltd. sells and services material handling equipment. The company has extensive knowledge in the areas of systems analysis, facilities and throughput planning, computer software, on-board communications, operator training and equipment maintenance. G. N. Johnston Equipment also offer a comprehensive line of materials handling equipment including narrow-aisle and counter-balanced trucks, orderpickers, horizontal and vertical carousels, plus racking and shelving. There are more than 100 employees at this location. Graduates most likely to be hired come from the following academic areas: Bachelor of Commerce/Business Administration (General, Marketing, Accounting), Certified Management Accountant, Certified General Accountant and Community College Diploma (Accounting, Business, Mechanic, Engineering Technician, Electrical Technician). Graduates would occupy Field Service Technician, Shop Mechanic, Junior/Intermediate Accountant and Salesperson positions. Company benefits are rated as industry standard. The potential for advancement is listed as being good. The average annual starting salary falls within the $25,000 to $30,000 range, and is commission based for Sales positions. The most suitable method for initial contact by those seeking employment is to mail a resume with a covering letter. *Contacts:* Beth McKenney, Director, Employee Relations or Ingrid Lambert, Employee Relations Assistant.

GARDENWORKS
6250 Lougheed Highway
Burnaby, BC V5B 2Z9

Tel.	604-299-9622
Fax	604-299-4403

Gardenworks operates six retail garden centre outlets which offer a full range of home and garden products. Open twelve months a year, Gardenworks is the leading independent retailer of garden supplies in British Columbia. There are more than 50 employees at this location and approximately 160 employees in the company. Graduates most likely to be hired come from the following academic areas: Bachelor of Arts (Horticulture), Bachelor of Science (Horticulture, Plant Sciences), Certified Management Accountant, Certified General Accountant, Community College Diploma (Business, Forestry, Horticulture) and High School Diploma. Graduates would occupy Sales Clerk and Management Trainee positions. Previous work experience in retail merchandising, team player and a genuine interest/hobby in gardening are all listed as desirable non-academic qualifications. Company benefits are rated as excellent. The potential for advancement is listed as being good. The average annual starting salary depends on the position being considered. The most suitable method for initial contact by those seeking employment is to mail a resume with a covering letter. Gardenworks does hire summer students. *Contact:* Bruce Meyers, Vice President Finance and Administration.

GATEWAY FREIGHT SYSTEMS
243 North Service Road West, Suite 302
Oakville, ON L6M 3E5

Tel. 905-842-3600
Fax 905-842-6210
Email .... gpo@gatewayfrt.com

Gateway Freight Systems is a truck transport and freight forwarding company. Graduates most likely to be hired come from the following academic areas: Community College Diploma (Business, Purchasing/Logistics, Secretarial). Graduates would occupy Dispatcher, Logistics Coordinator, Clerk, Bookkeeper and Customer Service Representative positions. Previous work experience in the truck transportation industry is listed as a desirable non-academic qualification. Company benefits are rated above average. The potential for advancement is listed as being good. The most suitable method for initial contact by those seeking employment is to fax a resume with a covering letter. Gateway Freight Systems does hire summer and co-op work term students. *Contact:* Bill Charney.

GE CANADA
2300 Meadowvale Blvd.
Mississauga, ON L5N 5P9

Tel. 905-858-6600
Fax 905-858-5641
Website .... www.ge.com

GE is a diversified and global technology, manufacturing, and services company. GE Canada is involved in the diverse business activities that GE operates worldwide. These include financial/capital services, hydro, electrical distribution and control, nuclear products, motors and industrial systems, industrial automation, aircraft engines, major home appliances, lighting, medical systems, plastics, silicones, transportation systems, meters, and information services. GE Canada operates facilities across Canada employing a total of 9,200 people. GE employs

over 250,000 people worldwide, and is one of the world's largest public companies. Graduates most likely to be hired come from the following academic areas: Bachelor of Science (Computer Science), Bachelor of Engineering (Chemical, Electrical, Mechanical, Computer Systems, Engineering Physics, Industrial Production, Power/Hydro), Bachelor of Commerce/Business Administration (General, Accounting, Finance, Human Resources, Information Systems, Marketing), Master of Business Administration (General, Human Resources, Marketing) and Master of Engineering. Graduates would occupy Design Engineer, Process/Manufacturing Engineer, Sales Engineer, Financial Analyst, Human Resources Specialist and Sales/Marketing Specialist positions. Initiative, self-motivated, change oriented, team player, good communication skills and an ability to inspire and influence others are all listed as desirable non-academic qualifications. Company benefits and the potential for advancement are both rated as excellent. The average annual starting salary falls within the $40,000 to $50,000 range. The most suitable method for initial contact by those seeking employment is to mail a resume with a covering letter. GE Canada does hire summer and co-op work term students. *Contact:* Mr. Terry Peach, University Recruitment.

GE CAPITAL FLEET SERVICES
2300 Meadowvale Boulevard
Mississauga, ON L5N 5P9

Tel. 905-858-6200
Website .... www.ge.com

GE Capital Fleet Services provides automobile leasing services for company car fleets. There are more than 100 employees at this location. Graduates most likely to be hired come from the following academic areas: Bachelor of Arts (General), Bachelor of Commerce/Business Administration and Master of Business Administration. Graduates would occupy Client Service and Administrative positions. Experience in the automotive industry or in leasing is considered a definite asset. Company benefits and the potential for advancement are both rated as excellent. The average annual starting salary falls within the $25,000 to $30,000 range. The most suitable method for initial contact by those seeking employment is to mail a resume with a covering letter. *Contact:* Susan Chisholm, Human Resources.

GE HARRIS ENERGY CONTROL SYSTEMS INC.
4525 Manilla Road SE
Calgary, AB T2G 4B6

Tel. 403-214-4400
Fax 403-287-9900
Email .... HR@hdap.com
Website .... www.geharris-ecs.com

GE Harris Energy Control Systems Inc. has more than 30 years experience in supplying the utility industry with the world's most technologically advanced monitoring and control systems. As pioneers of the supervisory control and data acquisitions business, GE HARRIS is the major force in the development of the most innovative systems for substation automation, distribution automation and hydro generation plant automation. Electric, gas and water utilities around the world use the company's systems to monitor, control and automate their operations effectively and efficiently. GE HARRIS records an installed base of over 12,000 systems in generation, transmission and distribution facilities in Canada coast to coast, throughout the United States, within Latin America, across Europe, in Africa, and widespread in Asia and the Pacific Rim. Customers range from national utilities to investor-owned corporations to rural and municipal utilities all employing the company's systems to ensure the best and most reliable service to their industrial, commercial and residential customers. GE HARRIS is part of a joint venture between General Electric Power Systems and Harris Corporation, Transcomm Division (Electronic Systems Sector). The company is based in Calgary, with sales support offices in Perth, Australia, Winnersh, England and Hong Kong. Graduates most likely to be hired come from the following academic areas: Bachelor of Engineering (Electrical, Mechanical, Computer Systems), Bachelor of Commerce/Business Administration (Accounting, Finance, Human Resources, Information Systems, Marketing), Certified Management Accountant, Certified General Accountant, Doctorate of Engineering, Community College Diploma (Accounting, Administration, Facility Management, Human Resources, Information Systems, Secretarial, CAD/CAM/Autocad, Computer Science, Electronics Technician, Engineering Technician) and High School Diploma. Graduates would occupy Software Developer, Analyst, Specialist, Coordinator and Engineering positions. Previous work term experience, good interpersonal skills, team player, creativity and excellent communication skills are all listed as desirable non-academic qualifications. Company benefits are rated above average. The potential for advancement is listed as excellent. The average annual starting salary falls within the $35,000 to $40,000 range. The most suitable method for initial contact by those seeking employment is to fax a resume with a covering letter. GE HARRIS does hire students for summer and co-op work terms. *Contact:* Judy Conrad, Manager, Human Resources.

GEC ALSTOM AMF TRANSPORT INC.
1830 rue Le Ber
Montreal, QC H3K 2A4

Tel.	514-925-3693
Fax	514-925-3514
Website	www.gecalsthom.com

GEC Alstom AMF Transport Inc. re-manufactures railroad cars and locomotives. GEC Alstom AMF Transport Inc. is a subsidiary of Paris, France based Alstom. The company is a leading supplier of components, systems and services to the energy, transport, industrial and marine infrastructure markets. Alstom is a global company employing over 100,000 people in more than 60 countries worldwide. GEC Alstom AMF Transport Inc. employs approximately 750 people at this location. Graduates most likely to be hired come from the following academic areas: Bachelor of Science (Chemistry, Computer Science, Environmental Science), Bachelor of Engineering (Chemical, Industrial Chemistry, Metallurgy, Pollution Treatment, Electrical, Mechanical), Bachelor of Commerce/Business Administration (General, Accounting, Finance, Human Resources, Information Systems, Marketing), Master of Business Administration and Community College Diploma (Purchasing/Logistics, Secretarial, Architecture/Drafting, CAD/CAM/Autocad, Computer Science, Welding). Graduates would occupy Engineer, Technician and Junior positions in Marketing, Human

Resources etc. Previous work experience in the railroad industry, hard working and team player are listed as desirable non-academic qualifications. Fluency in both French and English is a must. Company benefits and the potential for advancement are both rated as excellent. The average annual starting salary is dependent upon the type of position, experience and education of the applicant. The most suitable method for initial contact by those seeking employment is to mail a resume with a covering letter. *Contact:* Michel Martin, Manager, Human Resources.

GEMINI ENGINEERING INC.
5940 Macleod Trail SW, Suite 700
Calgary, AB T2H 2G4

Tel.	403-255-2006
Fax	403-252-5338
Email	hr@geminieng.com
Website	www.geminieng.com

Gemini Engineering Inc. provides quality engineering, project management and procurement services globally. Founded in 1982 and headquartered in Calgary, Gemini focuses on providing service to the upstream oil and gas sector. As a full discipline engineering firm, Gemini can supply EPCM as well as EPC services. There are 80 employees at this location and a total of 120 employees in Canada. Graduates most likely to be hired come from the following academic areas: Bachelor of Engineering (Chemical, Civil, Electrical, Mechanical), Bachelor of Commerce/Business Administration (Accounting, Human Resources) and Community College Diploma (Accounting, Secretarial, CAD/CAM/Autocad, Electronics Technician, Engineering Technician) and High School Diploma. Graduates would occupy Project Engineer, Design Engineer, Designer, Technologist, Technician, Clerical, Accountant and Secretarial positions. Team player and good communication skills are both listed as desirable non-academic qualifications. Company benefits are rated above average. The potential for advancement is listed as excellent. The average annual starting salary falls within the $25,000 to $30,000 range. The most suitable method for initial contact by those seeking employment is to e-mail a resume with a covering letter. Gemini Engineering Inc. does hire summer and co-op work term students. *Contact:* Stacy Smith, Manager, Human Resources.

GENDIS INC. / SAAN STORES LTD.
1370 Sony Place
Winnipeg, MB R3C 3C3

Tel.	204-474-5300
Fax	204-474-5471
Website	www.gendis.ca

Gendis Inc. / Saan Stores Ltd. operates retail department stores across Canada. There are approximately 350 employees at this location and a total of 3,000 employees in Canada. Graduates most likely to be hired come from the following academic areas: Bachelor of Commerce/Business Administration (General, Accounting, Finance, Human Resources, Information Systems, Marketing, Public Administration), Certified Management Accountant, Certified General Accountant, Master of Business Administration (General, Accounting, Finance, Human Resources, Information Systems, Marketing, Public Administration), Community College Diploma (Accounting, Administration, Advertising, Business, Financial Planning, Human Resources, Marketing/Sales, Secretarial) and High School Diploma. Previous work experience, good references, team player and a good attitude are all listed as desirable non-academic qualifications. Company benefits are rated as excellent. The potential for advancement is listed as being good. The most suitable method for initial contact by those seeking employment is to mail a resume with a covering letter. Gendis Inc./Saan Stores Ltd. does hire summer students. *Contact:* Ms. B. Scardina, Human Resources & Training.

GENESIS MICROCHIP INC.
165 Commerce Valley Dr. W.
Thornhill, ON L3T 7V8

Tel.	905-470-2742
Fax	905-470-2447
Email	hr@genesis-microchip.on.ca
Website	www.genesis-microchip.com

Genesis Microchip Inc. is a leader in digital video graphics technology. The company was established in 1987 and is publicly traded on Nasdaq. Genesis maintains offices in Markham, Ontario and Mountain View, California, setting the standard for high quality, state-of-the-art digital video scaling and line doubling IC's. Employing over 100 people worldwide, and with design wins in the digital projection and growing LCD monitor markets, in video editing, video teleconferencing, medical imaging, broadcast and avionics, Genesis' goal is to become the leading developer and provider of high quality video, graphics and image manipulation IC solutions that address evolving standards of digital display systems. Genesis' responsiveness and relationships with market leaders, together with its understanding of market trends, allows the Company to develop products more quickly. Genesis is also able to provide manufacture-ready reference designs that allow its customers to ramp into production quickly while controlling development costs. Graduates most likely to be hired come from the following academic areas: Bachelor of Engineering (Electrical), Bachelor of Commerce/Business Administration (Finance, Information Systems), Master of Business Administration (Marketing), Master of Engineering (Electrical) and Community College Diploma (Business, Journalism, Electronics Technician, Engineering Technician). Graduates would occupy Engineer, Technician, Technologist, and IS Support positions. Co-op work term or previous work experience, team player, initiative and good communication skills are all listed as desirable non-academic qualifications. Genesis offers a quality working environment with advanced up-to-date design tools, clean and modern work stations, healthy interactions, opportunities for continuous development and learning, flexible working hours, incentive initiatives and share options and purchase plans. Accordingly, company benefits and the potential for advancement are both rated as excellent. The average annual starting salary falls within the $45,000 to $50,000 range, and the company keeps track of pay levels in the industry to make sure that salaries remain competitive. The most suitable methods for initial contact by those seeking employment are to mail, fax or e-mail a resume with a covering letter, or by applying through the company's website at www.genesis-video.com. Genesis Microchip Inc. does hire summer and co-op work term students. *Contact:* Manager, Human Resources & Administration.

GENNUM CORPORATION
970 Fraser Drive, PO Box 489, Station A
Burlington, ON L7R 3Y3

Tel.	905-632-2996
Fax	905-632-2055
Email	career@gennum.com
Website	www.gennum.com

Gennum Corporation is a Canadian high technology company which designs, manufactures and markets electronic components. These are primarily silicon integrated circuits (IC's) and thick-film hybrid circuits, for specialized applications in the information world. Formed in 1973 and ISO9001-94 registered, the company's products include low voltage audio electronic amplifiers and analog signal processing circuitry supplied to the world hearing instrument industry, video signal distribution and processing components sold to the professional video and broadcast television markets, and user specific integrated circuits for a wide variety of specific applications where information is being conditioned, transmitted or interpreted. The company employs 400 people at this location and a total of 410 people worldwide. Graduates most likely to be hired come from the following academic areas: Bachelor of Engineering (Chemical, Electrical, Mechanical, Engineering Physics, Microelectronics, Telecommunications), Bachelor of Commerce/Business Administration (Accounting), Master of Business Administration (Marketing), Master of Engineering (Electrical, Engineering Physics), Doctorate of Engineering (Electrical) and Community College Diploma (Purchasing/Logistics, Secretarial, Graphic Arts, CAD/CAM/Autocad, Computer Science, Electronics Technician, Engineering Technician). Graduates would occupy Design Engineer, Technologist, Technician, Test Engineer, Process Engineer, Production Engineer, Product Definition Specialist, Marketing Specialist/Manager, Account Representative and Applications Engineer positions. Team skills, leadership abilities, creativity, business skills, innovation, and good interpersonal and communication skills are all listed as desirable non-academic qualifications. Company benefits and the potential for advancement are both rated as excellent. The average annual starting salary falls within the $40,000 to $50,000 range. The most suitable methods for initial contact by those seeking employment are to mail, fax or e-mail a resume with a covering letter, or by applying through the company's website at www.gennum.com. Gennum Corporation does hire students for summer and co-op work terms. *Contact:* Gary D. Gambacort, Director, Human Resources.

GEORGE BROWN COLLEGE
PO Box 1015, Station B
Toronto, ON M5T 2T9

Tel.	416-415-2000 / 800-265-2002
Fax	416-415-4795
Email	info@gbrownc.on.ca
Website	www.gbrownc.on.ca

George Brown College is a community college with locations throughout Toronto. The college employs approximately 1,700 staff and faculty. Graduates are hired from the entire academic spectrum for a wide variety of positions, including Professional, Technical, Trainee and Clerical and positions. Relevant work experience, and excellent oral and written communication skills are listed as desirable non-academic qualifications. Relevant work experience is emphasized as a critical qualification. Employee benefits and the potential for advancement are both rated as excellent. The average annual starting salary for support staff falls within the $20,000 to $25,000 range, and for faculty and administrative staff, the starting salary falls within the $30,000 to $35,000 range. The most suitable method for initial contact by those seeking employment is to mail a resume with a covering letter. George Brown College does hire summer and co-op work term students on a regular basis. *Contact:* Manager, Employment Services.

GEORGE KELK CORPORATION / KELK
48 Lesmill Road
Toronto, ON M3B 2T5

Tel. 416-445-5850
Fax 416-445-5972
Email .... personnel@kelk.com
Website .... www.kelk.com

George Kelk Corporation / KELK designs and manufactures state-of-the-art electronic measurement equipment, used mainly in steel and aluminum rolling mills and also in paper mills and mining applications. Equipment includes load, force and tension measuring equipment, optoelectronics gauges for the dimensional measurement of steel strip and plate, and laser velocimeters. Founded in 1953, the company operates from its modern Toronto plant that also houses the head office, engineering, manufacturing, research, and sales and service functions for the company. The sales and marketing sections are supported by a worldwide network of agents. KELK is a ISO 9002 registered company and employs approximately 100 people at this location. Graduates most likely to be hired come from the following academic areas: Bachelor of Engineering (Electrical, Software Development, Mechanical), Doctorate (Photonics) and Community College Diploma (Electronics, Software Development, Mechanical). Graduates would occupy Technician, Technologist, Field Service Representative and Design and Development Engineer positions. Reliability, creativity, interpersonal skills, team spirit and previous work experience are all listed as desirable non-academic qualifications. In addition to paying competitive salaries, company benefits are rated above average. The potential for advancement is listed as being good. The most suitable methods for initial contact by those seeking employment are to mail, fax or e-mail a resume with a covering letter, stating the position of interest. Additional information can be obtained from the company's website. *Contact:* Mrs. P. Worton - Personnel Manager.

GESCO INDUSTRIES INC.
1965 Lawrence Avenue West
Toronto, ON M9N 1H5

Tel. 416-243-0040
Fax 416-243-1263

Gesco Industries Inc. is a floorcovering manufacturer and distributor. There are approximately 150 employees at this location, with over 250 employees in Canada. Graduates most likely to be hired come from the following academic areas: Bachelor of Arts (General, Economics, Fine Arts), Bachelor of Engineering (Industrial), Certified Management Accountant, Certified General Accountant, Master of Business Administration and Community College Diploma (Accounting, Administration, Business). Graduates are hired to occupy Accounting Clerk, Financial Analyst, Accountant, Controller, and Marketing Assistant positions. Good communication skills and previous work experience are both listed as desirable non-academic qualifications. Company benefits are rated above average. The potential for advancement is listed as being good. The average annual starting salary is dependent upon the department and the position being considered. The most suitable method for initial contact by those seeking employment is to mail a resume with a covering letter. Gesco Industries Inc. does hire summer students, usually for specific projects in Accounting, Engineering

and Administration. *Contact:* Elaine MacIsaac, Human Resources Manager.

GESTION INFORMATIQUE OKA LTÉE
2075 University Street, Suite 750
Montreal, QC H3A 2L1

Tel. 514-282-9334
Fax 514-282-8060
Email .... oka@oka-info.com
Website .... www.oka-info.com

Gestion Informatique OKA Ltée / OKA Computer Systems Ltd. is a renowned and continuously expanding information technology consulting firm. Founded in 1977, OKA is one of Canada's leading information technology consulting firms and has been entrusted with large scale mandates in areas of business such as finance, transportation, manufacturing, food, insurance, telecommunications, retail distribution and sales, petrochemicals, aeronautics, pharmaceuticals, government and para-government. There are 140 employees at this location and a total of of 175 employees across Canada. Graduates most likely to be hired come from the following academic areas: Bachelor of Science (Computer Science, Mathematics), Bachelor of Engineering (Automation/Robotics, Computer Systems) and Bachelor of Commerce/Business Administration (Human Resources). Two years previous work or co-op experience, knowledge of French, willingness to move to Montréal, team player, autonomous and a high level of professionalism are all listed as desirable non-academic qualifications. Company benefits are rated as industry standard. The potential for advancement is listed as being excellent. The most suitable method for initial contact by those seeking employment is to e-mail a resume with a covering letter. *Contacts:* Sylvie Godin or Catherine Le Capitaine.

GIENOW BUILDING PRODUCTS LTD.
7140 - 40th Street SE
Calgary, AB T2C 2B6

Tel. 403-203-8200
Fax 403-279-2615
Email .... oneilll@gienow.com
Website .... www.gienow.com

Gienow Building Products Ltd. is one of Canada's premier manufacturers of custom windows and doors. The manufacturing of Gienow's products takes place at its head office (this location), with distribution worldwide. In addition, the company has several branches in Alberta and British Columbia. Gienow has been in business for over 50 years and today employs more than 450 people at this location and a total of 550 in Canada. Graduates most likely to be hired come from the following academic areas: Bachelor of Science (Computer Science), Bachelor of Engineering (Mechanical, Industrial Engineering, Industrial Production/Manufacturing), Bachelor of Commerce/Business Administration (General, Accounting, Finance, Human Resources, Marketing), Master of Business Administration (General) and Community College Diploma (Accounting, Human Resources, Marketing/Sales, Office Administration, Purchasing/Logistics, CAD/CAM/Autocad, Computer Science, Information Systems). Graduates would occupy Production Control, Engineering, Research and Development, System Analyst, Programmer, Junior Accountant, Cost Accounting, Buyer, Inside Sales, Customer Service and Administrative Assistant positions. Previous manufacturing experience, initiative, self-starter, a great attitude, excellent time management and communication skills and a strong desire to succeed are all listed as desirable non-academic qualifications. Company benefits are rated above average. The potential for advancement is listed as excellent. The most suitable methods for initial contact by those seeking employment are to mail, fax, or e-mail a resume with a covering letter, through the company's website, or via campus recruitment initiatives (visit your campus career centre). Gienow Building Products Ltd. does hire summer and co-op work term students. *Contact:* Leslie O'Neill, Human Resources Manager.

GIFFELS ASSOCIATES LIMITED
30 International Boulevard
Toronto, ON M9W 5P3

Tel. 416-675-5950
Fax 416-675-4620
Email .... info@giffels.com
Website .... www.giffels.com

Giffels Associates Limited is a full-service consulting and contracting organization offering a broad range of architectural, engineering, management and construction services worldwide. Canadian based, employee owned, and in business for 50 years, the company's services incorporate all aspects of design, construction and operations, from architecture, and engineering design, to infrastructure development project/construction management, process engineering and operations consulting. There are 300 employees at this location, a total of 350 in Canada and a total of 420 employees worldwide. Graduates most likely to be hired come from the following academic areas: Bachelor of Engineering (Civil, Architectural/Building, Surveying, Electrical, Automation/Robotics, Computer Systems, Instrumentation, Power, Mechanical, Industrial Design, Industrial Production, Mining), Bachelor of Architecture, Bachelor of Commerce/Business Administration (Information Systems) and Community College Diploma (Architecture/Drafting, CAD/CAM/MicroStation, Computer Science, Engineering Technician, HVAC Systems). Graduates would occupy Engineer-in-Training and Junior Technician or Technologist positions. Results-driven, team player, superb communication and interpersonal skills, natural leadership abilities, a demonstrated track record of success and hands-on management, design, engineering or consulting experience all listed as desirable non-academic qualifications. Company benefits are rated as good. The potential for advancement is listed as being good. The average annual starting salary falls within the $35,000 to $40,000 range. The most suitable methods for initial contact by those seeking employment are to mail, fax or e-mail a resume with a covering letter, or by applying through the company's website. Giffels Associates Limited does hire students for summer and co-op work terms. *Contacts:* John S. MacDonald, Director of Human Resources or Linda Janeway, Human Resources Administrator.

GLOBAL TRAVEL COMPUTER SERVICES
7550 Birchmount Road
Markham, ON L3R 6C6

Tel. 905-479-4949
Fax 905-479-5420
Email .... info@global-travel.on.ca
Website .... www.global-travel.on.ca

Global Travel Computer Services is North America's largest independent supplier of business processing software for travel professionals. Established in 1968, the company currently employs 59 people. Graduates most likely to be hired come from the following academic areas:

Bachelor of Science (Computer Science), Bachelor of Commerce/Business Administration (Accounting), Master of Business Administration (Accounting) and Community College Diploma (Computer Science). Graduates would occupy positions that relate directly to their academic backgrounds. Team player, initiative, and good communication skills are all listed as desirable non-academic qualifications. Company benefits are rated above average. The potential for advancement is listed as average. The average annual starting salary falls within the $30,000 to $35,000 range. The most suitable method for initial contact by those seeking employment is to mail a resume with a covering letter. Global Travel Computer Services occasionally hires summer students. *Contact:* Human Resources.

GLOBE AND MAIL, THE
444 Front Street West
Toronto, ON M5V 2S9

Tel. 416-585-5000
Fax 416-585-5675
Website .... www.theglobeandmail.com

The Globe and Mail, Canada's national newspaper, is produced at six regional printing plants across Canada, and publishes seven magazines. These include: Report on Business, Domino, Destinations, Broadcast Week, Toronto, Montreal Magazine and West. The Info Globe Division provides a variety of online news and financial database products and services and publishes specialized periodicals and books. There are more than 500 employees at this location. Graduates most likely to be hired come from the following academic areas: Bachelor of Arts (Journalism, General), Bachelor of Commerce/Business Administration, Master of Arts (Journalism, General) and Community College (General, Journalism). Applicants should possess appropriate experience and maintain a "good fit" with the corporate operating style. Company benefits and the potential for advancement are both rated as excellent. The average annual starting salary is dependent upon the position being considered. The most suitable method for initial contact by graduates seeking employment is to respond to positions advertised in The Globe and Mail. A small number of summer internships are available each year. Apply to the Deputy Managing Editor no later than October 31 of the prior year. *Contact:* Manager, Human Resources.

GMSI INC.
275 Michael Cowpland Drive
Kanata, ON K2M 2G2

Tel. 613-599-5161
Fax 613-599-6425
Email .... dthomson@gmsiworld.com
Website .... www.gmsiworld.com

GMSI Inc. develops fleet management and wireless communications systems for the transportation and service industries. GMSI's customers are organizations with fleets of 10 to 10,000 vehicles, in industries ranging from home services, couriers and taxis, to buses, distribution and long-haul trucking. Each uses GMSI's dispatch and tracking applications to optimize the usage and efficiency of their fleet by analyzing real-time work order and location information obtained over radio or satellite networks, from GMSI's in-vehicle radio modems and mobile terminals. Graduates most likely to be hired come from the following academic areas: Bachelor of Engineering (General, Computer Systems), Master of Engineering (Computer Systems) and Community College Diploma (Computer Science, Electronics Technician, Engineering Technician). Graduates would occupy Software Developer and Systems Installation positions. Team player and specialized knowledge of certain computer languages are listed as desirable non-academic qualifications. Company benefits are rated as industry standard. The potential for advancement is listed as being good. The average annual starting salary falls within the $45,000 to $50,000 range. The most suitable methods for initial contact by those seeking employment are to mail or fax a resume with a covering letter. *Contact:* Diahanne Thomson, Project Coordinator.

GOLDFARB CONSULTANTS
4950 Yonge Street, Suite 1700
Toronto, ON M2N 6K1

Tel.	416-221-9200
Fax	416-221-2214
Website	www.goldfarbconsultants.com

Goldfarb Consultants conducts custom research to gather, process and analyse data about a client's products or services and those segments of the population to which they are marketed. This includes research on attitudes, behaviours and opinions, as well as on advertising, media usage, customer satisfaction, brand equity and management, new product testing and package design. The company employs approximately 100 full-time and 350 part-time employees. Graduates most likely to be hired come from the following academic areas: Bachelor of Arts (Economics, Philosophy, Political Science, Psychology, Sociology), Bachelor of Commerce/Business Administration (Accounting, Finance, Human Resources, Marketing), Chartered Accountant, Certified Management Accountant, Certified General Accountant, Master of Business Administration (Marketing) and Community College Diploma (Business, Marketing/Sales, Secretarial, Computer Science). Graduates would occupy Market Research Analyst (qualitative/quantitative), Project Director, Accounting Clerk, Accounting Manager, Word Processor, Field Coordinator, Clinic Research Analyst and Clinic Project Director positions. Self starter, bright, energetic, competitive, curious, superior writing skills (for analyst positions), excellent skills with computer software (eg. Word, Excel, PowerPoint) and quality oriented are all listed as desirable non-academic qualifications. The most suitable method for initial contact by those seeking employment is to mail a resume with a covering letter. Goldfarb Consultants does hire summer students, applications should be made in the preceding February or March. *Contact:* Wendy Behm, Human Resources.

GOODWILL TORONTO
234 Adelaide Street East
Toronto, ON M5A 1M9

Tel.	416-362-4711
Fax	416-362-2369
Email	hr@goodwill.on.ca
Website	www.goodwill.on.ca

Goodwill Toronto is a not-for-profit, charitable organization that funds and provides work training and job-related services to people facing employment barriers. For more than 60 years, it has helped Toronto communities build better futures by helping people find gainful employment. With 187 Goodwills in North America and 52 international affiliates, Goodwill Toronto is part of a worldwide network of Goodwill agencies. All are not-for-profit, charitable agencies governed individually by local boards. Goodwills across Canada include Toronto, Hamilton, London, St. Catharines, Sarnia, Edmonton, and Montreal. Goodwill Toronto is 90% self-reliant through the sale of donated goods and other revenue-generating enterprises. Each year, over 25 million pounds of reusable clothing, housewares and furniture are sold in more than 30 Goodwill stores across southeastern Ontario. Beyond funds generated internally, Goodwill Toronto receives support through innovative partnerships with the government and corporate sector, allowing the agency to develop and offer a wide range of training programs that meet the changing employment needs of surrounding communities. With its three Employment Resource Centres, three Training Centres and 25 employment-related programs, Goodwill Toronto was able to help nearly 3,000 people reach their employment goals in 1997. Goodwill Toronto employs 1,100 people in the Greater Toronto Area. Graduates most likely to be hired come from the following academic areas: Bachelor of Arts (Social Work/BSW), Bachelor of Education (Special Needs) and Community College Diploma (Information Systems, Social Work/DSW, Carpentry, Welding). Graduates would occupy IT, Career Assessment Facilitator and Store Manager positions. Previous work experience in career/job counselling is listed as a definite asset. Company benefits are rated above average. The potential for advancement is listed as excellent. The most suitable method for initial contact by those seeking employment is to mail a resume with a covering letter. Goodwill Toronto does hire summer students. *Contact:* Human Resources Co-ordinator.

GOWLING, STRATHY & HENDERSON
160 Elgin Street, Suite 2600, PO Box 466, Station D
Ottawa, ON K1P 1C3

Tel.	613-233-1781
Fax	613-563-9869
Email	info@gowlings.com
Website	www.gowlings.com

Gowling, Strathy & Henderson was founded in 1887 and has grown to become one of the largest law firms in Canada with over 370 professionals. The firm maintains office locations in Ottawa, Toronto, Hamilton, Waterloo Region, Vancouver and Moscow. Gowling, Strathy & Henderson provides a full range of legal services in virtually every field of law, including environmental service, municipal planning, real estate, corporate finance, administrative tribunals and government agencies, banking, civil litigation, international trade, foreign investment, securities and taxation. Clients include a broad spectrum of corporations, public bodies, interest groups, professionals and individuals. There are 414 employees at this location, a total of 1,062 in Canada and a total of 1,077 employees worldwide. Graduates most likely to be hired come from the following academic areas: Bachelor of Science (Biology, Chemistry, Computer Science, Metallurgy), Bachelor of Engineering (Chemical, Electrical, Mechanical), Bachelor of Laws, Bachelor of Commerce/Business Administration (General, Finance, Human Resources, Information Systems), Community College Diploma (Accounting, Business, Office Administration, Secretarial) and High School Diploma. Graduates would occupy Lawyer, Patent Agent, Trade-Mark Agent, Legal Clerk, Data Processor, Accounting Clerk, Comptroller, Accounting Manager, Secretary, Assistant and Technical Support positions. Team player, enthusiasm and previous work experience are all listed as desirable non-academic qualifications. The most suitable method for initial contact by those seeking employment is to mail a resume with a covering letter to the Human Resources Coordinator. Gowling, Strathy & Henderson does hire summer students. *Contacts:* Sharon Mitchell, Chief Operating Officer; Holly Glenn, Human Resources Manager, Ottawa or Shannon O'Brien, Human Resources Manager, Toronto.

GRAND RIVER HOSPITAL
835 King Street West, PO Box 9065
Kitchener, ON N2G 1G3

Tel. 519-742-3611
Fax 519-749-4313

Grand River Hospital is an acute and chronic care facility serving the needs of a rapidly growing community of more than 300,000 people. Located in Kitchener-Waterloo, Grand River Hospital is one of the largest non-teaching medical centres in Canada with 2,500 employees, a medical staff of approximately 500 and an annual budget of $123 million. In order to meet the community's growing needs, the hospital has recently received approval for a MRI Unit and for the construction of a regional cancer treatment centre. Centrally located in southwestern Ontario, Kitchener-Waterloo is renowned as Canada's technology triangle and for its diverse and healthy economic base and quality of life, as well as being home to two internationally recognized universities and a community college. Graduates most likely to be hired at the Grand River Hospital come from the following academic areas: Bachelor of Science (Nursing, Nutritional Sciences, Occupational Therapy, Pharmacy, Physiotherapy, Psychology, Speech Pathology, Recreation Therapist), Bachelor of Commerce/Business Administration (Finance), Master of Science (Speech Pathology), Doctorate (Psychology) and Community College Diploma (Cook/Chef, Electronics Technician, Engineering Technician, Dietitian/Nutrition, Health/Home Care Aide, Laboratory Technician, Nursing RN/RNA, Radiology Technician, Rehabilitation Therapy, Respiratory Therapy, Ultrasound Technician, Pharmacy Technician, Recreation Therapist). Graduates would occupy Occupational Therapist, Physiotherapist, Dietitian, Pharmacist, Pharmacy Technician, Speech Language Pathologist, Psychotherapist, Psychologist, Biomedical Technician, Health Care Aide, Laboratory Technician, Radiology Technician, Rehabilitation Therapy Assistant, Respiratory Therapist, Ultrasound Technician, RPN, RN and Cook positions. Professionalism, team work skills, positive attitude, respect, patient focused and excellent communication skills are all listed as desirable non-academic qualifications. Company benefits are rated as industry standard. The potential for advancement is listed as being excellent. The most suitable methods for initial contact by those seeking employment are to mail or fax a resume with a covering letter. Grand River Hospital does hire summer and co-op work term students. *Contacts:* Human Resources Assistant, Recruitment & Selection or Human Resources Consultant, Recruitment & Selection.

GRANT THORNTON
200 Bay Street
10th Floor, North Tower, Royal Bank Plaza, Box 55
Toronto, ON M5J 2P9

Tel. 416-366-0100
Fax 416-360-4944
Email .... National@GrantThornton.ca
Website .... www.GrantThornton.ca

Grant Thornton (formerly Doane Raymond) is one of Canada's major chartered accounting firms providing professional accounting, taxation, business advisory and consulting services to growing entrepreneurial enterprises. The company maintains 50 offices across the country, with international affiliates in over 75 countries. There are approximately 2,300 employees across Canada and a total of 17,000 worldwide. Graduates most likely to be hired come from the following academic areas: Bachelor of Commerce/Business Administration (Accounting), Chartered Accountant and Master of Business Administration (Accounting). Graduates would be hired to occupy the position of Staff Accountant. Good interpersonal and problem solving skills, a high level of motivation, and a professional bearing and attitude are all listed as desirable non-academic qualifications. Company benefits are rated above average. The potential for advancement is listed as excellent. The average annual starting salary varies with location across Canada. The most suitable method for initial contact by those seeking employment is to mail a resume, covering letter and academic transcript. Grant Thornton does hire a small number of summer students. *Contact:* John Gunn, FCA National Human Resources Partner.

GREAT ATLANTIC & PACIFIC CO. OF CANADA LTD., THE
PO Box 68, Station A
Toronto, ON M5W 1A6

Tel. 416-239-7171
Fax 416-234-6583
Email .... furtadol@aptea.com
Website .... www.aptea.com

The Great Atlantic & Pacific Co. of Canada Ltd. is a food/grocery retailer operating approximately 260 stores, warehouses and bakery facilities across Canada. There are approximately 500 employees at the head office location. Graduates most likely to be hired come from the following academic areas: Bachelor of Arts (General, Criminology, Economics, Psychology), Bachelor of Science (Actuarial, Chemistry, Mathematics), Bachelor of Engineering (General), Chartered Accountant (Finance), Certified Management Accountant (Finance), Certified General Accountant (Finance), Master of Business Administration (Marketing), Community College Diploma (Accounting, Administration, Advertising, Business, Marketing/Sales, Secretarial, Human Resources, Security, Architecture/Drafting, Computer Science) and High School Diploma. Graduates are hired to occupy Financial Analyst, Accounting Clerk, Benefits Clerk, Computer Operator, Graphic/Layout Artist and Security positions. In addition to setting goals, applicants should possess related work experience. Company benefits and the potential for advancement are both rated as excellent. The average annual starting salary falls within the $20,000 to $30,000 range, ultimately depending upon the type of position being considered. The most suitable methods for initial contact by graduates seeking employment are to mail or fax a resume with a covering letter. Summer students are hired, beginning in March and April. *Con-*

tacts: Louisa Furtado, Personnel Manager or Mary Lajmanovski, Personnel Assistant.

GREAT PACIFIC COMPANY LTD.
1125 Howe Street
Vancouver, BC V6Z 2K8

Tel. 604-669-1143
Fax 604-669-0310
Website .... www.greatpacific.ca

Great Pacific Company Ltd. is a brokerage firm specializing in mutual funds and tax shelter sales. The company employs 100 people at this location and a total of 210 people in Canada. Graduates most likely to be hired come from the following academic areas: Bachelor of Commerce/Business Administration (Accounting, Information Systems, Marketing), Certified Management Accountant, Certified General Accountant, Master of Business Administration (Marketing) and Community College Diploma (Accounting, Administration, Financial Planning, Insurance, Marketing/Sales, Secretarial). Graduates would occupy Sales and Sales Assistant positions, and Clerical positions in Accounting, Administration and Data Entry. Team player and good communication skills are both listed as desirable non-academic qualifications. Company benefits are rated as industry standard. The potential for advancement is listed as average. The average annual starting salary for administrative positions ranges from $20,000 to $35,000, and is commission based for some sales positions. The most suitable method for initial contact by those seeking employment is to mail a resume with a covering letter. Great Pacific Company Ltd. does hire summer students. *Contacts:* Sandra Richard, Administration or Michael Peacock, Sales.

THE

Great-West Life
ASSURANCE ⚚ COMPANY

GREAT-WEST LIFE ASSURANCE COMPANY, THE
60 Osborne Street North
Winnipeg, MB R3C 1V3

Tel. 204-946-7693
Fax 204-946-4116
Email .... careers@gwl.ca
Website .... www.gwl.ca

The Great-West Life Assurance Company offers individuals, businesses and organizations a growing range of life and disability insurance, retirement savings, investment, and employee benefits plans. Great-West is an international corporation based in Winnipeg, and together with its subsidiary, London Life, the company employs 5,000 individuals serving the financial needs of more than eight million people through the network of Great-West and London Life field offices across Canada. Great-West has also joined the information systems (IS) divisions of Great-West, London Life and its sister company, Investors Group, to provide IS support to all three companies. This move has made the company's IS organization one of the largest in Canada. Graduates most likely to be hired come from the following academic areas: Bachelor of Arts (General, Economics, English, French), Bachelor of Science (General, Actuarial, Computer Science, Mathematics, Nursing, Occupational Therapy), Bachelor of Engineering (Computer Systems), Bachelor of Laws, Bachelor of Commerce/Business Administration (Accounting, Finance, Information Systems, Marketing), Chartered Accountant, Certified Management Accountant, Certified General Accountant, Master of Business Administration (Accounting, Finance, Information Systems), Master of Science (Actuarial), Community College Diploma (Accounting, Administration, Advertising, Business, Communications, Financial Planning, Insurance, Marketing, Purchasing/Logistics, Real Estate, Secretarial, Graphic Arts, Legal Assistant, Computer Science, HVAC, Nursing RN) and High School Diploma. Graduates would occupy Administrative, Clerical, Technical and Management positions. Leadership abilities, bilingualism and strong communication skills are all listed as desirable non-academic qualifications. Company benefits and the potential for advancement are both rated as excellent. The most suitable method for initial contact by those seeking employment is to mail a resume with a covering letter. The Great-West Life Assurance Company does hire summer and co-op work term students. *Contact:* Val Johnston, Manager, Human Resources.

GREATER EDMONTON FOUNDATION
10050 - 112 Street, Suite 810
Edmonton, AB T5K 2J1

Tel. 780-482-6561
Fax 780-488-3561
Website www.compusmart.ab.ca/gef/gefpage1.htm

Greater Edmonton Foundation supplies subsidized housing for functionally independent senior citizens. The foundation also offers a full range of services and creates full-fledged communities within the larger community for its residents. The foundation operates 14 lodges and 11 apartment buildings. There are 30 employees at this location and a total of 340 employees in Edmonton. Graduates most likely to be hired come from the following academic areas: Bachelor of Arts (Recreation Studies, Social Work), Bachelor of Science (Computer Science), Bachelor of Education (Adult, Physical and Health), Bachelor of Commerce/Business Administration (Accounting, Human Resources, Public Administration), Certified Management Accountant, Master of Business Administration (Human Resources, Public Administration), Community College Diploma (Accounting, Administration, Business, Human Resources, Marketing/Sales, Cooking, Hospitality) and High School Diploma. Graduates would occupy Activity Coordinator, Accountant, Marketing Coordinator, Director, Human Resource Administrator, Assistant Manager and Manager positions. Previous work experience, positive attitude, initiative, complete thought process and confidence are all listed as desirable non-academic qualifications. The most suitable methods for initial contact by those seeking employment are to mail a resume with a covering letter, via telephone, or through walk-in applications. The Greater Edmonton Foundation does hire summer students. *Contact:* Human Resources Administrator, Human Resources Department.

GROUP 4 CPS LIMITED
2 Lansing Square, Suite 204
Toronto, ON M2J 4P8

Tel. 416-490-8329

Group 4 CPS Limited provides protection and security services for various needs. The company employs more than 500 people. Although post-secondary education is not required for employment consideration, Group 4 CPS Limited has historically employed students at various stages of their educational programs as Security Officers. Company benefits are rated as industry standard. The potential for advancement is listed as being good.

The average annual starting salary falls in the $15,000 plus range. The most suitable methods for initial contact by those seeking employment are via telephone, or by applying in person. Group 4 CPS Limited does hire summer students on a regular basis. *Contact:* Personnel Manager.

GROUPE CONSEIL TS
325, de L'Espinay
Quebec, QC G1L 2J2

Tel. 418-647-1402
Fax 418-648-9288
Email .... gctsqc@total.net
Website .... www.groupets.com

Groupe Conseil TS is a subsidiary of Groupe TS, an association of eight companies working in fields of engineering, personnel training, and environment. The services offered by Groupe Conseil TS cover all aspects of the implementation of environmental characterization studies, of the development and implementation of decontamination and restoration programs, and the application of specific environmental techniques. Groupe Conseil TS employs 25 people at this location, and a total of 60 employees across Canada. Graduates most likely to be hired come from the following academic areas: Bachelor of Science (Geology), Bachelor of Engineering (Environmental/Resources, Geological, Industrial Chemistry, Pollution Treatment, Water Resources). Graduates would occupy Field Technician and Project Engineer positions. Company benefits are rated above average. The potential for advancement is listed as being good. The average annual starting salary for Technician positions falls within the $15,000 to $20,000 range. For Engineer positions, the average annual starting salary falls within the $30,000 to $35,000 range. The most suitable method for initial contact by those seeking employment is to mail a resume with a covering letter. Groupe Conseil TS does hire summer students. *Contacts:* Michel Drolet, Director or Richard Tardif, Assistant.

GROUPE HBA EXPERTS CONSEILS
150, Place Marchand
Drummondville, QC J2C 4N1

Tel. 819-478-8191
Fax 819-478-2994
Email .... hbadrv@hba.qc.ca
Website .... hba.qc.ca

Groupe HBA Experts Conseils is a engineering consulting company. Consulting activities include agriculture, environment, construction, urban infrastructure, transportation, geomatics, energy, telecommunications, and industry. There are 220 employees at this location, and a total of 250 employees worldwide. Graduates most likely to be hired come from the following academic areas: Bachelor of Science (Agriculture, Environmental, Forestry, Geography) and Bachelor of Engineering (Pollution Treatment, Electrical, Automation/Robotics, Biomedical Electronics, Computer Systems, Instrumentation, Microelectronics, Power, Telecommunications, Mechanical, Industrial Design, Industrial Production). Graduates would occupy Engineering positions. Applicants should be business minded. Company benefits are rated as industry standard. The potential for advancement is listed as average. The most suitable method for initial contact by those seeking employment is to mail a resume with a covering letter. Groupe HBA Experts Conseils does hire summer students, recruiting locally. *Contact:* Human Resources.

GSI LUMONICS INC.
105 Schneider Road
Kanata, ON K2K 1Y3

Tel. 613-592-4375
Fax 613-599-2550
Email .... hr@gsilumonics.com
Website .... www.gsilumonics.com

GSI Lumonics Inc. is a world leader in the development, design, manufacture and marketing of laser-based advanced manufacturing systems. These systems are for use in the semiconductor, electronics, aerospace, automotive and packaging markets, and are used in highly automated environments for applications such as cutting, drilling, welding and coding a wide range of products and materials. Global demand for the company's products has opened up new job opportunities in the Kanata facility. GSI Lumonics Inc. is a public company listed on the NASDAQ (GSLI) and the Toronto StockExchange (LSI). There are approximately 135 employees at this location. Graduates most likely to be hired come from the following academic areas: Bachelor of Science (Computer Science, Physics) and Bachelor of Engineering (Electrical, Mechanical, Engineering Physics). Team oriented, enthusiastic and flexible are listed as desirable non-academic qualifications. Company benefits are rated above average. The potential for advancement is listed as excellent. The average annual starting salary falls within the $35,000 to $40,000 range. The most suitable method for initial contact by those seeking employment is to e-mail a resume with a covering letter. GSI Lumonics Inc. does hire summer and co-op work term students. *Contacts:* Shelley Browne, Manager, Human Resources or Beth Typhair, Human Resources Administrator.

GUSDORF CANADA LTD.
2105, boul Dagnenais Ouest
Laval, QC H7L 5W9

Tel. 450-963-0808
Fax 450-963-4321
Website .... www.gusdorfonline.com

Gusdorf Canada Ltd. is a furniture manufacturer. The company employs approximately 200 people. Graduates most likely to be hired come from the following academic areas: Bachelor of Engineering (General, Mechanical, Computer Systems, Industrial Engineering, Transportation), Bachelor of Commerce/Business Administration (Accounting, Finance, Human Resources, Information Systems, Marketing), Chartered Accountant, Certified Management Accountant, Master of Business Administration (Accounting, Finance, Human Resources, Information Systems) and Community College Diploma (Accounting, Business, Human Resources, Office Administration, Secretarial, CAD/CAM/Autocad, Electronics Technician, Engineering Technician). The most suitable method for initial contact by those seeking employment is to mail a resume with cover letter. *Contact:* Nancy Leib, President.

GUTHRIE PHILLIPS GROUP INC. / GPG
1200 West 73rd Avenue, Suite 340, Airport Square
Vancouver, BC V6P 6G5

Tel. 604-263-9347
Fax 604-261-2336
Email .... gpg@gpg.bc.ca
Website .... www.gpg.bc.ca

The Guthrie Phillips Group Inc. / GPG is a firm of computer systems specialists providing customized applications to extend and enhance business systems. Incorporated in February 1990, GPG is a privately owned company, providing information systems consulting (strategic plans, system selection, etc.), custom systems development, project management, computer application systems and support, general computer systems services, and documentation services (reports, procedures, on-line help, websites). The company provides systems in a wide range of industries, specializing in areas where business systems typically do not support or adequately address. As one example, GPG has provided specialty banking systems for many large banks, trust companies, and credit unions. GPG solutions include: reconciliation, chequing and EFT, mortgage-backed securities, collections, utility bill payments, suspense, foreign exchange, and fraud detection. The company employs a total of 15 people. Graduates most likely to be hired come from the following academic areas: Bachelor of Science (Computer Science) and Community College Diploma (Marketing/Sales). Graduates would occupy Programmer, Systems Analyst, Business Analyst, Documentor, Quality Assurance, and Marketing positions. Previous work experience in banking and financial services, and experience in visual/object oriented programming are listed as desirable non-academic qualifications. Company benefits are rated as industry standard. The potential for advancement is listed as excellent. The average annual starting salary falls within the $40,000 to $45,000 range. The most suitable methods for initial contact by those seeking employment are to mail, fax or e-mail a resume with a covering letter. The Guthrie Phillips Group Inc. does hire co-op work term students. *Contacts:* David Phillips, President or Human Resources.

HALIFAX INSURANCE COMPANY, THE
75 Eglinton Avenue East
Toronto, ON M4P 3A4

Tel. 416-440-1000
Fax 416-440-0191
Email .... hrpool@halifaxinsurance.com
Website .... www.halifaxinsurance.com

The Halifax Insurance Company provides personal and commercial insurance products through the independent broker system. Halifax Insurance is a member of the Internationale Nederlanden Group / ING Group based in Amsterdam, the Netherlands. ING Group is active in the fields of banking, insurance and asset management in more than 60 countries, and has over 83,000 employees worldwide. Halifax Insurance maintains five regional offices and three service offices in Ontario as well as locations in Manitoba, Nova Scotia and New Brunswick. The company employs 318 people at this location and a total of 1,100 people across Canada. Graduates most likely to be hired come from the following academic areas: Bachelor of Arts (General, Criminology, Economics), Bachelor of Science (General, Actuarial, Computer Science), Bachelor of Engineering (Computer Systems), Bachelor of Education (General, Adult), Bachelor of Commerce/Business Administration (Accounting, Finance, Human Resources, Information Systems, Marketing), Chartered Accountant, Certified General Accountant, Master of Business Administration (Accounting, Finance, Human Resources, Information Systems, Marketing) and Community College Diploma (Accounting, Advertising, Business, Communications, Human Resources, Insurance, Marketing/Sales, Secretarial, Computer Science). Graduates would occupy Underwriting, Claims and Human Resources (Compensation and Training) positions. Relationship building skills, teamwork, cooperation, team leadership skills, innovation, initiative, a concern for or-

der and excellent customer service skills are all listed as desirable non-academic qualifications. Company benefits are rated above average. The potential for advancement is listed as being good. The average annual starting salary falls within the $20,000 to $25,000 range. The most suitable methods for initial contact by those seeking employment are to mail or fax a resume with a covering letter. The Halifax Insurance Company does hire summer students. *Contact:* Human Resources Manager.

HALIFAX SHIPYARD LIMITED
PO Box 9110
Halifax, NS B3K 5M7

Tel. 902-423-9271
Fax 902-494-5554

Halifax Shipyard Limited is involved in new ship construction and ship repair. The company employs approximately 750 people. Graduates most likely to be hired come from the following academic areas: Bachelor of Engineering (Civil, Electrical, Computer Systems, Mechanical, Industrial Design, Industrial Production, Marine, Welding), Bachelor of Commerce/Business Administration (General, Accounting, Finance, Human Resources, Information Systems), Master of Business Administration (Accounting, Finance, Human Resources, Information Systems), Master of Engineering and Community College Diploma (Accounting, Administration, Financial Planning, Human Resources, Purchasing/Logistics, Secretarial, Mechanic, Drafting, CAD/CAM/Autocad, Computer Science, Electronics Technician, Engineering Technician, HVAC Systems, Marine Engineering, Welding). An ability to work independently and with little supervision, previous work experience relating to position, team player, and a willingness to take on and learn new ideas and concepts are all listed as desirable non-academic qualifications. Company benefits are rated as industry standard. The potential for advancement is listed as average. The most suitable method for initial contact by those seeking employment is to mail a resume with a covering letter. Halifax Shipyard Limited does hire summer students. *Contact:* Human Resources.

HAMILTON HEALTH SCIENCES CORPORATION
237 Barton Street East
Hamilton, ON L8L 2X2

Tel. 905-527-0271
Fax 905-546-0412
Website .... www.hamcivhos.on.ca

Hamilton Health Sciences Corporation is Ontario's largest provider of comprehensive health services, serving a community of more than 1.9 million people. Hamilton Health Sciences Corporation was created in 1996 from the merger of Chedoke-McMaster Hospitals and Hamilton Civic Hospitals to continue to bring excellence in health care, research and teaching to the community. Through the affiliation with McMaster University's Faculty of Health sciences and partnerships with several health care providers and community agencies, Hamilton Health Science Corporation is at the forefront of innovation and excellence in health care delivery and health sciences. Hamilton Health Sciences Corporation is comprised of Chedoke Hospital Campus, General Hospital Campus (this address), Henderson Hospital Campus and McMaster Hospital Campus. Graduates most likely to be hired come from the following academic areas: Bachelor of Arts (General), Bachelor of Science (Chemistry, Computer Science, Microbiology, Nursing, Nutritional Sciences, Occupational Therapy, Pharmacy, Physical

Therapy), Bachelor of Engineering (Biomedical Electronics, Computer Systems), Bachelor of Commerce/Business Administration (Accounting, Finance, Human Resources, Information Systems), Chartered Accountant, Certified Management Accountant, Certified General Accountant, Master of Business Administration (Accounting, Human Resources), Master of Science (Speech Pathology), Master of Health Sciences and Community College Diploma (Accounting, Administration, Business, Human Resources, Purchasing/Logistics, Photography, Social Work, Computer Science, Electronics Technician, Engineering Technician, HVAC Systems, Dental Assistant, Dietician, Laboratory Technician, Nuclear Medicine Technician, Nursing RN/RNA, Radiology Technician, Respiratory Therapy, Ultrasound Technician). Possessing related work experience is listed as a desirable non-academic qualification. Company benefits are rated as excellent. The potential for advancement is rated as being good. The most suitable methods for initial contact by those seeking employment are to mail a resume with a covering letter, or in response to advertised positions. *Contact:* Human Resources.

HAMILTON-WENTWORTH CHILDREN'S AID SOCIETY
143 Wentworth Street South, PO Box 1170, Depot 1
Hamilton, ON L8N 4B9

Tel. 905-522-1121
Fax 905-572-9733
Email .... bsnider@hamiltoncas.com
Website .... www.hamiltoncas.com

Hamilton-Wentworth Children's Aid Society provides protection of children, family education, placement of children, visitation, and adoption services. The society employs 150 people. Graduates most likely to be hired come from the following academic areas: Master of Arts (Social Work) and Community College Diploma (Social Work/DSW). Graduates would occupy Frontline Social Worker positions. Good assessment, counselling, communication and investigative skills are all listed as desirable non-academic qualifications. Company benefits are rated as excellent. The potential for advancement is listed as being good. The average annual starting salary falls within the $30,000 to $35,000 range. The most suitable methods for initial contact by those seeking employment are to mail or fax a resume with a covering letter. Hamilton-Wentworth Children's Aid Society does hire summer students. *Contact:* Brenda Snider, Director of Human Resources.

HARROD & MIRLIN - FCB
245 Eglinton Avenue East, Suite 300
Toronto, ON M4P 3C2

Tel. 416-483-3600
Fax 416-489-8782

Harrod & Mirlin - FCB is a full-service advertising agency. The agency employs more than 100 people involved in all aspects of the advertising process, including costing, development of marketing strategies, research and strategic planning, marketing, creative development and the development of advertising copy. Graduates most likely to be hired come from the following academic areas: Bachelor of Arts (General/Related), Bachelor of Science, Bachelor of Commerce/Business Administration, Chartered Accountant, Certified Management Accountant, Master of Business Administration, Masters (Related/General) and Community College Diploma (Marketing, Advertising). The ability to handle a variety of responsi-

bilities, leadership qualities demonstrated through extracurricular activities, and good communication skills are all listed as desirable non-academic qualifications. In addition, previous summer/part-time work and academic grades are considered upon application. Company benefits and the potential for advancement are both rated as excellent. The most suitable method for initial contact by graduates seeking employment is to mail a resume with a covering letter. Harrod & Mirlin - FCB does hire summer students for clerical positions. *Contact:* Director of Human Resources.

HEALTH CARE CORPORATION OF ST. JOHNS / GRACE HOSPITAL SITE
241 LeMarchant Road, Main Floor, Room 144
St. John's, NF A1E 1P9

Tel. 709-778-6222
Fax 709-778-6640
Website .... www.hccsj.nf.ca

Health Care Corporation of St. Johns / Grace Hospital Site is an acute care hospital. The Grace Hospital employs approximately 1,000 people. Graduates most likely to be hired come from the following areas: Bachelor of Arts (Sociology/Social Work), Bachelor of Science (Biology, Chemistry, Computer Science, Microbiology, Audiology, Occupational Therapy, Pharmacy, Speech Pathology), Bachelor of Engineering (Architectural/Building, Biomedical Electronics, Computer Systems, Industrial Design, Welding), Bachelor of Education (General, Physical and Health), Bachelor of Commerce/Business Administration (Accounting, Human Resources, Information Systems, Public Administration), Master of Business Administration (Accounting, Human Resources, Information Systems, Public Administration) and Community College Diploma (Accounting, Administration, Business, Facility Management, Financial Planning, Human Resources, Purchasing/Logistics, Cooking, Social Work, Electronics Technician, Welding, Dental Assistant, Dietician, Laboratory Technician, Nuclear Medicine Technician, Nursing RN/RNA, Radiology Technician, Respiratory Therapy, Ultra-Sound Technician). Good communication skills, an ability to adapt to change, team player, enthusiasm and common sense are all listed as desirable non-academic qualifications. Company benefits are rated as industry standard. The potential for advancement is listed as average. The most suitable methods for initial contact by those seeking employment are to mail a resume with a covering letter, or via telephone to arrange an appointment with a Recruiting Officer. Health Care Corporation of St. Johns / Grace Hospital Site does hire summer students. *Contact:* Human Resources Manager, Human Resources Department.

HEALTH SCIENCES CENTRE / HSC
60 Pearl Street, 2nd Floor, Lennox Bell Lodge
Winnipeg, MB R3E 1X2

Tel. 204-787-3668
Fax 204-787-1376
Email .... employment@hsc.mb.ca
Website .... www.hsc.mb.ca

The Health Sciences Centre / HSC is an 850 bed comprehensive tertiary care facility and teaching hospital affiliated with the University of Manitoba. Winnipeg is western Canada's centre for health services development and research, and the HSC is the Trauma Centre for Manitoba's one million citizens. The centre's critical care facilities will be completely rebuilt over the next five years, thus ensuring an increase in the demand for health care professionals. Graduates most likely to be hired come from the following academic areas: Bachelor of Arts (Psychology, Recreation Studies, Social Work), Bachelor of Science (Computer Science, Environment/Ecology, Microbiology, Physics, Audiology, Dentistry, Nursing, Nutrition, Occupational Therapy, Pharmacy, Physiotherapy, Psychology, Speech Pathology), Bachelor of Engineering (Electrical, Mechanical, Architectural/Building, Biomedical Electronics, Computer Systems), Bachelor of Architecture, Bachelor of Education (Early Childhood), Bachelor of Commerce/Business Administration (General, Accounting, Finance, Human Resources, Information Systems, Public Administration), Chartered Accountant, Certified Management Accountant, Certified General Accountant, Master of Business Administration (General, Accounting, Finance, Human Resources, Information Systems, Public Administration), Master of Science, Master of Engineering, Doctorate (Medical/Related), Community College Diploma (Accounting, Business, Human Resources, Marketing/Sales, Office Administration, Purchasing/Logistics, Secretarial, Early Childhood Education, Graphic Arts, Journalism, Photography, Recreation Studies, Security/Enforcement, Audio/Visual Technician, CAD/CAM/Autocad, Carpentry, Computer Science, Cook/Chef Training, Electronics Technician, Engineering Technician, HVAC Systems, Information Systems, Plumber, Tool and Die/Machinist, Welding, Emergency Care, Diet/Nutrition, Health/Home Care Aide, Laboratory Technician, Massage Therapy, Nuclear Medicine, Nursing RN, Radiology, Rehabilitation Therapy, Respiratory Therapy, Social Work/DSW, Ultrasound Technician) and High School Diploma. Graduates would occupy a variety of positions relating directly to their particular academic background. Team player, a high level of motivation, excellent communication skills and the ability to manage change are all listed as desirable non-academic qualifications. Company benefits are rated as industry standard. The potential for advancement is listed as being average. The average annual starting salary is dependent upon the position being considered. The most suitable methods for initial contact by those seeking employment are to mail, fax or e-mail a resume with a covering letter, or by calling the Job Line at (204) 787-2007. The HSC does hire summer and co-op work term students. *Contacts:* Sandy Kellas, Nurse Recruiter (Nursing 204-787-1842); Darlene Bennett, Employment Officer or Randy Myrdal, Employment Officer (Non-Nursing 204-787-4048).

HEART
AND STROKE
FOUNDATION
OF ONTARIO

HEART AND STROKE FOUNDATION OF ONTARIO
1920 Yonge Street, 4th Floor
Toronto, ON M4S 3E2

Tel. 416-489-7100
Fax 416-482-0948
Email .... vlewis@hsf.on.ca
Website .... www.hsf.on.ca

Heart and Stroke Foundation of Ontario is a fundraising organization whose mandate is to reduce disability and death from heart disease and stroke. There are approximately 100 employees at this location. Graduates most likely to be hired come from the following academic areas: Bachelor of Arts (General, Recreation Studies), Bachelor of Science (General, Nutritional Sciences, Wellness), Bachelor of Education (General, Physical and Health), Bachelor of Commerce/Business Administration (Accounting, Finance, Human Resources, Information Systems, Marketing), Chartered Accountant, Certified Management Accountant, Certified General Accountant, Master of Business Administration (General, Marketing) Master of Science (Epidemiology) and Community College Diploma (Accounting, Administration, Advertising, Business, Human Resources, Secretarial, Recreation Studies, Dietician/Nutrition). Graduates would occupy Entry Level Clerk, Secretary/Assistant and Coordinator positions. Volunteer exposure, team player, positive attitude, self-starter, innovative, self-directed, planning and organization skills, and good interpersonal and leadership skills are all listed as desirable non-academic qualifications. Company benefits are rated as excellent. The potential for advancement is listed as average. The average starting salaries are listed as follows: Clerk - $20,000 to $22,000, Secretary/Assistant - $22,000 to $26,000, Coordinator - $28,000 to $33,000. The most suitable methods for initial contact by those seeking employment are to mail or fax a resume with a covering letter, or via telephone. The Heart and Stroke Foundation does hire summer students, depending upon HRDC grants. *Contact:* Manager, Human Resources.

HEBDO MAG INC.
130 de Liege Est
Montreal, QC H2P 1J1

Tel. 514-384-7902
Fax 514-384-2056
Email .... johanneg@hebdomag.com
Website .... www.hebdo.net

Hebdo Mag is a periodical publisher. The company employs 160 people at this location, a total of 700 in Canada, and a total of 3,000 people worldwide. Graduates most likely to be hired come from the following academic areas: Bachelor of Arts (Graphic Arts), Bachelor of Science (Computer Science), Bachelor of Commerce/Business Administration (General, Accounting, Finance, Human Resources, Information Systems, Marketing), Chartered Accountant, Certified Management Accountant, Certified General Accountant, Master of Business Administration (General, Accounting, Finance, Human Resources, Information Systems, Marketing) and Community College Diploma (Accounting, Administration, Business, Human Resources, Marketing/Sales, Purchasing/Logistics, Secretarial). Graduates would occupy Director, Manager, Clerk, Supervisor and Sales Representative positions. Company benefits are rated above average. The potential for advancement is listed as being good. The average annual starting salary falls within the $20,000 to $25,000 range. The most suitable method for initial contact by those seeking employment is to mail a resume with a covering letter. *Contact:* Johanne Gagnon, Human Resources Director - North America.

HERITAGE COLLEGE
325 Cité des Jeunes
Hull, QC J8Y 6T3

Tel. 819-778-2270
Fax 819-778-7364
Email .... hr@cegep-heritage.qc.ca
Website .... www.cegep-heritage.qc.ca

Heritage College is an English language, post-secondary institution. The college employs approximately 150 people. As an educational institution, graduates from almost all academic disciplines are hired for positions as Professors, Managers, Professionals, Technicians, and for Clerical and Administrative positions. Bilingualism, team player, initiative and previous work experience are all listed as desirable nonacademic qualifications. Company benefits are rated above average. The potential for advancement is listed as being average. The average annual starting salary falls within the $25,000 to $30,000 range. The most suitable methods for initial contact by those seeking employment are to mail or fax a resume with a covering letter. Heritage College does hire summer and co-op work term students. *Contact:* Michele Charlebois, Coordinator of Human Resouces.

HERMES ELECTRONICS INC.
40 Atlantic Street
Dartmouth, NS B2Y 4N2

Tel. 902-466-7491
Fax 902-463-6098
Email .... genadmin@hermes.ns.ca
Website .... www.hermes.ns.ca

Hermes Electronics Inc. is an internationally recognized defense electronics manufacturer. The company is a world leader in ASW sonobuoy technology, with a history of success in acoustic monitoring within challenging ocean environments. The company employs approximately 280 people. Graduates most likely to be hired come from the following academic areas: Bachelor of Science (Occupational Therapy), Bachelor of Engineering (Electrical, Mechanical, Industrial Production), Bachelor of Commerce/Business Administration (Accounting, Finance, Human Resources, Information Systems, Marketing), Chartered Accountant, Certified Management Accountant, Certified General Accountant, Master of Business Administration (Accounting, Finance, Human Resources, Information Systems, Marketing), Master of Engineering (Electrical, Mechanical), Doctorate (Engineering, Physics) and Community College Diploma (Accounting, Administration, Secretarial, Computer Science, Electronics, Engineering Technician, Quality Assurance, Tool & Die, Machinist). Graduates would occupy R&D Engineer, Design Engineer, Industrial Engineer, Quality Engineer, Purchasing Agent, Contracts Manager, Program Manager, Product Development Manager, Accountant, Electrician, Industrial Mechanic, Machinist and Assembler positions. Good problem solving skills, results driven, a value added doer, dynamic, team player, attitude and strong analytical and project management skills are all listed as desirable nonacademic qualifications. Company benefits are rated above average. The potential for advancement is listed as being good. The average salary for new graduates falls within the $30,000 to $40,000 range. The most suitable method for initial contact by those seeking employment is to mail a resume and covering letter. Hermes Electronics Inc. does hire summer and co-op work term students. *Contacts:* Donna Somerville, Director, Human Resources or Glenda Hill, Human Resources Generalist.

HERSHEY CANADA INC.
2350 Matheson Boulevard East
Mississauga, ON L4W 5E9

Tel. 905-602-9200
Fax 905-206-5022
Email .... jobreplies@hersheys.com
Website .... www.hersheys.com

Hershey Canada Inc. is involved in the manufacture and marketing of grocery and confectionery products. There are approximately 130 employees at this location. Graduates most likely to be hired come from the following academic areas: Bachelor of Arts (Social Sciences), Bachelor of Commerce/Business Administration (Marketing), Chartered Accountant, Certified Management Accountant, Master of Business Administration (Finance, Marketing), and Community College Diploma (Administration, Secretarial, Human Resources, Information Services). Graduates would occupy Marketing Coordinator, Sales Representative, Accountant, Accounting Clerk, Promotional Cost Analyst, Assistant Brands Manager and Associate Brands Manager positions. Reliable, good problem solving skills, goal oriented, determined and strong analytical skills are all listed as desirable nonacademic qualifications. Company benefits are rated above average. The potential for advancement is listed as being good. The average annual starting salary for most of the positions listed falls within the $30,000 to $35,000 range. The most suitable method for initial contact by those seeking employment is to mail a resume with a covering letter. Hershey Canada Inc. does hire summer students as the need arises. *Contact:* Human Resources Department.

HEWITT ASSOCIATES
25 Sheppard Avenue West
Toronto, ON M2N 6T1

Tel. 416-225-5001
Fax 416-228-6052
Website .... www.hewitt.com

Hewitt Associates is an international firm of consultants and actuaries. The firm specializes in the design, financing, administration and communication of benefits, compensation and human resources programs and strategies. Hewitt Associates employs more than 100 people at this location and more than 5,000 people worldwide. Graduates most likely to be hired come from the following academic areas: Bachelor of Science (Actuarial, Computer Science, Mathematics), Bachelor of Laws, Bachelor of Commerce/Business Administration (Finance, Information Systems), Master of Business Administration (General, Finance) and Community College Diploma (Human Resources, Secretarial). Within various practices there are available, from time to time, entry level Administrative Consultant positions for new graduates. New graduates should demonstrate strong quantitative, analytical and systems skills, as well as the ability to learn the business. In addition, strong communication and interpersonal skills, a willingness to work hard, team player, good project management skills and prior work experience in a financial consulting environment are all listed as desirable non-academic qualifications. The most suitable method for initial contact by those seeking employment is to mail a resume with a covering letter. Hewitt Associates occasionally hires summer students. *Contact:* Human Resources.

HILL & KNOWLTON CANADA
160 Bloor Street East, Suite 700
Toronto, ON M4W 3P7

Tel.	416-413-1218
Fax	416-413-1550
Email	careers@hillandknowlton.ca
Website	www.hillandknowlton.com

Hill & Knowlton Canada is an industry leader in the business of strategic communications. The company offers a complete range of communications services through its extensive network in Canada and around the world. Hill & Knowlton Canada was created in 1989 through the synergy of three specialist companies, including: PAI, Hill & Knowlton and Decima Research. Hill & Knowlton Canada is a subsidiary of New York based Hill & Knowlton, which in turn is a member of the WPP Group marketing and advertising services family. The group offers national, multinational and worldwide communications counsel to organizations of all industry sectors. The group maintains 54 offices in 32 countries around the world. In addition to the Toronto office, Hill & Knowlton Canada maintains office locations in Quebec City, Montreal, Ottawa, Calgary and Vancouver. The company employs approximately 85 people at this location and a total of 140 people in Canada. Graduates most likely to be hired come from the following academic areas: Bachelor of Arts (English, Journalism, Political Science), Bachelor of Science (Psychology), Bachelor of Commerce/Business Administration (Marketing), Master of Business Administration (Marketing), Master of Arts (Communications/Public Relations, Political Science, Social Sciences, Sociology), Master of Science (Consumer Behaviour) and Community College Diploma (Communications/Public Relations). Graduates would occupy Assistant Consultant and Research Analyst positions. Initiative, team work, good problem solving skills, and excellent organization, time management and presentation skills are all listed as desirable non-academic qualifications. Company benefits and the potential for advancement are both rated as excellent. The average annual starting salary falls within the $25,000 to $30,000 range. The most suitable methods for initial contact by those seeking employment are to mail, fax or e-mail a resume with a covering letter, or through the company's website. Hill & Knowlton Canada does hire summer and co-op work term students. *Contact:* Human Resources.

HINCKS-DELLCREST CENTRE, THE
1645 Sheppard Avenue West
Toronto, ON M3M 2X4

Tel.	416-633-0515
Fax	416-633-7141
Website	www.interlog.com/~hincks

The Hincks-Dellcrest Centre is a children's mental health centre providing a wide range of prevention, early intervention and treatment services to children, youth and their families. The centre focuses on helping clients deal with situations that are causing emotional and behavioural problems. Programs include outpatient counselling, day treatment and residential treatment services. With two locations, the centre employs more than 300 people. Graduates most likely to be hired come from the following academic areas: Bachelor of Arts (Psychology, Social Work), Bachelor of Science (Psychology) and Community College Diploma (Accounting, Secretarial, Early Childhood Education, Social Work). Graduates are hired as Social Workers, Child and Youth Workers, and Prevention Workers. Previous work experience in a social service setting, and knowledge and experience in differ-

ent modes of individual, group and family therapy are all listed as desirable non-academic qualifications. Company benefits are rated above average. The potential for advancement is listed as average. The average annual starting salary falls within the $25,000 to $30,000 range. The most suitable method for initial contact by those seeking employment is to mail a resume with a covering letter. The Hincks-Dellcrest Centre does hire summer and co-op work term students when government funding is available. (Other Location: 440 Jarvis Street, Toronto, ON, M4Y 2H6, Tel: 416-924-1164, Fax: 416-924-8208). *Contact:* Human Resources.

HOFFMANN-LA ROCHE LIMITED
2455 Meadowpine Boulevard
Mississauga, ON L5N 6L7

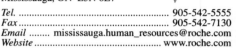

Tel.	905-542-5555
Fax	905-542-7130
Email	mississauga.human_resources@roche.com
Website	www.roche.com

Hoffmann-La Roche Limited is a global health care company focusing on sales, marketing and distribution activities in Canada. The company is a subsidiary of Basel, Switzerland based Roche Group, which is one of the world's leading research-based healthcare groups active in the discovery, development and manufacture of pharmaceuticals and diagnostic systems. The group is also one of the world's largest producers of vitamins and carotenoids and of fragrances and flavours. In addition to this location, the Hoffmann-La Roche Limited maintains a Pharmaceutical Division and Fine Chemicals Division in Cambridge, Ontario. The company employs 300 people at this location and a total of 600 people in Canada, including field staff. Graduates most likely to be hired come from the following academic areas: Bachelor of Arts (Economics), Bachelor of Science (Biology, Chemistry, Pharmacology, Computer Science), Bachelor of Commerce/Business Administration, Chartered Accountant, Certified Management Accountant, Certified General Accountant and Master of Science (Biology, Chemistry, Pharmacology). Graduates would occupy Medical Sales, Clinical Research, Quality Control, Regulatory Affairs and Medical Information positions. Possessing related work experience is listed as a desirable non-academic qualification. Compensation and other forms of remuneration such as group health benefits are highly competitive within the pharmaceutical industry. The opportunities for career and professional development are very good. To inquire about employment opportunities, send a resume with a covering letter describing career objectives or goals to the Human Resources Department. Hoffmann-La Roche Limited also operates a summer student hiring program. (Other Location: Hoffman-La Roche Limited - Fine Chemicals Division, P.O. Box 877, Cambridge, ON, N1R 5X9, Phone 519-622-2200, Fax 519-623-4849). *Contacts:* Lynn Butler, Manager, Human Resources or Kim Blake, Manager, Human Resources.

HOLDERBANK ENGINEERING CANADA LTD.
2310 Lakeshore Road West
Mississauga, ON L5J 1K2

Tel.	905-822-1693
Fax	905-822-1698
Email	general@holderbank.ca
Website	www.holderbank.ca

Holderbank Engineering Canada Ltd. offers a complete range of engineering services to cement industry producers throughout the Americas. This includes assisting manufacturers of cement, lime and related products in all aspects of the design, construction and operation of their plant facilities. As the Canadian-based engineering office of Holderbank Financière Glaris Ltd., Switzerland, the company is associated with more than 70 cement plants of the Holderbank Group. This international network of producers provides an unparalleled source of information and experience in all aspects of cement manufacture and plant operation, and helps make Holderbank a leader among cement-industry consultants. There are approximately 110 employees at this location and over 40,000 Holderbank employees worldwide. Graduates most likely to be hired come from the following academic areas: Bachelor of Science (Chemistry), Bachelor of Engineering (Chemical, Electrical, Mechanical), Master of Engineering (Civil) and Community College Diploma (CAD/CAM/Autocad, Electronics Technician). Graduates are hired for Technician and Trainee positions. Applicants should be team players. Company benefits are rated as industry standard. The potential for advancement is listed as being good. The average annual starting salary falls within the $35,000 to $40,000 range. The most suitable methods for initial contact by those seeking employment are to mail or fax a resume with a covering letter (no phone calls please). Holderbank Engineering Canada Ltd. does hire summer and co-op work term students. *Contact:* Wayne Gallant, Vice President, Finance & Administration.

HOLIDAY INN, EXPRESS
50 Estate Drive
Toronto, ON M1H 2Z1

Tel. 416-439-9666
Fax 416-439-4295
Website www2.basshotels.com/hiexpress

The Holiday Inn, Express is a full service hotel providing accommodation and banquet services. Operational activities also include administrative functions. The hotel employs more than 25 people. Graduates most likely to be hired come from the following academic areas: Bachelor of Commerce/Business Administration (Marketing), and Community College Diploma (Hospitality, Travel/Tourism, Marketing). Graduates would occupy Night Auditor, Banquet Porter, Room Attendant and Front Desk Clerk positions. Initiative, good interpersonal skills, friendly, outgoing and confidence are all listed as desirable non-academic qualifications. Company benefits are rated above average. The potential for advancement is listed as excellent. Employees are paid on an hourly wage scale. The most suitable method for initial contact by those seeking employment is to mail a resume with a covering letter. The Holiday Inn, Express Hotel does employ summer students. *Contact:* General Manager.

HONDA CANADA INC.
715 Milner Avenue
Toronto, ON M1B 2K8

Tel. 416-284-8110
Website .... www.honda.com

Honda Canada Inc. is involved in the sales, marketing, and distribution of auto, motorcycle, and power (e.g. lawn mowers) products. There are 300 employes at this location, a total of 2,500 in Canada and 80,000 Honda employees worldwide. Graduates most likely to be hired come from the following academic areas: Bachelor of Arts (Economics), Bachelor of Science (Computer Science, Mathematics), Bachelor of Engineering (Automation/

Robotics, Industrial Design, Industrial Production), Bachelor of Commerce/Business Administration (Accounting, Finance, Human Resources, Information Systems, Marketing), Chartered Accountant, Certified Management Accountant, Certified General Accountant, Master of Business Administration (Accounting, Finance, Information Systems, Marketing) and Community College Diploma (Accounting, Marketing/Sales, Auto Mechanic, Computer Science). Graduates would occupy Market Research Analyst, Product Planning, Field Sales Representative, Accounting Coordinator, Sales Operations Coordinator, Human Resources and Employee Relations positions. Strong communication skills, industrious, team player, international focus and an interest in the automotive industry are all listed as desirable non-academic qualifications. Company benefits are rated as excellent. The potential for advancement is listed as being good. The average annual starting salary falls within the $25,000 to $30,000 range. The most suitable method for initial contact by those seeking employment is to mail a resume with a covering letter. Summer students are hired for Honda's parts distribution centre, and manufacturing plant. *Contact:* Mr. J. Descoteaux, Manager, Human Resources.

HONEYWELL LIMITED
155 Gordon Baker Road
Toronto, ON M2H 3N7

Tel. 416-502-5200
Fax 416-502-4043
Website .... www.honeywell.ca

Honeywell Limited markets building controls that enhance comfort, improve productivity, save energy, protect the environment and increase security. These include HVAC systems for commercial buildings, residential heat and air conditioning controls, and industrial process controls. Honeywell Limited is a wholly-owned subsidiary of global controls company Honeywell Inc. of Minneapolis, Minnesota. Operating in Canada since 1930, Honeywell employs 2,800 in more than 50 locations across Canada. Graduates most likely to be hired come from the following academic areas: Bachelor of Engineering (Chemical, Electrical, Mechanical, Computer Systems, Food Processing, Industrial Chemistry, Industrial Engineering, Instrumentation, Petroleum/Fuels, Pulp and Paper), Bachelor of Commerce/Business Administration (Finance), Chartered Accountant, Certified Management Accountant, Certified General Accountant and Community College Diploma (CAD/CAM/Autocad, Electronics Technician, Engineering Technician, HVAC Systems, Information Systems). Graduates would occupy Systems Engineering, Technical Sales, Field Technician, Project Management and Financial Analyst positions. Team player, self empowered and a process orientation are listed as desirable non-academic qualifications. Company benefits are rated above average. The potential for advancement is listed as being good. The average annual starting salary varies with the position being considered. The most suitable method for initial contact by those seeking employment is to mail a resume with a covering letter. Honeywell Limited occasionally hires summer students (summer job seekers should inquire before applying). *Contact:* Human Resources.

HOSPITAL FOR SICK CHILDREN, THE
555 University Avenue, Room 5426
Toronto, ON M5G 1X8

Tel. 416-813-6680
Fax 416-813-5671

Email .... hr.recruiter@sickkids.on.ca
Website .... www.sickkids.on.ca

The Hospital For Sick Children is a major Canadian teaching and research centre dedicated exclusively to children. Affiliated with the University of Toronto, the hospital currently employs approximately 4,500 people. Graduates most likely to be hired come from the following academic areas: Bachelor of Arts (Psychology), Bachelor of Science (Biology, Chemistry, Computer Science, Microbiology, Audiology, Dentistry, Nursing, Nutritional Sciences, Occupational Therapy, Pharmacy, Physical Therapy, Psychology, Speech Pathology), Bachelor of Education (Early Childhood), Bachelor of Commerce/Business Administration (Accounting, Finance, Human Resources, Information Systems), Chartered Accountant, Certified Management Accountant, Certified General Accountant, Master of Business Administration (Accounting, Finance, Public Administration), Master of Science (General, Health Sciences), Medical Doctor and Community College Diploma (Administration, Human Resources, Hospitality, Security, Computer Science, Nursing RN/RNA, Radiology Technician, Respiratory Therapy, Ultra-Sound Technician). Prior work experience is listed as a desirable non-academic qualification. The most suitable method for initial contact by those seeking employment is to mail a resume with a covering letter. The Hospital For Sick Children does hire summer students. *Contact:* Human Resources.

HOTEL TORONTO EAST, CANADIAN PACIFIC HOTELS
2035 Kennedy Road
Toronto, ON M1T 3G2

Tel. 416-299-1500
Fax 416-299-8959
Website .... www.cphotels.com

Hotel Toronto East, a Canadian Pacific Hotel, is a full service hotel conveniently located just off of Highway 401 on Kennedy Road in Scarborough. Originally constructed in 1982, Hotel Toronto East has been a Canadian Pacific Hotel since 1998. Canadian Pacific Hotels is the largest owner-operated hotel company in Canada and one of the leading hotel companies in the world. Hotel Toronto East provides accommodation, food and beverage and convention services. The hotel is located close to downtown Toronto (25 to 30 minutes), 20 minutes away from the Pearson International Airport and is situated in a thriving business district with close proximity to the Toronto Zoo, Ontario Science Centre and shopping (Scarborough Town Centre). Hotel Toronto East employs approximately 400 people. Graduates most likely to be hired come from the following academic areas: Bachelor of Commerce/Business Administration and Community College Diploma (Administration, Hospitality). Graduates are hired to occupy Guest Service Agent, Sales Coordinator, Restaurant Supervisor, Security Officer/Supervisor and Accounting Clerk positions. Team player, enthusiastic, self-driven and a pleasant personality are all listed as desirable non-academic qualifications. Company benefits and the potential for advancement are both rated as excellent. The average annual starting salary falls within the $20,000 to $25,000 range. The most suitable methods for initial contact by those seeking employment are to mail a resume with a covering letter, or by applying in person at the office, Monday through Friday, 1:30 pm to 4:30 pm. Hotel Toronto East does hire summer students. *Contact:* Human Resources Department.

HOUSESITTERS CANADA
530 Queen Street East
Toronto, ON M5A 1V2

Tel. 416-947-9500
Fax 416-947-0075
Email .... email@to.housesitters.ca
Website .... www.housesitters.ca

Housesitters Canada provides house sitting, pet sitting, and general property management services. There are approximately 50 employees at this location and an additional 20 employees in Quebec. Graduates most likely to be hired come from the following academic areas: Bachelor of Arts (General), Bachelor of Engineering (Computer Systems), Bachelor of Commerce/Business Administration (General, Accounting, Finance) and Community College Diploma (Accounting, Administration, Advertising). Company benefits are rated as industry standard. The potential for advancement is listed as being good. The average annual starting salary falls within the $30,000 to $35,000 range. The most suitable methods for initial contact by those seeking employment are to mail or fax a resume with a covering letter. Housesitters Canada does hire summer and co-op work term students. *Contact:* William H. Murphy.

HOWARD JOHNSON PLAZA - HOTEL TORONTO EAST
40 Progress Court
Toronto, ON M1G 3T5

Tel. 416-439-6200
Fax 416-439-5689
Website .... www.hoteltorontoeast.com

Howard Johnson, Plaza Hotel Toronto East is a full service hotel. The hotel has 186 guest rooms, one restaurant, one lobby lounge, 16 meeting rooms, and employs more than 75 people. Graduates most likely to be hired come from the following academic areas: Bachelor of Arts (French Language), Community College Diploma (Administration, Cooking, Hospitality, Travel/Tourism) and High School Diploma. Graduates would occupy Front Desk, Secretary, Night Auditor, Sales and Supervisory positions. Enthusiastic, team player and an outgoing personality are listed as desirable non-academic qualifications. Company benefits and the potential for advancement are both rated as excellent. The average annual starting salary falls within the $15,000 to $20,000 range. The most suitable method for initial contact by those seeking employment is to mail a resume with a covering letter. The Plaza Hotel Toronto East does employ summer students. *Contact:* Human Resources.

HUDSON BAY MINING AND SMELTING CO. LIMITED
PO Box 1500
Flin Flon, MB R8A 1N9

Tel. 204-687-2054
Fax 204-687-3582

Hudson Bay Mining and Smelting Co. Limited is involved in both mining and smelting activities. The company employs approximately 2,140 people in total. Graduates most likely to be hired come from the following academic areas: Bachelor of Science (Chemistry, Metallurgy), Bachelor of Engineering (Chemical, Industrial Chemistry, Metallurgy, Electrical, Instrumentation, Mechanical, Mining), Bachelor of Commerce/Business Administration (Accounting, Finance, Information Systems), Certified Management Accountant, Certified General Accountant, Master of Business Administration (Accounting, Finance, Information Systems) and Community College Diploma (CAD/CAM/Autocad, Computer Science, Electronics Technician). Graduates would be hired to occupy Technician/Technologist, Junior Engineer Engineer, Planner, Accountant, Programmer/Analyst and Supervisor positions. Good communication skills, leadership abilities, team player and industrial experience are all listed as desirable non-academic qualifications. Company benefits are rated above average. The potential for advancement is listed as being good. The average annual starting salary ranges between $30,000 and $45,000 and is dependent upon the vacancy being filled, as well as being commensurate with the education and experience of the applicant. The most suitable method for initial contact by those seeking employment is to mail a resume with a covering letter. Hudson Bay Mining and Smelting Co., Limited does hire summer and co-op work term students (check with your campus career centre). *Contact:* Personnel Department.

HUDSON GENERAL AVIATION SERVICES INC.
Pearson Airport, P.O. Box 31, Toronto AMF
Mississauga, ON L5P 1A2
Fax 905-676-4894

Hudson General Aviation Services Inc. is an air transportation ground handling company. Hudson employs more than 500 people at Pearson Airport, and a total of 1,500 people in Canada. Graduates and non-graduates would occupy Aircraft Service Attendants, Check-In Agents, Equipment Maintenance Mechanics and Cabin Service Attendants. Company benefits are rated above average. The potential for advancement is listed as average. The most suitable methods for initial contact by those seeking employment are to mail or fax a resume with a covering letter. *Contact:* Dianne McEwan, Manager, Administration.

HUMBER COLLEGE OF APPLIED ARTS AND TECHNOLOGY
205 Humber College Boulevard
Toronto, ON M9W 5L7
Tel. 416-675-6622 ext.4685
Fax 416-675-4708
Email .... resumes@admin.humberc.on.ca
Website .... www.humberc.on.ca

Humber College of Applied Arts and Technology is one of Canada's largest and most diversified community colleges. The college is a leader in today's rapidly changing environment providing top quality programs to thousands of students each year. Humber College has two campuses in Toronto located in Rexdale and Etobicoke respectively, as well as the college's Business and Industry

Services Division found at different locations throughout the Toronto area. The division oversees various activities such as Transportation, Plastics, and Training and Job Finding Services. Humber College employs 900 full time employees and 1,600 contract full/part time employees. Graduates most likely to be hired come from the following academic areas: Bachelor of Arts (General, Economics, English, Languages, Music), Bachelor of Science (General, Nursing), Bachelor/Master of Engineering (General, Chemical, Civil, Electrical, Mechanical, Computer Systems, Industrial Design, Telecommunications), Bachelor of Education (General, Early Childhood), Bachelor of Commerce/Business Administration (Accounting, Finance, Human Resources, Information Systems), Chartered Accountant, Certified Management Accountant, Certified General Accountant, Master of Business Administration (General, Accounting, Finance, Information Systems, Public Administration), Community College Diploma (All Fields of Study), High School Diploma and other applicable accreditations. Graduates would occupy a wide variety of positions ranging from Support and Technical positions through to Instructor, Professor and Management positions. Strong written and oral communication skills, excellent interpersonal and organization skills and a knowledge of community college structures and processes are all listed as desirable non-academic qualifications. Company benefits are rated as industry standard. The potential for advancement is listed as being good. The average annual starting salary falls within the $25,000 to $30,000 range. The most suitable methods for initial contact by those seeking employment are to mail or fax a resume with a covering letter, via telephone, or through the college's website. Humber College does hire summer and co-op work term students, these are usually Humber College students. *Contacts:* Human Resources Department or the Department/Division of Interest.

HUMBER RIVER REGIONAL HOSPITAL
2111 Finch Avenue West
Toronto, ON M3N 1N1
Tel. 416-744-2500
Fax 416-747-3758
Email .... recruitment@hrrh.on.ca

Humber River Regional Hospital is a newly merged acute care hospital serving the culturally diverse northwest metropolitan Toronto area. The hospital is comprised of the former hospitals, Humber Memorial, Northwestern, and York Finch General. The hospital employs a total of 2,200 people. Graduates most likely to be hired come from the following academic areas: Bachelor of Arts (General, English, Fine Arts, Journalism, Psychology, Recreation Studies, Social Work), Bachelor of Science (General, Computer Science, Mathematics, Microbiology, Audiology, Nursing, Nutritional Sciences, Occupational Therapy, Pharmacy, Physio/Physical Therapy, Psychology, Speech Pathology), Bachelor of Engineering (General, Mechanical, Computer Systems, Environmental/Resources), Bachelor of Education (General, Adult), Master of Business Administration (General, Finance, Human Resources, Information Systems), Master of Science (Nursing), Community College Diploma (Accounting, Administration, Business, Communications/Public Relations, Facility Management, Financial Planning, Human Resources, Information Systems, Secretarial, Audio/Visual Technician, Graphic Arts, Recreation Studies, Security/Enforcement, Social Work/DSW, Computer Science, Plumber, Health/Home Care Aide, Laboratory Technician, Nuclear Medicine Technician, Nursing RN/RNA, Radiology, Respiratory Therapy, Ultra-Sound Technician) and High School Diploma. Graduates would occupy entry level positions relating to their academic backgrounds. Team work, collaborative, customer service skills, initiative and a non-discriminatory attitude are all listed as desirable non-academic qualifications. The average annual starting salary falls within the $20,000 to $25,000 range. The most suitable method for initial contact by those seeking employment is to mail a resume with a covering letter. Humber River Regional Hospital does hire summer and co-op work term students. *Contact:* Recruitment Specialist, Human Resoruces Planning (Phone Extension 2511).

HUMMINGBIRD COMMUNICATIONS LTD.

1 Sparks Avenue
Toronto, ON M2H 2W1

Tel.	416-496-2200
Fax	416-496-2207
Email	hr@hcl.com
Website	www.hummingbird.com

Hummingbird Communications Ltd. is Canada's fourth largest software development company and is growing quickly. The company has made its mark in enterprise network connectivity with products like Exceed, NFS-Maestro, and HostExplorer. In addition Hummingbird is active in developing new products for the rapidly growing data warehousing market. The company is on the leading edge of the network connectivity and business intelligence software business. For further details, please visit Hummingbird's website. Founded in 1989, the company has offices in 10 countries and currently employs 365 employees at this location, 522 in Canada and a total of 900 employees worldwide. Graduates most likely to be hired come from the following academic areas: Bachelor of Science (Computer Science, Mathematics), Bachelor of Engineering (Electrical, Computer Science, Telecommunications), Bachelor of Commerce/Business Administration (Information Systems, Marketing), Master of Business Administration (Marketing), Community College Diploma (Accounting, Advertising, Communications/Public Relations, Computer Science, Information Systems) and Microsoft Certified Systems Engineer (MCSE) accreditation. Graduates would occupy Technical Support Representative, Quality Assurance Analyst, Pretest Engineer, Programmer Analyst and Junior Software Developer positions. Strong interpersonal and communication skills, entrepreneurial, relevant work experience, excellent problem solving skills, energetic and motivated are all listed as desirable non-academic qualifications. Hummingbird offers a very competitive benefits package, including tuition, health club dues, RRSP's, bonuses, options, etc. The potential for advancement is listed as being good. The most suitable methods for initial contact by those seeking employment are to mail, fax or e-mail a resume with a covering letter. Hummingbird Communications Ltd. does hire summer and co-op work term students. *Contact:* Frank Nemeth, Manager, Human Resources.

HUSKY INJECTION MOLDING SYSTEMS LTD.

500 Queen Street South
Bolton, ON L7E 5S5

Tel.	905-951-5000
Fax	905-951-5323
Website	www.husky.ca

Husky Injection Molding Systems Ltd. is one of the leading suppliers of complete injection molding systems to the plastics industry. Bolton is Husky's corporate office, as well as one of its three manufacturing locations. This state-of-the-art facility comes complete with on-site fitness and wellness centres. Similar facilities are located in the United States and Europe. In addition, the company maintains offices in 25 countries around the world. Husky employs a total of 2,800 employees worldwide. Graduates most likely to be hired come from the following academic areas: Bachelor of Science (Computer Science, Mathematics), Bachelor of Engineering (General, Electrical, Mechanical, Automation/Robotics, Computer Systems, Environmental/Resources, Industrial Design, Industrial Engineering, Industrial Production/Manufacturing, Instrumentation) and Community College Diploma (CAD/CAM/Autocad, Computer Science, Electronics Technician, Engineering Technician, Tool and Die, Machinist, Welding). Graduates are hired to occupy Machine Design, Mold Design, Robotic Design, Assembly Technician and Test Technician positions in one of the following areas: Total Factory Solutions, Molds and Hot Runners, Injection Molding Machines, Information Services and Components Manufacturing. Husky also has opportunities for professionals to work in Sales and Service and other corporate and support positions. Quality-focused, committed to excellence, enjoy working in a fast-paced and changing environment, ambitious, self-motivated, team player, able to take pride in the work accomplished, a genuine desire to contribute and learn and a positive attitude are all listed as desirable non-academic qualifications. The most suitable method for initial contact by those seeking employment is to apply through the company's website. Husky Injection Molding Systems Ltd. does hire students for summer and co-op work terms. *Contacts:* Paul Pierroz, Manager, Human Resources - Components; Kathy Leeder, Manager, Human Resources - Machine Business or Glenn Cockfield, Manager, Human Resources - Molds Business.

HUSKY OIL LIMITED

PO Box 6525, Station D
Calgary, AB T2P 3G7

Tel.	403-298-6111
Fax	403-298-6799
Website	www.husky-oil.com

Husky Oil Limited is a Canadian-based, privately held integrated oil and gas company headquartered in Calgary. The company's operations include the exploration for and development of crude oil and natural gas, as well as the production, purchase, transportation, upgrading, refining and marketing of crude oil, natural gas, natural gas liquids, sulphur and petroleum coke, and the marketing of refined petroleum products, including gasoline, alternative fuels and asphalt. Husky ranks among Canada's top producers of crude oil, natural gas and sulphur. The company employs approximately 1,500 permanent employees located in Calgary, the Lloydminster and Prince George refineries, the Lloydminster Upgrader, and the Production Districts and Marketing Offices throughout Western Canada and Ontario. Graduates most likely to be hired come from the following academic areas: Bachelor of Science (Computer Science, Geology), Bachelor of Engineering (Chemical, Civil, Electrical, Power, Mechanical, Resources/Environmental, Petroleum), Bachelor of Laws, Bachelor of Commerce/Business Administration (General, Accounting, Finance, Human Resources, Marketing), Chartered Accountant, Certified Management Accountant, Master of Business Administration, Master of Engineering and Community College Diploma (Accounting, Administration, Communications). Good communication and interpersonal skills, flexibility, initiative, innovation, team work skills and knowledge of Microsoft Office are all listed as desirable non-academic qualifications. The most suitable method for initial contact by those seeking employment is to mail a resume with a covering letter. Husky Oil Limited is a dynamic employer that values workplace diversity. *Contact:* Human Resources Department.

IBM CANADA LTD.
3600 Steeles Avenue East, B2 / Y33
Markham, ON L3R 9Z7

Tel. 800-426-4968
Fax 905-316-5408
Email .... recruit@vnet.ibm.com
Website .... www.can.ibm.com

IBM Canada Ltd. is the largest Canadian company involved in the manufacture, design and marketing of computer hardware and software. IBM Canada Ltd. is the Canadian arm of IBM World Trade Corp. of New York. IBM Canada Ltd. and its wholly owned subsidiaries operate 143 facilities and employ over 17,000 employees across the country, including 3,000 in manufacturing and development. The company has 56 marketing locations covering all major cities, one manufacturing facility in Bromont, two software development laboratories in North York and Burnaby, one infrared wireless communications facility in Markham and one distribution warehouse in Markham. There are over 5,000 employees at this location. Graduates most likely to be hired come from the following academic areas: Bachelor of Science (Computer Science), Bachelor of Engineering (Electrical), Bachelor of Laws, Chartered Accountant and Master of Business Administration. Graduates would occupy entry-level Programmer, Systems Engineer and Marketing positions. Company benefits and the potential for advancement are both rated as excellent. The most suitable method for initial contact by those seeking employment is to mail a resume with a covering letter. IBM Canada Ltd. does hire summer and co-op work term students. *Contact:* Human Resource Department.

IHS PUBLISHING SOLUTIONS LIMITED
1 Antares Drive, Suite 200
Nepean, ON K2E 8C4

Tel. 613-225-2300
Fax 613-225-2304
Email .... hr.ihspsl@ihspsl.com
Website .... www.ihspsl.com

IHS Publishing Solutions Limited develops custom information retrieval and electronic publishing applications for organizations with significant investments in information. The company markets its software and service solutions directly in Canada and in distinct markets internationally. IHS is a demonstrated leader in enabling government, commercial and professional organizations to maximize their information investments. Incorporated in 1987, the company boasts over a decade of expertise and commitment to ensuring the quality and stability of its customer's information products. IHS Publishing Solutions is a self-contained operation employing 27 people. The company's team of highly skilled professionals consists of Technical Application Services; Sales and Marketing; Finance and Administration; and Support Services. Graduates most likely to be hired come from the following academic areas: Bachelor of Science (Computer Science), Bachelor of Engineering (Computer Sys-

tems), Bachelor of Commerce/Business Administration (Accounting, Finance, Information Systems, Marketing) and Community College Diploma (Accounting, Computer Science). Graduates would occupy Junior Software Developer, Software Developer, Accounting Clerk and Marketing Clerk positions. Good interpersonal and communication skills, and adaptable to working in a small company are listed as desirable non-academic qualifications. Company benefits are rated above average. The potential for advancement is listed as average. The average annual starting salary falls within the $30,000 to $35,000 range. The most suitable method for initial contact by those seeking employment is to e-mail a resume with a covering letter. IHS Publishing Solutions Limited does hire summer and co-op work term students. *Contact:* Carolyn Perkins, Human Resources.

ILCO UNICAN INC.
7301 Decarie Blvd.
Montreal, QC H4P 2G7

Tel. 514-735-5411
Fax 514-735-5732
Email .... cv@ilcounican.com
Website .... www.ilcounican.com

Ilco Unican Inc. operates internationally and is a world leader in the design and manufacture of key blanks, key machines, mechanical pushbutton and electronic access controls. With locations worldwide, the company reaches original equipment manufacturers, locksmiths, businesses, hotels, and hardware stores in over fifty countries on all continents. Ilco Unican maintains the Electronic Access Control Division and its head office in Montreal. There are 450 employees at this location, a total of 1,000 in Canada and 5,000 employees worldwide. Graduates most likely to be hired come from the following academic areas: Bachelor of Arts (Graphic Arts), Bachelor of Engineering (Electrical, Mechanical, Materials Science, Automation, Microelectronics, Telecommunications, Industrial Design/Production), Bachelor of Commerce/Business Administration (Accounting, Finance, Human Resources, Information Systems, Marketing), Chartered Accountant (Cost Accounting), Certified Management Accountant (Finance), Certified General Accountant (Finance), Master of Business Administration (Accounting, Finance, Human Resources, Information Systems, Marketing), Master of Engineering (Electrical, Electronics, Mechanical) and Community College Diploma (Accounting, Administration, Advertising, Business, Communications, Financial Planning, Human Resources, Marketing/Sales, Purchasing/Logistics, Secretarial, Security, CAD/CAM/Autocad, Computer Science, Electronics Technician, Engineering Technician). Graduates would occupy Mechanical Designer, Hardware Engineer, Programmer Analyst, Project Coordinator, Human Resources Coordinator, Assistant Divisional Controller, Administrative Assistant, Product Manager, Export Technician, Translator and Graphic Artist positions. Bilingualism, flexibility, team player and good communication skills are all listed as desirable non-academic skills. Company benefits are rated above average. The potential for advancement is listed as being excellent. The average annual starting salary falls within the $30,000 to $35,000 range. The most suitable method for initial contact by those seeking employment is to mail a resume with a covering letter. Ilco Unican Inc. does hire summer and co-op work term students. *Contacts:* Lise Pilon, Executive Director, Human Resources or Gaétan Olivier, Human Resources Consultant.

IMP GROUP INTERNATIONAL INC.
2651 Dutch Village Road, Suite 400
Halifax, NS B3L 4T1

Tel. 902-453-2400
Fax 902-453-6931
Email .... cheryl.deveaux@impgroup.com
Website .... www.impgroup.com

IMP Group International Inc. is a privately-owned, diversified company with three core operating divisions, including: Aerospace, Aviation and Commercial, as well as a corporate investment portfolio. The Aerospace Core Group is located at three sites within Nova Scotia where it provides engineering, depot level maintenance and many ancillary services to military aircraft, as well as avionics production, and the manufacture and assembly of metal and composite components for aircraft manufacturers. The Innotech-Execaire Aviation Group offers a full range of airline and corporate aircraft maintenance, modification, avionics, sales, interior refurbishment, flight management, and ground support including refueling. The group operates from eleven airports across Canada. The Commercial Core Group encompasses IMP's extensive industrial marine supply operations in Eastern Canada and in the United States, as well as Can-Med Surgical Supplies, Aerospace Machining Centre, IMP Fuels, foundry and other manufacturing operations. IMP's corporate portfolio includes the Moscow Aerostar Hotel in Russia and two hotels in Nova Scotia, the Holiday Inn Select Halifax and the Amherst Wandlyn Inn, as well as other corporate investments. Established in 1967 and headquartered in Halifax, the company employs 70 people at this location, 2,000 people in Canada and a total of 2,500 people worldwide. Graduates most likely to be hired come from the following academic areas: Bachelor of Engineering (Computer Systems, Instrumentation, Microelectronics, Mechanical, Aerospace, Industrial Design, Industrial Production, Marine, Welding), Bachelor of Laws, Bachelor of Commerce/Business Administration (Accounting, Finance, Human Resources, Information Systems), Master of Business Administration (Accounting, Finance, Human Resources, Information Systems, Marketing) and Community College Diploma (Accounting, Facility Management, Human Resources, Marketing/Sales, Aircraft Maintenance, Architecture/Drafting, CAD/CAM/Autocad, Computer Science, Electronics Technician, Engineering Technician, Marine Engineering, Welding). Computer skills, work experience, corporate fit and a multi-disciplined academic background are all listed as desirable attributes. Company benefits are rated as industry standard. The potential for advancement is listed as being good. The average annual starting salary depends upon the position being considered. The most suitable method for initial contact by those seeking employment is to mail a resume with a covering letter. IMP Group International Inc. occasionally hires summer students. Contact: Human Resources Administrator.

IMPERIAL OIL LIMITED
111 St. Clair Avenue West
Toronto, ON M5W 1K3

Tel. 416-968-8312
Fax 416-968-8129
Website .... www.imperialoil.com

Imperial Oil Limited has been a leading member of Canada's petroleum industry for more than a century. In addition to being the country's largest producer of crude oil and a major producer of natural gas, Imperial Oil is also the largest refiner and marketer of petroleum products, with a coast-to-coast supply network, and a major manufacturer of petrochemicals. Imperial's 7,500 employees

work in major cities and in communities across Canada. Graduates most likely to be hired from the following academic areas: Bachelor of Arts (Economics), Bachelor of Science (Chemistry, Computer Science, Geology, Mathematics, Metallurgy), Bachelor of Engineering (Chemical, Civil, Electrical, Mechanical, Resources/Environmental), Bachelor of Commerce/Business Administration (Accounting, Finance, Human Resources, Information Systems, Marketing), Certified Management Accountant, Certified General Accountant, Master of Business Administration (Accounting, Finance, Human Resources, Information Systems, Marketing), Master of Engineering and Community College Diploma (Engineering Technician). Previous work experience, mobility, team player and a high level of initiative are all listed as desirable non-academic qualifications. Company benefits are rated above average. The potential for advancement is listed as being good. The most suitable method for initial contact by those seeking employment is to mail a resume, covering letter, and a recent transcript (the months of August and September are best). On-campus recruitment requires CACEE forms and transcripts (see your career centre for opportunities with Imperial Oil). Imperial Oil Limited does hire students for summer and co-op work terms. Contact: Recruitment Co-ordinator.

IMPERIAL TOBACCO LIMITED
3810, rue Saint-Antoine Ouest, PO Box 6500
Montreal, QC H4C 1B5

Tel. 514-932-5952
Website .... www.imperialtobacco.com

Imperial Tobacco Limited is Canada's largest tobacco enterprise involved in all phases of the industry, from the raw leaf to the final product. Employing over 2,500 people, the company operates three manufacturing plants located in Montreal, Guelph, Ontario and Joliette, Quebec, in addition to two tobacco processing plants located in Aylmer, Ontario and LaSalle, Quebec. Imperial Tobacco Limited also maintains sales and distribution centres in six major Canadian cities including, Moncton, Montreal, Toronto, Winnipeg, Calgary and Vancouver. This location is the head office. The major corporate divisions are finance, marketing, manufacturing, materials management, human resources, and research and development. Graduates most likely to be hired come from the following academic areas: Bachelor of Arts (Psychology), Bachelor of Science (Chemistry, Computer Science, Health Sciences, Physics, Psychology), Bachelor of Engineering (Chemical, Civil, Environmental, Electrical, Industrial, Mechanical), Bachelor of Laws, Bachelor of Commerce/Business Administration (Accounting, Finance, Marketing), Chartered Accountant (Finance), Certified Management Accountant (Finance), Certified General Accountant (Finance), Master of Business Administration (Finance, Marketing) and Community College Diploma (Human Resources). Company benefits and the potential for advancement are both listed as excellent. The average annual starting salary falls within the $30,000 to $35,000 range. The most suitable method for initial contact by those seeking employment is to mail a resume with a covering letter. Imperial Tobacco Limited does hire summer students. Contact: Human Resources Department.

IMPRIMERIE INTERWEB INC.
1603 boulevard Montarville
Boucherville, QC J4B 5Y2

Tel. 450-655-2801
Fax 450-641-3650

Imprimerie Interweb Inc. is a commercial printing company that specializes in the production of magazines, newspapers and inserts. Founded in 1981, the company is a subsidiary of Groupe Transcontinentale. Interweb has about 300 permanent employees that work from their central office in Boucherville, Quebec and a total of 370 employees in Canada. Graduates most likely to be hired come from the following academic areas: Bachelor of Commerce/Business Administration (Marketing), Community College Diploma (Administration, Marketing/Sales, Purchasing/Logistics, Mechanic, Electronics Technician) and High School Diploma. Graduates would occupy Production (eg. General Help and Stackerman) and Customer Service positions. Creative, communicative, responsible, diligent, organized, enthusiastic and productive are all listed as desirable non-academic qualifications. Company benefits and the potential for advancement are both rated as excellent. The average annual starting salary falls within the $15,000 to $20,000 range. The most suitable method for initial contact by those seeking employment is to fax a resume with a covering letter. Imprimerie Interweb Inc. does hire summer and co-op work term students. *Contact:* Lucie Gérin, Human Resources.

IMPRIMERIES TRANSCONTINENTAL, DIVISION MÉTROPOLE LITHO
1201, rue Marie-Victorin
Saint-Bruno-de-Montarville, QC J3V 6C3

Tel. 450-441-1201
Fax 450-441-4242
Website .... www.transcontinental.ca

Imprimeries Transcontinental, Division Métropole Litho is active in book printing and binding. Division Métropole Litho is part of Imprimeries Transcontinental (Impression), the printing branch of GTC Transcontinental Group Ltd., based in Montréal. Founded in 1976, GTC is active across North America in printing, distribution, publishing, compact-disc production, electronic information and commerce and direct marketing services. Imprimeries Transcontinental, Division Métropole Litho employs approximately 200 people. Graduates most likely to be hired come from the following academic areas: Bachelor of Engineering (Electrical, Mechanical, Automation/Robotics, Industrial Production/Manufacturing), Bachelor of Commerce/Business Administration (General, Accounting, Finance, Human Resources), Chartered Accountant, Certified Management Accountant, Certified General Accountant, Community College Diploma (Accounting, Advertising, Purchasing/Logistics, Secretarial, Graphic Arts, Computer Science, Electronics Technician, Engineering Technician) and High School Diploma. Graduates would occupy related Junior Trainee positions. Previous work experience, leadership skills and industry knowledge are listed as desirable non-academic qualifications. Company benefits are rated above average. The potential for advancement is listed as being good. The average annual starting salary falls within the $25,000 to $30,000 range. The most suitable methods for initial contact by those seeking employment are to mail a resume with a covering letter. Imprimeries Transcontinental, Division Métropole Litho does hire summer students for production level positions. *Contact:* Sylvie Marceau, Coordonnatrice des ressources humaines.

INDUSTRIAL ACCIDENT PREVENTION ASSOCIATION / IAPA
250 Yonge Street, 28th Floor
Toronto, ON M5B 2N4

Tel. 416-506-8888
Fax 416-506-9092
Website .... www.iapa.on.ca

The Industrial Accident Prevention Association / IAPA is a non-profit association dedicated to helping firms achieve safe, healthy and productive workplaces. Established in 1917, IAPA has over 40,000 member firms across Ontario. The association's mission is the improvement of quality of life in workplaces and communities and works to fulfill this mission by providing publications, training, consulting, loss management services, an information centre, statistical services, an accident prevention magazine, the health and safety conference and trade show, regional conferences and through the help of IAPA volunteers. The IAPA employs 80 people at this location and a total of 210 employees in Ontario. Graduates most likely to be hired come from the following academic areas: Bachelor of Arts (English, Journalism, Psychology), Bachelor of Engineering (Industrial Chemistry, Industrial Production/Manufacturing, Telecommunications, Bachelor of Education (Adult), Bachelor of Commerce/Business Administration (Accounting, Finance, Human Resources, Information Systems, Marketing), Chartered Accountant, Certified General Accountant, Master of Business Administration (Finance, Human Resources, Information Systems, Marketing) and Community College Diploma (Accounting, Communications/Public Relations, Human Resources, Marketing/Sales, Office Administration, Purchasing/Logistics, Secretarial, Information Systems). Company benefits are rated above average. The potential for advancement is listed as being average. The average annual starting salary falls within the $40,000 to $45,000 range. The most suitable methods for initial contact by those seeking employment are to mail or fax a resume with a covering letter. The Industrial Accident Prevention Association does hire summer students. *Contact:* Human Resources Manager.

INDUSTRIES LASSONDE INC.
170 5 E Avenue
Rougemont, QC J0L 1M0

Tel. 450-469-4926
Fax 450-469-2505

Industries Lassonde Inc. is involved in food processing, primarily juices and drinks. The company employs 300 people at this location and a total of 500 people in Canada. Graduates most likely to be hired come from the following academic areas: Bachelor of Science (Chemistry, Microbiology, Nutritional Sciences), Bachelor of Engineering (Food Processing, Automation/Robotics, Computer Systems, Industrial Design, Industrial Production), Bachelor of Commerce/Business Administration (Accounting, Finance, Human Resources, Information Systems, Marketing, Public Administration), Chartered Accountant, Certified Management Accountant, Certified General Accountant and Community College Diploma (Accounting, Administration, Human Resources, Secretarial). Graduates would occupy Manager, Controller, Chief Accountant, Technician, Clerk, and Engineering positions. Good communication skills, leadership abilities, the ability to make decisions and team player are all listed as desirable non-academic qualifications. Company benefits are rated above average. The potential for advancement is listed as being good. The average annual starting salary falls within the $25,000 to $35,000 range. The most suitable method for initial contact by those seeking employment is to mail a resume with a covering letter. Industries Lassonde Inc. does hire summer students. *Contact:* Human Resources.

INFORMATION SYSTEMS CONSULTING GROUP / ISC
10665 Jasper Avenue, Suite 900
Edmonton, AB T5J 3S9

Tel.	780-428-3069
Fax	780-425-3301
Email	hr@isc-group.com
Website	www.isc-group.com

Information Systems Consulting Group / ISC is an information technology consulting firm based in Edmonton, providing all aspects of computing services to clients across North America. Services include application development and maintenance, network management, custom applications, training, user documentation, IVR, PeopleSoft/SAP consulting and full service web development. ISC provides long-term solutions which enable its clients to achieve maximum efficiency. There are 45 employees at this location, a total of 65 in Canada and a total of 87 employees worldwide. Graduates most likely to be hired come from the following academic areas: Bachelor of Science (Computer Science), Bachelor of Engineering (Computer Systems), Bachelor of Commerce/Business Administration (Accounting), Master of Business Administration (Accounting, Information Systems) and Community College Diploma (Computer Animation, Computer Science). Graduates would occupy Web Developer, Network/Help Desk, Programmer, Management Consultant, Systems Consultant, Mainframe Programmer, DBA and Technical Writer/Trainer positions. Team player, energetic, motivated, enthusiastic, a quick learner and good communication skills are all listed as desirable non-academic qualifications. Company benefits are rated as industry standard. The potential for advancement is listed as being good. The average annual starting salary falls within the $25,000 to $30,000 range. The most suitable method for initial contact by those seeking employment is to e-mail a resume with a covering letter. Information Systems Consulting Group does hire summer and co-op work term students. *Contact:* Tamezza Ratansi, Human Resources Department.

INFORMATION & TECHNOLOGY SERVICES / ITS
700 Lawrence Avenue West, Suite 370
Toronto, ON M6A 3B4

Tel.	416-314-5588
Fax	416-314-5758

Information & Technology Services / ITS is the technology division of the Ontario Housing Corporation. ITS develops in-house application systems for the client group, which is the Local Housing Authorities in Ontario. A help support centre is also provided. Systems developed are in the areas of accounting, human resources, budgeting and asset management. ITS employs a total of 60 personnel. Graduates most likely to be hired come from the following academic areas: Bachelor of Science (Com-

puter Science), Bachelor of Engineering (Computer Systems), Bachelor of Commerce/Business Administration (Information Systems) and Community College Diploma (Computer Science). Graduates would occupy Programmer/Analyst, Application Developer, Business Analyst, Software Tester, Software Implementer/Trainer and Help Centre Analyst positions. Good communication skills and flexibility are both listed as desirable non-academic qualifications. Company benefits are rated as industry standard. The potential for advancement is listed as being good. The average annual starting salary falls within the $40,000 to $45,000 range. The most suitable method for initial contact by those seeking employment is via telephone. ITS does hire summer and co-op work term students. *Contact:* Christopher Gomes, Human Resources Administrator.

INGENIUS ENGINEERING INC.
30 Rosemount Avenue, Suite 200
Ottawa, ON K1Y 1P4

Tel.	613-729-6400
Fax	613-729-6770
Email	recruit@ingenius.on.ca
Website	www.ingenius.on.ca

InGenius Engineering Inc. is a software engineering, technical consulting and recruiting firm specializing in information and telecommunications technology. Founded in 1986 as a software development company, InGenius began growing its consulting and recruiting business in the spring of 1993. The firm's technical expertise is based on core competencies in three technology areas: software development, computer networking, telecommunications systems and services. InGenius' services include technical contractor services, technical placement services, and custom software development services to clients within the telecommunications industry in North America and within the federal government. InGenius customizes its services according to the needs and business focus of each client. There are approximately 90 people at this location and a total of 100 people employed in Canada. InGenius provides project managers, full project teams, or individual team members on a contractual and permanent basis to meet the business and technical requirements of its clients. Graduates most likely to be hired come from the following academic areas: Bachelor of Science (Computer Science, Mathematics), Bachelor of Engineering (General, Electrical, Aerospace, Automation/Robotics, Computer Systems, Telecommunications), Master of Business Administration (Information Systems, Marketing) and Community College Diploma (Business, Human Resources, Marketing/Sales, Computer Science, Electronics Technician, Engineering Technician). InGenius hires people who possess special expertise in telecom software systems, multimedia applications, internet application, hardware development, systems administration, technical support, technical writing and project management. Good interpersonal and communications skills, good leadership capabilities, the ability to work either in a group or alone and relevant work experience are all desirable non-academic qualifications important to InGenius and its clients. Company benefits are rated as industry standard. The potential for advancement is listed as excellent. The average annual starting salary falls within the $45,000 to $50,000 range. The most suitable method for initial contact by those seeking employment is to e-mail a resume with a covering letter. InGenius Engineering Inc. does hire summer and co-op students. *Contacts:* Recruitment or Manager, Business Development.

INGERSOLL-RAND CANADA INC.
51 Worcester Road
Toronto, ON M9W 4K2

Tel.	416-213-4500
Fax	416-213-4616
Website	www.ingersoll-rand.com

Ingersoll-Rand Canada Inc. manufactures and sells industrial machinery such as air compressors, air tools, construction and mining machinery, hoists, bearings and architectural hardware. The company employs approximately 115 people at this location, a total of 750 across Canada, and 48,000 people worldwide. Graduates most likely to be hired come from the following academic areas: Bachelor of Engineering (Mechanical), Bachelor of Commerce/Business Administration (Accounting) and Community College Diploma (Accounting). Graduates would occupy Application Engineer and Financial/Accounting positions. Good communication skills, high integrity, team player and an ability to make decisions and follow through are all listed as desirable non-academic qualifications. Company benefits are rated above average. The potential for advancement is listed as being good. The average annual starting salary falls within the $35,000 to $40,000 range. The most suitable method for initial contact by those seeking employment is to mail a resume with a covering letter. *Contact:* Agako Nouch, Vice President, Finance & Administration.

INGLIS LIMITED
1901 Minnesota Court
Mississauga, ON L5N 3A7

Tel.	905-821-6400
Fax	905-821-3462
Website	inglislimited.com

Inglis Limited is involved in the sales, marketing and service of household appliances. Inglis employs approximately 225 people at this location, over 450 across Canada, and is a wholly owned subsidiary of Whirlpool Corporation, USA, which employs 40,000 people worldwide. Graduates most likely to be hired come from the following academic areas: Bachelor of Engineering, Chartered Accountant, Certified Management Accountant, Certified General Accountant, Master of Business Administration, Master (for different areas in organization) and Community College Diploma (Accounting, Administration, Advertising, Information Systems, Marketing/Sales, Purchasing/Logistics, Electronics Technician). Graduates are recruited for Sales and Marketing, Accounting, Clerical, and Customer Service positions in the company's call-centre. Inglis seeks high potential employees. Company benefits are rated as excellent. The potential for advancement is listed as being good. The average annual salary falls within the $30,000 to $35,000 range. The most suitable method for initial contact by those seeking employment is to mail a resume with a covering letter. Inglis Limited hires summer students depending upon their requirements. *Contact:* Human Resources.

INNOTECH-EXECAIRE AVIATION GROUP
10225 Ryan Avenue
Dorval, QC H9P 1A2

Tel.	514-636-7070
Fax	514-636-9659
Email	human.resources@innotech-execaire.com
Website	www.sabec.com/innotech

Innotech-Execaire Aviation Group is the largest general aviation organization in Canada. Headquartered in Montreal, the company is a fully integrated aircraft service company offering a full range of airline and corporate aircraft maintenance, modification, interior refurbishment, flight management, and ground support providing facilities, hangarage and refueling services. In Montreal, Toronto, Vancouver, Ottawa and St. John's, the company provides factory-authorized service for major airframe, engine and avionics manufacturers. In Dorval, Innotech's all-new aircraft maintenance and interior refurbishing facility accepts airplanes the size of Boeing 737 and Airbus A320, Gulfstream V, Global Express and other business jets. Based in Toronto, Montreal, and Ottawa, Execaire manages 19 business jets for Canadian corporations, making it the largest private operator and executive charter company in the country. Integral members of the Aviation Group include Air 500 in Toronto, Pacific Avionics & Instruments in Vancouver, Air Atlantic in St. John's and Innotech Aviation Services operating nine FBO's across Atlantic Canada, Ontario and Quebec. In business for more than 40 years and employing 500 people across Canada, Innotech-Execaire Aviation Group is a member of Halifax based IMP Group International Inc. Graduates most likely to be hired come from the following academic areas: Bachelor of Engineering (Mechanical, Aerospace), Bachelor of Commerce/Business Administration (Accounting, Human Resources, Information Systems, Marketing), Master of Business Administration (Accounting, Finance) and Community College Diploma (Accounting, Secretarial). Company benefits are rated as industry standard. The potential for advancement is listed as being good. The average annual starting salary falls within the $25,000 to $30,000 range. The most suitable methods for initial contact by those seeking employment are to mail, fax or e-mail a resume with a covering letter. Innotech-Execaire Aviation Group does hire summer students. *Contact:* Marie-Josée Caron.

INNOVEX, QUINTILES CANADA INC.
100 Alexis-Nihon, Suite 800
St. Laurent, QC H4M 2P4

Tel.	514-855-0888
Fax	514-855-1348
Website	www.innovexglobal.com

Innovex, a division of Quintiles Canada Inc., offers custom designed solutions to healthcare companies that allows them to accelerate their commercial success. As a world leader in contract pharmaceutical services, Innovex provides contract sales and marketing services, late phase clinical (IIIB -IV) services, as well as health management services. Graduates most likely to be hired come from Bachelor of Science (Biology, Microbiology, Nursing, Pharmacy) and Bachelor of Commerce/Business Administration programs. Innovex hires full-time employees across Canada, for Sales and Sales Management positions on specific customer projects, that may range from 6 to 18 months in duration. Enthusiasm, good communication skills, team player, initiative and a business acumen are all listed as desirable nonacademic qualifications. Company benefits are rated as industry standard. The potential for advancement is listed as being good. The average annual starting salary varies according to the applicants level of experience in pharmaceutical sales or clinical research. The most suitable method for initial contact by those seeking employment is through Innovex's website at www.innovexglobal.com (Fax Number 514-855-0880). *Contact:* Human Resources.

INSCAPE
67 Toll Road
Holland Landing, ON L9N 1H2

Tel.	905-836-7676
Fax	905-836-6000
Email	recruiting@inscapesolutions.com
Website	www.inscapesolutions.com

Inscape is a leading designer and manufacturer of office furniture. The company's product line includes furniture systems, filing, storage components, tables and seating. Originally founded in 1888, Inscape is a publicly traded company on the Toronto Stock Exchange with ISO9001 certification. Today, the company employs a total of 425 people. Graduates most likely to be hired come from the following academic areas: Bachelor of Arts (Economics, Psychology), Bachelor of Science (Environmental, Metallurgy), Bachelor of Engineering (General, Metallurgy, Architectural/Building, Industrial Design, Industrial Production, Welding), Bachelor of Commerce/Business Administration (Accounting, Finance, Human Resources, Information Systems, Marketing, Public Administration), Chartered Accountant, Certified Management Accountant, Certified General Accountant, Master of Business Administration (Accounting, Finance, Human Resources, Information Systems, Marketing, Public Administration), Community College Diploma (Accounting, Administration, Human Resources, Welding) and High School Diploma. Graduates would occupy Human Resources Administrator/Coordinator, Industrial Engineer, Mechanical Engineer, Product Engineer, Marketing Coordinator, Accountant, Controller, Cell Operator/Assembler, Fabrication Supervisor, Plant Supervisor and Production Manager positions. Strong interpersonal skills, team player, previous work experience, an ability to meet deadlines, detail oriented and strong organizational skills are all listed as desirable non-academic qualifications. The potential for advancement is listed as excellent. The most suitable method for initial contact by those seeking employment is to mail a resume with a covering letter. *Contacts:* Raihana Ansari, Human Resources Coordinator or Karen Copeland, Human Resources Coordinator.

Insight.

INSIGHT CANADA INC.
8600, boul. Decarie
Montreal, QC H4P 2N2

Tel.	514-344-3500
Fax	514-344-4244
Email	thamilto@insight.com
Website	www.insight.com

Insight Canada Inc. is one of North America's leading business suppliers of computers, hardware and software. Insight is a publicly traded company on NASDAQ (NSIT) with one billion dollars in annual sales and growing. Currently, the company is expanding its Canadian facility in Montreal to meet the demands of the growing market. Insight employs more than 150 people in Canada, and over 1,500 employees worldwide. Graduates most likely to be hired come from the following academic areas: Bachelor of Arts (General, Economics, English, Languages, Psychology), Bachelor of Science (General, Computer Science, Psychology), Bachelor of Engineering (General, Computer Systems, Telecommunications),

Bachelor of Commerce/Business Administration (General, Human Resources, Information Systems, Marketing, Public Administration), Master of Business Administration (General) and Community College Diploma (Administration, Business, Communications/Public Relations, Information Systems, Marketing/Sales, Television/Radio Arts, Computer Science). Graduates would occupy the position of Account Executive. A sales aptitude, good telephone speaking voice, team spirit and computer knowledge are all listed as desirable non-academic qualifications. Company benefits and the potential for advancement are both rated as excellent. The average annual starting salary falls within the $25,000 to $30,000 range. The most suitable methods for initial contact by those seeking employment are to mail, fax or e-mail a resume with a covering letter, via the company's website, or by applying in person. *Contact:* Tammy Hamilton, Recruiter.

INTELCAN TECHNOSYSTEMS INC.
69 Auriga Drive
Nepean, ON K2E 7Z2

Tel.	613-228-1150
Fax	613-228-1149
Email	hr@intelcan.com
Website	www.intelcan.com

Intelcan Technosystems Inc. is an integrator for telecommunications and civil aviation projects, primarily in emerging markets. The company employs approximately 35 people at this location and a total of 45 people worldwide. Graduates most likely to be hired come from the following academic areas: Bachelor of Engineering (Civil, Electrical, Telecommunications), Bachelor of Architecture, Bachelor of Commerce/Business Administration (Accounting, Human Resources, Information Systems), Chartered Accountant, Certified Management Accountant and Certified General Accountant. Graduates would occupy Electrical Engineer, Civil Engineer, Architect, Accountant and Accounting Clerk positions. A minimum of two years work experience for Junior Engineering positions, team player and the ability to travel are all listed as desirable non-academic qualifications. Company benefits are rated above average. The potential for advancement is listed as being good. The average annual starting salary is dependent on the position being considered. The most suitable methods for initial contact by those seeking employment are to mail or e-mail a resume with a covering letter. Intelcan Technosystems Inc. does hire co-op work term students. *Contact:* Tracy Hearty, Human Resources.

INTERACTIVE CHANNEL TECHNOLOGIES INC.
150 Dufferin Avenue, Suite 906
London, ON N6A 5N6

Tel.	519-669-4460
Fax	519-663-0339
Email	hr@ichanneltech.com
Website	www.sourcemedia.com

Interactive Channel Technologies Inc. is a dynamic hi-tech organization leading the industry in interactive television system development. The company's technology, VirtualModem, provides consumers with a variety of interactive television applications and on-demand services including: internet access, email, electronic program guide, electronic home shopping, and video-on-demand. The VirtualModem television system utilizes industry standard digital MPEG set-top boxes. Trials and deployments are ongoing with cable television and telephone companies, as well as in other commercial and business areas around the world. Interactive Channel Technologies employs 48 people at this location, and a total of 200 people worldwide. Graduates most likely to be hired come from the following academic areas: Bachelor of Science (Computer Science, Mathematics) and Bachelor of Engineering (Chemical, Mechanical, Computer Systems, Engineering Physics). Graduates would occupy Software and Hardware Programmer/Developer positions. Team player, good communication skills and previous work experience are all listed as desirable non-academic qualifications. Company benefits are rated as excellent. The potential for advancement is listed as average. The average annual starting salary falls within the $30,000 to $40,000 range. The most suitable method for initial contact by those seeking employment is to e-mail a resume with a covering letter. Interactive Channel Technologies Inc. does hire students for summer and co-op work terms. *Contact:* Mary Donnelly, Human Resources Manager.

INTERACTIVE MEDIA GROUP / IMG

10 Four Seasons Place, Suite 700
Etobicoke, ON M9B 6H7

Tel. 416-640-6300 x55660
Fax 416-640-1905
Email .... recruiting@interactivemedia.com
Website .... www.interactivemedia.com

Interactive Media Group / iMG is North America's largest provider of electronic meeting services. Operating since 1987, iMG is a fast growing Canadian company with a strong presence in markets across Canada, the United States, and Australia. iMG's state-of-the-art technology integrates computers, interactive voice response (IVR), and the world wide web. The company owns several well-known telephone services including Telepersonals, The Night Exchange and Manline, and the web based Webpersonals (www.webpersonals.com). Interactive Media Group employs 300 people at this location and a total of 540 people worldwide. Graduates most likely to be hired come from the following academic areas: Bachelor of Arts, Bachelor of Science, Community College Diploma and High School Diploma. Graduates would occupy Client Sales Team Associate (inbound customer service), Marketing, Finance, Call Centre Management, and various IT positions. Teamwork, open-minded, continuous learner, customer accountability, high level of performance and entrepreneurial are all listed as desirable non-academic qualifications. Company benefits are rated as industry standard. The potential for advancement is listed as being good. The average annual starting salary falls within the $25,000 to $30,000 range. The most suitable methods for initial contact by those seeking employment are to mail, fax or e-mail a resume with a covering letter. *Contact:* Recruiting Department.

INTERNATIONAL COMMUNICATIONS FOR MANAGEMENT GROUP / ICM

20 Toronto Street, 10th Floor
Toronto, ON M5C 2B8

Tel. 416-955-0375
Fax 416-955-0380
Email .... icm@thgto.com
Website .... www.icmworldwide.com

International Communications for Management Group / ICM is a global provider of business services including corporate hospitality at major sporting events, conferences and training courses, world congresses and management forums, business reports and contract publishing. ICM employs 1,000 people in offices located in 16 countries around the world. Graduates most likely to be hired come from the following academic areas: Bachelor of Arts (Economics), Bachelor of Science (Computer Science, Mathematics), Bachelor of Engineering (Computer Systems), Bachelor of Commerce/Business Administration (General, Human Resources, Information Systems, Marketing) and Community College Diploma (Business, Communications/Public Relations, Human Resources, Marketing/Sales, Office Administration, Secretarial, CAD/CAM/Autocad, Computer Science, Electronics Technician, Information Systems). Graduates would occupy Inside Sales, Operations Manager/Trainers, Producer (conferences), Reception and Administrative Assistant positions. Graduates should have an understanding of business and a strong desire to establish a successful sales career. In addition, good listening, communication, presentation and selling skills, self-motivated, positive, organized, proactive, ambitious and the ability to negotiate at the director level are all listed as desirable non-academic qualifications. A business degree is advantageous. Graduates hired would learn selling methods, and upon establishing a track record of sales would be appointed to Sales Management positions domestically or internationally. Company benefits are rated as industry standard. The potential for advancement is listed as excellent. The average annual starting salary falls within the $35,000 to $40,000 range, and is both salary and commission based. The most suitable method for initial contact by those seeking employment is to fax a resume with a covering letter. For further information visit ICM's website. *Contact:* Banti Abbott, Recruitment Director.

INTERNATIONAL FOREST PRODUCTS LIMITED / INTERFOR

1055 Dunsmuir St., Four Bentall Centre
Suite 3500, PO Box 49114
Vancouver, BC V7X 1H7

Tel. 604-681-3221
Fax 604-681-2092
Email .... itresumes@interfor.com
Website .... www.interfor.com

International Forest Products Limited / INTERFOR is one of western Canada's largest logging and sawmilling companies producing a diversified range of quality wood products for sale to world markets. The company harvests timber and manufactures and markets lumber products, logs, and wood chips. INTERFOR has 46 logging operations and six sawmills in the southern coastal region of British Columbia, and one logging operation and one sawmill in the central interior region of the province. The company employs approximately 2,100 people directly and a further 700 people through logging contractors operating under its direction. Graduates most likely to be hired come from the following academic areas: Bachelor of Science (Forestry), Bachelor of Engineering (Mechanical), Bachelor of Commerce/Business Administration (Accounting, Marketing), Master of Business Administration (Accounting, Marketing) and Community College Diploma (Forestry). Graduates would occupy Timber Cruiser, Assistant Forestry Engineer, Assistant Silviculturist, Manufacturing Management Trainee, Production and Sales positions. Applicants should be team players and self starters. Company benefits and the potential for advancement are both rated as excellent. The average annual starting salary falls within the $35,000 to $40,000 range. The most suitable methods for initial contact by those seeking employment are to mail or fax a resume and covering letter. INTERFOR does hire summer students. *Contact:* Human Resources Department.

INTERNATIONAL LEISURE SYSTEMS INC.
511 King Street West, Suite 303
Toronto, ON M5V 2Z4

Tel. 416-598-9494
Fax 416-598-0040
Email .... 103177.1014@compuserve.com

International Leisure Systems Inc. is a rapidly growing entertainment company. The company employs approximately 150 people worldwide. The company seeks graduates for training in the urban entertainment industry with the potential to work internationally. Graduates most likely to be hired come from the following academic areas: Bachelor of Arts (General), Master of Business Administration and Community College Diploma (Business, Facility Management, Financial Planning, Hospitality, Recreation Studies, Urban Planning). Graduates would be hired to occupy Assistant Manager positions. Enthusiasm, a willingness to travel, positive attitude, and a desire to gain experience in different areas of the urban entertainment industry are all listed as desirable non-academic qualifications. Company benefits are rated above average. The average annual starting salary is negotiable with the position and qualifications of the applicant. The most suitable method for initial contact by those seeking employment is to mail a resume with a covering letter. *Contact:* Laura Tweedy, Administration.

INTERTEC SECURITY & INVESTIGATION LIMITED
939 Eglinton Avenue East, Suite 119
Toronto, ON M4G 4E8

Tel. 416-424-2002

Intertec Security & Investigation Limited provides contract security services for condominium, industrial, commercial, and residential facilities, as well as providing investigation services. Graduates most likely to be hired come from the following academic areas: Bachelor of Arts, Bachelor of Commerce/Business Administration and Community College Diploma (Law Enforcement, Business). Graduates would occupy supervisory positions in the Security Division and possible management positions within the Personnel/Training or Operations Department. Good public relations, communication and English language skills are all listed as desirable non-academic qualifications. Company benefits are rated as industry standard. The potential for advancement is listed as excellent. The average annual starting salary falls within the $15,000 to $20,000 range, and is commission based for some positions. The most suitable methods for initial contact by those seeking employment are to mail a resume with a covering letter, or by applying in person. Intertec Security & Investigation Limited does hire summer students. *Contact:* Human Resources Manager.

INVESTORS GROUP
4 Westmount Square, Suite 250
Westmount, QC H3Z 2S6

Tel. 514-935-3520
Fax 514-935-2930
Website .... www.investorsgroup.com

Investors Group is one of the leading financial services companies in Canada. Investors Group is a dominant player in the mutual fund industry. In addition to mutual

funds, the company offers other individual and group investment products including life, health and disability insurance, mortgage financing, and tax preparation services. Investors Group employs approximately 60 people at the Westmount office and a total of 4,000 people in Canada. Graduates most likely to be hired for the Westmount office come from the following academic areas: Bachelor of Arts (Economics), Bachelor of Commerce/Business Administration (General, Accounting, Finance, Marketing), Chartered Accountant, Certified Management Accountant, Certified General Accountant, Master of Business Administration (Finance) and Community College Diploma (Accounting, Business, Financial Planning, Marketing/Sales). Graduates are hired as Sales Representatives in the financial planning field. The starting salary is commission based. Excellent human relations skills, self starter, ambitious, competitive and business oriented are all listed as desirable nonacademic qualifications. Company benefits and the potential for advancement are both rated as excellent. The most suitable methods for initial contact by those seeking employment are to mail or fax a resume with a covering letter. *Contact:* Babis Chronopoulos, Region Manager.

INVESTORS GROUP
447 Portage Avenue, One Canada Centre
Winnipeg, MB R3C 3B6

Tel. 204-956-8359
Fax 204-942-0967
Email .... humanresources@investorsgroup.com
Website .... www.investorsgroup.com

Investors Group is one of the leading financial services companies in Canada. Canadian owned and operated, Investors Group is a dominant player in the mutual fund industry. In addition to mutual funds, the company offers other individual and group investment products, including life, health and disability insurance, mortgage financing, and tax preparation services. Distribution of all services is handled by more than 3,300 representatives working from more than 95 sales offices across Canada. One Canada Centre is the corporate headquarters for Investors Group. Corporate functions are divided into 10 corporate divisions: Client Services, Corporate Affairs, Corporate Services and Internal Audit, Finance, Information Technology, Investment, Marketing, Property, Sales, and Strategic Initiatives. Graduates most likely to be hired come from the following academic areas: Bachelor of Arts (Economics), Bachelor of Science (Computer Science), Bachelor of Commerce/Business Administration (Accounting, Finance, Marketing), Certified Management Accountant, Certified General Accountant, Master of Business Administration (Accounting, Finance, Marketing) and Community College Diploma (Administration). Company benefits and the potential for advancement are rated as excellent. Starting salaries are based on a combination of education, experience, the position and its responsibilities. The most suitable method for initial contact by those seeking employment is to forward a resume with a covering letter. Investors Group does hire summer students. *Contact:* Colleen MacInnes, Human Resources Consultant.

IRVING OIL LIMITED
10 Sydney Street, PO Box 1421
Saint John, NB E2L 4K1

Tel. 506-632-2000
Fax 506-632-7161
Email .... iol-job@irvingoil.ca
Website .... www.irvingoil.com

Irving Oil Limited is recognized across Atlantic Canada as a leader in oil refining, and the sale and marketing of oil products. Graduates most likely to be hired come from the following academic areas: Bachelor of Engineering (Chemical, Civil, Environmental, Mechanical, Bachelor of Commerce/Business Administration (Accounting, Finance, Marketing, Information Systems), Chartered Accountant (Finance), Certified Management Accountant (Finance), Certified General Accountant (Finance), Master of Business Administration (Accounting, Finance, Marketing, Information Systems) and Community College Diploma (Accounting, Administration, Advertising, Business). The potential for advancement is rated as excellent. The most suitable methods for initial contact by those seeking employment are to mail or e-mail a resume with a covering letter. Irving Oil Limited does hire co-op work term students. Contact: Human Resources.

IRWIN TOY LIMITED
43 Hanna Street
Toronto, ON M6K 1X6

Tel. 416-533-3521
Fax 416-583-4578
Website .... www.irwin-toy.com

Irwin Toy Limited is a major Canadian manufacturer and distributor of toys and sporting goods. Activities also include importing and exporting, sales and marketing. There are more than 200 employees at this location. Post secondary education is not specified as a requirement for employment application. Excellent communication and organizational skills are both listed as desirable non-academic qualifications. Company benefits are rated as industry standard. The potential for advancement is listed as average. The most suitable method for initial contact by those seeking employment is to mail a resume with a covering letter. Irwin Toy Limited does hire summer students. Contact: Director Human Resources.

ISL INTERNATIONAL SURVEYS LTD.
151 Placer Court
Toronto, ON M2H 3R5

Tel. 416-495-0909
Fax 416-495-1369
Website .... www.npd.com

ISL International Surveys Ltd. provides a wide range of market research services from initial design, through data collection and collation, to tabulation and interpretation. There are more than 100 employees at this location. Graduates most likely to be hired come from the following academic areas: Bachelor of Arts (Statistics, General), Bachelor of Science, Bachelor of Commerce/Business Administration (Marketing), Certified Management Accountant, and Community College Diploma (Secretarial, Clerical). Graduates would occupy Report Preparations Processor/Programming, Intermediate Accounting Clerk, Data Entry Operator, Secretary and Management Assistant positions. Company benefits are rated above average. The potential for advancement is listed as being good. The average annual starting salary falls within the $20,000 to $25,000 range. The most suitable methods for initial contact by those seeking employment are to mail a resume with a covering letter, or via telephone. ISL International Surveys Ltd. does hire summer students, occasionally. Contacts: Human Resources Manager or Administrative Assistant, Human Resources.

IBM Global Services

ISM INFORMATION SYSTEMS MANAGEMENT CORPORATION
3600 Steeles Avenue East, B2
Markham, ON L3R 9Z7

Fax 905-316-5408
Website .... www.can.ibm.com/ism

ISM Information Systems Management Corporation is one of Canada's premier providers of information system management services. ISM is a wholly owned subsidiary of IBM Canada Ltd., and a member of the IBM Global Services team. There are 1,500 employees at this location, and a total of 6,500 employees in Canada. Graduates most likely to be hired come from the following academic areas: Bachelor of Science (Computer Science), Bachelor of Engineering (Computer Systems), Bachelor of Commerce/Business Administration (Information Systems), Master of Business Administration (Information Systems) and Community College Diploma (Computer Science). Graduates would occupy IT Specialist, Network Operations Analyst, Help Desk Support, Customer Service Representative, Software/Hardware Administrator, Disaster Recovery Analyst, and Programmer/Analyst positions. Team player, good written and verbal communication skills and a strong customer service orientation are all listed as desirable non-academic qualifications. Company benefits and the potential for advancement are both rated as excellent. The average annual starting salary falls within the $35,000 to $45,000 range. The most suitable methods for initial contact by those seeking employment are to apply online through the company's website, or to fax or mail a resume with a covering letter. ISM Information Systems Management Corporation does hire summer and co-op work term students. Contact: Recruitment Services - TCD.

ITS ELECTRONICS, INC.
200 Edgeley Boulevard, Units 24-26
Concord, ON L4K 3Y8

Tel. 905-660-0405
Fax 905-660-0406
Email .... itselectronics@sympatico.ca
Website .... www.itselectronics.com

ITS Electronics, Inc. a Canadian and ISO 9001 certified company, specializes in the development, design and manufacturing of RF Microwave and millimetre wave components (SSPAs, HPAs, LNAs) and subsystems (Ka-Band, Up/down converters). Customer driven and user specific for a wide variety of applications, ITS Electronics caters to numerous markets such as defence, satcom and wireless. The company's products are used in point-to-point microwave systems, LMCS/LMDS, MMDS and wireless loop applications. The newest addition to ITS Electronics' product line is InterWave 99, a family of products which are targeted towards wireless communication and internet needs. Graduates most likely to be hired come from the following academic areas: Bachelor of Engineering (Electrical, Mechanical, Engineering Physics, Microwave Telecommunications), Bachelor of Commerce/Business Administration (Marketing, Accounting), Master of Science, Master/Doctorate of Engineering (Electrical, Mechanical, Engineering Physics) and Community College Diploma (Electronics Engineering Technician, Electromechanical Technician). Graduates would occupy Analog/Digital Designer, RF/Microwave Assembler, Digital Engineer, Electrical Engineer, Mechanical Engineer, RF/Microwave Engineer, RF/Microwave Technicians/Technologist, Administrative Clerk, and Accounting Clerk positions. Team player, creative, self-motivated, results oriented, able to work under deadlines and at least two years previous work experience are all listed as desirable non-academic qualifications. Company benefits are rated industry standard. The potential for advancement is listed as excellent. The average annual starting salary is commensurate with industry experience and job requirements. The most suitable methods for initial contact by those seeking employment are to mail or e-mail a resume with a covering letter. ITS Electronics Inc. hires a few summer students annually. *Contact:* Ana P. Fini, Human Resources Administrator.

IVANHOÉ INC.
393, rue St-Jacques, bureau 800
Montreal, QC H2Y 3Z4

Tel. 514-841-7600
Fax 514-841-7795

Ivanhoé Inc. is a real estate management, development and investment company specializing in retail properties in Ontario, Quebec and the United States. The company employs approximately 150 employees at this location and a total of 200 full-time and 50 temporary employees in Canada. Graduates most likely to be hired come from the following academic areas: Bachelor of Engineering (Civil, Architectural/Building), Bachelor of Laws, Bachelor of Commerce/Business Administration (Accounting, Marketing), Chartered Accountant, Certified Management Accountant, Certified General Accountant and Community College Diploma (Accounting, Advertising, Secretarial, HVAC Systems). Graduates would occupy Secretary, Accounting Manager, Project Manager, Publicity and Promotions Administrator, Assistant Manager, and Technical positions in the shopping centres. Previous work experience, bilingualism, computer skills and service oriented are all listed as desirable non-academic qualifications. Company benefits are rated as excellent. The potential for advancement is listed as being good. The average annual starting salary falls within the $30,000 to $35,000 range. The most suitable method for initial contact by those seeking employment is to mail a resume with a covering letter. *Contact:* Human Resources Department.

IVL TECHNOLOGIES LTD.
6710 Bertram Place
Victoria, BC V8M 1Z6

Tel. 250-544-4091
Fax 250-544-4100

Email .... info@ivl.com
Website .... www.ivl.com

IVL Technologies Ltd. is a world leader in innovative vocal and musical signal processing. IVL designs and manufactures award winning products for the professional music, audio, and multimedia markets. The company has 80 creative employees working in engineering, manufacturing, sales and support at IVL's modern facilities located in Victoria, British Columbia. Graduates most likely to be hired come from the following academic areas: Bachelor of Science (Computer Science), Bachelor of Engineering (Electrical, Computer Systems, Industrial Design), Master of Science (Computer Science), Master of Engineering (Electrical, Computer Systems). Graduates would occupy Junior-Senior DSP Engineer, Junior-Senior Embedded Software Engineer and Junior-Senior Research Engineer positions. Excellent problem solving skills, strong team-players and a passion for music are all listed as desirable non-academic qualifications. Applicants with demonstrated related work experience, and real-time experience are preferred. Company benefits are rated as excellent. The potential for advancement is listed as average. The average annual starting salary falls within the $45,000 to $50,000 range. The most suitable method for initial contact by those seeking employment is to mail a resume with a covering letter. IVL Technologies Ltd. does hire co-op work term students. *Contact:* Human Resources.

J. D. SMITH AND SONS LIMITED
700 Flint Road
Downsview, ON M3J 2J5

Tel. 416-661-2500
Fax 416-661-7680
Email .... joel@jdsmith.com
Website .... www.jdsmith.com

J. D. Smith and Sons Limited specializes in truck transportation, including general common carrier and dedication contract. Services include warehousing, distribution and dedicated services. The company employs more than 300 people across Canada. Graduates most likely to be hired come from the following academic areas: Bachelor of Arts (General), Bachelor of Science (General), Bachelor of Commerce (General, Logistics), Master of Business Administration, Community College Diploma (Business, Facility Management, Human Resources, Purchasing/Logistics, Secretarial) and High School Diploma. Graduates would occupy Clerical, Supervisor Trainees for trucking and warehousing operations, Management Trainees and Business Analyst/Logistics positions. Honesty, dedication, good interpersonal skills, and a good attitude towards work and business environments are all listed as desirable non-academic qualifications. Company benefits are rated as excellent. The potential for advancement is listed as being good. The average annual starting salary falls within the $25,000 to $30,000 range. The most suitable method for initial contact by those seeking employment is to mail a resume with a covering letter. J. D. Smith and Sons Limited does hire summer students, traditionally for Clerical, Warehouse and Truck Driving positions. Summer students demonstrating appropriate skills may be considered for permanent positions upon graduation. *Contact:* Joseph Libralesso.

J.M. SCHNEIDER INC.
321 Courtland Avenue East
Kitchener, ON N2G 3X8

Tel. 519-741-5000

Fax 519-749-7414
Email .... hr@jms.ca
Website .... www.schneiders.ca

J. M. Schneider Inc. is a national food processor. The company is involved in the manufacture, distribution and sale of meat, poultry, grocery and baked goods products for the retail and foodservice markets as well as export markets. There are more than 1,000 employees at this location, and a total of 3,500 employees in Canada. Graduates most likely to be hired come from the following areas: Bachelor of Arts (General, English), Bachelor of Science (Chemistry, Computer Science, Mathematics), Bachelor of Commerce/Business Administration, Chartered Accountant, Master of Business Administration (Marketing) and High School Diploma. Graduates are hired to occupy positions relating to their specific specialty. Previous work experience, outside interests and related specialized qualifications are all listed as desirable non-academic qualifications. Company benefits are rated above average. The potential for advancement is listed as being good. The average annual starting salary ranges between $20,000 and $25,000 and will ultimately depend upon the position being considered. The most suitable method for initial contact by those seeking employment is to mail a resume with a covering letter. J. M. Schneider Inc. does hire summer students. *Contact:* Human Resources Team.

JACQUES WHITFORD AND ASSOCIATES LIMITED
3 Spectacle Lake Drive
Dartmouth, NS B3B 1W8

Tel. 902-468-7777
Fax 902-468-9009
Email .... info@jacqueswhitford.com
Website .... www.jacqueswhitford.com

Jacques, Whitford and Associates Limited provides consulting services in six disciplines in the engineering and environmental sciences. These disciplines are as follows: Environmental Engineering, Environmental Sciences, Geotechnical Engineering, Hydrogeology, Materials Engineering and Research, and Mining Services. Founded in 1972, there are approximately 100 employees at this location and a total of 325 across Canada. Graduates most likely to be hired come from the following academic areas: Bachelor of Arts (Geography, Urban Geography, Archeology), Bachelor of Science (Biology, Geography), Bachelor of Engineering (General, Chemical, Industrial Chemistry, Materials Science, Pollution Treatment, Civil, Environmental, Forest Resources, Water Resources, Petroleum, Geological, Geotechnical), Bachelor of Commerce/Business Administration (Accounting, Human Resources, Marketing), Certified Management Accountant, Master of Business Administration (Accounting, Finance), Master of Science (Biology, Geography), Master of Engineering (General, Chemical, Industrial Chemistry, Materials Science, Pollution Treatment, Civil, Environmental, Forest Resources, Water Resources, Petroleum, Geological, Geotechnical) and Community College Diploma (Accounting, Administration, CAD/CAM/Autocad, Engineering Technician, Laboratory Technician, Environmental Engineering Technician). Graduates would occupy Junior Engineer, Junior Scientist, Secretarial and Accounting positions. Good communication skills, community involvement and related work experience or completion of co-op work terms are all listed as desirable non-academic qualifications. Company benefits are rated above average. The potential for advancement is listed as excellent. The average annual starting salary falls within the $25,000 to $30,000 range. The most suitable method for initial contact by those seeking employment is to mail a resume with a covering letter. Jacques, Whitford and Associates Limited does hire summer students, mainly through organized co-op programs. *Contact:* Kim Crowell, Human Resources Coordinator.

JANNA SYSTEMS INC.
3080 Yonge Street, Suite 6020
Toronto, ON M4N 3N1

Tel. 416-483-7711
Fax 416-483-3220
Email .... hr@janna.com
Website .... www.janna.com

Janna Systems Inc. is a leading provider of enterprise-class Customer Relationship Management (CRM) solutions for the financial services and telecommunications industries. Janna Systems Inc. (CDN: JANA) provides enterprise CRM solutions that are scalable, mobile and web-enabled. Janna Contract Enterprise, Janna Remote and Janna Contact WebView put the customer at the centre of the computing paradigm allowing Janna to be the portal to enterprise customer knowledge, enabling the corporate enterprise to share all information about the client relationship across the entire organization. Headquartered in Toronto, the company has sales offices and partners worldwide. Janna employs approximately 140 people and offers an upstart attitude and an entrepreneurial environment where individuals are able to make a difference. Graduates most likely to be hired come from the following academic areas: Bachelor of Science (Computer Science, Mathematics), Bachelor of Engineering (General, Computer Systems) and equivalent backgrounds. Graduates would occupy Software Developer, Professional Services Consultant, Quality Assurance Analyst and Client Support Services positions. An ability to work with minimal supervision in a team environment, good communication skills, motivated, willing to make a commitment to success, and the ability to learn the skills of the "Big Five" consulting firms are all listed as desirable non-academic qualifications. Janna Systems offers an extremely competitive compensation package and excellent opportunities for professional growth. The most suitable method for initial contact by those seeking employment is to e-mail a resume with a covering letter. Janna Systems Inc. does hire summer and co-op students. *Contact:* Human Resources.

JAS F. GILLANDERS CO. LIMITED
33 Atomic Avenue
Toronto, ON M8Z 5K8

Tel. 416-259-5446
Fax 416-259-5614

Jas F. Gillanders Co. Limited is a custom millwork manufacturer of all types of cabinets, furniture, panelling, etc. The company employs more than 50 people. Graduates most likely to be hired come from the following academic areas: Community College Diploma (Accounting, Secretarial, Architecture/Drafting, Industrial Design) and High School Diploma. Possessing relevant work experience and technical trades would be a definite asset. Company benefits are rated as excellent. The potential for advancement is listed as being good. The average annual starting salary falls within the $15,000 to $20,000 range. The most suitable methods for initial contact by those seeking employment are to mail a resume with a covering letter, or via telephone. Jas F. Gillanders Co. Limited does hire summer students. *Contact:* Bill Vincent, Vice President, Administration.

JEWELSTONE SYSTEMS INC.
100 King Street West
1 First Canadian Place, Suite 2900
Toronto, ON M5X 1C8

Tel.	416-364-5800
Fax	416-364-5448
Email	positions@unitrax.com
Website	www.unitrax.com

Jewelstone Systems Inc. is a privately owned Canadian company that provides software solutions for the Canadian Investment Fund Industry. Incorporated in 1991, Jewelstone Systems Inc. has become well known in the investment fund, brokerage and banking industries for providing sound solutions complemented with commendable customer service. Jewelstone Systems Inc. employs a professional management team with extensive experience drawn from all facets within the financial services industry. There are a total of 75 employees in the company. Graduates most likely to be hired come from the following academic areas: Bachelor of Science (Computer Science), Bachelor of Commerce/Business Administration (General, Accounting, Finance, Information Systems, Marketing), Chartered Accountant, Certified Management Accountant, Certified General Accountant, Master of Business Administration (General) and Community College Diploma (Accounting, Administration, Information Systems, Marketing/Sales, Secretarial, Computer Science). Graduates would occupy Technical Support, Computer Programmer, Office Administration, Accounts Payable and Accounts Receivable positions. Previous work experience in the mutual fund industry, self-motivated, the ability to work well in a team environment and good communication skills are listed as desirable non-academic qualifications. Jewelstone offers competitive industry salaries and flexible working hours. Company benefits and the potential for advancement are both rated as excellent. The average annual starting salary falls within the $35,000 to $40,000 range. The most suitable method for initial contact by those seeking employment is to apply through the company's website. Jewelstone Systems Inc. does hire summer and co-op work term students. *Contact:* Human Resources Manager.

JML SHIRT LTD.
12 Long Street
Edmunston, NB E3V 3H3

Tel.	506-735-1920
Fax	506-735-1923
Website	www.jml.nb.ca

JML Shirt Ltd. is a manufacturer of men's and women's dress and uniform shirts and men's boxer shorts. Founded in 1953, the company employs approximately 215 people and produces over one million shirts and two million boxer shorts per year. Graduates most likely to be hired come from the following academic areas: Bachelor of Science (Computer Science), Bachelor of Engineering (Computer Systems, Industrial Production), Bachelor of

Commerce/Business Administration (Accounting, Finance, Human Resources, Information Systems, Marketing, Public Administration), Certified General Accountant (Accounting Comptroller), Community College Diploma (Accounting, Business, Secretarial, Computer Science, Engineering Technician) and High School Diploma. Graduates would occupy Accounting Clerk, Payroll Clerk and Receptionist positions. Good work ethic, team player and conscientious are listed as desirable non-academic qualifications. Company benefits are rated as industry standard. The potential for advancement is listed as average. The most suitable method for initial contact by those seeking employment is to mail a resume with a covering letter. *Contacts:* Jacques Mongeau or Dale Soucy.

JOHN DEERE CREDIT INC.
1001 Champlain Avenue, Suite 400
Burlington, ON L7L 5Z4

Tel.	905-319-5812
Fax	905-319-2147
Email	jdcredit@deere.com
Website	www.deere.com

John Deere Credit Inc. offers a wide variety of retail finance and lease products to the agricultural, construction, commercial, transportation, lawn and grounds care and materials handling equipment markets. The company also offers financing alternatives to marine and recreational vehicle customers, and provides a revolving credit product (AgLine), as well as operating loans, both designed to help farmers with the short-term financing of agricultural inputs and services. John Deere Credit Inc. is a wholly owned subsidiary of John Deere Limited and maintains offices in Burlington and Edmonton. John Deere Credit employs 100 people at this location, a total of 165 in Canada and a total of 2,000 people worldwide. Graduates most likely to be hired come from the following academic areas: Bachelor of Arts (Economics), Bachelor of Science (Agriculture/Horticulture, Computer Science, Mathematics), Bachelor of Laws, Bachelor of Commerce/Business Administration (General, Accounting, Finance, Human Resources, Information Systems, Marketing), Chartered Accountant, Certified Management Accountant, Certified General Accountant, Master of Business Administration (General, Finance) and Community College Diploma (Accounting, Business, Agriculture/Horticulture, Information Systems). Motivated and eager for the opportunity to contribute to a fast paced dynamic environment, and excellent communication, customer service and team skills are all listed as desirable non-academic qualifications. Company benefits and the potential for advancement are both rated as excellent. The average annual starting salary falls within the $25,000 to $30,000 range. The most suitable methods for initial contact by those seeking employment are to mail, fax or e-mail a resume with a covering letter. John Deere Credit Inc. does hire summer and co-op work term students. *Contact:* Tan Gill, Human Resources Recruiter.

JOHN FORSYTH COMPANY INC., THE
36 Horner Avenue
Toronto, ON M8Z 5Y1

Tel.	416-252-6231
Fax	416-253-4147

The John Forsyth Company Inc. is one of Canada's leading suppliers of apparel and has a growing presence in the United States. The company was started in 1903 by John Forsyth, a manufacturer of men's quality shirts and accessories. Today, Forsyth product lines include men's shirts, sweaters, overcoats, raincoats, jackets, activewear, casual pants, and jeans, pajamas, and robes, ties and scarves and women's shirts and blouses, sweaters, pants, skirts and activewear. The company's Penmans subsidiary produces T-shirts and fleece products for men, women, youths and children. The company maintains three warehouses in Toronto for distribution and processing, employing sales persons, merchandisers, sourcers, and artists. The company also maintains a manufacturing facility in Cambridge, Ontario. There are approximately 180 employees at this location and a total 1,000 employees in Canada. Graduates most likely to be hired come from the following academic areas: Bachelor of Arts (Economics), Bachelor of Commerce/Business Administration (Accounting, Finance) and Community College Diploma (Accounting, Merchandising, Secretarial, Artist, Fashion Design). Graduates would occupy Accounts Payable Clerk, Accounts Receivable Clerk, Secretary, Receptionist, Merchandiser, Sourcer and Artist positions. Team player, committed and enthusiastic are listed as desirable non-academic qualifications. Company benefits are rated as industry standard. The potential for advancement is listed as being good. The most suitable method for initial contact by those seeking employment is to mail a resume with a covering letter. John Forsyth Company Inc. does hire summer students for warehouse positions. *Contact:* Maria Rice, Benefits Administrator.

JOHN WILEY & SONS CANADA LIMITED
22 Worcester Road
Toronto, ON M9W 1L1

Tel. 416-236-4433
Fax 416-236-4447
Email .... canada@wiley.com
Website .... www.wiley.com

John Wiley & Sons Canada Limited is an educational and trade publishing company. There are more than 60 employees at this location, and a total of 78 people in Canada. Graduates most likely to be hired come from the following academic areas: Bachelor of Arts, Bachelor of Science, Bachelor of Education, Bachelor of Commerce/Business Administration, Chartered Accountant and Community College Diploma (Business). Graduates would occupy Editorial Assistant, Marketing Assistant, Sales Representative, Sales Assistant and Accounting positions. Good communication and interpersonal skills, strong work ethic, positive attitude, computer literacy and excellent organizational skills are all listed as desirable non-academic qualifications. Company benefits are rated as industry standard. The potential for advancement is listed as being good. The average annual starting salary falls within the $25,000 to $30,000 range. The most suitable method for initial contact by those seeking employment is to mail a resume with a covering letter. John Wiley & Sons Canada Limited does hire summer and co-op work term students. *Contact:* Human Resources.

JOHNSON & JOHNSON, MEDICAL PRODUCTS
1421 Lansdowne Street West
Peterborough, ON K9J 7B9

Tel. 705-741-6100
Fax 705-743-1545
Email .... csmith@medca.jnj.com
Website .... www.jnj.com

Johnson & Johnson, Medical Products is involved in the sales and distribution of medical devices. There are 95 employees at this location and a total of 350 employees in Canada. Graduates most likely to be hired come from

the following academic areas: Bachelor of Arts (General), Bachelor of Science (General, Biology, Computer Science), Bachelor of Commerce/Business Administration (General, Accounting, Finance, Human Resources, Information Systems, Marketing), Certified Management Accountant, Certified General Accountant and Community College Diploma (Accounting, Administration, Business, Human Resources, Information Systems, Secretarial, Computer Science). Graduates would occupy Product Specialist, Secretary, Product Manager, Accountant, Financial Controller, Associate Field Representative (nongrad), Sales Representative and Human Resources Manager positions. Previous work experience, assertive, innovative, self-directed, collaborative and good interpersonal skills are all listed as desirable non-academic qualifications. Company benefits are rated above average. The potential for advancement is listed as being good. The most suitable methods for initial contact by those seeking employment are to mail, fax or e-mail a resume with a covering letter. Johnson & Johnson, Medical Products does hire summer and co-op work term students. *Contact:* Carole Smith, Manager, Recruitment & Support Services.

JOHNSON MATTHEY LIMITED
130 Glidden Road
Brampton, ON L6W 3M8

Tel. 905-453-6120
Fax 905-454-6870
Website .... www.noble.matthey.com

Johnson Matthey Limited is a precious metals refiner and manufacturer. The company employs approximately 180 people at this location a total of 216 in Canada and 6,250 people worldwide. Graduates most likely to be hired come from the following academic areas: Bachelor of Science (Chemistry, Metallurgy), Bachelor of Engineering (Industrial Chemistry, Metallurgy, Industrial Production), Chartered Accountant and Community College Diploma (Marketing/Sales). Graduates would occupy Junior Engineering and Special Project positions. Team player, resourceful, dependable and an ability to work unsupervised are all listed as desirable non-academic qualifications. Company benefits are rated above average. The potential for advancement is listed as average. The average annual starting salary is dependent upon the position being considered. The most suitable method for initial contact by those seeking employment is to mail a resume with a covering letter. Johnson Matthey Limited does hire summer students when they are required. *Contacts:* Linda Szeli, Human Resources Assistant or Andy McCullough, Human Resources Manager.

JOSEPH BRANT MEMORIAL HOSPITAL
1230 North Shore Boulevard
Burlington, ON L7R 4C4

Tel. 905-632-3730
Fax 905-336-6486
Website .... www.jbmh.com

Joseph Brant Memorial Hospital, a 250 bed community hospital, has been providing integrated healthcare services to Burlington and surrounding areas since 1961. Conveniently located 40 minutes west of Toronto, the hospital employs 1,120 people in the provision of patient-focused care through a full range of medical specialties and caring compassionate teamwork. Graduates most likely to be hired come from the following academic areas: Bachelor of Arts (Psychology, Social Work), Bachelor of Science (Nursing, Occupational Therapy, Pharmacy,

Physiotherapy, Psychology, Speech Pathology), Bachelor of Commerce/Business Administration (Human Resources), Chartered Accountant and Community College Diploma (Secretarial, Recreation Studies, Carpentry, Electronics Technician, Plumber, Laboratory Technician, Nuclear Medicine, Nursing RN/RNA, Radiology, Respiratory Therapy, Social Work/DSW, Ultra-sound Technician). Graduates would occupy Unit Clerk, Finance Clerk, Secretary, Radiology, RN, RPN, Social Worker, Occupational Therapist, Physiotherapist, OTA/PTA, Speech Pathologist, Registered Technologist, Lab Technician, Millwright, Pharmacist, Recreationist and Respiratory Therapist positions. Team player, good customer service, assessment and problem solving skills, prior work experience in the field and the completion of specialized courses are all listed as desirable non-academic qualifications. Company benefits are rated as industry standard. The potential for advancement is listed as being average. The average annual starting salary falls within the $30,000 to $35,000 range. The most suitable methods for initial contact by those seeking employment are to mail or fax a resume with a covering letter. Joseph Brant Memorial Hospital does hire co-op work term students in some areas. *Contact:* Marlene Hall, Human Resource Coordinator.

JUNE WARREN PUBLISHING LTD.
9915 - 56 Avenue NW
Edmonton, AB T6E 5L7

Tel. 780-944-9333
Fax 780-944-9500
Website .... www.junewarren.com

June Warren Publishing Ltd. is a privately owned, Alberta company specializing in the development and distribution of trade publications for the Canadian oil, gas and construction industries. Utilizing leading edge in-house database and production technology, the company publishes a family of six premier trade publications. The Canadian Oilfield Service & Supply Directory, Oil & Gas Inquirer, and Canadian Oilfield Gas Plant Atlas are all geared to the needs of the Canadian oil and gas industry. Alberta Construction Service & Supply Directory, Alberta Construction '97, and Alberta Construction Association Membership Roster & Buyers Guide are geared towards the Alberta construction industry. June Warren employs over 35 people in offices located in Calgary and Edmonton. Graduates most likely to be hired come from the following academic areas: Bachelor of Arts (English, Journalism), Bachelor of Science (Computer Science), Bachelor of Commerce/Business Administration (Information Systems, Marketing), Master of Business Administration (Information Systems, Marketing) and Community College Diploma (Advertising, Marketing/Sales, Graphic Arts, Journalism). Company benefits are rated as industry standard. The potential for advancement is listed as being good. The average annual starting salary depends on the position being considered. The most suitable method for initial contact by those seeking employment is to mail a resume with a covering letter. *Contact:* Human Resources.

KEANE CANADA, INC.
2000 Barrington Street, Cogswell Tower, Suite 300
Halifax, NS B3K 3K1

Tel. 902-422-6036
Fax 902-422-6059
Email .... careers.hal@keane.com
Website .... www.keane.com

Keane Canada, Inc., a subsidiary of Keane Inc., is a leading information technology (IT) services firm that helps clients plan, build and manage application software to achieve business advantage. Keane delivers operational improvement and IT consulting, enterprise applications solutions and application management services, among other IT solutions. Founded in 1965, Keane is headquartered in Boston, Massachusetts and has 50 branch offices in major cities across Canada, the United States and the United Kingdom. In addition to Halifax, Canadian branch offices are found in Calgary and Toronto. The company employs 170 people at this location, a total of 350 in Canada and a total of 10,000 people worldwide. Graduates most likely to be hired at the Halifax location come from the following academic areas: Bachelor of Science (Computer Science), Bachelor of Commerce/Business Administration (Information Systems) and Community College Diploma (Computer Science). Graduates would occupy Consultant positions. Company benefits and the potential for advancement are both rated as excellent. The average annual starting salary falls within the $35,000 to $40,000 range. The most suitable method for initial contact by those seeking employment is to e-mail a resume with a covering letter. *Contact:* Human Resources.

KEANE CANADA, INC.
439 University Avenue, Suite 500
Toronto, ON M5G 1Y8

Tel. 416-596-1532
Fax 416-596-1546
Email .... careers.tor@keane.com
Website .... www.keane.com

Keane Canada, Inc., a subsidiary of Keane Inc., is a leading information technology (IT) services firm that helps clients plan, build and manage application software to achieve business advantage. Keane delivers operational improvement and IT consulting, enterprise applications solutions and application management services, among other IT solutions. Founded in 1965, Keane is headquartered in Boston, Massachusetts and has 50 branch offices in major cities across Canada, the United States and the United Kingdom. In addition to Toronto, Canadian branch offices are found in Halifax and Calgary. The company employs a total of 350 people in Canada and a total of 10,000 people worldwide. Graduates most likely to be hired at the Toronto location come from the following academic areas: Bachelor of Science (Computer Science), Bachelor of Engineering (Computer System Design), Master of Business Administration (Information Systems) and Master of Science (Computer Science). Graduates would occupy a Consultant role and should possess three to four years work experience (minimum) in a structural problem-solving environment working with structured analysis methods and tools. Company benefits are rated above average. The potential for advancement is listed as excellent. The average annual starting salary fall in the $35,000 plus range. The most suitable method for initial contact by graduates seeking employment is to mail or e-mail a resume with a covering letter. *Contact:* Human Resources.

KELOWNA, CITY OF
1435 Water Street
Kelowna, BC V1Y 1J4

Tel. 250-862-3376
Fax 250-862-3318
Website .... www.city.kelowna.bc.ca

The City of Kelowna provides a full range of municipal government services for the community. The city employs approximately 650 people. Graduates most likely to be hired come from the following academic areas: Bachelor of Arts (Recreation Studies, Urban Geography/ Planning), Bachelor of Science (Computer Science, Horticulture, Environment/Ecology), Bachelor of Engineering (Civil, Architectural/Building), Bachelor of Commerce/Business Administration (General, Public Administration), Certified General Accountant, Certified Management Accountant, Community College Diploma (Office Administration, Secretarial, Draftsperson/Autocad, Building Technician, Auto Mechanic, Painter, Carpenter, Plumber, Gas Technician, Welder) and High School Diploma for seasonal labourer positions. Graduates would occupy positions in Parks and Leisure Services, Works and Utilities, Planning and Development, Finance and Corporate Services and Human Resources. Good communication and customer service skills, teamwork oriented, strong ethics, innovative, creative and ambitious with a drive for personal success are all listed as desirable non-academic qualifications. Company benefits are rated above average. The potential for advancement is listed as average. The average annual starting salary for new graduates falls within the $30,000 to $35,000 range. The most suitable method for initial contact by those seeking employment is to mail a resume with a covering letter. For current information on job vacancies contact the Job Line at (250) 862-3339 ext. 562 (JOB). The City of Kelowna does hire summer students. *Contact:* Human Resources Department.

KELOWNA HOME SUPPORT
1340 Ellis Street
Kelowna, BC V1Y 1Z8

Tel. 250-712-3160

Kelowna Home Support provides in-home health care, personal care, light housekeeping, respite and meal program services. Graduates most likely to be hired come from the following academic areas: Bachelor of Science (Nursing), Community College Diploma (Health/Home Care Aide, Nursing RN) and High School Diploma. Company benefits are rated as excellent. The potential for advancement is listed as average. The average annual starting salary falls within the $25,000 to $30,000 range. The most suitable method for initial contact by those seeking employment is to apply in person at this location. Kelowna Home Support does hire summer students. *Contact:* Stuart Ballard, Human Resoruces.

KENNAMETAL LTD.
115 - B Matheson Boulevard West, Suite 211
Mississauga, ON L5R 3L1

Tel. 905-568-2288
Fax 905-568-4955

Kennametal Ltd. specializes in the design, manufacture and marketing of tungsten carbide cutting tools, tooling systems, supplies and services to the metal working industry. The Canadian subsidiary of the United States based multinational corporation, Kennametal Ltd. has six offices and plants in Canada employing a total of 200 people. Graduates most likely to be hired come from the following academic areas: Bachelor of Arts (General), Bachelor of Science (Metallurgy), Bachelor of Engineering (Mechanical, Design), Bachelor of Commerce/Business Administration (Accounting) and Community College Diploma (Engineering, Accounting, Business). Personable, good telephone manner and keyboard skills are listed as desirable non-academic qualifications. Com-

pany benefits are rated above average. The potential for advancement is listed as being good. The most suitable method for initial contact by graduates seeking employment is to mail a resume with a covering letter. *Contact:* Grant Adam, Manager of Human Resources.

KERNELS POPCORN LIMITED
40 Eglinton Avenue East, Suite 250
Toronto, ON M4P 3A2

Tel. 416-487-4194
Website .... www.kernelspopcorn.com

Kernels Popcorn Limited is a retailer of flavoured gourmet popcorn. There are 68 stores in Canada, located in major regional shopping malls. Kernels currently has four stores operating in South Korea. Approximately 25% of the stores are corporately owned, and 75% are franchised. Graduates most likely to be hired come from the following academic areas: Bachelor of Arts (General), Bachelor of Commerce/Business Administration (Accounting, Marketing), Certified Management Accountant, Certified General Accountant, Master of Business Administration (Marketing), and Community College Diploma (Accounting, Marketing/Sales). Graduates would be hired to occupy Clerical, Accounting, Marketing and Store Management positions. Hard working, a positive attitude, sharp, honest and ethical are all listed as desirable non-academic qualifications. Company benefits are rated above average. The potential for advancement is listed as being good. The average annual starting salary is dependent upon the position and the qualifications of the applicant. The most suitable method for initial contact by graduates seeking employment is to mail a resume with a covering letter. Kernels Popcorn Limited does hire summer students. *Contacts:* Paula Hurley, Store Positions or Loreta Miskinis, Office Positions.

KIMBERLY-CLARK INC.
90 Burnhamthorpe Road West
Mississauga, ON L5B 3Y5

Tel. 905-277-6500
Fax 905-277-6894

Kimberly-Clark Inc. is involved in the manufacture of consumer packaged goods. The company employs approximately 100 people at this location and a total of 230 people in Canada. Graduates most likely to be hired come from the following academic areas: Bachelor of Arts (General), Bachelor of Science (General), Bachelor of Engineering (Chemical, Electrical, Mechanical), Bachelor of Commerce/Business Administration (General, Marketing), Master of Business Administration (General, Marketing) and Community College Diploma (Business, Marketing/Sales). Graduates would occupy Sales Representative and Marketing Assistant positions. Initiative, adaptability and flexibility are all listed as desirable non-academic qualifications. Company benefits are rated above average. The potential for advancement is listed as being good. The average annual starting salary falls within the $30,000 to $35,000 range. The most suitable method for initial contact by graduates seeking employment is to mail a resume with a covering letter. Kimberly-Clark Inc. does hire summer students for Sales Intern positions. *Contact:* Recruiting/Personnel Services.

KINARK CHILD AND FAMILY CARE SERVICES
240 Duncan Mill Road, Suite 402
Toronto, ON M3B 3B2

Tel. 416-391-3884
Fax 416-444-8896

Email .... kinark@inforamp.net
Website .... www.kinark.on.ca

Kinark Child and Family Care Services is one of the largest child and family mental health service providers in Ontario. A non-profit organization established in 1984, Kinark operates six program centres in the province through the Ministry of Community and Social Services. Services provided include child, family and group counselling, professional assessments, residential treatment, family preservation, therapeutic foster care, and a special needs camp. Graduates most likely to be hired come from the following academic areas: Master of Social Work and Community College Diploma (Child and Youth Worker, Early Childhood Educator). Graduates would occupy Social Worker, Child and Youth Worker and Early Childhood Educator positions. Computer literacy, team player, leadership skills and excellent communication skills are all listed as desirable non-academic qualifications. Company benefits are rated as excellent. The potential for advancement is listed as being good. The average annual starting salary falls within the $35,000 to $40,000 range. The most suitable method for initial contact by those seeking employment is to mail a resume with a covering letter. Kinark does hire co-op work term students and summer students, usually for the Outdoor Camping Facility. *Contacts:* Lesley Ford, Manager Human Resources Services or Jane Dawes, Director Human Resources.

KINGSTON GENERAL HOSPITAL
76 Stuart Street
Kingston, ON K7L 2V7

Tel. 613-549-6666 x4200
Fax 613-548-1334
Email .... kghhr@kgh.kari.net
Website .... www.kgh.kari.net

Kingston General Hospital is a 446-bed teaching hospital affiliated with Queen's University. The hospital employs 2,600 people in the provision of critical care, trauma care, in-patient overnight stays, a full-service 24-hour emergency department and specialized programs and services. Graduates most likely to be hired come from the following academic areas: Bachelor of Science (Nursing) and Community College Diploma (Secretarial, Dietitian/ Nutrition, Health/Home Care Aide, Laboratory Technician, Nursing RN, Radiology, Rehabilitation Therapy, Respiratory Therapy, Social Worker/DSW, Ultra-Sound Technician. Graduates would occupy Registered Nurse, Social Worker, Respiratory Therapist, Health Care Aide, Lab Technician, etc. positions. Strong interpersonal skills and good problem solving and decision making abilities are all listed as desirable non-academic qualifications. Company benefits are rated above average. The potential for advancement is listed as being good. The average annual starting salary falls within the $30,000 to $35,000 range. The most suitable methods for initial contact by those seeking employment are to mail or fax a resume with a covering letter. Kingston General Hospital does hire summer students. *Contacts:* Hazel Gilchrist, Human Resources Consultant, Employment or Katherine Rudder, Human Resources Consultant, Employment.

KINKO'S CANADA
459 Bloor Street West, 2nd Floor
Toronto, ON M5R 1X9

Tel. 416-928-2745
Fax 416-928-2224
Email .... shelinas@kinkos.ca
Website .... www.kinkos.com

Kinko's Canada utilizes state-of-the-art technology to provide total document management solutions to its corporate and general clients across Canada. Kinko's Canada provides its customers with the most advanced communication tools and equipment available. Kinko's brand name and impressive service reputation has led to exceptional growth across the country. Worldwide, Kinko's operates operates 1,000 branch locations and has 20,000 employees. Graduates most likely to be hired come from the following academic areas: Bachelor of Arts (General), Bachelor of Commerce/Business Administration (General, Accounting, Human Resources, Information Systems), Master of Business Administration and Community College Diploma (Business, Human Resources, Office Administration, Graphic Arts, Computer Science). Graduates would occupy Computer Services Consultant, Corporate Account Manager, Branch Manager and Office Assistant positions. Team player, previous work experience and an excellent work ethic are all listed as desirable non-academic qualifications. Company benefits and the potential for advancement are both rated as excellent. The most suitable methods for initial contact by those seeking employment are to mail or fax a resume with a covering letter. Kinko's Canada does hire co-op work term students. *Contact:* Human Resources.

KIPLING ACRES HOME FOR THE AGED
2233 Kipling Avenue North
Toronto, ON M9W 4L3

Tel. 416-392-2300
Fax 416-392-3360

Kipling Acres Home for the Aged is a non-profit home for seniors run by the City of Toronto. The home provides a wide range of services for 335 residents in the home, and for nearly 200 seniors in the surrounding community. Kipling Acres employs approximately 450 full and part-time staff in the following departments: administration, social work, recreation, dietary, nursing, housekeeping, maintenance, rehabilitation, and staff development. Graduates most likely to be hired come from the following academic areas: Bachelor of Arts (Fine Arts, Psychology, Recreation Studies, Social Work, Gerontology), Bachelor of Science (Health Sciences, Nursing, Psychology), Bachelor of Commerce/Business Administration, Master of Arts (Social Work), Master of Science (Health Care Administration, Nursing, Dietary), Community College Diploma (Accounting, Facility Management, Cooking, Human Resources, Recreation, Social Work, Food/Nutrition, RN, RNA) and High School Diploma. Company benefits are rated as excellent. The potential for advancement is listed as being good. The average annual starting salary falls within the $25,000 to $30,000 range. The most suitable methods for initial contact by those seeking employment are to mail a resume with a covering letter, or by applying in person at this address. *Contact:* Personnel Department.

KITCHENER, CITY OF
200 King Street
Kitchener, ON N2G 4G7

Tel. 519-741-2260
Fax 519-741-2400
Email .... humres@city.kitchener.on.ca
Website .... www.city.kitchener.on.ca

The City of Kitchener provides municipal government services. Service operations are divided into seven departments, including: Corporate Services, City Clerk's and Chief Administrator's Office, Finance, Fire, Legal, Parks and Recreation, Business and Planning Services, and Public Works. The City Council consists of a Mayor and ten Ward Councillors who are responsible for the overall management of the City of Kitchener. The city employs 1,600 full time staff and approximately 600 part time/contract/student/temporary staff. Graduates most likely to be hired come from the following academic areas: Bachelor of Arts (Economics, Geography, Political Science, Recreation Studies, Urban Geography/Planning), Bachelor of Science (General, Computer Science, Environment/Ecology, Forestry, Geography, Mathematics), Bachelor of Engineering (Civil, Computer Systems, Environmental/Resources, Forest Resources, Surveying, Transportation), Bachelor of Landscape Architecture, Bachelor of Education (Special Needs), Bachelor of Laws, Bachelor of Commerce/Business Administration (General, Accounting, Finance, Human Resources, Information Systems, Marketing, Public Administration), Chartered Accountant, Certified Management Accountant, Certified General Accountant, Community College Diploma (Accounting, Business, Communications/Public Relations, Facility Management, Human Resources, Marketing/Sales, Office Administration, Purchasing/Logistics, Secretarial, Graphic Arts, Legal Assistant, Recreation Studies, Security/Enforcement, Urban Planning, Automotive Mechanic, Architectural Technician, CAD/CAM/Autocad, Carpentry, Computer Science, Electronics Technician, Engineering Technician, Forestry, HVAC Systems, Information Systems, Plumbing, Welding) and High School Diploma. Team player, creative thinker, dependable, flexible, positive attitude and a strong work ethic are all listed as desirable non-academic qualifications. Company benefits are rated as industry standard. The potential for advancement is listed as being good. The average annual starting salary falls within the $25,000 to $30,000 range. The most suitable methods for initial contact by those seeking employment are to mail, fax or e-mail a resume with a covering letter. The City of Kitchener does hire summer and co-op work term students. *Contact:* Human Resources.

KLAY INFORMATION MANAGEMENT CONSULTING LTD.

840 - 7th Avenue SW, Suite 1420
Calgary, AB T2P 3G2

Tel. 403-263-6463
Fax 403-263-6537
Email .... human.resources@kimc.com
Website .... www.kimc.com

Klay Information Management Consulting Ltd. provides a broad range of IT services ranging from from strategic planning to implementation, design and development and support and management. The company employs a total of 27 people in Canada. Graduates most likely to be hired come from the following academic areas: Bachelor of Science (General, Computer Science), Bachelor of Engineering (Computer Systems), Bachelor of Commerce/Business Administration (Information Systems, Marketing) and Community College Diploma (CAD/CAM/Autocad, Computer Animation, Computer Science, Engineering Technician, Information Systems). Graduates would occupy Junior Programmer, Junior Developer, Systems Analyst, Network Administrator and Technical Support positions. Integrity, attitude, team player, leadership qualities and a high level of confidence are all listed as desirable non-academic qualifications. Company benefits are rated above average. The potential for advancement is listed as being excellent. The average annual starting salary falls within the $35,000 to $40,000 range.

The most suitable methods for initial contact by those seeking employment are to mail, fax or e-mail a resume with a covering letter. *Contact:* Human Resources Department.

KLOCKNER STADLER HURTER LTD.

1400, rue du Fort, Bureau 900
Montreal, QC H3H 2T1

Tel. 514-932-4611
Fax 514-932-9700
Email .... hressources@ksh.ca

Klockner Stadler Hurter Ltd. is involved in the design and supply of pulp and paper mills and other industrial plants in Canada and internationally. The company employs 360 people. Graduates most likely to be hired come from the following academic areas: Bachelor of Engineering (Pollution Treatment, Pulp and Paper, Civil, Electrical, Instrumentation, Mechanical) and Community College Diploma (CAD/CAM/Autocad, Engineering Technician, HVAC Systems Technician). Bachelor of Engineering graduates would occupy Junior Engineer and Junior Specialist positions. Technical Diploma graduates would occupy Technician and Drafting positions. Company benefits are rated as excellent. The potential for advancement is listed as being good. The average annual starting salary for Technicians falls within the $20,000 to $25,000 range. The starting salary for Bachelor of Engineering graduates falls within the $30,000 to $35,000 range. The most suitable method for initial contact by those seeking employment is to mail a resume with a covering letter. *Contact:* Peter Almeida, Vice-President, Human Resources.

KNOLL NORTH AMERICA CORP.

1000 Arrow Road
Toronto, ON M9M 2Y7

Tel. 416-741-5453
Fax 416-741-7568
Website .... www.knoll.com

Knoll North America Corp. is a manufacturer of high end wood office furniture. Publicly traded on the New York Stock Exchange, Knoll's head office is located in East Greenville, Pennsylvania. The company operates three plants in Toronto with 75% of its production being exported to the United States. There are 950 employees at this location, a total of 1,000 employees in Canada and a total of 4,800 employees worldwide. Graduates most likely to be hired come from the following academic areas: Bachelor of Science (Wood Products Processing), Bachelor of Engineering (General, Chemical, Electrical, Mechanical, Automation/Robotics, Industrial Design, Industrial Engineering, Industrial Production/Manufacturing), Community College Diploma (Accounting, Human Resources, Purchasing/Logistics, Carpentry, Tool and Die/Machinist, Welding) and High School Diploma. Graduates would occupy Accounting, Management, and Technical positions in Plant Operations and Plant Support. A high energy level, enthusiasm, common sense, drive, initiative, decision making abilities and good communication skills are all listed as desirable non-academic qualifications. Company benefits are rated above average. The potential for advancement is listed as excellent. The average annual starting salary falls within the $40,000 to $45,000 range. The most suitable method for initial contact by those seeking employment is to fax a resume with a covering letter. Knoll North America Corp. does hire summer and co-op work term students. *Contact:* Human Resources.

KNOWLEDGE POWER INCORPORATED / KPI

34 Pippy Place, Suite 201
TAS Communications Building
St. John's, NF A1B 3X5

Tel.	709-726-8866
Fax	709-726-8868
Email	kpi@knowledgepower.com
Website	www.knowledgepower.com

Knowledge Power Incorporated / KPI is an information management and technology consulting firm providing information technology skills and services to organizations in the public and private sector. Services offered include marketing consulting for IT resource contracting services, IT training, and IT consulting. KPI offers the latest in technology skills to help its customers become more productive, efficient and effective. KPI employs a total of 12 professionals. Graduates most likely to be hired come from the following academic areas: Bachelor of Science (General, Computer Science, Mathematics), Bachelor of Engineering (Computer Systems, Instrumentation), Bachelor of Commerce/Business Administration (General, Information Systems, Marketing), Master of Business Administration (General, Information Systems) and Community College Diploma (Information Systems, CAD/CAM/Autocad, Computer Science). Graduates would occupy Junior Programmer, Programmer and Technical Support positions. Good written and oral communication skills, team player and self starter are all listed as desirable non-academic qualifications. Company benefits are rated as industry standard. The potential for advancement is listed as excellent. The average annual starting salary falls within the $30,000 to $35,000 range. The most suitable method for initial contact by those seeking employment is to e-mail a resume with a covering letter. Knowledge Power Incorporated does hire summer and co-op work term students. *Contact:* Human Resources.

KODAK CANADA INC.

3500 Eglinton Avenue West
Toronto, ON M6M 1V3

Tel.	416-766-8233
Fax	416-760-4462
Website	www.kodak.ca

Kodak Canada Inc. is Canada's only major manufacturer of photographic products and the leading supplier of business imaging products for commercial, industrial, government and health care markets. Kodak Canada Inc. is a subsidiary of Rochester, New York based Eastman Kodak Company. The company ranks as one of the 25 largest companies in the United States and employs 80,000 people worldwide. In 1999, Kodak Canada Inc. marked its 100th anniversary of operations in Canada. In addition to the head office location in Toronto, the company has offices in Montreal, Ottawa and Vancouver. Kodak Canada Inc. employs 1,200 people at this location and a total of 1,500 people in Canada. Graduates most likely to be hired come from the following academic areas: Bachelor of Science (General, Chemistry, Computer Science, Health Sciences), Bachelor of Engineering (General, Chemical, Electrical, Industrial, Mechanical), Bachelor of Commerce/Business Administration (Finance, Marketing), Master of Business Administration (Finance, Marketing), Community College Diploma (Accounting, Administration, Business, Electronics Technician) and High School Diploma. Graduates would occupy Service Technician, Financial Analyst, Systems Analyst, Chemical Engineer, Electrical Engineer, Industrial Engineer, Mechanical Engineer, Sales and Marketing, Manufacturing and Clerical positions. Possessing directly related work experience for the specific position is listed as a desirable non-academic qualification. Company benefits are rated above average. The potential for advancement is listed as being good. The average annual starting salary falls within the $25,000 to $35,000 range. The most suitable methods for initial contact by those seeking employment are to mail or fax a resume with a covering letter, or via the company's website. Kodak Canada Inc. does hire summer and co-op work term students. *Contact:* Mr. F.R. Fries, Human Resource Services.

KPMG

Suite 3300, Commerce Court West
PO Box 31, Station Commerce Court
Toronto, ON M5L 1B2

Tel.	416-777-8500
Fax	416-777-3286
Website	www.kpmg.ca

KPMG provides accounting, bookkeeping and related services to individuals and organizations. In Canada, practice areas include audit, tax, computer audit, forensics, solvency services, valuations/mergers and acquisitions and management consulting. In addition to maintaining offices across Canada, KPMG International maintains a global presence with more than 92,000 people collaborating worldwide, providing consulting, tax and legal, financial advisory and assurance services from 825 locations in 157 countries. KPMG Canada employs more than 500 people at this location. Graduates most likely to be hired come from the following academic areas: Bachelor of Arts (Economics, Business Related), Bachelor of Laws, Bachelor of Commerce/Business Administration (Accounting, Finance), Chartered Accountant, Master of Business Administration (Accounting), Master of Arts (Economics) and Community College Diploma (Accounting). Business and people oriented work experience, good interpersonal and communication skills and extra-curricular involvement are all listed as desirable non-academic qualifications. Company benefits and the potential for advancement are both rated as excellent. The average annual starting salary falls within the $25,000 to $30,000 range. The most suitable method for initial contact by those seeking employment is to mail a resume with a covering letter. KPMG does hire a limited number of summer students annually (traditionally summer is not the busiest season). *Contact:* Manager, Human Resources.

KRUG INC.

421 Manitou Drive
Kitchener, ON N2C 1L5

Tel.	519-748-5100
Fax	519-748-5177
Email	careers@krug.ca
Website	www.krug.ca

Krug Inc. is a leading furniture manufacturer. Krug employs 240 people at this location and an additional 140 people at locations in Stratford and Kitchener (Ahrens Street). Graduates most likely to be hired come from the following academic areas: Bachelor of Arts (General, Psychology), Bachelor of Engineering (Industrial Design, Industrial Engineering), Bachelor of Commerce/Business Administration (Human Resources, Marketing), Community College Diploma (Accounting, Human Resources, Marketing/Sales, Office Administration, Materials Management, Woodworking/Carpentry, CAD/CAM/Autocad, Computer Science, Information Systems) and High School Diploma. Graduates would occupy Marketing Coordinator, Information Services Technician/Administrator, Human Resources Administrator/Coordinator, Product Engineer (Autocad), Industrial Engineer, Maintenance Millwright and Woodworking Technician positions. A high level of emotional intelligence, team player and previous manufacturing experience are all listed as desirable non-academic qualifications. Company benefits are rated as above average. The potential for advancement is listed as being average. The average annual starting salary falls within the $30,000 to $35,000 range. The most suitable methods for initial contact by those seeking employment are to mail, fax or e-mail a resume with a covering letter. Krug Inc. does hire summer and co-op work term students. *Contacts:* Carolyn Hoffman, Human Resources Coordinator or Jennifer Horne, Human Resources Manager.

KUEHNE & NAGEL INTERNATIONAL LTD.
5935 Airport Road
Mississauga, ON L4V 1X3

Tel.	905-673-3981
Fax	905-673-0006
Website	www.kuehne-nagel.com

Kuehne & Nagel International Ltd. is a international transportation and logistics company active in freight forwarding, international logistics, customs brokerage, warehousing and distribution services. There are 200 employees at this location, a total of 1,000 employees in Canada, and 12,000 employees worldwide. Graduates most likely to be hired come from the following academic areas: Bachelor of Arts (General), Bachelor of Commerce/Business Administration (General, International Business), Community College Diploma (International Business, Purchasing/Logistics) and C.I.F.F.A., C.S.C.B., P.LOG. accreditations. Graduates would occupy Trainee/Apprentice, Clerk, Customer Service Representative and Sales Support positions. Good communication and problem solving skills, fluency in foreign languages (Spanish in particular) and previous experience in international freight movement are all listed as desirable non-academic qualifications. Company benefits and the potential for advancement are both rated as excellent. The average annual starting salary falls within the $20,000 to $25,000 range. The most suitable method for initial contact by those seeking employment is to mail a resume with a covering letter. Kuehne & Nagel International Ltd. does hire summer students. *Contacts:* Cathy Bilotta, Manager, Human Resources - Head Office or Ray Getson, Manager, Human Resources - KN Logistics.

LABELAD / SANDYLION STICKER DESIGNS
400 Cochrane Drive
Markham, ON L3R 8E3

Tel.	905-943-6623
Fax	905-943-6672
Email	esmith@labelad.com
Website	www.sandylion.com

Labelad / Sandylion Sticker Designs is a leader in the design, manufacturing and marketing of pressure-sensitive labels and novelty stickers. Founded in 1976, Labelad is a world-class manufacturer and supplier of pressure sensitive labels, offering innovative solutions for product promotion and packaging requirements. Labelad's client list, which includes many of the leading Fortune 500 companies, reflects the company's reputation for excellence. Labelad consistently works to the stringent printing specifications and service requirements of the food and beverage, pharmaceutical, personal care and consumer products industries. Founded in 1981, Sandylion is one of the world's leading sticker designers and manufacturers with over 1,000 sticker products and one of the world's most dynamic licensed sticker collections. The company serves the gift, stationery, craft, toy and educational markets in more than 50 countries worldwide. Labelad/Sandylion Sticker Designs employs a total of 376 people. Graduates most likely to be hired come from the following academic areas: Bachelor of Arts (General), Bachelor of Science (General, Computer Science), Bachelor of Engineering (Computer Systems), Bachelor of Commerce/Business Administration (General, Accounting, Finance, Human Resources, Information Systems, Marketing), Chartered Accountant, Certified Management Accountant, Certified General Accountant, Master of Business Administration (General, Accounting, Finance, Information Systems, Marketing), Community College Diploma (Accounting, Business, Human Resources, Marketing/Sales, Office Administration, Purchasing/Logistics, Secretarial, Graphic Arts, Computer Science, Information Systems, Tool and Die/Machinist) and High School Diploma. Graduates would occupy various entry level positions related directly to education, such as Human Resources Assistant, Marketing Clerk, Accounting Clerk and various IT positions. An entrepreneurial spirit, team oriented, independent work habits, creative and good people skills are all listed as desirable non-academic qualifications. Company benefits are rated as industry standard. The potential for advancement is listed as being good. The average annual starting salary falls within the $20,000 to $25,000 range. The most suitable method for initial contact by those seeking employment is to fax a resume with a covering letter. Labelad/Sandylion Sticker Designs does hire summer and co-op work term students. *Contact:* Elaine Cruise Smith, Human Resources Coordinator.

LAIDLAW INC.
3221 North Service Road, PO Box 5028
Burlington, ON L7R 3Y8

Tel.	905-336-1800
Fax	905-336-3900
Email	dblock@laidlaw.com
Website	www.laidlaw.com

Laidlaw Inc. is a leading North American service company providing school busing, public transit, emergency and non-emergency healthcare transportation, and the management of physician's practices within hospital emergency departments. Laidlaw's 94,500 employees operate from more than 900 locations throughout the United States and Canada. There are 150 employees at this location and a total of 9,500 employees in Canada. Laidlaw is dedicated to delivering predictable and growing returns to its shareholders. The company has grown through acquisition, by improving its operations, and by gaining new customers. Graduates most likely to be hired come from the following academic areas: Bachelor of Science (Computer Science), Bachelor of Commerce/Business Administration (Accounting, Finance, Human Resources, Information Systems), Chartered Accountant, Certified Management Accountant, Certified General Accountant, Master of Business Administration (Accounting, Finance), Community College Diploma (Accounting, Business, Communications/Public Relations, Human Resources, Information Systems, Secretarial, Legal Assistant, Computer Science, Ambulance/Emergency Care) and High School Diploma. Graduates would occupy Clerk, Accountant, Secretary, Computer Programmer, Systems Analyst, Business Analyst and Sales Representative positions. Previous related work experience, good oral and written communication skills, adaptable to change, team player, computer skills and an ability to think strategically are all listed as desirable non-academic qualifications. Company benefits are rated as industry standard. The potential for advancement is listed as average. The most suitable method for initial contact by those seeking employment is to mail a resume with a covering letter. Laidlaw Inc. does hire summer and co-op work term students, generally in the finance and tax department. *Contact:* Debbie Block, Manager, Human Resources.

LAKERIDGE HEALTH OSHAWA
1 Hospital Court
Oshawa, ON L1G 2B9

Tel.	905-576-8711
Fax	905-436-0193
Email	ctarrant@durham.net
Website	www.lakeridgehealth.on.ca

Lakeridge Health Oshawa is one of the busiest acute care community hospitals in Ontario responding to 70,000 emergency visits and over 20,000 surgeries a year. The hospital also delivers addiction services through Pinewood Centre programs throughout Durham Region, is the site of regional dialysis services, and provides comprehensive genetics, cancer, laboratory, diagnostic imaging, rehabilitation and base hospital/advanced life support services. Formerly the Oshawa General Hospital, the hospital merged in 1998 with Memorial Hospital Bowmanville, Port Perry Hospital, Uxbridge Hospital and Whitby General Hospital to form the Lakeridge Hospital Corporation. Lakeridge Health Corporation is one of the largest community hospitals in Ontario, serving over 500,000 residents and employing over 3,500 staff and physicians. Lakeridge Health Oshawa employs approximately 2,300 people. Graduates most likely to be hired come from the following academic areas: Bachelor of Arts (Social Work), Bachelor of Science (Nursing, Nutritional Sciences, Occupational Therapy, Pharmacy, Physical Therapy, Psychology, Speech Pathology), Bachelor of Engineering (Architectural/Building, Biomedical Electronics, Computer Systems), Chartered Accountant, Certified General Accountant, Master of Arts (Social Work), Master of Science (Nursing, Nutritional Sciences, Occupational Therapy, Pharmacy, Physical Therapy, Psychology, Speech Pathology) and Community College Diploma (Accounting, Human Resources, Purchasing/Logistics, Secretarial, Recreation Studies, Computer Science, Electronics Technician, HVAC Systems, Laboratory Technician, Nuclear Medicine Technician, Nursing RN/RNA, Radiology Technician, Respiratory Therapy, Ultrasound Technician). Excellent communication, interpersonal, organizational and written skills and computer literacy are all listed as desirable non-academic qualifications. Employee benefits are rated above average. The potential for advancement is listed as being good. The most suitable method for initial contact by those seeking employment is to mail a resume with a covering letter. *Contact:* Human Resources.

LAMBERT SOMEC INC.
1505 des Tanneurs
Quebec, QC G1N 4S7

Tel.	418-687-1640
Fax	418-688-7577

Lambert Somec Inc. is a specialized construction contractor providing electrical, plumbing, piping, HVAC and industrial mechanical services. The company employs approximately 400 people. Graduates most likely to be

hired come from the following academic areas: Bachelor of Science (Metallurgy, Physics), Bachelor of Engineering (General, Metallurgy, Pulp and Paper, Electrical, Instrumentation, Hydro-Power, Mechanical, Welding, Petroleum), Bachelor of Commerce/Business Administration, Chartered Accountant, Certified Management Accountant and Community College Diploma (Engineering Technician, HVAC Systems Technician, Welding). Work experience in the construction field, good team work habits and a willingness to learn are all listed as desirable non-academic qualifications. Company benefits are rated above average. The potential for advancement is listed as average. The average annual starting salary falls within the $25,000 to $30,000 range. The most suitable methods for initial contact by those seeking employment are to mail a resume with a covering letter, or through personal contacts. Lambert Somec Inc. does hire summer students. *Contact:* Human Resource Director.

LAMSON & SESSIONS OF CANADA LIMITED
5190 Bradco Boulevard
Mississauga, ON L4W 1G7

Tel.	905-624-4490
Fax	905-624-6195
Website	www.lamson-sessions.com

Lamson & Sessions of Canada Limited is involved in the manufacture and sale of industrial fasteners to the automotive industry. Lamson & Sessions of Canada Limited is a subsidiary of Cleveland, Ohio based Lamson & Sessions Co. The company is an industry-leading manufacturer and leading marketer of thermoplastic enclosures, fittings, conduit and pipe, and wiring devices for the electrical, construction, consumer, power and communications markets, and large diameter pipe for the waste-water markets. Lamson & Sessions of Canada Limited employs more than 50 people at this location. Graduates most likely to be hired are Community College graduates from Engineering Technology programs. Graduates would occupy Technician, Engineer and Manager positions. Able to translate theory into practical applications, independently motivated requiring no strong supervision, and good problem solving and supervisory skills are all listed as desirable non-academic qualifications. Company benefits are rated above average. The potential for advancement is listed as average. The most suitable method for initial contact by those seeking employment is to mail a resume with a covering letter. Lamson & Sessions of Canada Limited does hire summer students as required. *Contact:* Mr. C.L. Dahl, General Manager.

LANZAROTTA WHOLESALE GROCERS LTD.
10 Ronrose Drive
Concord, ON L4K 4R3

Tel.	905-669-9814
Fax	905-669-9570
Email	roberts@lanzarotta.com
Website	www.lanzarotta.com

Lanzarotta Wholesale Grocers Ltd. is a privately owned, wholesale grocery distributor of dry goods and frozen foods, including dairy products. Operating within Ontario are six cash and carry locations, five in Toronto and one in Barrie. Lanzarotta's main customers are independent grocers and grocery chains. There are approximately 150 employees at this location and a total of 365 employees in the company. Graduates most likely to be hired come from the following academic areas: Bachelor of Commerce/Business Administration (General, Accounting, Finance, Human Resources, Information Systems,

Marketing), Community College Diploma (Accounting, Administration, Business, Human Resources, Marketing/ Sales, Purchasing/Logistics) and High School Diploma. Graduates would occupy Accounts Payable Clerk, Accounts Receivable Clerk, Human Resources Assistant, Payroll Clerk, Data Entry Clerk, Accounting Clerk, Secretary/Receptionist, Customer Service Representative, Junior Buyer, Buyer, Administrative Assistant, Order Selector, Stock Clerk, Store Manager, Assistant Manager, and Grocery Manager positions. A positive attitude towards work, good interpersonal and communication skills, team player, organized, good problem solver and decision maker, related work experience and a willingness to learn and adapt to change are all listed as desirable non-academic qualifications. Company benefits are rated as industry standard. The potential for advancement is listed as average. The average annual starting salary falls within the $25,000 to $30,000 range. The most suitable methods for initial contact by those seeking employment are to mail or fax a resume with a covering letter. Lanzarotta Wholesale Grocers Ltd. does hire summer and co-op work term students. Summer students are hired at the cash and carry locations (check your white/yellow pages for the nearest location). *Contact:* Robert Santobuono, Human Resources Supervisor.

LAURA SECORD
1500 Birchmount Road
Toronto, ON M1P 2G5

Tel. 416-285-2505
Fax 416-751-8976
Email .... hr.birchmount@ca.nestle.com

Laura Secord is involved in the manufacturing and retailing of confectionery products. There are 300 employees at this location and a total of 2,500 employees across Canada. Graduates most likely to be hired come from the following academic areas: Bachelor of Arts (General), Bachelor of Science (General), Bachelor of Commerce/ Business Administration (Accounting, Finance, Human Resources, Information Systems, Marketing), Certified General Accountant and Community College Diploma (Accounting, Administration, Advertising, Business, Communications, Facility Management, Human Resources, Marketing/Sales, Purchasing/Logistics, Secretarial, Computer Science, Dietician/Nutrition, Laboratory Technician, Nursing RN). Good communication skills, leadership abilities and problem solving skills are all listed as desirable non-academic qualifications. Company benefits and the potential for advancement are both rated as excellent. The average annual starting salary falls within the $20,000 to $30,000 range. The most suitable methods for initial contact by those seeking employment are to mail or e-mail a resume with a covering letter. Laura Secord does hire a limited number of summer and co-op work term students. *Contacts:* Jo-Ann Latham, Human Resources Manager (Factory) or Rob Takimoto, Human Resources Manager (Office & Retail).

LAURENTIAN BANK OF CANADA
130 Adelaide Street West, 3rd Floor
Toronto, ON M5H 3P5

Tel. 416-947-5100
Fax 416-947-7442
Website .... www.laurentianbank.com

Laurentian Bank of Canada is a full service financial institution operating 256 branches and serving over one million customers. In business for over 150 years, the bank offers consumer banking products including deposit ac-

counts, GIC's, RRSP's, mutual funds, personal loans, mortgages and lines of credit. Laurentian's head office is located in Montreal. There are more than 25 employees at this location. Graduates most likely to be hired come from the following academic areas: Bachelor of Arts (Economics), Bachelor of Science (Computer Science, Mathematics), Bachelor of Commerce/Business Administration (Accounting, Marketing), Master of Business Administration and Community College Diploma (Accounting, Administration, Business, Communications, Marketing/Sales, Secretarial). A professional attitude and appearance, sales and marketing orientation and a quality customer service orientation are all listed as desirable non-academic qualifications. Graduates would occupy entry level Customer Service Representative positions, with the Management Training Program available after one year of service. Company benefits are rated above average. The potential for advancement is listed as being good. The average annual starting salary falls within the $20,000 to $30,000 range. The most suitable method for initial contact by those seeking employment is to mail a resume with a covering letter (no telephone calls please). Laurentian Bank of Canada does hire summer students. *Contact:* Cindy Gunderson, Human Resources.

LE CHATEAU
5695 Ferrier
Montreal, QC H4P 1N1

Tel. 514-738-7000
Fax 514-738-8288
Website .... www.lechateau.ca

Le Chateau is a leading retailer of apparel, accessories and footwear aimed at young spirited, fashion conscious men, women and kids. It is the company's vertically integrated approach, combined with its design strength, this gives Le Chateau a competitive edge and allows it to maintain its brand appeal in a rapidly changing market. The company's brand name clothing is sold mainly through its 150 retail stores. Stores average 3,000 square feet in size, and all are located in Canada with the exception of three which are located in the United States. The company is committed to research, design and product development, and manufactures approximately 65% of its goods in its own Canadian production facilities, located at the head office in Montreal. Le Château employs 300 people at this location and a total of 2,000 people. Graduates most likely to be hired come from the following academic areas: Bachelor of Commerce/Business Administration (Accounting), Community College Diploma (Fashion Arts, Graphic Arts, Computer Science) and High School Diploma. Enthusiastic, a high energy level and hard working are listed as desirable non-academic qualifications. Company benefits are rated as industry standard. The potential for advancement is listed as being very good. The most suitable method for initial contact by those seeking employment is to fax a resume with a covering letter. Le Chateau does hire summer students. *Contacts:* Coleen Main, Human Resources Director or Nicole Fortier, Human Resources Manager.

LEADER-POST, THE
1964 Park Street, PO Box 2020
Regina, SK S4P 3G4

Tel. 306-565-8211
Fax 306-565-7484
Website .... www.leader-post.sk.ca

The Leader-Post publishes Regina's daily newspaper and through Leader-Post Commercial Print, the company is one of the largest cold web printing suppliers in western Canada. Printing services range from creative to pre-press and platemaking, to pressroom and distribution. Printing capabilities include broadsheet and tabloid flyers, large and digest-size catalogues, TV book pony tabs, telephone directories, and large and small volume press runs. The Leader-Post employs approximately 400 people. Graduates most likely to be hired come from the following academic areas: Bachelor of Arts (English, Journalism, Political Science), Bachelor of Science (Computer Science), Bachelor of Engineering (Computer Systems), Bachelor of Commerce/Business Administration (Accounting), Certified Management Accountant and Community College Diploma (Accounting, Advertising, Marketing/Sales, Secretarial, Graphic Arts, Journalism, Computer Science, Electronics Technician, Engineering Technician). Good oral and written communications skills, flexibility, leadership potential, experience, attitude and focused personal objectives are all listed as desirable non academic qualifications. Company benefits are rated as excellent. The potential for advancement is listed as being good. The average entry level starting salary falls within the $20,000 range, and is commission based for some positions. The most suitable method for initial contact by those seeking employment is to mail a resume with a covering letter. The Leader-Post hires 4 month journalism interns twice a year. Also, the paper has contract positions that may become available during the summer months. *Contact:* Ms. J. Dockham, Human Resources Manager.

LEGO CANADA INC.
380 Markland Street
Markham, ON L6C 1T6

Tel. 905-887-5346
Fax 905-887-1171
Website .... www.lego.com

LEGO Canada Inc. is involved in the distribution of construction toys. There are 70 employees at this location, a total of 115 in Canada and a total of 10,000 employees worldwide. Graduates most likely to be hired come from the following academic areas: Bachelor of Arts (General), Bachelor of Science (General, Computer Science), Bachelor of Commerce/Business Administration (Accounting, Finance, Human Resources, Information Systems, Marketing), Chartered Accountant, Certified General Accountant and Community College Diploma (Accounting, Administration, Business, Human Resources, Marketing/Sales, Computer Science). Graduates would occupy Sales Planning Analyst, Credit Representative, Accountant, Programmer/Analyst, Consumer Services Representative and Assistant Brand Manager positions. Team player, able to work in fast paced environment, self-motivated, energetic and detail oriented are all listed as desirable non-academic qualifications. Company benefits are rated as excellent. The most suitable method for initial contact by those seeking employment is to mail a resume with a covering letter. LEGO Canada Inc. hires summer students for the LEGO Creative Play Centre at Ontario Place in Toronto. *Contact:* Wendy LaValle, Human Resources Manager.

LEHNDORFF TANDEM MANAGEMENT INC.
390 Bay Street
Toronto, ON M5H 2Y2

Tel. 416-869-0656
Fax 416-869-7851

Lehndorff Tandem Management Inc. is a real estate development company. Activities include, property management, real estate investment, risk management, asset management, development, re-development, syndication and mutual fund management. The company employs approximately 80 staff at this location and a total of 280 employees across Canada. Graduates most likely to be hired come from the following academic areas: Bachelor of Engineering (Computer Systems, Mechanical), Bachelor of Laws (Corporate), Bachelor of Commerce/Business Administration (Accounting, Finance, Human Resources, Information Systems), Chartered Accountant, Certified Management Accountant, Certified General Accountant, Community College Diploma (Accounting, Administration, Business, Human Resources, Insurance, Secretarial, Computer Science, HVAC Systems) and High School Diploma. Graduates would be hired to occupy Managerial, Clerical, Technical, Secretarial and Administrative positions. Related work experience, team player, positive work attitude, professionalism and good problem solving skills are all listed as desirable non-academic qualifications. Company benefits are rated above average. The potential for advancement is listed as average. The average annual starting salary falls within the $30,000 to $35,000 range. The most suitable method for initial contact by those seeking employment is to mail a resume with a covering letter. Lehndorff Tandem Management Inc. does hire summer students. *Contact:* Michelle Ziegler, Manager, Human Resources.

LENNOX INDUSTRIES (CANADA) LTD.
400 Norris Glen Road
Toronto, ON M9C 1H5

Tel. 416-621-9302
Fax 416-621-6303
Email .... employment.services@lennoxind.com
Website .... www.davelennox.com

Lennox Industries (Canada) Ltd. is an ISO 9000 certified world-class manufacturer of high quality heating, ventilation and air conditioning products. The corporate head office is located in Dallas, Texas. Sales and distribution districts are located throughout Canada in most major cities. There are more than 150 employees at the Canadian head office located in Toronto. Graduates most likely to be hired come from the following academic areas: Bachelor of Arts (General, Psychology), Bachelor of Science (Computer Science, Psychology), Bachelor of Engineering (Mechanical, Industrial), Bachelor of Commerce/Business Administration (General, Accounting, Finance), Chartered Accountant, Certified Management Accountant, Certified General Accountant (Finance), Master of Engineering and Community College Diploma (Administration, Marketing/Sales, HVAC Systems, Industrial Design). An exciting blend of Technical and Administrative opportunities are available for graduates. Leadership potential, computer literacy, and good communication, interpersonal and organizational skills are all listed as desirable non-academic qualifications. Company benefits are rated above average. The potential for advancement is listed as being good. The average annual starting salary falls within the $30,000 to $35,000 range. The most suitable method for initial contact by those seeking employment is to mail a resume with a covering letter. *Contact:* Barbara Thornton, Human Resources Consultant.

LENWORTH METAL PRODUCTS LIMITED
275 Carrier Drive
Toronto, ON M9W 5Y8

Tel. 416-675-9390
Fax 416-675-6874

Email .... lenworth@spectranet.ca
Website .... www.lenworth.com

Lenworth Metal Products Limited manufactures custom and standard metal products for the material handling industry. In business for over 30 years, the company maintains 100,000 square ft. of working plant space with full production lines employing state of the art machinery. Graduates most likely to be hired come from the following academic areas: Bachelor of Engineering, Bachelor of Commerce/Bachelor Business Administration, Chartered Accountant and Certified Management Accountant. Graduates would occupy Office Manager, Controller, Quality Assurance and Drafting/Estimator positions. Aggressiveness, reliability, initiative, dedication and promptness are all listed as desirable non-academic qualifications. Company benefits are rated as industry standard. The potential for advancement is listed as being good. The average annual starting salary falls within the $20,000 to $25,000 range. The most suitable method for initial contact by graduates seeking employment is to mail a resume with a covering letter. Contact: Payroll Department.

LEVI STRAUSS & CO. (CANADA) INC.
1725 - 16th Avenue
Richmond Hill, ON L4B 4C6

Tel. 905-763-4400
Fax 905-763-4401
Website .... www.levistrauss.com

Levi Strauss & Co. (Canada) Inc. is the country's leading manufacturer and marketer of jeans and casual apparel with brand names such as Levi's and Dockers. Levi Strauss & Co. (Canada) Inc. is a subsidiary of San Francisco, California based Levi Strauss & Co. Inc. Founded in 1853, the company is one of the world's largest brand-name apparel marketers employing 35,000 people worldwide. Levi Strauss & Co. (Canada) Inc. employs approximately 250 people at this location and a total of 1,800 people in Canada. Graduates most likely to be hired come from the following academic areas: Bachelor of Arts (General), Bachelor of Science (Textiles), Bachelor of Commerce/Business Administration, Chartered Accountant, Certified Management Accountant, Certified General Accountant, Master of Business Administration, Community College Diploma (Accounting, Administration, Business, Human Resources, Marketing/Sales, Purchasing/Logistics, Secretarial, CAD/CAM/Autocad, HVAC Systems) and High School Diploma. Graduates would occupy various positions relating to their academic backgrounds. Team player and initiative are both listed as desirable non-academic qualifications. Company benefits are rated above average. The potential for advancement is listed as being good. The most suitable method for initial contact by those seeking employment is to mail a resume with a covering letter. Levi Strauss & Co. (Canada) Inc. does hire summer students. Contact: Human Resources Specialist.

LEVY PILOTTE, CHARTERED ACCOUNTANTS
5250 Decarie Blvd., 7th Floor
Montreal, QC H3X 3Z6

Tel. 514-487-1566
Fax 514-488-5145
Email .... rguirgui@levypilotte.com
Website .... www.levypilotte.com

Levy Pilotte, Chartered Accountants is a chartered accountancy firm. The firm employs approximately 45 people in Montreal. Graduates most likely to be hired come from the following academic areas: Bachelor of Commerce/Business Administration (Accounting, Information Systems), Chartered Accountant, Certified General Accountant, Master of Business Administration (Accounting) and Community College Diploma (Accounting). Graduates would occupy Audit Trainee and Junior Accountant positions. Team player, leadership qualities and previous accounting work experience are all listed as desirable non-academic qualifications. Company benefits are rated above average. The potential for advancement is listed as excellent. The average annual starting salary falls within the $25,000 to $30,000 range. The most suitable method for initial contact by those seeking employment is to fax a resume with a covering letter. Levy Pilotte, Chartered Accountants does hire students for summer and co-op work terms. Contacts: Raouf Guirguis, Partner or Nick Vannelli, Partner.

LGS GROUP INC.
1155 Metcalfe Street, 12th Floor
Montreal, QC H3B 2V6

Tel. 514-861-3835
Fax 514-877-4435
Email .... jbergeron@lgs.ca
Website .... www.lgs.com

LGS Group Inc. is one of Canada's leading systems integration firms, providing consulting in all aspects of information technology and management. The company's aim is to establish state-of-the-art solutions, adapted and suited to the business environments of its clients. LGS Group Inc. employs approximately 300 people at this location, a total of 1,100 people in Canada and a total of 1,200 people worldwide. Graduates most likely to be hired come from the following academic areas: Bachelor of Science (Computer Science, Mathematics), Bachelor of Engineering (Computer Systems), Master of Business Administration (Finance, Information Systems), Master of Science (Computer Science), Master of Engineering (Electrical, Computer Systems) and Doctorate (Information/Computer Systems). Graduates would occupy Programmer/Analyst, Technical Support Technician, Analyst and Technical Analyst. Excellent written and spoken and communication skills, and the practical application of academic courses are listed as desirable non-academic qualifications. Company benefits and the potential for advancement are both rated as excellent. The average annual starting salary falls within the $30,000 to $35,000 range. The most suitable method for initial contact by those seeking employment is to mail a resume with a covering letter. LGS Group Inc. does hire summer students. Contact: Lisa Gabrielle.

LICHTMAN'S NEWS AND BOOKS
24 Ryerson Avenue, Suite 400
Toronto, ON M5T 2P3

Tel. 416-703-7773
Fax 416-703-1078
Email .... lichtman@ican.net
Website .... www.lichtmans.com

Lichtman's News and Books is a Canadian owned and operated independent chain of bookstores that has been in business for over 75 years. Based in Toronto, the company has a tradition of providing its customers with both imported and domestic newspapers, magazines and books from around the world. Lichtman's features over 240 newspapers from around the world, 4,400 magazine titles and over 60,000 book titles. The company employs 13 people at its head office and a total of 165 people throughout the company. Graduates most likely to be hired come from the following academic areas: Bachelor of Arts (General) and Bachelor of Science (General). Graduates would occupy Management Trainee, Book Buyer, Operations Co-ordinator and Store Manager positions. An entrepreneurial spirit coupled with unparalleled customer service skills are listed as desirable non-academic qualifications. Company benefits are rated above average. The potential for advancement is listed as being good. The average annual starting salary falls within the $15,000 to $20,000 range. The most suitable method for initial contact by those seeking employment is to mail a resume with a covering letter. Lichtman's News and Books hires summer students for store positions. *Contact:* General Manager.

LILY CUPS INC.
2121 Markham Road
Toronto, ON M1B 2W3

Tel.	416-691-2181
Fax	416-691-3665

Lily Cups Inc. manufactures paper cups, polystyrene cups and food containers for the food service industry. Lily Cups Inc. is a leader within the industry on environmental issues. The company is committed to the concepts of waste reduction, reuse, recycling and recovery in the context of environmental stewardship. The company employs a total of 450 people. Graduates most likely to be hired come from the following academic areas: Bachelor of Science (Chemistry, Computer Science), Bachelor of Engineering (General), Bachelor of Commerce/Business Administration (Accounting, Finance, Information Systems, Marketing) and Community College Diploma (Accounting, Administration, Human Resources, Marketing/Sales, Secretarial). Graduates would occupy Laboratory Technician, Engineer, Junior and Intermediate Accountant, Human Resources Administration, Secretarial, and Junior Sales and Marketing positions. Applicants must be team players, organized, possess appropriate work experience, knowledge of Total Quality Management, and be able to work independently and manage pressure/deadline situations. Company benefits are rated above average. The potential for advancement is listed as being good. The average annual starting salary falls within the $25,000 to $30,000 range. The most suitable method for initial contact by those seeking employment is to mail a resume with a covering letter (no telephone calls please). Lily Cups does hire summer students for plant positions and occasionally for office positions, as well as occasionally hiring co-op work term students. *Contacts:* Diane Budd, Human Resources Co-ordinator (Salaried Personnel) or Suzanne Ruffo, Benefits Administrator (Hourly Personnel).

LINCOLN PLACE NURSING HOME
429 Walmer Road
Toronto, ON M5P 2X9

Tel.	416-967-6949
Fax	416-928-1965

Lincoln Place Nursing Home operates a nursing home for the aged. The home employs approximately 260 people. Graduates most likely to be hired come from the following academic areas: Bachelor of Arts (Music, Recreation Studies, Social Work), Bachelor of Science (Nursing, Nutritional Sciences, Occupational Therapy, Physical Therapy, Speech Pathology), Bachelor of Education (Adult), Bachelor of Commerce/Business Administration (Human Resources, Information Systems, Marketing,

Public Administration), Master of Business Administration (Human Resources, Information Systems, Marketing) and Community College Diploma (Recreation Studies, Health Promotion, Massage Therapy, Nursing RN/RNA, Social Work). Graduates would occupy Nurse, Nurses Aide, Music Therapist, Art Therapist, Recreational Therapist, Nurse Educator, Information Management Specialist, Nurse Manager and Health Promotion Therapist positions. Team player (very important), group skills, innovative problem solving skills and creativity are all listed as desirable non-academic qualifications. Company benefits are rated as industry standard. The potential for advancement is listed as average. The average annual starting salary falls within the $15,000 to $50,000 range, depending on the position being considered. The most suitable method for initial contact by those seeking employment is to mail a resume with a covering letter. *Contacts:* Tulia Ferreira, Administration or Nursing Department.

LINMOR TECHNOLOGIES INC.
177 Colonnade Road
Nepean, ON K2E 7J4

Tel.	613-727-2757
Fax	613-727-2627
Email	hr@linmor.com
Website	www.linmor.com

Linmor Technologies Inc. is a leading developer of network performance management, fault management, and customer network management systems for ATM, frame relay and IP data networks. Linmor's NEBULA product line provides network management solutions to the telecommunications and network service provider industries. NEBULA is widely renowned for its advanced architecture and high scalability. NEBULA's proactive approach to network management provides comprehensive solutions for web-based performance reporting and analysis, real-time fault monitoring of all network devices and applications, and intelligent, automated management of network resources. Linmor employs 30 people at this location and a total of 32 people worldwide. Graduates most likely to be hired come from the following academic areas: Bachelor of Science (Computer Science), Bachelor of Engineering (Computer Systems, Telecommunications), Master of Science (Computer Science) and Doctorate (Computer Science). Graduates would occupy Junior Software Developer, Junior Software Verification and Technical Support Analyst positions. Team player, work experience with C++ in Unix environment, Perl, ATM and Frame Relay and previous work experience with telecommunication or IP companies are listed as desirable non-academic qualifications. Company benefits are rated above average. The potential for advancement is listed as being excellent. The average annual starting salary falls within the $55,000 to $60,000 range. The most suitable methods for initial contact by those seeking employment are to e-mail a resume with a covering letter. Linmor Technologies Inc. does hire summer and co-op work term students. *Contact:* Michelle Graham, Manager, Human Resources.

LOCKHEED MARTIN CANADA INC.
6111 avenue Royalmount
Montreal, QC H4P 1K6

Tel.	514-340-8317
Fax	514-340-8314
Email	lmcda.hr@lmco.ca
Website	www.lmco.com/canada

Lockheed Martin Canada Inc. is a leader in systems integration, software development, and large-scale program management and Canada's premier supplier of electronic defence and sonar systems. The company has emerged as the leading naval supplier to Canada's Navy. Lockheed Martin Canada Inc. is a division of Lockheed Martin, headquartered in Bethesda, Maryland. The company is one of the world's leading diversified technology companies employing 190,000 people worldwide. The company researches, designs, develops, manufactures and integrates advanced technology systems, products, and services for government and commercial customers around the world. Core businesses span aeronautics, electronics, energy, information and services, space, systems integration and telecommunications. Lockheed Martin Canada Inc. employs 175 people at this location a total of 700 people in Canada. The company's head office is located in Kanata and supporting operations are located in Montreal (this location), Toronto, Halifax, Winnipeg and Victoria. Graduates most likely to be hired at this location come from the following academic areas: Bachelor of Science (Computer Science, Mathematics, Physics), Bachelor of Engineering (Electrical, Mechanical, Aerospace, Computer Systems), Master of Science (Computer Science), Master of Engineering (Electrical Engineering, Computer Systems) and Community College Diploma (Computer Science). Graduates would occupy Software Engineering Specialist, Hardware Engineering Specialist and Systems Engineering Specialist positions. Team player, initiative and creativity are listed as desirable non-academic qualifications. Company benefits are rated above average. The potential for advancement is listed as being good. The average annual starting salary falls within the $35,000 to $40,000 range. The most suitable methods for initial contact by those seeking employment are to mail, fax or e-mail a resume with a covering letter. Lockheed Martin Canada Inc., Montreal does hire summer and co-op work term students. *Contact:* Lucie-Marie Gauthier, Human Resources, Montreal.

LOCKHEED MARTIN CANADA INC.

3001 Solandt Road
Kanata, ON   K2K 2M8

Tel. 613-599-3270
Fax 613-599-3282
Email .... Human_Resources@kan.lmcda.lmco.com
Website .... www.lmco.com/canada

Lockheed Martin Canada Inc. is a leader in systems integration, software development, and large-scale program management and Canada's premier supplier of electronic defence and sonar systems. The company has emerged as the leading naval supplier to Canada's Navy. Lockheed Martin Canada Inc. is a division of Lockheed Martin, headquartered in Bethesda, Maryland. The company is one of the world's leading diversified technology companies employing 190,000 people worldwide. The company researches, designs, develops, manufactures and integrates advanced technology systems, products, and services for government and commercial customers around the world. Core businesses span aeronautics, electronics, energy, information and services, space, systems integration and telecommunications. Lockheed Martin Canada employs over 700 people across Canada with its head office in Kanata and supporting operations in Montreal, Toronto, Halifax, Winnipeg, and Victoria. Graduates most likely to be hired come from the following academic areas: Bachelor of Arts (General), Bachelor of Science (Computer Science), Bachelor of Engineering (Electrical, Mechanical, Computer Systems), Bachelor of Commerce/Business Administration (General, Finance), Certified Management Accountant, Certified General Accountant and Community College Diploma (Electronics Technician, Engineering Technician). Graduates would occupy Junior Engineer, Engineer, Software Engineer, Technician and Technical Specialist positions. Previous work experience, good communication skills, adaptability and team work skills are all listed as desirable non-academic qualifications. Company benefits are rated above average. The potential for advancement is listed as being good. The average annual starting salary falls within the $35,000 to $40,000 range. The most suitable methods for initial contact by those seeking employment are to fax or e-mail a resume with a covering letter. Lockheed Martin Canada Inc. does hire summer and co-op work term students. *Contact:* Jackie Plant, Human Resources.

LOMBARD CANADA LTD.

105 Adelaide Street West
Toronto, ON   M5H 1P9

Tel. 416-350-4389
Fax 416-350-4106
Email .... diddon@lombard.ca
Website .... www.lombard.ca

Lombard Canada Ltd. is one of Canada's top ten general, property and casualty insurance companies. The company is 100% Canadian owned, employs 425 people at this location and a total of 675 people across the country. Graduates most likely to be hired come from the following academic areas: Bachelor of Arts (General, Economics, Sociology), Bachelor of Science (General, Actuarial, Computer Science, Mathematics), Bachelor of Engineering (General, Computer Systems, Mechanical), Bachelor of Commerce/Business Administration (General, Accounting, Finance, Information Systems, Marketing), Chartered Accountant (General, Insurance), Certified Management Accountant (General, Insurance), Certified General Accountant (General, Insurance), Master of Business Administration and Community College Diploma (Accounting, Business, Insurance). Graduates would occupy Underwriting Trainee, Claims Trainee, Financial Analyst Trainee, Business Analyst, Human Resources Consultant, Computer Technician, Accounting and Customer Service Representative positions. Previous related work experience, good communication skills, customer focus, commitment, positive attitude, accountable, team player, leadership skills, motivated, creative and innovative are all listed as desirable non-academic qualifications. Company benefits are rated as excellent. The potential for advancement is listed as being good. The average annual starting salary falls within the $29,000 to $35,000 range. The most suitable methods for initial contact by those seeking employment are to mail or fax a resume with a covering letter. Lombard Canada Ltd. does hire summer students and a limited number of co-op work term students. *Contact:* Diana Iddon, Human Resources Consultant.

LONG & MCQUADE LIMITED

1744 Midland Avenue
Toronto, ON   M1P 3C2

Tel. 416-751-9785
Fax 416-751-4765
Website .... www.long-mcquade.com

Long & McQuade Limited is Canada's largest chain of music instrument sales and rental stores. Founded in Toronto in 1956, Long & McQuade has grown to a company which employs over 300 people in 15 locations from

British Columbia to Ontario. The stores are known for their variety and range of musical instruments and professional audio products. Graduates most likely to be hired at this location are Bachelor of Commerce/Business Administration and Chartered Accountant graduates. Graduates would occupy various Accounting and Administration positions. Graduates should possess a strong business background. The most suitable method for initial contact by graduates seeking employment is to mail a resume with a covering letter. *Contact:* Controller.

LOTEK ENGINEERING INC.
115 Pony Drive
Newmarket, ON L3Y 7B5

Tel. 905-836-6680
Fax 905-836-6455
Email .... positions@lotek.com
Website .... www.lotek.com

Lotek Engineering Inc. designs and manufactures wildlife telemetry products for use in biological research. Lotek's sister company, Lotek Marine Technologies, is located in St. John's, Newfoundland and specializes in marine applications. The company's technology is considered leading edge and its customer base is worldwide. Lotek employs 60 people at this location and a total of 100 people in Canada. Graduates most likely to be hired come from the following academic areas: Bachelor of Science (Biology), Bachelor of Engineering (Electrical, Microelectronics), Bachelor of Commerce/Business Administration (Marketing), Community College Diploma (Accounting, Marketing/Sales, Electronics Technician) and High School Diploma. Graduates would occupy Marketing and Sales Specialist, Sales Person, Accounting Clerk, Software Engineer, Hardware Engineer, Assembler, and Electronics Technician positions. Organized, good communication skills, confidence, energetic, team player, initiative and adaptability are all listed as desirable non-academic qualifications. Company benefits are rated above average. The potential for advancement is listed as being good. The average annual starting salary falls within the $25,000 to $30,000 range. The most suitable method for initial contact by those seeking employment is to mail a resume with a covering letter. Lotek Engineering Inc. does hire summer and co-op work term students. *Contact:* Human Resources Manager.

LOVAT INC.
441 Carlingview Drive
Etobicoke, ON M9W 5G7

Tel. 416-675-3293
Fax 416-675-6702
Email .... tbm@lovat.com

Lovat Inc. is a Canadian-based world leader in the manufacture of customized tunnel boring machines (TBMs). TBMs are utilized for the construction of tunnels in the transportation, sewer, water main, mining and telecommunications industries. The company was founded in 1972 to improve safety and efficiency of tunnelling operations. Since then, Lovat has built over 180 TBMs which have completed more than 350 tunnelling projects on six continents. From Seattle to Cairo to Bangkok, Lovat machines have excavated more than 825,000m of tunnel in over twenty countries. Lovat specializes in shield rock, mixed face, soft ground, EPB and Slurry TBMs, and open face tunnel shields ranging from 1.5 metres to 14 metres in diameter. Continually expanding with market demands, the company presently employs 276 specialized engineering, production, sales, service support, and marketing personnel at its head office and manufacturing facilities in Toronto. Even with more than 98 percent of sales being exports, 90 percent of all Lovat products are built at the Toronto plant. Throughout Europe and Asia, first-line support of all TBMs operation on the continents is provided by Lovat's Europe office (based near Birmingham, United Kingdom), and Lovat's Asia office (based in Alexandria, Australia). Elsewhere, an international network of Representatives assist to monitor global tunnelling activity, open new markets and support operating TBMs within their territories. Graduates most likely to be hired come from the following academic areas: Bachelor of Arts (General), Bachelor of Engineering (Electrical, Mechanical), Certified Management Accountant, Certified General Accountant and Community College Diploma (CAD/CAM/Autocad, Fluid Power Technologist, Mechanical Technologist, Electrical Technologist). Graduates would occupy Junior Draftsperson, Junior Designer, Intern Accountant, Receptionist, Administrative Assistant and Plant Helper positions. Creativity, innovation, team player and flexibility are all listed as desirable non-academic qualifications. Company benefits are rated above average. The potential for advancement is listed as being good. The average annual starting salary falls within the $30,000 to $35,000 range. The most suitable methods for initial contact by those seeking employment are to mail or fax a resume with a covering letter. Lovat Inc. does hire summer and co-op work term students. *Contact:* Human Resources.

LOYALTY GROUP, THE
4110 Yonge Street, Suite 200
Toronto, ON M2P 2B7

Tel. 416-228-6500
Fax 416-733-9712
Website .... www.airmiles.ca

The Loyalty Group is the owner of the Air Miles rewards program in Canada. Loyalty's data driven organization is recognized for its leading edge database capabilities, as well as its insight on the motivations and actions of its Air Miles collectors. Founded in 1991 as a data management company, the company's business has grown to include expertise in loyalty programs (Air Miles), direct marketing, marketing research and analysis, retail systems technical development, retail database warehouse development consulting services and the company's very own full service travel agency, Extra Mile Travel. The company employs 580 people at this location and a total of 602 people in Canada. Graduates most likely to be hired come from the following academic areas: Bachelor of Arts (Economics), Bachelor of Science (Computer Science, Geography, Mathematics), Bachelor of Engineering (Telecommunications), Bachelor of Commerce/Business Administration (General, Accounting, Finance, Human Resources, Information Systems, Marketing), Master of Business Administration (General, Accounting, Finance, Human Resources, Information Systems, Marketing), Master of Science (Statistics), Doctorate (Statistics, Mathematics) and Community College Diploma (Human Resources). Graduates would occupy Business Analyst, Financial Analyst, Programmer Analyst, Telecommunications Analyst, Marketing Coordinator and Account Management Coordinator positions. Team player, professional, articulate, results oriented, driven, ambitious, entrepreneurial, the ability to balance work with outside interests and previous related work experience are all listed as desirable non-academic qualifications. Company benefits and the potential for advancement are both rated as excellent. The average annual starting salary falls within the $35,000 to $40,000 range. The most suitable methods for initial contact by those seeking employment are to mail or fax a resume with a covering letter. The Loyalty Group does hire college and university students for summer and co-op work terms. *Contact:* Corporate Recruiter, Human Resources.

M3I SYSTEMS INC.
1111, rue St. Charles Ouest, 11th Floor, East Tower
Longueuil, QC J4K 5G4

Tel.	450-928-4600
Fax	450-442-5076
Email	resume@m3isystems.com
Website	www.m3isystems.com

M3i Systems Inc. is a world leader in the development, implementation and support of integrated software systems for distribution operations and dispatch management. Specializing in command centre support systems, M3i provides innovative operational solutions for electric, gas and water utilities, for emergency response organizations, and for the transportation and telecommunications industries. Initially created within the operations of Hydro-Québec, M3i Systems Inc. was incorporated in 1990 and has since grown from seven to over 400 employees, and today has offices in Ottawa, Los Angeles, Chicago, Pittsburgh, Seattle, Birmingham (United Kingdom), Paris, and Singapore. Graduates most likely to be hired come from the following academic areas: Bachelor of Arts (English), Bachelor of Science (Computer Science), Bachelor of Engineering (Computer Systems, Microelectronics) and Community College Diploma (Computer Science, Electronics Technician). Graduates would occupy Programmer (all levels, in all categories), Technical Writer, Hardware Specialist, Network Specialist, Applications Specialist, Systems Architect and Project Manager positions. Creativity, flexibility, initiative, autonomy, team player, dedication, working knowledge of latest programming tools and methods, and previous relevant work or co-op experience are all listed as desirable non-academic qualifications. Company benefits and the potential for advancement are both rated as excellent. The average annual starting salary for those with previous work experience, falls within the $30,000 to $35,000 range. The most suitable method for initial contact by those seeking employment is to mail a resume with a covering letter. M3i Systems Inc. does hire summer students. *Contact:* Human Resources Director.

MACDONALD DETTWILER & ASSOCIATES / MDA
13800 Commerce Parkway
Richmond, BC V6V 2J3

Tel.	604-278-3411
Fax	604-278-2281
Email	jobs@mda.ca
Website	www.mda.ca

MacDonald Dettwiler is a leading Canadian space company and provider of information, products and services. Through a diverse range of applied technologies and services, the company provides systems and information to help a growing segment of the global society manage their activities. MDA is diversified across multiple domestic and international systems, services and information product markets. The company plays an active role in virtually every phase of information delivery, from Earth observation satellite missions and space-borne communications to ground reception, processing and distribution systems. MDA's involvement in the value-added services and electronic commerce sectors complete the chain of information delivery to consumers. The company is organized into four primary groups: Space Missions, Systems, Services and Electronic Commerce. This structure provides the central control needed to ensure cost-effective systems, products and services, while giving each group the autonomy required to keep pace with changing technologies and customer needs. There are 665 employees at this location, a total of 1,374 in Canada and 1,414 employees worldwide. Graduates most likely to be hired come from the following academic areas: Bachelor of Science (General, Computer Science, Geography, Mathematics, Physics), Bachelor of Engineering (General, Electrical, Computer Systems, Engineering Physics), Bachelor of Commerce/Business Administration (General, Marketing), Chartered Accountant, Certified Management Accountant, Certified General Accountant, Master of Business Administration (Accounting, Finance) and Community College Diploma (Accounting, Business, Human Resources, Engineering Technician, Information Systems). Company benefits and the potential for advancement are both rated as excellent. The average annual starting salary falls within the $40,000 to $45,000 range. The most suitable methods for initial contact by those seeking employment are to e-mail a resume with a covering letter, or via the company's website. MacDonald Dettwiler & Associates does hire summer and co-op work term students. *Contact:* Recruiting Office.

MACKENZIE FINANCIAL CORPORATION
150 Bloor Street West
Toronto, ON M5S 3B5

Tel.	416-922-5322
Fax	416-922-1278
Email	hr@mackenziefinancial.com
Website	www.mackenziefinancial.com

Mackenzie Financial Corporation is one of Canada's leading mutual fund companies, managing over $20 billion in assets on behalf of more than 800,000 investors across Canada. There are 800 employees at this location, and a total of 1,200 employees in Canada. Graduates most likely to be hired come from the following academic areas: Bachelor of Arts (Economics, English, French, Psychology), Bachelor of Science (Computer Science), Bachelor of Commerce/Business Administration (General, Finance, Information Systems, Marketing), Chartered Accountant, Certified Management Accountant, Certified General Accountant, Master of Business Administration (General, Accounting, Finance, Information Systems, Marketing) and Community College Diploma (Accounting, Administration, Business, Information Systems, Secretarial). Graduates would occupy Data Processing Clerk, Customer Service Representative, Training and Documentation Coordinator, Trust Accountant, Accounting Clerk, Computer Operator, Junior Programmer, Desktop Publisher, Graphic Designer, Receptionist, and Secretary positions. Good organizational skills, team player, a willingness to do any kind of work and strong problem solving skills are all listed as desirable non-academic qualifications. Company benefits and the potential for advancement are both rated as excellent. The average annual starting salary falls within the $25,000 to $30,000 range. The most suitable methods for initial contact by those seeking employment are to mail, fax or e-mail a resume with a covering letter, or by applying through Mackenzie's website at www.mackenziefinancial.com. Mackenzie Financial Corporation does hire co-op work term students during the winter season, January through May. *Contact:* Human Resources Consultant.

MACLEAN HUNTER PUBLISHING LTD.
777 Bay Street, 9th Floor
Toronto, ON M5W 1A7

Tel.	416-596-5270
Fax	416-596-5967
Website	www.rogers.com/media/publishing

Maclean Hunter Publishing Ltd., a Rogers Communications company, publishes some of Canada's leading business and consumer magazines including Maclean's, Canada's weekly newsmagazine. There are approximately 800 employees at this location, and a total of 1,000 employees in Canada. Graduates most likely to be hired come from the following academic areas: Bachelor of Arts (General, English, Journalism, Political Science), Bachelor of Science (Computer Science), Bachelor of Commerce/Business Administration (General, Information Systems, Marketing) and Community College Diploma (Accounting, Administration, Advertising, Graphic Arts, Journalism). Graduates would occupy Editorial Assistant, Assistant Editor, Sales Coordinator, Inside Sales Representative, Administrative Assistant, Marketing Coordinator, PC Specialist, and Assistant Art Director positions. Good communication and organizational skills, detail oriented, able to work well in a team environment, high energy level, computer software knowledge (word processing and spreadsheets) and previous work experience are all listed as desirable non-academic qualifications. The most suitable methods for initial contact by those seeking employment are to mail or fax a resume with a covering letter. Maclean Hunter Publishing Ltd. hires a limited number of summer students each year, the type and number of summer positions is generally known by May (sometimes late April). Maclean Hunter also hires co-op work term students. *Contact:* Receptionist, Human Resources.

MACMILLAN BATHURST
220 Water Street, PO Box 150
Whitby, ON L1N 5R7

Tel.	905-686-2600
Fax	905-427-0892

MacMillan Bathurst, Whitby Plant is a corrugated box manufacturer. There are approximately 185 employees at the Whitby plant, and a total of 1,800 employees in Canada. Graduates most likely to be hired come from the following academic areas: Bachelor of Science (Biology, Chemistry, Computer Science, Environmental, Forestry), Bachelor of Engineering (Chemical, Materials Science, Pulp and Paper, Electrical, Instrumentation, Mechanical, Industrial Design, Industrial Production), Bachelor of Commerce/Business Administration (General, Accounting, Human Resources) and Community College Diploma (Accounting, Human Resources, Secretarial, Electronics Engineering, Engineering Technician, Production Engineering). Graduates would occupy Quality Facilitator, Production Leadhand and Accounting positions. Previous work experience in the paper and corrugated box industry would be a definite asset. Company benefits and the potential for advancement are both rated as excellent. The average annual starting salary falls within the $25,000 to $30,000 range. The most suitable method for initial contact by those seeking employment is to mail a resume with a covering letter. MacMillan Bathurst does hire summer students, applications must be received before April 30th. *Contacts:* Steve Ashby, Employee Relations or Ken Gills, Production Manager.

MACMILLAN BLOEDEL LIMITED
925 West Georgia Street, 7th Floor
Vancouver, BC V6C 3L2

Tel.	604-661-8000
Fax	604-681-5469
Email	hr.services@mbltd.com
Website	www.mbltd.com

MacMillan Bloedel Limited is one of Canada's largest forest products companies with integrated operations in Canada, the United States and Mexico. The company manages 2 million hectares of productive timberlands that supply most of its fibre requirements, and of these timberlands, 1.1 million hectares are in British Columbia. The products of MacMillan Bloedel and its affiliated companies are marketed throughout the world and include lumber, panel boards, engineered lumber, containerboard and corrugated containers. MacMillan Bloedel is a publicly held company (Toronto Stock Exchange: MB; NASDAQ: MMBL) with approximately 65 percent of the company's stock held in Canada and 30 percent held in the United States. MacMillan Bloedel Limited employs approximately 450 people. Graduates most likely to be hired come from the following academic areas: Bachelor of Science (Environmental, Forestry), Bachelor of Engineering (Pulp and Paper, Forest Resources), Bachelor of Commerce/Business Administration (Accounting, Finance, Human Resources, Information Systems, Marketing), Master of Business Administration (Accounting, Finance, Human Resources) and Community College Diploma (Accounting, Financial Planning, Human Resources, Marketing/Sales, Secretarial). Graduates would be hired to occupy a broad range of positions, from Forester to Accountant, depending upon their academic backgrounds. The most suitable method for initial contact by those seeking employment is to mail a resume with a covering letter. MacMillan Bloedel Limited does hire Engineering students for summer positions. *Contact:* Human Resources Department.

MAGNA PROJECTS INC.
4393 - 14 Street NE, Suite 200
Calgary, AB T2E 7A9

Tel.	403-250-4676
Fax	403-219-3149
Email	christinecole@projcalmagnaiv.com
Website	www.projcalmagnaiv.com

Magna Projects Inc. is a Canadian based engineering firm providing single or multidiscipline engineering, procurement and construction management services to the oil and gas, utility and industrial sectors. The firm is a leader in technologies related to infrastructure, power, process industries and systems. Services range from feasibility studies to complete detailed design, construction management and start-up. After start-up Magna can provide training, troubleshooting, and plant optimization services. Magna is comprised of learned individuals who collectively deliver a wealth of experience and information to every project. The company's history of quality and commitment to service depicts a foundation from which the firm continually strives to build and excel upon. Graduates most likely to be hired come from the following academic areas: Bachelor of Engineering (Civil, Electrical, Mechanical, Computer Systems, Instrumentation, Petroleum/Fuels, Power/Hydro, Pulp and Paper, Telecommunications) and Community College Diploma (Administration, Human Resources, Information Systems, Secretarial). Team player, computer literacy and previous engineering experience are all listed as desirable non-academic qualifications. Company benefits and the potential for advancement are both rated as excellent. The most suitable methods for initial contact by those seeking employment are to mail, fax or e-mail a resume with a covering letter. Magna Projects Inc. does hire summer and co-op work term students. *Contact:* Christine Cole.

MANAC, A DIVISION OF THE CANAM MANAC GROUP INC.
51 Centennial Road
Orangeville, ON L9W 3R1

Tel. 519-941-2018
Fax 519-941-2108
Website .... www.canammanac.com

Manac, a division of The Canam Manac Group Inc. is the largest manufacturer of quality, custom built semitrailers in North America. Manac specializes in the design, manufacture and marketing of custom products tailored to the specific needs of its customers. The company's head office is located in Saint-Georges de Beauce, Quebec. Manac employs over 1,000 people, and The Canam Manac Group Inc. employs over 4,400 throughout Canada, the United States, Mexico, and France. Graduates most likely to be hired come from the following academic areas: Bachelor of Arts (General), Bachelor of Engineering (General, Industrial Design, Industrial Production), Bachelor of Commerce/Business Administration, Chartered Accountant, Certified Management Accountant, Certified General Accountant, Community College Diploma (Technicians, Technologists Accounting, Administration) and High School Diploma. Graduates would occupy a variety of unskilled, semi-skilled and entry level professional positions in the following functional areas: Production, Engineering, Human Resources, Finance, and Administration. Customer orientation, team players, capacity to adapt to change, results oriented achievers, innovators, analytical thinkers and problem solving skills are all listed as desirable traits. The average starting salary reaches up to $30,000 plus range. The most suitable methods for initial contact by those seeking employment are to mail, fax or e-mail a resume with a covering letter, stating geographic and positions preferences. Manac does hire summer students. *Contact:* Human Resources Team.

MANITOBA AGRICULTURE
401 York Avenue, Suite 803
Winnipeg, MB R3C 0P8

Tel. 204-945-3308
Fax 204-945-5024
Email .... humanresources@agr.gov.mb.ca
Website .... www.gov.mb.ca/agriculture

Manitoba Agriculture sustains and enhances the economic and personal well-being of participants within the agriculture and food chain. In support of this mission the department's role is to provide leadership and a range of services to assist agriculture and food participants in creating a sustainable economic climate to improve their net income and general well-being. Manitoba Agriculture is composed of four divisions which are called the Management and Operations Division, Regional Agricultural Services Division, Agricultural Development and Marketing Division, and the Policy and Economics Division. The department employs 575 people throughout the province of Manitoba. Graduates most likely to be hired come from the following academic areas: Bachelor of Arts (General), Bachelor of Science (General, Agriculture, Computer Science, Microbiology, Human Ecology), Bachelor of Commerce/Business Administrator (General, Accounting, Finance, Human Resources, Marketing), Chartered Accountant, Certified Management Accountant, Certified General Accountant, Master of Business Administration (Finance, Human Resources, Marketing), Master of Science (Agriculture), Doctor of Veterinary Medicine and Community College Diploma (Administration, Agriculture/Horticulture). Graduates would occupy Administrative Clerk, Financial Clerk, Agrologist (Agricultural Representative, Specialist, etc.), Information Technologist, Medical Technologist, Agricultural Engineer, Financial Manager, Financial Analyst, Manager, Director, Home Economist, Veterinary Medical Officer, Livestock Technician and Laboratory Technician positions. Excellent oral and written communication skills, able to work cooperatively in a team environment and the ability to provide leadership are all listed as desirable non-academic qualifications. Company benefits are rated above average. The potential for advancement is listed as being good. The most suitable method for initial contact by those seeking employment is to mail a resume with a covering letter. Manitoba Agriculture does hire summer and co-op work term students. *Contact:* Mrs. Angie Kudlak, Personnel Administrator, HR Management Services.

MANITOBA HYDRO
PO Box 815
Winnipeg, MB R3C 2P4

Tel. 204-474-4294
Fax 204-474-4985
Website .... www.hydro.mb.ca

Manitoba Hydro is a major electric utility headquartered in Winnipeg and serving over 394,000 customers throughout the province. Activities involve forecasting the province's future energy requirements, to designing, constructing, maintaining and operating the numerous facilities needed to meet those requirements. Virtually all electricity generated by the utility is from self-renewing water power. Manitoba Hydro is the fourth largest electrical utility in Canada. Graduates most likely to be hired are: Bachelor of Science (Chemistry, Computer, Forestry), Bachelor of Engineering (Civil, Electrical, Mechanical), Bachelor of Laws, Bachelor of Commerce/Business Administration (Accounting, Finance, Marketing, Personnel), Chartered Accountant, Certified Management Accountant, Certified General Accountant, Master of Business Administration (Accounting, Finance, Marketing), Master of Engineering (Electrical, Mechanical, Civil), Community College Diploma (Accounting, Administration, Business, Communications, Marketing, Graphic Arts, Human Resources, Drafting, Computer Science, Electronics Technician, Engineering Technician, CAD/CAM/Autocad, Industrial Design) and High School Diploma. Graduates would occupy Clerk, Technician, Engineering Aid, Application Programmer Analyst, Accountant, Marketing Officer, Personnel Officer, Engineer-in-Training, Junior Engineer, Chemist, Forester, Auditor, Lawyer and Apprenticeship Trainees (Power Line, Electrical, Mechanical and Station Operator) positions. Strong interpersonal and communication skills are both listed as desirable non-academic qualifications. Company benefits are rated above average. The potential for advancement is listed as good. The most suitable methods for initial contact by those seeking employment are to mail a resume with a covering letter, or by applying in person at this location. Summer students are hired through Step Services (a Manitoba Government service). Manitoba

Hydro is an employment equity employer. *Contact:* Rachelle Woodard, Personnel Officer, Employment Department.

MAPLE LEAF MEATS, A MEMBER OF MAPLE LEAF FOODS INC.
150 Bartor Road
Toronto, ON M9M 1H1

Tel.	416-741-7181
Fax	416-741-7693
Website	www.mlfi.com

Maple Leaf Meats, A Member of Maple Leaf Foods Inc., is a major meat processing company. The company employs approximately 400 people at this location. Graduates most likely to be hired come from the following academic areas: Bachelor of Science (Biology, Chemistry, Microbiology), Bachelor of Engineering (Industrial), Bachelor of Commerce/Business Administration and Community College Diploma (Laboratory Technician). Graduates would occupy Laboratory Technician, Microbiologist and Industrial Engineer positions. Possessing related food industry experience is listed as a definite asset. Company benefits and the potential for advancement are both rated as excellent. The average starting salary falls between the $25,000 to $40,000 plus range, and ultimately depends upon the position being considered. The most suitable method for initial contact by individuals seeking employment is to mail a resume with a covering letter. Maple Leaf Meats does hire a limited number of summer students annually. *Contact:* Marilyn Broderick, Manager, Human Resources.

MAPLE LODGE FARMS LTD.
RR#2
Norval, ON L0P 1K0

Tel.	905-455-8340
Fax	905-455-8370

Maple Lodge Farms Ltd. is a food processing company, primarily involved in poultry processing. The company employs approximately 1,600 people. Graduates most likely to be hired come from the following academic areas: Bachelor of Science (Biology, Chemistry, Computer Science, Environmental, Nursing, Nutritional Sciences), Bachelor of Engineering (General, Chemical, Food Processing, Industrial Chemistry, Pollution Treatment, Electrical, Computer Systems, Mechanical, Industrial Design, Industrial Production, Welding, Resources/Environmental, Water Resources), Bachelor of Commerce/Business Administration (General, Accounting, Finance, Human Resources, Marketing), Chartered Accountant, Certified Management Accountant, Certified General Accountant, Master of Business Administration (Accounting, Finance, Human Resources, Information Systems, Marketing, Public Administration), Master of Science, Master of Engineering, Community College Diploma (Accounting, Administration, Business, Financial Planning, Human Resources, Insurance, Marketing/Sales, Purchasing/Logistics, Secretarial, Cooking, Graphic Arts, Security, CAD/CAM/Autocad, Computer Science, Electronics Technician, Engineering Technician, Welding, Dietician, Nursing RN/RNA) and High School Diploma. Graduates would occupy Food Technologist, Water/Waste Treatment, Microbiologist, Plant Nurse, Electrician, Maintenance, Welder, Refrigeration, Engineering Manager, Maintenance Manager, Computer Programmer, Accountant, Controller, Accounts Payable/Receivable Clerk, Human Resource Professional, Marketing, Sales Representative, Secretary, Purchasing Agent, Security Personnel and Cafeteria Worker positions. Previous work experience, good references, team player, attitude and enthusiasm are all listed as desirable non-academic qualifications. Company benefits are rated above average. The average annual starting falls within the $25,000 to $30,000 range. The most suitable method for initial contact by those seeking employment is to mail a resume with a covering letter. Maple Lodge Farms Ltd. does hire summer students. *Contact:* Personnel Officer.

MARK'S WORK WEARHOUSE LTD.
1035 - 64 Avenue SE, Suite 30
Calgary, AB T2H 2J7

Tel.	403-255-9220
Fax	403-258-7575
Website	www.marks.com

Mark's Work Wearhouse Ltd. is a Canadian retailer of clothing and footwear. The company employs approximately 100 people at this location and a total of 1,800 people across Canada. Graduates most likely to be hired come from the following academic areas: Bachelor of Arts (Graphic Arts), Bachelor of Engineering (Computer Systems, Telecommunications, Industrial Design), Chartered Accountant, Certified Management Accountant, Certified General Accountant, Master of Business Administration (Accounting, Finance), Community College Diploma (Accounting, Administration, Facility Management, Financial Planning, Marketing/Sales, Purchasing/Logistics) and High School Diploma. Graduates would occupy Store Manager, Department Manager, Trainee and Clerical positions. Team player, dedicated, and dependable are all listed as desirable non-academic qualifications. Company benefits and the potential for advancement are both rated as excellent. The average annual starting salary falls within the $30,000 to $35,000 range and is commission based for some positions. The most suitable method for initial contact by those seeking employment is to mail a resume with a covering letter. Mark's Work Wearhouse Ltd. does hire summer and co-op work term students. *Contact:* Human Resources.

MARKEL INSURANCE COMPANY OF CANADA
105 Adelaide Street West, 7th Floor
Toronto, ON M5H 1P9

Tel.	416-364-7800
Fax	416-364-1625
Website	www.markelcorp.com

Markel Insurance Company of Canada is the largest commercial insurance company specializing in long haul trucking insurance. The company maintains branches in Montreal, Edmonton and Calgary, as well as subsidiary tractor trailer driver schools in Guelph and Exeter (Ontario). There are more than 70 employees at this location and a total of 115 employees in Canada. Graduates most likely to be hired come from the following academic areas: Bachelor of Science (Actuarial, Mathematics), Bachelor of Commerce/Business Administration (Accounting, Finance), Master of Business Administration (Accounting, Finance) and Community College Diploma (Accounting, Business, Insurance). Graduates would occupy Underwriting Technical Assistant, Junior Underwriter, Junior Claims Examiner, Administrative Services Clerk, Secretary, Technician and Computer Operator positions. Company benefits are rated above average. The potential for advancement is listed as being good. The average annual starting salary falls within the $30,000 to $35,000 range. The most suitable method for initial contact by those seeking employment is to mail a resume with a covering letter. Markel Insurance Company of Canada occasionally hires summer and co-op work term students. *Contact:* Delores Johnson, Personnel Manager.

MARKHAM STREET SERVICES DEPARTMENT
101 Town Centre Boulevard
Markham, ON L3R 9W3

Tel. 905-475-4700
Fax 905-479-7774
Website .... www.city.markham.on.ca

The Town of Markham's Street Services Department is responsible for infrastructure, long-term planning and daily operations. This includes municipal roads, bridges, sidewalk, all drainage features, fresh water and waste water management traffic, and transportation systems. The Street Services Department employs approximately 80 people. Graduates most likely to be hired come from the following academic areas: Bachelor of Arts (Urban Geography/Planning), Bachelor of Engineering (Civil, Surveying, Water Resources), Bachelor of Commerce/Business Administration (Accounting, Public Administration), Certified Management Accountant, Community College Diploma (Accounting, Administration, Secretarial, CAD/CAM/Autocad, Computer Science, Engineering Technician) and High School Diploma. Employee benefits are rated as excellent. The potential for advancement is listed as average. The average annual starting salary falls within the $30,000 plus range. The most suitable methods for initial contact by those seeking employment are to mail or fax a resume with a covering letter. The Town of Markham's Street Services Department does hire summer students on a regular basis. *Contact:* Human Resources Department.

MARKHAM TRANSIT
101 Town Centre Boulevard
Markham, ON L3R 9W3

Tel. 905-475-4888
Fax 905-475-4709

The Town of Markham Transit Department is involved in the planning for and operation of municipal public transit in Markham. Transit services include conventional bus operation and services for physically disabled persons. There are approximately 25 employees at this location. Graduates most likely to be hired come from the following academic areas: Bachelor of Arts (Urban Geography/Planning), Bachelor of Engineering (Transportation) and Community College Diploma (Transportation Technology). The types of positions these graduates would occupy are as follows: Transit Planner, Transit Technician and Operations Supervisor. Good interpersonal skills, previous work experience and a geographic knowledge of the area are listed as desirable non-academic qualifications. Employee benefits are rated as excellent. The potential for advancement is listed as average. The average annual starting salary falls within the $25,000 to $30,000 range. The most suitable method for initial contact by graduates seeking employment is to mail a resume with a covering letter. *Contact:* Manager, Human Resources.

MARSHALL MACKLIN MONAGHAN LIMITED
80 Commerce Valley Drive East
Thornhill, ON L3T 7N4

Tel. 905-882-1100
Fax 905-882-0055
Email .... mmm@mmm.ca
Website .... www.mmm.ca

Marshall Macklin Monaghan Limited provides comprehensive consulting services to government and private sector clients across Canada and overseas. Established in 1952, the company is a privately held Canadian company, owned and managed by its practitioners, and currently employs more than 350 personnel, of whom one third are registered professionals. The company provides a multidisciplinary consulting service. The traditional discipline skills include engineering, surveying, and planning. Offices are located in Toronto and Edmonton, with additional offices established as required for local or project needs. Graduates most likely to be hired come from the following academic areas: Bachelor of Arts (Urban Geography/Planning, General), Bachelor of Science (Geography, Chemistry), Bachelor of Engineering (Civil, Electrical, Mechanical, Environmental), Bachelor of Architecture, Bachelor of Landscape Architecture, Bachelor of Commerce/Business Administration (Accounting), Chartered Accountant, Certified Management Accountant, Masters (Environmental Studies, Chemistry) and Community College Diploma (Civil Engineering Technology). Excellent written and oral communication skills are listed as desirable non-academic qualifications. Company benefits are rated as excellent. The potential for advancement is listed as being good. The most suitable method for initial contact by graduates seeking employment is to mail a resume with a covering letter. Marshall Macklin Monaghan Limited does hire summer and co-op work term students. *Contact:* Manager, Human Resources.

MARUSYK, MILLER & SWAIN / MBM & CO.
PO Box 809, Station B
Ottawa, ON K1P 5P9

Tel. 613-567-0762
Fax 613-563-7671
Email .... mbm@mbm-law.com
Website .... www.mbm-law.com

Marusyk, Miller & Swain is a law firm that practices exclusively in the arena of intellectual property, including the commercialization of technology and the exploitation of knowledge, while MBM & Co. is a patent and trademark agency firm that is associated with the law firm. There are a total of 20 employees at this location. Graduates most likely to be hired come from the following academic areas: Bachelor of Science (Biology, Chemistry), Bachelor of Engineering (Biotechnology/Bioengineering), Bachelor of Laws (Intellectual Property), Bachelor of Commerce/Business Administration (Marketing), Master of Business Administration (Marketing), Doctorate and Community College Diploma (Office Administration, Legal Assistant). Graduates would occupy Articling Student-at-Law, Patent Agent Trainee, Lawyer, Patent Agent, Trademark Agent, Marketing Director, Paralegal and Legal Support positions. Team player, quick learner and a high level of initiative are all listed as desirable non-academic qualifications. Company benefits are rated above average. The potential for advancement is listed as being good. The average annual starting salary falls within the $20,000 to $25,000 range. The most suitable method for initial contact by those seeking employment is to mail a resume with a covering letter. Marusyk, Miller & Swain / MBM & Co. does hire summer and co-op work term students. *Contact:* Elizabeth Schroeder, Office Manager.

MATROX ELECTRONIC SYSTEMS LTD.
1055 St-Regis Blvd.
Dorval, QC H9P 2T4

Tel.	514-822-6000
Fax	514-822-6274
Email	personnel@matrox.com
Website	www.matrox.com

Matrox Electronic Systems Ltd. designs and manufactures ASICs, hardware and software for computer graphics, desktop video, PC-based image processing and computer networking applications. The company produces state-of-the-art products, known worldwide for their quality and price-performance ratio. In addition to the 1,200 employees based in Montreal, Matrox has design centres in Markham, Ontario and in Boca-Raton, Florida. Graduates most likely to be hired come from the following academic areas: Bachelor of Engineering (Robotics, Computer Systems, Microelectronics, Telecommunications), Bachelor of Science (Computer Science, Mathematics, Physics), Bachelor of Commerce/Business Administration/MBA (Accounting, Finance, Human Resources, Information Systems, Marketing), Chartered Accountant, Bachelor of Arts (Graphic Art, Journalism), Master of Science (Physics), Master of Engineering (Electrical), Doctorate (Electrical Engineering) and Community College Diploma (Computer Science, Electronics Technician, Engineering Technician). Graduates would occupy Hardware Designer, Software Designer, New Product Introduction Specialist, ASIC Designer, ASIC Architect, Validation Specialist, Engineering Sales Representative, Applications/OEM Support Representatives, Quality Assurance Specialist, Production Support Specialist, Product Manager, Technical Support Representative, Software Quality Assurance Technician, Project Coordinator, Junior Buyer, Sales and Marketing Coordinator, Customer Service Representative, Technical Writer and Inside Sales Representative positions. Team player, a high level of initiative and motivation, computer literacy, and strong interpersonal and communication skills are all listed as desirable non-academic qualifications. Company benefits are rated as excellent and include group insurance, profit sharing, on-site daycare, free parking, a fully equipped gym, a heated outdoor pool and volleyball and basketball courts. The potential for advancement is also rated as excellent. The average annual starting salary for engineering positions falls within the $35,000 to $40,000 range, and the average starting salary for non-engineering positions falls within the $25,000 to $30,000 range. The most suitable methods for initial contact by those seeking employment are to mail a resume with a covering letter, or by applying through the company's website at www.matrox.com/hrweb. Matrox also offers summer positions, internships, cooperative education terms, and part-time positions. *Contacts:* Anita Salvador, Human Resources Manager; Andrea Di Domenico, Recruiting Specialist or Catherine Masson, Recruiting Specialist.

MAVES INTERNATIONAL SOFTWARE, INC.
90 Allstate Parkway, Suite 400
Markham, ON L3R 6H3

Tel.	905-475-1300
Fax	905-475-9878
Email	ackcha@tor.maves.ca
Website	www.maves.com

Maves International Software, Inc. has been a leading provider of software solutions for the logistics industry for more than 25 years. Maves has over 100 employees at offices in Toronto and Vancouver, serving more than 250 clients in Canada, the United States, and the United Kingdom, with installations in over 1,100 warehouse locations. Graduates most likely to be hired come from the following academic areas: Bachelor of Science (Computer Science), Bachelor of Commerce/Business Administration (Computer Systems) and Community College Diploma (Information Systems, Purchasing/Logistics, Computer Science). Graduates would occupy Consulting/Project Management, Quality Assurance Testing, Technical/Programming and Trainee positions. Bright, self-motivated, hard working, multitasked, good verbal and written communication skills, able to work independently as well as within a team and excellent problem solving skills are all listed as desirable non-academic qualifications. Company benefits are rated above average. The potential for advancement is listed as being good. The average annual starting salary falls within the $35,000 to $40,000 range. Employment opportunities at Maves are ongoing, in the Toronto and Vancouver offices, and on a contract basis. The most suitable method for initial contact by those seeking employment is to e-mail a resume with a covering letter. *Contact:* Charmaine Ackerman, Manager, Human Resources.

MAXAM M & S INC.
1 Holiday Street, East Tower, 5th Floor
Pointe-Claire, QC H9R 5N3

Tel.	514-694-3326
Fax	514-694-3126
Email	maxam@total.net

MAXAM M & S Inc. is involved in the development of computer based data management systems. The company employs a total of four people. Graduates most likely to be hired come from the following academic areas: Bachelor of Science (Computer Science), Bachelor of Engineering (Computer Systems) and Community College Diploma (Computer Science). Graduates would be hired to occupy S/W Application Specialist and Database Administrator positions. Applicants should be familiar with Unix, Oracle and SQL programming languages. Company benefits are rated as industry standard. The potential for advancement is listed as being excellent. The average annual starting salary falls within the $30,000 to $35,000 range. The most suitable method for initial contact by those seeking employment is to mail a resume with a covering letter. MAXAM M & S Inc. does hire summer students. *Contact:* Magdy Boghdady, Director of Operations.

MAYA HEAT TRANSFER TECHNOLOGIES LTD.
4999 St. Catherine Street W., Suite 400
Montreal, QC H3Z 1T3

Tel.	514-369-5706
Fax	514-369-4200
Email	jobs@mayahtt.com
Website	www.mayahtt.com

MAYA Heat Transfer Technologies Ltd. is a leading developer of advanced analysis and simulation software applications for mechanical engineering. MAYA is one of the world's leading developers of advanced heat transfer and fluid flow simulation software for electronics, aerospace, automotive and manufacturing applications. Established in 1982, MAYA is a private Canadian company headquartered in Montreal with offices in Cincinnati, Boston, Dallas, and Ottawa. There are 45 employees in Canada and a total of 50 employees worldwide. Graduates most likely to be hired come from the following academic areas: Bachelor of Engineering (Mechanical) and Master of Engineering (Mechanical). Graduates would occupy Applications Engineer and Developer positions. Graduates should be comfortable and able to work within an informal structure. Company benefits are rated as industry standard. The potential for advancement is listed as being good. The average annual starting salary falls within the $40,000 to $45,000 range. The most suitable methods for initial contact by those seeking employment are to e-mail a resume with a covering letter or via the company's website. MAYA Heat Transfer Technologies Ltd. does hire summer and co-op work term students. *Contact:* Dan Dupras, Human Resources.

MCCARNEY GREENWOOD LLP
1300 Central Parkway West, Suite 300
Mississauga, ON L5C 4G8

Tel. 905-276-3891
Fax 905-896-8959
Email .... rdinshaw@mgca.com

McCarney Greenwood LLP is a chartered accounting firm providing a full range of public accounting services. Services include audits, reviews, compilations, and tax returns, as well as providing tax consulting and management consulting services. McCarney Greenwood employs 25 people at this location and an additional 15 people in Toronto. Graduates most likely to be hired come from the following academic areas: Bachelor of Commerce/Business Administration (General, Accounting, Finance), Chartered Accountant, Certified General Accountant and Master of Business Administration (Accounting). Graduates would occupy CA Student or Accountant positions. Strong analytical skills, organized, good verbal and written communication skills, personable and professional are all listed as desirable non-academic qualifications. Company benefits are rated as industry standard. The potential for advancement is listed as being good. The average annual starting salary falls within the $30,000 to $35,000 range. The most suitable methods for initial contact by those seeking employment are to mail or fax a resume with a covering letter. McCarney Greenwood does hire co-op work term students. *Contact:* Ms. R. Dinshaw, Human Resources.

MCCORMICK CANADA INC.
316 Rectory Street, PO Box 5788
London, ON N6A 4Z2

Tel. 519-432-1166
Fax 519-432-4648
Email .... london_hr@mccormick.ca
Website .... www.mccormick.com

McCormick Canada Inc. is the industry leader in the area of processing, packaging and selling of spices, seasonings and flavourings. McCormick Canada Inc. is a subsidiary of Baltimore, Maryland based McCormick & Company, Inc. Founded in 1889, McCormick is one of the world's leading spice companies employing 8,500 people worldwide. McCormick Canada Inc. employs approximately 225 people at this location and a total of 450 people across Canada. Graduates most likely to be hired come from the following academic areas: Bachelor of Arts (General, Economics), Bachelor of Science (Microbiology, Nutritional Sciences), Bachelor of Engineering (Chemical, Food Processing, Electrical, Industrial Production), Bachelor of Commerce/Business Administration (Accounting, Finance, Human Resources, Information Systems, Marketing), Chartered Accountant, Certified Management Accountant, Certified General Accountant, Master of Business Administration (Accounting, Finance, Human Resources), Professional Designa-tions CHRP and PMAC, Community College Diploma (Accounting, Communications, Human Resources, Marketing/Sales, Purchasing/Logistics, CAD/CAM/Autocad, Electronics Technician, Engineering Technician, HVAC Systems, Dietician) and High School Diploma. New graduates would occupy entry level Finance, Administration, Information Resources, Manufacturing, Technical and Laboratory positions. Graduates with relevant work experience would occupy positions throughout the organization at every level. The ability to adapt and work in a team oriented environment, commitment to continuous improvement of both self and company, successful work experience and stability of previous employment are all listed as desirable non-academic qualifications. Company benefits and the potential for advancement are both rated as excellent. The most suitable method for initial contact by those seeking employment is in response to advertised positions. McCormick Canada Inc. hires summer students, primarily recruited from within the company. *Contacts:* George Ward, Human Resources Manager or Barb Stotts, Human Resources Co-ordinator.

MCDONALD'S RESTAURANTS OF CANADA LIMITED
McDonald's Place
Toronto, ON M3C 3L4

Tel. 416-433-1000
Fax 416-446-3429
Website .... www.mcdonalds.com

McDonald's is one of the most recognized brands in the world and the largest global foodservice retailer. McDonald's Restaurants of Canada Limited and its franchisees operate over 1,000 restaurants across Canada and employ more than 70,000 Canadians. University and Community College graduates are hired from a wide variety of academic areas for the McDonald's Management Trainee Program as well as for a variety of disciplines related to McDonald's business (eg. Marketing, Information Services, Human Resources, Purchasing, Customer Relations, etc.). Leadership abilities, good communication and people skills, a high energy level and enthusiasm are all considered desirable non-academic qualifications. Starting salaries are competitive within the industry and company benefits and the potential for advancement are both rated as excellent. Resumes for Restaurant Management Trainee positions are welcome by fax or mail to the attention of the Human Resources Department. If inquiring about availability of summer and part-time positions, contact the individual restaurant location. *Contact:* Human Resources Department.

MCELHANNEY CONSULTING SERVICES LTD.
780 Beatty Street, Suite L100
Vancouver, BC V6B 2M1

Tel. 604-683-8521
Fax 604-683-4350
Email .... humanresources@mcelhanney.com
Website .... www.mcelhanney.com

McElhanney Consulting Services Ltd. is an employee owned, Canadian consulting company specializing in engineering, surveying and mapping / GIS services. The company employs 70 people at this location and a total of 200 people in Canada. Graduates most likely to be hired come from the following academic areas: Bachelor of Science (Forestry), Bachelor of Engineering (Civil, Surveying, Transportation, Water Resources), Bachelor of Commerce/Business Administration (Human Resources, Information Systems), Certified General Accountant and Community College Diploma (Accounting, Human Resources, Office Administration, Secretarial, CAD/CAM/Autocad, Engineering Technician, Information Systems). Graduates would occupy Engineer (EIT), Engineering Technician, Project Land Surveyor, Project Manager, Draftsperson, Survey Engineer, Accounting Clerk, Accountant, Secretary/Clerk, Computer Analyst and Human Resources Assistant positions. Related work experience, flexible and a willingness to relocate are all listed as desirable non-academic qualifications. Company benefits are rated above average. The potential for advancement is listed as being good. The average annual starting salary falls within the $35,000 to $40,000 range. The most suitable method for initial contact by those seeking employment is to e-mail a resume with a covering letter. McElhanney Consulting Services Ltd. does hire summer students. *Contact:* Human Resources.

MCGILL UNIVERSITY HEALTH CENTRE / MONTREAL CHILDREN'S HOSPITAL
2300 Tupper Street
Montreal, QC H3H 1P3

Tel. 514-934-4403
Fax 514-934-4387

The McGill University Health Centre (MUHC) represents the first and largest voluntary merger of university teaching hospitals in Canada. The McGill University Health Centre (MUHC) represents the first and largest voluntary merger of university teaching hospitals in Canada. The five partners include the Faculty of Medicine of McGill University, three institutions serving adult patients: the Montreal General Hospital, the Royal Victoria Hospital (including the Montreal Chest Institute) and the Montreal Neurological Hospital, as well as one institution serving children, the Montreal Children's Hospital. The partner hospitals provide a high level and broad scope of specialized services, focusing on the kind of expertise that has helped them attain their international reputation for excellence. At the same time, the MUHC is renowned as a world class research institution, operating at the forefront of new knowledge, innovations, trends and technologies. It is a bilingual institution and serves a diversified community. More than 1,000 doctors and 11,000 employees are part of this centre. The Montreal Children's Hospital offers a full range of health care services to children and adolescents, and is the teaching and research site for McGill's pediatric programs. It has particular strengths in specialized surgery, trauma, intensive care, injury prevention, developmental problems, ambulatory care and home-based programs, and has been designated as a Pediatric Trauma Centre. The Montreal Children's site is a major pediatric, research and teaching centre employing approximately 2,000 people. Graduates most likely to be hired come from the following academic areas: Bachelor of Arts (Psychology, Sociology, Social Work), Bachelor of Science (Audiology, Biology, Chemistry, Computer Science, Microbiology, Nursing, Nutritional Sciences, Occupational Therapy, Pharmacy, Physical Therapy, Psychology, Speech Pathology), Bachelor of Engineering (Architectural/Building, Biomedical Electronics, Civil, Computer Systems, Electrical, Instrumentation, Mechanical, Telecommunications, Welding), Bachelor of Architecture, Bachelor of Education (General, Special Needs), Bachelor of Commerce/Business Administration (Accounting, Finance, Human Resources, Information Systems, Public Administration), Certified Management Accountant, Certified General Accountant, Master of Business Administration, Master of Arts (Psychology), Master of Science (Health Sciences), Master of Social Work, Master of Nursing Science, Medical Doctor,

Community College Diploma (Accounting, Administration, Architecture/Drafting, Dental Assistant, Dental Hygienist, Dietician, Electronics Technician, Engineering Technician, Facility Management, Human Resources, Laboratory Technician, Nursing RN/RNA, Purchasing, Nutrition, Radiology, Respiratory Therapy, Secretarial, Social Work, Ultra-Sound Technician, Welding) and High School Diploma. Previous work experience, bilingualism, good interpersonal, communication and organizational skills, a customer service orientation, motivation, flexibility, initiative, good judgement, the ability to be autonomous and a team player and an interest in/experience working with a pediatric population are all listed as desirable non-academic qualifications. Company benefits are rated above average. The potential for advancement is listed as average to good. The average starting salary is dependent upon the position being considered, and according to government scales. The most suitable methods for initial contact by those seeking employment are to mail or fax a resume with a covering letter. The Montreal Children's Hospital does hire summer students. *Contact:* Manpower Management Sector, Human Resources.

MCGILL UNIVERSITY HEALTH CENTRE / MONTREAL GENERAL HOSPITAL
1650 Cedar Avenue
Montreal, QC H3G 1A4

Tel. 514-934-8077
Fax 514-934-8274
Website .... www.muhc.mcgill.ca

The McGill University Health Centre (MUHC) represents the first and largest voluntary merger of university teaching hospitals in Canada. The McGill University Health Centre (MUHC) represents the first and largest voluntary merger of university teaching hospitals in Canada. The five partners include the Faculty of Medicine of McGill University, three institutions serving adult patients: the Montreal General Hospital, the Royal Victoria Hospital (including the Montreal Chest Institute) and the Montreal Neurological Hospital, as well as one institution serving children, the Montreal Children's Hospital. The partner hospitals provide a high level and broad scope of specialized services, focusing on the kind of expertise that has helped them attain their international reputation for excellence. At the same time, the MUHC is renowned as a world class research institution, operating at the forefront of new knowledge, innovations, trends and technologies. It is a bilingual institution and serves a diversified community. More than 1,000 doctors and 11,000 employees are part of this centre. The Montreal General Hospital is a Level 1 Trauma Centre and has a wide range of specialties including cardiology, rheumatic diseases, oncology, dialysis and a number of surgical subspecialties. It is also a nationally designated Centre of Excellence in neuroscience, genetics and bacterial physiology. The hospital's Research Institute has accomplished many major scientific advances. The Montreal General Hospital employs approximately 3000 people. Graduates most likely to be hired come from the following academic areas: Bachelor of Arts (Psychology, Sociology, Social Work), Bachelor of Science (Audiology, Biology, Chemistry, Computer Science, Microbiology, Nursing, Nutritional Sciences, Occupational Therapy, Pharmacy, Physical Therapy, Psychology, Speech Pathology), Bachelor of Engineering (Architectural/Building, Biomedical Electronics, Civil, Computer Systems, Electrical, Instrumentation, Mechanical, Telecommunications, Welding), Bachelor of Architecture, Bachelor of Education (General, Special Needs), Bachelor of Commerce/Business Administration (Accounting, Finance, Human Resources, Information Systems, Public Administration), Certified Management Accountant, Certified General Accountant, Master of Business Administration, Master of Arts (Psychology), Master of Science (Health Sciences), Master of Social Work, Master of Nursing Science, Medical Doctor, Community College Diploma (Accounting, Administration, Architecture/Drafting, Dental Assistant, Dental Hygienist, Dietician, Electronics Technician, Engineering Technician, Facility Management, Human Resources, Laboratory Technician, Nursing RN/RNA, Purchasing, Nutrition, Radiology, Respiratory Therapy, Secretarial, Social Work, Ultra-Sound Technician, Welding) and High School Diploma. Previous work experience, bilingualism, good interpersonal, communication and organizational skills, a customer service orientation, motivation, flexibility, initiative, good judgement, and the ability to be autonomous and a team player are all listed as desirable non-academic qualifications. Company benefits are rated above average. The potential for advancement is listed as average to good. The average starting salary is dependent upon the position being considered, and according to government scales. The most suitable methods for initial contact by those seeking employment are to mail or fax a resume with a covering letter. The Montreal General Hospital does hire summer students. *Contact:* Manpower Management Sector, Human Resources.

MCGILL UNIVERSITY HEALTH CENTRE / MONTREAL NEUROLOGICAL HOSPITAL
3801 University Street
Montreal, QC H3A 2B4

Tel. .... 514-398-6644 ext. 3227
Fax 514-398-4513

The McGill University Health Centre (MUHC) represents the first and largest voluntary merger of university teaching hospitals in Canada. The McGill University Health Centre (MUHC) represents the first and largest voluntary merger of university teaching hospitals in Canada. The five partners include the Faculty of Medicine of McGill University, three institutions serving adult patients: the Montreal General Hospital, the Royal Victoria Hospital (including the Montreal Chest Institute) and the Montreal Neurological Hospital, as well as one institution serving children, the Montreal Children's Hospital. The partner hospitals provide a high level and broad scope of specialized services, focusing on the kind of expertise that has helped them attain their international reputation for excellence. At the same time, the MUHC is renowned as a world class research institution, operating at the forefront of new knowledge, innovations, trends and technologies. It is a bilingual institution and serves a diversified community. More than 1,000 doctors and 11,000 employees are part of this centre. The Montreal Neurological Hospital specializes in treating patients with diseases of the nervous system, including Epilepsy, Parkinson's disease and ALS among many others, as well as injuries to the spine and to the brain. The The Montreal Neurological Hospital employs approximately 600 people. Graduates most likely to be hired come from the following academic areas: Bachelor of Arts (Psychology, Sociology, Social Work), Bachelor of Science (Audiology, Biology, Chemistry, Computer Science, Microbiology, Nursing, Nutritional Sciences, Occupational Therapy, Pharmacy, Physical Therapy, Psychology, Speech Pathology), Bachelor of Engineering (Architectural/Building, Biomedical Electronics, Civil, Computer Systems, Electrical, Instrumentation, Mechanical, Telecommunications, Welding), Bachelor of Architecture, Bachelor of Educa-

tion (General, Special Needs), Bachelor of Commerce/ Business Administration (Accounting, Finance, Human Resources, Information Systems, Public Administration), Certified Management Accountant, Certified General Accountant, Master of Business Administration, Master of Arts (Psychology), Master of Science (Health Sciences), Master of Social Work, Master of Nursing Science, Medical Doctor, Community College Diploma (Accounting, Administration, Architecture/Drafting, Dental Assistant, Dental Hygienist, Dietician, Electronics Technician, Engineering Technician, Facility Management, Human Resources, Laboratory Technician, Nursing RN/ RNA, Purchasing, Nutrition, Radiology, Respiratory Therapy, Secretarial, Social Work, Ultra-Sound Technician, Welding) and High School Diploma. Previous work experience, bilingualism, good interpersonal, communication and organizational skills, a customer service orientation, motivation, flexibility, initiative, good judgement, and the ability to be autonomous and a team player are all listed as desirable non-academic qualifications. Company benefits are rated above average. The potential for advancement is listed as average to good. The average starting salary is dependent upon the position being considered, and according to government scales. The most suitable methods for initial contact by those seeking employment are to mail or fax a resume with a covering letter. The Montreal Neurological Hospital does hire summer students. *Contact:* Manpower Management Sector, Human Resources.

MCGILL UNIVERSITY HEALTH CENTRE / ROYAL VICTORIA HOSPITAL
687 Pine Avenue, Room M3-15
Montreal, QC H3A 1A1

Tel. .... 514-842-1231 ext. 1546
Fax 514-849-3681

The McGill University Health Centre (MUHC) represents the first and largest voluntary merger of university teaching hospitals in Canada. The McGill University Health Centre (MUHC) represents the first and largest voluntary merger of university teaching hospitals in Canada. The five partners include the Faculty of Medicine of McGill University, three institutions serving adult patients: the Montreal General Hospital, the Royal Victoria Hospital (including the Montreal Chest Institute) and the Montreal Neurological Hospital, as well as one institution serving children, the Montreal Children's Hospital. The partner hospitals provide a high level and broad scope of specialized services, focusing on the kind of expertise that has helped them attain their international reputation for excellence. At the same time, the MUHC is renowned as a world class research institution, operating at the forefront of new knowledge, innovations, trends and technologies. It is a bilingual institution and serves a diversified community. More than 1,000 doctors and 11,000 employees are part of this centre. The Royal Victoria Hospital (RVH), together with the Montreal Chest Hospital, which merged with the RVH in 1994 to become an institute of the RVH, offers a wide range of specialized and ultra-specialized services, and is a leader in basic and clinical research. It is recognized as Quebec's major transplant centre, has developed the major treatment for Parkinson's disease and has established the first palliative care unit in Canada. The Royal Victoria Hospital employs approximately 5000 people. Graduates most likely to be hired come from the following academic areas: Bachelor of Arts (Psychology, Sociology, Social Work), Bachelor of Science (Audiology, Biology, Chemistry, Computer Science, Microbiology, Nursing, Nutritional Sciences, Occupational Therapy, Pharmacy, Physical

Therapy, Psychology, Speech Pathology), Bachelor of Engineering (Architectural/Building, Biomedical Electronics, Civil, Computer Systems, Electrical, Instrumentation, Mechanical, Telecommunications, Welding), Bachelor of Architecture, Bachelor of Education (General, Special Needs), Bachelor of Commerce/Business Administration (Accounting, Finance, Human Resources, Information Systems, Public Administration), Certified Management Accountant, Certified General Accountant, Master of Business Administration, Master of Arts (Psychology), Master of Science (Health Sciences), Master of Social Work, Master of Nursing Science, Medical Doctor, Community College Diploma (Accounting, Administration, Architecture/Drafting, Dental Assistant, Dental Hygienist, Dietician, Electronics Technician, Engineering Technician, Facility Management, Human Resources, Laboratory Technician, Nursing RN/RNA, Purchasing, Nutrition, Radiology, Respiratory Therapy, Secretarial, Social Work, Ultra-Sound Technician, Welding) and High School Diploma. Previous work experience, bilingualism, good interpersonal, communication and organizational skills, a customer service orientation, motivation, flexibility, initiative, good judgement, and the ability to be autonomous and a team player are all listed as desirable non-academic qualifications. Company benefits are rated above average. The potential for advancement is listed as average to good. The average starting salary is dependent upon the position being considered, and according to government scales. The most suitable methods for initial contact by those seeking employment are to mail or fax a resume with a covering letter. The Royal Victoria Hospital does hire summer students. *Contact:* Manpower Management Sector, Human Resources.

MCGRAW-HILL RYERSON LIMITED
300 Water Street
Whitby, ON L1N 9B6

Tel. 905-430-5000
Fax 905-430-5020
Website .... www.mcgrawhill.ca

McGraw-Hill Ryerson Limited is a leading Canadian publisher of educational textbooks, teaching materials, reference books and general interest books. The range of books published by McGraw-Hill Ryerson covers all levels and types of educational institutions: elementary, secondary and tertiary; academic, business and vocational. The company's professional and trade publishing program offers to the general public a wide range of non-fiction books, from wine guides to RRSPs, from cooking to sports, from business handbooks to military history. McGraw-Hill Ryerson has more than 1,000 Canadian produced books in print, representing about 800 authors and publishes an average of 100 English language books per year. Publicly traded on the Toronto Stock Exchange, McGraw-Hill Ryerson Limited is a subsidiary of New York based The McGraw-Hill Companies, Inc. There are 200 employees at this location and a total of 250 employees in Canada. Graduates most likely to be hired come from the following academic areas: Bachelor of Arts (English, Geography, History, Psychology), Bachelor of Science (Geography, Mathematics), Bachelor of Education (Primary Junior, Junior Intermediate, Intermediate Senior, Adult), Bachelor of Commerce/Business Administration (Accounting, Finance, Human Resources, Information Systems, Marketing), Chartered Accountant, Certified Management Accountant, Certified General Accountant and Community College Diploma (Accounting, Book and Magazine Publishing, Business, Human Resources, Marketing/Sales, Office Administration, Secretarial, Graphic Arts, Information Systems). Graduates would

occupy Sales Representative, Editorial Assistant, Marketing Assistant, Inside Sales Representative, Graphic Designer, Customer Service Representative, Accounting Clerk, Administrative Assistant and Inventory Coordinator positions. Team player, creativity, customer service oriented, personal development, strong values, a high level of integrity and knowledge of Excel, Word, PageMaker and other applications are all listed as desirable non-academic qualifications. Company benefits are rated above average. The potential for advancement is listed as average. The average annual starting salary falls within the $25,000 to $30,000 range, and is base and bonus structured for sales positions. The most suitable method for initial contact by those seeking employment is to mail a resume with a covering letter. McGraw-Hill Ryerson Limited does hire summer and co-op work term students with the total number varying from year to year. *Contact:* Manager, Human Resources.

MCMAN YOUTH, FAMILY AND COMMUNITY SERVICES ASSOCIATION
11821 - 123 Street
Edmonton, AB T5L 0G7

Tel. 780-482-4461
Fax 780-482-2686

McMan Youth Family and Community Services Association is a not-for-profit, provincial, multi-service organization that helps individuals and families across Alberta develop the skills and supports to function effectively as members of their communities. The association employs a total of 530 people throughout the province. Graduates most likely to be hired come from the following academic areas: Bachelor of Arts (Psychology, Social Work), Bachelor of Science (Psychology), Bachelor of Education (Special Needs), Bachelor of Commerce/Business Administration (Accounting, Finance, Human Resources), Certified Management Accountant, Master of Business Administration (Accounting, Finance, Human Resources), Master of Arts (Social Work) and Community College Diploma (Accounting, Human Resources, Secretarial, Rehabilitation Therapy, Social Work). Health Sciences Diploma and Bachelor of Arts/Science/Education graduates would occupy Child and Youth Care Worker, Family Support Worker, Program Supervisor/Manager, Rehabilitation Worker and Community Resource Worker positions. Business Diploma and Bachelor of Commerce/Business Administration graduates would occupy Administration, Finance and Human Resource positions. MBA and MSW graduates would occupy Executive Director, Assistant Executive Director and Manager positions. Strong leadership skills, related work experience, team player, and good interpersonal, verbal and written communication skills are all listed as desirable non-academic qualifications. Company benefits are rated above average. The potential for advancement is listed as being average. The average annual starting salary falls within the $25,000 to $30,000 range. The most suitable method for initial contact by those seeking employment is to mail a resume with a covering letter. McMan Youth, Family and Community Services Association does hire summer and co-op work term students. *Contact:* Human Resources Department.

MCMILLAN BINCH
Royal Bank Plaza, South Tower, Suite 3800
Toronto, ON M5J 2J7

Tel. 416-865-7947
Fax 416-865-7048
Website .... www.mcbinch.com

McMillan Binch is one of Canada's leading business law firms. Since 1903, McMillan Binch has provided definitive legal advice to Canadian and international businesses, financial institutions, governments and private individuals. The firm is committed to understanding its clients' needs and objectives and working with them to achieve effective and creative solutions. Today, McMillan Binch comprises approximately 160 lawyers with a total staff of 474 in Toronto. Graduates most likely to be hired come from the following academic areas: Bachelor of Laws and Community College Diploma (Accounting, Information Systems, Secretarial, Legal Assistant, Computer Science). Graduates would occupy Associate Lawyer, Legal Secretary, Law Clerk and a limited number of Accounting and Systems Technology positions. Team player, strong communication skills and good organizational skills are all listed as desirable non-academic qualifications. Company benefits and the potential for advancement are both rated as excellent. The average annual starting salary depends on the position being considered. The most suitable method for initial contact by those seeking employment is to mail a resume with a covering letter. McMillan Binch does hire summer and co-op work term students. *Contacts:* Stephanie Willson, Director, Student & Associate Programs or Nisha Mullick, Manager, Human Resources.

MCW CONSULTANTS LTD.
156 Front Street West, Suite 600
Toronto, ON M5J 2L6

Tel. 416-598-2920
Fax 416-598-5394

MCW Consultants Ltd. provides engineering consulting services. The company employs approximately 40 people at this location and a total of 100 people in Canada. Graduates most likely to be hired are Bachelor of Engineering (Electrical, Mechanical) graduates. Company benefits are rated as industry standard. The potential for advancement is listed as average. The average annual starting salary falls within the $25,000 to $30,000 range. The most suitable method for initial contact by those seeking employment is to mail a resume with a covering letter. MCW Consultants Ltd. does hire summer students. *Contact:* Virgilio De Melo.

MEDIA EXPRESS CUSTOMER CONTACT CENTRE
1134, rue Ste-Catherine Ouest, Suite 101
Montreal, QC H3B 1H4

Tel. 514-876-8760 x243
Fax 514-876-8746
Website .... www.media-express.com

Media Express Customer Contact Centre is one of Canada's leading providers of outsourced call centre services. The company provides inbound and outbound teleservices, customized training programs and call centre consulting services. Through telephone, internet or e-mail, Media Express provides a unified customer contact centre maximizing every medium used to effectively communicate with its customer's clients. There are 600 employees at this location and a total of 1,000 employees across Canada. Graduates most likely to be hired come from the following academic areas: Bachelor of Engineering (Computer Systems, Telecommunications), Bachelor of Education (General, Primary Junior, Junior Intermediate, Intermediate Senior, Adult), Bachelor of Commerce/Business Administration (General, Accounting, Human Resources, Information Systems, Marketing), Chartered Accountant, Certified Management Accountant, Master of Business Administration (General, Accounting, Finance, Human Resources, Information Systems, Marketing), Community College Diploma (Accounting, Business, Communications/Public Relations, Facility Management, Human Resources, Insurance, Marketing/Sales, Office Administration, Secretarial, Computer Science, Information Systems) and High School Diploma. Graduates would occupy Inbound/Outbound Telephone Sales Representative, Technical Support, Programming and Development, Sales and Marketing, Human Resources and Training, Accounting and Administration positions. Previous sales experience, team player, bilingual, dynamic, motivated, computer literate and excellent communication skills are all listed as desirable non-academic qualifications. Company benefits are rated as industry standard. The potential for advancement is listed as being excellent. The average annual starting salary falls within the $20,000 to $25,000 range. The most suitable method for initial contact by those seeking employment is via telephone. Media Express Customer Contact Centre does hire co-op work term students. *Contact:* Recruiting Officer, Human Resources Department.

MEDIA SYNERGY
260 King Street East, Building C
Toronto, ON M5A 1K3

Tel. 416-369-1100
Fax 416-369-9482
Email .... hresources@mediasynergy.com
Website .... www.mediasynergy.com

Media Synergy is a fast-growing internet software company providing innovative online marketing solutions to corporations internationally. The company's clients include Hallmark Cards, National Geographic, CBS Sportsline, Travelocity, and Teletoon. Media Synergy currently employs 35 people. Graduates most likely to be hired come from the following academic areas: Bachelor of Science (Computer Science, Mathematics), Bachelor of Engineering (Computer Systems) and Community College Diploma (Advertising). Graduates would occupy Software Developer, Software Engineer, Project Manager, Program Manager and Account Executive positions. Team player, work experience, good problem solving and communication skills, self-motivated, energetic and creative are all listed as desirable non-academic qualifications. Company benefits and the potential for advancement are both rated as excellent. The average annual starting salary falls within the $40,000 to $45,000 range. The most suitable methods for initial contact by those seeking employment are to fax or e-mail a resume with a covering letter. *Contact:* Jessica Gelberg, Human Resources Manager.

MEDIASOFT TELECOM INC.
8600 Decarie Blvd., Suite 215
Mont Royal, QC H4P 2N2

Tel. 514-731-3838
Fax 514-731-3833
Email .... admin@mediasoft.com
Website .... www.mediasoft.com

MediaSoft Telecom Inc. provides computer telephony and web solutions as a strategic technology partner to OEMs, systems integrators and application developers worldwide. The company's core product IVS allows developers to build, run and manage small to large-scale interactive CT-Web solutions quickly and easily integrating voice, fax, web and multimedia technologies. MediaSoft employs approximately 50 people. Graduates most likely to be hired come from the following academic areas: Bachelor of Science (Computer Science), Bachelor of Engineering (Computer Systems, Telecommunications), Bachelor of Commerce/Business Administration (Marketing) and Community College Diploma (Advertising, Marketing/Sales, Secretarial). Graduates would occupy Programmer/Developer, Secretary/Receptionist, Marketing Secretary, Sales Representative, Technical Support, Advertising and Technical Writer positions. Team player, communicative, flexible, experienced, imaginative and creative are all listed as desirable non-academic qualifications. Company benefits are rated as industry standard. The most suitable methods for initial contact by those seeking employment are to mail, fax or e-mail a resume with a covering letter. *Contacts:* Linda Villeneuve, Administrative Assistant or Ahmed Aina.

MEI GROUP INC.
9001, boul. L'Acadie, 7th Floor
Montreal, QC H4N 3H5

Tel.	514-384-6411
Fax	514-384-6410
Email	resume@mei.ca
Website	www.mei.ca

MEI Group Inc. is the world leader in sales and marketing automation systems for the consumer goods industry. The company is dedicated to providing national and international organizations with powerful, innovative information systems. These systems are designed to enable organizations to reshape their marketing and sales activities, and to become more focused, more effective, more efficient and thus more profitable. In addition to the Montreal location, MEI has offices in Lisle, Illinois and Roissy, France. The company employs a total of 130 people worldwide. Graduates most likely to be hired come from the following academic areas: Bachelor of Engineering (Electrical, Computer Systems), Bachelor of Commerce/Business Administration (Information Systems), Master of Business Administration (Information Systems), Community College Diploma (Computer Science, Information Systems), MCSE, MCSD and MCP accreditations. Graduates would occupy Analyst/Programmer and Technician positions. Team player, bilingual and good communication skills are all listed as desirable non-academic qualifications. Company benefits are rated above average. The potential for advancement is listed as being excellent. The average annual starting salary falls within the $45,000 to $50,000 range. The most suitable methods for initial contact by those seeking employment are to fax or e-mail a resume with a covering letter, or through the company's website. MEI Group Inc. does hire summer and co-op work term students. *Contact:* Human Resources Department.

MEMOTEC

CONNECTING. COMMUNICATING. CONVERGING.

MEMOTEC COMMUNICATIONS INC.
600 McCaffrey Street
St-Laurent, QC H4T 1N1

Tel.	514-738-4781
Fax	514-738-4436
Email	careers@memotec.com
Website	www.memotec.com

Memotec Communications Inc. is an industry leading provider of data, voice and video convergence solutions for telecommunications carriers, internet service providers and corporate customers. The company employs 150 people at this location and a total of 200 people worldwide. Graduates most likely to be hired come from the following academic areas: Bachelor of Science (Computer Science, Mathematics, Physics), Bachelor of Engineering (Electrical, Computer Systems, Microelectronics, Telecommunications, Mechanical, Industrial Design), Bachelor of Commerce/Business Administration, Chartered Accountant, Certified Management Accountant, Certified General Accountant, Master of Business Administration (General, Accounting), Master/Doctorate of Science, Master/Doctorate of Engineering, Community College Diploma (CAD/CAM/Autocad, Computer Science, Electronics Technician, Engineering Technician) and High School Diploma. Graduates would occupy Technician, Test Technician, CAD Technician, Electrical Designer, Software Designer, Mechanical Designer, Clerk, Secretary, and Receptionist positions. Team player, organized, leadership qualities, innovative, client dedicated, and good interpersonal skills are all listed as desirable non-academic qualifications. Company benefits are rated above average. The potential for advancement is listed as average. The most suitable methods for initial contact by those seeking employment are to mail, fax or e-mail a resume with a covering letter. Memotec Communications Inc. does hire summer and co-op work term students. *Contact:* Sandra Aguzzi, Human Resources Manager.

MERAK
322 - 11 Avenue SW, Suite 600
Calgary, AB T2R 0C5

Tel.	403-294-4300
Fax	403-294-4301
Email	resume@merak.com
Website	www.merak.com

Merak develops and markets a wide variety of software applications, as well as related training and consulting services for the Canadian, U.S. and international energy markets. Presently, more than 600 companies use Merak's software applications in over 30 countries. The company's record of embracing the right technology has helped establish it as a leader in energy software development. Originally founded in Calgary in 1980, Merak has grown from a three-person company in 1987 to a company with over 160 employees in Canada and over 220 professionals worldwide. Graduates most likely to be hired come from the following academic areas: Bachelor of Science (Computer Science), Bachelor of Engineering (General, Computer Systems, Geological Engineering, Petroleum/Fuels), Master of Business Administration (Information Systems), Master of Engineering (Petroleum/Fuels, Computer Systems) and Community College Diploma (Information Systems). Graduates would occupy Client Technical Service, Software Support, Software Developer, Project Manager and Field Consultant positions. Team player, positive attitude, keen intellect, enthusiasm and a dynamic personality are all listed as desirable non-academic qualifications. Company benefits are rated as excellent. The potential for advancement is listed as being good. The average annual starting salary falls within the $35,000 to $45,000 range. The most suitable method for initial contact by those seeking employment is to e-mail a resume with a covering letter. Merak does hire summer and co-op work term students. *Contact:* Merak Hiring Team.

MERCK FROSST CANADA INC.
PO Box 1005
Pointe Claire, QC H9R 4P8

Tel.	514-428-3189
Fax	514-428-4940
Email	hr_montreal@merck.com
Website	www.merckfrosst.ca

Merck Frosst is Canada's largest integrated pharmaceutical company. Founded in Montreal at the turn of the century, the company employs 1,500 people in Canada and is a leader in pharmaceutical research. Merck Frosst's research and development investments place it among the top five R & D corporations in all of Canada. The company's main activities include basic research (medicinal chemistry, pharmacology, biochemistry, molecular biology), process research and development, medical research (clinical research, medical services and regulatory affairs), operations (quality assurance, manufacturing, material management, engineering, safety and industrial hygiene), sales and marketing, corporate affairs, human resources, finance and MIS. Graduates most likely to be hired come from the following academic areas: Bachelor of Science (Biology, Chemistry, Computer Science, Microbiology, Nursing, Pharmacy), Bachelor of Engineering (Chemical, Civil, Mechanical, Industrial Production/Manufacturing, Materials Science), Bachelor of Laws, Bachelor of Commerce/Business Administration (General, Accounting, Finance, Human Resources, Information Systems, Marketing), Chartered Accountant, Master of Business Administration (General, Accounting, Finance, Human Resources, Information Systems, Marketing), Master of Science, Doctorate (Sciences) and Community College Diploma (Office Administration, Secretarial, CAD/CAM/Autocad, Engineering Technician, Laboratory Technician, Nursing RN). Graduates would occupy Research Chemist, Clinical Research Associate, Biomedical Research Associate, Laboratory Technician, Chemical Engineer, Professional Sales Representative, Health Science Associate, Market Research Analyst, Promotion Production Specialist, Purchasing Agent, Microbiologist, Quality Assurance Auditor and Pharmaceutical Operator positions. Team player, fast learner and previous pharmaceutical experience are all listed as desirable non-academic qualifications. Company benefits and the potential for advancement are both rated as excellent. The average annual starting salary falls within the $25,000 to $30,000 range. The most suitable method for initial contact by those seeking employment is to fax a resume with a covering letter. Merck Frosst Canada Inc. does hire summer and co-op work term students. *Contacts:* Sylvie Lepage, Staffing Associate; Tina Scalera, Staffing Associate or Marie-Josée Trudel, Staffing Associate.

MESSAGINGDIRECT LTD.
10117 Jasper Ave., Suite 900
Edmonton, AB T5J 1W8

Tel.	780 424 4922
Fax	780-424-4925
Email	recruitment@messagingdirect.com
Website	www.messagingdirect.com

MessagingDirect Ltd. is one of the world's leading developers of standards based electronic messaging and directory software for the e-business market. The company's business to business and business to consumer solutions are based on a secure embedded messaging foundation. MessagingDirect was formed in 1999, resulting from the merger of Isode, a leading developer of Internet/X.400 messaging and LDAP/X.500 directory servers, and Execmail, a leading developer of IMAP messaging clients and message stores. The company's worldwide customer base includes solution providers, large multinational corporations, telecommunications service providers, educational establishments and government agencies. Customers include: AT&T, BT, Bell-Emergis, Bull, Nortel, Notre Dame University, Siemens Nixdorf and Wal Mart. In addition to the Edmonton office, MessagingDirect has offices in Richmond, United Kingdom and Wilmington, Delaware. There are 40 employees at this location and a total of 70 employees worldwide. Graduates most likely to be hired come from the following academic areas: Bachelor of Science (Computer Science), Bachelor of Engineering (Computer Systems), Bachelor of Commerce/Business Administration (Marketing), Certified Management Accountant, Master of Engineering (Computer Science) and Community College Diploma (Marketing/Sales, Office Administration, Computer Science, Information Systems). Graduates would occupy Computer Programmer, Systems Analyst, Software Developer and Marketing Coordinator positions. Team player, work experience, flexibility and a high level of initiative are all listed as desirable non-academic qualifications. Company benefits and the potential for advancement are rated as excellent. The average annual starting salary falls within the $35,000 to $40,000 range. The most suitable method for initial contact by those seeking employment is to e-mail a resume with a covering letter. MessagingDirect Ltd. does hire summer and co-op work term students. *Contact:* Human Resources Manager.

METAFORE
154 Sheldon Drive
Cambridge, ON N1R 7K9

Tel.	519-623-9800
Fax	519-623-7400
Email	recruiter@metaforegroup.com
Website	www.metaforegroup.com

Metafore is an enterprise technology services provider and application developer. The company delivers comprehensive information technology (IT) services, education services, skill sourcing and application development offerings. With over 100 associates, headquartered in Cambridge, Ontario, Metafore has professional education centres, and a global network of business partners. Graduates most likely to be hired come from the following academic areas: Bachelor of Science (Computer Science), Bachelor of Engineering (Computer Systems), Bachelor of Commerce/Business Administration (Information Systems), Community College Diploma (Computer Science), as well as other Information Technology accreditations. Graduates would occupy Senior Technical Analyst, Application Developer, Programmer and Systems Analyst, Project Leader, Technical Support Specialist, and Help Desk positions. Superior written and oral communication skills, team work, bilingual, and multi-tasking abilities are all listed as desirable non-academic qualifications. Company benefits are rated as excellent. The potential for advancement is listed as being good. The most suitable methods for initial contact by those seeking employment are to fax or e-mail a resume with a covering letter. Metafore does hire students for summer and co-op work term positions. *Contacts:* Brent Davidson, Director; Christina Laughren, IT Resource Specialist or Lars Pastrik, IT Resource Specialist.

METRO ORTHOPAEDIC REHAB CLINICS / MORC
909 Jane Street, Suite 202
Toronto, ON M6N 4C6

Tel.	416-604-4404
Fax	416-604-4406

Metro Orthopaedic Rehab Clinics / MORC offers individualized assessment and ongoing patient education using a complete multi-disciplinary approach to rehabilitation and pain management. Applying a proactive approach to the rehabilitation of muscular-skeletal injuries, the multi-disciplinary treatment approach optimizes input from each branch of expertise in order to provide an individualized rehabilitative package for each patient. MORC operates six clinics in Toronto, employing a total of 25 people. Graduates most likely to be hired come from the following academic areas: Bachelor of Arts (General, Economics), Bachelor of Science (General, Physio/Physical Therapy, Psychology) and Community College Diploma (Accounting, Business, Health/Home Care Aide, Massage Therapy). Punctuality, team player, innovative, culturally sensitive, good people skills and excellent customer service skills are all listed as desirable non-academic qualifications. Company benefits are rated as excellent. The potential for advancement is listed as average. The average annual starting salary falls within the $15,000 to $45,000 plus range, depending on the position being considered. The most suitable method for initial contact by those seeking employment is to mail a resume with a covering letter. Metro Orthopaedic Rehab Clinics occasionally hires summer and co-op work term students. *Contact:* Kash Handy, Manager.

MÉTRO-RICHELIEU INC.
11011, boul Maurice Duplessis
Montreal, QC H1C 1V6

Tel.	514-643-1055
Fax	514-643-1215
Email	metrorichelieu@metro.ca
Website	www.metro-richelieu.com

Métro-Richelieu Inc. is a leader in Quebec's food distribution industry supplying customers with grocery products, fruits and vegetables, fish and seafood as well as meat and frozen foods from its distribution centres throughout Quebec. The company is a leader in the Quebec supermarket segment with its Métro banner and in neighbourhood market with the Marché Richelieu banner and is well positioned in the discount segment with Super C stores. Through its Éconogros, Pêcheries Atlantiques and Distagro divisions, Métro-Richelieu also serves more than 4,000 customers in the food services industry as well as a large network of convenience stores. In addition, the company is active in the pharmaceutical segment through its subsidiary McMahon distributeur pharmaceutique Inc., a wholesaler acting as franchisor for the Brunet chain of drugstores. Métro-Richelieu is a public company trading on The Montreal Exchange and The Toronto Stock Exchange under the symbol MRU.A. The company directly employs some 6,700 people as well as creating 15,000 jobs through its affiliated and franchised retailers. Graduates most likely to be hired come from the following academic areas: Bachelor of Arts (Industrial Relations), Bachelor of Engineering (Industrial), Bachelor of Commerce/Business Administration (Accounting, Finance, Marketing), Certified Management Accountant (Finance), Certified General Accountant (Finance), Master of Business Administration and Community College Diploma (Human Resources, Security/En-

forcement, Computer Science). Previous work experience is listed as a desirable non-academic qualification. The most suitable method for initial contact by those seeking employment is to mail a resume with a covering letter (no telephone calls please). Métro-Richelieu Inc. does hire summer students. *Contact:* Ressources humaines.

MEYERS NORRIS PENNY & CO.
1661 Portage Avenue, Suite 508
Winnipeg, MB R3J 3T7

Tel.	204-775-4531
Fax	204-772-5917
Website	www.mnp.ca

Meyers Norris Penny & Co. is one of western Canada's leading chartered accountancy and business advisory firms with 25 offices located throughout the three prairie provinces. There are 30 employees at this location and a total of 250 employees in the company. Graduates most likely to be hired come from the following academic areas: Bachelor of Commerce/Business Administration (Accounting, Human Resources, Information Systems, Marketing), Chartered Accountant, Certified Management Accountant, Certified General Accountant, Master of Business Administration (Accounting, Human Resources, Information Systems, Marketing) and Community College Diploma (Accounting, Human Resources, Marketing, Secretarial, Computer Science). The most suitable method for initial contact by those seeking employment is to mail a resume with a covering letter. Meyers Norris Penny & Co. does hire summer students. *Contact:* Human Resources Department.

MICROAGE / CACHET ATLANTIC INC.
61 Raddall Avenue, Unit J
Dartmouth, NS B3B 1T4

Tel.	902-468-7195
Fax	902-468-7196
Email	hrecruiter@hfx.microage.ca
Website	www.microage.ca

MicroAge / Cachet Atlantic Inc. is a branch of Montreal based MicroAge, a leading global technology services integrator providing multi-vendor products and integrated services worldwide. Through a network of branches and alliance partners spanning 34 countries, MicroAge services the local, national, and international requirements of corporate organizations and government agencies. The MicroAge global network includes 1,200 branches worldwide. International connections provide clients with access to world-class technology and technical support, while local branch focus provide personalized attention and timely service. The MicroAge / Cachet Atlantic Inc. branch employs 15 people while MicroAge employs a total of 500 people in Canada. Graduates most likely to be hired at the Cachet Atlantic branch come from the following academic areas: Bachelor of Science (Computer Science), Bachelor of Commerce/Business Administration (General, Information Systems) and Community College Diploma (Computer Science). Graduates would occupy Technician and Sales Representative positions. Self directed and goal driven are both listed as desirable non-academic qualifications. Company benefits and the potential for advancement are both rated as excellent. The average annual starting salary falls within the $30,000 to $35,000 range. The most suitable method for initial contact by those seeking employment is to e-mail a resume with a covering letter. *Contact:* Frank Fricker, President.

MICROSOFT CANADA INC.
320 Matheson Boulevard West
Mississauga, ON L5R 3R1

Tel.	905-568-0434
Fax	905-568-1527
Email	msjobs@microsoft.com
Website	www.microsoft.com

Microsoft Canada Inc. is involved in the sales, support, marketing and distribution of Microsoft software products in Canada. Microsoft Canada Inc. is a subsidiary of Redmond, Washington based Microsoft Corporation. Founded in 1975, Microsoft is the world's leading software provider, producing innovative products designed to meet customers' evolving needs. The company's products are available in more than 30 languages and sold in more than 50 countries around the world. Microsoft Corporation employs 22,000 people worldwide. Microsoft Canada Inc. employs approximately 350 people in Canada. Graduates most likely to be hired come from the following academic areas: Bachelor of Science (Computer Science, Mathematics) and Bachelor of Engineering (Computer Systems, Electrical). Graduates would be hired to occupy Product Support and Systems Engineering positions. Applicants should be enthusiastic, self-starters, love PC's and possess excellent written and verbal communication skills. Company benefits and the potential for advancement are both rated as excellent. The average annual starting salary is dependent upon the position being considered. The most suitable method for initial contact by graduates seeking employment is to mail a resume with a covering letter. Microsoft Canada Inc. hires students for co-op work terms. *Contact:* Renee Reynolds, Recruiter.

MILGRAM GROUP OF COMPANIES
407, rue McGill, Suite 500
Montreal, QC H2Y 2G7

Tel.	514-288-2161
Fax	514-288-6829
Website	www.milgram.com

Milgram Group of Companies are freight forwarders and customs brokers. The company's head office is in Montreal, with branch office locations found in Dorval, Lacolle, Mississauga and Richmond. Milgram employs approximately 162 employees at this location and a total of 219 employees in Canada. Graduates most likely to be hired come from the following academic areas: Bachelor of Science (General, Computer Science), Bachelor of Engineering (Computer Systems), Bachelor of Commerce/Business Administration (General, Accounting, Finance, Human Resources, Information Systems, Marketing, Public Administration), Master of Business Administration and Community College Diploma (Accounting, Administration, Business, Marketing/Sales, Secretarial). Graduates would occupy Secretarial, Clerk and Technician positions. Previous work experience, team player and a good attitude are listed as desirable non-academic qualifications. Company benefits are rated above average. The potential for advancement is listed as being good. The average annual starting salary falls within the $15,000 to $20,000 range. The most suitable methods for initial contact by those seeking employment are to mail or fax a resume with a covering letter, or by applying through the company's website. Milgram Group of Companies occasionally hires summer students. *Contact:* Human Resources.

MILLTRONICS LTD.
1954 Technology Drive, PO Box 4225
Peterborough, ON K9J 7B1

Tel.	705-745-2431
Fax	705-740-7566
Email	cahr@milltronics.com
Website	www.milltronics.com

Milltronics Ltd. designs and manufactures advanced, electronics-based instrumentation and sensors for customers in 93 countries. The company has two main product lines: continuous and point level measurement products, and weighing, feeding and motion sensing systems from the Mass Dynamics Division. These product lines are proven in over 200,000 applications in primary and secondary industries. Founded in 1954 and headquartered in Peterborough, Milltronics Ltd. has 16 locations in 11 countries around the world. There are 268 employees at this location, a total of 300 in Canada and a total of 600 employees worldwide. Graduates most likely to be hired come from the following academic areas: Bachelor of Science (Computer Science), Bachelor of Engineering (Electrical, Mechanical, Computer Systems, Engineering Physics, Instrumentation), Bachelor of Commerce/Business Administration (Accounting, Human Resources, Marketing), Master of Business Administration (Marketing) and Community College Diploma (Human Resources, Marketing/Sales, Electronics Technician). Graduates would occupy Engineering Analyst, Advisor and Coordinator positions. Team player, previous work experience and excellent interpersonal skills are all listed as desirable non-academic qualifications. Company benefits and the potential for advancement are both rated as excellent. The average annual starting salary falls within the $35,000 to $40,000 range. The most suitable method for initial contact by those seeking employment is to e-mail a resume with a covering letter. Milltronics Ltd. does hire summer and co-op work term students. *Contact:* Human Resources Department.

MINISTRY OF EDUCATION / MINISTRY OF TRAINING, COLLEGES & UNIVERSITIES, ONTARIO
900 Bay Street, 19th Floor, Mowat Block
Toronto, ON M7A 1L2

Tel.	416-327-9045
Fax	416-327-9043
Email	info@edu.gov.on.ca
Website	www.edu.gov.on.ca

The Ministry of Education and the Ministry of Training, Colleges and Universities are responsible for the administration of laws relating to education and skills training in the province of Ontario. The Ministry of Education is responsible for elementary and secondary education, and the Ministry of Training, Colleges and Universities is responsible for post secondary education and training. The Ministry of Education and the Ministry of Training, Colleges and Universities employ approximately 2,500 people. Graduates most likely to be hired come from the following academic areas: Bachelor of Arts, Bachelor of Science, Bachelor of Engineering, Bachelor of Education, Bachelor of Commerce/Business Administration, Master of Business Administration, Community College Diploma and High School Diploma. Graduates are hired to occupy a wide variety of administrative, clerical, secretarial, and policy, etc. positions. Excellent written and verbal communication skills, team player, good interpersonal skills and good organizational skills are all listed as desirable non-academic qualifications. Company benefits are rated above average. The potential for advancement is listed as being good. The average annual starting salary falls within the $30,000 to $35,000 range. The most suitable method for initial contact by those seeking employment is to mail a resume with a covering letter. The Ministry of Education and the Ministry of Training, Colleges and Universities hire summer students. *Contact:* Human Resources Planning and Services Branch.

MINISTRY OF NATURAL RESOURCES, ONTARIO
300 Water Street, PO Box 7000
Peterborough, ON K9J 8M5

Fax 705-755-3108
Website .... www.mnr.gov.on.ca/MNR

The Ministry of Natural Resources is responsible for the management of the renewable and non-renewable natural resources in the province of Ontario. This involves a wide variety of resource activities, including forest, wildlife and fisheries management, cartography, public education, provincial park operation, forest fire prevention, water resource management, as well as a multitude of administrative functions. In addition to this main office there are eight regional and forty-seven district offices spread across the province. Graduates most likely to be hired come from the following academic areas: Bachelor of Arts (Sociology, Recreation/Planning), Bachelor of Science (Forestry, Biology, Geography), Bachelor of Landscape Architecture, Bachelor of Commerce/Business Administration, Chartered Accountant, Certified Management Accountant, Certified General Accountant, Master of Business Administration, Master of Arts (Related), Master of Science (Related) and Community College Diploma (Forestry Technology). Graduates would occupy a wide variety of related positions including: Forester, Biologist, Resource Technician, Conservation Officer, Planner and Administrative positions. Employee benefits and the potential for advancement are both rated as excellent. The most suitable method for initial contact by those seeking employment is to mail a resume with a covering letter. The Ministry of Natural Resources does hire summer students. *Contact:* Human Resources Branch.

MINISTRY OF THE SOLICITOR GENERAL & CORRECTIONAL SERVICES, ONTARIO
171 Judson Street, Building C
Toronto, ON M8Z 1A4

Tel. 416-314-8381
Fax 416-314-2838
Website .... www.sgcs.gov.on.ca

The Correctional Services Division is responsible for the supervision of adults awaiting trial, sentence, deportation or transfer to a correctional institution. In addition, the division is responsible for the supervision of offenders sentenced to terms of probation or institutional custody of less than two years, and under the Young Offenders Act, the division is responsible for young offenders. The Correctional Services Division employs more than 1,000 people in the province. Graduates most likely to be hired come from the following academic areas: Bachelor of Arts (General, Criminology, Psychology, Recreation, Sociology, Social Work), Bachelor of Science (Nursing, Psychology), Community College Diploma (Early Childhood Education, Recreation Studies, Security/Enforcement, Social Work/DSW, Nursing RN) and High School Diploma. Graduates would occupy Correctional Officer, Probation Officer, Nurse, Recreation Officer, Social Worker, Youth Officer positions. Good interpersonal skills, an ability to use tact and judgement, and able to recognize and react to abnormal situations are all listed as desirable non-academic qualifications. Employee benefits are rated as excellent. The potential for advancement is listed as being good. The average annual starting salary falls within the $30,000 to $35,000 range. The most suitable method for initial contact by those seeking employment is to mail a resume with a covering letter. The Correctional Services Division does hire summer students through the summer experience program, see your campus career centre for details. *Contact:* Central Recruitment Unit (Toll Free 1-888-412-8111).

MINOLTA BUSINESS EQUIPMENT (CANADA), LTD.
369 Britannia Road East
Mississauga, ON L4Z 2H5

Tel. 905-890-6600
Fax 905-890-2339
Email .... tbradshaw@minolta.ca
Website .... www.minolta.ca

Minolta Business Equipment (Canada), Ltd. is involved in the sales and service of business equipment, including photocopiers, facsimiles, and printers. There are 35 employees at this location, and a total of 730 employees in Canada. Graduates most likely to be hired come from the following academic areas: Bachelor of Arts (Economics, English, History, Political Science, Sociology), Bachelor of Commerce/Business Administration (Accounting, Finance, Marketing) and Community College Diploma (Electronics Technician, Engineering Technician). Graduates would occupy Sales Representative, Technician, Clerical and Accounting positions. Previous work experience and a positive attitude are listed as desirable non-academic qualifications. Company benefits are rated above average. The potential for advancement is listed as average. The average annual starting salary falls within the $25,000 to $30,000 range. The most suitable methods for initial contact by those seeking employment are to mail, fax or e-mail a resume with a covering letter. *Contact:* Tracie Bradshaw, Corporate Manager of Human Resources.

MINTZ & PARTNERS
1446 Don Mills Road, Suite 100
Toronto, ON M3B 3N6

Tel. 416-391-2900
Fax 416-391-2748
Email .... hr@mintzca.com
Website .... www.mintzca.com

Mintz & Partners is a chartered accounting firm providing a full range of financial and consulting services for the entrepreneurial, owner-managed client. The firm is small enough to provide a personal touch to their services and large enough to be able to provide a full range of services on a national and international scale. Mintz & Partners employs more than 100 people. Graduates most likely to be hired come from the following academic areas: Bachelor of Commerce/Business Administration (Accounting), Chartered Accountant, Certified Management Accountant, Certified General Accountant and Master of Business Administration (Accounting). Graduates would occupy Staff Accountant, Students-in-Accounts and Accounting Technician positions. Chartered Accountant training is provided. Small business work experience and strong interpersonal and communication skills are listed as desirable non-academic qualifications. Company benefits are rated above average. The potential for advancement is listed as being good. The average annual starting salary falls within the $30,000 to $35,000 range.

The most suitable method for initial contact by those seeking employment is to mail a resume with a covering letter. Mintz & Partners does hire summer and co-op work term students. These are primarily third year Bachelor of Commerce and Bachelor of Business Administration/ Management students. *Contact:* Annette Plorins, Manager of Human Resources.

MISSISSAUGA, CITY OF

300 City Centre Drive, 5th Floor
Mississauga, ON L5B 3C1

Tel. 905-896-5023
Fax 905-615-4185
Email .... hr.info@city.mississauga.on.ca
Website .... www.city.mississauga.on.ca

The City of Mississauga provides a full range of municipal government services through various departments and affiliates. The city employs 2,500 full time and 1,900 temporary employees. Departments include the City Manager's Office, Corporate Services, Transportation and Works, Community Services, and Planning and Building. Affiliates include Art Gallery of Mississauga, Mayor's Youth Advisory Committee, Mississauga Arts Council, Mississauga Heritage Foundation, and the Mississauga Sports Council. Graduates most likely to be hired come from the following academic areas: Bachelor of Arts (Geography, Urban Geography/Planning), Bachelor of Science (Computer Science, Geography), Bachelor of Engineering (Civil, Electrical, Mechanical, Architectural/ Building, Computer Systems, Environmental/Resources, Surveying, Water Resources), Bachelor of Architecture, Bachelor Landscape Architecture, Bachelor of Commerce/Business Administration (Accounting, Finance, Human Resources, Information Systems, Marketing, Public Administration) and Community College Diploma (Accounting, Administration, Communications/Public Relations, Facility Management, Financial Planning, Human Resources, Information Systems, Recreation Studies, Security/Enforcement, Urban Planning, Agriculture/Horticulture, CAD/CAM/Autocad, Computer Science, Electronics Technician, Engineering Technician, Forestry, HVAC Systems). Good communication skills, team player, enthusiasm and work experience are all listed as desirable non-academic qualifications. Company benefits are rated as industry standard. The potential for advancement is listed as average. The most suitable method for initial contact by those interested in working for the City of Mississauga is to mail, fax or drop off a resume, cover letter and an application form to the Corporate Services Department, Human Resources Division at this address. The Human Resources Division receives all applications submitted to the City and is responsible for reviewing them and maintaining the Applications Inventory File. All applications are kept on file for six months to be reviewed continuously for suitable vacancies that come open to external applicants. The City of Mississauga does hire students for summer and co-op work terms. *Contact:* Corporate Services Department, Human Resources Division.

MISTAHIA HEALTH REGION

10320 - 99 Street, 2nd Floor, Provincial Building
Grande Prairie, AB T8V 6J4

Tel. 780-538-5387
Fax 780-538-5455
Website .... www.mhr.ab.ca

The Mistahia Health Region is dedicated to ensuring quality health care and promoting healthy lifestyles. Mistahia Health Region was established as a part of regionalization to coordinate health services within an area in northwestern Alberta that includes Grande Prairie, Fairview, Grimshaw, Worsley, Grande Cache, Hythe, Beaverlodge, Spirit River, and Valleyview. Mistahia Health Region directly serves 85,000 residents and employs a total of 2,200 people. Mistahia Health Region provides excellent opportunities for new graduates to gain experience in general and specialized areas of health care. Graduates most likely to be hired come from the following academic areas: Bachelor of Arts (Social Work), Bachelor of Science (Computer Science, Audiology, Nursing, Nutritional Sciences, Occupational Therapy, Pharmacy, Physical Therapy, Recreation Therapy), Bachelor of Commerce/Business Administration (Finance, Human Resources, Information Systems), Certified Management Accountant, Certified General Accountant, Master of Business Administration (Finance, Human Resources), Master of Science (Speech Pathology, Psychology), Medical Doctor (Psychiatry, General Medicine) and Community College Diploma (Accounting, Human Resources, Purchasing/Logistics, Secretarial, Recreation, Computer Science, Dental Assistant/Hygienist, Nutrition, Laboratory Technician, Nuclear Medicine Technician, Nursing RN/RNA, Radiology Technician, Respiratory Therapy, Ultra-Sound Technician). Graduates from the Health Sciences would occupy positions related directly to their academic backgrounds. Other graduates would occupy Financial Analyst, Human Resources Officer, Labour Relations Consultant, Technical Support Analyst and Programmer/Analyst positions. Team player, adaptable to change and good communication skills are all listed as desirable non-academic qualifications. Company benefits are rated as industry standard. The potential for advancement is listed as being good. The most suitable method for initial contact by those seeking employment is to mail a resume with a covering letter. The Mistahia Health Region does hire a small number of summer students depending on programs available. In addition, Mistahia does hire co-op work term students. For more information visit the Mistahia Health Region's website. When telephoning long distance Mistahia can be reached toll free at 1-800-732-8981. *Contacts:* Human Resources (all Other Health Care Occupations) or Regional Medical Director (for Physicians).

MITEC TELECOM INC.

9000 Trans-Canada Highway
Pointe-Claire, QC H9R 5Z8

Tel. 514-694-6666
Fax 514-694-3731
Email .... opportunities@mitectelecom.com
Website .... www.mitectelecom.com

Mitec Telecom Inc. is an industry leader in the design and manufacture of microwave and telecom products. Mitec designs and develops microwave communications components and subsystems; satellite communications equipment for earth stations; monitoring, alarm and control products, in both generic and dedicated forms; and PCS and cellular base station subsystems and components. Founded in 1972, the company employs approximately 157 people at this location and a total of 279 worldwide. Graduates most likely to be hired are Bachelor of Engineering graduates from Electrical, Microelectronics and Telecommunications programs. Graduates would occupy Development Engineer, Process Engineer, Controller, Process Planner, Electrical Test Technician, Typist and CAD Operator positions. Previous related work experience is listed as a desirable non-academic qualification. Company benefits are rated above average. The potential for advancement is listed as being good. The most suitable method for initial contact by those seeking employment is to mail a resume with a covering letter. Mitec Telecom Inc. does hire summer students. *Contact:* Human Resources.

MITRA IMAGING INC.
455 Phillip Street
Waterloo, ON N2L 3X2

Tel.	519-746-2900
Fax	519-746-3745
Email	hr@mitra.com
Website	www.mitra.com

Mitra Imaging Inc. develops systems that allow hospitals to capture, store, transmit and display medical images and other clinical information on computer networks. Mitra is a family of companies that is making an impact on healthcare services worldwide. The company's goals are improved productivity, faster access to data, shorter hospital stays and more rational use of experts and resources, all of which is aimed at providing better care for the patient. In association with multinational partners such as Agfa, General Electric and others, Mitra's products are improving healthcare at more than 2,000 hospitals worldwide. Founded in 1991, the company has division in Eindhoven, The Netherlands and Milwaukee, U.S.A in addition to the Waterloo location. Mitra employs 125 people at this location and a total of 150 people worldwide. Graduates most likely to be hired come from the following academic areas: Bachelor of Science (Computer Science, Mathematics, Physics), Bachelor of Engineering (Biomedical Electronics, Computer Systems), Master of Science (Computer Science) and Master of Engineering (Biomedical Electronics, Computer Systems). Graduates would occupy Software Designer, Integration Specialist, Product Manager, Technical Support Analyst, Systems Engineer and Software Verification Specialist positions. Team player, responsible, dedicated, quick learner, problem solver and bright are listed as non-academic qualifications. Company benefits and the potential for advancement are both rated as excellent. The most suitable methods for initial contact by those seeking employment are to e-mail a resume with a covering letter, or via the company's website. Mitra Imaging Inc. does hire co-op work term students. *Contact:* Julie Symons, Human Resources Administrator.

MOHAWK OIL CO. LTD.
6400 Roberts Street, Suite 325
Burnaby, BC V5G 4G2

Tel.	604-293-4114
Fax	604-293-7126

Mohawk Oil Co. Ltd. is involved in the retail of gasoline, convenience store marketing, and the manufacturing of lubricants and ethanol. The company employs 96 people at this location and a total of 282 people across Western Canada. Graduates most likely to be hired come from the following academic areas: Bachelor of Commerce/Business Administration (Accounting, Finance, Human Resources, Information Systems, Marketing), Certified Management Accountant, Community College Diploma (Accounting, Administration, Advertising, Business, Human Resources, Marketing/Sales, Legal Assistant) and High School Diploma. Graduates would occupy Entry Level Marketing and District Manager Trainee positions. Retail experience, industry experience, a willingness to move within western Canada, a positive outlook, team player and strong leadership qualities are all listed as desirable non-academic qualifications. Company benefits are rated as excellent. The potential for advancement is listed as being good. The most suitable method for initial contact by those seeking employment is to mail a resume with a covering letter. Mohawk Oil Co. Ltd. does hire a limited number of summer students. *Contacts:* Neil B. Zambik, Director, People Development and Communications or Lucille Wright, Leader, People Support Services.

MONARCH COMMUNICATIONS INC.
361 First Street SE
Medicine Hat, AB T1A 0A5

Tel.	403-526-4529
Fax	403-526-4000

Monarch Communications Inc. is involved in the operation of radio, television and cable television systems. The company employs 300 people. Graduates most likely to be hired come from the following academic areas: Bachelor of Arts (Journalism), Bachelor of Engineering (Microelectronics, Telecommunications), Bachelor of Commerce/Business Administration (Marketing) and Community College Diploma (Accounting, Communications, Journalism, Television/Radio Arts, Electronics Technician). Graduates would occupy On-Air Announcer, News Reporter, Creative Writer, Production Editor, VTR Operator, Salesperson, Administrative Assistant, Master Control Operator, Electronic Technician, Data Processing and Computer Technician positions. Creative, self-motivated, team player and able to communicate in a professional manner are all listed as desirable non-academic qualifications. Company benefits and the potential for advancement are both rated as excellent. The average annual starting salary varies depending upon the position being considered. The most suitable method for initial contact by those seeking employment is to mail a resume with a covering letter. *Contact:* Heather Lemeshuk, Supervisor, Human Resources.

MONTAGE
10130 - 103 Street, Suite 1900
Edmonton, AB T5J 3N9

Tel.	780-423-4553
Fax	780-423-7088
Email	hr@montage.ca
Website	www.montage.ca

Montage is an information technology (IT) firm providing IT services throughout North America. The company specializes in the application of internet, Microsoft, Oracle and Oracle Financials technologies. In addition to the company's Edmonton headquarters, Montage maintains regional offices in Ottawa, Toronto, Calgary and Raleigh, North Carolina. Graduates most likely to be hired come from the following academic areas: Bachelor of Science (Computer Science) and Community College Diploma (Computer Science). Graduates would occupy Junior Developer positions. Team player, a high level of initiative and excellent interpersonal skills are all listed as desirable non-academic qualifications. Company benefits and the potential for advancement are both rated as excellent. The average annual starting salary falls within the $35,000 to $40,000 range. The most suitable method for initial contact by those seeking employment is to e-mail a resume with a covering letter. MONTAGE does hire summer students. *Contact:* Deanna Fuoco, Recruiter.

MOORE NORTH AMERICA
5500 Explorer Drive
Mississauga, ON L4W 5C3

Tel. 905-602-1727
Fax 905-602-1731

Moore North America is a leading manufacturer of business forms and is also involved in a variety of business activities. Activities include business information handling and processing support services, telesales, direct-mail marketing, data processing, and a variety of specialized services. There are approximately 138 employees at this location with a total of over 1,300 employees across Canada in over fifty sales offices and six manufacturing facilities. Graduates most likely to be hired come from the following academic areas: Bachelor of Arts (General), Bachelor of Commerce/Business Administration, Chartered Accountant, Certified Management Accountant, Master of Business Administration and Community College Diploma (Administration, Business, Marketing/Sales). Graduates would occupy Sales Assistant, Accounting Clerk, Customer Service Representative, Programmer and Sales Representative positions. Adaptable, team-oriented, self-motivated, quality-conscious and a high level of initiative are all listed as desirable non-academic qualifications. Company benefits are rated above average. The potential for advancement is listed as being good. The average annual starting salary falls within the $25,000 to $30,000 range, and is commission based for sales positions. The most suitable method for initial contact by those seeking employment is to mail a resume with a covering letter. Moore North America does hire summer students. Contact: Human Resources.

MORELAND RESOURCES INC.
717 - 7th Avenue SW, Suite 1480
Calgary, AB T2P 0Z3

Tel. 403-263-2330
Fax 403-313-1001
Email .... moreland@cadvision.com

Moreland Resources Inc. is a junior oil and gas company. Graduates most likely to be hired are Bachelor of Engineering graduates from Chemical, Mechanical, Geological, and Petroleum/Fuels disciplines. Successful applicants would occupy Senior Engineer, Staff Engineer and Senior Staff Engineer positions. Previous work experience, team player and good human relations skills are listed as desirable non-academic qualifications. Company benefits are rated as excellent. The potential for advancement is listed as average. The average annual starting salary falls in the $60,000 plus range. The most suitable method for initial contact by those seeking employment is to mail a resume with a covering letter. (See listing for Veba Oil Operations BV). Contacts: Kam Fard, P.Eng. or Human Resources.

MORRISON HERSHFIELD LIMITED
4 Lansing Square
Toronto, ON M2J 1T1

Tel. 416-499-3110
Fax 416-499-9658
Website .... www.mhgroup.ca

Morrison Hershfield Limited is a prominent multi-disciplinary consulting engineering and management firm. The company's focus is in providing clients with expertise in communications infrastructure, civil and structural engineering, building science, facility management, fire and safety, transportation infrastructure, project and construction management, and specialized services in management and marketing consulting. There are approximately 150 employees at this location with a total of 250 employees in five office locations across Canada. Graduates most likely to be hired come from the following academic areas: Bachelor of Engineering (Civil, Architectural/Building, Electrical, Telecommunications, Mechanical) and Community College Diploma (CAD/CAM/Autocad, Engineering Technician). Graduates would occupy Engineers in Training, Junior Technician and Technologist and CAD Operator positions. Previous work experience in the consulting field or in engineering are both listed as desirable non-academic qualifications. Company benefits are rated above average. The potential for advancement is listed as excellent. The average annual starting salary falls within the $35,000 to $40,000 range. The most suitable method for initial contact by those seeking employment is to mail a resume with a covering letter. Morrison Hershfield Limited does hire summer and co-op work term students, the number varies annually with requirements. Contact: Dennis Comand, Human Resources Officer.

MOTOROLA CANADA LIMITED
3900 Victoria Park Avenue, Suite 2
Toronto, ON M2H 3H7

Tel. 416-499-1441
Fax 416-499-6994
Website .... www.motorola.ca

Motorola Canada Limited is a leading provider of wireless communications, semiconductors and advanced electronic systems and services. Major equipment businesses include cellular telephone, two-way radio paging and data communications, personal communications, automotive, defence and space electronics and computers. Communication devices, computers and millions of other products are powered by Motorola semiconductors. Motorola Canada Limited's parent company, Motorola Inc., maintains sales, service and manufacturing facilities throughout the world, conducts business on six continents and employs more than 140,000 people worldwide. Graduates most likely to be hired come from the following academic areas: Bachelor of Engineering (Electrical, Computer Systems, Telecommunications) and Community College Diploma (Electronics Technician, Engineering Technician). Graduates would occupy Electrical Engineering and Computer Science positions. Previous work experience that is relevant to position, telecommunications knowledge, and a willingness to learn new skills through constant training are all listed as desirable non-academic qualifications. Company benefits are rated above average. The potential for advancement is listed as excellent. The most suitable method for initial contact by those seeking employment is to mail a resume. Motorola Canada Limited does recruit Bachelor of Engineering students for co-op work terms (contact your campus career centre). Contacts: Staffing Department or Human Resources.

MOUNT SINAI HOSPITAL
600 University Avenue
Toronto, ON M5G 1X5

Tel. 416-586-5040
Fax 416-586-5045
Email .... mgaul@mtsinai.on.ca
Website .... www.mtsinai.on.ca

Mount Sinai Hospital is at the forefront of the Canadian health care arena in the areas of patient care, teaching and research. Presently the hospital employs approximately 3,000 people. Graduates most likely to be hired come from the following academic areas: Bachelor of Science (Biology, Chemistry, Dentistry, Nursing, Nutritional Sciences, Occupational Therapy, Pharmacy, Physiotherapy, Speech Pathology), Bachelor of Engineering (General, Electrical, Mechanical, Biomedical Electronics, Computer Systems), Chartered Accountant, Certified Management Accountant, Certified General Accountant, Master of Business Administration (General, Health Care Administration) and Community College Diploma (Administration, Communications/Public Relations, Human Resources, Information Systems, Secretarial, Cook/Chef, Electronics Technician, Engineering Technician, HVAC Systems, Plumber, Animal Health, Dental Assistant, Dental Hygiene, Dietitian/Nutrition, Health/Home Care Aide, Nuclear Medicine, Radiology, Respiratory Therapy, Ultrasound Technician). Graduates would occupy Pharmacist, Physiotherapist, Occupational Therapist, Registered Nurse, Medical Secretary, Administrative Secretary, Research Technician, Biomedical Engineer, Computer Analyst, Electrician, etc. positions. Company benefits are rated as industry standard. The potential for advancement is listed as being good. The average annual starting salary falls within the $25,000 to $30,000 range. The most suitable methods for initial contact by those seeking employment are to mail or fax a resume with a covering letter. Mount Sinai Hospital does hire summer and co-op work term students. *Contacts:* Marilyn Gaul, Employment Relations Manager or Kerri McKenzie, Employment Relations Officer.

MTD PRODUCTS LIMITED
97 Kent Avenue, PO Box 1386
Kitchener, ON N2G 4J1

Tel. 519-579-5500
Fax 519-579-5730

MTD Products Limited manufactures and assembles outdoor power equipment, including all types of power mowers, yard tractors, and snow throwers. MTD Products Limited also has significant exposure as an OEM supplier of automotive stampings, primarily to the Ford Motor Company. The company employs approximately 750 people at this location, a total of 800 people in Canada, and 8,000 people worldwide. Graduates most likely to be hired come from the following academic areas: Bachelor of Science (Mathematics), Bachelor of Engineering (Robotics, Computer Systems, Instrumentation, Microelectronics, Mechanical, Industrial Design/Production), Bachelor of Commerce/Business Administration (Accounting, Finance, Information Systems, Human Resources, Marketing), Chartered Accountant, Certified Management Accountant, Certified General Accountant, Master of Business Administration (Accounting, Finance, Human Resources, Information Systems, Marketing), Community College Diploma (Accounting, Administration, Business, Advertising, Facility Management, Financial Planning, Human Resources, Marketing, Purchasing, CAD/CAM/Autocad, Computer Science, Electronics Technician, Engineering Technician, HVAC Technician, Welding) and High School Diploma. Positions would range from hourly rated unionized production positions, through junior and senior supervisors, all the way to senior management positions. Relevant work experience and good communication skills are listed as desirable non-academic qualifications. Preference in hiring would likely be shown to graduates of cooperative education programs.

Company benefits are rated as industry standard. The potential for advancement is listed as average. The average annual starting salary falls within the $30,000 to $35,000 range. The most suitable method for initial contact by those seeking employment is mail a resume with a covering letter. MTD Products Limited does hire co-op work term students. *Contact:* Mark Schneider, Human Resources Manager.

MTS COMMUNICATIONS INC.
489 Empress Street, PO Box 6666
Winnipeg, MB R3C 3V6

Tel. 204-941-5096
Fax 204-772-0617
Website .... www.mts.mb.ca

MTS Communications Inc. is the major supplier of telecommunications products and services in the province of Manitoba. MTS employs 3,500 people throughout the province. Graduates most likely to be hired come from the following academic areas: Bachelor of Science (Computer Science), Bachelor of Engineering (Electrical, Telecommunications), Bachelor of Commerce/Business Administration (Finance, Information Systems, Marketing), Chartered Accountant, Certified Management Accountant, Certified General Accountant, Master of Business Administration (Marketing) and Community College Diploma (Information Systems, Marketing/Sales, Computer Science). Graduates would occupy Engineer, Product Manager, Business Sales Representative, Account Manager, Programmer/Analyst and System Analyst positions. Leadership, teamwork, innovation and good communication skills are all listed as desirable non-academic qualifications. Company benefits are rated above average. The potential for advancement is listed as being good. The average annual starting salary falls within the $30,000 to $35,000 range. The most suitable method for initial contact by those seeking employment is to mail a resume with a covering letter. MTS Communications Inc. does hire summer and co-op work term students. *Contact:* Olga Ford, Manager, Employment Services.

MUELLER CANADA
8069 Lawson Road, PO Box 1001
Milton, ON L9T 4B6

Tel. 905-878-0541
Fax 905-878-3888

Mueller Canada, a Tyco International Ltd. company, manufactures gas and water flow equipment. This includes valves, hydrants, and pipe fittings (eg. nipples, plugs, bushings). In addition, Mueller Canada provides installation and servicing of fire protection equipment including sprinklers, alarms, and extinguishers. Graduates most likely to be hired come from the following academic areas: Bachelor of Engineering (Industrial Design, Industrial Production), Bachelor of Commerce/Business Administration (Marketing), Certified General Accountant (Manufacturing) and Community College Diploma (Accounting, Marketing/Sales). Graduates would occupy Cost Accountant, Sales Representative, Design Engineer and Manufacturing Engineer positions. Company benefits are rated as excellent. The potential for advancement is listed as being good. The average annual starting salary depends upon the position being considered. The most suitable methods for initial contact by those seeking employment are to mail or fax a resume with a covering letter. Mueller Canada does hire summer students. *Contact:* Human Resources Manager.

MULTIVIEW INC.
36 Antares Drive, Suite 500
Nepean, ON K2E 7W5

Tel.	613-225-5050
Fax	613-225-0505
Website	www.multiviewcorp.com

Multiview Inc. is a premier independent supplier of full-featured financial applications for the HP 3000, HP 9000, and Windows NT operating environments. With 1,800 applications installed, Multiview supports more than 500 clients worldwide representing more that 42 industries. Customers employ Multiview's integrated applications to improve the analysis of their financial information, better understand the details of their operations and improve the performance of their companies. Graduates most likely to be hired come from the following academic areas: Bachelor of Science (Computer Science), Bachelor of Engineering (Computer Systems) and Community College Diploma (Accounting). Graduates would occupy Software Engineer and Software Consultant positions. Company benefits are rated above average. The potential for advancement is listed as excellent. The most suitable methods for initial contact by those seeking employment are to mail or fax a resume with a covering letter. Multiview Inc. does hire summer and co-op work term students. *Contact:* John Leslie.

MUSTANG SURVIVAL CORP.
3810 Jacombs Road
Richmond, BC V6V 1Y6

Tel.	604-270-8631
Fax	604-270-0489
Email	mustang@mustangsurvival.com
Website	www.mustangsurvival.com

Mustang Survival Corp. is a leader in the design, development, manufacturing and marketing of personal safety and survival equipment. Mustang Survival has created an extensive range of products to meet the specific needs of recreational, industrial and military uses. Based on a tradition of excellence built over 31 years, Mustang is driven by its commitment to continuous improvement and innovation through ongoing research and testing, total quality management and world class manufacturing practices, as well as developing strong partnerships with its employees and customers. The company employs 350 people in five locations in Canada, the United States and the United Kingdom. Graduates most likely to be hired come from the following academic areas: Bachelor of Arts (General), Bachelor of Science (Computer Science), Bachelor of Engineering (Chemical, Mechanical, Engineering Physics, Industrial Engineering, Industrial Production), Bachelor of Commerce/Business Administration (Accounting, Human Resources, Information Systems, Marketing), Certified Management Accountant, Certified General Accountant, Community College Diploma (Accounting, Business, Communications/Public Relations, Human Resources, Purchasing/Logistics, Secretarial, Graphic Arts, CAD/CAM/Autocad, Computer Science, Engineering Technician) and High School Diploma. Graduates would occupy Customer Service Representative, Credit Assistant, Engineering Technologist, Quality Assurance Technician, Junior Engineer, Junior Scientist, Industrial Engineer, Operations and Production positions. Adaptable, confident, productive, analytical, creative, efficient, innovative, dependable, communicative, team player and leadership skills are all listed as desirable non-academic qualifications. Company benefits are rated above average. The potential for advancement is listed as being good. The average annual starting salary falls within the $25,000 to $35,000 range, depending on the education level of the applicant and the position being considered. The most suitable methods for initial contact by those seeking employment are to mail, fax or e-mail a resume with a covering letter, or via the company's website. Mustang Survival Corp. does hire students for summer and co-op work terms. *Contacts:* Janice Robinson, Director, Human Resources; Caroline Mitchell, Human Resources Advisor or Kelly Chung, Human Resources Assistant.

N.D. LEA CONSULTANTS LTD.
1455 West Georgia Street, 6th Floor
Vancouver, BC V6G 2T3

Tel.	604-685-9381
Fax	604-685-8655
Email	lea@bc.sympatico.ca

N.D. Lea Consultants Ltd. is a consulting engineering firm active in the transportation sector. There are 50 employees at this location, a total of 72 in Canada and a total of 89 employees worldwide. Graduates most likely to be hired come from the following academic areas: Bachelor of Engineering (Civil, Transportation) and Community College Diploma (CAD/CAM/Autocad). Graduates would occupy Engineer and Autocad Operator positions. Company benefits are rated as industry standard. The potential for advancement is listed as being average. The most suitable methods for initial contact by those seeking employment are to fax or e-mail a resume with a covering letter. *Contact:* H. Copeland, Office Manager.

NACAN PRODUCTS LIMITED
60 West Drive
Brampton, ON L6T 4W7

Tel.	905-454-4466
Fax	905-796-1450
Email	monica.wanner@nstarch.com
Website	www.nationalstarch.com

Nacan Products Limited is a manufacturer and supplier to industry of adhesives, resins, specialty chemicals, specialty industrial food starches, seasonings and flavourings. The company maintains plant locations in Toronto, Collingwood, Surrey, and Boucherville. The Brampton location is Nacan's Corporate Office and R & D Centre employing over 100 people. There are total of 300 employees across Canada. Nacan Products Limited is part of the US based National Starch and Chemical Corporation which in turn is part of the ICI Group, one of the world's largest specialty products, coatings and material companies with an impressive record in innovation. Graduates most likely to be hired come from the following academic areas: Bachelor of Science (Chemistry), Bachelor of Engineering (Chemical), Bachelor of Commerce/Business Administration and Community College Diploma (Accounting, Business, Secretarial, Human Resources, Engineering Technician). Maturity, stability, a positive attitude, motivation, aptitude, and good communication, leadership and listening skills are all listed as desirable non-academic qualifications. Company benefits are rated above average. The potential for advancement is listed as excellent. The average starting salary falls within the $30,000 to $40,000 range, depending upon the position being considered. The most suitable methods for initial contact by those seeking employment are to mail, fax or e-mail a resume with a covering letter. Nacan Products Limited does hire summer students and NSERC eligible students for 4 and 8 month work term placements. Nacan is an equal opportunity employer. *Contact:* Monica A. Wanner, Manager, Employee Relations.

NATIONAL GROCERS COMPANY LTD. / LOBLAWS COMPANIES LIMITED
6 Monogram Place
Toronto, ON M9R 4C4

Tel.	416-245-5050
Fax	416-240-3866
Website	www.loblaw.com

National Grocers Company Ltd. / Loblaws Companies Limited is at the heart of Canada's most successful grocery retail and wholesale organization. The company is recognized by many as the leader in bringing unique and innovative products, such as G.R.E.E.N., President's Choice and No Name products, to the marketplace. There are more than 1,000 employees between this and the 22 St. Clair Avenue East (Toronto) locations and approximately 60,000 employees across Canada. Graduates most likely to be hired come from the following academic areas: Bachelor of Arts (Economics, Psychology, Urban Planning), Bachelor of Science (Computer Science, Nutritional Sciences, Pharmacy, Psychology), Bachelor of Engineering (Computer Systems, Industrial), Bachelor of Laws (Labour Law), Bachelor of Commerce/Business Administration (Finance, Human Resources, Information Systems), Master of Business Administration (Accounting, Finance, Human Resources, Information Systems), Community College Diploma (Accounting, Business, Human Resources, Purchasing/Logistics, Secretarial, Computer Science) and High School Diploma. Graduates would occupy Human Resources Manager/Specialist, Project Engineer, Analyst, Secretary, Warehouse Assistant, Consultant, Legal Advisor, I.R. Consultant, Food Product Development Specialist, Store Management Trainee, Departmental Manager and Continuous Process Improvement positions. Results oriented, innovative, leadership skills, proven track record of success, team player and previous grocery store experience are all listed as desirable non-academic qualifications. Company benefits are rated as excellent. The potential for advancement is listed as being good. The most suitable method for initial contact by those seeking employment is to mail a resume with a covering letter. National Grocers Company Ltd. / Loblaws Companies Limited hires summer students, applications should be made prior to the summer season. *Contact:* Human Resources.

NATIONAL LIFE ASSURANCE COMPANY OF CANADA
522 University Avenue, 7th Floor
Toronto, ON M5G 1Y7

Tel.	416-598-2122
Fax	416-598-4574
Email	hr@nationallife.ca
Website	www.nationallife.ca

National Life Assurance Company of Canada designs, markets and sells individual and group life and health insurance products, and retirement income plans. In business since 1899, National Life has office locations across Canada and in the Caribbean. There are approximately 360 employees at the Toronto head office. Candidates with a background in the following academic areas may be interested in career opportunities with the company: Bachelor of Arts (General), Bachelor of Science (General, Actuarial, Computer Science, Mathematics), Bachelor of Commerce/Business Administration, an Accounting Designation and Community College Diploma (Accounting, Administration, Business, Communications, Insurance, Secretarial, Human Resources). Career opportunities would include Sales Representative, Claims Examiner, Trainee Underwriter, Administrator, Accountant, Actuarial Student and Trainee Programmer/Analyst positions. Starting salaries are competitive and vary depending on the position being considered. National Life offers a comprehensive benefits package. Accordingly, company benefits are listed as excellent. Commitment to quality is an important part of the company's philosophy. The most suitable methods for initial contact by those seeking employment are to mail a resume with a covering letter, or by calling the Employment Information Line at (416) 585-8090. *Contacts:* Ana Cimolai, Administrator, Human Resources or Kellee Wells, Administrator, Human Resources.

NATIONAL SILICATES LIMITED
429 Kipling Avenue
Toronto, ON M8Z 5C7

Tel.	416-255-7771
Fax	416-201-4343

National Silicates Limited is involved in the manufacturing of inorganic chemicals, sodium silicates. The company employs more that 50 people. Graduates most likely to be hired come from the following academic areas: Bachelor of Science (Chemistry), Bachelor of Engineering (Mechanical, Chemical) and Bachelor of Commerce/Business Administration. Engineering and Science graduates would occupy Laboratory Technician positions. Company benefits are rated as excellent. The potential for advancement is listed as being good. The average annual starting salary falls within the $25,000 to $30,000 range. The most suitable method for initial contact by graduates seeking employment is to mail a resume with a covering letter. National Silicates Limited does hire summer students on a regular basis. *Contact:* Employee Relations Manager.

NATIONAL TRUST, A MEMBER OF THE SCOTIABANK GROUP
1 Adelaide Street East, One Financial Place, 9th Floor
Toronto, ON M5C 2W8

Tel.	416-361-3611
Fax	416-361-3906
Website	www.scotiabank.ca

National Trust, A member of the Scotiabank Group is a full service financial institution. Financial services provided include banking, retail lending, mortgage lending, as well as personal trust services and corporate trust services including pensions and mutual funds. National Trust employs more than 500 employees at this location. Graduates most likely to be hired come from the following academic areas: Bachelor of Arts (Business, Economics), Bachelor of Commerce/Business Administration, Chartered Accountant, Certified Management Accountant, Certified General Accountant and Community College

Diploma (Business, Marketing, Accounting). Graduates would occupy positions in Finance, Accounting, Client Services and Administration. Company benefits are rated above average. The potential for advancement is listed as being good. The average annual starting salary falls within the $20,000 to $30,000 range. The most suitable methods for initial contact by those seeking employment are to mail a resume with a covering letter, or via telephone. National Trust does hire summer students. *Contact:* Human Resources Advisor.

NATREL INC.
7100 Woodbine Avenue, Suite 400
Markham, ON L3R 5J2

Tel. 905-947-5600
Fax 905-947-5705

Natrel Inc., a subsidiary of Quebec based Agropur, is a leader in the Canadian dairy industry. Agropur is a leading Canadian cooperative owned by 4,800 milk producers and employing 2,800 people. The cooperative has a strategic foothold in the cheese and milk ingredients sector, the yogurt and fresh cheese sector, through Ultima Foods (manufacturers of Yoplait products) and in the fluid milk sector through Natrel. Natrel Inc. employs 80 people at this location and a total of 1,800 people worldwide. Graduates most likely to be hired come from the following academic areas: Bachelor of Arts (Economics), Bachelor of Science (Microbiology), Bachelor of Engineering (Mechanical), Bachelor of Laws, Bachelor of Commerce/Business Administration (Accounting, Finance, Human Resources, Information Systems, Marketing), Chartered Accountant, Certified Management Accountant, Certified General Accountant, Master of Business Administration (Finance, Marketing), Community College Diploma (Accounting, Business, Human Resources, Marketing/Sales, Office Administration, Purchasing/Logistics, Secretarial, Information Systems, Laboratory Technician) and High School Diploma. Computer skills, bilingual, team player and excellent communication skills are all listed as desirable non-academic qualifications. Company benefits are rated above average. The potential for advancement is listed as being average. The average annual starting salary falls within the $40,000 to $45,000 range. The most suitable method for initial contact by those seeking employment is to mail a resume with a covering letter. Natrel Inc. does hire summer and co-op work term students. *Contact:* Human Resources Department.

NATURAL SCIENCES & ENGINEERING RESEARCH COUNCIL / NSERC
350 Albert Street, PO Box 1610, Station B
Ottawa, ON K1P 6G4

Tel. 613-995-5992
Fax 613-992-5337
Email .... recruiting@nserc.ca
Website .... www.nserc.ca

The Natural Sciences and Engineering Research Council of Canada / NSERC is the national instrument for making strategic investments in Canada's capability in science and technology. The NSERC's role is to secure a healthy research base in universities and as a corollary, to secure a sound balance between the diversified research base and more targeted programs of research. The council supports both basic university research through research grants and project research through partnerships of universities with industry as well as the advanced training of highly qualified people in both areas. In addition, the NSERC works to secure an adequate supply of highly qualified personnel who have been well educated in basic science as well as trained with state-of-the-art facilities, and to facilitate collaboration between research and development performing sectors in Canada. This role is exercised through the delivery of the program of scholarships and grants in aid of research. The NSERC employs 190 people. Graduates most likely to be hired come from the following academic areas: Bachelor of Science (Biology, Chemistry, Computer Science, Forestry, Geology, Geography, Mathematics, Metallurgy, Microbiology, Oceanography, Physics, Zoology), Bachelor of Engineering (Chemical, Civil, Electrical, Mechanical, Resources/Environmental), Master of Science, Master of Engineering and Community College Diploma (Computer Science). A knowledge of the scientific community, administrative experience, team player and strong interpersonal skills are all listed as desirable non-academic qualifications. Company benefits are rated above average. The potential for advancement is listed as being good. The average annual starting salary falls within the $30,000 to $35,000 range. The most suitable method for initial contact by those seeking employment is to mail a resume with a covering letter. The NSERC does hire summer students. *Contact:* Human Resources.

NCR CANADA LTD.
320 Front Street West
Toronto, ON M5V 3C4

Tel. 416-599-4627
Fax 416-351-2159
Website .... www.ncr.com

NCR Canada Ltd., a subsidiary of NCR Corporation, is a recognized world leader in data warehousing solutions, ATMs, point-of-sale, high performance scanners, and support services for retail, financial and national accounts markets. Headquartered in Dayton, Ohio, NCR Corporation employs over 33,000 employees in 130 countries. Companies worldwide trust NCR with their transactions, interactions and relationships by providing technology enabled business solutions. These solutions allow companies to capture and analyze data to maximize customer acquisition, retention, and profitability. The company has over a century of experience and today has the industry expertise, software, consulting services and hardware to build integrated solutions for businesses. NCR offers an unique capability to help businesses understand and market their products and services to individual customers at each and every point of interaction. NCR Canada Ltd. employs over 1,200 people across the country in IT, sales, professional services, finance, marketing and administration. Graduates most likely to be hired come from the following academic areas: Bachelor of Science (Computer Science, Mathematics), Bachelor of Engineering (General, Computer Systems, Telecommunications) and Bachelor of Commerce/Business Administration (General). Graduates would occupy Accounts Manager, Systems Engineer, Finance and Administration Trainee, Administration Clerk, Financial Analyst, Information Systems, Programmer/Analyst and Field Engineer positions. Company benefits and the potential for advancement are both rated as excellent. The most suitable methods for initial contact by those seeking employment are to mail, fax or e-mail a resume with a covering letter, or via on-campus recruitment initiatives (see your campus career centre for details). NCR Canada Ltd. does hire summer and co-op work term students. *Contact:* Human Resources Manager.

NCR CANADA LTD.
580 Weber Street North
Waterloo, ON N2J 4G5

Tel.	519-884-1710
Fax	519-884-0610
Email	employment.specialist@Waterloo.NCR.com
Website	www.ncr.com

NCR Canada Ltd., a subsidiary of NCR Corporation, is a leader in data warehousing solutions, ATMs, point-of-sale, high performance scanners, and support services for retail, financial and national accounts markets. NCR Canada Ltd. is a subsidiary of NCR Corporation, headquartered in Dayton, Ohio and employing over 33,000 employees in 130 countries. Companies worldwide trust NCR with their transactions, interactions and relationships by providing technology enabled business solutions. These solutions allow companies to capture and analyze data to maximize customer acquisition, retention, and profitability. The company has over a century of experience and today has the industry expertise, software, consulting services and hardware to build integrated solutions for businesses. NCR offers an unique capability to help businesses understand and market their products and services to individual customers at each and every point of interaction. NCR Canada Ltd. employs 550 employees at this location and over 1,200 people across the country in IT, sales, professional services, finance, marketing and administration. Graduates most likely to be hired come from the following academic areas: Bachelor of Science (Computer Science), Bachelor of Engineering (Electrical, Mechanical, Computer Systems, Industrial Engineering), Bachelor of Commerce/Business Administration (Accounting, Finance, Human Resources), Certified Management Accountant, Certified General Accountant, Master of Business Administration (Accounting, Finance, Human Resources, Marketing), Master of Engineering and Community College Diploma (Financial Planning, Human Resources). Graduates would occupy Manufacturing Engineer, Programmer Analyst, Mechanical Engineer, Electrical Engineer, Financial Analyst and Human Resources Generalist positions. Team player, multi-tasking abilities, good communication skills and a high level of enthusiasm are all listed as desirable non-academic qualifications. Company benefits are rated as above average. The potential for advancement is listed as being good. The average annual starting salary falls within the $40,000 to $45,000 range. The most suitable method for initial contact by those seeking employment is to apply through the company's website. NCR Canada Ltd. does hire summer and co-op work term students. *Contact:* Barb Sills, Employment Specialist.

NEDCO, A DIVISION OF WESTBURNE INDUSTRIAL ENTERPRISES LTD.
5600 Keaton Crescent
Mississauga, ON L5R 3G3

Tel.	905-712-4004
Fax	905-507-1129
Website	www.nedco.ca

Nedco, a Division of Westburne Industrial Enterprises Ltd. is Canada's largest distributor of electrical and industrial products. Westburne Industrial Enterprises Ltd. / Nedco Division is a subsidiary of Montreal based Westburne Inc. Westburne Inc.'s stock is traded on the Toronto and Montreal Stock Exchanges. Westburne Inc. has 94 branches and a total of 1,450 employees in Ontario and employs 5,200 staff across North America. There are approximately 375 employees at the Nedco Division. Graduates most likely to be hired at this location come from the following academic areas: Bachelor of Arts (General), Bachelor of Engineering (Electrical, Automation/Robotics, Telecommunications), Bachelor of Commerce/Business Administration, Chartered Accountant, Certified Management Accountant, Certified General Accountant, Master of Business Administration and Community College Diploma (Accounting, Administration, Business, Human Resources, Marketing/Sales, Purchasing/Logistics, Secretarial, Computer Science, HVAC Systems). Graduates would occupy Outside/Inside Sales, Counter, Warehouse, Purchasing, Quotations and Office Administration positions, as well as Head Office positions in Accounting (Receivable and Payable), Finance, Credit, Information Systems, Total Quality Management, Human Resources, and Payroll and Administration. Related distribution experience in the electrical, plumbing, waterworks, HVAC/R, wire and cable, drives and automation, lighting and telecommunications industries is preferred. Company benefits and the potential for advancement are both rated as excellent. The average annual starting salary is dependent upon the position being considered. The most suitable method for initial contact by those seeking employment is to mail or fax a resume with a covering letter. Westburne Industrial Enterprises Ltd. / Nedco Division does hire summer students. *Contact:* Human Resources.

NELVANA LIMITED
32 Atlantic Avenue
Toronto, ON M6K 1X8

Tel.	416-588-5571
Fax	416-588-5252
Email	hr@nelvana.com
Website	www.nelvana.com

Nelvana Limited is a leading producer and distributor of animated children's and family entertainment. The company's areas of programming include animated television series, specials and feature films. Nelvana's Toronto head office houses one of North America's largest animation studios. The company also has operations in Los Angeles, London and Paris. Nelvana employs approximately 250 people at this location, a total of 450 in Canada and a total of 480 people worldwide. Graduates most likely to be hired come from the following academic areas: Bachelor of Arts (General, Graphic Arts), Bachelor of Commerce/Business Administration (Accounting, Finance, Marketing) and Community College Diploma (Accounting, Marketing/Sales, Secretarial, Graphic Arts, Legal Assistant, Television/Radio Arts, Classical Animation, Computer Animation). Graduates would occupy Storyboard Artist, Timing Director, Production Manager, Location Designer, Prop Designer, Animator, Producer, Digital Painter, Digital Compositor, Background Artist, Character Designer, Layout Artist, Poser and Assistant Animator positions. Team player, strong interpersonal skills, previous work experience (not necessarily within the industry) and good computer skills are all listed as desirable non-academic qualifications. Company benefits are rated above average. The potential for advancement is listed as excellent. The average annual starting salary falls within the $25,000 to $30,000 range. The most suitable method for initial contact by those seeking employment is to mail a resume with a covering letter. For certain positions, applicants should include portfolio when mailing resume with covering letter. *Contact:* Human Resources Manager.

NEON PRODUCTS
555 Ellesmere Road
Toronto, ON M1R 4E8

Tel. 416-759-1111
Fax 416-759-4965
Website .... www.neon-products.com

Neon Products is the premiere manufacturer of illuminated signage in Canada. The company's expertise in the industry dates back to the turn of the century. As a member of The Jim Pattison Sign Group, Neon Products represents the largest electrical sign company in the world, employing over 600 people, with manufacturing facilities in 5 locations across Canada and sales and service facilities in a further 18 locations. The company provides comprehensive coverage to all areas of the country. Graduates most likely to be hired at this location come from the following academic areas: Bachelor of Arts (Economics), Bachelor of Science (Metallurgy), Bachelor of Commerce/Business Administration (Accounting, Marketing), Chartered Accountant, Certified Management Accountant, Certified General Accountant, Master of Business Administration (Marketing), Community College Diploma (Accounting, Advertising, Business, Marketing/Sales) and High School Diploma. Graduates would occupy Accounting, Artist, Sales Representative, Draftsman and Estimator positions. Community involvement and possessing related work experience are both listed as desirable non-academic qualifications. Company benefits are rated above average. The potential for advancement is listed as average. The average annual starting salary is dependent upon the position being considered. The most suitable method for initial contact by graduates seeking employment is to mail a resume with a covering letter. Neon Products does hire summer students. *Contact:* Human Resources.

NESTE RESINS CANADA
5865 McLaughlin Road, Suite 3
Mississauga, ON L5R 1B8

Tel. 905-712-0900
Fax 905-712-0901
Email .... deborah.journeaux@neste.com
Website .... www.neste.com

Neste Resins Canada manufactures chemicals and adhesives (eg. formaldehyde resins) for the pulp and paper industry. Neste Resins Canada, is a member of the Neste Group based in Finland. Neste Group is an international oil, energy, and chemicals company. Neste employs 40 people at this location, a total of 250 in Canada, and 9,000 people worldwide. Graduates most likely to be hired come from the following academic areas: Bachelor of Science (Chemistry, Forestry), Bachelor of Engineering (Chemical, Environmental/Resources, Industrial Chemistry), Bachelor of Commerce/Business Administration (Accounting, Finance, Human Resources, Information Systems, Marketing), Master of Business Administration (Finance, Human Resources, Information Systems, Marketing), Master of Science, Master of Engineering, Community College Diploma (Accounting, Financial Planning, Human Resources, Information Systems, Marketing/Sales) and High School Diploma. Graduates would occupy Chemist, Laboratory Technician, Technical Sales, Technical Service, Accountant, EHS, Human Resources, Information Technology and Systems, Marketing Manager, Sales Manager, Laboratory Technician and Research Chemist positions. Dedicated, challenges the status quo, professional and honesty are all listed as desirable non-academic qualifications. Company benefits are rated above average. The potential for advancement is listed as being good. The average annual starting salary falls within the $30,000 to $35,000 range. The most suitable method for initial contact by those seeking employment is to e-mail a resume with a covering letter. Neste Resins Canada does hire student for summer and co-op work terms. *Contact:* Human Resources.

NESTLE CANADA INC.
25 Sheppard Avenue West
Toronto, ON M2N 6S8

Tel. 416-512-9000
Fax 416-218-2828
Website .... www.nestle.com

Nestlé Canada Inc. is involved in the manufacture and sales of a wide variety of food products. Activities encompass manufacturing, distribution, logistics, purchasing, marketing, sales, financial planning, accounting, information services, human resources, and other related activities. There are more than 400 employees at this location. Graduates most likely to be hired come from the following academic areas: Bachelor of Arts (General, Economics, Psychology, Sociology, English), Bachelor of Science (Biology, Biochemistry, Chemistry, Computer, Nutrition), Bachelor of Engineering (Mechanical, Electrical, Industrial), Bachelor of Commerce/Business Administration (Marketing, Accounting, Finance), Certified Management Accountant, Master of Business Administration (Marketing, Finance), Master of Arts (Economics, English) and Community College (Laboratory Technician, Administration). Excellent verbal and written communication skills, customer service oriented, initiative, loyalty, proactive, good organizational skills and a working knowledge of MS Office are all listed as desirable non-academic qualifications. Company benefits are rated above average. The potential for advancement is listed as being good. The average annual starting salary falls within the $25,000 to $30,000 range. The most suitable methods for initial contact by those seeking employment are to mail or fax a resume with a covering letter (no telephone calls please). Nestlé Canada Inc. does hire summer and co-op work term students. *Contact:* Human Resources.

NET-WORTH ADVERTISING
14 Elmwood Avenue
St. Catharines, ON L2R 2T7

Tel. 888-765-9506
Fax 905-765-9424
Email .... ewieler@yahoo.com
Website .... www.vaxxine.com/networth

Net-Worth Advertising provides a wide range of advertising services, including website design, internet advertising, catalogues, promotional packages, wedding advertising and special occasion features. The company publishes The Weddingmarch Magazine and Focus, Niagara's Lifestyle Magazine, as well as the Internet based www.onlinephonebook.com and www. thewedding marchcom. All designs are created in house by a highly trained and advanced design team. Established in 1996, Net-Worth Advertising serves over 200 clients in Canada and the United States. Graduates most likely to be hired come from the following academic areas: Bachelor of Arts (General), Bachelor of Commerce/Business Administration (Marketing) and Community College Diploma (Marketing/Sales). Graduates would occupy Area Sales Director and Area Account Executive positions. Team player, consistent, self motivated and self-confident are all listed as desirable non-academic qualifications. Company benefits are rated above average. The potential for advancement is listed as being excellent. The average annual starting salary varies and is commission based. The most suitable methods for initial contact by those seeking employment are to mail, fax or e-mail a resume with a covering letter. Net-Worth Advertising does hire summer and co-op work term students. *Contact:* Eveline Wieler, Sales Director.

NETT TECHNOLOGIES INC.
PO Box 43134
Mississauga, ON L5B 4A7

Tel.	905-602-7747
Fax	905-602-4545
Email	hr@nett.ca
Website	www.nett.ca

Nett Technologies Inc. manufactures engine emission control products. The company specializes in exhaust pollution control for construction and mining machinery, industrial forklifts, gen-sets, urban buses and trucks. Nett Technologies has world wide distributorship network to sell its products. There are 25 employees at this location. Graduates most likely to be hired come from the following academic areas: Bachelor of Arts (Economics, Journalism, Sociology), Bachelor of Science (Chemistry, Physics), Bachelor of Engineering (Chemical, Mechanical, Mining, Welding), Bachelor of Commerce/Business Administration (Marketing), Master of Business Administration (Marketing) and Community College Diploma (Administration, Business, Marketing/Sales). Graduates would occupy Marketing and Sales Coordinator, Export Coordinator, Research and Development Engineer, Application Engineer, Territorial Sales Manager, National Sales Manager and Inside Sales Representative positions. Company benefits are rated as industry standard. The potential for advancement is listed as being excellent. The most suitable methods for initial contact by those seeking employment are fax or e-mail a resume with a covering letter. Nett Technologies Inc. does hire co-op work term students. *Contacts:* John Popik or Mark Daugela.

NETWORK DESIGN AND ANALYSIS / NDA
60 Gough Road, 2nd Floor
Markham, ON L3R 8X7

Tel.	905-477-9534
Fax	905-477-9572
Email	nda@ndacorp.com
Website	www.ndacorp.com

Network Design and Analysis / NDA is a software company specializing in the development of telecommunications network optimization, performance analysis and cost control tools. The company has been servicing large scale international corporations since its foundation in 1983. NDA employs a total of 21 people in Canada. Graduates most likely to be hired come from the following academic areas: Bachelor of Science (Computer Systems, Telecommunications), Master of Business Administration (Information Systems), Master of Science (Computer Science, Operations) and Doctorate (Operations Research). Graduates would occupy Project Engineer, Scientist and Product Manager positions. Good communication skills, able to use own initiative and two years previous work experience are all listed as desirable non-academic qualifications. Company benefits and the potential for advancement are both rated as excellent. The average annual starting salary falls within the $40,000 to $45,000 range. The

most suitable method for initial contact by those seeking employment is to fax a resume with a covering letter. *Contact:* Maureen Tracey, Administrator.

NEW AUTOMATION CORPORATION / NAC
5280 South Service Road
Burlington, ON L7L 5H5

Tel.	905-333-3606
Fax	905-333-1477
Email	nac@newautomation.com
Website	www.newautomation.com

New Automation Corporation / NAC designs and manufactures custom automated manufacturing and material-handling systems. These systems include welded beam manufacturing lines, automated punching / drilling lines, transfer machines, drilling centres, continuous beam welders, profile cutters, robotic palletizers / pick and places, as well as motion control projects requiring specialized robotics and or CNC control. The company was founded in 1982 in response to the introduction of the microprocessor to industry and the accompanying need for control system specialists. From these roots NAC has achieved significant growth by staying in the forefront of technology, addressing new and existing processes with state of the art solutions. Today, the company's strength lies with the skill of it's engineering and manufacturing staff and the continuing application of emerging technologies in a variety of industries. Graduates most likely to be hired come from the following academic areas: Bachelor of Engineering (Electrical, Mechanical, Automation/Robotics, Industrial Production/Manufacturing), Community College Diploma (Accounting, Business, Marketing/Sales, Office Administration, CAD/CAM/Autocad, Electronics Technician, Engineering Technician, Tool and Die, Machinist, Millwright, Welding) and High School Diploma. Graduates would occupy Mechanical Designer, Project Leader, Drafting Technician, Electrician, Millwright, Machinist, Assembler, Accounting Clerk, Customer Service Representative and Purchasing Assistant positions. Team player, motivated, customer oriented and excellent leadership skills are all listed as desirable non-academic qualifications. Company benefits are rated as industry standard. The potential for advancement is listed as being good. The most suitable methods for initial contact by those seeking employment are to mail, fax or e-mail a resume with a covering letter. New Automation Corporation does hire co-op work term students. *Contact:* Human Resources.

NEW BRUNSWICK POWER CORPORATION / NB POWER
515 King Street, PO Box 2000
Fredericton, NB E3B 4X1

Tel.	506-458-4004
Fax	506-458-4000
Email	employment@nbpower.com

New Brunswick Power Corporation / NB Power is a provincial crown corporation responsible for the generation, transmission and distribution of electricity. Electricity is generated using a variety of fuels and technologies, including hydro, nuclear, coal, orimulsion, oil and combustion turbines. The corporation participates in a program that shares training and technology with developing countries, and is a leader in technology throughout North America. There are approximately 2,500 employees throughout the province. Graduates most likely to be hired come from the following academic areas: Bachelor of Science (Computer Science), Bachelor of Engineering

(Electrical, Computer Systems, Nuclear Power, Mechanical), Bachelor of Commerce/Business Administration (Accounting, Finance, Human Resources, Information Systems), Master of Business Administration (Accounting, Finance, Human Resources, Information Systems) and Community College Diploma (Administration, Human Resources, Computer Science, Electronics Technician). Graduates would occupy Accounting, Business, Administration, Programming, Technical and Engineering positions. Customer service orientation, positive attitude towards new experiences, good verbal and written communication skills and related work experience are all listed as desirable non-academic qualifications. The potential for advancement is listed as being good. The most suitable methods for initial contact by those seeking employment are to mail or e-mail a resume with a covering letter. New Brunswick Power Corporation actively recruits individuals for summer and co-op work term positions. *Contacts:* Jill Doucett, Manager, Employment or Karen Stafford, Director, Personnel Services.

NEW BRUNSWICK TELEPHONE CO., THE
One Brunswick Square, PO Box 1430
Saint John, NB E2L 4K2

Tel. 506-658-7439
Fax 506-694-2392

The New Brunswick Telephone Co. is the prime provider of telephone service, and data-information systems in the province of New Brunswick. The company employs approximately 2,300 people throughout the province. Graduates most likely to be hired come from the following academic areas: Bachelor of Science (Computer Science) and Bachelor of Engineering (General, Electrical, Industrial Engineering). Leadership skills, entrepreneurial, team player, risk taker, and analytical are all listed as desirable non-academic qualifications. In addition, the ability to communicate in New Brunswick's two official languages would be an asset. Company benefits and the potential for advancement are both listed as excellent. The most suitable method for initial contact by those seeking employment is to mail a resume with a covering letter. The New Brunswick Telephone Co. does hire summer and co-op work term students. *Contact:* John Hebert, Human Resources Consultant.

NEW HOLLAND CANADA LTD.
1260 Clarence Avenue, PO Box 7300
Winnipeg, MB R3C 4E8

Tel. 204-477-2545
Fax 204-477-2325
Website .... www.newholland.com

New Holland Canada Ltd. manufactures agricultural implements, including two wheel and four wheel drive tractors. New Holland Canada Ltd. is a subsidiary of the Netherlands based New Holland N.V., a publicly traded company on the New York Stock Exchange under the symbol NH. New Holland N.V. is a global company employing 18,000 people in the design, manufacture and selling of agricultural tractors, combine harvesters, hay and forage equipment, grape harvesters and industrial equipment. New Holland Canada Ltd. has 700 employees at this location and a total of 800 employees across Canada. Graduates most likely to be hired come from the following academic areas: Bachelor of Science (Computer Science), Bachelor of Engineering (Mechanical, Industrial Design, Industrial Production), Bachelor of Commerce/Business Administration (Accounting, Finance, Information Systems), Chartered Accountant, Cer-

tified Management Accountant, Certified General Accountant, Master of Business Administration and Community College Diploma (Accounting, CAD/CAM/Autocad, Computer Science, Engineering Technician). Engineering graduates would occupy Industrial Engineer and Manufacturing Engineering Analyst positions. Relevant work experience, vision, creativity, team player and an interest in process improvements are all listed as desirable non-academic qualifications. Company benefits are rated above average. The potential for advancement is listed as being good. The average annual starting salary for recent graduates falls within the $32,000 to $36,000 range. The most suitable method for initial contact by those seeking employment is to mail a resume with a covering letter. New Holland Canada Ltd. does hire summer students on a limited basis. *Contact:* Human Resources Manager.

NEWBRIDGE NETWORKS CORPORATION
600 March Road, PO Box 13600
Kanata, ON K2K 2E6

Tel. 613-591-3600
Fax 613-599-3615
Email .... staffing@newbridge.com
Website .... www.newbridge.com

Newbridge Networks Corporation is a leading international designer, manufacturer, marketer and service provider for a comprehensive family of networking products and systems that deliver the power of multimedia communications solutions to organizations worldwide. Newbridge Kanata is the company's corporate headquarters, and is active in research and development, marketing, manufacturing, finance and general administration, and with its state-of-the-art manufacturing operations supplies 85% of Newbridge's global customers. The company employs 3,470 people at this location, a total of 3,730 in Canada and 6,400 people worldwide. Graduates most likely to be hired come from the following academic areas: Bachelor of Science (Computer Science, Mathematics), Bachelor of Engineering (General, Electrical, Mechanical, Computer Systems, Engineering Physics, Industrial Engineering, Industrial Production/Manufacturing, Telecommunications), Master of Engineering (Electrical Engineering, Computer Systems) and Community College Diploma (Computer Science, Electronics Technician, Engineering Technician). Graduates would occupy Software Designer, Hardware Designer and Business Systems Analyst positions. Risk taking and effective communication skills are listed as desirable non-academic qualifications. Company benefits and the potential for advancement are both rated as excellent. The average annual starting salary falls within the $40,000 to $45,000 range. The most suitable method for initial contact by those seeking employment is to apply through the company's website. Newbridge Networks Corporation (Kanata) does hire summer and co-op work term students. *Contact:* Carolyn Gill, Manager of Recruitment Operations, Global Human Resources.

NEWBRIDGE NETWORKS CORPORATION
4190 Still Creek Drive, Suite 400
Burnaby, BC V5C 6C6

Tel. 604-421-2643
Fax 604-421-2644
Email .... bcstaff@newbridge.com
Website .... www.newbridge.com

Newbridge Networks Corporation is a leading international designer, manufacturer, marketer and service provider for a comprehensive family of networking products and systems that deliver the power of multimedia communications solutions to organizations worldwide. The Burnaby office is the company's third largest research and development facility worldwide with 150 employees, 30% of whom are devoted to research and development activities. The Burnaby research and development office includes three core groups: ATM Product Development, Network and Services Management and ASIC design. Graduates most likely to be hired come from the following academic areas: Bachelor of Science (Computer Science), Bachelor of Engineering (Electrical, Computer Systems, Engineering Physics, Telecommunications) and Community College Diploma (Computer Science, Electronics Technician, Engineering Technician). Graduates would occupy Feature Test Designer, Software Designer, Hardware Designer and ASIC Designer positions. Team work, good communication and interpersonal skills are all listed as desirable non-academic qualifications. Company benefits are rated above average. The potential for advancement is listed as being excellent. The average annual starting salary falls within the $40,000 to $50,000 range. The most suitable method for initial contact by those seeking employment is to apply through the company's website. Newbridge Networks Corporation (Burnaby) does hire summer and co-op work term students. *Contact:* Shannon Clements, Human Resources.

NEWFOUNDLAND & LABRADOR HYDRO
PO Box 12400
St. John's, NF A1B 4K7

Tel. 709-737-1400
Fax 709-737-1231
Website .... www.nlh.nf.ca

Newfoundland & Labrador Hydro is responsible for the generation and transmission of electricity throughout the province. The company employs a total of 1,250 people throughout the province. Graduates most likely to be hired come from the following academic areas: Bachelor of Engineering (Civil, Electrical, Power, Telecommunications, Mechanical, Industrial Design), Bachelor of Commerce/Business Administration (Accounting, Human Resources, Information Systems), Chartered Accountant, Certified Management Accountant, Certified General Accountant, Master of Business Administration (Human Resources) and Community College Diploma (Accounting, Human Resources, CAD/CAM/Autocad, Computer Science, Electronics Technician, Engineering Technician). Graduates would occupy Technician, Clerk, Human Resources, Accounting and Engineering positions. Team player and good communication skills are both listed as desirable non-academic qualifications. Company benefits are rated as excellent. The potential for advancement is listed as average. The average annual starting salary falls within the $30,000 to $35,000 range. The most suitable method for initial contact by those seeking employment is to mail a resume with a covering letter. Newfoundland & Labrador Hydro does hire co-op work term and summer students. These students must be enrolled in a post secondary institute for the year prior and must be returning the following autumn. *Contact:* Mr. Alan Evans, Human Resources Specialist.

NEWFOUNDLAND POWER
55 Kenmount Road, PO Box 8910
St. John's, NF A1B 3P6

Tel. 709-737-5776
Fax 709-737-2967
Website .... www.newfoundlandpower.com

Newfoundland Power is an electrical distribution company providing service to almost 250,000 customers on the island portion of the province of Newfoundland. There are more than 800 employees at this location. Graduates most likely to be hired come from the following academic areas: Bachelor of Engineering (Civil, Environmental, Electrical, Industrial, Mechanical), Bachelor of Laws, Bachelor of Commerce/Business Administration (Accounting, Information Systems), Chartered Accountant (Finance), Certified Management Accountant (Finance), Certified General Accountant (Finance), Master of Business Administration (Finance) and Community College Diploma (Human Resources, Computer Science, Electronic Technician, Engineering Technician, Mechanic Technician). Graduates would occupy Analyst, Engineer, Technician and Programmer, etc. positions. Strong interpersonal and communications skills are both listed as desirable non-academic qualifications. Company benefits are rated as excellent. The potential for advancement is listed as being good. The average annual starting salary falls within the $25,000 to $30,000 range. The most suitable method for initial contact by those seeking employment is to mail a resume with a covering letter. Newfoundland Power does hire summer students. *Contact:* Douglas Chafe, Director, Employee Services.

NIKON CANADA INC.
1366 Aerowood Drive
Mississauga, ON L4W 1C1

Tel. 905-625-9910
Fax 905-625-0103
Website .... www.nikon.ca

Nikon Canada Inc. is the Canadian distributor of photographic goods and accessories, ophthalmic measuring instruments, microscopes, electronic image engineering products. There are more than 25 employees at this location. Graduates most likely to be hired come from the following academic areas: Bachelor of Arts and Bachelor of Commerce/Business Administration. Graduates are hired as Clerks, Repair Technicians or Trainees. A basic knowledge of office routines, computer oriented background and accounting experience at various levels are all listed as desirable non-academic qualifications. Also, for Repair Technician positions, possessing a basic knowledge of cameras is desirable. Company benefits are rated above average. The potential for advancement is listed as being good. The average annual starting salary falls within the $15,000 to $20,000 range. The most suitable method for initial contact by graduates seeking employment is to mail a resume with a covering letter. Nikon Canada Inc. does hire summer students, occasionally. *Contact:* Mr. H.K.S. Surty, Treasurer & Controller.

NLK CONSULTANTS INC.
855 Homer Street
Vancouver, BC V6B 5S2

Tel. 604-689-0344
Fax 604-443-1000
Email .... info@nlkvcr.nlkeng.com
Website .... www.nlkeng.com

NLK Consultants Inc. is a consulting engineering firm active in the pulp and paper industry. There are 200 employees at this location, a total of 300 in Canada, and a total of 325 employees worldwide. Graduates most likely to be hired come from the following academic areas: Bachelor of Engineering (Chemical, Pulp and Paper, Civil, Architectural/Building, Electrical, Instrumentation, Power, Mechanical, Industrial Production) and Community College Diploma (Architecture/Drafting, CAD/CAM/Autocad, Engineering Technician). Graduates would occupy Engineer (in all disciplines), CAD Designer and Drafting positions. Previous work experience in the pulp and paper industry, team player and a strong work ethic are all listed as desirable non-academic qualifications. Company benefits are rated as excellent. The potential for advancement is listed as being good. The average annual starting salary depends on the position being considered. The most suitable methods for initial contact by those seeking employment are to mail, fax or e-mail a resume with a covering letter. NLK Consultants Inc. does hire summer and co-op work term students. (Montreal Office: NLK Consultants Inc., 1425 boul. Réné Lévesque ouest, 8e étage, Montreal, QC, H3G 1T7, Phone 514-875-7950, Fax 514-397-1535). *Contacts:* Patricia Marion, Manager, Administration - Montreal or Barbara MacDonald, Office Manager - Vancouver.

NOR-MAN REGIONAL HEALTH AUTHORITY
PO Box 240
The Pas, MB R9A 1K4

Tel. 204-623-9240
Fax 204-623-9263

The NOR-MAN Regional Health Authority provides service which include acute care, long term care, rehabilitation services and community services. The NOR-MAN region is situated 630 km north of Winnipeg and extends from Grand Rapids in the southeast corner of the region to Flin Flon in the extreme northwest of the region. The NOR-MAN Regional Health Authority is a dynamic organization that continuously works to improve the health of the residents in the NOR-MAN region. There are 700 employees within the organization. Graduates most likely to be hired come from the following academic areas: Bachelor of Science (Nursing, Physical Therapy), Medical Doctor and Community College Diploma (Dietician/Nutrition, Laboratory Technician, Nursing RN/RNA, Radiology Technician, Ultra-Sound Technician). Graduates would occupy Nurse, Health Care Aide, Dietary Aide, Laboratory Technician, Radiology Technician and related positions. The health authority offers an excellent benefits package. The potential for advancement is listed as being good, with the authority actively supporting regular training and encouraging employees to pursue professional and personal goals. The average annual starting salary falls within the $30,000 to $35,000 range. The most suitable method for initial contact by those seeking employment is to mail a resume with a covering letter. The NOR-MAN Regional Health Authority does hire summer students. *Contact:* Human Resources.

NORANDA MINING AND EXPLORATION INC., BRUNSWICK DIVISION
PO Box 3000
Bathurst, NB E2A 3Z8

Tel. 506-547-3442
Fax 506-547-6162

Noranda Mining and Exploration Inc., Brunswick Division in involved in mining activities. The Brunswick Division employs 990 people. Graduates most likely to be hired come from the following academic areas: Bachelor of Arts (Economics), Bachelor of Science (Chemistry, Computer Science, Environmental, Geology, Metallurgy), Bachelor of Engineering (Chemical, Industrial Chemistry, Metallurgy, Surveying, Automation/Robotics, Computer Systems, Instrumentation, Microelectronics, Power, Industrial Design, Industrial Production, Welding, Min-

ing), Bachelor of Commerce/Business Administration (Accounting, Finance, Human Resources, Information Systems), Chartered Accountant, Certified Management Accountant, Master of Business Administration (Accounting, Finance), Master of Science, Master of Engineering and Community College Diploma (Human Resources, Purchasing/Logistics, Architecture/Drafting, CAD/CAM/Autocad, Computer Science, Electronics Technician, Engineering Technician, HVAC Systems, Welding). Graduates would occupy Professional, Engineer and Technician positions. Team player, flexibility and bilingualism (French/English) are all listed as desirable non-academic qualifications. Company benefits and the potential for advancement are both rated as excellent. The average annual starting salary falls within the $40,000 to $45,000 range. The most suitable method for initial contact by those seeking employment is to mail a resume with a covering letter. Brunswick Mining Division does hire summer and co-op work term students. *Contact:* Bruno Couteille, Human Resources Supervisor.

NORBORD INDUSTRIES INC.
1 Toronto Street, Suite 500
Toronto, ON M5C 2W4

Tel. 416-365-0710
Fax 416-360-2243

Norbord Industries Inc. is an international manufacturer of wood and wood composite products for construction and industrial uses. A wholly-owned subsidiary of Nexfor Inc., Norbord employs 1,300 people in the manufacture of lumber and panel board products (eg. oriented strand board, medium density fibreboard, hardwood plywood, softwood lumber), and 1,300 people through its 50% interest in CSC Forest Products of Cowie, Scotland. Graduates most likely to be hired come from the following academic areas: Bachelor of Science (Forestry), Bachelor of Engineering (Environmental, Mechanical), Bachelor of Commerce/Business Administration (Finance, Human Resources, Marketing), Chartered Accountant (Finance), Certified Management Accountant (Finance), Master of Business Administration (Accounting, Human Resources, Marketing) and Community College Diploma (Secretarial, Human Resources, Forestry). Team player, flexibility, adaptability, excellent interpersonal and communication skills, enthusiasm, drive to continually improve self and quality of work, and fluency in French as well as other languages, including Japanese and German are all listed as desirable non-academic qualifications. Company benefits and the potential for advancement are both rated as excellent. The most suitable method for initial contact by those seeking employment is to mail a resume with a covering letter. Norbord Industries Inc. does hire summer students. *Contact:* Human Resources Department.

NORTEL NETWORKS
PO Box 3511, Station C
Ottawa, ON K1Y 4H7

Tel. 613-763-8232
Fax 613-765-3900
Website .... www.nortelnetworks.com

Nortel Networks is the world's most diversified provider of digital network solutions and is active in shaping the standards for internet access and high-speed data transmission. Nortel Networks has earned a reputation for its expertise in networks, designing, building and integrating information, entertainment and communications networks globally. The company's environment is innovative, challenging, dynamic, culturally diverse, flexible and fun. The atmosphere inspires teamwork, breakthrough thinking and a passion for work. Nortel Networks recruits recent graduates who thrive on creativity and individuality, and hold a degree in Engineering, Computer Science, Business or Marketing. Nortel employs 80,000 people worldwide, 25 percent of whom work in research and development. Key lines of business include Enterprise Networks, Enterprise Data Networks, Wireless Networks, Broadband Networks and Public Carrier Networks. Nortel owns and operates R&D, sales and manufacturing facilities across Canada. The corporate headquarters is located in Brampton, Ontario. Unique opportunities exist in Ottawa, Montreal, Belleville, Toronto, Calgary, and Vancouver. Exciting opportunities also exist in the United States, where the company has a presence in North Carolina, Texas, Georgia, California and Tennessee. Graduates would occupy positions in Software Design and Development, Test and Verification, Hardware Design and Development, Network Engineer, Radio Systems Development, Technical Support Engineer, Installation Engineer, Information Technology, Systems Engineer and Architecture, Component Engineer, Marketing/Product Marketing, Finance and Business/Information Systems. Company benefits and the potential for advancement are both rated as excellent. Co-op and non co-op students are hired during the fall, winter and summer terms. Other programs that support students include the High School Co-op Program and the Career Edge Program. For detailed information about available positions access the company's website, mail or e-mail a resume with a cover letter and a copy of the most recent transcripts to the National Resourcing Centre. *Contact:* National Resourcing Centre.

NORTEL NETWORKS, TORONTO MULTIMEDIA APPLICATIONS CENTRE

c/o National Resourcing Centre, PO Box 3511, Station C
Ottawa, ON K1Y 4H7

Fax 800-906-5554
Website .... www.nortelnetworks.com

The Nortel Networks, Toronto Multimedia Applications Centre (TorMAC) develops global products in high-growth, internet business areas, including computer telephony integration, multimedia messaging, call centre applications and interactive voice response. Through the development of industry-leading technology, Nortel Networks is achieving its goal of being a global leader in the data market for telecommunications networks. The Toronto Multimedia Applications Centre's creative and casual atmosphere, located in downtown Toronto, offers the opportunity to help chart the future of global communications. As a result of its success, the centre has experienced a fifty percent growth in staff over the last three years and today employs 400 people. The Toronto Multimedia Applications Centre's fast paced environment attracts very talented people, who bring integrity, intelligence, enthusiasm and a customer focus to their work. Graduates most likely to be hired are those with degrees in Science (Computer Science), Engineering (Electrical) and Business Administration. Opportunities for graduates include positions such as Application Designer, Operating Systems Designer, Hardware Design Engineer and Digital Signal Processing Software Engineer, as well as Multimedia Designer and Information Developer. With 80,000 employees and offices in 27 countries, Nortel Networks values diversity and offers an evolving range of opportunities to highly motivated individuals. The most

suitable methods for initial contact by those seeking employment are to mail or fax a resume with a covering letter to the National Resourcing Centre in Ottawa, via the company's website or through your campus career centre (no phone calls please). The Toronto Multimedia Applications Centre also hires students for co-op work term and internship placements. *Contact:* National Resourcing Centre.

NORTH AMERICAN DETECTORS INC. / NADI

100 Tempo Avenue
Toronto, ON M2H 3S5

Tel. 416-496-5900
Fax 416-496-5931
Email .... hr@nadi.com
Website .... www.nadi.com

North American Detectors Inc. / NADI is the fourth-largest manufacturer and marketer of residential carbon monoxide alarms, smoke alarms and explosive gas detectors in the world. NADI has achieved a high level of success through an ongoing dedication to research and development, cost effective manufacturing, quality products and world class customer services. The company employs 100 people at this location and a total of 100 people worldwide. Graduates most likely to be hired come from the following academic areas: Bachelor of Engineering (Electrical, Mechanical), Bachelor of Commerce/Business Administration (Accounting, Finance, Human Resources, Information Systems, Marketing), Certified Management Accountant, Certified General Accountant, Community College Diploma (Accounting, Business, Financial Planning, Human Resources, Marketing/Sales, Office Administration, Purchasing/Logistics, Secretarial, CAD/CAM/Autocad, Electronics Technician, Engineering Technician, Information Systems) and High School Diploma. Team player, self motivated and excellent organizational skills are all listed as desirable non-academic qualifications. Company benefits are rated as industry standard. The potential for advancement is listed as being good. The most suitable methods for initial contact by those seeking employment are to mail or fax a resume with a covering letter. North American Detectors Inc. / NADI does hire co-op work term students. *Contact:* Human Resources.

NORTH SHORE NEWS

1139 Lonsdale Avenue
North Vancouver, BC V7M 2H4

Tel. 604-985-2131
Fax 604-985-1157

North Shore News publishes a community newspaper in one of Canada's richest markets. The company employs 95 people. Graduates most likely to be hired come from the following academic areas: Bachelor of Arts (Graphic Arts, Journalism), Bachelor of Engineering (General) and Community College Diploma (Advertising, Business, Communications, Marketing/Sales, Journalism). Graduates would occupy Trainee Sales Representative, Freelance Journalist and Sales Representative positions. Energy, enthusiasm, drive, determination and good communication skills are all listed as desirable non-academic qualifications. Company benefits and the potential for advancement are both rated as excellent. The average annual starting salary falls within the $20,000 to $25,000 range. The most suitable method for initial contact by those seeking employment is to mail a resume with a covering letter. *Contact:* Dee Dhaliwal.

NORTH YORK COMMUNITY CARE ACCESS CENTRE
45 Sheppard Avenue East, 7th Floor
Toronto, ON M2N 5W9

Tel. 416-222-2241
Fax 416-224-1470
Email .... hr@nyccac.on.ca
Website .... www.nyccac.on.ca

The North York Community Care Access Centre is a nonprofit corporation involved in the planning, coordination and delivery of a full range of services required to support clients and their caregivers in their homes. In addition, services are also provided in schools throughout North York. These services include: nursing, nutritional counselling, occupational therapy, physiotherapy, social work, speech-language pathology, personal support, drug, hospital equipment, laboratory services, medical supplies and transportation for medical appointments. The centre employs approximately 200 people. Graduates most likely to be hired come from the following academic areas: Bachelor of Arts (Social Work), Bachelor of Science (Nursing, Occupational Therapy, Physiotherapy), Bachelor of Commerce/Business Administration (Accounting, Finance, Human Resources, Information Systems), Masters (Speech/Language Pathology, Social Work), Community College Diploma (Accounting, Communications, Human Resources, Secretarial) and High School Diploma. Graduates would occupy Secretary, Supervisor, Case Manager Coordinator, Physiotherapist, Speech-Language Pathologist, Social Worker, Clerk, Network Administrator and Human Resources positions. Team player, strong customer service skills, knowledge of commercial software applications, keyboard skills, analytical, able to handle concurrent tasks without close supervision, sound knowledge of medical terminology, multilingual, and good organizational, problem solving and communication skills are all listed as desirable non-academic qualifications. Company benefits are rated above average. The potential for advancement is listed as being average. Starting salary falls within the $24,000 to $29,000 range for clerical positions, and is $43,000 plus for professional positions. The most suitable methods for initial contact by those seeking employment are to mail, fax or e-mail a resume with a covering letter, or via the centre's website. The North York Community Care Access Centre does hire summer students on a regular basis. Contact: Suzanne Jones, Human Resources Department.

NORTH YORK GENERAL HOSPITAL, BRANSON DIVISION
555 Finch Avenue West
Toronto, ON M2R 1N5

Tel. 416-635-2524
Fax 416-635-2413
Email .... hr@nybh.org
Website .... www.nygh.on.ca

North York General Hospital, Branson Division is a general community hospital that is being redeveloped into an ambulatory care centre. The North York General Hospital is a multi-site regional teaching hospital. The hospital serves people in north central Toronto and southern York Region. In addition to the Branson Division the North York General Hospital consists of the General Division, which is a regional teaching hospital and the Seniors' Health Centre, which is a long term care facility and day hospital for seniors. North York General Hospital is also affiliated with the University of Toronto and is a partner with Sunnybrook & Women's College Health Sciences Centre in the Peters-Boyd Academy. The Branson Division employs approximately 1,100 people. Graduates most likely to be hired come from the following academic areas: Bachelor of Arts (General, Social Work), Bachelor of Science (Nursing, Nutritional Sciences, Occupational Therapy, Pharmacy, Physical Therapy), Bachelor of Commerce/Business Administration (Accounting, Finance), Master of Business Administration (Accounting), Master of Arts (Social Work) and Community College Diploma (Accounting, Administration). Graduates would occupy Secretary, Clerk, Nurse, Paramedic, Technologist and Technician positions. Employee benefits are rated as industry standard. The potential for advancement is listed as average. The average annual starting salary falls within the $25,000 to $30,000 range. The most suitable method for initial contact by those seeking employment is to mail a resume with a covering letter. North York General Hospital, Branson Division does hire summer students. Contact: Ashton White, Human Resources Manager.

NORTHERN ALBERTA INSTITUTE OF TECHNOLOGY / NAIT
11762 - 106 Street
Edmonton, AB T5G 2R1

Tel. 780-471-7018
Fax 780-471-7533
Website .... www.nait.ab.ca

The Northern Alberta Institute of Technology / NAIT is one of Canada's foremost institutes of technical training dedicated to offering quality career education that fulfills the goals and expectations of students while serving the needs of the economy. NAIT employs approximately 700 instructional and 700 support staff. Graduates most likely to be hired come from the following academic areas: Bachelor of Arts (General, English, Graphic Arts), Bachelor of Science (General, Biology, Chemistry, Computer Science, Forestry, Geology, Mathematics, Metallurgy, Microbiology, Physics, Dentistry, Nutrition), Bachelor of Engineering (General, Industrial Chemistry, Materials Science, Metallurgy, Building, Surveying, Electrical, Biomedical Electronics, Computer Systems, Instrumentation, Microelectronics, Power, Telecommunications, Mechanical, Aeronautical, Industrial Design, Welding, Fish/Wildlife, Forest Resources, Mining, Petroleum, Water Resources), Bachelor of Architecture, Bachelor of Landscape Architecture, Bachelor of Education (General, Adult), Bachelor of Commerce/Business Administration (General, Accounting, Finance, Human Resources, Information Systems Marketing, Public Administration), Certified Management Accountant, Certified General Accountant, Master of Business Administration (General, Accounting, Finance, Human Resources, Information Systems, Marketing) and Community College Diploma (Accounting, Business, Financial Planning, Television/Radio Arts, Mechanic, Drafting, Animal Health, Dental Assistant/Hygienist). Graduates would be hired to occupy support and instructional (no teaching qualifications required) positions. Five to ten years previous work experience, empathy with students, team player, and quality/customer orientation are all listed as desirable non-academic qualifications. Company benefits are rated above average. The potential for advancement is listed as being good. The average annual starting salary for instructional positions falls within the $30,000 to $35,000 range. The most suitable methods for initial contact by those seeking employment are to mail a resume with a covering letter, or via telephone. Contacts: Mike Maitre; Donna Foerster or Marian Pangburn.

NORTHERN COMPUTER SYSTEMS, INC. / NCS
93 James Street
Parry Sound, ON P2A 1T7

Tel.	705-746-5873
Fax	705-746-5178
Email	ncs@northerncomputer.com
Website	www.northerncomputer.com

Northern Computer Systems, Inc. / NCS was established in 1983, and developed the world's first finite capacity scheduling solution for manufacturing and fabrication companies. Some of NCS' clients include INCO, the world's largest nickel supplier, who achieved a 25% increase in throughput in divisional shops through the implementation of NCS' scheduling technology. Vision 4000 is easily tailored through user features that allow a diverse range of industries to utilize and benefit from the company's technology. Some of these industries include the General Motors Proving Ground, The Timken Company, American Cast Iron Pipe Company, and both divisions of the second largest supplier to the Boeing Company, Menasco Aerospace. Northern Computer Systems, Inc. employs a total of 17 people. Graduates most likely to be hired come from the following academic areas: Bachelor of Science (Computer Science, Mathematics), Bachelor of Engineering (General, Chemical, Mechanical), Master of Engineering (Industrial Engineering) and Community College Diploma (Information Systems, Computer Science). Graduates would occupy Industrial Engineer, Applications Engineer and Software Systems Engineer. Able to work well on individual projects as well as in a team environment, manufacturing knowledge and experience, results oriented, able to meet deadlines and excellent communication skills are all listed as desirable non-academic qualifications. Company benefits are rated as industry standard. The potential for advancement is listed as excellent. The average annual starting salary falls within the $35,000 to $40,000 range. The most suitable method for initial contact by those seeking employment is to e-mail a resume with a covering letter. *Contacts:* Geoff Osborne, Manager, Applications Engineering or David Cox, President and Manager of Development.

NORTHERN TELEPHONE LIMITED
PO Box 4000
New Liskeard, ON P0J 1P0

Tel.	705-647-3288
Fax	705-647-3587
Email	tdeighton@ntl.nt.net
Website	www.northerntel.on.ca

Northern Telephone Limited is a leading provider of progressive telecommunications services designed to meet the changing needs of its customer base in Northeastern Ontario. Established in 1905, the company operates 32 exchanges and more than 66,000 telephone numbers over an 83,000 square kilometre service area. Northern Telephone serves the communities of Timmins, Kirkland Lake, Kapuskasing, Hearst and the Tri-Towns, along with many smaller population centres. In addition to a comprehensive range of local access and broad band transmission, Northern Telephone provides Sympatico Internet services, as well as cellular, paging and mobile satellite telephone services through its subsidiary, NorTel Mobility. Northern Telephone Limited is a subsidiary of Bell Canada and today employs 250 people throughout Northeastern Ontario. Graduates most likely to be hired come from the following academic areas: Bachelor of Engineering (Electrical, Computer Systems, Telecommunications), Bachelor of Commerce/Business Administration (Accounting, Information Systems, Marketing) and Community College Diploma (Electronics Technician, Information Systems). Graduates would occupy Telecommunications Engineer, Telecommunications Technician, Computer Programmer, Network Support Analyst, Marketing Manager and Accounting positions. Leadership skills, team player, customer focus, computer literacy, and excellent interpersonal and communication skills are all listed as desirable non-academic qualifications. Company benefits are rated as excellent. The potential for advancement is listed as being good. The average annual starting salary falls within the $35,000 to $40,000 range. The most suitable methods for initial contact by those seeking employment are to fax or e-mail a resume with a covering letter. Northern Telephone Limited does hire summer and co-op work term students. *Contact:* Terry Deighton, Human Resources Manager.

NORTHWEST GTA HOSPITAL CORPORATION, BRAMPTON CAMPUS
20 Lynch Street
Brampton, ON L6W 2Z8

Tel.	905-796-4477
Fax	905-451-9888
Email	nwgtahr@pmh.on.ca
Website	www.egh.on.ca

Northwest GTA Hospital Corporation is Ontario's largest community hospital. The hospital corporation employs over 3,800 people across its three campuses, Brampton Campus, Etobicoke Campus and Georgetown Campus. The hospital provides unparalleled health care services, and as driven advocates of community wellness, the hospital and its staff continually work to improve and develop unique services and facilities to meet the growing needs of the community. Graduates most likely to be hired at the Brampton Campus come from the following academic areas: Bachelor of Arts (Psychology), Bachelor of Science (Nursing, Occupational Therapy, Pharmacy, Physiotherapy), Bachelor of Commerce/Business Administration (Accounting), Chartered Accountant, Certified Management Accountant, Certified General Accountant, Master of Education, Master of Social Work and Community College Diploma (Accounting, Business, Office Administration, Secretarial, Health/Home Care Aide, Laboratory Technician, Nursing RN/RNA, Radiology, Respiratory Therapy, Ultra-sound Technician). Graduates would occupy Registered Nurse, Accountant, Physiotherapist, Occupational Therapist, Speech Therapist, Technicians and Secretarial positions. Employee benefits are rated as excellent. The potential for advancement is listed as being good. The most suitable methods for initial contact by those seeking employment are to mail or fax a resume with a covering letter, or via telephone. Northwest GTA Hospital Corporation, Brampton Campus does hire summer students on a regular basis. *Contact:* Employee Services Department.

NORTHWESTEL INC.
PO Bag 2727
Whitehorse, YT Y1A 4Y4

Tel.	867-668-5300
Fax	867-668-3236
Email	recruitment@nwtel.ca
Website	www.nwtel.ca

Northwestel Inc. is a telecommunications company, providing voice, data, cellular, satellite, mobile, cable television and internet services in the Yukon, Northwest Territories and Northern British Columbia. The company employs approximately 600 people. Graduates most likely to be hired come from the following academic areas: Bachelor of Arts (Economics), Bachelor of Science (Computer Science), Bachelor of Engineering (Civil, Electrical, Computer Systems, Telecommunications), Bachelor of Commerce/Business Administration (General, Accounting, Finance, Human Resources, Information Systems, Marketing, Chartered Accountant, Certified Management Accountant, Certified General Accountant, Master of Business Administration (General, Accounting, Finance, Human Resources, Information Systems, Marketing), Master of Engineering (Electrical), and Community College Diploma (Accounting, Administration, Business, Communications/Public Relations, Human Resources, Information Systems, Marketing/Sales, Legal Assistant, Computer Science, Electronics Technician, Engineering Technician) and High School Diploma. Team player, highly motivated, adaptable, focused on quality customer service, and strong interpersonal and communication skills are all listed as desirable non-academic qualifications. Company benefits and the potential for advancement are both rated as excellent. The average annual starting salary falls in the $45,000 plus range. The most suitable method for initial contact by those seeking employment is to mail a resume with a covering letter. Northwestel Inc. does hire summer students. *Contact:* Human Resources.

NOVA CHEMICALS CORPORATION
PO Box 5006
Red Deer, AB T4N 6A1

Tel. 403-314-8611
Fax 403-314-8787
Email .... resumes@novachem.com
Website .... www.novachem.com

NOVA Chemicals Corporation is a petrochemicals company which operates two commodity chemicals businesses, olefins / polyolefins and styrenics. The company operates two commodity chemicals businesses, olefins/ polyolefins and styrenics. NOVA Chemicals has more than a dozen petrochemical and plastics plants in Canada and the United States. There are 600 employees at this location, a total of 2,680 in Canada, and 3,600 employees worldwide. Graduates most likely to be hired come from the following academic areas: Bachelor of Science (Computer Science, Nursing), Bachelor of Engineering (Chemical, Civil, Electrical, Mechanical, Computer Systems, Instrumentation), Bachelor of Commerce/Business Administration (Finance, Human Resources, Information Systems, Marketing), Certified Management Accountant, Certified General Accountant, Master/Doctorate of Engineering (Process Control) and Community College Diploma (Accounting, Administration, Information Systems, Secretarial, Computer Science, Ambulance/Emergency Care, Laboratory Technician, Power Engineering - Minimum 4th Class, Chemical Technology). Graduates would occupy Programmer, Desktop Support, Occupational Health Nurse, Graduate Engineer, Secretarial, Accountant, Human Resources Consultant, Systems Analyst, Buyer, Loss Prevention Technician, Laboratory Technician, and Operating Technician positions. Good communication skills, a customer service orientation, leadership skills, problem solving and decision making abilities, self management skills, team player, change management skills and good interpersonal skills are all listed as desirable non-academic qualifications. Company benefits and the potential for advancement are both rated as excellent. Accordingly, NOVA Chemicals supports diversity initiatives, offers alternative work arrangements, leadership programs and a flexible benefits program. The average annual starting salary depends on the applicant and the position being considered. Career opportunities at NOVA Chemicals appear on the FWJ job board at www.fwj.com, or can by listened to by calling 1-888-371-0161 (toll free). The most suitable methods for initial contact by interested and qualified job seekers are to mail or fax a resume with a covering letter, or by applying through campus career centres. NOVA Chemicals Corporation does hire summer and co-op work term students. *Contacts:* Connie Maundrell, Human Resources Consultant or Melody Jones, Human Resources Consultant.

NOVA SCOTIA REHABILITATION CENTRE
1341 Summer Street
Halifax, NS B3H 4K4

Tel. 902-422-1787
Fax 902-425-6466
Website www.qe2-hsc.ns.ca/rehab.html

The Nova Scotia Rehabilitation Centre is an active treatment centre employing the broad concept of total rehabilitation for the physically disabled through a multidisciplinary approach. Although possessing certain characteristics of a hospital, its approach and method are more functional than clinical and in many cases concerned with adjustment rather than cure. The centre employs more than 250 people. Graduates most likely to be hired come from the following academic areas: Bachelor of Arts (Recreation), Bachelor of Science (Nursing), Bachelor of Education (Adult), Bachelor of Commerce/Business Administration, Master of Business Administration (Finance), Master of Science (Physiotherapy, Occupational Therapy), Master of Engineering (Biomedical), Doctorate (Psychology) and Community College Diploma (Accounting, Secretarial, Human Resources, Recreation, Social Work, Food/Nutrition, Nursing RN/RNA, Orthotic/ Prosthetic Technician, Orthotic Footwear Technician). Graduates would occupy entry level positions relating to their specific area of study. Excellent communication skills, team player, adaptable and a commitment to patient care are all listed as desirable non-academic qualifications. Company benefits are rated as industry standard. The potential for advancement is listed as average. The average annual starting salary falls within the $20,000 to $35,000 range and ultimately depends upon the position being considered. The most suitable method for initial contact by those seeking employment is to mail a resume with a covering letter. The Nova Scotia Rehabilitation Centre does hire summer students. *Contact:* Joy Stevens, Human Resources Services Manager.

NOVARTIS PHARMACEUTICALS CANADA INC.
385, boul Bouchard
Dorval, QC H9R 4P5

Tel. 514-631-6775
Fax 514-631-1867
Website .... www.pharma.novartis.com

Novartis Pharmaceuticals Canada Inc., a subsidiary of Novartis Pharma AG, serves medical professionals and patients through the provision of a broad range of prescription medicines and pursuing the discovery and development of new and future innovative medicines. Novartis Pharma AG is headquartered in Basel, Switzerland and is located in more than 60 countries through 126 affiliates and employs more than 36,000 people worldwide. Novartis was created in 1996 by the merger of Ciba and Sandoz. A world leader in the life sciences arena, the company focuses on healthcare, agribusiness and nutrition. Novartis Pharmaceuticals Canada Inc. maintains one of Canada's broadest programs of clinical research in immunology, neurology, endocrinology, asthma and cardiovascular diseases. Graduates most likely to be hired come from the following academic areas: Bachelor of Arts (Journalism, Languages, Psychology), Bachelor of Science (Biology, Chemistry, Computer Science, Health Sciences, Microbiology, Nursing, Pharmacy, Physics, Psychology), Bachelor of Engineering (Chemical), Bachelor of Commerce/Business Administration (Accounting, Finance, Information Systems, Marketing), Chartered Accountant (Finance), Certified Management Accountant (Finance), Certified General Accountant (Finance), Master of Business Administration (Accounting, Finance, Information Systems, Marketing), Master/Doctorate of Science (Immunology, Oncology, Central Nervous System, Cardiovascular, Neurology) and Community College Diploma (Marketing, Purchasing/Logistics, Secretarial, Human Resources, Journalism, Computer, Nursing RN/RNA). Graduates would occupy Sales Representative, Regional/National Sales Manager, Marketing Research Analyst, Product Manager, Associate Product Manager, Training Manager, Analyst, Technical Support, Medical Liaison Associate, New Product Manager and Clinical Research positions. Bilingual, an ability to work in a team environment, and excellent interpersonal and communication skills are listed as desirable non-academic qualifications. Company benefits and the potential for advancement are both rated as excellent. The most suitable methods for initial contact by those seeking employment are to mail or fax a resume with a covering letter. Novartis Pharmaceuticals Canada Inc. does hire summer students. *Contact:* Human Resources.

NOWSCO WELL SERVICE LTD.
801 - 6th Avenue SW, Suite 1300
Calgary, AB   T2P 4E1

Tel.	403-531-5151
Fax	403-296-1575
Email	HR@nowsco.com
Website	www.nowsco.com

Nowsco Well Service Ltd. supplies technical expertise, specialized services, products, and equipment to upstream and downstream operations in the oil and gas industry. Nowsco has achieved international recognition as a leading provider of well, pipeline, process and industrial services, and has fostered an aggressive approach towards the development and implementation of new technologies. In 1996, Nowsco was purchased by Houston, Texas based BJ Services Company. Together the combined companies provide well services around the world and employ more than 7,000 people worldwide. Nowsco Well Service Ltd. employs approximately 300 people at this location and a total of 800 people in Canada. Graduates most likely to be hired come from the following academic areas: Bachelor of Science (Chemistry, Computer Science, Geology), Bachelor of Engineering (Chemical, Metallurgy, Computer Systems, Welding, Petroleum), Bachelor of Commerce/Business Administration (Accounting, Finance, Human Resources, Information Systems, Marketing) and Community College Diploma (Accounting, Administration, Business, Communications, Financial Planning, Human Resources, Insurance, Marketing/Sales, Secretarial, CAD/CAM/Autocad, Computer Science, Engineering Technician, Laboratory Technician). Graduates would occupy Accounting Clerk, Petroleum Engineer, Sales and Marketing and Human Resource positions. Team player, creativity and enthusiasm are listed as desirable non-academic qualifications. Company benefits and the potential for advancement are both rated as excellent. The average

annual starting salary falls within the $25,000 to $35,000 range. The most suitable method for initial contact by those seeking employment is to mail a resume with a covering letter. Nowsco Well Service Ltd. does hire summer students. *Contact:* Human Resources.

NRI INDUSTRIES
394 Symington Avenue
Toronto, ON   M6N 2W3

Tel.	416-657-1111
Fax	416-652-4213
Email	careers@nriindustries.com
Website	www.nriindustries.com

NRI Industries Inc. was founded in 1927 and currently operates five manufacturing plants in Canada and the United States. Through its expertise in rubber compounding and product design the company has become North America's leading manufacturer of automotive and industrial rubber parts based on recycled materials. Annual sales exceed $60 million with more than 80% from export sales. The company's objective is to remain the lowest total cost producer of value-added products using recycled materials and meet the highest specifications for quality. NRI achieved QS9000 certification in 1997. There are 350 employees at this location, a total of 450 in Canada, and a total of 600 employees in Canada and the United States. Graduates most likely to be hired come from the following academic areas: Bachelor of Science (Chemistry), Bachelor of Engineering (Chemical, Industrial Chemistry, Materials Science, Instrumentation, Industrial Design, Industrial Production) and Master of Business Administration (Marketing). Graduates would occupy Marketing, Production Management, Chemical Engineering, Mechanical Engineering and Electrical Engineering positions. Applicants should be enthusiastic and active participants. Company benefits are rated as industry standard. The potential for advancement is listed as being good. The average annual starting salary falls within the $30,000 to $35,000 range. The most suitable method for initial contact by those seeking employment is to mail a resume with a covering letter. NRI Industries Inc. does hire summer students. *Contacts:* Sheila Kendall, Manager, Human Resources or Randy Garrett, Vice President, Human Resources.

NSI COMMUNICATIONS
4610, chemin Bois Franc
St-Laurent, QC   H4S 1A7

Tel.	514-956-8880
Fax	514-956-8251
Email	nsi@nsicomm.com
Website	www.nsicomm.com

NSI Communications manufactures, designs and markets state of the art satellite based telecommunications equipment and services worldwide. There are approximately 40 employees at this location, 50 across Canada, and a total of 60 employees worldwide. Graduates most likely to be hired come from the following academic areas: Bachelor of Science (Computer Science, Mathematics, Physics), Bachelor of Engineering (General, Electrical, Computer Systems, Telecommunications, Mechanical, Industrial Design), Bachelor of Commerce/Business Administration (Accounting, Finance, Human Resources, Information Systems, Marketing), Chartered Accountant, Master of Business Administration (Marketing), Master of Science (Computer Science), Master of Engineering (Electronic Circuits, Computer Science), Doctorate (Engineering) and Community College Diploma (Accounting, Business, Human Resources, Marketing, Purchasing/Logistics, Secretarial, Graphic Arts, CAD/CAM/ Autocad, Computer Science, Electronics Technician, Engineering Technician). Graduates would occupy Technical positions in Research and Development, Production, and Systems, as well as positions in Marketing and Accounting. Depending upon the level of experience and academic background of the applicant, positions would range from the Junior to Director levels. An ability to speak and write properly in both official languages where applicable, good work ethic, self-starter, proactive, reliable, punctual, non-smoker and good presentation skills are all listed as desirable non-academic qualifications. Company benefits are rated as industry standard. The potential for advancement is listed as being good. The average annual starting salary depends upon the level and function of the position being considered. The most suitable method for initial contact by those seeking employment is to mail a resume with a covering letter. NSI Communications does hire summer students. *Contact:* Human Resources Manager.

NTI NEWSPAPER TECHNOLOGIES INC.
500 - 4th Avenue SW, Suite 3100
Calgary, AB T2P 2V6

Tel.	403-234-0230
Fax	403-234-7897
Email	hr@nti.ca
Website	www.nti.ca

NTI Newspaper Technologies Inc. markets and develops circulation management software for the newspaper industry. The NTI Newsline suite of products include: Home Delivery, Single Copy, Total Market Coverage, Collections, Mapping, Telephony and Internet. NTI Newsline products are based on Windows, client/server technology, and are year 2000 compliant. With language, database and platform independence, NTI Newsline allows any size of publication, anywhere in the world, to design a circulation management system to fit their specific corporate standards. Newspapers ranging in size from 2,000 to 650,000 circulation daily, have joined NTI's growing user-base. NTI currently employs 55 people. Graduates most likely to be hired come from the following academic areas: Bachelor of Science (Computer Science), Bachelor of Engineering (Electrical, Computer Systems), Bachelor of Commerce/Business Administration (Information Systems) and Community College Diploma (Information Systems). Graduates would occupy Software Engineer and Technical Support positions. Team player and good people skills are both listed as desirable non-academic qualifications. Company benefits are rated as industry standard. The potential for advancement is listed as being good. The average annual starting salary falls within the $30,000 to $35,000 range. The most suitable methods for initial contact by those seeking employment are to mail, fax or e-mail a resume with a covering letter, or via the company's website. NTI Newspaper Technologies Inc. does hire summer and co-op work term students. *Contact:* Leon Perrier, Technical Recruiter.

NUMAC ENERGY INC
321 - 6th Avenue SW, Suite 400
Calgary, AB T2P 3H3

Tel.	403-260-9400
Fax	403-294-3402
Email	recruit@numac.com
Website	www.numac.com

Numac Energy Inc. is one of Canada's top 25 oil and gas producing companies. The company's major strengths include a balanced inventory of long-life reserves and production, and competitive advantages in oil field infrastructure and marketing. There are 160 employees at this location, and a total of 240 employees in Canada. Graduates most likely to be hired come from the following academic areas: Bachelor of Arts (Economics), Bachelor of Science (Computer Science, Geology, Geography), Bachelor of Engineering (Industrial Production, Petroleum), Bachelor of Laws, Bachelor of Commerce/Business Administration (Accounting, Finance, Human Resources, Information Systems, Marketing), Chartered Accountant, Certified Management Accountant, Certified General Accountant, Master of Business Administration (Accounting, Finance, Human Resources, Information Systems, Marketing), Master of Science, Master of Engineering, Community College Diploma (Accounting, Administration, Business, Human Resources, Computer Science, Engineering Technician) and High School Diploma. Graduates would occupy Facilities Engineer, Production Engineer, Reservoir Engineer, Operations Engineer, Drilling Engineer, Geologist, Geophysicist, Marketing, Computer/IS Department, Human Resources, Land Acquisitions/Divestitures, Finance, Tax and General Accounting positions. Team player, self motivated, independent thinker and previous industry experience are all listed as desirable non-academic qualifications. Company benefits are rated as excellent. The potential for advancement is listed as being good. The average annual starting salary for new graduates falls within the $25,000 to $30,000 range. The most suitable methods for initial contact by those seeking employment are to mail a resume with a covering letter, or through networking contacts. Numac Energy Inc. hires 15 to 20 students per year for summer and co-op work terms. *Contact:* Patti Lou Barron.

NYGARD INTERNATIONAL INC.
1771 Inkster Boulevard
Winnipeg, MB R2X 1R3

Tel.	204-982-5000
Fax	204-697-1254
Website	www.nygard.net

Nygard International Inc. manufactures and retails ladies apparel. There are 1,300 employees at this location, and a total of 2,000 employees worldwide. Graduates most likely to be hired come from the following academic areas: Bachelor of Engineering (Industrial), Bachelor of Commerce/Business Administration (Finance, Human Resources, Information Systems), Chartered Accountant, Certified Management Accountant, Certified General Accountant, Master of Engineering (Industrial) and Community College Diploma (Administration, Business, Human Resources, Legal Assistant, Security/Enforcement, Travel/Tourism, CAD/CAM/Autocad, Computer Science, Electronics Technician). Garment manufacturing, design and construction experience, computer literacy, team oriented, able to work with a minimum of supervision and deadline oriented are all listed as desirable non-academic qualifications. Company benefits and the potential for advancement are both rated as excellent. The average annual starting salary falls within the $20,000 to $25,000 range. The most suitable method for initial contact by those seeking employment is to mail a resume with a covering letter. Nygard International Inc. does hire a limited number of summer students annually. *Contact:* Human Resources.

OERLIKON AEROSPACE INC.
225, boul du Séminaire Sud
St-Jean-sur-Richelieu, QC J3B 8E9

Tel.	450-358-2000
Fax	450-358-7707
Email	recrutement@oerlikon.ca

Oerlikon Aerospace Inc. is a world-class integrator of complex systems with a reputation for leadership in the field of real-time and embedded systems. The company employs a total of 300 people. Graduates most likely to be hired come from the following academic areas: Bachelor of Science (Computer Science), Bachelor of Engineering (Electrical, Aerospace, Telecommunications), Master of Business Administration (Information Systems) and Community College Diploma (Electronics Technician, Engineering Technician). The majority of new graduates hired would occupy the position of Software Engineer. Previous military and work experience in the aerospace industry are listed as a desirable non-academic qualifications. The potential for advancement is listed as being excellent. The average annual starting salary falls within the $35,000 to $40,000 range. The most suitable methods for initial contact by those seeking employment are to mail, fax or e-mail a resume with a covering letter. Oerlikon Aerospace Inc. does hire co-op work term students. *Contacts:* Lise Forté, Recruiter, Human Resources Department or Thérèse Ménard, Human Resources Supervisor.

OFFICE OF THE AUDITOR GENERAL OF CANADA
240 Sparks Street
Ottawa, ON K1A 0G6

Tel.	613-995-3708 ext: 4229
Fax	613-954-0441
Email	emploi@oag-bvg.gc.ca
Website	www.oag-bvg.gc.ca

The Office of the Auditor General's mission is to conduct independent audits and examinations that provide objective information, advice and assurance to Parliament. The office promotes accountability and best practices in government operations. The Auditor General offers a variety of work in government departments, Crown corporations and agencies touching all aspects of national life. Transportation, finance, culture, the environment, foreign aid, broadcasting and scientific research are just a few of the areas covered by auditors. The office is recognized internationally as a leader in developing innovative approaches, software packages and applications to assist in auditing government activities. The office maintains a vision of making a difference for the Canadian people by promoting, in all its work for Parliament, answerable, honest, and productive government. The Office of the Auditor General employs a total of 550 people across Canada in offices located in Halifax, Montreal, Ottawa, Winnipeg, Edmonton and Vancouver (450 in Ottawa). Graduates with a Bachelor level degree would enter the Financial Audit Trainee program. These graduates would be required to obtain an accounting designation, with preference given to candidates who have successfully completed or enrolled in advanced courses in financial accounting, management accounting or auditing. Undergraduate degree specialization must be in accounting, commerce, administration, finance, or other related disciplines. Graduates with a Master degree or Professional qualification in public/business administration, social science, applied science, applied science (including environmental science), mathematics, computer science, law, engineering or other disciplines related to the work of the Office, would enter the Value-for-Money Audit Trainee program. The Office maintains a commitment to Audit Trainees by offering high quality and lively training, both on the job and in the classroom, and has designed an extensive professional development curriculum for all its staff, ranging from technical knowledge courses to training in management skills. Audit Trainees also have the opportunity to enter into the mentoring program. Bilingualism is listed as a definite asset. The average annual starting salary falls within the $25,000 to $30,000 range. The most suitable methods for initial contact by those seeking employment are to mail, fax or e-mail a resume, cover letter and most recent transcript. The Office of the Auditor General does hire summer and co-op work term students. *Contacts:* Dominique Martel or Lucie Smith.

OLAND BREWERIES LIMITED
3055 Agricola Street
Halifax, NS B3K 4G2

Tel.	902-453-3821
Fax	902-453-5664

Oland Breweries Limited brews and markets beer. The company employs 196 people at this location and approximately 3,000 in Canada. Graduates most likely to be hired come from the following academic areas: Bachelor of Arts (General), Bachelor of Science (Chemistry), Bachelor of Engineering (Food Processing, Industrial Production), Bachelor of Commerce/Business Administration (Accounting, Finance, Human Resources, Information Systems, Marketing), Master of Business Administration (Accounting, Finance, Human Resources, Information Systems, Marketing) and Community College Diploma (Accounting, Business, Human Resources, Marketing/Sales, Laboratory Technician). The positions graduates would occupy depend upon the specific openings, but usually they are entry level Clerical, Technical or Sales positions. Results oriented, analytical, team work, and good communication, people, leadership, problem solving and decision making skills are all listed as desirable non-academic qualifications. Company benefits are rated as excellent. The potential for advancement is listed as being good. The average annual starting salary falls within the $25,000 to $30,000 range. The most suitable method for initial contact by those seeking employment is to mail a resume with a covering letter. Oland Breweries Limited occasionally hires summer students. *Contacts:* John Stacey, Director of Human Resources or Eleanor Grodett, Human Resources Co-ordinator.

OLYMEL
2200, rue Leon Pratte, Suite 400
St. Hyacinthe, QC J2S 4B6

Tel.	450-771-0400
Fax	450-771-0519
Website	www.olymel.com

Olymel is a major meat processing and packaging company. There are approximately 2,200 employees at separate locations in Canada. Graduates most likely to be hired come from the following academic areas: Bachelor of Science (Biology, Computer Science), Bachelor of Engineering (Civil), Bachelor of Commerce/Business Administration (Accounting, Marketing), Chartered Accountant (Finance), Certified General Accountant and Community College Diploma (Computer Science). Company benefits are rated above average. The potential for advancement is listed as average. The average annual starting salary falls within the $30,000 to $35,000 range. The most suitable method for initial contact by those seeking employment is to mail a resume with a covering letter. *Contact:* Human Resources Manager.

OMNIMARK TECHNOLOGIES CORPORATION
1400 Blair Place, 4th Floor
Ottawa, ON K1J 9B8

Tel.	613-745-4242
Fax	613-745-5560
Email	hr@omnimark.com
Website	www.omnimark.com

OmniMark Technologies Corporation develops, markets and supports technologies for maximizing enterprise and e-commerce web performance. OmniMark's SureSpeed, is a software network system for delivering secure, consistent performance from all high-traffic online applications, and OmniMark 5 is a high-level network programming language. Founded in 1986 and privately owned by its management, OmniMark Technologies Corporation is a profitable, financially sound company, with over 50 full-time employees at its corporate headquarters in Ottawa, as well as direct sales and technical support offices in the United States, France, Belgium and the United Kingdom. The company has more than 1,200 customers in over 35 countries and has powered some of the world's most innovative websites, including The Wall Street Journal Interactive Edition, Hewlett-Packard and Airbus Industries. Graduates most likely to be hired come from the following academic areas: Bachelor of Science (Computer Science, Mathematics), Bachelor of Engineering (Computer Systems), Master of Science (Computer Science), Master of Engineering (Computer Science) and Community College Diploma (Computer Science). Graduates would occupy Programming Language Specialist and Software Developer positions. Team player, interest in web technology, initiative and strong communication skills are all listed as desirable non-academic qualifications. Company benefits and the potential for advancement are both rated as excellent. The average annual starting salary ranges widely, depending on the position, the applicant's experience and skill set. The most suitable method for initial contact by those seeking employment is to e-mail a resume with a covering letter. OmniMark Technologies Corporation does hire students for co-op work terms. *Contact:* Doris Kiffner, Human Resources Generalist.

ONTARIO COLLEGE OF ART AND DESIGN / OCAD
100 McCaul Street
Toronto, ON M5T 1W1

Tel.	416-977-6000
Fax	416-977-3034
Website	www.ocad.on.ca

The Ontario College of Art and Design / OCAD is the oldest and largest college of art and design in Canada. The college provides post-secondary students with a 4 Year Diploma Program in such areas as Fine Art, Industrial and Environmental Design, Ceramics, Wood and Metal Work, Film and Photography. OCAD employs approximately 350 people. Graduates most likely to be hired come from the following academic areas: Bachelor of Arts (Fine Art/Design, Journalism), Bachelor of Education (Arts/Design), Bachelor of Commerce (Account-

ing, Finance, Human Resources, Information Systems, Marketing), Masters (Fine Art/Design), Community College Diploma (Accounting, Administration, Advertising, Communications, Financial Planning, Human Resources, Marketing/Sales, Purchasing/Logistics, Secretarial, Fine Art/Graphics/Design, Journalism, Photography, Security/Enforcement) and High School Diploma. Good oral and written communication skills, able to work as a member of a team, detail oriented, able to prioritize and meet deadlines, computer skills (word processing, spreadsheet and database) and good interpersonal skills are all listed as desirable non-academic qualifications. Employee benefits are rated as excellent. The potential for advancement is listed as being good. The most suitable method for initial contact by those seeking employment is to mail a resume with a covering letter. The Ontario College of Art & Design hires summer students depending on need. *Contact:* Human Resources.

ONTARIO FOOD TERMINAL BOARD
165 The Queensway
Toronto, ON M8Y 1H8

Tel.	416-259-5479
Fax	416-259-4303
Website	www.oftb.com

The Ontario Food Terminal Board is a Schedule II Ontario Government agency responsible for operating the Ontario Food Terminal which is located at this address. The board rents space to tenants who in turn sell their produce to retailers. There are more than 25 employees with the board. Graduates most likely to be hired come from the following academic areas: Bachelor of Commerce/Business Administration (Accounting) and Community College Diploma (Engineering Technician, HVAC Systems, Plumber, Security/Enforcement). Graduates would occupy security, office, HVAC and maintenance positions. Company benefits are rated as excellent. The average annual starting salary falls within the $25,000 to $30,000 range. The most suitable method for initial contact by those seeking employment is to mail a resume with a covering letter. The Ontario Food Terminal Board does hire summer students. *Contact:* Mr. C.E. Carsley, General Manager.

ONTARIO HOSPITAL ASSOCIATION / OHA
200 Front Street West, Suite 2800
Toronto, ON M5V 3L1

Tel.	416-205-1300
Fax	416-205-1392
Email	recruit@oha.com
Website	www.oha.com

The Ontario Hospital Association / OHA is a voluntary non-profit organization of hospitals and health care institutions in Ontario. The OHA's mission is to promote excellence in the delivery of health care through effective utilization of available resources. The OHA employs approximately 85 people. Graduates most likely to be hired come from the following academic areas: Bachelor of Arts (Journalism, Political Science), Bachelor of Laws (Health), Bachelor of Commerce/Business Administration (Accounting, Finance, Human Resources, Public Administration), Chartered Accountant, Certified Management Accountant, Certified General Accountant, Master of Business Administration (Finance, Human Resources, Health Administration), Masters (Health Administration, Industrial Relations) and Community College Diploma (Accounting, Business, Communications/Public Relations, Human Resources, Office Administration,

Secretarial). Graduates would occupy Public Affairs Specialist, Hospital Consultant, Labour Relations Consultant, Accountant/Financial Analyst, Program Planner (Education) and Administrative Assistant positions. Previous work experience in the hospital sector and excellent computer, negotiation, interpersonal, oral and written communication, analytical, organizational and project management skills are all listed as desirable non-academic qualifications. Company benefits are rated as excellent. The potential for advancement is listed as being good. The most suitable methods for initial contact by those seeking employment are to mail, fax or e-mail a resume with a covering letter. Current employment opportunities are posted at 'HireHealthcare' at the association's website. Ontario Hospital Association does hire summer and co-op work term students. *Contact:* Human Resources.

ONTARIO HYDRO SERVICES COMPANY
483 Bay Street, 9th Floor
Toronto, ON M5G 2P5

Tel.	416-592-5111
Website	www.ohsc.com

Ontario Hydro Services Company is one of the largest, most reliable and cost-efficient energy providers in the world. Ontario Hydro Services Company with over $9 billion worth of assets, operates one of the largest transmission and distribution systems in North America. Ontario Hydro's "wires company" is comprised of a 29,000 kilometre transmission grid and a 120,000 kilometre distribution system spread throughout the province. The company currently services 106 large industrial customers and about one million retail customers, including homes, farms and small businesses. With the company's enormous pool of existing assets and 7,000 professional and dedicated employees, Ontario Hydro Services Company is well positioned to compete effectively in Ontario and beyond, to capitalize on the ongoing market convergence phenomenon, to extend its asset base and to better serve its customers. Graduates most likely to be hired come from the following academic areas: Bachelor of Arts (Criminology), Bachelor of Science (Computer Science, Forestry), Bachelor of Engineering (Civil, Electrical, Mechanical, Computer Systems, Power/Hydro, Telecommunications), Bachelor of Commerce/Business Administration (Accounting, Finance, Human Resources, Information Systems, Chartered Accountant, Certified Management Accountant, Certified General Accountant, Master of Business Administration (Accounting, Finance, Human Resources) and Community College Diploma (Electronics Technician). Company benefits and the potential for advancement are both rated as excellent. The average annual starting salary falls within the $40,000 to $45,000 range. The most suitable methods for initial contact by those seeking employment are to apply through the company's website or through your campus career centre. Ontario Hydro Services Company does hire summer and co-op work term students. *Contact:* Staffing Department.

ONTARIO JOCKEY CLUB, THE
555 Rexdale Boulevard, PO Box 156
Toronto, ON M9W 5L2

Tel.	416-675-7223
Fax	416-213-2130
Email	smk@ojc.com
Website	www.ojc.com

The Ontario Jockey Club is a sports entertainment organization and a respected player in Canada's horse racing heritage. The Ontario Jockey Club employs a total of 2,100 people worldwide. Graduates most likely to be hired come from the following academic areas: Bachelor of Arts (General), Bachelor of Science (General, Computer Science), Bachelor of Commerce/Business Administration (Accounting, Finance, Human Resources, Information Systems, Marketing), Chartered Accountant, Certified Management Accountant, Certified General Accountant, Master of Business Administration (Accounting, Finance), Community College Diploma (Accounting, Advertising, Business, Communications, Facility Management, Human Resources, Marketing/Sales, Purchasing/Logistics, Secretarial, Cooking, Hospitality, Security/Enforcement, Television/Radio Arts, Computer Science) and High School Diploma. Team player, adaptable to change, good communication skills, initiative, attention to detail, customer service focus, good organizational skills and previous work experience are all listed as desirable non-academic qualifications. Company benefits are rated as industry standard. The potential for advancement is listed as being good. The most suitable method for initial contact by those seeking employment is to mail a resume with a covering letter. The Ontario Jockey Club hires summer students for maintenance and customer service positions. *Contact:* Human Resources Services.

ONTARIO MARCH OF DIMES
10 Overlea Boulevard
Toronto, ON M4H 1A4

Tel.	416-425-3463
Fax	416-425-1920
Email	bmatthaes@dimes.on.ca
Website	www.dimes.on.ca

Ontario March of Dimes is a multi-service, charitable organization delivering a wide range of programs that enrich the lives of over 10,000 men and women with physical disabilities each year in communities across Ontario. Through programs and services, Ontario March of Dimes enables adults with physical disabilities to participate more fully in community life, providing them with the tools needed to enhance their independence. The Ontario March of Dimes employs a total of 1,100 people, of which approximately 750 are engaged directly in the provision of support services. Graduates most likely to be hired come from the following academic areas: Bachelor of Arts (General, Psychology, Social Work), Chartered Accountant, Certified General Accountant and Master of Business Administration (Accounting). Graduates would occupy Secretarial, Clerical, Finance, Accounting, Attendant and Support Service positions. Team player, flexible and empathetic to client needs are all listed as desirable non-academic qualifications. Company benefits are rated as industry standard. The potential for advancement is listed as average. The average annual starting salary for full-time positions falls within the $25,000 to $30,000 range. The most suitable method for initial contact by those seeking employment is to mail a resume with a covering letter. Ontario March of Dimes does hire a few summer students annually. *Contacts:* Birgit Matthaes, Human Resources Assistant (x 385) or Jim Davidson, Director of Human Resources & Quality (x 334).

ONTARIO POWER TECHNOLOGIES
800 Kipling Avenue
Toronto, ON M8Z 5S4

Tel.	416-207-6550
Fax	416-207-5875

Ontario Power Technologies is one of the largest single source technology centres in the world. The company's mandate is to support the technology development needs of Ontario Hydro and its business units and, in addition, to commercialize promising technologies and to market its technical services more broadly throughout the energy and process industries. Graduates most likely to be hired come from the following academic areas: Bachelor of Science (Chemistry, Biology, Computer Science, Mathematics, Metallurgy, Materials Science), Bachelor of Engineering (Mechanical, Civil, Electrical, Computer Systems, Materials Science), Bachelor of Commerce/Business Administration (Marketing), Master/Doctorate of Science (Chemistry, Biology, Computer Science, Mathematics, Metallurgy, Materials Science) and Master/Doctorate of Engineering (Mechanical, Civil, Electrical, Computer Systems, Materials Science). Graduates are hired as Technicians, Scientists, Engineers and Researchers. Creativity, commitment, flexibility and strong communication skills are all listed as desirable non-academic qualifications. Company benefits are rated as excellent. The potential for advancement is listed as being good. The average starting salary falls within the $35,000 plus range. The most suitable method for initial contact by those seeking employment is to mail a resume with a covering letter. Ontario Power Technologies does hire summer students. *Contact:* Human Resources Officer.

OPAL MANUFACTURING LTD.
105 Brisbane Road, Suite 12
Toronto, ON M3J 2K6

Tel. 416-665-6605
Fax 416-665-5631
Website .... www.opal.on.ca

Opal Manufacturing Ltd. designs and manufactures vending machines and liquid dispensing devices. The company is a small but aggressive and fast growing company with international distribution. Opal Manufacturing employs approximately 40 people. Graduates most likely to be hired are Bachelor of Engineering graduates specializing in Electrical and Mechanical engineering. Graduates would occupy Service Manager, Technician, Designer, Production Manager and Casual Labour positions. Company benefits are rated above average. The potential for advancement is listed as excellent. The most suitable method for initial contact by those seeking employment is to mail a resume with a covering letter. Opal Manufacturing Ltd. does hire summer students, depending upon production demand. *Contact:* Garnet Rich.

OPEN LEARNING AGENCY / OLA
4355 Mathissi Place
Burnaby, BC V5G 4S8

Tel. 604-431-3000
Fax 604-431-3384
Email .... hrinfo@ola.bc.ca
Website .... www.ola.bc.ca

Open Learning Agency / OLA is a non-profit, fully accredited educational institution. OLA provides flexible and innovative education and training to British Columbians through a variety of technologies (that are among the most advanced used anywhere in the world) and a variety of services, including the Knowledge Network, Open University, Open College, Open School and Workplace Training Systems. To ensure that OLA's offerings reach the broadest possible audience, it works with a wide variety of partners from industry, government, and other educational institutions. OLA is funded by the British Columbia government and by grants, tuition fees, sales, donations, sponsorships, and partnerships. Employing approximately 600 people, OLA is headquartered in Burnaby, British Columbia. Graduates most likely to be hired come from the following academic areas: Bachelor of Science (Biology, Chemistry, Computer Science, Mathematics, Metallurgy), Bachelor of Engineering (Civil, Electrical, Mechanical, Computer Systems, Materials Science, Metallurgy), Bachelor of Commerce/Business Administration (Accounting, Finance, Human Resources, Information Systems, Marketing) and Community College Diploma (Accounting, Business, Communications/Public Relations, Human Resources, Office Administration, Secretarial, Computer Science, Information Systems). Good communication, interpersonal and organizational skills, ability to work in a team environment, high energy level, positive attitude, creative, motivated, computer skills and related work experience are all listed as desirable non-academic qualifications. Company benefits are rated above average. The potential for advancement is listed as being good. The average annual starting salary depends upon the level and function of the position being considered. The most suitable methods for initial contact by those seeking employment are to mail or fax a resume with a covering letter, quoting the relevant competition number (OLA does not accept unsolicited resumes). *Contact:* Human Resources.

Optel

OPTEL COMMUNICATIONS CORPORATION
111 Peter Street, Suite 300
Toronto, ON M5V 2H1

Tel. 416-586-0333
Fax 416-586-0350
Website .... www.optel.ca

Established in 1995, Optel provides both local and long-distance telecommunication services to small and medium sized businesses. Optel currently serves over 11,000 customers and has grown rapidly to over 350 employees with offices in Toronto and Montreal. Graduates most likely to be hired come from the following academic areas: Bachelor of Arts (General), Bachelor of Science (Computer Science, Mathematics), Bachelor of Engineering (Electrical, Computer Systems, Telecommunications), Bachelor of Commerce/Business Administration (Finance, Information Systems, Marketing), Certified General Accountant and Community College Diploma (Marketing/Sales). Graduates may be hired for positions in Network Operations, Network Engineering, Information Systems, Customer Care, Sales, Marketing and Finance. Successful candidates bring a combination of academic and business experience (preferably in a telecom environment), possess a "can-do" attitude, a strong work ethic and proven abilities as team players. Company benefits and the potential for advancement are both rated as excellent. The average annual starting salary for those in non-professional or non-technical positions, falls within the $25,000 to $30,000 range. The most suitable methods for initial contact by those seeking employment are to fax a resume with a covering letter, or by applying through Optel's website. *Contact:* Human Resources Department.

OPTIMAL ROBOTICS CORP.
4700 de la Savane, Suite 101
Montreal, QC H4P 1T7

Tel. 514-738-8885
Fax 514-738-2284
Email .... techjobs@optimal-robotics.com
Website .... www.optimal-robotics.com

Optimal Robotics Corp. is the leader in the development and implementation of automated self-checkout systems for retail applications. The U-Scan Express system is designed to reduce the cost of checkout transactions to retailers and increase shopper's convenience by providing a level of service and convenience similar to that provided in the banking industry by ATMs. Optimal Robotics employs a total of 85 people. Graduates most likely to be hired come from the following academic areas: Bachelor of Science (Computer Science), Bachelor of Engineering (Electrical) and Community College Diploma (Computer Science). Graduates would occupy Programmer, Technician, Help Desk and Quality Assurance positions. Previous work experience, flexible and a willingness to travel are listed as desirable non-academic qualifications. Company benefits are rated as industry standard. The potential for advancement is listed as excellent. The average annual starting salary falls within the $35,000 to $40,000 range. The most suitable methods for initial contact by those seeking employment are to fax or e-mail a resume with a covering letter. Optimal Robotics Corp. does hire a limited number of summer students. Contacts: Charles Morris, Programmers or Brett Johnson, Technicians.

ORGANIZATION METRICS INC. / OMI
10 Winchester Road East, PO Box 550
Brooklin, ON L0B 1C0

Tel. 905-655-8414
Fax 905-655-8570
Email .... lpiebalgs@orgmetrics.com
Website .... www.orgmetrics.com

Organization Metrics Inc. / OMI is an internationally recognized provider of custom designed human resource systems. OMI has worked with some of North America's largest public and private organizations to ensure the development of human resources in direct support of business strategies. Founded in 1982, the company currently employs 10 people. Graduates most likely to be hired come from the following academic areas: Bachelor of Arts (General), Bachelor of Science (General), Bachelor of Engineering (General, Computer Systems), Bachelor of Commerce/Business Administration (General) and Community College Diploma (Computer Science). Graduates would occupy Computer Programmer and Software Developer positions. Self-motivated, team player, hands-on computer programming work experience and excellent communication skills are all listed as desirable non-academic qualifications. Company benefits are rated as excellent. The potential for advancement is listed as being good. The most suitable method for initial contact by those seeking employment is to e-mail a resume with a covering letter. Organization Metrics Inc. does hire summer and co-op work term students. Contact: Monika Schmidt (mschmidt@orgmetrics.com).

ORTHOPAEDIC & ARTHRITIC CAMPUS / SUNNYBROOK
43 Wellesley Street East
Toronto, ON M4Y 1H1

Tel. 416-967-8647

Fax 416-967-8593
Email .... recruitment@ortharth.toronto.on.ca
Website .... ortharth.toronto.on.ca

The Orthopaedic & Arthritic Campus of Sunnybrook & Women's College Health Sciences Centre is an acute care hospital specializing in orthopaedics and arthritic type disorders. The Orthopaedic and Arthritic Hospital amalgamated in 1998 with Sunnybrook Health Science Centre and Women's College Hospital to form the Sunnybrook and Women's College Health Sciences Centre. Fully affiliated with the University of Toronto, the Orthopaedic and Arthritic Campus continues to build on the established leadership of the Orthopaedic & Arthritic Hospital in the field of musculoskeletal care and services. The Orthopaedic and Arthritic Campus employs more than 250 people. Graduates most likely to be hired come from the following academic areas: Bachelor of Science (Chemistry, Health Sciences, Nursing, Pharmacy), Bachelor of Engineering (Computer Systems), Chartered Accountant (Finance) and Community College Diploma (Accounting, Secretarial, Human Resources, Laboratory Technician, Nursing RN/RNA, Radiology Technician). Graduates would be hired to occupy Service positions (Housekeeping, Dietary), Technical positions (Lab, X-ray) and Professional positions (RN, Physiotherapy). Friendly, good with people, polite, good communication skills and related customer service work experience are all listed as desirable non-academic qualifications. Employee benefits are rated as excellent. The potential for advancement is listed as being good. The average annual starting salary falls within the $25,000 to $35,000 range, and ultimately depends upon the position being considered. The most suitable method for initial contact by those seeking employment is to mail a resume with a covering letter. The Orthopaedic & Arthritic Campus does hire summer students. Contacts: Laurette Sauer, Supervisor, Human Resources or Marilyn Reddick, Director, Human Resources.

OSRAM SYLVANIA LTD.
2001 Drew Road
Mississauga, ON L5S 1S4

Tel. 905-671-5605
Fax 905-671-5594
Website .... www.sylvania.com

Osram Sylvania Ltd. provides general lighting sales, marketing, distribution and related services to the Canadian market. Osram Sylvania Ltd., is the Canadian subsidiary of Osram Sylvania Inc. based in Danvers, Massachusetts, which is the North American operation of Osram GmbH, a wholly owned subsidiary of Munich based Siemens AG. With regional offices across the country, Osram's sales staff work as partners with a significant distributor base in Canada to service customers. Osram Sylvania Ltd. manufactures lighting products in a facility in Drummondville, Quebec. There are approximately 180 employees at this location, a total of 800 in Canada, and 27,000 Osram employees worldwide. Graduates most likely to be hired come from the following academic areas: Bachelor of Science (Computer Science), Bachelor of Engineering (Electrical, Power/Hydro), Bachelor of Commerce (Accounting, Finance, Human Resources, Information Systems, Marketing), Chartered Accountant, Certified Management Accountant, Certified General Accountant, Master of Business Administration (General, Accounting, Finance, Human Resources) and Community College Diploma (Engineering Technician, Forklift Driver). Graduates would occupy Engineering Co-op and Trainee positions. Team player, a customer service orientation, flexible, adaptable and a commitment to continuous improvement are all listed as desirable non-academic qualifications. Company benefits are rated as industry standard. The potential for advancement is listed as excellent. The average annual starting salary falls within the $25,000 to $30,000 range, depending upon the position being considered. The most suitable method for initial contact by those seeking employment is to e-mail a resume with a covering letter to yoav.kaplun@sylvania.com. Osram Sylvania Ltd. does hire student interns through CareerEdge for 6 to 9 month work terms. *Contacts:* Yoav Kaplun, Recruiter or Donna Harding, Human Resources Administrative Assistant.

OTTAWA HOSPITAL, CIVIC CAMPUS
1053 Carling Avenue
Ottawa, ON K1Y 4E9

Tel.	613-798-5555
Fax	613-761-5374
Website	www.civich.ottawa.on.ca

The Ottawa Hospital, Civic Campus is a major academic health sciences centre affiliated with the University of Ottawa. The hospital is dedicated to the provision of quality patient care in an atmosphere of academic and research excellence. The hospital employs approximately 7,000 people. Graduates most likely to be hired come from the following academic areas: Bachelor of Arts (French, Graphic Arts, Psychology, Recreation, Social Work), Bachelor of Science (Biology, Chemistry, Computer Science, Audiology, Nursing, Nutritional Sciences, Occupational Therapy, Pharmacy, Physical Therapy, Psychology, Speech Pathology), Bachelor of Commerce/Business Administration (Accounting, Finance, Human Resources, Information Systems, Marketing, Public Administration), Certified Management Accountant, Certified General Accountant, Master of Business Administration, Master of Science, Master of Health Sciences, Community College Diploma (Accounting, Administration, Advertising) and High School Diploma. Excellent communication and interpersonal skills are both listed as desirable non-academic qualifications. Company benefits and the potential for advancement are both rated as excellent. The most suitable method for initial contact by those seeking employment is to mail a resume with a covering letter. The Ottawa Hospital, Civic Campus occasionally hires summer students. *Contacts:* Sandii Paquette, Employment Services Officer or Adele Savoie, Employment Services Officer.

OWENS-CORNING CANADA
3450 McNicoll Avenue
Toronto, ON M1V 1Z5

Tel.	416-292-4000
Fax	416-292-5837
Website	www.owenscorning.com

Owens-Corning Canada is the largest manufacturer of glass fibre insulation products for the Canadian market. Owens-Corning Canada is a wholly owned subsidiary of Toledo, Ohio based Owens Corning. Owens-Corning is a broad-based, global organization with more than 20,000 employees around the world and manufacturing, sales and research facilities including joint venture and licensee relationships in more than 30 countries on six continents. Owens-Corning Canada employs more than 100 people in its Toronto plant. Graduates most likely to be hired come from the following academic areas: Bachelor of Science (Chemistry), Bachelor of Engineering (Mechanical), Chartered Accountant, Certified Management Accountant (Finance, Accounting) and Community College

Diploma (Architectural Technician, Sciences). Graduates are hired to occupy Accounting, Engineering and Technical positions. Good communication skills, an interest in team work and previous job experience in a manufacturing environment are all listed as desirable non-academic qualifications. Company benefits are rated as excellent. The potential for advancement is listed as being good. The most suitable method for initial contact by those seeking employment is to mail a resume with a covering letter. Owens-Corning Canada does hire a limited number of summer students. *Contact:* Employee Relations Manager.

OXFORD PROPERTIES GROUP INC.
120 Adelaide Street West, Suite 1700
Toronto, ON M5H 1T1

Tel.	416-865-8300
Fax	416-868-0701
Email	hrrecruit@oxfordproperties.com
Website	www.oxfordproperties.com

Oxford Properties Group Inc. is one of North America's leading real estate corporations. The company was formed in 1960, and manages approximately 56 million square feet of prime real estate assets throughout North America. There are 400 employees at this location, 1,200 in Canada and a total of 1,250 employees worldwide. Graduates most likely to be hired come from the following academic areas: Bachelor of Commerce/Business Administration (Accounting), Chartered Accountant, Certified Management Accountant, Certified General Accountant and Community College Diploma (Accounting). Graduates would occupy Property Accountant, Financial Analyst, Assistant Property Manager and Operations Supervisor positions. Relevant work experience, team player and a high energy level are all listed as desirable non-academic qualifications. Company benefits are rated above average. The potential for advancement is listed as being good. The average annual starting salary depends upon the specific position being considered and the qualifications of each individual applicant. The most suitable method for initial contact by those seeking employment is to mail a resume with a covering letter. *Contact:* Human Resources Department.

OXY VINYLS CANADA INC.
PO Box 1027
Niagara Falls, ON L2E 6V9

Tel.	905-357-3131
Fax	905-374-5614
Website	www.oxyvinyls.com

Oxy Vinyls Canada Inc. is a manufacturer of vinyl (VCM) resins. There are approximately 120 employees at this location, a total of 200 in Canada and 2,000 employees worldwide. Graduates most likely to be hired come from the following academic areas: Bachelor of Engineering (Chemical, Industrial Chemistry), Master of Business Administration and Community College Diploma (Accounting, Computer Science, Engineering Technician). Graduates would occupy Process Engineer, Project Engineer, Chemical Technician and Accounting positions. An entrepreneurial drive, accountability and a positive attitude are all listed as desirable non-academic qualifications. Company benefits and the potential for advancement are both rated as excellent. The average annual starting falls within the $40,000 to $45,000 range. The most suitable method for initial contact by those seeking employment is to mail a resume with a covering letter. *Contact:* Manager, Human Resources.

PAFCO INSURANCE COMPANY LIMITED
1243 Islington Avenue, Suite 300
Toronto, ON M8X 2Y3

Tel.	416-231-2835
Fax	416-231-2806
Website	www.pafco.com

Pafco Insurance Company Limited underwrites and settles claims for a variety of specialty insurance lines and comprehensive packages. The company employs more than 150 people across Canada. Graduates most likely to be hired come from the following academic areas: Chartered Accountant, Certified General Accountant (Accounting, Finance), Community College Diploma (Clerical, Underwriting, Claims, Marketing, Secretarial), A.I.I.C Designation and F.I.I.C. designation preferred. Graduates would occupy general positions such as Telephone Adjuster, Claims Examiner, Underwriter, Marketing Representative, Secretary, Accountant, Reinsurance Clerk and Clerical Support positions, and managerial positions in Underwriting, Marketing, Claims, Administration/Personnel and Accounting. Insurance knowledge, computer skills, mathematical aptitude, initiative, ability to work independently or as part of a team, good communication skills, ability to meet deadlines, a mature attitude and reliability are all listed as desirable non-academic qualifications. Company benefits are rated above average. The potential for advancement is listed as being good. The average annual starting salary is dependent upon the position being considered. The most suitable method for initial contact by those seeking employment is to mail or fax a resume with a covering letter. Pafco Insurance Company Limited does hire summer students. *Contact:* Manager, Human Resources.

PAGE + STEELE INCORPORATED, ARCHITECTS PLANNERS
95 St. Clair Avenue West, Suite 200
Toronto, ON M4V 1N6

Tel.	416-924-9966
Fax	416-924-9067

Page + Steele Incorporated is a full service architectural firm involved in urban planning and design of the architectural built environment in commercial, residential, entertainment and institutional spheres. Both new construction and renovations are executed. Page + Steele employs a total of 80 people. Graduates most likely to be hired come from the following areas: Bachelor/Master of Architecture, Bachelor of Arts (Urban Planning) and Community College Diploma (Architecture/Drafting, Interior Design, Architectural Technician, CAD/CAM Autocad, Urban Planning). Graduates would occupy CADD Technician/Operator, Junior Architectural Designer and Interior Designer positions. Team player, attention to detail, good communication skills and a high level of initiative are all listed as desirable non-academic qualifications. Company benefits are rated as industry standard. The potential for advancement is listed as being good. The average annual starting salary falls within the $27,000 to $35,000 range, and is dependent upon skills and previous work experience. The most suitable method for initial contact by those seeking employment is to mail a resume with a covering letter. Page + Steele Incorporated does hire summer students, primarily University students. *Contacts:* Tim Gorley, Associate / Production or Robin Clarke, Vice President / Design.

PALLISER FURNITURE LTD.
80 Furniture Park
Winnipeg, MB R2G 1B9

Tel.	204-988-0827
Fax	204-988-5657
Website	www.palliser.com

Palliser Furniture Ltd. is Canada's largest furniture manufacturer, specializing in leather upholstery and wood products. The company employs approximately 3,000 people in Manitoba, 3,200 in Canada and at total of 3,600 people worldwide. With its corporate head office located in Winnipeg, Palliser is a team based, multicultural company dedicated to leadership in design, service and customer value. Graduates most likely to be hired come from the following academic areas: Bachelor of Arts (Criminology), Bachelor of Science (Computer Science), Bachelor of Engineering (Electrical, Mechanical, Computer Systems, Industrial Engineering, Industrial Production), Bachelor of Commerce/Business Administration (Accounting, Finance, Human Resources, Marketing), Chartered Accountant, Certified Management Accountant, Certified General Accountant and Community College Diploma (Accounting, Administration, Human Resources, Information Systems, Marketing/Sales, Secretarial, Graphic Arts, Journalism, CAD/CAM/Autocad, Carpentry, Computer Science, Tool and Die, Machinist, Welding). Palliser has many opportunities for those seeking career changes and for new graduates. Team player, honesty, integrity and a solid work ethic are all listed as desirable non-academic qualifications. Company benefits and the potential for advancement are both rated as excellent. The average annual starting salary falls within the $20,000 to $30,000 range. The most suitable methods for initial contact by those seeking employment are to mail or fax a resume with a covering letter, or by applying in person. Palliser Furniture Ltd. does hire summer and co-op work term students. *Contact:* Corporate Human Resources, Employment Services.

PALLISER FURNITURE LTD.
Box 3520
Airdrie, AB T4B 2B7

Tel.	403-948-5931
Fax	403-948-4532
Website	www.palliser.com

Palliser Furniture Ltd.'s Airdrie location manufactures upholstered motion furniture. The company employs approximately 165 people at this location, 3,200 in Canada and a total of 3,600 people worldwide. Graduates most likely to be hired at this location come from the following academic areas: Community College Diploma (Upholstery) and High School Diploma. These graduates would occupy Upholsterer, Sewer and Woodshop Worker positions. Company benefits are rated above average. The potential for advancement is listed as being good. The most suitable methods for initial contact by those seeking employment are to mail or fax a resume with a covering letter, or by applying in person. Palliser Furniture Ltd.'s Airdrie location does hire summer students. *Contact:* Shawna Vince, Human Resources Manager.

PAPINEAU GROUP
CP 100
St-Jerome, QC J7Z 5T7

Tel.	450-432-7555
Fax	450-538-7304

Papineau Group provides general merchandise transportation services in Quebec, Ontario, and the United States. There are approximately 384 employees at this location and a total of 512 employees in Canada. Graduates most likely to be hired come from the following academic areas: Bachelor of Science (Computer Science), Bachelor of Commerce/Business Administration (General, Accounting, Finance, Human Resources, Information Systems, Marketing), Chartered Accountant, Community College Diploma (Accounting, Administration, Business, Human Resources, Secretarial, Computer Science) and High School Diploma. Bilingualism, good judgement, dedication, good work skills and two years previous work experience are all listed as desirable non-academic qualifications. Company benefits are rated as industry standard. The potential for advancement is listed as being good. The average annual starting salary falls within the $20,000 to $25,000 range. The most suitable method for initial contact by those seeking employment is to mail a resume with a covering letter. Papineau Group does hire summer students. *Contact:* Christine Arcad, Human Resource Services.

PARAGON PROTECTION LTD.
1210 Sheppard Avenue East
Toronto, ON M2K 1E3

Tel. 416-498-4000
Fax 416-498-1648

Paragon Protection Ltd. provides protection of people, property and information for select clientele. There are 550 employees at this location, and a total of 650 employees in Canada. Graduates most likely to be hired come from the following academic areas: Bachelor of Arts (General, Criminology, Psychology, Sociology), Bachelor of Science (General), Bachelor of Engineering (General), Bachelor of Education (General), Bachelor of Laws, Bachelor of Commerce/Business Administration (General) and Community College Diploma (Administration, Security/Enforcement, Nursing RN/RNA). Graduates are hired to occupy the position of Security Officer. Excellent communication and interpersonal skills, good decision making abilities, physically fit, good public relations and customer service skills, able to work under stress and with or without supervision, calm during emergency situations, good conflict resolution and problem solving skills, team and individual worker, computer literacy, attention to detail, goal oriented, and excellent time management and report writing skills are all listed as desirable non-academic qualifications. Company benefits are rated above average. The potential for advancement is listed as being good. The average annual starting salary falls within the $15,000 to $20,000 range. The most suitable methods for initial contact by those seeking employment are to mail a resume with a covering letter, or by applying in person at this location. Paragon Protection Ltd. does hire summer students. *Contact:* Human Resources.

PARK PROPERTY MANAGEMENT INC.
16 Esna Park Drive, Suite 200
Markham, ON L3R 5X1

Tel. 905-940-1718
Fax 905-940-2898

Park Property Management Inc. is involved in residential and industrial property management activities. The company employs more than 25 people. Positions requiring post-secondary academic qualifications are very few. Park Property generally hires semi-qualified people who can be trained accordingly. When graduates are hired, those most likely to be hired come from the following academic areas: Chartered Accountant (Finance, Real Estate), Certified Management Accountant (In-training), Certified General Accountant (In-training), Community College Diploma (HVAC Systems, Mechanic Technician) and High School Diploma. Graduates are hired to occupy Accountant, Accounts Receivable Clerk, Accounts Payable Clerk, Secretary, Property Manager and Maintenance Department positions. Company benefits are rated above average. The potential for advancement is listed as average. The average annual starting salary falls within the $20,000 to $25,000 range. The most suitable method for initial contact by those seeking employment is to mail a resume with a covering letter. *Contact:* Human Resources.

PARKLAND SAVINGS AND CREDIT UNION LTD.
4901 - 48th Street, Suite 601
Red Deer, AB T4N 6M4

Tel. 403-343-0144
Fax 403-347-6686
Email .... pquesnel@parklandsavings.com
Website .... www.parklandsavings.com

Parkland Savings and Credit Union Ltd. provides a variety of financial services to its customers. The credit union employs approximately 275 people in 16 branches located throughout central Alberta. Graduates most likely to be hired come from the following academic areas: Bachelor of Commerce/Business Administration (General, Accounting, Finance, Information Systems, Marketing), Chartered Accountant, Certified Management Accountant, Master of Business Administration (Accounting, Finance, Information Systems), Community College Diploma (Accounting, Administration, Business, Communications/Public Relations, Financial Planning, Human Resources, Information Systems, Insurance, Marketing/Sales, Computer Science), and High School Diploma. Graduates would occupy Accountant, Human Resources Consultant, Marketing Specialist, Financial Planner, Lending Specialist and Investment Specialist positions. Good communication skills, entrepreneurial and strong interpersonal skills are listed as desirable non-academic qualifications. Company benefits and the potential for advancement are both listed as excellent. The average annual starting salary falls within the $20,000 to $25,000 range for entry level positions, $25,000 to $35,000 range for permanent staff positions, and $40,000 to $55,000 for management positions. The most suitable method for initial contact by those seeking employment is to mail a resume with a covering letter. Parkland Savings and Credit Union Ltd. does hire summer and co-op work term students. *Contacts:* Herb Der, General Manager or Mr. Pat Quesnel, Vice President, Human Resources.

PASTEUR MERIEUX CONNAUGHT CANADA
1755 Steeles Avenue West
Toronto, ON M2R 3T4

Tel. 416-667-2701
Fax 416-667-9391
Website .... www.ca.pmc-vacc.com

Pasteur Mérieux Connaught Canada is Canada's leading producer of vaccines for human health and a member of the Rhône-Poulenc Group. Pasteur Mérieux Connaught's operations are fully integrated and include research and development, manufacturing and Canadian marketing. The company's history dates back more than 80 years to the beginning of vaccine production in Canada. Today, Pasteur Mérieux Connaught's fully-integrated research and manufacturing facility in Toronto employs more than 950 people. Over 300 of those employees hold university, graduate or post-graduate degrees. Graduates most likely to be hired come from the following academic areas: Bachelor of Science (Biology, Chemistry, Microbiology), Bachelor of Engineering (Chemical), Master of Business Administration (Accounting, Finance, Marketing), Master of Science (Biology, Chemistry, Microbiology) and Community College Diploma (Animal Health, Biotechnology). Graduates would occupy Technician and Technologist positions. Previous work experience and the practical application of theory are both listed as desirable non-academic qualifications. Company benefits are rated above average. The potential for advancement is listed as being good. The average annual starting salary falls within the $30,000 to $35,000 range. The most suitable methods for initial contact by those seeking employment are to mail or fax a resume with a covering letter, or through on-campus recruitment programs (see your campus career centre for details). Pasteur Merieux Connaught Canada does hire summer students. *Contact:* Employment Office - Human Resources.

PC WORLD (DIVISION OF CIRCUIT WORLD CORP.)
250 Finchdene Square
Toronto, ON M1X 1A5

Tel.	416-299-4000
Fax	416-292-4308
Email	dkeeping@circtwrld.com

PC World (Division of Circuit World Corp.) is a manufacturer of printed circuit boards. The company employs approximately 160 people. Graduates most likely to be hired come from the following academic areas: Bachelor of Arts (General), Bachelor of Science (Chemistry, Computer Science), Bachelor of Engineering (Chemical, Civil, Electrical, Mechanical, Environmental/Resources, Industrial Chemistry, Industrial Engineering, Metallurgy), Bachelor of Commerce/Business Administration (Accounting, Finance, Information Systems, Marketing), Certified Management Accountant, Certified General Accountant and Community College Diploma (Accounting, Administration, Business, Facility Management, Marketing/Sales, CAD/CAM/Autocad, Computer Science, Electronics Technician, Engineering Technician). Graduates would occupy Product Engineer, Process Engineer, Operations Analyst, Systems Engineer, Environmental Coordinator, Accountant and CAM Operator positions. Computer literacy, team player, strong people skills, multitasking abilities, organized and excellent communication skills are all listed as desirable nonacademic qualifications. Company benefits are rated above average. The potential for advancement is listed as being good. The average annual starting salary falls within the $30,000 to $35,000 range. The most suitable method for initial contact by those seeking employment is to fax a resume with a covering letter. PC World does hire co-op work term students on occasion. *Contact:* Delphine Keeping, Human Resources Administrator.

PEACOCK INC.
8600, rue St. Patrick
Montreal, QC H8N 1V1

Tel.	514-366-5900
Fax	514-366-9804
Website	www.peacock.ca

Peacock Inc. supplies Canadian industry with a wide range of industrial products and services. Established in 1897, the company markets leading, industrial process, instrumentation and pumping products and mechanical equipment repair, maintenance and refurbishment services. Peacock's activities largely serve the mining, pulp and paper, oil and gas, and power generation industries. Peacock Inc. is a subsidiary of Glasgow, Scotland based Weir Group PLC. The company is a leading mechanical engineering company that manufactures in 14 countries from 44 plant locations and employs 10,000 people worldwide. Peacock Inc. employs 280 people at this location and more than 650 people across Canada. Graduates most likely to be hired come from the following academic areas: Bachelor of Science (Metallurgy), Bachelor of Engineering (Materials Science, Metallurgy, Pollution Treatment, Pulp and Paper, Instrumentation, Mechanical, Industrial Production, Welding), Bachelor of Commerce/Business Administration (General, Accounting, Finance, Human Resources, Information Systems, Marketing), Chartered Accountant, Certified Management Accountant, Certified General Accountant, Master of Business Administration (Accounting, Information Systems), Master of Engineering, Community College Diploma (Accounting, Administration, Business, Human Resources, Secretarial, Engineering, Forestry, Machinist, Millwright, Welding) and High School Diploma. Bilingualism is a definite asset. Company benefits are rated excellent. The potential for advancement is listed as being good. The average annual starting salary is dependent upon the position being considered. The most suitable method for initial contact by those seeking employment is to mail a resume with a covering letter. Peacock Inc. does hire summer students. *Contacts:* Carole Proulx, Human Resources Administrator or Louis Tassé, Director of Human Resources.

PEEL CHILDREN'S AID SOCIETY
8 Nelson Street W., Suite 204
Brampton, ON L6X 4J2

Tel.	905-796-2121
Fax	905-796-2293
Website	www.peelcas.org

Peel Children's Aid Society is involved in child protection work, mandated by the Child and Family Services Act. This involves investigations and assessments of children at risk from harm, and placement and family court involvement for children (and families) in need of protection. Graduates most likely to be hired come from the following academic areas: Bachelor of Arts (Social Work) and Master of Arts (Social Work). Graduates would occupy Front-Line Social Worker and Intake or Family Worker positions. Applicants should possess child welfare or children's aid society work experience. Employee benefits are rated as excellent. The potential for advancement is listed as average. The average annual starting salary falls within the $34,000 to $37,000 range. The most suitable method for initial contact by those seeking employment is to mail a resume with a covering letter. Peel Children's Aid Society does hire approximately three summer students annually as recreation aids. *Contact:* Human Resources.

PEOPLES JEWELLERS LIMITED
1440 Don Mills Road
Toronto, ON M3B 3M1

Tel.	416-441-1515
Fax	416-391-7756
Website	www.peoplesjewellers.com

Peoples Jewellers Limited is Canada's largest jewellery retailer, with over 200 stores nationally. There are more than 130 employees at this location. Graduates most likely to be hired come from the following academic areas: Bachelor of Commerce/Business Administration (General, Accounting, Finance, Marketing) and Community College Diploma (Accounting, Administration, Business, Architectural Technician). Graduates would occupy Sales Representative, Store Manager, Clerk, Financial Analyst and Information Systems positions. Company benefits and the potential for advancement are both rated as excellent. The average annual starting salary depends upon the position being considered. The most suitable methods for initial contact by graduates seeking employment are to mail or fax a resume with a covering letter. Peoples Jewellers Limited does hire summer and co-op work term students. *Contact:* Human Resources.

PEPSI-COLA CANADA LTD.
5205 Satellite Drive
Mississauga, ON L4W 5J7

Tel. 905-212-7377
Fax 905-212-7327
Website .... www.pepsico.com

Pepsi-Cola Canada Ltd. is the Canadian division of PepsiCo Inc., based in Purchase, New York. PepsiCo is among the most successful consumer products companies in the world. Pepsi-Cola Canada Ltd. employs more than 100 people at this location, primarily involved in administration and marketing activities. Recent graduates most likely to be hired are Community College graduates from Secretarial and Administrative programs. These graduates are hired for Clerical and Secretarial positions. A minimum of 3 to 5 years experience in the packaged-goods industry is required for management positions in Marketing, Sales, and Trade Development. Company benefits and the potential for advancement are both rated as excellent. The most suitable method for initial contact by graduates seeking employment is to mail a resume with a covering letter. Pepsi-Cola Canada Ltd. does hire summer students at this location. *Contact:* Human Resources Representative.

PERREAULT, WOLMAN, GRZYWACZ & CO.
5250 Ferrier, Suite 814
Montreal, QC H4P 2N7

Tel. 514-731-7987
Fax 514-731-8782
Email .... pwgca@aol.com

Perreault, Wolman, Grzywacz & Co. is a chartered accounting and management consulting firm. The firm employs a total of 35 people. Graduates most likely to be hired come from the following academic areas: Bachelor of Commerce/Business Administration (General, Accounting), Chartered Accountant, Certified Management Accountant, Certified General Accountant and Master of Business Administration (Accounting). Graduates would occupy Audit Manager, Auditor, Tax Manager and Business Consultant positions. Previous work experience in a chartered accounting firm is listed as a desirable non-academic qualification. Company benefits are rated as industry standard. The potential for advancement is listed as being excellent. The average annual starting salary falls within the $50,000 to $55,000 range. The most suitable methods for initial contact by those seeking employment are to fax a resume with a covering letter, or via telephone. Perreault, Wolman, Grzywacz & Co. does hire summer students. *Contacts:* William Grzywacz, CA or Don Wolman, CA.

PET VALU CANADA INC.
121 McPherson Street
Markham, ON L3R 3L3

Tel. 905-946-1200
Fax 905-946-1860
Website .... www.petvalu.com

Pet Valu Canada Inc. is a subsidiary of Pet Valu International Inc., which operates 390 stores in Canada and the United States. Pet Valu Canada Inc. operates corporate owned stores, while the majority of stores are franchised operations. Pet Valu carries both private label and brand name products. Pet Valu Canada Inc. employs 135 people at the Markham head office and an additional 155 store and warehouse employees across Canada. Graduates most likely to be hired come from the following academic areas: Bachelor of Science (Mathematics), Bachelor of Engineering (General, Chemical, Civil, Electrical, Mechanical) and Bachelor of Commerce/Business Administration (General, Accounting, Finance, Information Systems). Graduates would occupy Inventory Analyst and Pricing and Promotions Analyst positions. Logical reasoning, retail work experience and good academic grades in quantitative courses are listed as desirable non-academic qualifications. Company benefits are rated as industry standard. The potential for advancement is listed as being excellent. The average annual starting salary falls within the $35,000 to $40,000 range. The most suitable method for initial contact by those seeking employment is to apply via your campus career centre. Presently, the company recruits through Wilfrid University, University of Waterloo, University of Western Ontario, McMaster University, University of Toronto, Queen's University, Ryerson University and York University. Pet Valu Canada Inc. does hire summer and co-op work term students for Accounting, Human Resources and Information Technology positions. *Contact:* Human Resources Department.

PETER KIEWIT SONS CO. LTD.
2600 Skymark Avenue, Building 2, Suite 201
Mississauga, ON L4W 5B2

Tel. 905-206-1490
Fax 905-206-1513
Email .... serge.gagnon@kiewit.qc.ca
Website .... www.jobweb.org/employer/kiewit.htm

Peter Kiewit Sons Co. Ltd. is engaged in heavy civil engineering construction, mining and related businesses throughout Canada. The company has been in the contracting business for 115 years and is one of North America's largest and most respected, employee-owned construction firms. Headquartered in Omaha, Nebraska, Peter Kiewit Sons', Inc. serves clients through a network of Kiewit and affiliate locations across the United States and Canada. In addition to the Mississauga office, Canadian offices are located in Vancouver, Edmonton and Montreal. The company employs over 3,600 staff employees and more than 14,000 craft workers worldwide. There are 42 staff employees at this location and a total of 200 in Canada. Graduates most likely to be hired come from the following academic areas: Bachelor of Engineering (Civil, Mechanical, Geological, Mining). Graduates would occupy Field Engineer, Field Supervisor, Maintenance Engineer, Project Engineer, Project Manager, Engineer/Estimator, Job Superintendent and Office Engineer positions. Initiative, mobility, strong leadership and interpersonal skills and extra-curricular involvement while at school are all listed as desirable non-academic qualifications. Company benefits are rated as industry standard. The potential for advancement is listed as being good.

The average annual starting salary falls within the $35,000 to $40,000 range. The most suitable methods for initial contact by those seeking employment are to mail or e-mail a resume with a covering letter. Peter Kiewit Sons Co. Ltd. does hire summer and co-op work term students. *Contacts:* Louis Chapoelaine, District Manager or John Neal, Area Manager.

PETO MACCALLUM LTD.
165 Cartwright Avenue
Toronto, ON M6A 1V5

Tel. 416-785-5110
Fax 416-785-5120
Website .... www.petomac.on.ca

Peto MacCallum Ltd. is an independent, Canadian consulting engineering company. The company provides a broad range of specialized engineering and technical services related to the following fields of activity: geotechnical engineering, geo-environmental and hydrogeological services, construction materials engineering, quality control - testing and inspection and building science services. Peto MacCallum employs a total of 200 people in Ontario. In addition to the Toronto head office, the company maintains offices in Aurora, Barrie, Brampton, Hamilton, Kitchener and Oshawa. Graduates most likely to be hired come from the following academic areas: Bachelor of Science (Chemistry, Geology), Bachelor of Engineering (Chemical, Civil, Environmental, Materials Science, Geotechnical), Master of Engineering (Geotechnical, Hydrogeology, Environmental) and Community College Diploma (Engineering Technician). Graduates would be hired to occupy related positions as Engineers, Technologists and Technicians. Company benefits and the potential for advancement are both rated as excellent. The most suitable method for initial contact by graduates seeking employment is to mail a resume with a covering letter. Peto MacCallum Ltd. does hire summer students. *Contact:* Manager, Human Resources.

PETRO-CANADA PRODUCTS
5140 Yonge Street, Suite 200
Toronto, ON M2N 6L6

Tel. 416-730-2000
Fax 416-730-2151
Website .... www.petro-canada.ca

Petro-Canada Products is the division of Petro-Canada involved in the refining, marketing and distribution of downstream petroleum products. Graduates most likely to be hired come from the following academic areas: Bachelor of Science (Computer Science), Bachelor of Engineering (Mechanical, Chemical), Bachelor of Commerce/Business Administration (Accounting), Certified Management Accountant, Certified General Accountant and Master of Business Administration. Graduates would occupy Accountant, Credit Representative, Marketing Representative Trainee, Marketing Analyst Trainee, Engineer and Computer Programmer positions. Leadership and good communication skills, team player, continuous improvement and service mindset, ability to adapt to an ever changing environment, and the ability to manage a number of priorities within tight time frames are all listed as desirable attributes. Company benefits are rated as excellent. The potential for advancement is listed as average. The average annual starting salary falls within the $30,000 to $36,000 range. The most suitable method for initial contact by those seeking employment is to mail a resume with a covering letter. Petro-Canada Products does hire summer students who are returning to full-time post secondary studies in the fall. *Contact:* Human Resources, Central.

PHILIP ENVIRONMENTAL INC.
PO Box 423, Depot 1
Hamilton, ON L8L 7W2

Tel. 905-544-6687

Philip Environmental Inc. is active in waste management and recycling. There are approximately 200 employees at this location and a total of 1,500 employees in Canada. Graduates most likely to be hired come from the following academic areas: Bachelor of Science (Chemistry), Bachelor of Engineering (Architectural/Building, Industrial Production, Welding), Bachelor of Commerce/Business Administration (Accounting, Marketing), Chartered Accountant, Certified Management Accountant, Master of Business Administration (Accounting), Master of Engineering (Construction), Community College Diploma (Accounting, Administration, Business, Purchasing/Logistics, Secretarial, Truck Mechanic, Architecture/Drafting, CAD/CAM/Autocad, Welding) and High School Diploma. Graduates would occupy Welder, Mechanic, Millwright, Electrician, Accountant (with/without designation) and Secretarial positions. A positive attitude, flexibility, an ability to work well with others, and three to five years related work experience (depending upon the position) are all listed as desirable non-academic qualifications. Company benefits are rated as excellent. The potential for advancement is listed as being good. The average annual starting salary for Clerical positions falls within the $20,000 to $25,000 range. The starting salary for Technical positions falls within $35,000 to $40,000 range. The most suitable methods for initial contact by those seeking employment are to mail a resume with a covering letter, or by responding to advertised positions in the paper. Philip Environmental Inc. hires a few summer students each year. *Contact:* Mr. Rennie Mohammed, Human Resources Supervisor.

PHOENIX INTERNATIONAL
2350 Cohen Street
Montreal, QC H4R 2N6

Tel. 514-333-0033
Fax 514-335-8340
Email .... emp_recruit@pils.com
Website .... www.pils.com

Phoenix International is a world leader among contract research organizations, serving the pharmaceutical and biotechnology industries. In June 1999, its innovative and high-tech scientific environment comprised of a highly educated worldwide staff of 1,800, including 160 PhDs and MD's, 220 Masters and 720 Bachelor level personnel who help to bring new drugs to the marketplace. At its head office in Montreal, Phoenix has the largest bioanalytical laboratories in the world and is a leading provider of clinical study services with 416 beds in four specialized clinics. This represents an explosion of growth in only 10 years since the company began. Phoenix provides a unique opportunity to work with, and learn from, many of the world's top scientists and IT professionals. Graduates most likely to be hired come from the following academic areas: Bachelor of Science (Chemistry, Computer Science, Mathematics), Bachelor of Engineering (Electrical, Biotechnology/Bioengineering, Instrumentation), Bachelor of Commerce/Business Administration (Information Systems), Master of Business Administration (General Information Systems, Marketing), Master of Science (General, Computer Science), Doctorate (Sciences), Community College Diploma (Accounting, Secretarial, Electronics Technician, Medical Technician) and High School Diploma. Graduates would occupy Help Desk/IT Support, Developer, Volunteer Recruiter, Lab Analyst, Scientist, Instrument Specialist, Clinical Research Assistant and Project Manager positions. Candidates must have a minimum of two years related experience and be computer literate. Company benefits are rated as above average. The potential for advancement is listed as being good. The most suitable methods for initial contact by those seeking employment are to mail, fax or e-mail a resume with a covering letter. Phoenix International does hire summer students and co-op work term students. *Contact:* Human Resources.

PICARD TECHNOLOGIES INC. / PTI

9916 Cote de Liesse
Lachine, QC H8T 1A1

Tel.	514-422-8404
Fax	514-422-8406
Email	bferris@picardtech.com
Website	www.picardtech.com

Picard Technologies Inc. / PTI is a systems integration and project management company servicing the pharmaceutical industry. Employing approximately 10 people, PTI provides resources that are well-versed in industrial communications, controls and automation for the manufacturing and process industries. PTI focuses on the pharmaceutical industry extending these services to where experience with GMP approaches to automation and equipment is critical. Graduates most likely to be hired are Bachelor of Engineering graduates from Chemical, Electrical and Mechanical Engineering programs. Graduates would occupy the position of Project Specialist. Team player, versatile and committed are listed as desirable non-academic qualifications. Company benefits are rated above average. The potential for advancement is listed as being good. The average annual starting salary falls within the $45,000 to $50,000 range. The most suitable method for initial contact by those seeking employment is to e-mail a resume with a covering letter. Picard Technologies Inc. does hire co-op work term students. *Contact:* Brenda Ferris.

PICKERING PLANNING DEPARTMENT

1 The Esplanade, Pickering Civic Complex
Pickering, ON L1V 6K7

Tel.	905-420-4617
Fax	905-420-7648
Email	planning@town.pickering.on.ca
Website	www.town.pickering.on.ca

The Town of Pickering, Planning Department is primarily concerned with planning, development and the redevelopment of land in the town of Pickering. Activities include processing development applications, setting of official plan and development guidelines for the municipality, providing information (written and oral) on public inquiries concerning land use and other planning related concerns. The department employs approximately 25 people. Graduates most likely to be hired come from the following academic areas: Bachelor of Arts (Urban Planning/Geography) and Master of Arts (Urban Planning/Geography). Recent graduates would occupy entry-level positions as a Planning Technician or Draftsperson. Good oral and written communication skills, independent work habits and the ability to handle a wide variety of tasks are all listed as desirable non-academic qualifications. Company benefits are rated above average. The potential for advancement is listed as average. The average annual starting salary falls within the $20,000 to $25,000 range. The most suitable method for initial contact by those seeking employment is to mail a resume with a covering letter to the Human Resources Department. The Planning Department hires three students annually, each for four month work terms. *Contact:* Director of Human Resources.

PINE FALLS PAPER COMPANY LIMITED

PO Box 10
Pine Falls, MB R0E 1M0

Tel.	204-367-5205
Fax	204-367-2442
Email	pfpcwoods@mts.net
Website	www.pinefallspaper.com

Pine Falls Paper Company Limited is a newsprint manufacturer and Manitoba's only newsprint mill. The company is the largest recycler of old newspapers and magazines in Manitoba, and its geographic location enables the company to serve a wide range of customers in the midwestern regions of Canada and the United States. Pine Falls Paper Company Limited is a subsidiary of Témiscaming, Quebec based Tembec Inc. Pine Falls Paper Company Limited employs approximately 475 people. Graduates most likely to be hired come from the following academic areas: Bachelor of Arts (General), Bachelor of Science (Biology, Chemistry), Bachelor of Engineering (Chemical, Pulp and Paper, Electrical, Mechanical, Forest Resources), Bachelor of Commerce/Business Administration (Accounting, Finance, Human Resources), Certified Management Accountant and Master of Business Administration (Accounting). Graduates are hired to occupy non-union supervisory positions. Team player and previous work experience are both listed as desirable non-academic qualifications. Company benefits are rated above average. The potential for advancement is listed as being good. The average annual starting salary falls within the $25,000 to $30,000 range. The most suitable method for initial contact by those seeking employment is to mail a resume with a covering letter. Pine Falls Paper Company Limited does hire local students for summer positions. *Contact:* Human Resources.

PINK ELEPHANT INC.

5575 North Service Road
Burlington, ON L7P 1J9

Tel.	905-331-5060
Fax	905-331-5070
Email	resume@pinkelephant.com
Website	www.pinkelephant.com

Pink Elephant Inc. is a leading information technology (IT) service management provider in the areas of consulting, education and outsourcing. With offices in the United States, Canada, Australia, the Netherlands and the United Kingdom, the company employs 2,000 people worldwide and is currently experiencing significant growth. Graduates most likely to be hired come from the following academic areas: Bachelor of Science (Computer Science), Bachelor of Engineering (Computer Systems), Bachelor of Commerce/Business Administration (Information Systems) and Community College Diploma (Business, Computer Science, Electronics Engineering). Pink Elephant seeks full-time IT Support Professionals with experience in technical support. Graduates would begin developing careers working on special projects at the company's client sites beginning with Desktop and Network Support, moving to future opportunities that range from Network Migration and Project Management to Consulting and IT Management. Able to thrive in an environment with unlimited opportunities and challenges, and a high level of motivation and initiative are listed as desirable non-academic qualifications. Company benefits are rated above average. The potential for advancement is listed as being excellent. The most suitable method for initial contact by those seeking employment is to e-mail a resume with a covering letter. *Contact:* Human Resources.

PIONEER GRAIN COMPANY, LIMITED
One Lombard Place, Suite 2800
Winnipeg, MB R3B 0X8

Tel. 204-934-5961

Pioneer Grain Company, Limited handles all major grains and oilseeds and provides a complete range of crop input (fertilizer, chemicals, seed) sales and services at over 100 locations throughout western Canada. The company employs more than 500 people. Graduates most likely to be hired come from the following academic areas: Bachelor of Science (Computer Science), Bachelor of Engineering (General), Bachelor of Commerce/Business Administration (Accounting, Finance, Marketing, Information Systems), Chartered Accountant (Finance), Certified Management Accountant (Finance), Certified General Accountant (Finance), Master of Business Administration (Accounting, Finance, Marketing, Information Systems) and Community College Diploma (Accounting, Administration, Business, Marketing/Sales, Purchasing/Logistics, Secretarial, Human Resources, Architecture/Drafting, Computer Science, Engineering, Industrial Design). Company benefits are rated as excellent. The potential for advancement is listed as being good. The most suitable method for initial contact by those seeking employment is to mail a resume with a covering letter. Pioneer Grain Company, Limited does hire summer students. *Contacts:* Sherrie Rauth, Human Resource Administrator (Staffing & Recruiting) or Colleen Johnston, Manager, Human Resources.

PIONEER STANDARD CANADA INC.
3415 American Drive
Mississauga, ON L4V 1T4

Tel. 905-405-8300

Pioneer Standard Canada Inc. maintains locations across Canada and is involved in the distribution of electronic components. There are two divisions within the company. The first deals with electronic semi-conductors, passive and non passive products while the second serves the computer marketplace. The company employs approximately 75 people at this location. Graduates most likely to be hired come from the following academic areas: Bachelor of Arts (General), Bachelor of Science (Computer Science), Bachelor of Engineering (Electrical) and Bachelor of Commerce/Business Administration.

Graduates would occupy Technician, Sales Representative, Buyer and various head office positions. Applicants should possess drive, motivation and sales skills, accordingly. Company benefits and the potential for advancement are both rated as excellent. The average annual starting salary varies according to the position being considered. The most suitable method for initial contact by those seeking employment is to mail a resume with a covering letter. *Contact:* John Turner.

PIXSTREAM INCORPORATED
180 Columbia St. West
Waterloo, ON N2L 3L3

Tel. 519-884-4196
Fax 519-884-9892
Email .... jobs@pixstream.com
Website .... www.pixstream.com

PixStream Incorporated develops, manufactures and globally markets hardware and software solutions that enable network service providers and enterprises to reliably distribute and manage digital video. By using PixStream solutions, high quality video and audio can be transported more efficiently over broadband networks, optimizing bandwidth and enabling customers to introduce leading-edge video services and applications. Founded in 1996, PixStream is based in Waterloo and today employs a total of 90 people. Graduates most likely to be hired come from the following academic areas: Bachelor of Engineering (Electrical, Mechanical, Computer Systems, Telecommunications), Bachelor of Commerce/Business Administration (Marketing), Master of Business Administration (Marketing), Master of Engineering and Community College Diploma (Communications/Public Relations, Marketing/Sales, CAD/CAM/Autocad, Computer Science, Engineering Technician, Information Systems). Graduates would occupy Software Designer, Hardware Designer, Firmware Designer, Test Engineer and Test Technician positions. Team player, work experience and a high level of enthusiasm are all listed as desirable non-academic qualifications. Company benefits and the potential for advancement are both rated as excellent. The most suitable methods for initial contact by those seeking employment are to fax or e-mail a resume with a covering letter. PixStream Incorporated does hire co-op work term students. *Contact:* Jennifer Patterson, Human Resources.

PIZZA PIZZA LIMITED
580 Jarvis Street
Toronto, ON M4Y 2H9

Tel. 416-967-1010
Fax 416-967-3566

Pizza Pizza Limited is one of Canada's leading pizza chains, a franchised operation consisting mainly of takeout and delivery stores. The head office provides services and administration for a network of franchised and company operated stores throughout Ontario. After more than 30 years in business, the company continues to be a fast-paced, entrepreneurial corporation - a market leader. Part of this success can be attributed to its famous leading-edge marketing programs and technology systems. Activities at the Head Office include Accounting, Marketing, Architecture and Real Estate, Customer Service, Commissary, Operations, Franchising, Warehousing and Training. Graduates most likely to be hired come from the following academic areas: Bachelor of Commerce/Business Administration, Certified Management Accountant and Community College Diploma (Administration,

Advertising, Business, Marketing/Sales, Secretarial, Hospitality). Graduates would occupy Store Manager, Area Representative, Secretarial, Accounting and Marketing positions. Flexibility, enthusiasm, initiative, a high energy level, leadership skills and good communication skills are all listed as desirable non-academic qualifications. Company benefits are rated above average. The potential for advancement is listed as excellent. The average annual starting salary falls within the $20,000 to $28,000 range. The most suitable methods for initial contact by those seeking employment are to mail a resume with a covering letter, or via telephone. *Contact:* Human Resources.

PLACER DOME NORTH AMERICA LTD.
1055 Dunsmuir St.
Suite 600, PO Box 49305, Bentall Postal station
Vancouver, BC V7X 1L3

Tel.	604-661-1991
Fax	604-661-3722
Website	www.placerdome.com

Placer Dome North America Ltd. is a wholly owned subsidiary of international mining corporation Placer Dome Inc. Headquartered in Vancouver, Placer Dome operates six mines across the country. With five gold mines in Ontario and Quebec and a molybdenum mine in British Columbia, Placer Dome is one of the largest gold producers in Canada. Graduates most likely to be hired come from the following academic areas: Bachelor of Arts (Economics), Bachelor of Science (Computer Science, Geology, Metallurgy), Bachelor of Engineering (Mining, Environmental, Electrical, Mechanical), Bachelor of Laws, Bachelor of Commerce/Business Administration (Accounting, Finance, Marketing, Information Systems), Chartered Accountant (Finance), Certified Management Accountant (Finance), Certified General Accountant (Finance), Master of Business Administration (Accounting, Finance, Marketing), Master of Engineering (Mining, Geology, Metallurgy), Doctorate (Geostatistics, Geology) and Community College Diploma (Accounting, Administration, Secretarial, Human Resources, Computer Science, Electronic Technician, Engineering Technician, Mechanic, Industrial Design). Graduates would develop careers in Geology, Mining, Engineering, Metallurgy, Mechanical and Electrical Maintenance and related fields, as well as corporate functions in Finance and Administration. Company benefits and the potential for advancement are both listed as excellent. The average annual starting salary is dependent upon position and performance. The most suitable method for initial contact by those seeking employment is to mail a resume with a covering letter. Placer Dome North America Ltd. does hire summer and co-op work term students. *Contacts:* Karen Walsh, Manager, Human Resources Department or Human Resources Department.

PMC-SIERRA, INC.
8555 Baxter Place, Suite 105
Burnaby, BC V5A 4V7

Tel.	604-415-6000
Fax	604-415-6209
Email	careers@pmc-sierra.com
Website	www.pmc-sierra.com

PMC-Sierra, Inc. is a leading provider of high speed internetworking component solutions emphasizing ATM, SONET/SDH, TI/EI and ethernet applications. The company's quality system is registered with Quality Management Institute to the ISO 9001 standard. As co-founder of the SATURN Development Group, PMC-Sierra works with over 40 other member companies to define and develop interoperable, standard-compliant solutions for high speed networking applications. Headquartered near Vancouver, British Columbia, PMC-Sierra offers technical and sales support in California, Texas, Illinois, Massachusetts, Europe and Asia. In addition, continuing growth has added to development capabilities that now include a Beaverton, Oregon facility that is developing ethernet switching solutions and new Design Centres in Montreal, Quebec; Saskatoon, Saskatchewan; San Jose, California; and Gaithersburg, Maryland. There are 350 employees in Burnaby, a total of 375 in Canada and a total of 475 employees worldwide. Graduates most likely to be hired come from the following academic areas: Bachelor of Engineering (Electrical, Microelectronics, Telecommunications) and Master of Engineering (Microelectronics, Telecommunications). Graduates would occupy Digital Designer, Analog Designer, CAD Engineer, Physical Design Engineer, I/O Library Engineer, Validation Engineer, Application Engineer, Product Marketing Engineer, DSP H/W Designer, Product Engineer and Test Engineer positions. Team building skills and good interpersonal skills are both listed as desirable non-academic qualifications. Company benefits and the potential for advancement are both rated as excellent. The average annual starting salary falls within the $40,000 to $45,000 range. The most suitable methods for initial contact by those seeking employment are to mail, fax or e-mail a resume with a covering letter. PMC-Sierra, Inc. does hire summer students. *Contact:* Teri McNaughton, Manager, Employment Services.

PNG GLOBE ENVELOPES
400 Humberline Drive
Toronto, ON M9W 5T3

Tel.	416-675-9370
Fax	416-675-3724

PNG Globe Envelopes is involved in the manufacture, printing, and distribution of envelopes. The company employs more than 100 people. Post-secondary education is not a prerequisite for employment application. Intelligent, motivated, committed, adaptable, able to work well with colleagues, and related work experience are all listed as a desirable non-academic qualification. Applicants would occupy Accounting, Sales, Marketing, Operations Management and Traffic positions. Company benefits are rated above average. The potential for advancement is listed as being good. The average annual starting salary falls within the $20,000 to $30,000 range. The most suitable method for initial contact by those seeking employment is to mail or fax a resume with a covering letter. PNG Globe Envelopes does hire summer students. *Contact:* Mary Neto, Human Resources Manager.

POLYGRAM CANADA INC.
1345 Denison Street
Markham, ON L3R 5V2

Tel.	905-415-9900
Fax	905-415-7369
Website	
polygram.capolygram.capolygram.capolygram.ca	

PolyGram Canada Inc. is a music and film entertainment company. The company employs approximately 150 people at this location and a total of 254 people across Canada. Graduates most likely to be hired come from the following academic areas: Bachelor of Arts (General, Graphic Arts, Journalism, Music), Bachelor of Laws (Entertainment/Contract), Bachelor of Commerce/Business Administration (Accounting, Finance, Human Resources, Information Systems, Marketing), Chartered Accountant, Certified Management Accountant, Certified General Accountant, Master of Business Administration (Accounting, Finance), Community College Diploma (Accounting, Administration, Business, Communications, Human Resources, Marketing/Sales, Secretarial, Graphic Arts, Television/Radio Arts) and High School Diploma. Graduates would occupy Clerk and Assistant positions. Previous music or film industry experience, team player, enthusiastic, motivated and good interpersonal and communications skills are all listed as desirable non-academic qualifications. Company benefits and the potential for advancement are both rated as excellent. The average annual starting salary for entry level positions falls within the $20,000 to $30,000 range. The most suitable method for initial contact by those seeking employment is to mail a resume with a covering letter. PolyGram Canada Inc. does hire one or two summer students for office services and mailroom positions. In addition, PolyGram also hires co-op students for unpaid work terms. *Contacts:* Lorie McMackin, Vice President of Human Resources or Voula Vagdatis, Human Resources Administrator.

POSTAL PROMOTIONS LTD.
1100 Birchmount Road
Toronto, ON M1K 5H9

Tel. 416-752-8100
Fax 416-752-8239
Email .... hr1@postalpro.com

Postal Promotions Limited provides direct mail advertising services. Activities include, data processing, data base management, printing, and direct mail advertising. The company employs more than 100 people. Graduates most likely to be hired come from the following academic areas: Chartered Accountant, Master of Business Administration and Community College Diploma (Graphic Arts, Data Processing). Graduates would occupy Accounting, Client Service, and Sales and Marketing positions. Adaptability to specific training, a willingness to accept a challenge, and good communication skills are all listed as desirable non-academic qualifications. Company benefits are rated above average. The potential for advancement is listed as being good. The average annual starting salary falls within the $20,000 to $25,000 range, and is based upon commission for sales positions. The most suitable method for initial contact by graduates seeking employment is to mail a resume with a covering letter. Postal Promotions Limited does employ summer students on a regular basis. *Contact:* Operations Manager.

POTACAN MINING COMPANY
PO Box 5005
Sussex, NB E0E 1P0

Tel. 506-839-2146
Fax 506-839-6415

Potacan Mining Company is involved in the mining of potash. The company employs approximately 500 people. Graduates most likely to be hired come from the following academic areas: Bachelor of Arts (Economics), Bachelor of Engineering (Electrical, Computer Systems, Instrumentation, Mechanical, Industrial Design, Welding, Mining), Master of Business Administration (Accounting, Finance, Human Resources, Information Systems) and Community College Diploma (Accounting, Administration, Business, Human Resources, Auto Mechanic, CAD/CAM/Autocad, Computer Science, Electronics

Technician, Engineering Technician, Welding, Nursing RNA). Company benefits are rated above average. The potential for advancement is listed as being good. The average annual starting salary falls within the $35,000 to $40,000 range. The most suitable method for initial contact by those seeking employment is to mail a resume with a covering letter. *Contact:* Employee Relations, Personnel & Benefits Administrator.

PPG CANADA INC., WORKS 81, OSHAWA
155 First Avenue, PO Box 340
Oshawa, ON L1H 7L3

Tel. 905-725-1144
Fax 905-725-3422
Email .... recalla@ppg.com
Website .... www.ppg.com

PPG Canada Inc., Works 81 in Oshawa is a manufacturer of automotive safety glass. The company employs approximately 400 people at Works 81, while PPG employs a total of 3,200 people in Canada and a total of 30,000 worldwide. PPG Canada Inc. is a subsidiary of PPG Industries Inc., based in Pittsburgh, Pennsylvania. Established in 1883, the company is a leading global manufacturer supplying products for manufacturing, construction, automotive, chemical processing and numerous other world industries. PPG operates approximately 110 major manufacturing and seven research & development facilities worldwide. The company makes protective and decorative coatings, flat glass, fabricated glass products, continuous-strand fiber glass products, and industrial and specialty chemicals. Graduates most likely to be hired at the Oshawa location come from the following academic areas: Bachelor of Engineering (Electrical, Mechanical, Automation/Robotics, Computer Systems, Industrial Engineering, Industrial Production/Manufacturing, Bachelor of Commerce/Business Administration (Accounting, Human Resources, Information Systems) and Community College Diploma (Human Resources). Team player and good communication skills are both listed as desirable non-academic qualifications. Company benefits are rated above average. The potential for advancement is listed as being good. The average annual starting salary falls within the $40,000 to $45,000 range. The most suitable method for initial contact by those seeking employment is to mail a resume with a covering letter. PPG Canada Inc., Works 81, Oshawa does hire summer and co-op work term students. *Contact:* Director, Human Resources.

PRATT & WHITNEY CANADA INC. / P&WC
1801 Courtney Drive
Mississauga, ON L5T 1J3

Tel. 905-564-7500
Fax 905-564-4114
Email .... human.resources@pwc.ca
Website .... www.pwc.ca

Pratt & Whitney Canada Inc. / P&WC is the world's leading manufacturer of small and medium sized gas turbine engines. As a member of The Pratt & Whitney Group and a subsidiary of United Technologies Corporation / UTC of Hartford, Connecticut, P&WC operates with a world mandate to design, develop, manufacture, market and support small and medium sized gas turbine engines. The company employs 1,000 people at this location, a total of 7,760 people in Canada and 9,050 people worldwide. Graduates most likely to be hired come from the following academic areas: Bachelor of Science (Computer Science), Bachelor of Engineering (Electrical, Mechanical, Aerospace, Industrial Engineering), Master of Engineering (Mechanical, Aerospace) and Community College Diploma (Aircraft Maintenance, CAD/CAM/Autocad, Electronics Technician). Graduates would occupy Trainee positions. Company benefits and the potential for advancement are both rated as excellent. The most suitable method for initial contact by those seeking employment is to mail a resume with a covering letter. Pratt & Whitney Canada does hire co-op work term students. *Contact:* Ed Wyzykowski, Manager, Human Resources.

PRE PRINT INC.
12520 - 104 Avenue, Suite 200
Edmonton, AB T5N 3Z9

Tel.	780-424-1234
Fax	780-424-4728
Email	hr@pre-print.com
Website	www.pre-print.com

Pre Pint Inc. is an internationally renowned software developer for the telecommunications and yellow pages publishing industry. The corporate head office is located in Edmonton, with a sister company in Dresden, Germany. Pre Print is positioned as the leading supplier of client/server solutions and has well-established worldwide clients. There are 125 employees at this location and an additional 75 employees at the Dresden location. Graduates most likely to be hired come from the following academic areas: Bachelor of Science (Computer Science), Bachelor of Engineering (Computer Systems), Bachelor of Commerce/Business Administration (Information Systems), Master of Science (Computer Science), Doctorate (Computer Science) and Community College Diploma (Information Systems, Computer Science). Graduates would occupy Software Developer, Tester, Business Analyst, Technical Support Analyst, Technical Systems Analyst, Database Administrator and Project Manager positions. A customer oriented focus, initiative, quality conscious, team work skills, accountability and commitment are all listed as desirable non academic qualifications. Company benefits are rated as industry standard. The potential for advancement is listed as being good. The average annual starting salary for a new graduate falls within the $35,000 to $40,000 range. The most suitable methods for initial contact by those seeking employment are to e-mail a resume with a covering letter, or via telephone. Pre Print Inc. occasionally hires summer and co-op work term students. *Contacts:* Diane Golchert, Human Resources Consultant or Gary Nikipilo, Human Resources Manager.

PRECISION DRILLING CORPORATION
112 - 4th Avenue SW, Suite 700
Calgary, AB T2P 0H3

Tel.	403-716-4500
Fax	403-716-4869
Email	info@precisiondrilling.com
Website	www.precisiondrilling.com

Precision Drilling Corporation is a premier provider of land drilling services and a leading integrated oilfield and industrial service contractor. The company serves oil and gas exploration and production companies in western Canada and abroad. There are approximately 100 employees at this location, and a total of 2,000 employees across Canada. Graduates most likely to be hired come from the following academic areas: Bachelor of Arts (English), Bachelor of Science (Computer Science), Bachelor of Engineering (Industrial Design, Petroleum), Bachelor

of Commerce/Business Administration (Accounting, Finance, Human Resources, Information Systems, Marketing), Chartered Accountant, Certified Management Accountant, Certified General Accountant, Master of Business Administration (Accounting, Human Resources, Information Systems, Marketing) and Community College Diploma (Accounting, Administration, Business, Communications, Human Resources, Marketing, Secretarial, Computer Science). Graduates would occupy Accounts Payable Clerk, Accounts Receivable Clerk, Accountant, Payroll and Benefits Clerk, Personnel Administrator, Purchaser and Engineer positions. Computer literacy, team player, inquisitive, adaptable and versatile are all listed as desirable non-academic qualifications. Company benefits and the potential for advancement are both rated as excellent. The average annual starting salary varies widely between the $20,000 to $45,000 range, depending upon the position being considered. The most suitable method for initial contact by those seeking employment is to mail a resume with a covering letter. Precision Drilling Corporation does hire summer students. *Contact:* Jackie Swartout, Manager, Human Resources.

PREMIS SYSTEMS CANADA
3500 Steeles Avenue East, Suite 1300
Markham, ON L3R 0X1

Tel.	905-477-4155
Fax	905-477-9949
Website	www.premis.com

Premis Systems Canada develops retail software, including POS, Back Office, Head Office, and communications products. There are 40 employees at this location, and a total of 75 employees worldwide. Graduates most likely to be hired come from the following academic areas: Bachelor of Science (Computer Science), Bachelor of Engineering (Computer Systems) and Community College Diploma (Computer Science, Information Systems). Graduates would occupy Programmer, Business Analyst and Customer Support Analyst positions. Team player, independent worker, high caliber, POS experience, professional and co-op work experience are all listed as desirable non-academic qualifications. Company benefits are rated above average. The potential for advancement is listed as excellent. The average annual starting salary falls within the $50,000 to $55,000 range, depending upon experience. The most suitable method for initial contact by those seeking employment is to mail a resume with a covering letter. *Contact:* Human Resources.

PRICEWATERHOUSECOOPERS
Royal Trust Tower, Suite 3000, Box 82, TD Centre
Toronto, ON M5K 1G8

Tel.	416-863-1133
Fax	416-947-8993
Website	www.pwcglobal.com/ca

PricewaterhouseCoopers Canada offers a unique approach to providing solutions for organizations that conduct business in Canada and throughout the global marketplace. The firm operates globally with over 150,000 people working out of 150 countries worldwide. PricewaterhouseCoopers Canada employs approximately 1,300 people in the Toronto area and maintains office locations across Canada. Graduates most likely to be hired come from the following academic areas: Bachelor of Arts (General, Economics), Bachelor of Science (General, Computer Science), Bachelor of Engineering (General), Bachelor of Commerce/Business Administration (General, Accounting), Chartered Accountant, Master of Business Administration (General, Accounting, Finance, Human Resources, Information Systems, Marketing, Public Administration) and Community College Diploma (Accounting, Administration, Business, Communications, Facility Management, Financial Planning). Recent graduates are primarily hired for Staff Accounting positions and occasionally for more senior positions. Strong interpersonal and communication skills are both listed as desirable non-academic qualifications. Company benefits are rated above average. The potential for advancement is listed as excellent. The average annual starting salary falls in the $30,000 plus range. The most suitable method for initial contact by those seeking employment is to mail a resume, covering letter, and a transcript of academic marks. PricewaterhouseCoopers does hire a limited number of summer students. *Contact:* Manager, Human Resources.

PRINCE ALBERT, CITY OF
1084 Central Avenue
Prince Albert, SK S6V 7P3

Tel.	306-953-4330
Fax	306-953-4353
Email	cityp@sk.sympatico.ca
Website	www.citylightsnews.com/pacity.htm

The City of Prince Albert is involved in the provision of municipal government services for the community, including fire and police services. The city employs 520 people. Graduates most likely to be hired come from the following academic areas: Bachelor of Arts (General, Criminology, Geography, Recreation Studies, Urban Geography), Bachelor of Science (Computer Science), Bachelor of Engineering (General, Civil), Bachelor of Commerce/Business Administration (Accounting, Finance, Human Resources, Information Systems, Public Administration), Certified Management Accountant, Master of Business Administration (Human Resources, Public Administration) and Community College Diploma (Accounting, Human Resources, Information Systems, Secretarial, Urban Planning, CAD/CAM/Autocad, Engineering Technician). Company benefits are rated above average. The potential for advancement is listed as being good. The average annual starting salary falls within the $30,000 to $35,000 range. The most suitable method for initial contact by those seeking employment is to mail a resume with a covering letter. The City of Prince Albert does hire summer and co-op work term students. *Contact:* Laurent Mougeot, Director, Human Resources.

PRINCE ALBERT HEALTH DISTRICT
1220 - 25th Street West
Human Resources Department, Box 3000
Prince Albert, SK S6V 5T4

Tel.	306-953-0207
Fax	306-764-2818
Website	citylightsnews.com/pahealth.htm

Prince Albert Health District provides health care and related services. The health district employs 1,800 people. Graduates most likely to be hired come from the following academic areas: Bachelor of Arts (Recreation Studies, Social Work), Bachelor of Science (Computer Science, Audiology, Nursing, Nutritional Sciences, Occupational Therapy, Pharmacy, Physiotherapy, Psychology, Speech Pathology), Bachelor of Commerce/Business Administration (Accounting, Finance, Human Resources), Master of Business Administration (Accounting, Finance, Human Resources) and Community College Diploma (Dietitian/Nutrition, Health/Home Care Aide, Laboratory

Technician, Nuclear Medicine Technician, Nursing RN/RNA, Rehabilitation Therapy, Respiratory Therapy, Ultrasound Technician). Graduates would occupy positions relating to their academic backgrounds, from labour positions (housekeeping, maintenance), semi-professional positions (finance, human resources, health records), to professional positions (doctor, nurse, social worker, psychologist). A positive mental attitude, a willingness and desire to work, and the ability to get along with other people are all listed as desirable non-academic qualifications. Company benefits are rated above average. The potential for advancement is listed as being good. The average annual starting salary falls within the $30,000 to $35,000 range, depending on the position being considered. The most suitable methods for initial contact by those seeking employment are to mail or fax a resume with a covering letter, or by completing an application with the Human Resources Department. The Prince Albert Health District does hire summer students. *Contact:* Bette Hartsfield, Employment Officer, Human Resources.

PRINT KEY INC., THE
7621 Bath Road
Mississauga, ON L4T 3T1

Tel.	905-677-5699
Fax	905-677-8274
Email	jobs@printkey.com
Website	www.printkey.com

The Print Key Inc. is a manufacturer of computer business forms with locations in Mississauga and Montreal. Founded in 1981 with the recognition that more and more small businesses were investing in computers, the company recognized a growing need for quality, custom printed computer forms in short-run quantities and established a shorter standard 2 week turnaround time. Since its establishment, The Print Key has continued to grow by developing long-term partnerships with customers and has expanded its product line and ventured into longer print runs. In 1986 the company opened a second plant in Montreal and today employs a total of 102 people. Graduates most likely to be hired come from the following academic areas: Community College Diploma (Graphic Arts, Printing Technician). Graduates would occupy Pre-Press and Press Operator positions. Team player, dependable, self-motivated, enthusiastic and hard working are all listed as desirable non-academic qualifications. Company benefits are rated above average. The potential for advancement is listed as being average. The average annual starting salary falls within the $20,000 to $25,000 range. The most suitable methods for initial contact by those seeking employment are to fax or e-mail a resume with a covering letter. The Print Key Inc. does hire summer students. *Contact:* Human Resources.

PROCTER & GAMBLE INC.
8th Floor, PO Box 355, Station A
Toronto, ON M5W 1C5

Tel.	416-730-4711
Fax	416-730-4684
Website	www.pg.com

Procter & Gamble Inc. is a recognized leader in the development, manufacture and marketing of a broad range of quality consumer products. Procter & Gamble markets more than 300 brands to nearly five billion consumers in over 140 countries. These brands include: Tide, Ivory, Cover Girl, Pantene Pro-V, Crest, Always, Folgers,

Pringles, Pampers, and Oil of Olay. The company employs approximately 600 people at this location, over 2,000 in Canada and more than 100,000 people worldwide. Graduates most likely to be hired come from the following academic areas: Bachelor of Arts (General), Bachelor of Science (General), Bachelor of Engineering (General, Civil, Electrical, Mechanical), Bachelor of Commerce/Business Administration (Accounting, Finance, Information Systems, Marketing) and Master of Business Administration (Accounting, Finance, Information Systems, Marketing). Graduates would occupy entry level management positions in Marketing, Sales, Product Supply, Finance and Information Technology. The ability to work effectively with others, leadership skills, follow through, and excellent thinking and problem solving skills are all listed as desirable non-academic qualifications. Company benefits and the potential for advancement are both rated as excellent. The average annual starting salary falls within the $40,000 to $45,000 range. The most suitable methods for initial contact by those seeking employment are to mail a resume with a covering letter, or through on-campus recruitment initiatives (see your campus career centre for details). Procter & Gamble Inc. does hire summer and co-op work term students. *Contact:* Corporate Recruiting, Human Resources Department.

PURDUE FREDERICK
575 Granite Court
Pickering, ON L1W 3W8

Tel. 905-420-6400
Fax 905-420-5430

Purdue Frederick is a research-based pharmaceutical company providing superior health care products to people worldwide. The company employs 110 people at this location, and a total of 155 people in Canada. Graduates most likely to be hired come from the following academic areas: Bachelor of Arts (General, Economics, English), Bachelor of Science (General, Chemistry, Computer Science, Mathematics, Nursing, Nutritional Sciences, Pharmacy, Psychology), Bachelor of Engineering (General, Chemical, Computer Systems, Industrial Chemistry), Bachelor of Education (General, Adult, Physical and Health), Bachelor of Commerce/Business Administration (General, Finance, Human Resources, Information Systems, Marketing), Chartered Accountant, Certified Management Accountant, Certified General Accountant, Master of Business Administration (General, Finance, Human Resources, Information Systems, Marketing), Master of Science, Community College Diploma (Accounting, Facility Management, Human Resources, Purchasing/Logistics, Secretarial, CAD/CAM/Autocad, Computer Science, Laboratory Technician, Nursing RN), CHRP designation and High School Diploma. Graduates would occupy entry level and more advanced positions, including Chemist, Technician, Product Manager, Human Resources Manager, Assistant Controller, Controller, Accounting Clerk, Secretarial, and Clerical positions. Previous work experience, team player, good work ethic, initiative, organized, and leadership skills are all listed as desirable non-academic qualifications. Company benefits are rated as excellent. The potential for advancement is listed as being good. The average annual starting salary is dependent upon the position being considered. The most suitable methods for initial contact by those seeking employment are to mail or fax a resume with a covering letter. Summer students are hired. These are usually University level students recruited from within the company. *Contact:* Manager, Human Resources.

PUROLATOR COURIER LTD.
11 Morse Street, 2nd Floor, Training & Recruitment
Toronto, ON M4M 2P7

Tel. .... 416-461-9031 ext. 301
Fax 416-461-3994
Email .... careers@purolator.com
Website .... www.purolator.com

Purolator Courier Ltd. is Canada's largest overnight courier company. The company provides its customers with automated solutions, round-the-clock pick up and delivery along with services and customized solutions designed to move its customers shipments "across town or around the world". Originally founded in 1960, Purolator is a 100% Canadian owned and operated company and today employs approximately 12,000 people across Canada, 4,000 of whom are couriers. Over 375,000 envelopes and parcels are funnelled through the company's system each night, and Purolator now serves over 175 countries worldwide. Graduates most likely to be hired come from the following academic areas: Bachelor of Arts (General, English, French, Psychology), Bachelor of Science (General, Computer Science), Bachelor of Engineering (Mechanical, Computer Systems, Industrial Design, Transportation), Bachelor of Education (General, Adult), Bachelor of Commerce/Business Administration (General, Accounting, Finance, Human Resources, Information Systems, Marketing, Public Administration), Chartered Accountant, Certified Management Accountant, Certified General Accountant, Community College Diploma (Accounting, Advertising, Business, Communications/Public Relations, Facility Management, Financial Planning, Human Resources, Marketing/Sales, Office Administration, Purchasing/Logistics, Secretarial, Legal Assistant, Security/Enforcement, Aircraft Maintenance, Automotive Mechanic, Computer Science, Information Systems) and High School Diploma. Graduates would occupy Sales Professional, Human Resources Assistant, Human Resources Consultant, Customer Service Manager, Customer Service Representative, Junior Accounts Payable Clerk, Manager National Accounts, Administrative Assistant, Senior Marketing Manager, Loss Prevention Professional, Senior Buyer, Internal Audit Manager, Support Representative, Customer Automation Support Representative, Financial Analyst, Public Relations Specialist, Senior PC/QA Analyst, Database Administrator, Training Specialist and Senior Programmer Analyst positions. Exceptional people and coaching skills, team player and excellent interpersonal, organizational and leadership skills are all listed as desirable non-academic qualifications. Purolator offers employees competitive compensation and benefits packages. Accordingly, company benefits and the potential for advancement are both rated as excellent. The most suitable methods for initial contact by those seeking employment are to mail or fax a resume with a covering letter, via telephone, or by applying in person at this location. Purolator Courier Ltd. does hire summer and co-op work term students. *Contacts:* Debbie Kamino, Human Resources, Metro Recruiter or Lise Comeau, Human Resources, Corporate.

QLT PHOTOTHERAPEUTICS INC.
520 West 6th Avenue, Suite 200
Vancouver, BC V5Z 4H5

Tel. 604-872-7881
Fax 604-871-1308
Email .... hr@qlt-pdt.com
Website .... www.qlt-pdt.com

QLT PhotoTherapeutics Inc. is a world leader in the development and commercialization of proprietary pharmaceutical products for photodynamic therapy. Photodynamic therapy is a field of medicine that uses light activated drugs for the treatment of cancer diseases of the eye and other medical conditions. The company employs a total of 122 people. Graduates most likely to be hired come from the following academic areas: Bachelor of Science (Biology, Chemistry), Bachelor of Engineering (Biomedical Electronics, Mechanical), Bachelor of Commerce/Business Administration (Accounting, Finance, Human Resources, Information Systems, Marketing), Chartered Accountant, Certified General Accountant, Master of Business Administration (Marketing), Master of Science (Biology, Biochemistry, Chemistry), Doctorate (Biology, Biochemistry, Chemistry), Community College Diploma (Accounting, Human Resources, Computer Science) and High School Diploma. Graduates would occupy Clerk, Technician, Associate, Scientist, Manager, Engineer and Analyst positions. Team player, good interpersonal skills, work experience, supervisory skills, adaptability, and good written and verbal communication skills are all listed as desirable non-academic qualifications. Company benefits are rated above average. The potential for advancement is listed as being good. The most suitable method for initial contact by those seeking employment is to mail a resume with a covering letter. QLT PhotoTherapeutics Inc. does hire summer students. *Contact:* Human Resources.

QSR LIMITED
166 Pearl Street
Toronto, ON M5H 1L3

Tel. 416-597-0969
Fax 416-597-1776

QSR Limited is involved in gold mining and milling. There are approximately 100 people employed at this location and locations in Timmins, Ontario and Bachelor Lake, Quebec. Graduates most likely to be hired come from the following academic areas: Bachelor of Science (Geology), Bachelor of Engineering (Mining), Bachelor of Commerce/Business Administration (Accounting) and Chartered Accountant. Graduates would be hired for positions located at on-site operations and for administrative positions at this location in Toronto. Applicants should be willing and able to work in remote areas. Company benefits are rated as industry standard. The potential for advancement is listed as average. The average annual starting salary falls within the $20,000 to $25,000 range. The most suitable method for initial contact by those seeking employment is to mail a resume with a covering letter. *Contact:* Human Resources.

QUAKER OATS COMPANY OF CANADA LIMITED, THE
Quaker Park
Peterborough, ON K9J 7B2

Tel. 705-743-6330
Fax 705-876-4141
Website .... www.quakeroats.ca

The Quaker Oats Company of Canada Limited manufactures and markets oat-based food products, as well as Gatorade beverages for retail stores and the food service industry. There are approximately 200 employees at this location and a total of 900 employees in Canada. Graduates most likely to be hired come from the following academic areas: Bachelor of Arts (Economics), Bachelor of Science (Computer Science, Mathematics), Bachelor of Engineering (Food Processing, Electrical, Mechanical), Bachelor of Commerce/Business Administration (General, Accounting, Finance, Human Resources, Information Systems, Marketing, Public Administration), Chartered Accountant, Certified Management Accountant, Master of Business Administration (General, Accounting, Finance, Human Resources, Information Systems, Marketing) and Community College Diploma (Accounting, Human Resources, Marketing/Sales, Purchasing/Logistics, Secretarial, CAD/CAM/Autocad, Engineering Technician). Graduates would occupy Financial Manager (CA's), Financial Analyst, Programmer Analyst, Computer Operator, Buyer, Customer Service Representative, Sales Representative, Project Engineer, Cost Accountant, Marketing Assistant, Quality Assurance Technician and Production Line Supervisor positions. Company benefits are rated as excellent. The potential for advancement is listed as being good. The average annual starting salary is dependent upon position and previous experience. The most suitable method for initial contact by those seeking employment is to mail a resume with a covering letter. *Contacts:* Denise Kouri, Human Resources or Sonia Crook, Human Resources.

QUEBEC BLUE CROSS
550, rue Sherbrooke Ouest, Suite 160
Montreal, QC H3A 1B9

Tel. 514-286-8471
Fax 514-286-8475
Email .... resshum@qc.croixbleue.ca
Website .... www.qc.croixbleue.ca

Québec Blue Cross provides health insurance, travel insurance and related assistance products and services. Established in 1942, Québec Blue Cross is the oldest health insurance company in Québec. The company is a non-profit, legally independent organization which is wholly Québec-owned. Québec Blue Cross employs more than 300 people at this location. Graduates most likely to be hired come from the following academic areas: Bachelor of Science (Actuarial, Computer Science, Mathematics, Nursing), Bachelor of Commerce/Business Administration (Accounting, Marketing), Chartered Accountant, Certified Management Accountant, Certified General Accountant and Community College Diploma (Accounting, Administration, Communications, Insurance, Secretarial, Hospitality, Travel/Tourism, Nursing RN). Graduates would occupy Customer Service Agent, Actuary, Claims Agent and Underwriter positions. Team player, a dynamic person, customer service oriented and previous work experience are all listed as desirable non-academic qualifications. The average annual starting salary falls within the $20,000 to $30,000 range. The most suitable method for initial contact by those seeking employment is to mail a resume with a covering letter. Québec Blue Cross does hire summer students. *Contacts:* Claude Soucy, Human Resources Director or Caroline Sirois, Human Resources Advisor.

QUESTOR INDUSTRIES INC.
6961 Russell Avenue
Burnaby, BC V5J 4R8

Tel. 604-454-1134
Fax 604-454-1137
Email .... info@questorinc.com
Website .... www.questorinc.com

Questor Industries Inc. is a developer and manufacturer of a range of ultra compact, high efficiency gas separation systems for industries, vehicles, medical and aerospace applications. The company employs 37 people in Canada. Graduates most likely to be hired come from the following academic areas: Bachelor of Science (Chemistry, Physics), Bachelor of Engineering (Chemical, Mechanical, Automation/Robotics, Engineering Physics, Industrial Engineering), Bachelor of Commerce/Business Administration (Marketing), Master of Business Administration (General, Marketing), Master/Doctorate of Science, Master/Doctorate of Engineering and Community College Diploma (Marketing/Sales, Purchasing/Logistics, CAD/CAM/Autocad, Computer Science, Engineering Technician). Graduates would occupy Design Engineer, Project Engineer, Project Technologist/Technician and Sales Clerk positions. Flexible, team worker and imaginative are all listed as desirable non-academic qualifications. Company benefits and the potential for advancement are both rated as excellent. The average annual starting salary falls within the $30,000 to $35,000 range. The most suitable methods for initial contact by those seeking employment are to mail or e-mail a resume with a covering letter. Questor Industries Inc. does hire summer and co-op work term students. *Contacts:* Sharon MacLellan (Sales and Administrative Positions) or Carl Hunter (Technical Positions).

R.V. ANDERSON ASSOCIATES LIMITED
2001 Sheppard Avenue East, Suite 400
Toronto, ON M2J 4Z8

Tel. 416-497-8600
Fax 416-497-0342
Email .... toronto@rvanderson.com
Website .... www.rvanderson.com

R.V. Anderson Associates Limited is a consulting engineering and technology management firm. Consultation activities include water pollution control, water supply, water resources, environmental planning, transportation, tunnels and shafts, municipal services, land development, structural and architectural consulting services. Established in 1948, the company is owned by its principals and associates, with a staff complement of 175, providing services to the public and private sectors, in Canada and overseas. Graduates most likely to be hired come from the following academic areas: Bachelor of Engineering (Environmental, Transportation, Structural, Water Resources), Master of Engineering (Environmental, Transportation, Structural, Water Resources) and Community College Diploma (Engineering Technician). Graduates are hired as Junior Engineers (In-Training). The ability to work well with others, solid work ethic and independent work habits, are listed as desirable non-academic qualifications. Company benefits and the potential for advancement are both rated as excellent. The most suitable method for initial contact by those seeking employment is to mail a resume with a covering letter. R. V. Anderson Associates Limited does hire summer students on a regular basis, primarily for field work. *Contact:* Human Resources.

RADISSON PLAZA HOTEL ADMIRAL
249 Queens Quay West
Toronto, ON M5J 2N5

Tel. 416-203-3333
Fax 416-203-3100
Website .... www.radisson.com

Radisson Plaza Hotel Admiral is a hotel and restaurant, located on Toronto's waterfront. The hotel employs 110 people. Hotel Admiral is part of Radisson Hotels Worldwide which operates 385 hotels in 50 countries worldwide. Graduates most likely to be hired are Community College graduates from Hospitality and Travel/Tourism programs. Graduates would occupy Front Office, Food and Beverage Waitstaff and Supervisory positions. Applicants should be outgoing and service oriented. The most suitable method for initial contact by those seeking employment is to mail a resume with a covering letter. Radisson Plaza Hotel Admiral does hire a few summer students annually. *Contact:* Human Resources Manager.

RADISSON PLAZA HOTEL TORONTO
90 Bloor Street East
Toronto, ON M4W 1A7

Tel. 416-961-8000
Fax 416-961-9581

Radisson Plaza Hotel Toronto is a 256 room, "Four Diamond" hotel. The hotel employs approximately 150 people. Graduates most likely to be hired come from the following academic areas: Bachelor of Arts (General) and Community College Diploma (Hospitality, Hotel Administration, Tourism, Culinary/Cooking). Graduates would occupy Waiter, Kitchen and Housekeeping staff positions, as well as front office Clerk positions. The ability to work shifts (including weekends), a strong command of the English language, good customer service and communication skills, and a strong interest in the hospitality and service industry are all listed as desirable non-academic qualifications. Company benefits are rated as industry standard. The potential for advancement is listed as average. The average annual starting salary falls within the $18,000 to $23,000 range. The most suitable methods for initial contact by those seeking employment are to mail a resume with a covering letter, or via telephone. Radisson Plaza Hotel Toronto does hire summer students depending upon the level of business. Summer students must also be available to work on weekends. *Contact:* Human Resources Manager.

RAMADA HOTEL, TORONTO AIRPORT EAST CONFERENCE & CONVENTION CENTRE
1677 Wilson Avenue
Toronto, ON M3L 1A5

Tel. 416-249-8171
Fax 416-243-7342
Email .... ramadata@total.net
Website .... www.ramada.ca

Ramada Hotel, Toronto Airport East Conference & Convention Centre is a 200 bedroom, full service hotel with conference facilities to accommodate 1,500 guests. The hotel employs more than 100 people catering to corporate business conventions, small and large banquet functions, sports groups, tour groups, and individual travellers. Graduates most likely to be hired are Community College graduates from Hospitality/Hotel Administration and Food and Beverage programs. Able to interact well with the public, enjoy working in a service oriented industry, and the ability to speak French, German and/or Spanish are all listed as desirable non-academic qualifications. Company benefits are rated above average. The potential for advancement is listed as being good. The average annual starting salary falls within the $20,000 to $25,000 range, and varies a great deal depending upon the positions being considered. The most suitable method for initial contact by those seeking employment is to mail a resume with a covering letter. Ramada Hotel, Toronto Airport East Conference & Convention Centre does hire summer students. *Contact:* Wenli Ho, General Manager.

RBC DOMINION SECURITIES INC.
PO Box 50, Royal Bank Plaza
Toronto, ON M5J 2W7

Tel.	416-842-8000
Fax	416-842-8033
Email	careers@rbcds.com
Website	www.rbcds.com

RBC Dominion Securities Inc. is a leading Canadian investment dealer with operations in all facets of corporate and government finance, mergers and acquisitions, sales and trading of equities, bonds, money market instruments, foreign exchange, futures and options, research and investment management. Originally founded in 1901, RBC Dominion Securities is a business unit of the Royal Bank of Canada. The company maintains over 200 offices, 32 part-time branches in smaller communities and 1600 Registered Representatives. RBC Dominion Securities is well represented nationally as well as internationally with offices in New York, Boston, Chicago, London, Paris, Frankfurt, Hong Kong, Singapore, Tokyo, Sydney, Bermuda, Grand Cayman, Lausanne, Nassau and Turks & Caicos. Graduates most likely to be hired come from the following academic areas: Bachelor of Arts, Bachelor of Science (Computer Science) Bachelor of Commerce/Business Administration, Chartered Accountant, Master of Business Administration, Masters (General/Related) and Community College (General/Related). Graduates would occupy a wide variety of entry-level positions in Corporate Finance, Clerical and Computer Programming. Company benefits are rated above average. The potential for advancement is listed as being good. The average annual starting salary is dependent upon the level of position. The most suitable method for initial contact by those seeking employment is to mail a resume with a covering letter. RBC Dominion Securities Inc. does hire summer students. *Contact:* Human Resources.

READER'S DIGEST ASSOCIATION (CANADA) LTD.
1100, boul René Lévesque Ouest
Montreal, QC H3Z 2V9

Tel.	514-940-0751
Fax	514-940-7360
Website	www.readersdigest.ca

Reader's Digest Association (Canada) Ltd. is a major publisher and direct marketer of published materials. There are approximately 265 employees at this location, an additional 20 employees at the Toronto office and a total of 5,000 employees in 50 locations around the world. Graduates most likely to be hired come from the following academic areas: Bachelor of Arts (General, English, French, Graphic Arts, Journalism), Bachelor of Science (Computer Science, Mathematics), Bachelor of Commerce/Business Administration (General, Accounting, Finance, Human Resources, Information Systems, Marketing), Chartered Accountant, Certified Management Accountant, Certified General Accountant, Community College Diploma (Accounting, Administration, Advertising, Business, Communications, Marketing/Sales, Purchasing/Logistics, Secretarial, Graphic Arts, Journalism, Computer Science) and High School Diploma. Graduates would occupy Secretary, Clerk, Programmer Trainee, Programmer Analyst, Marketing Coordinator, Marketing Assistant, Marketing Analyst, Accounting Clerk, Financial Analyst, Statistician, Junior Copywriter, Assistant Editor, Customer Relations Representative, PC Support Technician, Research Analyst, Graphic Artist and Graphic Designer positions. Initiative, adaptability, flexibility, thoroughness, energy, results oriented, motivation, good communication skills, team player and a curious mind are all listed as desirable non-academic qualifications. Company benefits are rated as excellent. The potential for advancement is listed as very good. The average annual starting salary falls within the $25,000 to $30,000 range. The most suitable methods for initial contact by those seeking employment are to mail a resume with a covering letter, or through industry contacts and employee referrals. The Reader's Digest Association (Canada) Ltd. does hire summer and co-op work term students. *Contact:* Patrick Colavecchio, Human Resources Manager.

REBEL.COM INC.
150 Isabella Street, Suite 1000
Ottawa, ON K1S 5R3

Tel.	613-788-6000
Fax	613-230-8300
Email	hr@rebel.com
Website	www.rebel.com

Rebel.com inc. is a leading manufacturer and supplier of Linux, Unix and Windows-based systems. The company's product line includes the Netwinder family of Linux-based computers, Horizon Sparc/Unix based systems and PC products that are manufactured by Rebel.com's wholly owned subsidiary, Mask Systems. Incorporated in 1987 as Hardware Canada Computing, the company was recently named one of Canada's fastest growing companies by Profit Magazine. Rebel.com's impressive client list includes Nortel Networks, Newbridge Networks Corporation, Data General, Mitel Corporation, Government of Canada and Fortune 500 companies. Based in Ottawa, the company employs 65 people at this location and a total of 150 people in Canada. Graduates most likely to be hired come from the following academic areas: Bachelor of Engineering (Electrical, Mechanical, Computer Systems, Materials Science), Bachelor of Commerce/Business Administration (Accounting, Finance, Human Resources, Marketing, Chartered Accountant, Certified Management Accountant and Community College Diploma (Communications/Public Relations, Marketing/Sales, Secretarial). Graduates would occupy Mechanical Design, Hardware Design, Software Design, Software Development, Product Management, Accounting Clerk and Administrative Assistant positions. Team player, a strong work ethic, energetic, bright, and previous experience in the high tech industry are all listed as desirable non-academic qualifications. Company benefits are rated above average. The potential for advancement is listed as being excellent. The average annual starting salary falls within the $35,000 to $40,000 range. The most suitable method for initial contact by those seeking employment is to apply through the company's website. Rebel.com does hire summer and co-op work term students. *Contact:* Human Resources Department.

RECKITT & COLMAN CANADA INC.
2 Wickman Road
Toronto, ON M8Z 5M5

Tel.	416-201-7104
Fax	416-255-1964
Website	www.reckitt.com

Reckitt & Colman Canada Inc. is a manufacturer and distributor of a variety of household and food products. Popular brand categories include Airwick, Wizard, Black Flag, Easy-Off, Sani-Flush, Sanifoam, Neet, Chore-Boy, Dettol, Down-to-Earth (environmental products), Mr. Bubble, Carpet Fresh, French's Mustard, Keen's Mustard and French's Assorted Sauces and Gravies. Reckitt & Colman Canada Inc. is a subsidiary of London, United Kingdom based Reckitt & Colman PLC. Reckitt & Colman PLC is a world-class consumer products company with principal activities being the manufacture and sale of household and over-the-counter pharmaceutical brands. The company has operating sites in more than 50 countries, markets its products in over 170 countries and employs a total of 15,900 people worldwide. Graduates most likely to be hired come from the following academic areas: Bachelor of Science (Chemistry), Bachelor of Engineering (Chemical), Bachelor of Commerce/Business Administration (Accounting, Finance, Marketing, Information Systems), Master of Business Administration (Finance, Marketing) and Community College Diploma (Accounting, Business, Marketing/Sales, Purchasing/Logistics, Secretarial, Human Resources). Graduates would occupy Laboratory Technician, Plant Engineer, Accounting Manager, Product Manager, Systems Analyst, Human Resources Associate, Credit Clerk, Accounts Payable Clerk, Buyer, Vendor Scheduler, and Secretarial positions. Team player, dedicated, self motivated, good communication skills, a professional image, initiative and an interest in continual improvement and challenging the status quo are all listed as desirable non-academic qualifications. Company benefits and the potential for advancement are both rated as excellent. The most suitable method for initial contact by those seeking employment is to telephone directly. Reckitt & Colman Canada Inc. does hire summer students. *Contact:* Human Resources Department.

RECOCHEM INC.
850 montée de Liesse
Montreal, QC H4T 1P4

Tel.	514-341-3550
Fax	514-341-1292
Website	www.recochem.com

Recochem Inc. manufactures, packages and distributes automotive and specialty chemicals for industry and individual consumers. The company is also an important worldwide exporter of bulk chemicals. There are 225 employees at this location, at total of 425 in Canada, and a total of 525 employees worldwide. Graduates most likely to be hired come from the following academic areas: Bachelor of Science (Chemistry, Computer Science), Bachelor of Engineering (Chemical, Industrial Chemistry, Computer Systems, Mechanical), Bachelor of Commerce/Business Administration (Accounting, Finance, Human Resources, Information Systems), Certified Management Accountant, Master of Business Administration (Accounting, Finance, Human Resources, Information Systems, Marketing) and Community College Diploma (Accounting, Computer Science, Electronics Technician, Engineering Technician). Graduates would occupy Network Integrator, Accounting Clerk, Human Resource Manager, Payroll Supervisor, Plant Manager, Warehouse Manager and Chemist positions. Company benefits are rated above average. The potential for advancement is listed as average. The average annual starting salary depends upon the position being considered. The most suitable method for initial contact by those seeking employment is to mail a resume with a covering letter, specifying salary and range. *Contact:* Eva Kuchar, Vice President, Administration.

RED COAT TRAIL SCHOOL DIVISION #69
PO Box 1330
Assiniboia, SK S0H 0B0

Tel.	306-642-3341
Fax	306-642-3455
Email	redcoat@sk.sympatico.ca

Red Coat Trail School Division #69 is a school board operating nine schools in rural Saskatchewan. The division employs approximately 130 people. Graduates most likely to be hired come from the following academic areas: Bachelor of Arts (General, Psychology, Social Work), Bachelor of Science (General, Computer Science, Audiology, Psychology, Speech Pathology), Bachelor of Engineering (Computer Systems), Bachelor of Education (General, Early Childhood, Primary Junior, Junior Intermediate, Intermediate Senior, Physical and Health, Special Needs), Bachelor of Commerce/Business Administration (General), Community College Diploma (Accounting, Facility Management, Office Administration, Secretarial, Automotive Mechanic, Computer Science, Electronics Technician, Information Systems) and High School Diploma. Depending upon academic background, graduates would occupy Teacher, Principal, Teacher's Aide, Secretarial, Administration, School Bus Driver, and Mechanic positions. Related work experience, enthusiasm, an ability to get along with children and adults, and knowledge and training in area of employment are all listed as desirable non-academic qualifications. Company benefits are rated as industry standard. The potential for advancement is listed as average. The average annual starting salary falls within the $15,000 to $20,000 range for non-academic positions, and within the $25,000 to $30,000 range for academic positions. The most suitable method for initial contact by those seeking employment is to mail a resume with a covering letter. Red Coat Trail School Division #69 does hire summer students, although rarely. *Contacts:* Edward H. Maksymiw, Director of Education or Arthur J. Warnecke, Secretary Treasurer.

RED DEER COLLEGE
PO Box 5005
Red Deer, AB T4N 5H5

Tel.	403-342-3300
Fax	403-340-8940
Email	hro@admin.rdc.ab.ca
Website	www.rdc.ab.ca

Established in 1963, Red Deer College is a learning-centered college committed to excellence and educational leadership. The goal of Red Deer College is to provide a wide range of quality educational opportunities which promote success of learners and the enrichment of life in the communities served. Red Deer College is located in the City of Red Deer, Alberta, but also offers off-campus programming through distance delivery in many areas of the province. Programs include adult development, career oriented studies, apprenticeship training, and university undergraduate studies. Red Deer College also offers the citizens of Central Alberta the opportunity to complete degrees while remaining in Red Deer. Baccalaureate programs in Nursing and Elementary Education (middle years major) are offered in collaboration with the University of Alberta. A Bachelor of Arts degree is offered in collaboration with the University of Calgary. The College's comprehensive mandate together with its reputation as an excellent teaching institution with quality instruction attracts students. Graduates most likely to be hired come from the following academic areas: Bachelor of Arts (General, Economics, English, French, Geography, Fine Arts, History, Philosophy, Political Science, Psychology, Recreation Studies, Sociology/Social Work), Bachelor of Science (General, Biology, Chemistry, Computer Science, Mathematics, Microbiology, Physics, Nursing, Pharmacy, Psychology), Bachelor of Engineering (General, Electrical, Mechanical, Computer Systems, Water Resources, Welding), Bachelor of Education (General, Early Childhood, Adult, Special Needs), Bachelor of Commerce/Business Administration (General, Accounting, Finance, Human Resources, Information Systems, Marketing), Chartered Accountant, Certified Management Accountant, Certified General Accountant and Master of Business Administration (General, Accounting, Finance, Human Resources, Information Systems, Marketing). Company benefits and the potential for advancement are both rated as excellent. The average annual starting salary falls within the $30,000 to $35,000 range. The most suitable method for initial contact by those seeking employment is to mail a resume with a covering letter. Red Deer College does hire summer students. *Contact:* Employee Support and Development.

REENA
927 Clark Avenue West
Thornhill, ON L4J 8G6

Tel. 905-889-6484
Fax 905-763-8272
Website .... www.reena.org/socialwork.html

Reena is a non-profit, social service agency providing support to people who are developmentally handicapped. This primarily involves assisting in community integration. Reena has over 300 employees. Graduates most likely to be hired come from the following academic areas: Bachelor of Arts (Psychology, Recreation Studies, Social Work), Bachelor of Education (Special Needs), Bachelor of Commerce/Business Administration (Accounting, Finance, Human Resources), Chartered Accountant, Certified Management Accountant, Certified General Accountant and Community College Diploma (Recreation Studies, Social Work). Graduates would occupy Support Worker, Social Worker, Supervisor and Accountant positions. Previous experience in a supporting and teaching environment with those who have special needs is listed as a desirable non-academic qualification. Company benefits are rated above average. The potential for advancement is listed as average. The average annual starting salary falls within the $20,000 to $30,000 range. The most suitable methods for initial contact by graduates seeking employment are to mail or fax a resume with a covering letter, or by phoning the Human Resources Department directly. Reena does hire summer students to occupy positions with their summer cottage program. *Contact:* Human Resources Manager.

REGAL CONSTELLATION HOTEL
900 Dixon Road
Toronto, ON M9W 1J7

Tel. 416-675-1500
Fax 416-673-1737

The Regal Constellation Hotel boasts one of the largest hotel convention and tradeshow facilities in Canada, enabling service to over 3,000 people. The hotel offers extensive recreation facilities, 708 guestrooms, and a variety of lounges and restaurants. The hotel employs approximately 575 people. Graduates most likely to be hired come from the following academic areas: Bachelor of Science (Computer Science), Chartered Accountant, Certified Management Accountant, Master of Business Ad-

ministration (Accounting, Human Resources), Community College Diploma (Business, Human Resources, Marketing/Sales, Cooking, Hospitality, Travel/Tourism) and High School Diploma. Graduates would occupy Room Attendant, Front Desk Clerk, Reservations Agent, Accounting Clerk, Sales/Catering Coordinator and Restaurant Staff Management positions. Previous hotel experience, team player and a customer service orientation are listed as desirable non-academic qualifications. Company benefits are rated above average. The potential for advancement is listed as excellent. The average annual starting salary falls within the $15,000 to $25,000 range. The most suitable method for initial contact by those seeking employment is to visit the Human Resource Department at the hotel from 2:00pm to 4:00pm, weekdays. The Regal Constellation Hotel hires 3 to 6 summer students annually. *Contact:* Human Resources Department.

REGENT HOLIDAYS LIMITED
6205 Airport Road, Building A, Suite 200
Mississauga, ON L4V 1E1

Tel. 905-673-0777
Fax 905-673-1717
Website .... www.regentholidays.com

Regent Holidays Limited is primarily involved in placing travel reservations and taking bookings from travel agents. Operational areas include, customer service, product development, documentation, sales, and accounting. There are 116 employees at this location, and a total of 125 worldwide. Graduates most likely to be hired come from the following academic areas: Bachelor of Arts (Languages), Bachelor of Commerce/Business Administration (Accounting, Finance, Human Resources, Information Systems, Marketing), Master of Business Administration (Accounting, Finance, Human Resources, Information Systems) and Community College Diploma (Accounting, Administration, Advertising, Business, Hospitality, Travel/Tourism). Graduates would occupy positions ranging from entry-level Reservation, Sales and Clerical positions to Supervisory positions. Applicants should possess good communication skills. Company benefits are rated as industry standard. The potential for advancement is listed as being good. The average annual starting salary falls within the $15,000 to $20,000 range. The most suitable method for initial contact by graduates seeking employment is to mail a resume with a covering letter. *Contact:* Linda Johnston, Manager, Human Resources.

REGION 3 HOSPITAL CORPORATION
PO Box 9000
Fredericton, NB E3B 5N5

Tel. 506-452-5063
Fax 506-452-5680
Website www.gov.nb.ca/hospital/region3

Region 3 Hospital Corporation is a major health care corporation, operating 15 healthcare facilities. The corporation employs a total of 3,200 people throughout the region. Graduates most likely to be hired come from the following academic areas: Bachelor of Science (Audiology, Nursing, Nutritional Sciences, Occupational Therapy, Pharmacy, Physical Therapy, Speech Pathology), Bachelor of Engineering (Biomedical Electronics), Bachelor of Education (Adult), Master of Arts (Social Work), Master of Science (Clinical Psychology, Speech Pathology), and Community College Diploma (Dietician/Nutrition, Ambulance/Emergency Care Technician, Laboratory

Technician, Nuclear Medicine Technician, Nursing RN/ RNA, Radiology Technician, Respiratory Therapy). Graduates are hired to occupy Registered Nurse, Occupational Therapist, Physiotherapist, Speech Language Pathologist, Dietician, Clinical Psychologist and related positions. Demonstrated communication, interpersonal and team building skills are all listed as desirable non-academic qualifications. Company benefits are rated above average. The potential for advancement is listed as being good. The average annual starting salary depends upon the position being considered. The most suitable method for initial contact by those seeking employment is to mail a resume with a covering letter. The Region 3 Hospital Corporation does hire summer students. *Contact:* Human Resources Officer.

REICHHOLD LTD.
1919 Wilson Avenue
Toronto, ON M9M 1B1

Tel. 416-742-0262
Website .... www.reichhold.com

Reichhold Ltd. is involved in the research, development, manufacture and the bulk sale of liquid and powder chemicals to industrial companies. For more than 70 years, Reichhold has been providing its customers with innovative solutions that are based upon creative chemistry. The company provides advanced polymers, adhesives and polymer systems based upon the most comprehensive technology found in a single company in the industry. Products include forest product adhesives for plywood and waferboard, and products such as base paints and plastic resins. The company supplies to leading producers of products from carpets to boats, books to boxes, and paper to paint. Reichhold Ltd. employs more than 100 people at this location and a total of 500 people across Canada. Graduates most likely to be hired come from the following academic areas: Bachelor of Science (Chemistry, Forestry), Bachelor of Engineering (Chemistry, Forestry), Bachelor of Commerce/Business Administration, and Master of Business Administration (Marketing), Master of Science (Chemistry), Doctorate of Science (Chemistry) and Community College Diploma (Laboratory Technician). Good writing skills, entrepreneurial abilities, a strong work ethic, integrity and being "down to earth" are all listed as desirable non-academic qualifications. Company benefits are rated above average. The potential for advancement is listed as excellent. The average annual starting salary falls between the $25,000 to $35,000 plus range. The most suitable method for initial contact by those seeking employment is to mail a resume with a covering letter. Reichhold Ltd. hires a small number students for summer and co-op work terms, primarily co-op students. *Contact:* Manager, Human Resources.

REID'S CONSTRUCTION GROUP INCORPORATED
Highway 55 West, Bag 5000
Cold Lake, AB T9M 1P7

Tel. 780-639-3368
Fax 780-639-2123

Reid's Construction Group Incorporated is comprised of five different operating companies spread throughout western Canada involved in modular construction, shop fabrication, pipeline construction, civil construction, facilities construction, facilities maintenance, equipment sales and rentals and management consulting. Established in 1953, the Reid's Group of Companies has become a respected name in northern Alberta's oil and gas and business communities. The company employs from 400 to 1,200 employees, with the number fluctuating throughout the year. There are over 200 employees at this location. Graduates most likely to be hired come from the following academic areas: Bachelor of Engineering (General, Civil, Electrical, Mechanical, Industrial Design, Industrial Engineering, Industrial Production/Manufacturing, Petroleum/Fuels, Welding), Community College Diploma (Automotive Mechanic, Carpentry, Steamfitter, Pipefitter, Crane Operator, Heavy Equipment Operator, Heavy Duty Mechanic, Boiler Maker, Ironworker, Machinist, Millwright, Welding) and High School Diploma. Previous work experience, team player, hard worker, outgoing personality, good communicator, ambitious, excellent organizational skills and a strong work ethic are all listed as desirable non-academic qualifications. Company benefits and the potential for advancement are both rated as excellent. The average annual starting salary falls within the $20,000 to $25,000 range. The most suitable methods for initial contact by those seeking employment are to mail or fax a resume with a covering letter. Reid's Construction Group Incorporated does hire summer and co-op work term students. *Contact:* Jason Beaman, Human Resources.

RENAISSANCE VANCOUVER HOTEL HARBOURSIDE
1133 West Hastings
Vancouver, BC V6E 3T3

Tel. 604-689-9211
Fax 604-689-4358
Website .... www.renaissancehotels.com/YVRRD

Renaissance Vancouver Hotel Harbourside is a major Vancouver hotel with restaurant. The hotel employs approximately 300 people. Graduates most likely to be hired come from the following academic areas: Bachelor of Arts (Languages), Bachelor of Engineering (Food Processing, Electrical, Mechanical, Welding), Bachelor of Commerce/ Business Administration (General, Accounting, Finance, Human Resources, Marketing), Chartered Accountant, Certified Management Accountant, Certified General Accountant, Master of Business Administration (Accounting, Finance, Human Resources, Marketing), Community College Diploma (Accounting, Administration, Business, Facility Management, Financial Planning, Human Resources, Marketing/Sales, Purchasing/Logistics, Secretarial, Cooking, Hospitality, Travel/Tourism, HVAC Systems, Welding, Nutrition) and High School Diploma. Graduates would occupy Line Staff positions such as Cook, Front Desk Clerk, Reservations, General Maintenance, Server, Bartender, and Cleaner, and Management positions in Accounting, Sales, Human Resources, Secretarial, Food and Beverage and Purchasing. Excellent customer service skills, prior work experience, an ability to balance many work tasks simultaneously, outgoing, professional and computer literacy are all listed as desirable non-academic qualifications. Company benefits are rated above average. The potential for advancement is listed as being good. The average annual starting salary falls within the $20,000 to $25,000 range. The most suitable method for initial contact by those seeking employment is to mail a resume with a covering letter. Renaissance Vancouver Hotel Harbourside hires summer students from March to September. *Contact:* Human Resources.

RESEARCH IN MOTION LIMITED / RIM
295 Phillip Street
Waterloo, ON N2L 3W8

Tel.	519-888-7465
Fax	519-888-7884
Email	careers@rim.net
Website	www.rim.net

Research in Motion is a world leader in designing, manufacturing and marketing wireless electronic access technology for the mobile communications market. RIM is a knowledge-based company with proven, leading technologies and has a history of developing breakthrough wireless data solutions. The company's current product portfolio includes revolutionary wireless email solutions, two-way pagers, wireless personal computer card adapters and embedded radio-modems. These products are sold to a diverse range of major multinational companies including wireless network suppliers, original equipment manufacturers and value-added resellers. Headquartered in Waterloo, Ontario and founded in 1984, RIM currently employs over 330 people. Graduates most likely to be hired come from the following academic areas: Computer Science, Electrical, Computer, Systems Design, Mechanical Engineering, Electronics Engineering Technology and Business Administration. Graduates would occupy a variety of positions within either Software Engineering, Hardware Engineering, Manufacturing or Sales and Marketing. A strong interest in technology, flexibility, creativity, initiative, demonstrated team player skills, enthusiasm, time management and a positive attitude are all listed as desirable non-academic qualifications. Company benefits and the potential for advancement are both rated as excellent. The average annual starting salary depends upon the position being considered and the applicants background. The preferred method for initial contact by those seeking employment is to e-mail a resume with a covering letter to the attention of Organizational Development. Research in Motion Limited hires co-op students in all areas of the organization on four month rotating terms all year round. *Contact:* Organizational Development.

RESTAURANTS NORMANDIN INC., LES
2335, boul Bastien
Quebec, QC G2B 1B3

Tel.	418-842-9160
Fax	418-842-8916

Les Restaurants Normandin Inc. is a restaurant company with 27 locations, including corporate and franchise locations. There are approximately 45 employees at the head office and 1,300 throughout the province of Quebec. Head office, located in Quebec will recruit and select Restaurant Managers and Assistant Managers for each facility as well as support staff and management. Graduates most likely to be hired come from the following academic areas: Bachelor of Arts (Sociology), Bachelor of Science (Computer Science, Nutritional Sciences), Bachelor of Engineering (Food Processing, Automation/Robotics, Instrumentation), Bachelor of Commerce/Business Administration (General, Accounting, Finance, Human Resources, Marketing), Chartered Accountant, Certified Management Accountant, Certified General Accountant and Community College Diploma (Accounting, Admin-

istration, Advertising, Business, Communications, Facility Management, Human Resources, Marketing/Sales, Purchasing/Logistics, Secretarial, CAD/CAM/Autocad, Computer Science). Graduates are hired to occupy Manager, Associate Manager, Assistant Manager, Marketing Assistant, Human Resources Assistant and Computer Programmer positions. Restaurant or food market experience is listed as a desirable non-academic qualification. The most suitable method for initial contact by those seeking employment is to mail a resume with a covering letter to the Human Resource Department. *Contacts:* Jean Dénommé, Director, Human Resources or Maude Gallichand, Assistant Director, Human Resources.

REUTERS INFORMATION SERVICES (CANADA) LIMITED
121 King Street West, Suite 2000
Toronto, ON M5H 3T9

Tel.	416-941-8000
Fax	416-941-9064
Email	canada.employment@reuters.com
Website	www.reuters.ca

Reuters Information Services (Canada) Limited, Reuters Canada Division is the Canadian arm of Reuters Holdings PLC, the world's leading news and information organization. For the financial community, Reuters provides real-time and delayed price information on every financial market in the world, and global coverage of business and market news. Reuters obtains information from exchanges and over-the-counter markets and from a vast network of journalists, photographers and camera persons. Reuters distributes this information through video terminals and teleprinters, using the latest technology to inform the world. The division employs approximately 123 people across Canada. Graduates most likely to be hired come from the following academic areas: Master of Business Administration (General), Bachelor of Arts (General), Bachelor of Science (General, Computer Science), Bachelor of Commerce/Business Administration, Chartered Accountant, Certified Management Accountant and Community College Diploma (Accounting, Business, Journalism). Graduates would occupy Account Executive, Account Support Representative, Sales Specialist, Client Administrator, Technician and Journalist positions. Strategic thinking, dynamic, energetic, entrepreneurial, innovative and creativity are all listed as desirable non-academic qualifications. Company benefits are rated above average. The potential for advancement is listed as average. The average annual starting salary falls within the $45,000 to $50,000 range, dependent on the position being considered. The most suitable methods for initial contact by those seeking employment are to mail, fax or e-mail a resume with a covering letter. *Contact:* Sharon E. Greenholt, Director, Human Resources and Facilities.

REUTERS INFORMATION SERVICES (CANADA) LIMITED
130 King Street West, Suite 2000, The Exchange Tower
Toronto, ON M5X 1E3

Tel.	416-350-5427
Fax	416-364-9017
Website	www.reuters.com

Reuters Information Services (Canada) Limited, Data Services Division provides up-to-the-second information to the international financial markets. Reuters is the world's leading provider of financial information, providing quality data to analysts and key decision makers in business, finance and government. Located in downtown Toronto, the Data Services Division builds timeseries databases in the areas of equities, energy, commodities, options, fixed income, foreign exchange, money markets and economics. The division consists of the Data Group, the Numeric Database Technology Group and the Technical Operations Group. There are 230 employees at this location and a total of 500 employees in Canada. Graduates most likely to be hired come from the following academic areas: Bachelor of Arts (Economics), Bachelor of Science (Computer Science, Mathematics), Bachelor of Engineering (Electrical, Computer Systems) and the Canadian Securities Course accreditation. Graduates would occupy Data Analyst and Programmer/Analyst positions. Team player, detail oriented, analytical and excellent written and oral communication skills are all listed as desirable non-academic qualifications. Company benefits and the potential for advancement are both rated as excellent. The average annual starting salary falls within the $40,000 to $45,000 range. The most suitable method for initial contact by those seeking employment is to fax a resume with a covering letter. Reuters Information Services (Canada) Limited, Data Services Division does hire co-op work term students. *Contact:* Human Resources Department.

REVENUE CANADA, INFORMATION TECHNOLOGY BRANCH
875 Heron Road, Suite 5082
Ottawa, ON K1A 0L8

Tel. 613-954-9105
Fax 613-941-3799
Website .... www.rc.gc.ca

Revenue Canada is responsible for Canadian tax, trade, and border administration. The department draws its mandate from a federal statute, the Department of National Revenue Act, which gives the Minister of National Revenue federal responsibility for controlling, regulating, managing and supervising income and consumption taxes, as well as customs and excise duties. The Minister is also responsible for controlling the movement of people and goods into Canada. Revenue Canada carries out its mandate through four business lines: revenue generation, trade policy administration, customs border services, and income redistribution. Graduates most likely to be hired for the Information Technology Branch of Revenue Canada must have an University Degree from a recognized institution in Information Systems, Computer Science or Software Engineering. Graduates would occupy Programmers/Analyst, Technology Specialist, Database Administrator, Systems Programmer/Analyst, and LAN Support Specialist positions. Team player, strong interpersonal skills, good judgment, reliability and motivation are all listed as desirable non-academic qualifications. Company benefits are rated as industry standard. The potential for advancement is listed as being good. The average annual starting salary falls within the $30,000 to $35,000 range. The most suitable method for initial contact by those seeking employment is to apply through Revenue Canada's website. Revenue Canada - Information Technology Branch does hire students for summer and co-op work terms. *Contact:* Career Opportunities.

REYNOLDS AND REYNOLDS (CANADA) LTD.
2470 Milltower Court
Mississauga, ON L5N 7W5

Tel. 905-813-7992
Fax 905-813-6101
Email .... hr@reyrey.com
Website .... www.reyrey.com

Reynolds and Reynolds (Canada) Ltd. is a recognized leader in providing information systems, information management products and value added services for its customers in the automotive marketplace. Reynolds and Reynolds employs approximately 311 people in Canada and 4,500 people worldwide. Graduates most likely to be hired come from the following academic areas: Bachelor of Arts (General, Economics), Bachelor of Science (Computer Science), Bachelor of Engineering (Computer Systems), Bachelor of Commerce/Business Administration (Human Resources, Information Systems, Marketing), Master of Business Administration (Human Resources, Information Systems, Marketing) and Community College Diploma (Administration, Business, Human Resources, Marketing/Sales, Secretarial, Computer Science), and High School Diploma. Graduates would occupy various positions in manufacturing and computer systems/operations. Related work experience, initiative, drive, self starter, positive attitude, attendance and punctuality and involvement in community and career related associations are all listed as desirable non-academic qualifications. Company benefits are rated as industry standard. The potential for advancement is listed as average. The average annual starting salary falls within the $25,000 to $30,000 range. The most suitable method for initial contact by those seeking employment is to mail a resume with a covering letter. *Contacts:* Christine Pascoe, Manager, Human Resources/Payroll or Christine Smith, Human Resources Specialist.

RICHARD & B. A. RYAN LIMITED
78 Logan Avenue
Toronto, ON M4M 2M8

Tel. 416-461-0791
Fax 416-461-7606

Richard & B. A. Ryan Limited is a general contractor and construction management firm. Activities include industrial, commercial and institutional construction. The company employs more than 50 people. Graduates most likely to be hired come from the following academic areas: Bachelor of Engineering (Civil, Architectural/Building), Bachelor of Commerce/Business Administration (Accounting), Chartered Accountant, Certified General Accountant, Community College Diploma (Accounting, Engineering Technician) and High School Diploma. Graduates would occupy Project Manager, Estimator and Superintendent positions. Company benefits are rated as excellent. The potential for advancement is listed as being good. The average annual starting salary falls within the $20,000 to $30,000 range. The most suitable method for initial contact by those seeking employment is to mail a resume with a covering letter. Richard & B. A. Ryan Limited does hire summer students on a regular basis. *Contacts:* Mr. Y. Loisel, President & C.E.O. or Mr. B. Bridle, Purchasing Manager.

RICHTER, USHER & VINEBERG
2 Place Alexis Nihon, Suite 2230
Montreal, QC H3Z 3C2

Tel. 514-934-3400
Fax 514-934-3408

Email .... mtlinfo@richter.ca
Website .... www.richter.ca

Richter, Usher & Vineberg was founded in 1926 and today has grown to offer a wide range of business services. Services provided include accounting, auditing, management consulting, taxation, insolvency consulting, business counselling, financial litigation and business valuation. Graduates most likely to be hired come from the following academic areas: Bachelor of Engineering (Computer Systems), Bachelor of Commerce/Business Administration (General, Accounting, Finance, Information Systems), Chartered Accountant, Certified Management Accountant, Certified General Accountant, Master of Business Administration (General, Information Systems) and Community College Diploma (Accounting, Administration, Secretarial). Graduates would occupy Audit Trainee, Audit Technician, Tax Technician, Chartered Accountant, Secretary, Typist, Clerk, Systems Analyst, Programmer, Project Leader, Systems Trainer and Customer Service Technician positions. Good communication skills, team player, dynamic, self-starter and strong interpersonal skills are all listed as desirable non-academic qualifications. The most suitable method for initial contact by those seeking employment is to mail a resume with a covering letter. Richter, Usher & Vineberg does hire summer students. (Toronto Location: 90 Eglinton Avenue East, Toronto, Ontario, M4P 2Y3; Phone 416-932-8000; Fax 416-932-6200). *Contact:* Human Resources Department.

RICOH/SAVIN CANADA INC., DOCUMENT DIRECTION LTD.
4100 Yonge Street, Suite 414
Toronto, ON M2P 2B5

Tel. 416-218-4360
Fax 416-218-4381
Website .... www.ricoh.ca

Ricoh/Savin Canada Inc., Document Direction Ltd. is a leader in the fast-growing color copier market and major supplier of copiers and facsimile products, digital duplicators and management services. Ricoh/Savin Canada Inc., Document Direction Ltd.'s parent company, Ricoh Corporation was founded in 1936 and has long been regarded as a leading manufacturer in the office equipment industry. Graduates most likely to be hired come from the following academic areas: Bachelor of Arts (General, Economics, English, History, Political Science), Bachelor of Science (General), Bachelor of Engineering (General), Bachelor of Commerce/Business Administration (General, Information, Marketing), Master of Business Administration (General, Information Systems, Marketing), Master of Arts (Economics) and Community College Diploma (Advertising, Business, Marketing/Sales, Information Systems). Graduates would occupy Account Manager and Sales Representative positions. Self starter, highly motivated, articulate, personable, well organized, focused and previous sales experience are all listed as desirable non-academic qualifications. Company benefits are rated as industry standard. The potential for advancement is listed as being good. The average annual starting salary falls within the $25,000 to $30,000 range. The most suitable method for initial contact by those seeking employment is to fax a resume with a covering letter. *Contacts:* David Armstrong or Toni Filipelli.

RIDLEY COLLEGE
PO Box 3013
St. Catharines, ON L2R 7C3

Tel. 905-684-8193

Fax 905-684-8875
Email .... admission@ridley.on.ca
Website .... www.ridley.on.ca

Ridley College is an independent, co-educational, residential school offering an advanced academic program in grades 5 through 13 (OAC). The college employs approximately 150 personnel, including teaching, administration and support staff. Graduates most likely to be hired come from the following academic areas: Bachelor of Education (General, Primary Junior, Junior Intermediate, Intermediate Senior, Physical and Health). Company benefits are rated above average. The potential for advancement is listed as being good. The average annual starting salary falls within the $35,000 to $40,000 range for teaching positions. The most suitable method for initial contact by those seeking employment is to mail a resume with a covering letter. Ridley College does hire summer students. *Contacts:* Rupert Lane, Headmaster or Lowell Scott, Director of Academics.

RIO ALTO EXPLORATION LTD.
205 - 5th Avenue SW, Suite 2500
Calgary, AB T2P 2V7

Tel. 403-264-8780
Fax 403-261-7626
Email .... lizg@ rioalto.com

Rio Alto Exploration Ltd. is an oil and gas production company based in Calgary, Alberta. The company's focus is on exploration, development and production, with an emphasis on meeting production and financial targets. This emphasis makes Rio Alto one of the lowest cost operators in the industry. There are 97 employees at this location and a total of 236 employees in Canada. Graduates most likely to be hired come from the following academic areas: Bachelor of Science (Geology), Bachelor of Engineering (General, Mechanical, Environmental/Resources, Geological Engineering, Petroleum/Fuels), Bachelor of Commerce/Business Administration (Accounting, Human Resources, Marketing), Chartered Accountant, Certified Management Accountant, Master of Business Administration (Accounting, Marketing), Master of Engineering and Community College Diploma (Accounting, Administration, Financial Planning, Human Resources). Graduates would occupy Accountant, Accounting Clerk, Human Resources Assistant, Engineer and Geologist positions. Competent, team player, and good verbal and written communication skills are all listed as desirable non-academic qualifications. Company benefits are rated above average. The potential for advancement is listed as excellent. The average annual starting salary is dependent upon the position being considered. The most suitable method for initial contact by those seeking employment is to fax a resume with a covering letter. Rio Alto Exploration Ltd. does hire summer and co-op work term students. *Contact:* Liz Ganton.

RISDON AMS (CANADA) INC.
137 John Street
Barrie, ON L4N 2L1

Tel. 705-726-6571
Fax 705-726-2812

Risdon AMS (Canada) Inc. specializes in the manufacture of plastic lipstick containers using the injection molding, hot die stamping and auto assembly processes. Risdon AMS (Canada) Inc. is part of the global Health and Beauty Division of Crown Cork & Seal Company, Inc. Headquartered in Philadelphia, Pennsylvania, Crown Cork & Seal currently operates 223 plants located in 49 countries and employs 38,459 people worldwide. Risdon AMS (Canada) Inc. operates three shifts on a five, six or seven day basis and employs a total of 270 people. Graduates most likely to be hired come from the following academic areas: Bachelor of Engineering (Automation/Robotics, Mechanical, Industrial Design, Industrial Production, Quality Engineer - ASQC), Master of Business Administration (Finance, Human Resources), Community College Diploma (Accounting, Administration, Business, Human Resources, Marketing/Sales, Purchasing/Logistics, Engineering Technician, Mold Maker) and High School Diploma. Graduates would occupy Moldmaker, Injection Molding Technician, Automation/Robotics Technician, Engineer and various Administrative positions. Previous injection molding experience, a high energy level, self starter and team player are all listed as desirable non-academic qualifications. Company benefits are rated above average. The potential for advancement is listed as average. The most suitable method for initial contact by those seeking employment is to mail a resume with a covering letter. Risdon AMS (Canada) Inc. does hire summer students. *Contact:* Human Resources Manager.

ROAD RESCUE CANADA INC. / MR. RESCUE
16 Four Seasons Place, Suite 206
Etobicoke, ON M9B 6E7

Tel. 416-626-0191
Fax 416-626-9998
Email .... est_cyr@mrrescue.com

Road Rescue Canada Inc. / Mr. Rescue provides call centre services. The company employs 13 people in Canada and a total of 220 people worldwide. Graduates most likely to be hired come from the following academic areas: Bachelor of Arts (General, Geography), Bachelor of Science (General), Bachelor of Engineering (Computer Systems), Bachelor of Education (General) and Bachelor of Commerce/Business Administration (General, Accounting, Human Resources). Graduates would occupy CSR, Accounts Payable and Quality Assurance Representative positions. Two years previous call centre experience, energetic, results oriented, detailed, professional, reliable, bilingual, excellent communication skills and a good knowledge of Canada's geography are all listed as desirable non-academic qualifications. Company benefits are rated as industry standard. The potential for advancement is listed as being excellent. The average annual starting salary falls within the $25,000 to $30,000 range. The most suitable method for initial contact by those seeking employment is to fax a resume with a covering letter. Road Rescue Canada Inc. / Mr. Rescue does hire summer and co-op work term students. *Contacts:* Edwin St-Cyr, Assistant Manager or Marisa Perrone.

ROBCO INC.
7200 St. Patrick
La Salle, QC H8N 2W7

Tel. 514-368-2723
Fax 514-367-4884

Robco Inc. manufactures and distributes industrial sealing and maintenance repair products for all sorts of industry. Robco Inc. employs 160 people at this location, and a total of 225 people across Canada. Graduates most likely to be hired come from the following academic areas: Bachelor of Arts (General), Bachelor of Science (General, Chemistry, Computer Science, Forestry), Bachelor of Engineering (General, Chemical, Industrial Chemistry, Materials Science, Metallurgy, Pollution Treatment,

Pulp and Paper, Computer Systems, Mechanical, Industrial Design, Industrial Production, Marine, Forest Resources, Mining, Petroleum, Water Resources), Bachelor of Commerce/Business Administration (Accounting, Finance, Information Systems, Marketing), Chartered Accountant, Certified Management Accountant, Certified General Accountant, Master of Business Administration (Accounting, Finance, Marketing) and Community College Diploma (Accounting, CAD/CAM/Autocad, Forestry). Self-starter and entrepreneurial are both listed as desirable non-academic qualifications. Company benefits are rated as industry standard. The potential for advancement is listed as excellent. The average annual starting salary falls within the $20,000 to $25,000 range. The most suitable method for initial contact by those seeking employment is to mail a resume with a covering letter. Robco Inc. does hire summer students. *Contacts:* Mr. R. Duguay or Mr. J. T. White.

ROBERTS COMPANY CANADA LIMITED
2070 Steeles Avenue
Bramalea, ON L6T 1A7

Tel. 905-791-4444
Fax 905-791-1998

Roberts Company Canada Limited is a manufacturer of floor covering installation products and accessories, including adhesives, smoothedge, and tape. The company employs more than 25 people. Graduates most likely to be hired come from the following academic areas: Bachelor of Science (Chemistry), Bachelor of Engineering (Industrial), Bachelor of Commerce/Business Administration (Marketing), Chartered Accountant (Finance), Certified General Accountant, Community College Diploma (Administration, Business) and High School Diploma. Graduates would occupy Laboratory Technician, Marketing Assistant and Accounting positions. Applicants should be a suitable match with the company. Company benefits are rated above average. The potential for advancement is limited due to the company's size, and is therefore listed as average. Although job vacancies in the areas listed are rare, the most suitable method for initial contact by graduates seeking employment is to mail a resume with a covering letter. Roberts Company Canada Limited does hire 2 to 3 summer students annually for general labour positions. *Contact:* Human Resources Manager.

ROCKWELL AUTOMATION CANADA
135 Dundas Street
Cambridge, ON N1R 5X1

Tel. 519-740-4100
Fax 519-740-4111
Email .... racambhumanresources@ra.rockwell.com
Website .... www.automation.rockwell.com

Rockwell Automation Canada, a subsidiary of Milwaukee, Wisconsin based Rockwell Automation, creates automation solutions for companies worldwide. The company produces more than 500,000 products carrying brand names that have been providing automation solutions for nearly a century. Rockwell's brands include Allen-Bradley, Reliance Electric, Dodge and Rockwell Software. These brands are known for their leading-edge technology and responsiveness to customers' needs. Rockwell Automation is represented in over 80 countries and employs over 25,000 employees worldwide. Rockwell Automation Canada employs 850 people at this location and a total of 1,300 people in Canada. Graduates most likely to be hired come from the following academic areas:

Bachelor of Arts (Economics), Bachelor of Science (Computer Science), Bachelor of Engineering (Electrical, Mechanical, Automation/Robotics, Industrial Engineering), Bachelor of Commerce/Business Administration (Accounting, Finance, Information Systems, Marketing), Master of Engineering (Power Electronics) and Community College Diploma (Accounting, Human Resources, Marketing/Sales, Purchasing/Logistics, CAD/CAM/Autocad, Electronics Technician, Engineering Technician). Graduates would occupy Trainee, Manufacturing Specialist, Application Engineering Specialist, Programmer, Network Analyst, Financial Analyst, Product Support Specialist and Designer positions. Team working skills are listed as desirable non-academic qualifications. Company benefits and the potential for advancement are both rated as excellent. The average annual starting salary falls within the $35,000 to $40,000 range. The most suitable method for initial contact by those seeking employment is to fax a resume with a covering letter. Rockwell Automation Canada does hire summer and co-op work term students. *Contacts:* Rob Page, Senior Human Resources Representative or Ross Russell, Senior Human Resources Representative.

ROCTEST LTEE
665, avenue Pine
St-Lambert, QC J4P 2P4

Tel.	450-465-1113
Fax	450-465-1938
Email	info@roctest.com
Website	www.roctest.com

Roctest Ltée specializes in the manufacture and marketing of high-technology instruments designed for monitoring major civil engineering and environmental projects. By measuring parameters such as pressure, bearing capacity, permeability, displacement, deformation and inclination, its instruments can assess the stability and potential risks of failure of large-scale construction works. Roctest instruments and monitoring systems are incorporated into hundreds of dams, mines, tunnels, nuclear power stations, buildings and bridges in over 75 countries. Founded in 1967, the company employs 55 people at this location, a total of 75 in Canada and 120 people worldwide. Graduates most likely to be hired come from the following academic areas: Bachelor of Science (General, Environment/Ecology, Geology, Meteorology/Climatology) and Bachelor of Engineering (Environment/Resources, Geological, Industrial Engineering, Instrumentation, Mining, Petroleum/Fuels, Pollution Treatment, Power/Hydro, Water Resources). Graduates would occupy Production Technician, R&D Technician, Production Engineer, R&D Engineer, Junior Accountant, Sales Representative and Project Director positions. Company benefits are rated above average. The potential for advancement is listed as being good. The average annual starting salary falls within the $20,000 to $30,000 range. The most suitable methods for initial contact by those seeking employment are to mail, fax or e-mail a resume with a covering letter. Roctest Ltée does hire summer students. *Contact:* Human Resources.

ROGERS BROADCASTING LIMITED
36 Victoria Street
Toronto, ON M5C 1H3

Tel.	416-864-2000
Fax	416-864-2133
Website	www.rogers.com

Rogers Broadcasting Limited is a radio and television broadcaster. Broadcasting activities includes both AM and FM stations across Canada, the multicultural television station CFMT in Toronto and The Shopping Channel. There are 120 employees at this location, and a total of 1,200 employees across Canada. Graduates most likely to be hired come from the following academic areas: Bachelor of Engineering (Computer Systems), and Community College Diploma (Accounting, Administration, Marketing/Sales, Secretarial, Graphic Arts, Television/Radio Arts). Graduates would occupy Accountant, Accounting Clerk, Administrator, Administrative Assistant, Sales Representative, Copy Writer, Radio Talent, and Television/Radio Technical Crew positions. Natural talent (for on-air work), industry related work experience (eg. radio/television station experience), flexibility, commitment and aptitude are all listed as desirable non-academic qualifications. Company benefits are rated as excellent. The potential for advancement is listed as being good. The average annual starting salary falls within the $20,000 to $25,000 range, depending on the position being considered, geographic location, and the experience of the applicant. For certain positions the salary is commission based. The most suitable method for initial contact by those seeking employment is to mail a resume with a covering letter. *Contact:* Human Resources Administrator.

ROGERS CABLESYSTEMS LIMITED
855 York Mills Rd.
Toronto, ON M3B 1Z1

Tel.	416-466-6500
Fax	877-935-5627
Website	www.rogers.com

Rogers Cablesystems Limited is Canada's largest cable television company, serving more than two million customers in Ontario and British Columbia. Rogers provides a full suite of cable products and services, including Rogers@Home high speed access to the internet via cable. Rogers Cablesystems Limited employs 3,000 people in Canada. Graduates most likely to be hired come from the following academic areas: Bachelor of Arts (General), Bachelor of Science (Computer Science), Bachelor of Engineering (Electrical, Computer Systems, Telecommunications), Bachelor of Commerce/Business Administration (Accounting, Finance, Human Resources, Information Systems, Marketing), Chartered Accountant, Certified Management Accountant, Certified General Accountant, Master of Business Administration (Accounting, Finance, Human Resources, Information Systems, Marketing) and Community College Diploma (Accounting, Business, Human Resources, Television/Radio Arts/Broadcasting). Graduates would occupy Finance, Sales, Marketing, Human Resources, Administration, Customer Service, Technical Service, Maintenance, Network Management and Television Programming positions. Company benefits and the potential for advancement are both rated as excellent. The average annual starting salary depends upon the position being considered. The most suitable method for initial contact by those seeking employment is through the company's website. Rogers Cablesystems Limited does hire summer students. *Contact:* Human Resources.

ROGERS CANTEL INC.
333 Bloor Street East, 3rd Floor
Toronto, ON M6W 1G9

Tel.	416-935-3112
Fax	416-935-3111

Email .... cjaswal@rci.rogers.com
Website .... www.cantelatt.com

Rogers Cantel Inc. is Canada's largest national wireless telecommunications company. The company offers customers a broad spectrum of wireless products and services and is currently the only company in Canada licensed to provide cellular, digital PCS, paging and wireless data services nationwide. Rogers Cantel Inc. has offices in Montreal, Toronto, Halifax, Vancouver, Calgary and Winnipeg. There are 1,600 employees at this location and a total of 2,800 employees across Canada. Graduates most likely to be hired come from the following academic areas: Bachelor of Arts (General), Bachelor of Science (Computer Science), Bachelor of Engineering (Electrical, Computer Systems, Telecommunications), Bachelor of Commerce/Business Administration (General, Finance, Human Resources, Information Systems, Marketing), Master of Business Administration (Marketing) and Community College Diploma (Business, Human Resources, Office Administration, Electronics Technician, Engineering Technician). Graduates would occupy Network Technician, Programmer/Analyst, Switch Engineer, Radio Engineer, Customer Service Consultant, Financial Analyst and Human Resource Administrator positions. Team work skills, achievement and customer service oriented, and good listening, understanding and responding skills are all listed as desirable non-academic qualifications. Company benefits are rated above average. The potential for advancement is listed as being excellent. The average annual starting salary falls within the $30,000 to $35,000 range. The most suitable methods for initial contact by those seeking employment are to fax a resume with a covering letter, or through the company's website. Rogers Cantel Inc. does hire summer and co-op work term students. *Contact:* Corporate Recruiter.

ROGERS VIDEO
10100 Shellbridge Way, Suite 100
Richmond, BC V6X 2W7

Tel. 604-270-9200
Fax 604-270-4530

Rogers Video is Canada's largest Canadian-owned video retailer, with more than 200 video retail stores located in British Columbia, Alberta, Saskatchewan, Manitoba and Ontario. A division of Rogers Cablesystems Limited, Rogers Video employs over 2,600 people across the country. Graduates most likely to be hired come from the following academic areas: Bachelor of Arts (General), Bachelor of Science (General, Computer Science), Bachelor of Commerce/Business Administration (General, Accounting, Finance, Human Resources, Information Systems, Marketing, Public Administration) and Community College Diploma (Accounting, Advertising, Business, Communications/Public Relations, Facility Management, Human Resources, Marketing/Sales, Office Administration, Purchasing/Logistics, Real Estate Sales, Secretarial, Information Systems). Excellent team work, communication and customer service skills are all listed as desirable non-academic qualifications. Company benefits are rated above average. The potential for advancement is listed as being good. The average annual starting salary falls within the $20,000 to $25,000 range. The most suitable method for initial contact by those seeking employment is to fax a resume with a covering letter. Rogers Video does hire summer and co-op work term students. *Contacts:* Vice President, Human Resources or Regional Human Resources Manager.

ROSEMOUNT INSTRUMENTS LIMITED
808 - 55th Avenue NE
Calgary, AB T2E 6Y4

Tel. 403-275-8400
Fax 403-275-2856

Rosemount Instruments Limited is the Canadian division of Fisher-Rosemount, the world's leading manufacturer of industrial process instrumentation. Rosemount Instruments has sales offices across Canada, with headquarters and a manufacturing plant in Calgary. Through Fisher-Rosemount, and its parent corporation, Emerson Electric Co., Rosemount employees have the opportunity to take on assignments around the world. There are approximately 70 employees here at the Calgary location, a total of 150 employees across Canada, and through Emerson Electric Co., there are 60,000 employees worldwide. Graduates most likely to be hired come from the following academic areas: Bachelor of Science (Chemistry, Environmental), Bachelor of Engineering (Chemical, Instrumentation, Resources/Environmental), Chartered Accountant, Certified Management Accountant, Certified General Accountant and Community College Diploma (Accounting, Secretarial, Industrial Instrumentation). Graduates would occupy Inside/Outside Instrument Sales, Product Marketing Specialist, Accountant, Secretary, Service and Technical positions. Relevant work experience, personal initiative, positive outlook and a customer focus are all listed as desirable non-academic qualifications. The most suitable method for initial contact by those seeking employment is to mail a resume with a covering letter. *Contact:* Human Resources Manager.

ROSS ROY COMMUNICATIONS CANADA LIMITED
1737 Walker Road, PO Box 2235
Windsor, ON N8Y 4R8

Tel. 519-258-7584
Fax 519-258-4242

Ross Roy Communications Canada Limited is a below-the-line advertiser and merchandiser for large automobile clients. Activities include training, direct marketing, telemarketing, print production and new car announcement shows for sales personnel. The company employs approximately 130 people. Graduates most likely to be hired come from the following academic areas: Bachelor of Arts (English, French, Fine Arts/Graphic Arts, Journalism), Bachelor of Science (Computer Science), Bachelor of Engineering (Mechanical, Computer Systems), Bachelor of Commerce/Business Administration (General, Accounting, Finance, Human Resources, Information Systems, Marketing, Public Administration), Chartered Accountant, Certified Management Accountant, Certified General Accountant, Master of Business Administration (General, Accounting, Finance, Human Resources, Information Systems, Marketing, Public Administration) and Community College Diploma (Accounting, Advertising, Business, Communications/Public Relations, Human Resources, Marketing/Sales, Office Administration, Secretarial, Audio/Visual Technician, Automotive Mechanic, Computer Science, Electronics Technician). Graduates would occupy positions in the following areas: Accounting, Human Resources, Administration, Operations, Marketing, Information Services, Creative Writing and Creative Art/Design. Positions include: Administrative Assistant, English and French Proofreader, Bilingual Telephone Service Representative, Technical Analyst/Specialist, Programmer, Payroll Administrator, Billing Clerk, Human Resources Assistant, Account Administrator, Account Executive, Shows/Meeting Administrator, Shows/Meeting Executive, Copy Writer and Art Director. Relevant work experience, excellent interpersonal and communication skills, a strong work ethic and an ability to work under pressure are core competencies required and preferred in successful candidates. Ross Roy offers market competitive salaries, an attractive benefits package and is committed to providing a work environment conducive to employee development, advancement and retention. The most suitable methods for initial contact by those seeking employment are to mail a resume with a covering letter, or through recruitment agencies. Ross Roy Communications Canada Limited does hire summer and co-op work term students. *Contacts:* Sairoz Kovacs, Director, Human Resources or Jean Winn, Human Resources Consultant.

Rouge Valley

Health System

Centenary Health Centre

ROUGE VALLEY HEALTH SYSTEM
2867 Ellesmere Road
Toronto, ON M1E 4B9

Tel.	416-281-7271
Fax	416-281-7417

The Rouge Valley Health System is renowned for providing quality health care services to the communities in which it operates. The Rouge Valley Health System was formed through the amalgamation of the Centenary Health Centre and the Ajax and Pickering Health Centre. There are 2,200 employees at the Centenary Health Centre Site (this location) and 750 employees at the Ajax and Pickering Health Centre Site (address listed below). Graduates most likely to be hired come from the following academic areas: Bachelor of Science (Audiology, Nursing, Nutritional Sciences, Occupational Therapy, Pharmacy, Physiotherapy, Speech Pathology), Bachelor of Education (Early Childhood), Bachelor of Commerce/Business Administration (Finance, Human Resources, Information Systems), Chartered Accountant (Finance), Certified Management Accountant (Finance), Certified General Accountant (Finance), Master of Business Administration (General), Master of Science (Nursing, Psychology), Master of Social Work and Community College Diploma (Accounting, Communications/Public Relations, Human Resources, Secretarial, Security/Enforcement, Electronics Technician, Health/Home Care Aide, Laboratory Technician, Nuclear Medicine, Nursing RN/RNA, Radiology, Respiratory Therapy, Ultrasound Technician). Excellent organizational, communication and interpersonal skills, previous experience in a health care or hospital setting, computer skills and the ability to work within a team and in a hectic environment are all listed as desirable non-academic qualifications. Company benefits are rated as excellent. The potential for advancement is listed as being good. The average annual starting salary is dependent upon the position being considered. The most suitable method for initial contact by graduates seeking employment is to mail a resume with a covering letter. (Ajax and Pickering Health Centre Site: 580 Harwood Avenue South, Ajax, Ontario, L1S 2J4; Phone 905-683-2320; Fax 905-683-2618). *Contact:* Employment Services.

ROYAL BANK FINANCIAL GROUP
970 Lawrence Avenue West, Suite 110
Toronto, ON M6A 3B6

Tel.	416-256-0088
Fax	416-256-0169
Email	emp@rb-erc.com
Website	www.royalbank.com

Royal Bank Financial Group is Canada's premier financial services group and one of North America's largest financial institutions. Royal Bank and its key subsidiaries, Royal Trust, RBC Dominion Securities, RBC Insurance and Royal Bank Action Direct employ 58,134 people who serve 10 million clients through 1,500 branches and offices in 36 countries. Graduates most likely to be hired come from the following academic areas: Bachelor of Arts (General, Economics), Bachelor of Science (Actuarial, Computer Science, Mathematics), Bachelor of Commerce/Business Administration (General, Accounting, Finance, Human Resources, Information Systems, Marketing), Chartered Accountant, Certified Management Accountant, Certified General Accountant, Master of Business Administration (General, Accounting, Finance, Human Resources, Information Systems, Marketing, Public Administration), Master of Arts (Economics), Master of Science (Computer Science) and Community College Diploma (Accounting, Administration, Advertising, Business, Human Resources, Information Systems, Marketing/Sales, Computer Science). Graduates would enter Career Management Programs. In 1997, Royal Bank invested more than $100 million in employee training. Achievement, motivation, impact and influence, customer service skills, initiative, leadership skills, teamwork and adaptability are all listed as desirable non-academic qualifications. Company benefits and the potential for advancement are both rated as excellent. The average annual starting salary varies with the position being considered, and the education and experience of the applicant. The most suitable methods for initial contact by those seeking employment are to mail, fax or e-mail a resume with a covering letter, or by applying through the Royal Bank's website. Interested applicants should visit Royal Bank's website to learn more about products, services and career opportunities. Royal Bank Financial Group does hire summer and co-op work term students. The company values diversity in the workplace and is committed to employment equity. *Contact:* Employment Resources Centre.

ROYAL HOST CORPORATION/TRAVELODGE CANADA
5940 Macleod Trail South, Suite 500
Calgary, AB T2H 2G4

Tel.	403-259-9800
Fax	403-255-6981
Email	bannon@royalhost.com
Website	www.travelodge.com

Royal Host Corporation is a specialist entity of the Royal Host Real Estate Investment Trust / REIT, dedicated to hotel and resort management. The company seeks to develop standards and an improved bottom line for investors in the Royal Host Real Estate Investment Trust and other private owners/investors. The REIT is also the parent company for Travelodge Canada, the master franchiser of Travelodge and Thriftlodge. There are over 80 employees at the corporate office in Calgary with responsibilities for managing hotels in Canada and the United States. Graduates most likely to be hired come from the following academic areas: Bachelor of Commerce/Business Administration (Hotel and Food Administration),

Community College Diploma (Travel and Tourism, Hotel and Catering) and High School Diploma. Graduates are hired to occupy Trainee Manager positions at the Hotel locations. Successful applicants would participate in a 12 to 18 month training program. Good interpersonal skills, leadership potential, organization skills, deadline orientation, initiative, practical hands-on ability and an enthusiasm for the hotel and catering industry are all listed as desirable non-academic skills. Company benefits are rated as industry standard. The potential for advancement is listed as excellent. The average annual starting salary falls within the $20,000 to $25,000 range. The most suitable method for initial contact by those seeking employment is to mail a resume with a covering letter. Summer students are hired, subject to the business demands of individual property locations. *Contact:* Sue Wadland, Vice President, Human Resources.

ROYAL LEPAGE REAL ESTATE SERVICES LTD.
39 Wynford Drive
Toronto, ON M3C 3K5

Tel. 416-510-5800
Fax 416-510-5667
Email .... humanresources@royallepage.ca
Website .... www.royallepage.ca

Royal LePage Real Estate Services Ltd. is the largest full service real estate company in Canada. Activities include residential, commercial and investment real estate, property management, consulting, mortgage administration and real estate appraisal. Royal LePage maintains numerous locations throughout Canada. Graduates most likely to be hired come from the following academic areas: Bachelor of Arts, Bachelor of Commerce/Business Administration, Chartered Accountant, Certified Management Accountant, Master of Business Administration, Community College Diploma (General/Related) and Real Estate courses (contact your local Real Estate Board). Graduates would occupy Finance, Computer Operations, Systems, Human Resources, Appraisal, Marketing, Mortgage Administration, Consulting and commission based Sales positions. Company benefits are rated above average. The potential for advancement is listed as being good. The average annual starting salary within the $15,000 and $35,000 range, depending greatly upon the position being considered. The most suitable method for initial contact by those seeking employment is to mail a resume with a covering letter. Royal LePage Real Estate Services Ltd. does hire summer students. *Contacts:* Employment Services Co-ordinator or Human Resources.

ROYAL MERIDIEN KING EDWARD HOTEL, LE
37 King Street East
Toronto, ON M5C 1E9

Tel. 416-863-9700
Fax 416-863-3244

Le Royal Meridien King Edward Hotel is a luxury hotel located in downtown Toronto. The hotel employs more than 300 people. Graduates most likely to be hired come from the following academic areas: Bachelor of Arts (General, Languages), Community College Diploma (Business, Cook/Chef Training, Hospitality, Travel/Tourism) and Cles D'Or (Concierge). Graduates would occupy Front Office Agent, Food and Beverage Server, Chef, Kitchen Help, and Professional positions in the Business Office. Team player, proactive, quick learner, flexible and able to manage change well are all listed as desirable non-academic qualifications. Company benefits are rated above average. The potential for advancement is listed

as being good. The average annual starting salary falls within the $20,000 to $25,000 range. The most suitable method for initial contact by graduates seeking employment is to mail a resume with a covering letter. Le Royal Meridien King Edward Hotel does hire summer students, depending upon the position and the area of employment. *Contacts:* Laurie Hewson, Human Resources Director or Anne Hardacre, Human Resources Consultant.

RUBBERMAID CANADA INC.
2562 Stanfield
Mississauga, ON L4Y 1S5

Tel. 905-279-1010
Fax 905-279-2993
Website .... www.rubbermaid.com

Rubbermaid Canada Inc. is a leading manufacturer of plastic household products. Rubbermaid Canada Inc. is a subsidiary of Wooster, Ohio based Newell Rubbermaid Inc. The company is a multinational, leading-brand manufacturer and marketer of high quality, innovative products. The company is publicly-held and trades on the New York Stock Exchange under the symbol NWL. In addition to Canada, the company has operating facilities in Australia, France, Great Britain, Ireland, Japan, Korea, Luxembourg, Mexico, Poland, South Africa and the United States, and employs a total of 12,000 people around the world. Rubbermaid Canada Inc. employs approximately 310 people. Graduates most likely to be hired come from the following academic areas: Bachelor of Arts (General, Economics), Bachelor of Science (Chemistry), Bachelor of Engineering (Electrical, Industrial Production), Bachelor of Commerce/Business Administration (Finance, Human Resources, Marketing), Certified Management Accountant, Community College Diploma (Accounting, Business, Secretarial, Computer Science, Engineering Technician) and High School Diploma. Graduates would occupy Marketing Manager, Production Supervisor, Industrial Engineer, Customer Service Representative, Administrative Assistant and Production Worker positions. Community involvement and previous related work experience are listed as desirable non-academic qualifications. Company benefits are rated above average. The potential for advancement is listed as being good. The average annual starting salary falls within the $35,000 to $40,000 range. The most suitable method for initial contact by those seeking employment is to mail a resume with a covering letter. Rubbermaid Canada Inc. does hire students for summer and co-op work terms. *Contact:* Human Resources Department.

RUSSEL METALS INC.
1900 Minnesota Court, Suite 210
Mississauga, ON L5N 3C9

Tel. 905-567-8500
Fax 905-819-7292
Email .... hrdept@russelmetals.com
Website .... www.russelmetals.com

Russel Metals Inc. is involved in the processing, warehousing and distribution of steel. The company employs approximately 2,000 people worldwide. Graduates most likely to be hired come from the following academic areas: Bachelor of Science (General, Metallurgy), Bachelor of Engineering (General, Mechanical), Bachelor of Commerce/Business Administration (Accounting, Finance, Marketing, Information Systems), Chartered Accountant (Finance), Certified Management Accountant (Finance), Certified General Accountant (Finance) and Community College Diploma (Accounting, Administration, Business). Graduates would occupy Sales, Accounting and Administration positions. Team player and strong people skills are listed as desirable non-academic qualifications. The potential for advancement is listed as average. The average annual starting salary falls within the $30,000 to $35,000 range, and is ultimately dependent upon position, qualifications, and experience. The most suitable method for initial contact by graduates seeking employment is to mail a resume with a covering letter. Russel Metals Inc. does hire summer students. *Contact:* Human Resources Department.

RYDER TRANSPORTATION SERVICES
4308 Village Centre Court
Mississauga, ON L4Z 1S2

Tel.	905-276-4392
Fax	905-276-7486
Email	alagrant@ryder.com
Website	www.ryder.com

Ryder Transportation Services (Canada) provides cost-effective transportation solutions for both small and large businesses. Ryder Canada is a subsidiary of Ryder Systems Inc., which is headquartered in Miami, Florida and employs over 42,000 people in operations in Canada, the United States, South America and Europe. Ryder Transportation Services has operated in Canada for over 40 years and today employs over 800 people in a national network of 35 company operated facilities, providing services to local, regional and national companies. Headquartered in Mississauga, the company has over 8,000 vehicles, from small trucks to tractors, trailers, refrigerated and specialized equipment. Graduates most likely to be hired come from the following academic areas: Bachelor of Arts (General), Bachelor of Science (General), Bachelor of Engineering (Transportation), Bachelor of Commerce/Business Administration (General, Marketing), Master of Business Administration, Community College Diploma (Business, Marketing/Sales, Office Administration, Automotive Mechanic) and High School Diploma. Graduates would occupy Apprentice Mechanic, Rental Representative, Fuel Island Attendant, Clerical and Office Administration positions. Team player, multilingual, strong interpersonal and communication skills, and previous work experience in customer service, sales or an office environment are all listed as desirable non-academic qualifications. Company benefits are rated as competitive within the industry. The potential for advancement is listed as being excellent. The average annual starting salary falls within the $20,000 to $25,000 range. The most suitable methods for initial contact by those seeking employment are to mail, fax or e-mail a resume with a covering letter. Ryder Transportation Services does hire summer and co-op work term students. *Contact:* Al Grant, National Human Resources Manager.

S & C ELECTRIC CANADA LTD.
90 Belfield Road
Toronto, ON M9W 1G4

Tel.	416-249-9171
Fax	416-249-1893
Email	dpatten@scelectric.ca
Website	www.sandc.com

S & C Electric Canada Ltd. is a recognized leader in the manufacturing of high voltage switching and protection equipment for the electric power industry. S & C Electric Canada Ltd. is a wholly owned subsidiary of S & C Electric Company, Chicago, Illinois. There are approxi-

mately 260 employees at the Toronto location, and a total of 1,800 employees worldwide. Graduates most likely to be hired come from the following academic areas: Bachelor of Science (Computer Science), Bachelor of Engineering (Electrical, Mechanical, Computer Systems, Industrial Engineering, Industrial Production/Manufacturing, Power/Hydro), Bachelor of Commerce/Business Administration (Accounting, Finance) and Community College Diploma (Accounting, CAD/CAM/Autocad, Computer Science, Engineering Technician, Information Systems). Graduates would occupy Engineer, Technician, Technologist and Specialist positions. Self motivated, team player, positive attitude and an ability to focus on the job and the company are all listed as desirable non-academic qualifications. Company benefits are rated above average. The potential for advancement is listed as being good. The average annual starting salary for college graduates falls within the $25,000 to $30,000 range, and for university graduates it falls within the $30,000 to $35,000 range. The most suitable method for initial contact by those seeking employment is to mail a resume with a covering letter. S & C Electric Canada Ltd. does hire summer and co-op work term students. *Contacts:* Douglas J. Patten, Director Human Resources or Carmel Foster, Personnel Administrator.

SAFEHAVEN PROJECT FOR COMMUNITY LIVING, THE
3910 Bathurst Street, Suite 302
North York, ON M3H 5Z3

Tel.	416-398-6022
Fax	416-398-6026
Website	www.safehavenproj.org

The Safehaven Project for Community Living is a parent run, charitable, organization dedicated to providing community residential alternatives, respite and day programs for children and young adults who face severe physical, mental and health challenges. Incorporated in 1997, the Safehaven Project for Community Living employs 18 full time and 35 part time staff. Graduates most likely to be hired come from the following academic areas: Bachelor of Arts (General) and Community College Diploma (Social Work). Graduates would occupy Residential Support Worker positions. Team player, good communication skills, knowledge of community, and experience in paediatrics and with persons with disabilities are all listed as desirable non-academic qualifications. Company benefits are rated as industry standard. The potential for advancement is listed as being average. The average annual starting salary falls within the $25,000 to $30,000 range. The most suitable methods for initial contact by those seeking employment are to mail or fax a resume with a covering letter. The Safehaven Project for Community Living does hire summer and co-op work term students. *Contact:* Program Manager.

SAJO INC.
1212, rue Louvain Ouest
Montreal, QC H4N 1G5

Tel.	514-385-0333
Fax	514-389-8622

SAJO Inc. operates throughout Canada, the United States and Europe, providing a full range of services in the construction, renovation and project management sectors. Since 1977, SAJO has established itself as one of the most trusted specialized contractors in the construction industry and has developed into one of the largest interior finishing companies. The company's Montreal office is supported by millwork operations, architectural metal manufacturing facilities and warehouse distribution facilities. SAJO's principal services are general contracting, project management, sourcing and distribution of store fixtures. The general contracting of the firm is concentrated in the high-end fashion retail chains (interior finishing). The company also manages its customers' capital expenditure budgets. The sourcing and distribution of store fixtures involves coordinating and installing store fixtures for multiple sites. Yearly, SAJO executes more than 250 projects and 750 soft shops. The company employs a total of 100 people. Graduates most likely to be hired come from the following academic areas: Bachelor of Science (Computer Science), Bachelor of Engineering (Civil, Architectural/Building, Computer Systems, Industrial Design), Bachelor of Architecture and Community College Diploma (Architectural Technician, CAD/CAM/Autocad, Carpentry, Computer Science, Engineering Technician). Graduates would occupy Assistant Project Manager, Project Manager, Superintendent and Information Systems Technician. Good communication skills, strong interpersonal skills, multi-task oriented, eagerness to learn and improve and excellent time management skills are all listed as desirable non-academic qualifications. Company benefits are rated as industry standard. The potential for advancement is listed as excellent. The average annual starting salary falls within the $30,000 to $35,000 range. The most suitable methods for initial contact by those seeking employment are to mail or fax a resume with a covering letter, or via telephone. SAJO Inc. does hire summer and co-op work term students. *Contact:* Director of Human Resources.

SALOMON SMITH BARNEY CANADA INC.
161 Bay Street, BCE Place, Suite 4600
Toronto, ON M5J 2S1

Tel. 416-866-2300
Fax 416-866-7484
Website .... www.smithbarney.com

Salomon Smith Barney Canada Inc. is a full service global investment banking firm. Salomon Smith Barney Canada Inc. is a subsidiary of New York, New York based Salomon Smith Barney, the second largest brokerage and investment firm in the United States. Salomon Smith Barney has over 500 offices worldwide and employs over 35,000 people. Salomon Smith Barney Canada Inc. employs approximately 30 people in its Toronto office. Graduates most likely to be hired come from the following academic areas: Bachelor of Arts (Economics, Political Science), Bachelor of Science (Mathematics), Bachelor of Engineering (General), Bachelor of Commerce/Business Administration (General, Marketing), Master of Business Administration (General, Finance) and Community College Diploma (Business, Marketing/Sales). In Corporate Finance, graduates could occupy Analyst, Associate and Vice President positions. In Sales and Trading, graduates would occupy Fixed Income Sales, Fixed Income Trading and Training positions. Applicants must possess a high degree of intelligence, excellent analytical skills, aggressiveness, excellent sales skills, knowledge of the industry and very high ethical standards. Company benefits and the potential for advancement are both rated as excellent. The most suitable method for initial contact by those seeking employment is to mail a resume with a covering letter. Salomon Smith Barney Canada Inc. does hire summer students. *Contact:* Human Resources.

SANFORD CANADA
2670 Plymouth Drive
Oakville, ON L6H 5R6

Tel. 905-829-5051
Fax 905-829-3074
Website .... www.sanfordcorp.com

Sanford Canada, a division of Newell Rubbermaid, is a wholesaler of writing instruments and related products. The company employs approximately 40 people in Canada. Graduates most likely to be hired come from the following academic areas: Bachelor of Arts (General), Bachelor of Commerce/Business Administration, Chartered Accountant, Certified Management Accountant, Certified General Accountant, Master of Business Administration (General, Marketing) and Community College Diploma (Accounting, Administration, Business, Human Resources, Marketing/Sales, Secretarial). Graduates would occupy Clerical, Customer Service, Marketing and Administration positions. Self motivated, independent worker, team player and excellent communication skills are all listed as desirable non-academic qualifications. Company benefits are rated above average. The potential for advancement is listed as being good. The most suitable method for initial contact by those seeking employment is to mail a resume with a covering letter. Sanford Canada does hire summer students. *Contact:* Fiona Morrison, Human Resources and Payroll.

SAPUTO GROUP INC.
6869, boul Metropolitain Est
St-Leonard, QC H1P 1X8

Tel. 514-328-3325
Fax 514-328-3322
Email .... saprh@cam.org
Website .... www.saputo.com

Saputo Group Inc. is one of Canada's leading producers and distributors of cheese and other food products. There are 75 employees at this location and a total of 1,000 employees across Canada. Graduates most likely to be hired come from the following academic areas: Bachelor of Science (Biology, Computer Science, Microbiology), Bachelor of Engineering (General, Chemical, Mechanical, Environmental/Resources, Food Processing, Industrial Engineering, Industrial Production/Manufacturing, Instrumentation), Bachelor of Commerce/Business Administration (General, Accounting, Finance, Human Resources, Information Systems, Marketing), Chartered Accountant, Certified Management Accountant, Certified General Accountant, Community College Diploma (Accounting, Information Systems, Laboratory Technician) and High School Diploma. Graduates would occupy Clerk, Technician, Engineer, Accountant and Assistant Manager positions. Previous work experience, entrepreneurial skills, team player and creativity are all listed as desirable non-academic qualifications. Company benefits and the potential for advancement are both rated as excellent. The average annual starting salary falls within the $20,000 to $25,000 range. The most suitable method for initial contact by those seeking employment is to mail a resume with a covering letter. Saputo Group Inc. does hire summer and co-op work term students. *Contacts:* Pierre Leroux, Executive VP, Quality and Human Resources or Sylvie Gazaille, Director, Human Resources.

SASKATCHEWAN CROP INSURANCE CORPORATION / SCIC

PO Box 3000
Melville, SK S0A 2P0

Tel. 306-728-7200
Fax 306-728-7260

Saskatchewan Crop Insurance Corporation / SCIC provides crop insurance to growers in Saskatchewan. The main purpose of crop insurance is to provide customers peace of mind while they farm. SCIC employs approximately 550 people. In addition to the head office in Melville there are 21 Customer Service Offices located across the province. Within the head office there are several divisions, these include: Audits, Communications, Field Operations, Finance and Administration, Systems, Processing, Planning and Development, and Human Resources. Graduates most likely to be hired come from the following academic areas: Bachelor of Science (Actuarial, Agriculture, Computer Science), Bachelor of Engineering (Computer Systems), Bachelor of Commerce/ Business Administration (Accounting, Finance, Human Resources, Information Systems, Public Administration), Master of Business Administration (Accounting, Finance, Human Resources, Information Systems, Marketing, Public Administration), Master of Science (Agriculture, Actuarial Studies), Master of Engineering (Computer Systems), Community College Diploma (Accounting, Administration, Business, Communications, Human Resources, Secretarial, Journalism, Computer Science, Engineering Technician) and High School graduates with sufficient related work experience. Excellent interpersonal and communication skills, ambition, team player, confidence and an ability to deal with customers and fellow employees in a business setting are all listed as desirable non-academic qualifications. The most suitable method for initial contact by those seeking employment is to mail a resume with a covering letter. SCIC does hire summer students, though the number varies with program and workload changes. *Contacts:* Louise Sawyer, Manager, Employee Relations, Human Resources or Sharon Granquist, Personnel Officer, Human Resources.

SASKATCHEWAN RESEARCH COUNCIL / SRC

15 Innovation Boulevard
Saskatoon, SK S7N 2X8

Tel. 306-933-5400
Fax 306-933-7446
Website .... www.src.sk.cawww.src.sk.ca

The Saskatchewan Research Council / SRC exists to help the people of Saskatchewan develop a viable economy with quality jobs and a secure environment. A member of the Association of Provincial Research Organizations, the SRC employs 235 people, and is a leader in the province's science and technology infrastructure, through technology development, implementation and innovation. Graduates most likely to be hired come from the following academic areas: Bachelor of Science (Biology, Chemistry, Geography, Geology, Microbiology), Bachelor of Engineering (Chemical, Electrical, Mechanical), Bachelor of Commerce/Business Administration, Chartered Accountant, Certified Management Accountant, Certified General Accountant, Master of Business Administration, Master of Science (Geology, Biology, Chemistry, Microbiology), Master of Engineering (Industrial, Mechanical), Doctorate of Science (Geology, Biology, Chemistry, Microbiology), Doctorate of Engineering (Chemical, Electrical, Industrial, Mechanical) and Community College Diploma (Facility Management, CAD/CAM/ Autocad, Electronics Technician, Engineering Technician,

Laboratory Technician). Graduates would occupy Research Scientist I-IV, Research Engineer I-IV, Research Technician I-IV, Controller, Administrative Support, Human Resources, Marketing, and Facilities Manager positions. Team player, work and supervisory experience, and good interpersonal and communication skills are all listed as desirable non-academic qualifications. Company benefits are rated as industry standard. The potential for advancement is listed as good. The most suitable method for initial contact by those seeking employment is to mail a resume with a cover letter. The Saskatchewan Research Council does hire summer students. *Contact:* Human Resources.

SASKPOWER

2025 Victoria Avenue, 10SE
Regina, SK S4P 0S1

Tel. 306-566-2121
Fax 306-566-2087
Email .... hr@saskpower.com
Website .... www.saskpower.com

SaskPower is a crown-owned electrical utility which operates a number of generating stations to meet the province of Saskatchewan's demands for energy. This includes coal-fired and multi-fuel steam powered stations, as well as hydro and gas facilities. SaskPower employs a total of 2,200 people in the province. Graduates most likely to be hired come from the following academic areas: Bachelor of Arts (Journalism), Bachelor of Science (Chemistry, Computer Science, Environmental, Metallurgy), Bachelor of Engineering (Chemical, Industrial Chemistry, Metallurgy, Civil, Electrical, Instrumentation, Power, Mechanical, Welding, Environmental, Water Resources), Bachelor of Education (Adult), Bachelor of Commerce/ Business Administration (Accounting, Finance, Human Resources, Information Systems, Marketing), Chartered Accountant, Certified Management Accountant, Certified General Accountant, Master of Business Administration (Accounting, Finance, Human Resources, Information Systems, Marketing, Public Administration), Master of Engineering and Community College Diploma (Accounting, Administration, Business, Financial Planning, Human Resources, Marketing/Sales, Secretarial, Graphic Arts, Journalism, Industrial Mechanic, Instrument Mechanic, CAD/CAM/Autocad, Computer Science, Electrician, Engineering, Power Engineer, Welding, Chemical Laboratory Technician, Millwright). Graduates would occupy Engineer, Analyst, Coordinator, Consultant, Technologist, Clerk, Stenographer, Secretary, Electrician, Industrial Mechanic, Welder, Machinist, Instrument Mechanic, Chemical Technician, Power Line Technician, Power Engineer, Drafting Technician and Apprentice positions. Knowledge of business, leadership, problem solving skills, innovative, good interpersonal skills, entrepreneurial and computer literacy are all listed as desirable non-academic qualifications. Company benefits are rated as excellent. The potential for advancement is listed as being good. The average annual starting salary falls within the $25,000 to $30,000 range. The most suitable methods for initial contact by those seeking employment are to mail or e-mail a resume with a covering letter. SaskPower does hire summer and co-op work term students. *Contact:* Laurel Kopeck, Human Resources.

SASKTEL

2121 Saskatchewan Drive, Main Floor
Regina, SK S4P 3Y2

Tel. 306-777-2755
Fax 306-359-0653

Email .... human.resources@sasktel.sk.ca
Website .... www.sasktel.com

SaskTel is a highly competitive technology leader committed to delivering outstanding customer service and cost-effective communications solutions for customers in the province of Saskatchewan. The company serves 450,000 customers across Saskatchewan and employs 4,200 people who live and work in communities across the province. Graduates most likely to be hired come from the following academic areas: Bachelor of Arts (English), Bachelor of Science (Computer Science), Bachelor of Engineering (Electrical, Telecommunications), Bachelor of Commerce/Business Administration (Accounting, Finance, Human Resources, Infomation Systems, Marketing, Chartered Accountant, Certified Management Accountant, Certified General Accountant, Master of Business Administration, Community College Diploma (Accounting, Advertising, Business, Human Resources, Marketing/Sales, Secretarial, Electronics Technician, Engineering Technician) and High School Diploma. Team player, positive attitude, creative, flexible, highly skilled and focused on excellence are all listed as desirable non-academic qualifications. Company benefits are rated as excellent. The potential for advancement is listed as being good. The average annual starting salary falls within the $30,000 to $35,000 range. The most suitable methods for initial contact by those seeking employment are to mail, fax or e-mail a resume with a covering letter, or by applying through campus recruitment initiatives (see your campus career centre for details). SaskTel does hire summer and co-op work term students. *Contacts:* Allison Wills, Recruiter; Lewanna Dobray, Recruiter or Sherry Moe, Recruiter.

SBR INTERNATIONAL
14 College Street, Suite 300
Toronto, ON M5G 1K2

Tel. 416-962-7500
Fax 416-962-7503
Email .... hr@sbr-global.com
Website .... www.sbr-global.com

SBR International is a growing professional services provider focused on delivering strategic and business process solutions to a Fortune 500 client base. Practice areas include financial services, decision support services, operations support services, networks and human resources. The company employs 20 people at this location and a total of 75 people in Canada. Graduates most likely to be hired come from the following academic areas: Bachelor of Arts (Economics, Political Science, Psychology), Bachelor of Science (General, Actuarial, Chemistry, Computer Science, Mathematics), Bachelor of Engineering (General, Chemical, Civil, Electrical, Mechanical, Industrial), Bachelor of Laws, Bachelor of Commerce/Business Administration (General, Accounting, Finance, Human Resources, Information Systems, Marketing), Chartered Accountant, Certified Management Accountant, Certified General Accountant, Master of Business Administration (General, Accounting, Finance, Marketing), Master of Arts, Master of Science, Master of Engineering and Doctorate (Engineering/P.Eng). Graduates would occupy Program Manager, Project Manager, Lead Analyst, Financial Analyst, Market Analyst, Research Analyst, Process Analyst, Desktop Publisher, Administrative Assistant and Human Resource Professional positions. Strong oral and written communication skills, team player, and previous consulting and project management experience are all listed as desirable non-academic qualifications. Company benefits are rated above average. The potential for advancement is listed as being excellent. The average

annual starting salary falls within the $55,000 to $60,000 range. The most suitable methods for initial contact by those seeking employment are to fax or e-mail a resume with a covering letter, or through the company's website. *Contact:* Human Resources.

SC INFRASTRUCTURE INC.
1177 - 11th Avenue SW, Suite 700
Calgary, AB T2R 1K9

Tel. 403-244-9090
Fax 403-228-8643
Email .... johnf@groupsci.com
Website .... www.groupsci.com

SC Infrastructure Inc. is a construction management group dedicated to infrastructure design, build and operation of construction projects. The company is the builder of the Confederation Bridge and is involved in construction management projects in Canada, the United States and Europe. There are 25 employees at this location and a total of 35 employees in Canada. Graduates most likely to be hired come from the following academic areas: Bachelor of Engineering (Civil, Electrical, Mechanical, Environmental/Resources), Bachelor of Commerce/Business Administration (Finance), Master of Business Administration (Finance) and Community College Diploma (CAD/CAM/Autocad, Engineering Technician). Graduates would occupy Field Engineer, Office Engineer, Surveyor and Draftsmen positions. Team player, analytical and hard working are all listed as desirable non-academic qualifications. Company benefits are rated as industry standard. The potential for advancement is listed as being good. The average annual starting salary falls within the $45,000 to $50,000 range. The most suitable methods for initial contact by those seeking employment are to mail or fax a resume with a covering letter. SC Infrastructure Inc. does hire summer and co-op work term students, depending on the projects available. *Contact:* John Forgeron, Manager, Human Resources.

SCARBOROUGH GENERAL HOSPITAL
3050 Lawrence Avenue East
Toronto, ON M1P 2V5

Tel. 416-431-8126
Fax 416-431-8186
Email .... sghhr@netrover.com
Website .... www.sgh.net

Scarborough General Hospital is a full service general hospital. The hospital employs approximately 2,200 professional and non-professional staff. Graduates most likely to be hired come from the following academic areas: Bachelor of Arts (Psychology, Recreation Studies), Bachelor of Science (Audiology, Nursing, Occupational Therapy, Pharmacy, Physio/Physical Therapy, Psychology), Bachelor of Engineering (Computer Science), Bachelor of Education (Adult), Bachelor of Commerce/Business Administration (Accounting, Finance, Human Resources, Information Systems), Master of Business Administration (General), Master of Science (Health Sciences), Master of Education and Community College Diploma (Human Resources, Recreation Studies, Laboratory Technician, Nuclear Medicine, Nursing RN/RPN, Radiology, Respiratory Therapy, Ultra-Sound Technician). Graduates would occupy Nursing RN/RPN, Service Technical Aide, Engineer, Unit Clerk, Dietician, Food Services Supervisor, Occupational Therapist, Physiotherapist, Clerk and Technician positions. Team work, customer service skills, accountability, professionalism and a dedication to continuous improvement are all listed as desirable non-academic qualifications. Employee benefits are rated above average. The potential for advancement is listed as average. The average annual starting salary ranges widely over professional and non-professional positions. The most suitable methods for initial contact by individuals seeking employment are to mail or fax a resume with a covering letter. The Scarborough General Hospital does hire co-op work term students. *Contact:* Human Resources Department.

SCHERING-PLOUGH HEALTHCARE PRODUCTS CANADA

6400 Northam Drive
Mississauga, ON L4V 1J1

Tel. 905-673-6242
Fax 905-671-0997
Website .... www.schering-plough.com

Schering-Plough Healthcare Products Canada is a leading manufacturer and marketer of brand name products, including Coppertone, Dr. Scholl's, Correctol, and Muskol. There are more than 100 employees at this location. Graduates most likely to be hired come from the following academic areas: Bachelor of Arts (General), Bachelor of Science (General), Bachelor of Commerce/Business Administration (Finance, Marketing), Certified Management Accountant and Master of Business Administration. Graduates are hired to occupy Sales and Marketing Assistant, Sales Representative, Accounting Clerk and Customer Service Representative positions. Teamwork, a positive attitude, competitiveness and assertiveness are listed as desirable non-academic qualifications. Company benefits are rated as excellent. The potential for advancement is listed as being good. The average annual starting salary falls within the $30,000 to $35,000 range. The most suitable method for initial contact by those seeking employment is to mail a resume with a covering letter. Schering-Plough Healthcare Products Canada does hire summer students. *Contact:* Director, Human Resources.

SCHLUMBERGER OILFIELD SERVICES

525 - 3rd Avenue SW, Eau Claire Place I
Calgary, AB T2P 0G4

Tel. 403-509-4000
Fax 403-509-4016
Website .... www.slb.com

Schlumberger Oilfield Services is a recognized technology leader which provides engineering services in the energy industry. The company utilizes complex technology to design, execute and evaluate optimized solutions for energy companies. The technology areas include: seismic data acquisition, processing and interpretation; drilling; measurements and logging while drilling; fluids engineering and pumping; wireline well evaluation; testing and production; and data services and software. Schlumberger is an international company employing 64,000 people in over 100 countries. There are 250 employees at this location and a total of 1,100 employees in Canada. Graduates most likely to be hired come from the following academic areas: Bachelor of Science (Geology), Bachelor of Engineering (Chemical, Civil, Electrical, Mechanical, Engineering Physics, Geological Engineering, Industrial Engineering, Mining, Petroleum/Fuels) and Community College Diploma (Electronics Technician, Engineering Technician). Bachelor of Engineering graduates would occupy Field Engineering trainee positions. Engineering Technology graduates would occupy Field Service Supervisor/Specialist Trainee posi-

tions. Team player, communication skills, adaptability, flexibility, leadership skills, willingness to relocate, decision-making abilities and outdoors/field work experience. Company benefits and the potential for advancement are both rated as excellent. The average annual starting salary for Engineering Technology graduates falls within the $30,000 to $35,000 range, and for Bachelor of Engineering graduates the starting salary falls within the $40,000 to $45,000 range. The most suitable methods for initial contact by those seeking employment are to mail or fax a resume with a covering letter, or via campus career centres.

SCHOLARSHIP CONSULTANTS OF NORTH AMERICA INC.

PO Box 3084, South
Halifax, NS B3J 3G6

Tel. 902-425-1100
Fax 902-425-1915
Website .... www.resp-usc.com

Scholarship Consultants of North America Inc. provides group and individual presentations, explaining a special savings plan (RESP) for children's future post-secondary education and assistance in applying for additional Canada Education Savings Grant. The company's business is focused on marketing and financial planning. Scholarship Consultants employs approximately 30 people at this location. Graduates most likely to be hired come from the following academic areas: Bachelor of Commerce/Business Administration (Finance, Marketing) and Master of Business Administration (Finance, Human Resources, Marketing). Graduates would occupy Enrollment Representative, Sales Manager, and Agency Director positions. Working in partnership with USC, which has agencies and sales professionals across Canada, Enrollment Representatives will receive support and training to ensure that their business succeeds. USC provides sales support materials, state-of-the-art computer based training, local agency support, conferences and seminars, and ongoing recognition and award programs. Entrepreneurial attitude, extremely self-motivated, previous sales and marketing work experience, computer literacy, honest, mature and professional are all listed as desirable non-academic qualifications. All representatives are licensed by their Provincial Securities Commissions, while the company provides a comprehensive training program designed to ensure that all representatives are well prepared to represent USC's leading edge education savings plans. Company benefits are rated as industry standard. The potential for advancement is listed as excellent, with the level of success ultimately determined by the individual's effort. The average annual starting is commission based following a industry leading, and very generous compensation structure. The most suitable method for initial contact by those seeking employment is to fax a resume with a covering letter. *Contacts:* Laura Coulombe, Executive Agency Director or Mark Corkum, Director of Marketing.

SCIENTIFIC-ATLANTA INC.

120 Middlefield Road
Toronto, ON M1S 4M6

Tel. 416-299-6888
Fax 416-754-4266
Email .... hr.stnd@sciatl.com
Website .... www.sciatl.com

Scientific-Atlanta Inc. is a leading supplier of broadband communications systems, satellite-based video, voice and data communications networks and worldwide customer service and support. The Satellite Television Networks Division leads in the design and manufacture of video processing equipment for the encryption and transmission of satellite signals. Scientific-Atlanta employs 5,000 people worldwide. Graduates most likely to be hired come from the following academic areas: Bachelor of Engineering (Electrical, Computer Systems, Engineering Physics) and Community College Diploma (Computer Science). Graduates would occupy Design Engineer positions. Company benefits are rated as industry standard. The most suitable method for initial contact by those seeking employment is to e-mail a resume with a covering letter. Scientific-Atlanta Inc. does hire co-op work term students. *Contact:* Human Resources Manager.

SDL OPTICS INC.
6703 Rajpur Place
Saanichton, BC V8M 1Z5

Tel. 250-544-2244
Fax 250-544-2225
Email .... hroptics@sdli.com
Website .... www.sdli.com

SDL Optics Inc. designs and markets fibre-coupled laser diodes for a wide range of fibre optic applications. These are used in telecommunications, CATV, data communications, sensing and various industrial and scientific applications. The company's primary area of focus is the communications industry. SDL is recognized for innovation in product design and manufacturing yielding high quality, reliable devices at competitive prices. The company combines stringent quality standards with extensive experience in order to meet the quality, reliability and performance requirements of its customers. SDL Optics Inc. employs 150 people at this location, and is a wholly owned subsidiary of SDL, Inc., based in San Jose, California, and traded on the Nasdaq Exchange under the symbol SDLI. Graduates most likely to be hired come from the following academic areas: Bachelor of Science (Physics), Bachelor of Engineering (Electrical, Mechanical, Engineering Physics, Telecommunications), Master of Science (Physics) and Master of Engineering (Electrical, Mechanical, Engineering Physics, Telecommunications). Graduates would occupy Process Engineer, Product Engineer and Project Engineer positions. Excellent team skills, SPC, DOE, ISO and ESD experience, and five years experience in fibre optics and telecommunications are all listed as desirable non-academic qualifications. Company benefits and the potential for advancement are both rated as excellent. The most suitable methods for initial contact by those seeking employment are to mail, fax or e-mail a resume with a covering letter, apply through the company's website at www.sdli.com, or via telephone. SDL Optics Inc. does hire co-op work term students. *Contact:* Kathy Neeves, Human Resources Manager.

SECOND CUP LTD., THE
175 Bloor Street East, South Tower, Suite 801
Toronto, ON M4W 3R8

Tel. 416-975-5541
Fax 416-975-5207
Email .... second@secondcup.com
Website .... www.secondcup.com

The Second Cup Ltd. is a North American leader in retailing specialty coffees. The company is the market leader with more than 375 stores in Canada. There are 45 employees at this location and a total of 160 employees across the country. Graduates most likely to be hired

come from the following academic areas: Bachelor of Arts (General, French, Geography, Urban Geography/Planning), Bachelor of Commerce/Business Administration (General, Accounting, Finance, Marketing), Certified General Accountant and Community College Diploma (Administration, Marketing/Sales, Real Estate, Hospitality). Graduates would occupy Administration and Trainee positions. Quick learner and team player are both listed as desirable non-academic qualifications. Company benefits are rated as industry standard. The potential for advancement is listed as being good. The average annual starting salary falls within the $30,000 to $35,000 range. The most suitable methods for initial contact by those seeking employment are to mail or fax a resume with a covering letter (no phone calls please). *Contact:* Human Resources Department.

SED SYSTEMS INC.
18 Innovation Boulevard, PO Box 1464
Saskatoon, SK S7K 3P7

Tel. 306-931-3425
Fax 306-933-1582
Email .... hr@sedsystems.ca
Website .... www.sedsystems.ca

SED Systems Inc. is a Canadian advanced technology company with a worldwide reputation for excellence in space, communications, satellite test and control, defense systems engineering and in custom electronic system manufacturing. Operating for over 34 years, SED has 260 employees and is a wholly owned subsidiary of Calian Technology Ltd., which is located in Ottawa and trades on the Toronto Stock Exchange under the symbol CTY. Graduates most likely to be hired come from the following academic areas: Bachelor of Science (Computer Science, Physics), Bachelor of Engineering (Electrical, Aerospace), Master of Science (Computer Science), Master of Engineering (Electrical) and Community College Diploma (Accounting, Human Resources, Office Administration, Purchasing/Logistics, Secretarial, CAD/CAM/Autocad, Computer Science, Electronics Technician, Engineering Technician, Information Systems). Graduates would occupy Programmer, System Engineer, Technologist, Clerk, Secretary and Buyer positions. Flexibility and good presentation and communication skills are all listed as desirable non-academic qualifications. Company benefits are rated above average. The potential for advancement is listed as being good. The average annual starting salary falls within the $30,000 to $35,000 range. The most suitable methods for initial contact by those seeking employment are to mail, fax or e-mail a resume with a covering letter. SED Systems Inc. does hire summer and co-op work term students. *Contact:* Judy Adams, Manager, Human Resources.

SEDGWICK LIMITED
PO Box 439, Toronto Dominion Centre
Toronto, ON M5K 1M3

Tel. 416-361-6700
Fax 416-361-6777
Website .... www.sedgwick.com

Sedgwick Limited is an insurance broker for both general insurance and group benefits. Sedgwick employs more than 250 people. Graduates most likely to be hired come from the following academic areas: Bachelor of Science (Mathematics, Actuarial Science, Computer Science), Bachelor of Engineering (Civil), Bachelor of Laws, Chartered Accountant, Masters (Library Science) and Community College Diploma (Business, Human Resources, Computer, Accounting, Secretarial). Technical Positions exist in Computer Programming, Benefits Administration, Pension Administration, Accounting, Customer Service, Marketing and Sales. Consulting positions exist in Risk Management, Actuary, Research, Legal Counsel and Administration. Company benefits are rated above average. The potential for advancement is listed as being good. The average starting salary falls within the $25,000 to $30,000 range. The most suitable methods for initial contact by those seeking employment are to mail a resume with a covering letter, or through on-campus recruitment initiatives (see your campus career centre for details). Sedgwick Limited does hire summer students. *Contact:* Nazaneen Parson, Human Resources.

SEMICONDUCTOR INSIGHTS INC.
3000 Solandt Drive
Kanata, ON K2K 2X2

Tel.	613-599-6500
Fax	613-599-6501
Email	hr@semiconductor.com
Website	www.semiconductor.com

Semiconductor Insights Inc. provides microelectronics services and products to major corporations on a global basis. The company's consulting services division serves the semiconductor industry with competitive analysis, intellectual property services and product design services. Established as an independent company in 1989, Semiconductor Insights Inc. has provided industry leading insights to a wide array of major semiconductor and information technology companies all over the world. Employee owned, the company currently employs 110 people. Graduates most likely to be hired come from the following academic areas: Bachelor of Science (Computer Science), Bachelor of Engineering (Electrical, Engineering Physics) Master of Engineering (Electrical) and Community College Diploma (CAD/CAM/Autocad, Electronics Technician). Graduates would occupy Patent Analysis Engineer and Design Analysis Engineer positions. Strong interpersonal skills, team player, good communication skills and co-op internship experience are all listed as desirable non-academic qualifications. Company benefits are rated as excellent. The potential for advancement is listed as being good. The most suitable method for initial contact by those seeking employment is to apply through the company's website. Semiconductor Insights Inc. does hire co-op work term students. *Contact:* Cindy Hansen, Recruiting Specialist.

SEN
698 King Street West, Cathedral Square
Hamilton, ON L8P 1C7

Tel.	905-522-6887
Fax	905-522-5579
Email	sen@bestnet.org
Website	www.bestnet.org/~sen

SEN provides in-home nursing, supportive housing services and volunteer visiting in the communities of Hamilton-Wentworth and Halton. Established in 1921, the mandate of the organization is to provide health care and support to clients and their families during times of illness, palliation and rehabilitation. SEN is a member of the St. Joseph's Health Care System which includes partnership and collaboration with St. Joseph's Hospital in Hamilton, St. Joseph's Hospital in Brantford, St. Joseph's Villa in Dundas, St. Joseph's Hospital and Home in Guelph, and St. Mary's Hospital in Kitchener. SEN employs 250 full and part-time staff, providing care 24 hours per day, 7 days a week. Graduates most likely to be hired come from the following academic areas: Bachelor of Arts (Psychology, Social Work), Bachelor of Science (Nursing), Bachelor of Education (Adult), Bachelor of Commerce/Business Administration (Human Resources, Information Systems), Master of Business Administration (Accounting), Master of Health Sciences, Community College Diploma (Accounting, Administration, Business, Secretarial, Social Work, Computer Science, Nursing RN/RNA, HCA, HSW2, HSW3) and High School Diploma. Graduates would occupy Home Support Worker in the community, Nursing in the community and Clerk positions. Previous work experience, excellent verbal and communication skills, conscientious, team player and strong organizational skills are all listed as desirable nonacademic qualifications. Company benefits are rated as industry standard. The potential for advancement is listed as average. The most suitable method for initial contact by those seeking employment is to mail a resume with a covering letter. SEN does hire summer students. *Contact:* Human Resources.

SENECA COLLEGE OF APPLIED ARTS AND TECHNOLOGY
1750 Finch Avenue East
Toronto, ON M2J 2X5

Tel.	416-491-5050
Fax	905-479-4162
Website	www.senecac.on.ca

Seneca College of Applied Arts and Technology is a major educational institution offering post-secondary courses, certificates, diplomas, post-diplomas and contract training. Seneca employs approximately 1,200 staff (all campuses) and offers more than 120 diploma programs. Graduates most likely to be hired come from the following academic areas: Bachelor of Arts (General, Economics, English, Geography, Fine Arts, Journalism, Political Science, Psychology, Recreation Studies, Social Work, Sociology), Bachelor of Science (Biology, Chemistry, Computer Science, Microbiology, Zoology, Nursing, Psychology), Bachelor of Engineering (General, Chemical, Civil, Electrical, Computer Systems, Instrumentation, Microelectronics, Telecommunications), Bachelor of Education (General, Early Childhood, Adult), Bachelor of Laws, Bachelor of Commerce/Business Administration (General, Accounting, Finance, Human Resources, Information Systems, Marketing), Chartered Accountant, Certified Management Accountant, Certified General Accountant, Master of Business Administration (General, Accounting, Finance, Human Resources, Information Systems, Marketing), Master of Arts (English), Master of Science (Biology, Chemistry), Master of Engineering, Community College Diploma (Accounting, Advertising, Business, Communications/Public Relations, Facility Management, Human Resources, Marketing/Sales, Office Administration, Secretarial, Audio/Visual Technician, Early Childhood Technician, Fashion Arts, Graphic Arts, Journalism, Recreation Studies, Social Work, Aircraft Maintenance, Computer Science, Electronics Technician, HVAC Systems, Information Systems, Animal Health, Laboratory Technician) and High School Diploma. Graduates are hired to occupy a diverse range of positions in three main staff groups, including Administrative, Faculty and Support Staff. Good communication skills, relevant work experience, team player, good interpersonal skills, an ability to relate effectively with a multicultural, multiracial and multiable student population, good problem solving skills, strong analytical skills and competency with a variety of computer software applications are all listed as desirable non-academic qualifications. Company benefits are rated above average. The potential for advancement is listed as average. The average annual starting salary, depending upon the staff group, falls within the $25,000 to $60,000 range. The most suitable methods for initial contact by those seeking employment are to mail or fax a resume with a covering letter, or via telephone. Seneca College does hire summer and co-op work term students through their own and through government sponsored programs. *Contact:* Jane Wilson, Personnel Officer, Employee Relations.

SERNAS GROUP, THE
110 Scotia Court, Unit 41
Whitby, ON L1N 8Y7

Tel.	905-686-6402
Fax	905-432-7877
Email	hr@sernas.com
Website	www.sernas.com

The Sernas Group of companies provide consulting services in municipal, water resources, power distribution, and transportation engineering, as well as land use and transportation planning. In business for more than 35 years, G.M. Sernas & Associates Limited has developed a strong reputation for providing urban land use planning, municipal infrastructure planning, design, and implementation for residential, commercial and industrial developments in southern Ontario. RGP Transtech Inc. specializes in the field of transportation and transit planning and implementation. SRM Associates Inc. was recently created to specifically provide transportation planning and engineering project design and implementation for the public sector. With offices in Whitby and Mississauga, The Sernas Group employs a total of 75 people. Graduates most likely to be hired come from the following academic areas: Bachelor of Arts (Urban Geography), Bachelor of Engineering (Civil, Environmental, Electrical), Master of Engineering (Transportation) and Community College Diploma (Engineering Technician). During the initial years of employment, graduates are placed on personally-tailored development programs to expose them to all aspects of the company's consulting work within their field of specialization. Depending upon the individuals capabilities and interests, careers may lead to specialized technical work, supervisory responsibilities or project management in the long term. Applicants should be interested in working with the deadlines and interpersonal contacts experienced in consulting work. Good organizational skills, strong written and oral communication skills, ability to work on multiple projects at once and to work with minimal supervision are all required to excel in consulting. Company benefits are rated above average. The potential for advancement is listed as being good. The average annual starting salary depends upon the position being considered, and the qualifications and experience of the applicant. The most suitable methods for initial contact by those seeking employment are to mail or fax a resume with a covering letter. The Sernas Group does hire summer and work term students. *Contact:* Mrs. Jone Webster, Human Resources Manager.

SHARP ELECTRONICS OF CANADA LTD.
335 Britannia Road East
Mississauga, ON L4Z 1W9

Tel.	905-890-2100
Website	www.sharp.ca

Sharp Electronics of Canada Ltd. distributes electronic products in Canada. Sharp Electronics of Canada Ltd. is a subsidiary of Osaka, Japan based Sharp Corporation. In operation in Canada for over 25 years, Sharp Electronics of Canada Ltd. employs approximately 200 people at its Canadian headquarters. Graduates most likely to be hired come from the following academic areas: Bachelor of Arts (General, Economics), Bachelor of Science (Mathematics), Bachelor of Engineering (General), Bachelor of Commerce/Business Administration (Accounting, Finance, Marketing, Information Systems), Chartered Accountant (Finance), Certified Management Accountant (Finance), Certified General Accountant (Finance), Master of Business Administration (Accounting, Finance, Marketing) and Community College Diploma (Accounting, Advertising, Administration, Business, Communications, Facility Management, Marketing/Sales, Purchasing/Logistics, Secretarial, Human Resources, Computer Science, Electronics, Engineering). Graduates would occupy a variety of head office positions. Excellent presentation skills, outgoing and strong communication skills are listed as desirable non-academic qualifications. Company benefits are rated above average. The potential for advancement is listed as being good. The average annual starting salary falls within the $30,000 to $35,000 range, and is commission based for certain positions. The most suitable method for initial contact by graduates seeking employment is to mail a resume with a covering letter. Sharp Electronics of Canada Ltd. does hire a small number of summer students annually. *Contact:* Tracy Savage, Recruitment, Employment Practices & Training Specialist.

SHAW INDUSTRIES LTD.
25 Bethridge Road
Toronto, ON M9W 1M7

Tel.	416-743-7111
Fax	416-743-8194
Email	hr@shawind.com

Shaw Industries Ltd. is a global energy services company specializing in products and services for the exploration and production, pipeline and downstream sectors of the oil and gas industry. Through its 50/50 joint venture with Dresser Industries, Inc., the company is the world leader in the design and manufacture of corrosion insulation and weight coating products utilized in the pipeline industry for oil and gas gathering and long distance transmission applications. The joint venture operates 29 plants located in all major energy producing markets, and in addition to these permanent facilities, employs its engineering expertise to install temporary project-specific plants anywhere in the world. The company's wholly owned divisions and subsidiaries also provide proprietary ultrasonic weld inspection services and heat shrinkable sleeves utilized for corrosion protection applications by the global pipeline industry. In the exploration and production sector, the company provides seismic equipment for gathering geophysical data, drill string components for drilling oil and gas wells, and inspection and refurbishment services for drill pipe production tubing and casing. For petrochemical, utility and industrial markets, the company manufactures wire and cable for use in process instrumentation and control systems and heat shrinkable tubing used for electrical, electronic and telecommunications applications. There are 280 employees at this location, a total of 702 in Canada and a total of 1,592 employees worldwide. Graduates most likely to be hired come from the following academic areas: Bachelor of Science (Metallurgy), Bachelor of Engineering (Chemical, Electrical, Mechanical, Environmental/Resources, Industrial Engineering, Industrial Production/Manufacturing, Instrumentation, Power/Hydro), Bachelor of Commerce/Business

Administration (Accounting, Human Resources, Marketing), Chartered Accountant, Certified Management Accountant, Certified General Accountant, Master of Business Administration (Accounting, Finance, Human Resources, Marketing), Master of Science, Master of Engineering and Community College Diploma (Accounting, Administration, Business, Marketing/Sales, Secretarial, Computer Science, Electronics Technician, Engineering Technician). Computer literacy, excellent negotiation skills, previous work experience, and good written and verbal communication skills are all listed as desirable non-academic qualifications. The average annual starting salary falls within the $35,000 to $40,000 range. The most suitable method for initial contact by those seeking employment is to fax a resume with a covering letter. Shaw Industries Ltd. does hire summer and co-op work term students. *Contact:* Mr. J.M. Lamb, Corporate Human Resources Manager.

SHELL CANADA PRODUCTS LIMITED
PO Box 2000, Sarnia Manufacturing Centre
Corunna, ON N0N 1G0

Tel.	519-481-1100
Fax	519-481-1288
Website	www.shell.ca

Shell Canada Products Limited is involved in the refining of petrochemicals. There are more than 300 employees at this location. Graduates most likely to be hired come from the following academic areas: Bachelor of Science (Chemistry), Bachelor of Engineering (Chemical, Mechanical), Bachelor of Commerce/Business Administration (Accounting) and Community College Diploma (Electronics Technician, Engineering Technician, Mechanic, Instrumentation, Process Operations). Graduates would occupy positions as Process Operators, Chemists, and positions in Engineering. Previous work experience, motivated, innovative, excellent problem solving skills, an ability to work in a team environment, and strong communication and interpersonal skills are all listed as desirable non-academic qualifications. Company benefits and the potential for advancement are both rated as excellent. The average annual starting salary falls within the $30,000 to $35,000 range, and ultimately depends upon the position being considered. The most suitable methods for initial contact by those seeking employment are to mail or fax a resume with a covering letter, by responding to campus recruitment listings and programs (see your campus career centre for details), or by responding to advertised positions in newspapers. Shell Canada Products Limited does hire summer and co-op work term students. *Contact:* Human Resources Analyst.

SHERATON CENTRE TORONTO HOTEL
123 Queen Street West
Toronto, ON M5H 3M9

Tel.	416-947-4900
Fax	416-361-6223
Website	www.sheratonctr.toronto.on.ca

Sheraton Centre Toronto Hotel provides lodging, food and beverage services, and large convention service facilities. The hotel employs a total of 960 people. Graduates most likely to be hired come from the following academic areas: Bachelor of Arts (General, Hospitality and Tourism), Bachelor of Science (Computer Science), Bachelor of Commerce/Business Administration (General, Human Resources, Marketing), Chartered Accountant, Certified Management Accountant, Certified General Accountant, Master of Business Administration, Community College

Diploma (Accounting, Business, Facility Management, Human Resources, Cooking, Hospitality, Computer Science) and High School Diploma. Graduates would occupy Guest Service Agent in Reception, Sales Coordinator, Food and Beverage Supervisor, Trainee positions, and Entry Level Management and Non-Management positions. Friendly, enthusiastic, problem solving skills, outgoing, initiative, quality awareness, business savvy, entrepreneurship and customer service oriented are all listed as desirable non-academic qualifications. Company benefits are rated above average. The potential for advancement is listed as being good. The starting salary and benefit level varies with the position. The most suitable method for initial contact by those seeking employment is by calling the Job Hotline at (416) 947-4900. Sheraton Centre Toronto Hotel hires a limited number of students, these are mostly part-time term contract positions. *Contacts:* Anthony Hopkins, Director, Human Resources; Tracey Kraus, Human Resources Consultant or Anna Salvati, Human Resources Consultant.

SHERATON PARKWAY HOTEL, TORONTO NORTH
600 Highway 7 East
Richmond Hill, ON L4B 1B2

Tel.	905-881-2121
Fax	905-882-3112

Sheraton Parkway Hotel, Toronto North provides accommodation, food and beverage, and convention services to tourists, corporations and associations. The hotel employs more than 250 people. Graduates most likely to be hired come from the following academic areas: Bachelor of Arts, Bachelor of Science, Bachelor of Commerce/Business Administration, Chartered Accountant, Certified Management Accountant and Community College Diploma (Travel/Tourism, Hotel/Hospitality, Culinary/Cooking). Graduates are hired to occupy Managerial positions for the following departments: Front Office, Lounge and Restaurants, Kitchen, Banquets, Housekeeping, Maintenance, Security, Accounting, Human Resources, Catering, and Sales and Marketing. Computer literacy, outgoing, friendly, a helpful attitude and excellent communication and public relations skills are all listed as desirable non-academic qualifications. Company benefits and the potential for advancement are both rated as excellent. The average annual starting salary falls within the $15,000 to $20,000 range. The most suitable method for initial contact by those seeking employment is to mail a resume with a covering letter. The Sheraton Parkway Hotel does hire summer students, depending upon the level of business. *Contact:* Human Resources Manager.

SHERWOOD CREDIT UNION
PO Box 1960, Station Main
Regina, SK S4P 4M1

Tel.	306-780-1649
Fax	306-780-1521
Email	lynn.hunter@sherwoodcu.com

Sherwood Credit Union is a financial institution offering a variety of financial services and products. The company employs 145 people at this location and a total of 325 people within Saskatchewan. Graduates most likely to be hired come from the following areas: Bachelor of Arts (General, Economics, English), Bachelor of Science (Computer Science), Bachelor of Education (Adult), Bachelor of Commerce/Business Administration (Accounting, Finance, Human Resources, Information Systems, Marketing, Public Administration), Chartered Accountant, Certified Management Accountant, Certified

General Accountant and Community College Diploma (Accounting, Administration, Business, Communications, Financial Planning, Human Resources, Insurance, Marketing/Sales). Graduates would occupy Financial Services Representative, Lending Representative, Service Centre Manager, Sales and Service Leader and Information Technology Specialist positions. An ability to work with the public, friendliness, team player and sales experience are all listed as desirable non-academic qualifications. Company benefits and the potential for advancement are both rated as excellent. The average annual starting salary falls within the $20,000 to $25,000 range. The most suitable method for initial contact by those seeking employment is to mail a resume with a covering letter. Sherwood Credit Union does hire summer and co-op students. *Contact:* Human Resource Coordinator, Human Resources Department.

SHIRMAX FASHIONS LTD.
3901 Jarry Street East
Montreal, QC H1Z 2G1

Tel. 514-729-3333
Fax 514-729-3018
Email .... hr@shirmax.com

Shirmax Fashions Ltd. is a leading retail specialist in maternity and plus-size women's fashions. The company maintains 140 stores and 2,200 employees across Canada. Graduates most likely to be hired come from the following academic areas: Bachelor of Science (Computer Science), Bachelor of Engineering (Computer Systems), Bachelor of Architecture, Bachelor of Commerce/Business Administration (Accounting, Finance, Human Resources, Information Systems, Marketing), Chartered Accountant, Master of Business Administration (Accounting, Finance, Marketing), Community College Diploma (Accounting, Administration, Advertising, Business, Human Resources, Marketing/Sales, Secretarial, Graphic Arts, Architecture/Drafting, Computer Science) and High School Diploma. Company benefits are rated as excellent. The potential for advancement is listed as being good. The average annual starting salary falls within the $20,000 to $25,000 range. The most suitable method for initial contact by those seeking employment is to mail a resume with a covering letter. Shirmax Fashions Ltd. does hire summer students. *Contact:* Human Resources.

SHOPPING CHANNEL, THE - TELEMARKETING/ WAREHOUSE
1400 Castlefield Avenue
Toronto, ON M6B 4H8

Tel. 416-785-3500
Fax 416-785-0493
Email .... tkatz@rci.rogers.com
Website .... www.tSc.ca

The Shopping Channel, Telemarketing/Warehouse produces a Canadian televised home shopping service. The service is video taped live from the broadcast centre in Mississauga. The Shopping Channel sells jewellery, fashions, fitness equipment, home decorating items, cosmetics, etc. There are a total of 500 employees at the Toronto and Mississauga locations. Graduates most likely to be hired come from the following academic areas: Bachelor of Engineering (Electrical), Bachelor of Commerce/Business Administration (General, Accounting, Finance, Human Resources, Information Systems, Marketing), Certified Management Accountant, Certified General Accountant, and Community College Diploma (Accounting, Administration, Communications/Public

Relations, Audio Visual Technician, Graphic Arts, Television/Radio Arts, Broadcasting, Electronics Technician, Engineering Technician). Graduates would occupy Merchandising Assistant, AIP Clerk, Controller, General Accounting and Camera Operator positions. Previous work experience and an ability to work flexible hours are listed as desirable non-academic qualifications. Company benefits are rated above average. The potential for advancement is listed as being good. The most suitable methods for initial contact by those seeking employment are to mail or fax a resume with a covering letter, or by applying in person. The Shopping Channel does hire summer students. (Head Office Location: The Shopping Channel, 59 Ambassador Drive, Mississauga, Ontario, L5T 2P9). *Contact:* Recruitment Specialist.

SIDUS SYSTEMS INC.
66 Leek Crescent
Richmond Hill, ON L4B 1H1

Tel. 905-882-1600
Fax 905-882-2430
Website .... www.sidus.ca

Sidus Systems Inc. is involved in computer manufacturing, sales and customer support. Graduates most likely to be hired come from the following academic areas: Bachelor of Engineering (Computer Systems, Industrial Production/Manufacturing), Bachelor of Commerce/Business Administration (Accounting, Finance), Chartered Accountant, Certified Management Accountant, Certified General Accountant, Community College Diploma (Computer Science, Electronics Technician, Engineering Technician), and graduates with Microsoft Certified Systems Engineer (MCSE), Certified Novell Administrator (CNA 3, 4), and Certified Novell Engineer (CNE 3) accreditations. Graduates would occupy Systems Engineer, Computer Technician, Technical Service Representative, Manufacturing Engineer, Credit and Collections, Accounting, Computer Assembly and Sales positions. Previous experience, team player, team builder, initiative, motivation and the ability to work independently are all listed as desirable non-academic qualifications. Company benefits are rated as industry standard. The potential for advancement is listed as being good. The average annual starting salary falls within the $20,000 to $25,000 range. The most suitable method for initial contact by those seeking employment is to fax a resume with a covering letter. Sidus Systems Inc. does hire summer and co-op work term students. *Contact:* Carolyn Jaswal, Human Resources.

SIEMENS CANADA LIMITED
2185 Derry Road West
Mississauga, ON L5N 7A6

Tel. 905-819-8000
Fax 905-819-5777
Email .... jobs@siemens.ca
Website .... www.siemens.ca

Siemens is one of the largest and most diversified companies in the world, working in areas such as healthcare, energy and power, industry, information and communications, transportation, construction and lighting. The company employs approximately 400,000 people worldwide. In Canada, Siemens is headquartered in Mississauga and has 80 offices and 13 manufacturing facilities across the country. Locations span from coast to coast staffed by 5,900 employees. Graduates most likely to be hired come from the following academic areas: Bachelor of Arts (Economics, Psychology), Bachelor of

Engineering (Electrical, Mechanical, Automation/Robotics, Biomedical Electronics, Biotechnology/Bioengineering, Computer Systems, Industrial Design, Industrial Engineering, Industrial Production/Manufacturing, Instrumentation, Mining, Power/Hydro, Pulp and Paper, Telecommunications, Transportation), Bachelor of Commerce/Business Administration (General, Accounting, Finance, Human Resources, Information Systems, Marketing), Chartered Accountant, Certified Management Accountant, Certified General Accountant, Master of Business Administration (Accounting, Finance) and Community College Diploma (Accounting, Advertising, Business, Communications/Public Relations, Human Resources, Marketing/Sales, Purchasing/Logistics, CAD/CAM/Autocad, HVAC Systems, Nuclear Medicine, Radiology, Respiratory Therapy, Ultrasound Technician). Graduates would Administrative/Clerical, Junior Sales, Marketing, Technical/Service and PC/IT Support positions. Leadership skills, team player, flexibility, ownership, customer partnership, good analytical and problem solving skills are all listed as desirable non-academic qualifications. Company benefits are rated above average. The potential for advancement is listed as being good. The most suitable methods for initial contact by those seeking employment are to mail, fax or e-mail a resume with a covering letter, or via the company's website. Siemens Canada Limited does hire summer and co-op work term students. These may be referrals from present employees or through job placement programs (contact your campus career centre). *Contact:* Corporate Relations.

SIERRA SYSTEMS CONSULTANTS INC.
880 Douglas Street, Suite 500
Victoria, BC V8W 2B7

Tel. 250-385-1535
Fax 250-385-4761
Email .... erutherford@sierrasys.com
Website .... www.sierrasys.com

Sierra Systems Consultants Inc. offers high quality, cost effective information technology based business solutions. The extensive range of services Sierra provides includes business and technical consulting, systems integration and delivery, technology management, and internet development and delivery. While working in large variety of industries and business functional areas, Sierra's main areas of focus are human resources and payroll, finance, government, health care, education, and justice. Since its establishment in 1966, Sierra has offered practical advice and technical expertise to clients in a myriad of industries including government, health care, banking, hospitality, insurance, utilities, airlines and unions. Sierra's growth has been substantial, yet managed in a controlled fashion to ensure financial stability and long-term viability. Based in British Columbia, Sierra is a $66 million company with over 620 employees and 11 branches in both the United States and Canada. Graduates most likely to be hired come from the following academic areas: Bachelor of Science (Computer Science), Bachelor of Commerce/Business Administration (Information Systems), Master of Business Administration (Information Systems) and Community College Diploma (Information Systems, Computer Science). Graduates would occupy Applications Developer, Business Analyst, Technical Architect, and Technical Analyst positions. Excellent oral and written communication skills, able to think in business terms, a willingness to travel, and enjoy the challenge of solving business problems are all listed as desirable non-academic qualifications. Sierra provides an innovative remuneration plan, including profit sharing and

a comprehensive benefits package. The company is committed to ongoing education and career development for its employees. The average annual starting salary falls within the $35,000 to $40,000 range for Junior positions and for those with two to three years experience. The most suitable method for initial contact by those seeking employment is to e-mail a resume with a covering letter. Sierra Systems Consultants Inc. does hire co-op work term students. *Contact:* Evelyn Rutherford, Human Resources Director.

SILK FM BROADCASTING LTD. / SILK INTERNET MEDIA LTD.
1598 Pandosy Street
Kelowna, BC V1Y 1P4

Tel. 250-860-1010
Fax 250-860-0505
Email .... cindy@silk.net

Silk FM Broadcasting Ltd. is Kelowna's soft rock radio station. The station's demographic is adults between the ages 25 to 54, primarily women between the ages 35 to 44. Silk FM Broadcasting Ltd. / Silk Internet Media Ltd. was established in 1985 and currently employs more than 30 people. Graduates most likely to be hired come from the following academic areas: Bachelor of Arts (Journalism), Bachelor of Science (Computer Science), Bachelor of Engineering (Computer Systems), Bachelor of Commerce/Business Administration (General, Accounting, Human Resources, Marketing) and Community College Diploma (Accounting, Administration, Advertising, Business, Communications/Public Relations, Human Resources, Marketing/Sales, Secretarial, Computer Science). Graduates would occupy News Reporter, Internet Support Technician, Accountant, Bookkeeper, Sales, Promotions, Receptionist, Sales Assistant and Technical Engineer positions. Ambitious, organized, professional, friendly, proactive and goal oriented are all listed as desirable non-academic qualifications. Company benefits are rated as industry standard. The potential for advancement is listed as being good. The average annual starting salary falls within the $25,000 to $30,000 range. The most suitable methods for initial contact by those seeking employment are to mail, fax or e-mail a resume with a covering letter. Silk FM Broadcasting Ltd. / Silk Internet Media Ltd. does hire summer and co-op work term students. *Contact:* Cindy Kindret, Personnel Manager.

SIMON FRASER HEALTH REGION
260 Sherbrooke Street
New Westminster, BC V3L 3M2

Tel. 604-524-2845
Fax 604-520-4204
Website .... www.sfhr.com

The Simon Fraser Health Region is a major teaching and referral facility consisting of six hospitals. These include the Royal Columbian Hospital and Queen's Park Care Centre in New Westminster, Eagle Ridge Hospital in Port Moody, Ridge Meadows Hospital in Maple Ridge,

Burnaby Hospital and Fellburn Care Centre in Burnaby. In addition, the health region operates community programs and services within these communities. The Simon Fraser Health Region employs more than 8,000 people in total. Graduates most likely to be hired come from the following areas: Bachelor of Arts (Recreation Studies, Social Work), Bachelor of Science (Biology, Chemistry, Computer Science, Microbiology, Nursing, Nutritional Sciences, Occupational Therapy, Pharmacy, Physiotherapy, Speech Pathology), Bachelor of Commerce/Business Administration (Accounting, Finance, Human Resources, Information Systems, Marketing), Chartered Accountant, Certified Management Accountant, Certified General Accountant, Master of Business Administration (General, Accounting, Finance, Human Resources, Information Systems), Master of Arts (Social Work) and Community College Diploma (Business, Communications/Public Relations, Financial Planning, Human Resources, Secretarial, Cook/Chef Training, Journalism, Carpentry, Computer Science, HVAC Systems, Information Systems, Plumber, Tool and Die/Machinist, Welding, Laboratory Technician, Nuclear Medicine, Nursing RN/RNA, Radiology, Ultrasound Technician, Medical Transcription). Graduates would occupy Clerk, Computer Systems Programmer/Analyst, Accountant, Human Resources Advisor, Public Relations/Communications, Cook, Trades (various), Medical Transcription, Lab Technologist, Nurse, Dietitian, Occupational Therapist, Pharmacist, Physiotherapist, Speech Pathologist, Social Worker, Nuclear Medicine Technician, Radiology Technician, Respiratory Technician and Ultrasound Technician positions. Team player, previous work experience, good communication, organization and problem solving skills, leadership abilities, good attendance record, and the ability to work in an environment subject to frequent changes and a high volume of work are all listed as desirable non-academic qualifications. The average annual starting salary falls with the $30,000 to $35,000 range. Company benefits are rated above average. The potential for advancement is listed as being good. The most suitable methods for initial contact by those seeking employment are to mail or fax a resume with a covering letter. The Simon Fraser Health Region does hire summer and co-op work term students. *Contact:* Employment Services.

SIMPLEX
6300 Viscount Road
Mississauga, ON L4V 1H3
Tel. 905-677-7000
Fax 905-677-7812
Website .... www.simplexnet.com

Simplex is involved in the manufacturing, distribution, sales and service of fire detection, security and time data systems. Simplex is a subsidiary of Gardner, Massachusetts based Simplex Time Recorder Co. The company is a recognized expert in delivering integrated solutions for fire detection, security, building communications and workforce information applications. In addition to an extensive branch network located in major cities throughout North America, Simplex Time Recorder Co. maintains offices in Australia, the Far East, Europe and Latin America, with a presence in 65 countries around the world and employing a total of 7,000 people worldwide. Simplex employs 100 people at this location and a total of 250 people in Canada. Graduates most likely to be hired come from the following academic areas: Bachelor of Arts (Economics, Journalism, Psychology), Bachelor of Science (Computer Science, Mathematics, Psychology), Bachelor of Engineering (Computer Systems, Instrumentation, Microelectronics), Bachelor of Commerce/Business Administration (Accounting, Finance, Human Resources, Information Systems, Marketing), Certified Management Accountant, Certified General Accountant, Master of Business Administration (Accounting, Finance, Human Resources, Information Systems, Marketing), Master of Engineering (Electronics), Community College Diploma (Accounting, Administration, Business, Financial Planning, Human Resources, Marketing/Sales, Purchasing/Logistics, Secretarial, CAD/CAM/Autocad, Computer Science, Electronics Technician) and High School Diploma. Graduates would occupy Electronic Technician, Electronic Project Engineer, Network Administrator, Sales Representative, Human Resources Administrator, Purchasing, Accounting, Secretarial, Administration, Payroll and Accounts Payable positions. Excellent communication and leadership skills, team player, driven, determined and good people skills are all listed as desirable non-academic qualifications. Company benefits are rated as excellent. The potential for advancement is listed as being good. The average annual starting salary falls within the $30,000 to $35,000 range. The most suitable method for initial contact by those seeking employment is to mail a resume with a covering letter. *Contact:* Human Resources.

SIMWARE INC.
2 Gurdwara Road
Ottawa, ON K2E 1A2
Tel. 613-228-5109
Fax 613-224-3804
Email .... hr@simware.com
Website .... www.simware.com

Simware Inc. helps companies create corporate extranets that bring business applications closer to company stakeholders. For more than 16 years, the company has provided software solutions that have enabled their global 2000 customers to leverage their enterprise systems to dramatically improve service delivery, reduce costs, increase revenues and gain strategic advantages. Simware Inc. is a publicly traded company (NASDAQ:SIMWF), headquartered in Ottawa, with offices the United Kingdom and Belgium, and alliances with leading customer solution providers globally. There are 110 employees at the Ottawa location, and a total of 125 employees worldwide. Graduates most likely to be hired come from the following academic areas: Bachelor of Science (Computer Science), Bachelor of Engineering (Computer Systems), Bachelor of Commerce/Business Administration (Accounting, Finance, Human Resources, Marketing), Certified Management Accountant, Master of Business Administration (Marketing) and Community College Diploma (Accounting, Communications/Public Relations, Human Resources, Marketing/Sales, Secretarial, Computer Science). Graduates would occupy Accountant, Clerical, Finance, Marketing Specialist, Sales Manager, Software Developer, Technical Support Technician, Technical Consultant, Programmer and Network Analyst positions. Team player, good oral and written communication skills, innovative and a high energy level are all listed as desirable nonacademic qualifications. Company benefits are rated above average. The potential for advancement is listed as excellent. The average annual starting salary falls within the $30,000 to $35,000 range. The most suitable methods for initial contact by those seeking employment are to mail, fax or e-mail a resume with a covering letter, or by applying through the company's website at www.simware.com. *Contact:* Human Resources.

SITEL CANADA
350 Bloor Street East, 5th Floor
Toronto, ON M4W 3J6

Tel.	416-932-2000
Fax	416-964-8966
Email	nas.to@hrads.com
Website	www.sitel.com

SITEL Canada is Canada's leading provider of dedicated, outsourced telephone based sales and customer service solutions to large and fast growing corporations worldwide. SITEL Canada has coast to coast coverage of the Canadian and U.S. marketplaces, with offices and call centre operations in Montreal, Toronto and Calgary. SITEL Canada employs 450 people at this location, and a total of 1,200 people in Canada. SITEL Canada's parent company, SITEL Corporation, employs 22,000 people worldwide and is a global leader in providing outsourced teleservices to Fortune 500 companies worldwide. The company has 70 call centres in more than 17 countries. Graduates most likely to be hired come from the following academic areas: Bachelor of Commerce/ Business Administration (Human Resources, Information Systems) and Community College Diploma (Business, Financial Planning, Human Resources, Information Systems). Graduates would occupy Systems Analyst, Client Services Manager/Analyst, Operations Supervisor, Quality Assurance Representative, Human Resources Recruiter, Trainer and Sales/Customer Services Representative positions. Great communication skills, experience, a willingness to learn and a "can-do attitude" are all listed as desirable non-academic qualifications. Company benefits are rated above average. The potential for advancement is listed as being excellent. The average annual starting salary falls within the $25,000 to $30,000 range. The most suitable methods for initial contact by those seeking employment are to mail, fax or e-mail a resume with a covering letter, or via telephone. SITEL Canada does hire summer and co-op work term students. (Other Canadian Locations: Montreal 514-482-6188, Toronto 416-932-2000, and Calgary 403-269-3333). *Contacts:* Vice President, Human Resources (for Client Services, Human Resources, Training, and Finance positions) or Manager, Human Resources (for Operations positions).

SKYJACK INC.
55 Campbell Road
Guelph, ON N1H 1B9

Tel.	800-265-2738
Fax	519-837-3102
Email	johndykstra@skyjackinc.com
Website	www.skyjackinc.com

Skyjack Inc. is a world leader in the design, assembly, manufacturing, marketing and distribution of self propelled scissors lifts and booms, as well as push around personal lifts. Skyjack began in 1969 as an industrial machine shop in Brampton, Ontario. The company started production of scissor lifts in 1985 and in order to expand production capacity the plant moved to Guelph in 1989. In 1994 the company went public and has expanded. Today, Skyjack has eight manufacturing, product support, sales and warehousing facilities in Canada, USA and Europe. The company exports to customers in the USA, Europe and Asia markets. Skyjack has received many awards for its success, including the 1995 Canada Export Award for excellence in entrepreneurship, and the 1995 Canada Export Award. There are approximately 700 employees at the corporate headquarters in its Guelph facilities and a total of 1,400 employees worldwide. Graduates most likely to be hired come from the follow- ing academic areas: Bachelor of Engineering (Electrical, Mechanical), Bachelor of Commerce/Business Administration (Accounting, Finance, Human Resources), Chartered Accountant, Certified Management Accountant, Certified General Accountant and Community College Diploma (Accounting, Business, Human Resources, Office Administration, Purchasing/Logistics, Mechanic, CAD/CAM/AutoCAD, Engineering Technician, Welding). Graduates would occupy Mechanical Engineer, AutoCAD Mechanical Designer, Electrical Engineer, Hydraulics/Fluid Power Designer, Test Engineer, Product Engineer, Welder/Fitter, Robotics Welding Specialist, Equipment Assembler, Industrial Spray Painter, CNC Lathe Operator, Accountant, Accounting Clerk and Buyer positions. Manufacturing experience, team player, excellent problem solving skills, common sense and good computer skills are all listed as desirable non-academic qualifications. Company benefits are rated as excellent. The potential for advancement is listed as being good. The average annual starting salary falls within the $25,000 to $30,000 range. The most suitable methods for initial contact by those seeking employment are to mail or e-mail a resume with a covering letter. Skyjack Inc. does hire students for summer and co-op work terms. Co-op students are recruited through various university and college co-op programs while summer students are largely recruited internally. *Contact:* John Dykstra, Recruiter.

SMED INTERNATIONAL INC.
10 Smed Lane SE
Calgary, AB T2C 4T5

Tel.	403-203-6000
Fax	403-203-6001
Email	resumes@smednet.com
Website	www.smednet.com

SMED International Inc. is a Calgary-based manufacturer and marketer of creative interior office environments. The company's products include cellular flooring, office furniture systems and moveable, reusable wall systems. SMED employs 1,535 people at this location, a total of 1,600 people in Canada and an additional 200 people outside of the country. Graduates most likely to be hired come from the following academic areas: Bachelor of Science (Computer Science), Bachelor of Engineering (Mechanical, Industrial Design, Industrial Engineering, Industrial Production/Manufacturing), Bachelor of Commerce/Business Administration (Finance, Information Systems, Marketing, Operations Management), Community College Diploma (Architectural Technician, Computer Science, Engineering Technician, Information Systems) and High School Diploma. Team skills, self motivation and a solid work history are all listed as desirable non-academic qualifications. Company benefits are rated above average. The potential for advancement is listed as excellent. The average annual starting salary falls within the $20,000 to $30,000 range, depending on the position and area of employment (Production: $9.00/hour, Administration: $30,000 plus range). The most suitable methods for initial contact by those seeking employment are to e-mail or fax a resume with a covering letter. SMED International Inc. does hire summer and co-op work term students. *Contact:* Human Resources.

SMITH INTERNATIONAL CANADA LTD.
335 - 8th Avenue SW, Suite 1600
Calgary, AB T2P 1C9

Tel.	403-264-6077
Fax	403-269-3269
Website	www.smith-intl.com

Smith International Canada Ltd. is involved in the manufacturing and sales of drill bits. Smith International Canada Ltd. is a subsidiary of Houston, Texas based Smith International, Inc. The company is is a leading worldwide supplier of products and services to the oil and gas exploration, production and petrochemical industries. Smith International Canada Ltd. employs 35 people at this location and a total of 85 people in Canada. Graduates most likely to be hired come from the following academic areas: Bachelor of Science (Geology), Bachelor of Engineering (General, Industrial Design, Industrial Production, Welding, Petroleum), Certified Management Accountant, Certified General Accountant, Master of Business Administration (Information Systems) and Community College Diploma (Financial Planning, Purchasing/Logistics, Engineering Technician, Welding). Graduates would occupy entry level Clerk, Technician, Sales, Information Systems and Assistant positions. Outgoing, self-motivated, diverse, easy-going and a positive attitude are all listed as desirable non-academic qualifications. Company benefits are rated as excellent. The potential for advancement is listed as average. The average annual starting salary falls within the $25,000 to $30,000 range. The most suitable method for initial contact by those seeking employment is by telephone. Smith International Canada Ltd. does hire summer students. *Contact:* Office Administrator.

SMITHKLINE BEECHAM

2030 Bristol Circle
Oakville, ON L6H 5V2

Tel.	905-829-2030
Fax	905-829-6063
Website	www.sb.com

Smithkline Beecham is one of the world's leading healthcare companies. The company is involved in the discovery, development, manufacturing and marketing of pharmaceuticals, vaccines, over-the-counter medicines and health-related consumer products. Smithkline Beecham also provides healthcare services, including disease management, clinical laboratory testing, and pharmacy benefit management. The company employs a total of 53,000 employees worldwide. Graduates most likely to be hired come from the following academic areas: Bachelor of Science (General, Biology, Chemistry, Nursing, Pharmacy, Psychology), Bachelor of Commerce/Business Administration and Master of Business Administration. Graduates would occupy Medical Sales Representative, Specialist Sales Representative, Oncology Sales Representative, and Biological Sales Representative positions. Previous experience in sales (especially pharmaceutical sales), detail oriented and able to work with little supervision are all listed as desirable non-academic qualifications. Company benefits are rated above average. The potential for advancement is listed as excellent. The average annual starting salary falls within the $40,000 to $45,000 range. The most suitable method for initial contact by those seeking employment is to mail a resume with a covering letter. Smithkline Beecham does hire summer students. *Contact:* Human Resources.

SNC-LAVALIN INC., CHEMICALS & PETROLEUM BUSINESS UNIT

909 - 5 Avenue SW
Calgary, AB T2P 3G5

Tel.	403-294-2100
Fax	403-294-2193
Email	cval@snc-lavalin.com
Website	www.snc-lavalin.com

SNC-Lavalin Inc., Chemicals and Petroleum Business Unit is a leader in process design, engineering procurement and construction of facilities for the chemicals and petroleum industries. The Chemicals and Petroleum Business Unit is headquartered in Alberta with offices in Calgary and Edmonton, and has demonstrated a commitment to quality project excellence that has earned it a world-class reputation. The business unit is a member of SNC-Lavalin Inc.. Founded 80 years ago, SNC-Lavalin Inc. is one of the largest engineering and construction management firms in the world. The company has successfully implemented major projects in over 120 countries. In addition to offices across Canada, SNC-Lavalin operates from strategically located bases in Africa, Asia, Europe, Latin America and the Middle East. Graduates most likely to be hired for the Chemicals and Petroleum Business Unit come from the following academic areas: Bachelor of Engineering (Chemical, Civil, Electrical, Mechanical, Instrumentation, Metallurgy, Mining, Telecommunications) and Community College Diploma (CAD/CAM/Autocad, Engineering Technician). Graduates would occupy Technician and Engineer positions. Generic competency is listed as desirable non-academic qualifications. Company benefits are rated above average. The potential for advancement is listed as average. The average annual starting salary falls within the $40,000 to $45,000 range. The most suitable method for initial contact by those seeking employment is to e-mail a resume with a covering letter. The Chemicals and Petroleum Business Unit does hire summer and co-op work term students. (Head Office: SNC-Lavalin Inc., 455 Rene-Levesque Boulevard West, Montreal, Quebec, H2Z 1Z3; Tel: 514-393-1000; Fax: 514-866-0795). *Contact:* Human Resources.

SNC-LAVALIN INC., ONTARIO DIVISION

2235 Sheppard Avenue East
Toronto, ON M2J 5A6

Tel.	416-756-2300
Fax	416-756-2266
Website	www.snc-lavalin.com

SNC-Lavalin Inc., Ontario Division provides engineering consulting services in environmental, municipal (eg. water, waste water, sewage), transportation, bridges and structures, and highway lighting. Founded 80 years ago, SNC-Lavalin Inc. is one of the largest engineering and construction management firms in the world. The company has successfully implemented major projects in over 120 countries. In addition to offices across Canada, SNC-Lavalin operates from strategically located bases in Africa, Asia, Europe, Latin America, and the Middle East. The Ontario Division employs approximately 175 people. Graduates most likely to be hired at the division come from the following academic areas: Bachelor of Arts (Urban Geography), Bachelor of Science (Biology, Chemistry, Environmental, Geology), Bachelor of Engineering (Architectural/Building, Instrumentation, Industrial Design), Bachelor of Commerce/Business Administration (Human Resources), Certified Management Accountant, Certified General Accountant and Community College Diploma (Accounting, Human Resources, Architectural Technician, CAD/CAM/Autocad, HVAC Systems Technician). Graduates would occupy Engineer-in-Training, Technician, Drafting/Designing, Engineer, Librarian and Human Resource positions. Entrepreneurial, self-starter, time oriented, team player, creative and dedication are all listed as desirable non-academic qualifications. Company benefits are rated above average. The potential for advancement is listed as being good. The average annual starting salary falls within the $20,000 to $40,000 range, depending on the position being considered. The most suitable methods for initial contact by those seeking employment are to mail or e-mail a resume with a covering letter. SNC-Lavalin Inc., Ontario Division does hire summer and co-op work term students. (Head Office: SNC-Lavalin Inc., 455 Rene-Levesque Boulevard West, Montreal, Quebec, H2Z 1Z3; Tel: 514-393-1000; Fax: 514-866-0795). *Contacts:* Keri Christensen, Human Resources or Marcy Principio, Human Resources.

SNC-LAVALIN INC., POWER DEVELOPMENT DIVISION

1100, boul René Lévesque Ouest
Montreal, QC H3B 4P3

Tel.	514-393-1000
Fax	514-871-4913
Website	www.snc-lavalin.com

SNC-Lavalin Inc., Power Development Division provides turnkey services for engineering, procurement and construction of power generation and transmission projects, as well as investment and debt financing, greenfield sites and rehabilitation and extension of existing facilities. The Power Development Division is an operating division of SNC-Lavalin Inc. Founded 80 years ago, SNC-Lavalin Inc. is one of the largest engineering and construction management firms in the world. The company has successfully implemented major projects in over 120 countries. In addition to offices across Canada, SNC-Lavalin operates from strategically located bases in Africa, Asia, Europe, Latin America and the Middle East. The Power Development Division employs approximately 300 employees. Graduates most likely to be hired at the division come from the following academic areas: Bachelor of Science (Geology), Bachelor of Engineering (Civil, Electrical, Automation/Robotics, Instrumentation, Power, Telecommunications, Mechanical, Industrial Design, Hydraulics, Geotechnical) and Community College Diploma (CAD/CAM/Autocad). The most suitable method for initial contact by those seeking employment is to mail a resume with a covering letter. (Head Office: SNC-Lavalin Inc., 455 Rene-Levesque Boulevard West, Montreal, Quebec, H2Z 1Z3; Tel: 514-393-1000; Fax: 514-866-0795). *Contact:* Human Resources.

SNS/ASSURE CORP.

5090 Orbitor Drive
Mississauga, ON L4W 5B5

Tel.	905-602-8374
Fax	905-602-7831
Email	jill_ellis@sns.ca
Website	www.sns.ca

SNS/Assure Corp. is a leading Canadian based provider of electronic commerce products and value added services. Services are provided primarily to the financial, health care, transportation, logistics, retail and manufacturing industries. The company offers a broad range of customized and proprietary solutions in the areas of point-of-sale (POS) transaction processing, health benefits processing, electronic data interchange (EDI) and workflow and document management. These solutions are designed to automate and accelerate the creation, use, communication and transmission, electronically, of traditionally paper-based information, both within an organization and in its relationships with customers and suppliers. To provide a complete customer solution, SNS/Assure also offers specialized consulting, implementation, training and technical or business support services across

its four business segments. SNS/Assure has 436 employees at this location, a total of 445 in Canada, and a total of 509 employees worldwide. Graduates most likely to be hired come from the following academic areas: Bachelor of Science (Computer Science, Mathematics, Nursing), Bachelor of Engineering (General, Computer Science, Telecommunications), Bachelor of Commerce/Business Administration (General, Accounting, Finance, Human Resources, Information Systems, Marketing), Master of Science (Computer Science), Master of Engineering (Computer Systems) and Community College Diploma (Accounting, Administration, Business, Financial Planning, Human Resources, Information Systems, Marketing/Sales, Secretarial, Computer Science, Electronics Technician). Graduates would occupy Programmer/Analyst, System Architect, Occupational Health Nurse, Sales, Accounts Payable/Receivable and Administration positions. Previous work experience is listed as a desirable non-academic qualifications. Company benefits are rated as excellent. The potential for advancement is listed as being good. The average annual starting salary falls within the $35,000 to $40,000 range. The most suitable method for initial contact by those seeking employment is to e-mail a resume with a covering letter. SNS/Assure Corp. does hire summer and co-op work term students. *Contacts:* Jill Ellis, Human Resources Coordinator or Darlene LeGree, Human Resources Manager.

SOBEYS CANADA INC.

123 Foord Street
Stellarton, NS B0K 1S0

Tel.	902-752-8371
Fax	902-928-1671
Email	customer.service@sobeys.ca
Website	www.sobeysweb.com

Sobeys Canada Inc. is a major food retailer, wholesaler and food service distributor. The company is comprised of two main business segments: Sobeys Inc. is Canada's largest food retail franchisor and second largest food distributor with sales of $10 billion annually, and SERCA Foodservice Inc. is the country's only national foodservice wholesaler. Sobeys is known for its many banners such as IGA, Price Chopper, Knechtel, Food Town, Sobeys, Lofoods, Tra Foods and Green Gables convenience stores. SERCA distributes nationally to restaurants, hospitals, hotels and institutional accounts. The company employs a total of 30,000 people across Canada. Graduates most likely to be hired come from the following academic areas: Bachelor of Arts (General), Bachelor of Science (Computer Science), Bachelor of Engineering (Industrial Engineering), Bachelor of Commerce/Business Administration (General, Accounting, Finance, Human Resources, Information Systems, Marketing), Chartered Accountant, Master of Business Administration (General), Community College Diploma (Accounting, Business, Human Resources, Information Systems, Marketing/Sales, Purchasing/Logistics, Computer Science) and High School Diploma. Action and results driven, innovative, excellent problem solving skills, customer driven and the ability to build positive relationships are all listed as desirable non-academic qualifications. Company benefits are rated above average. The potential for advancement is listed as being good. The average annual starting salary depends on the position being considered. The most suitable methods for initial contact by those seeking employment are to fax or e-mail a resume with a covering letter to the nearest regional office. Sobeys Canada Inc. does hire summer and co-op work term students. *Contact:* Human Resources.

SOCIÉTÉ LAURENTIDE INC.
4660 - 12e Avenue
Shawinigan-Sud, QC G9N 6T5

Tel. 819-537-6636
Fax 819-537-5293
Website .... www.societelaurentide.com

Société Laurentide Inc. manufactures chemicals such as wood finishes, paints, antifreeze, solvents and plastics. The company employs approximately 125 people at this location and a total of 300 employees in Canada. Graduates most likely to be hired come from the following academic areas: Bachelor of Science (Chemistry), Bachelor of Engineering (Industrial Chemistry, Industrial Production), Bachelor of Commerce/Business Administration (General, Accounting, Finance, Human Resources, Marketing), Certified Management Accountant, Certified General Accountant and Community College Diploma (Business, Secretarial). Graduates would occupy Clerk, Technician and Director positions. Bilingual, positive attitude and determination are all listed as desirable non-academic qualifications. Company benefits and the potential for advancement are both rated as excellent. The most suitable method for initial contact by those seeking employment is to mail a resume with a covering letter. Société Laurentide Inc. does hire summer students. *Contact:* Denis Hogue.

SODEXHO MARRIOTT SERVICES CANADA LTD. / SMSC
774, rue St-Paul Ouest
Montreal, QC H3C 1M5

Tel. 514-866-7070
Fax 514-866-2212
Website .... www.sodexomarriott.com

Sodexho Marriott Services Canada Ltd. / SMSC is one of Canada's leading providers of outsourced food and facilities management services. Formed through an amalgamation of Montreal based Sodexho Canada and Burlington based Marriott Corporation of Canada, SMSC provides outsourcing services, including food service, laundry, housekeeping, groundskeeping and other facilities management services to approximately 260 clients in corporate, healthcare, education, recreation, leisure and remote-site markets. SMSC employs 1,500 people in Quebec and a total of 5,000 people in Canada and is a wholly owned subsidiary of Sodexho Marriott Services, Inc., based in Bethesda, Maryland, which is the largest provider of outsourced food and facilities management services in North America. Graduates most likely to be hired come from the following academic areas: Bachelor of Arts (General), Bachelor of Science (Nutritional Sciences), Bachelor of Commerce/Business Administration (General, Accounting, Marketing), Community College Diploma (Accounting, Administration, Business, Facility Management, Marketing/Sales, Secretarial, Cook/Chef Training, Hospitality, Nutrition) and High School Diploma. Graduates would occupy Account Manager, Secretary, Accounting Clerk, Chef, Dietician and Sales Representative positions. Organized, a good attitude, creative and service oriented are all listed as desirable non-academic qualifications. Company benefits are rated above average. The potential for advancement is listed as being good. The average annual starting salary falls within the $25,000 to $30,000 range. The most suitable methods for initial contact by those seeking employment are to mail or fax a resume with a covering letter. Sodexho Marriott does hire summer students. *Contact:* Stéphane Rivet, Directeur, Ressources Humaines.

SODEXHO MARRIOTT SERVICES CANADA LTD. / SMSC
3350 South Service Road
Burlington, ON L7N 3M6

Tel. 905-632-8592
Fax 905-681-3021
Email .... jalaw@sodexhomarriott.com
Website .... www.sodexomarriott.com

Sodexho Marriott Services Canada Ltd. / SMSC is one of Canada's leading providers of outsourced food and facilities management services. Formed through an amalgamation of Montreal based Sodexho Canada and Burlington based Marriott Corporation of Canada, SMSC provides outsourcing services, including food service, laundry, housekeeping, groundskeeping and other facilities management services to approximately 260 clients in corporate, healthcare, education, recreation, leisure and remote-site markets. SMSC is a wholly owned subsidiary of Sodexho Marriott Services, Inc., based in Bethesda, Maryland, which is the largest provider of outsourced food and facilities management services in North America. Graduates most likely to be hired come from the following academic areas: Bachelor of Science (Nutritional Sciences), Bachelor of Commerce/Business Administration (General, Accounting, Finance, Human Resources, Marketing), Master of Business Administration (Accounting, Finance, Human Resources) and Community College Diploma (Accounting, Facility Management, Human Resources, Marketing/Sales, Secretarial, Hospitality, Cook/Chef, HVAC Systems, Dietitian/Nutrition). Graduates would occupy Cook, Chef, Assistant Manager, Manager, General Manager, Operations Director, Financial Analyst and Controller positions. Team player, self-starter, customer focused and the drive to succeed and exceed expectations are all listed as desirable non-academic qualifications. Company benefits are rated as industry standard. The potential for advancement is listed as being excellent. The average annual starting salary falls within the $25,000 to $35,000 range. The most suitable method for initial contact by those seeking employment is to e-mail a resume with a covering letter. Sodexho Marriott Services Canada Ltd. occasionally hires summer students on a project specific basis and hires co-op work term students for the company's Student Manager Program. *Contact:* Human Resources Department.

SOLCORP
5925 Airport Road, 9th Floor
Mississauga, ON L4V 1W1

Tel. 905-672-9444
Fax 905-672-1322
Email .... recruiting@solcorp.com
Website .... www.solcorp.com

SOLCORP is a leading provider of software and solutions to life insurance companies. Over the past two decades, SOLCORP has established an unique partnership with many of the world's major players in the industry. Today, the company is a global organization with customers ranging across five continents. Well over 150 project implementations for more than 75 companies, including a long list of industry leaders, have been successfully completed. SOLCORP is dedicated to serving the life insurance industry by providing customer-driven solutions that give companies the flexibility to launch innovative policies, bring new products quickly to market and to increase revenue by distributing customer and policy information directly to the point-of-sale. SOLCORP is a wholly-owned subsidiary of EDS, and employs 500 people worldwide, in offices in Mississauga, Montreal, Downers Grove, Illinois, West Sussex, England and North Sydney, Australia. Graduates most likely to be hired come from the following academic areas: Bachelor of Science (General, Actuarial, Computer Science, Forestry, Mathematics), Bachelor of Engineering (General, Computer Systems), Bachelor of Commerce/Business Administration (Information Systems, Marketing), Master of Business Administration (Information Systems, Marketing), Master of Engineering (General, Information Systems) and Community College Diploma (Information Systems, Insurance, Marketing/Sales, Computer Science, Electronics Technician, Engineering Technician). SOLCORP seeks talented Programmer Analysts and Business Analysts with extensive COBOL, CICS, VisualC++, and individual life insurance administration systems experience (eg. CAPSIL, Life 70, Paxus) to work on research and development of their products and implementation at client sites throughout the world. In addition to Analyst positions, graduates would occupy Database Administrator, Project Manager, Team Leader and Technical Support Analyst positions. Team player, life insurance knowledge, customer service skills, a willingness to travel for extended periods of time and strong communication skills are all listed as desirable non-academic qualifications. Company benefits and the potential for advancement are both rated as excellent. The average annual starting salary falls within the $50,000 to $55,000 range. The most suitable methods for initial contact by those seeking employment are to fax or e-mail a resume with a covering letter, or through the company's website. SOLCORP does hire summer, intern and co-op work term students. *Contact:* Human Resources.

SONY MUSIC CANADA
1121 Leslie Street
Toronto, ON M3C 2J9

Tel. 416-391-3311
Fax 416-391-7969
Website .... www.sonymusic.ca

Sony Music Canada is involved in the production and distribution of recorded music, music publishing, as well as sales and marketing of their products and related support services. The company maintains regional branches across Canada in Toronto, Vancouver, Calgary and Montreal with representatives in Edmonton, Moncton, and Halifax. Sony Music Canada employs approximately 300 people at this location, and an additional 100 people across Canada. Graduates most likely to be hired come from the following areas: Bachelor of Arts (General, English, Graphic Arts, Journalism, Music), Bachelor of Engineering (Chemical, Civil, Electrical, Automation/Robotics, Computer Systems, Telecommunications, Mechanical, Welding), Bachelor of Architecture, Bachelor of Commerce/Business Administration (Accounting, Finance, Human Resources, Information Systems, Marketing, Public Administration), Chartered Accountant, Certified Management Accountant, Certified General Accountant and Community College Diploma (Accounting, Administration, Advertising, Business, Communications, Facility Management, Financial Planning, Human Resources, Marketing, Purchasing/Logistics, Secretarial, Graphic Arts, Journalism, Photography, Television/Radio Arts, CAD/CAM/Autocad, Computer Science, Electronics Technician, Engineering Technician, HVAC Systems, Welding). Graduates would occupy Mechanical Technician, Electrical Technician, General Operator, Chemical Engineer, Administrative Assistant, Account Service Representative, Accountant, Financial Analyst, Computer Operator, Accounts Payable Clerk and Warehouse Clerk positions. Company benefits and the potential for advancement are both rated as excellent. The most suitable method for initial contact by those seeking employment is to mail a resume with a covering letter. Sony Music Canada does hire summer students. *Contact:* Human Resources.

SOUTH-EAST HEALTH CARE CORPORATION
135 MacBeath Avenue
Moncton, NB E1C 6Z8

Tel. 506-857-5585
Fax 506-857-5590

South-East Health Care Corporation is dedicated to the provision and promotion of quality health care services to the communities served. The corporation is made up of the following facilities in the following New Brunswick communities: The Albert County Hospital in Riverside-Albert, Health Services Centre in Rexton, Petitcodiac Health Centre in Petitcodiac, The Sackville Memorial Hospital in Sackville, The Moncton Hospital in Moncton, Addiction Services in Moncton, Katherine Wright Family Wellness Centre in Moncton and Extra-Mural Services in Moncton. Together, these facilities form the South-East Health Care Corporation and employ a total of 2,400 people. Graduates most likely to be hired come from the following academic areas: Bachelor of Arts (Psychology, Social Work), Bachelor of Science (Computer Science, Audiology, Nursing, Occupational Therapy, Pharmacy, Psychology, Speech Pathology), Bachelor of Commerce/Business Administration (Accounting, Human Resources, Information Systems, Chartered Accountant, Certified Management Accountant, Certified General Accountant, Master of Business Administration (Information Systems), Community College Diploma (Secretarial, Computer Science, Electronics Technician, HVAC Systems, Information Systems, Plumber, Ambulance/Emergency Care, Dietitian/Nutrition, Health/Home Care Aide, Laboratory Technician, Nuclear Medicine Technician, Nursing RN/RNA, Radiology Technician, Rehabilitation Therapy, Respiratory Therapy) and High School Diploma. Graduates from health related disciplines would occupy positions related to the staffing of health care facilities (eg. Nurses, Pharmacists, Social Workers, Laboratory Technicians, etc.), while graduates from other disciplines are hired for positions related to the functioning of the health care facilities (eg. Food Services, Administrative Staff, Maintenance Staff, etc.). Team player, good organizational skills, positive attitude and excellent communication skills are all listed as desirable non-academic qualifications. Company benefits are rated above average. The potential for advancement is listed as average. The average annual starting salary varies widely depending on the position being considered. The most suitable methods for initial contact by those seeking employment are to mail a resume with a covering letter, or via telephone. The South-East Health Care Corporation does hire summer and co-op work term students. *Contact:* Human Resources.

SOUTHAM INC.
1450 Don Mills Road
Toronto, ON M3B 2X7

Tel. 416-445-6641
Fax 416-442-2208
Email .... careers@corporate.southam.ca
Website .... www.southam.com

Southam Inc. is a leading Canadian information company with interests in daily and community newspapers and business-to-business information. Southam is a subsidiary of Hollinger International Inc., an international newspaper company. Southam is Canada's largest publisher of daily newspapers with average daily circulation of 1.6 million. The company also publishes 48 free circulation and 16 paid circulation non-daily community papers. In addition, Southam operates a business communications division, Southam Magazine and Information Group, which produces over 30 trade publications as well as industry-specific directories, newsletters, seminars and conferences. The company also hosts a national consumer website, Canada.com, that provides a variety of news content and searching capabilities through the internet. A number of Southam's business communications products host online services as well. Southam employs more than 500 staff at the head office location. Graduates most likely to be hired come from the following academic areas: Bachelor of Arts (Economics, English, French, Journalism, Languages, Psychology), Bachelor of Science (Mathematics), Bachelor of Engineering (Computer Systems, Mining, Telecommunications), Bachelor of Commerce/Business Administration (General, Accounting, Finance, Human Resources, Information Systems, Marketing), Chartered Accountant, Certified Management Accountant, Certified General Accountant, Master of Business Administration (General, Accounting, Finance, Human Resources, Information Systems, Marketing, Public Administration) and Community College Diploma (Accounting, Advertising, Business, Communications/Public Relations, Facility Management, Financial Planning, Human Resources, Marketing/Sales, Graphic Arts, Journalism). Graduates would occupy Editorial Assistant, Inside Sales Representative, Junior Sales Representative, Accounting Clerk, Administrative Assistant and Clerical Support Staff positions. Team player, initiative, flexibility and creativity are all listed as desirable non-academic qualifications. Company benefits are rated above average. The potential for advancement is listed as being good. The average annual starting salary falls within the $25,000 to $30,000 range. The most suitable method for initial contact by those seeking employment is to mail a resume with a covering letter. Southam Inc. does hire summer and co-op work term students. *Contact:* Human Resources.

SPACEBRIDGE NETWORKS CORPORATION
115 Champlain Street
Hull, QC J8X 3R1

Tel. 819-776-2848
Fax 819-776-4179
Email .... hr@spacebridge.com
Website .... www.spacebridge.com

SpaceBridge Networks Corporation develops broadband satellite network solutions, products and technologies for both today's satellite systems and the advanced global networks of the future. SpaceBridge was formed in 1997 through a joint venture between COM DEV, a market leader in space-qualified equipment, and Newbridge Networks Corporation, a market leader in advanced networking equipment. This unique teaming gives SpaceBridge access to a wide range of market-leading networking technology, products and applications that directly complement the company's satellite networking products. SpaceBridge employs a total of 70 people. Graduates most likely to be hired come from the following academic areas: Bachelor of Science (Computer Science), Bachelor of Engineering (Electrical, Computer Systems, Telecommunications) and Master of Engineering (Electrical). Graduates would occupy ASIC Designer, Software Designer, Hardware Designer and DSP Designer positions. Team player, entrepreneurial, initiative, enthusiastic and strong leadership skills are all listed as desirable non-academic qualifications. Company benefits and the potential for advancement are both rated as excellent. The most suitable methods for initial contact by those seeking employment are to e-mail a resume with a covering letter, or by applying through the company's website. SpaceBridge Networks Corporation does hire summer and co-op work term students. *Contact:* Human Resources.

SPECTRA COMPUTER SERVICES LTD.
383 Dovercourt Drive, Suite 200
Winnipeg, MB R3Y 1G4

Tel. 204-489-9790
Fax 204-489-1667
Email .... info@spectra.ca
Website .... www.spectra.ca

Spectra Computer Services Ltd. is a North American leader in developing real estate management software. Spectra's professional team of software developers continues to expand due to corporate growth and expansion. Currently, the company employs 20 people. Graduates most likely to be hired are Bachelor of Science graduates in Computer Science. Graduates are hired as Software Developers using Microsoft development tools. Initiative, self-motivated, team player and good communication skills are all listed as desirable non-academic qualifications. Company benefits are rated as industry standard. The potential for advancement is listed as average. The average annual starting salary falls within the $35,000 to $40,000 range. The most suitable method for initial contact by those seeking employment is to mail a resume with a covering letter. Spectra Computer Services Ltd. does hire co-op work term students. *Contact:* Vice President of Development.

SPECTRUM SIGNAL PROCESSING INC.
8525 Baxter Place, Suite 100
Burnaby, BC V5A 4V7

Tel. 604-421-5422
Fax 604-421-1764
Email .... jobs@spectrumsignal.com
Website .... www.spectrumsignal.com

Spectrum Signal Processing Inc. leads the worldwide market in the development and integration of superior quality digital signal processing (DSP) products. Spectrum designs, develops and markets programmable DSP solutions which are incorporated into high-performance applications. All of the product solutions possess a very unique quality: they are all based on software programmable DSPs, rather than fixed function DSPs. This allows maximum system flexibility and provides a better more flexible system for customers. By incorporating these high-end programmable processors into all of their hardware products, Spectrum offers their customers the option to simply upgrade their old system, rather than completely replacing it. The company's proven engineering capabilities and expertise in programmable DSP software, hardware and ASIC designs, position it as the leading provider of programmable DSP system solutions worldwide. Founded in 1987, Spectrum employs 150 people at this location and a total of 175 people worldwide. Graduates most likely to be hired come from the following academic areas: Bachelor of Science (Computer Science) and Bachelor of Engineering (Electrical, Computer Systems, Engineering Physics). Graduates would occupy Development Engineer and Field Application Engineers. Team player, related DSP experience, innovative and good problem solving skills are all listed as desirable non-academic qualifications. Company benefits and the potential for advancement are both listed as excellent. The average annual starting salary falls within the $40,000 to $45,000 range. The most suitable method for initial contact by those seeking employment is to mail a resume with a covering letter. Spectrum Signal Processing Inc. does hire co-op work term students. *Contact:* Carol Schulz, Human Resources Committee Chairperson.

SPEEDWARE CORPORATION
9999 Cavendish Boulevard, Suite 100
St-Laurent, QC H4M 2X5

Tel.	514-747-7007
Fax	514-747-3380
Email	HR@speedware.com
Website	www.speedware.com

Speedware Corporation develops and markets rapid application development tools that enable their customers to create specialized computer applications for their businesses. The company also sells client server applications for accounting, database reporting and executive information systems. Speedware products run on stand alone and networked computers under most popular operating systems. There are 130 employees at this location, a total of 150 in Canada, and 230 worldwide. Graduates most likely to be hired come from the following academic areas: Bachelor of Science (Computer Science, Mathematics), Bachelor of Engineering (Computer Systems, Telecommunications), Bachelor of Commerce/Business Administration (Information Systems), Master of Business Administration (Information Systems), Master of Science (Computer Science), Master of Engineering (Computer Systems) and Community College Diploma (Accounting, Administration, Computer Science). Graduates would occupy Programmer, Software Developer, Systems Analyst, Software Systems Tester, Quality Assurance Specialist, Software Systems Support, Customer Support Specialist, Technical Product Manager, Marketing Specialist, Technical Writer, Training Course Developer and Administrative Clerk positions. Flexible, organized, detail oriented, fast learner, work with minimal supervision and to tight deadlines, willing to accept a variety of assignments, interested in maintaining up-to-date technical knowledge, and experience with business systems, internet and networked computers are all listed as desirable non-academic skills. Company benefits are rated above average. The potential for advancement is listed as being good. The average annual starting salary falls within the $30,000 to $35,000 range, depending upon qualifications. The most suitable methods for initial contact by those seeking employment are to mail or e-mail a resume with a covering letter. Speedware Corporation occasionally hires summer and co-op work term students for programming, technical writing and graphic design positions. (Other Canadian Locations: Speedware, Quebec City: 2600 boul. Laurier, Suite 2350, Sainte Foy, QC, G1V 4M6, Phone 418-650-6567, Fax 418-650-5887;

Speedware, Toronto: 150 John Street, 10th Floor, Toronto, ON, M5V 3E3, Phone 416-408-2880, Fax 416-408-2872.)   *Contact:* Rose Church, Manager, Human Resources.

SPORT MART DISCOUNT SUPERSTORES
945 Columbia, Suite 214
Kamloops, BC V2C 1L5

Tel.	250-372-3128
Fax	250-828-2558
Email	sportmart@wkpowerlink.com
Website	www.sportmart.ca

Sport Mart Discount Superstores operates sporting goods retail superstores in western Canada. There are approximately 18 employees at this location and a total of 450 employees in the company. Graduates with a High School Diploma are hired, post secondary education is not listed a prerequisite for employment application. Company benefits are rated above average. The potential for advancement is listed as being excellent. The average annual starting salary falls within the $15,000 to $20,000 range. The most suitable methods for initial contact by those seeking employment are to mail a resume with a covering letter, or via the company's website. Sport Mart Discount Superstores does hire summer students. *Contacts:* Shawn Fiddick, Prairies & Ontario; James Marchand, Alberta; Rob Hillier, Vancouver; or John Campbell, Interior BC & Island.

SPRINT CANADA INC.
2235 Sheppard Avenue East, Suite 600
Toronto, ON M2J 5G1

Tel.	416-496-1644
Website	www.sprintcanada.ca

Sprint Canada Inc. is Canada's leading alternative long-distance telecommunications company, offering voice and data services nationwide. The company offers a full range of telecommunications products and services to all market segments, from long distance to virtual private networks and data networking. Sprint Canada provides service to residential customers, small businesses, major corporations and governments. The company operates 18 offices and employs more than 2,600 people across the country. There are more than 580 employees at this location. Graduates most likely to be hired come from the following academic areas: Bachelor of Arts (General, French, Languages), Bachelor of Science (Computer Science, Mathematics), Bachelor of Engineering (General, Telecommunications), Bachelor of Laws, Bachelor of Commerce/Business Administration (General, Accounting, Finance, Human Resources, Information Systems), Chartered Accountant, Master of Business Administration (Human Resources, Information Systems, Marketing) and Community College Diploma (Human Resources). Graduates would occupy Financial Analyst, Programmer/Analyst, Human Resources Assistant, Recruiter, Computer Operator and Customer Services Representative positions. Adaptable, flexible, positive, team player and able to work well independently are all listed as desirable non-academic qualifications. Company benefits are rated above average. The potential for advancement is listed as excellent. The average annual starting salary falls within the $30,000 to $35,000 range. The most suitable methods for initial contact by those seeking employment are to mail a resume with a covering letter, or via the company's website. Sprint Canada Inc. does hire summer and co-op work term students. *Contact:* Marianne Carruthers, Manager, Recruitment Centre.

SQL TECHNOLOGIES INC. / SQL TECH
2323 Yonge Street, Suite 605
Toronto, ON M4P 2C9

Tel.	416-483-7383
Fax	416-483-8102
Website	www.sql-tech.com

SQL Technologies Inc. / SQL Tech is an organization specializing in the planning and delivery of client server solutions. Employing more than 45 people, SQL is a sales organization and supplier of contract IT professionals. Graduates most likely to be hired come from the following academic areas: Bachelor of Science (Computer Science), Master of Business Administration (Marketing) and Human Resources Management Diploma. Graduates would occupy Consultant, Marketing and Human Resources positions. Integrity, a forthright manner, self-motivation, excellent communication skills, a high energy level and customer relations skills are all listed as desirable non-academic qualifications. Company benefits are rated as industry standard. The potential for advancement is listed as being good. The average annual starting salary falls within the $30,000 to $35,000 range and is commission based for certain positions. The most suitable method for initial contact by those seeking employment is to mail a resume with a covering letter. SQL Technologies Inc. does hire summer students. *Contact:* Frank McCrea, President.

ST. JOHN'S REHABILITATION HOSPITAL
285 Cummer Avenue
Toronto, ON M2M 2G1

Tel.	416-226-6780
Fax	416-226-1598
Website	www.stjohnsrehab.com

The St. John's Rehabilitation Hospital provides quality short term rehabilitation services to adolescent and adult populations. Patients are referred to St. John's from active treatment hospitals where they have undergone surgery/treatment in orthopaedics, amputation, and general surgery. St. John's focuses on interdisciplinary patient care including nursing, social work, patient education, physical and occupational therapy. The hospital employs 350 people. Graduates most likely to be hired come from the following academic areas: Bachelor of Arts (General, Recreation Studies, Social Work), Bachelor of Science (General, Zoology, Nursing, Occupational Therapy, Pharmacy, Physiotherapy, Speech Pathology), Bachelor of Commerce/Business Administration (General), Master of Business Administration (Human Resources, Public Administration), Master of Arts (Social Work), Master of Science (Health Administration, Nursing, Occupational Therapy, Physiotherapy, Speech Pathology) and Community College Diploma (Massage Therapy, Nursing RNA, Rehabilitation Therapy). Graduates would occupy positions relating directly to their particular academic background. Team based skills, a positive attitude, good interpersonal skills and previous work experience in a health care or social service setting are all listed as desirable non-academic qualifications. Company benefits are rated above average. The potential for advancement is listed as being good. The average annual starting salary falls within the $30,000 to $35,000 range. The most suitable method for initial contact by graduates seeking employment is to mail a resume with a covering letter. St. John's Rehabilitation Hospital does hire summer students and occasionally hires co-op work term students. *Contacts:* Terry McMahon, Director of Human Resources or Mita Saha, Human Resources Assistant.

ST. JOSEPH PRINTING LIMITED
50 MacIntosh Boulevard
Concord, ON L4K 4P3

Tel.	905-660-3111
Fax	905-660-6820

St. Joseph Printing Limited is a high quality commercial printer on the cutting edge in the application of new technologies. It is the largest privately owned printing corporation in Canada employing approximately 425 people. Network Studios, a division of St. Joseph Printing provides state of the art photography and pre-press activities. Together, St. Joseph Printing and Network Studios offer services from concept to doorstep. Graduates most likely to be hired come from the following academic areas: Bachelor of Arts, Bachelor of Science (Computer Science), Bachelor of Commerce/Business Administration, Certified Management Accountant, Community College Diploma (Business, Graphic Arts, Commercial Photography) and High School Diploma. Career opportunities for graduates exist in Creative and Art Direction, Customer Service, Accounting, Administration and Operations. Possessing previous work experience in the printing or fashion photography industries would be desirable. St. Joseph Printing Limited is a growing company committed to employee and business excellence. Graduates interested in a career with St. Joseph Printing Limited should mail a resume with covering letter to the above address. The company does hire summer students. *Contact:* Helen Ploumis, Director of Human Resources.

ST. JOSEPH'S HEALTH CENTRE
30 The Queensway
Toronto, ON M6R 1B5

Tel.	416-530-6460
Fax	416-530-6034

St. Joseph's Health Centre is a community teaching hospital sponsored by the Sisters of St. Joseph and affiliated with the University of Toronto. The centre is one of the largest hospitals in Toronto and offers a broad range of primary and secondary level programs as well as selected tertiary care programs. Services include general medical and surgical, mental health, rehabilitation, obstetrical and paediatric, emergency and out-patient, family support and health promotion, and illness prevention. Facilities include a Women's Health Centre, Family Medicine Centre, Detoxification Unit, Just For Kids Clinic, a Community Health Centre, Elderly Community Health Services and a Renal Therapy Centre. St. Joseph's Health Centre employs approximately 2,000 people. Graduates most likely to be hired come from the following academic areas: Bachelor of Arts (General), Bachelor of Science (Nursing, Pharmacy), Bachelor of Education (Adult/Nursing), Masters (Nursing/Health Administration, Human Resources) and Community College Diploma (General, Nursing, Food/Nutrition, Health Technicians, Secretarial). Graduates would occupy a wide variety of positions in Administration, Nursing, Technical Services, Nutrition Services, and Human Resources. High School graduates are also hired for clerical and service related positions. Excellent written and verbal communication skills and reliability are listed as desirable non-academic qualifications. Company benefits are rated above average. The most suitable method for initial contact by those seeking employment is to mail a well prepared resume with a covering letter. St. Joseph's Health Centre does hire a few summer students each year. *Contact:* Human Resources.

ST. MICHAEL'S HOSPITAL
30 Bond Street
Toronto, ON M5B 1W8

Tel. 416-867-7401
Fax 416-867-7488
Website .... www.smh.toronto.on.ca

St. Michael's Hospital, a Catholic teaching hospital affiliated with the University of Toronto, is recognized for its excellence and leadership in the prevention and treatment of heart disease, prevention and rehabilitation of trauma victims and inner city health. Through the new Wellesley Central Site, it is also a recognized leader in the care and treatment of people living with HIV and AIDS, and cystic fibrosis. Originally established in 1892, the hospital currently employs more than 3,000 people. Graduates most likely to be hired come from the following academic areas: Bachelor of Arts (Social Work), Bachelor of Science (Computer Science, Audiology, Nursing, Nutritional Sciences, Occupational Therapy, Pharmacy, Physiotherapy, Speech Pathology), Bachelor of Engineering (Biomedical Electronics, Telecommunications), Bachelor of Commerce/Business Administration (Information Systems), Master of Science (Nurse Practitioner), Post Graduate programs (Critical Care RN, Cardiovascular Perfusionist) and Community College Diploma (Laboratory Technician, Nuclear Imaging Technologist, Personal Support Worker, Medical Imaging Technologist, Respiratory Technician, Nursing RN, Office/Medical Administration). Graduates would occupy positions which are directly related to their academic field of study. Previous work experience in a hospital environment, team player and a commitment to the mission and values of a hospital are all listed as desirable non-academic qualifications. The most suitable methods for initial contact by those seeking employment are to mail or fax a resume with a covering letter. Contact: Human Resources.

STAGE WEST ALL SUITE HOTEL & THEATRE RESTAURANT
5400 Dixie Road
Mississauga, ON L4W 4T4

Tel. 905-238-0159
Fax 905-238-9820

Stage West All Suite Hotel & Theatre Restaurant is a full service hotel and live theatre restaurant that has mounted more than 50 major productions and numerous one-night shows over the past decade. In addition to showcasing many celebrity personalities, Stage West is also known for its huge buffet and sumptuous dessert table. Stage West maintains 224 suites, an aquatic centre, as well as meeting rooms and a 240-person capacity ballroom. Stage West All Suite Hotel & Theatre Restaurant is part of the Stage West chain based in Calgary. There are approximately 250 employees at this location. Graduates most likely to be hired come from the following academic areas: Bachelor of Arts (General), Bachelor of Commerce/Business Administration (Marketing, Finance), Certified Management Accountant and Community College Diploma (Hotel/Restaurant, Culinary/Cooking). Graduates with relevant experience would be hired for Chef/Cook, Controller, and Middle Management positions in the Front Office, Restaurant, Administration, Food and Beverages, and Sales and Marketing. Punctual, reliable, excellent communication and public relations skills, and a willingness to work shifts and extra hours are all listed as desirable non-academic qualifications. Company benefits are rated as industry standard. The potential for advancement is listed as being good. The most suitable method for initial contact by those seeking employment is to mail

a resume with a covering letter. Stage West does hire summer students. Contact: Sylvia Gimenez, Human Resources Co-ordinator.

STANDARD AERO LIMITED
33 Allen Dyne Road
Winnipeg, MB R3H 1A1

Tel. 204-775-9711
Fax 204-788-2333
Email .... human_resources@standardaero.ca
Website .... www.standardaero.com

Standard Aero is one of the world's largest gas turbine engine and accessory repair and overhaul companies. With facilities located around the globe, Standard Aero serves the ever-changing needs of aircraft, marine and industrial engine operators in over eighty countries. The company's customers include corporate and charter aircraft organizations, governments/militaries, power generation and gas line pumping companies, and some of the largest regional airlines in the world. Standard Aero is headquartered in Winnipeg and employs over 1,550 people in facilities worldwide. Graduates most likely to be hired come from the following academic areas: Bachelor of Science (Computer Science), Bachelor of Engineering (Chemical, Mechanical, Aerospace, Metallurgy), Bachelor of Education (Adult), Bachelor of Commerce/Business Administration (General, Accounting, Human Resources, Information Systems, Marketing), Chartered Accountant, Certified Management Accountant, Certified General Accountant, Master of Engineering, Doctorate of Engineering and Community College Diploma (Accounting, Business, Human Resources, Purchasing/Logistics, Aircraft Maintenance, Computer Science, Engineering Technician, Tool and Die, Machinist). Team player, proficient with Microsoft Office and excellent communication skills are all listed as desirable non-academic qualifications. Company benefits and the potential for advancement are both rated as excellent. The average annual starting salary falls within the $20,000 to $25,000 range. The most suitable method for initial contact by those seeking employment is to e-mail a resume with a covering letter. Standard Aero Limited does hire students for summer and co-op work term positions. Contacts: Alex Yoong, Director of Human Resources or Sandra Hawryluk, Human Resources Assistant.

STANDARD LIFE ASSURANCE COMPANY
1245 rue Sherbrooke Ouest
Montreal, QC H3G 1G3

Tel. 514-499-8855
Fax 514-499-8897
Email .... recruitment@standardlife.ca
Website .... www.standardlife.ca

Standard Life Assurance Company provides group life and health insurance, individual life and health insurance, group pension, individual pension, mutual funds and other investment vehicles. The company employs approximately 900 people at this location and a total of 2,000 people in Canada. Graduates most likely to be hired come from the following academic areas: Bachelor of Arts (General), Bachelor of Science (Actuarial, Nursing), Chartered Accountant, Certified Management Accountant, Certified General Accountant, Master of Business Administration (General, Finance, Information Systems, Marketing), Master of Science (Computer Science), Community College Diploma (Accounting, Administration, Financial Planning, Human Resources, Information Systems, Insurance, Marketing/Sales, Purchasing/Logistics, Secretarial, Graphic Arts, Computer Science). Leadership skills, teamwork, action oriented, business acumen, and a customer focus are all listed as desirable non-academic qualifications. Company benefits and the potential for advancement are both rated as excellent. The average annual starting salary is dependent upon the position being considered. The most suitable method for initial contact by graduates seeking employment is to mail a resume with a covering letter. Standard Life Assurance Company does hire summer students. *Contact:* Staffing Officer.

STANDENS LIMITED
PO Box 67, Station T
Calgary, AB T2H 2G7

Tel.	403-258-7000
Fax	403-258-7808
Email	employment@standens.com
Website	www.standens.com

Standen's Limited manufactures leaf springs, as well as other industrial, automotive and agricultural machinery parts. Products include leaf springs, air beams, trailer axles, cultivator shanks, stabilizer bars, u-bolts, suspension components, draw bars and specialty steel products. Headquartered in Calgary, the company employs a total of 500 people. Graduates most likely to be hired come from the following academic areas: Community College Diploma (Administration, Purchasing/Logistics, Mechanic, Engineering Technician, Welding, Tool and Die Maker, Millwright) and High School Diploma. Graduates would occupy Administrative, Clerical and Skilled Trade positions. Previous work experience, good communication skills, self-starter and focused career objectives are all listed as desirable non-academic qualifications. The most suitable method for initial contact by those seeking employment is to mail a resume with a covering letter. Standen's Limited does hire summer students for manufacturing positions. *Contact:* Roland Osske, Manager, Human Resources.

STANTEC CONSULTING LTD.
10160 - 112 Street, Suite 200
Edmonton, AB T5K 2L6

Tel.	780-917-7000
Fax	780-917-7330
Email	hr@stantec.com
Website	www.stantec.com

Stantec Consulting Ltd. is a consulting engineering firm offering a broad range of engineering and professional consulting services. The company provides services to private and public sector clients in Canada, the United States and internationally. The principal services offered include environmental consulting, infrastructure design and development, industrial engineering, and land development services and project management. Founded in 1954, Stantec operates out of 45 different locations across North America, and has completed over 35,000 projects for some 3,500 clients in more than 80 countries around the world. The company employs 450 people at this location, a total of 1,700 in Canada and a total of 2,000 people worldwide. Graduates most likely to be hired come from the following academic areas: Bachelor of Arts (General, Economics, Journalism, Urban Geography/Planning), Bachelor of Science (General, Biology, Chemistry, Computer Science, Environment/Ecology, Geology), Bachelor of Engineering (General, Chemical, Civil, Electrical, Mechanical, Computer Systems, Geological Engineering, Industrial Chemistry, Industrial Design, Indus-

trial Engineering Surveying, Transportation, Water Resources), Bachelor of Landscape Architecture, Bachelor of Commerce/Business Administration (General, Accounting, Finance, Human Resources, Information Systems, Marketing, Public Administration, Chartered Accountant, Certified Management Accountant, Certified General Accountant, Master of Business Administration (General, Accounting, Finance, Human Resources, Information Systems, Marketing, Public Administration), Master of Engineering and Community College Diploma (Accounting, Advertising, Business, Communications/Public Relations, Financial Planning, Human Resources, Marketing/Sales, Office Administration, Purchasing/Logistics, Architectural Technician, CAD/CAM/Autocad, Electronics Technician, Engineering Technician, Information Systems). Graduates would occupy Clerk, Administrator, Technician, Trainee (with professional component), Junior Engineering and Information Systems positions. Those with a Masters degree may be hired at the Project Management level if they possess a number of years experience. A positive attitude, team player, flexibility and a high level of initiative are all listed as desirable non-academic qualifications. Company benefits are rated above average. The average annual starting salary falls within the $25,000 to $30,000 range. The most suitable methods for initial contact by those seeking employment are to mail or e-mail a resume with a covering letter. Stantec Consulting Ltd. hires summer and co-op work term students. *Contacts:* Alan Gee, Manager, Employment Services or Anne Marie Lakusta, Employment Services Advisor.

STAR DATA SYSTEMS INC.
7030 Woodbine Avenue, 8th Floor
Markham, ON L3R 1A2

Tel.	905-479-7827
Fax	905-479-0736
Email	hr@stardata.ca
Website	www.stardata.com

Star Data Systems Inc. provides high tech delivery of online, real-time financial information systems, solutions and data to over 16,000 wealth managers in Canada. The Applications Service Division provides a comprehensive range of administrative, investment and asset management services to the financial services industry. Star Data's head office is in Markham, with additional office locations in Vancouver, Calgary, Winnipeg, Toronto, Montreal, Halifax and London, United Kingdom. There are 300 employees at this location, a total of 500 employees in Canada and a total of 505 employees in the United Kingdom and Canada. Graduates most likely to be hired come from the following academic areas: Bachelor of Arts (General, Economics, English, French, Psychology, Sociology), Bachelor of Science (General, Computer Science, Mathematics), Bachelor of Engineering (General, Computer Systems, Telecommunications), Bachelor of Laws, Bachelor of Commerce/Business Administration (Accounting, Finance, Human Resources, Information Systems, Marketing), Chartered Accountant, Certified General Accountant, Master of Business Administration (Accounting, Finance, Information Systems) and Community College Diploma (Accounting, Administration, Human Resources, Computer Science, Electronics Technician). Graduates would occupy Finance and Administration, Programming, High Technology/Telecommunications, Sales and Marketing, Human Resource, Training and Technology Assisted Learning positions. Strong interpersonal skills and PC literacy (Word/Spreadsheet/PowerPoint) are listed as desirable non-academic qualifications. Company benefits and the potential for advancement are both rated as excellent. The average annual starting salary is based upon the position being considered. The most suitable method for initial contact by those seeking employment is via referrals through employees. Star Data Systems Inc. does hire summer students. *Contacts:* Vaugnn McIntyre, SVP Organization and Professional Development or Brenda Arcangeli, Manager, Organization and Professional Development.

STATE FARM INSURANCE COMPANIES
100 Consilium Place, Suite 102
Toronto, ON M1H 3G9

Tel.	416-290-4100
Website	www.statefarm.com

State Farm Insurance Companies are involved in the sale and service of automobile, life, and homeowners insurance policies. State Farm's parent company is based in Bloomington, Illinois. Founded in 1922, the company is one of the world's largest property and casualty insurance company. State Farm Insurance Companies employs more than 500 people at this location. Graduates most likely to be hired come from the following academic areas: Bachelor of Arts, Bachelor of Science, Bachelor of Engineering, Bachelor of Education, Bachelor of Laws, Bachelor of Commerce/Business Administration and Community College Diploma (Business). Graduates would occupy Claims Service Representative, Underwriter, Computer Operator, Accounting Trainee and Accounting Clerk positions. Good communication skills and a customer service background are both listed as desirable non-academic qualifications. Company benefits and the potential for advancement are both rated as excellent. The average annual starting salary falls within the $25,000 to $30,000 range. The most suitable method for initial contact by those seeking employment is to mail a resume with a covering letter. State Farm Insurance Companies does hire summer students on a limited basis. *Contact:* Human Resources.

Steelcase

STEELCASE CANADA LTD.
1 Steelcase Road West
Markham, ON L3R 0T3

Tel.	905-475-6333
Fax	905-475-6073
Website	www.steelcase.com

Steelcase Canada Ltd. is the country's leading provider of office furnishings and knowledge about workplace performance. The company is a subsidiary of Steelcase Inc., headquartered in Grand Rapids, Michigan, the world's leader in the industry. There are approximately 650 employees at this location, while Steelcase Inc. employs 19,000 people worldwide. Graduates most likely to be hired come from the following academic areas: Bachelor of Engineering (Mechanical), Bachelor of Architecture, Bachelor of Commerce/Business Administration (Finance, Human Resources), Certified Management Accountant, Master of Business Administration (Finance) and Community College Diploma (Engineering Technician, Information Systems). Graduates would occupy Sales/Consulting, Integrated Interiors Consultant, Product Engineer, Manufacturing Engineer and Manufactur-

ing Technologist positions. Applicants should enjoy working in a team based environment. Company benefits and the potential for advancement are both rated as excellent. The average annual starting salary falls within the $35,000 to $40,000 range. The most suitable methods for initial contact by those seeking employment are to mail or fax a resume with a covering letter. Steelcase Canada Ltd. does hire summer and co-op work term students. For more information about Steelcase please visit the company's website. *Contact:* Human Resources.

STERLING PULP CHEMICALS, LTD.
2 Gibbs Road
Toronto, ON M9B 1R1

Tel.	416-239-7111
Fax	416-237-0431
Website	www.clo2.com

Sterling Pulp Chemicals, Ltd. is one of the world's largest producers of sodium chlorate, an industrial salt used primarily for the manufacture of chlorine dioxide. Chlorine dioxide is the cornerstone of an important bleaching process that reduces pollution. This process, known as elemental chlorine-free bleaching, has a superior environmental track record and yields high quality, environmentally friendly white paper products. The company also licenses and constructs large-scale chlorine dioxide generators, used in the bleaching process by the pulp and paper industry. In addition, Sterling Pulp Chemicals produces sodium chlorite, caustic, chlorine, hydrochloric acid, and calcium hypochlorite. There are 150 employees in Toronto, 465 across Canada, and a total of 500 worldwide. The company operates facilities in Buckingham QC, Thunder Bay ON, Saskatoon, Grande Prairie AB, Vancouver, and Valdosta, Georgia. The company's business headquarters, its research and development facilities and the ERCO Systems Group are located at this address in Toronto. Sterling Pulp Chemicals, Ltd. is owned by Sterling Chemicals Holdings, Inc. based in Houston, Texas. Graduates most likely to be hired come from the following academic areas: Bachelor of Science (Chemistry), Bachelor of Engineering (Chemical, Environmental, Electrical, Mechanical), Bachelor of Commerce/Business Administration (Accounting, Finance, Marketing), Chartered Accountant (Finance), Certified Management Accountant (Finance), Certified General Accountant (Finance) and Community College Diploma (Secretarial, Human Resources, Computer Science). Graduates would occupy R & D Laboratory, Instrumentation, Technical Service, Process Engineering, Project Engineering, Finance, Accounting, Sales and Marketing, Purchasing, Clerical, Secretarial and Human Resource positions. Company benefits and the potential for advancement are both rated as excellent. The most suitable methods for initial contact by those seeking employment are to mail a resume with a covering letter, or via the company's website. Sterling Pulp Chemicals, Ltd. does hire summer and co-op students for R & D Laboratory positions. *Contact:* Human Resources Department.

STIKEMAN, ELLIOTT
Commerce Court West, Suite 5300
Toronto, ON M5L 1B9

Tel.	416-869-5500
Fax	416-947-0866
Email	cbleakley@tor.stikeman.com
Website	www.stikeman.com

Stikeman, Elliott is one of Canada's leading business law firms, drawing on the skills of more than 300 lawyers with a wealth of experience in Canada and around the world. Founded in 1952, the firm maintains Canadian offices in Montreal, Toronto, Vancouver, Calgary and Ottawa, and internationally in New York, Washington, London, Hong Kong, Singapore and Sydney. Graduates most likely to be hired come from the following academic areas: Bachelor of Laws, Bachelor of Commerce/Business Administration (Accounting, Human Resources, Information Systems, Marketing), Master of Business Administration (Accounting, Human Resources, Information Systems) and Community College Diploma (Accounting, Advertising, Facility Management, Human Resources, Secretarial, Information Systems). Graduates would occupy Legal Secretary, Accounting Clerk, Human Resources Manager/Assistant, Systems Staff/Manager, Law Clerk and Office Service Clerk positions. Team player, word processing skills, good oral and written communication skills and previous work experience are all listed as desirable non-academic qualifications. Company benefits are rated as industry standard. The potential for advancement is listed as being good. The average annual starting salary falls within the $25,000 to $40,000 range, depending on the level of position. The most suitable methods for initial contact by those seeking employment are to mail, fax or e-mail (Word, Wordperfect or ASCII formats only), or through the firm's website. Stikeman, Elliott does hire summer and co-op work term students. *Contact:* Cathy Bleakley.

STONE & WEBSTER CANADA LIMITED
2300 Yonge Street
Toronto, ON M4P 2W6

Tel. 416-932-4400
Fax 416-482-2865
Email .... swcl.hr@stoneweb.com
Website .... www.stoneweb.com

Stone & Webster Canada Limited is a full service engineering, procurement and construction management firm. The company operates in the petrochemical, refining, power generation, and heavy industrial sectors. There are approximately 450 employees at this location and a total of 550 employees in Canada. The parent company of Stone & Webster Canada Limited employs approximately 8,000 people worldwide. Graduates most likely to be hired come from the following academic areas: Bachelor of Engineering (Chemical, Civil, Electrical, Instrumentation, Mechanical), Bachelor of Commerce/Business Administration (Accounting, Human Resources, Information Systems), Master of Engineering (Mechanical, Electrical, Civil) and Community College Diploma (Architecture/Drafting, CAD/CAM/Autocad, Computer Science). Graduates would occupy Engineer in Training, Drafter and Designer positions. A willingness to travel, team oriented and effective communication skills are all listed as desirable non-academic qualifications. The most suitable methods for initial contact by those seeking employment are to mail or e-mail a resume with a covering letter. Stone & Webster Canada Limited does hire summer and co-op work term students. *Contacts:* Lisa Dantas, Human Resources Representative or Paul Farkas, Human Resources Manager.

STRESSGEN BIOTECHNOLOGIES CORP.
4243 Glanford Avenue, Suite 350
Victoria, BC V8Z 4B9

Tel. 250-744-2811
Fax 250-744-2877
Email .... jobs@stressgen.com
Website .... www.stressgen.com

StressGen Biotechnologies Corp. is a growing biopharmaceutical company developing medical applications of the cellular stress response. StressGen's research and development programs focus on utilizing stress proteins as immunomodulatory agents in therapeutic applications. The company's biochemical division is an international leader in the development, manufacture and sale of stress protein-related and other research reagents. Based in Victoria, StressGen was the first company to focus exclusively on developing medical treatments based on the cellular stress response and remains at the forefront of this burgeoning field. The company employs 72 people at this location and an additional 4 people in Collegeville, PA, USA. Graduates most likely to be hired come from the following academic areas: Bachelor of Science (General, Biology, Chemistry, Microbiology) and Master of Science. Graduates would occupy Research Technician, Research Assistant and Research Associate positions. Multi-tasking skills, previous work experience in a lab setting, team player, good time management skills and research experience are all listed as desirable non-academic qualifications. Company benefits are rated above average. The potential for advancement is listed as being good. The average annual starting salary falls within the $25,000 to $30,000 range. The most suitable method for initial contact by those seeking employment is to mail a resume with a covering letter. StressGen Biotechnologies Corp. does hire summer and co-op work term students. *Contact:* Dana Quarry, Human Resources.

STRONGCO MATERIAL HANDLING, DIVISION OF STRONGCO INC.
29 Regan Road
Brampton, ON L7A 1B2

Tel. 905-846-5910
Fax 905-846-3368

Strongco Material Handling, Division of Strongco Inc. is involved in the sales and service of material handling equipment. The division employs more than 50 people. Post-secondary education is not listed as a prerequisite for employment application. Strongco Material Handling hires people to occupy Service Technician positions. Relevant work experience and applied education would be a definite asset. Company benefits are rated as excellent. The potential for advancement is listed as being good. The most suitable method for initial contact regarding employment opportunities is to mail a resume with a covering letter. *Contacts:* Grant McCarole, General Manager or Patty McArthur, Human Resources.

STURGEON LAKE BOARD OF EDUCATION
Bag #5
Valleyview, AB T0H 3N0

Tel. 780-524-4590
Fax 780-524-3696
Email .... sturglke@telusplanet.net

Sturgeon Lake Board of Education is the primary controlling body of Sturgeon Lake School, located 365 km north of Edmonton. Sturgeon Lake School has 24 employees, both teachers and paraprofessionals. The school has an enrollment of 250 students in ECS to grade 12. Graduates most likely to be hired are Bachelor of Education (General, Early Childhood, Primary Junior - Grades 0-6, Junior Intermediate - Grades 4-10, Intermediate Senior - Grades 7 - 12, Physical and Health, Special Needs) graduates. Graduates are hired to occupy Teacher positions. Experience teaching Native students, team player, and a willingness to get involved in the community are all listed as desirable non-academic qualifications. Company benefits are rated above average. The school is located near two provincial parks, Williamson's and Young's Point, for those who enjoy various outdoor pursuits. The potential for advancement is listed as average. The average annual starting salary falls within the $30,000 to $35,000 range. The most suitable method for initial contact by those seeking employment is to mail a resume with a covering letter. *Contacts:* Tim Martens, Principal or Carol Goodswimmer, Education Administrator.

SUN LIFE OF CANADA
225 King Street West, 8th Floor
Toronto, ON M5V 3C5

Tel.	416-408-7585
Fax	416-595-1587
Email	hr@sunlife.com
Website	www.sunlife.com/canada

Sun Life of Canada is one of Canada's leading financial institutions, offering a variety of insurance and financial products and services. The company has built its reputation through its core group of products and services offered to individuals, employee groups, employers, organizations and associations, these include: life, health and disability insurance; annuities; savings, investment and retirement plans; and reinsurance. Founded in 1871, Sun Life has representatives and offices located from coast to coast. The company's headquarters are located in Montreal and Toronto and regional offices are located in Vancouver, Edmonton, Calgary, Ottawa and Moncton. Sun Life employs approximately 5,200 people in Canada and a total of 10,000 employees worldwide. Graduates most likely to be hired come from the following academic areas: Bachelor of Arts (Economics), Bachelor of Science (Actuarial, Computer Science, Mathematics), Bachelor of Commerce/Business Administration (Accounting, Finance, Human Resources, Information Systems), Master of Business Administration (Accounting, Finance, Human Resources, Information Systems, Marketing) and Community College Diploma (Legal Assistant). Excellent organizational skills, creative, innovative, good verbal and written communication skills, flexibility, adaptability, team player, and good interpersonal, consultative and negotiating skills are all listed as desirable non-academic qualifications. Company benefits are rated above average. The potential for advancement is listed as being good. The most suitable method for initial contact by those seeking employment is to mail a resume with a covering letter. Sun Life of Canada does hire summer students. *Contact:* Human Resources.

SUNBURY TRANSPORT LIMITED
PO Box 905, Station A
Fredericton, NB E3B 5B4

Tel.	506-453-1133
Fax	506-453-7658
Website	www.sunburytransport.com

Sunbury Transport Limited is a transportation company providing full truck load carrier services. Safety conscious and aiming to be the best possible carrier, Sunbury Transport uses the most advanced satellite technology in the industry to communicate with their vehicles on the road. There are 90 employees at this location and a total of 110 employees in Canada. Graduates most likely to be hired come from the following academic areas: Bachelor of Engineering (General), Bachelor of Education (Adult), Bachelor of Commerce/Business Administration

(Accounting, Human Resources, Information Systems, Marketing), Certified Management Accountant and Community College Diploma (Administration, Marketing/Sales). Graduates would occupy Management Trainee, Operations Trainee and Sales Associate positions. Team player, positive attitude, good communication skills, initiative and relevant work experience are all listed as desirable non-academic qualifications. Company benefits and the potential for advancement are both rated as excellent. The average annual starting salary falls within the $20,000 to $25,000 range, depending upon the position being considered. The most suitable method for initial contact by those seeking employment is to mail a resume with a covering letter. Sunbury Transport Limited occasionally hires summer students. *Contacts:* Cathy Colpitts or Todd Stewart.

SUNOCO INC.
36 York Mills Road
Toronto, ON M2P 2C5

Tel.	416-733-7238
Fax	416-733-1233
Website	www.suncor.com

Sunoco Inc. is a fully owned subsidiary of Suncor Energy Inc. which is a 100% publicly owned Canadian integrated oil and gas company. Headquartered in Toronto, Sunoco manufactures, distributes and markets transportation fuels, petrochemicals and heating oils in Ontario. Sunoco also markets natural gas to Ontario households. Sunoco's main refinery is located in Sarnia, Ontario. Graduates most likely to be hired come from the following academic areas: Bachelor of Science (Computer Science), Bachelor of Engineering (Chemical, Electrical, Environmental/Resources), Bachelor of Commerce/Business Administration (Accounting) and Community College Diploma (Accounting, Business, Information Systems). Graduates would occupy Business Analyst, Business Development Specialist, and Distribution Analyst positions. Analytical skills, customer focus and good problem solving skills are listed as desirable non-academic qualifications. Company benefits are rated above average. The potential for advancement is listed as excellent. The average annual starting salary falls within the $40,000 to $45,000 range. The most suitable method for initial contact by those seeking employment is to mail a resume with a covering letter. Sunoco Inc. does hire summer and co-op work term students. *Contact:* Julia Anderson.

SUPER FITNESS CENTRES INC.
2336 Bloor Street West, PO Box 84539
Toronto, ON M6S 1T0

Tel.	416-762-6070
Fax	416-762-6870

Super Fitness Centres Inc. operates commercial health clubs. The company employs more than 250 people. Graduates most likely to be hired come from the following academic areas: Bachelor of Arts, Bachelor of Science, Bachelor of Education (Physical Education) and Chartered Accountant. Graduates would occupy positions in Membership Enrollment, Fitness Instruction, Reception/Clerical and Managerial functions. An athletic background, good personality, a people-person and an athletic appearance are all listed as desirable non-academic qualifications. Company benefits are rated as industry standard. The potential for advancement is listed as excellent. Most employee positions are salary based plus commission. The average starting salary falls within the $15,000 to $20,000 range, and may be supplemented through commission earnings (potential earnings can be high). The most suitable methods for initial contact by those seeking employment are to mail a resume with a covering letter, or via telephone. Super Fitness Centres Inc. does hire summer students on a regular basis. *Contact:* Christine Steiger, Vice President.

SUR-GARD SECURITY SYSTEMS LTD.
401 Magnetic Drive, Unit 25
Toronto, ON M3J 3H9

Tel. 416-665-4494
Fax 416-665-4222
Email .... hrgroup@sur-gard.com
Website .... www.sur-gard.com

Sur-Gard Security Systems Ltd., a member of the DSC Group of companies, is a leader in the development of security communications products. As a principal development resource for the DSC Group, Sur-Gard's alarm communications technology is incorporated into a diverse array of products marketed under the DSC and Sur-Gard nameplate. Today, DSC which is also based in Toronto, is one of the world's most recognized names in the security manufacturing industry selling into 68 countries around the globe. There are 80 employees at this location and a total of 2,000 employees worldwide. Graduates most likely to be hired come from the following academic areas: Bachelor of Engineering (Electrical) and Community College Diploma (CAD/CAM/Autocad, Electronics Technician, Engineering Technician, Information Systems). A positive attitude, team player and a high level of motivation are all listed as desirable non-academic qualifications. Company benefits are rated above average. The potential for advancement is listed as being excellent. The average annual starting salary falls within the $30,000 to $35,000 range. The most suitable methods for initial contact by those seeking employment are to fax or e-mail a resume with a covering letter. *Contact:* Ms N. Belperio, HR Services.

SWIFT CURRENT HEALTH DISTRICT
429 - 4th Avenue NE
Swift Current, SK S9H 2J9

Tel. 306-778-5105
Fax 306-773-9513
Email .... smonti@scdhb@sk.ca
Website .... www.city.swift-current.sk.ca

The Swift Current Health District is a multifaceted health care delivery organization dedicated to excellence in community health, long term care, acute care and home based services. It is the host district for southwestern Saskatchewan and supplies outreach services to the two neighbouring health districts. The district employs a total of 1,000 people, serving approximately 20,000. residents. Graduates most likely to be hired come from the following academic areas: Bachelor of Science (Nursing, Nutritional Sciences, Occupational Therapy, Pharmacy, Physio/Physical Therapy, Psychology, Speech Pathology), Bachelor of Education (Early Childhood), Bachelor of Commerce/Business Administration (General, Accounting, Finance, Human Resources), Chartered Accountant and Community College Diploma (Accounting, Administration, Human Resources, Secretarial, Social Work/DSW, Dietitian/Nutrition, Health/Home Care Aide, Laboratory Technician, Nursing RN, Radiology Technician, Ultra-Sound Technician). Graduates would occupy So-

cial Worker, Psychologist, RN, RPN, Physiotherapist, Medical Radiation Technician, Laboratory Technician, and Accounting positions. Good written and verbal communication skills, computer literacy, team player, strong interpersonal and leadership skills, and previous work experience are all listed as desirable non-academic qualifications. Company benefits are rated as excellent. The potential for advancement is listed as being good. The average annual starting salary falls within the $20,000 to $25,000 range. The most suitable method for initial contact by those seeking employment is to mail a resume with a covering letter. The Swift Current Health District does hire summer students. *Contacts:* Cheryl James, Manager of Human Resources or Katy Wasiak, Communications.

SYNERVISION DIGITAL PRODUCTIONS
47 Clarence Street, Suite 200
Ottawa, ON K1N 9K1

Tel. 613-562-0464
Fax 613-562-0116
Email .... hr@synervisiondpi.com
Website .... www.synervisiondpi.com

Synervision Digital Productions is a leading developer of learning and performance improvement and measurement technology. Synervision products are delivered across server based intranet and internet environments. Traditional CD-ROM and satellite technology is also available. The company's work is entirely focused on training and corporate performance improvement. Synervision is an innovator in their field, working to exceed customer expectations in the areas of human resources development, strategic planning, learning systems design, instructional design, programming integrity, graphic design, and learning measurement. The company directly serves three main vertical markets: financial services, telecommunications, and transportation, as well as using indirect channels to serve other vertical markets. Synervision employs a total of 52 people worldwide. Graduates most likely to be hired come from the following academic areas: Bachelor of Science (Computer Science), Bachelor of Engineering (Computer Systems), Bachelor of Education (Adult), Bachelor of Commerce/Business Administration (Accounting, Finance, Human Resources, Information Systems, Marketing, Public Administration), Chartered Accountant, Certified Management Accountant, Master of Business Administration (General, Accounting, Finance, Human Resources, Marketing), Masters (Educational Technology) and Community College Diploma (Accounting, Administration, Advertising, Business, Communications/Public Relations, Human Resources, Information Systems, Marketing/Sales, Graphics Arts/Design, Computer Science). Graduates would occupy Instructional Designer, Programmer, Learning Consultant (Sales), Senior Software Engineer, Software Applications Engineer, Product Manager, Marketing, Graphic Designer, Accounting Clerk, Client Services and Office Administrator positions. Team player, motivated, previous experience in the educational technology area, and experience in Synervision's vertical markets are all listed as desirable non-academic qualifications. The most suitable methods for initial contact by those seeking employment are to mail or e-mail a resume with a covering letter, or by applying through the company's website at www.synervisiondpi.com/main.html. Synervision does hire co-op work term students. *Contacts:* Peter McKercher, Vice President, Operations or Human Resources Department.

SYSTEMATIX INFORMATION TECHNOLOGY INC.
320 Front Street West, Suite 830
Toronto, ON M5V 3B6

Tel. 416-595-5331
Fax 416-595-1525
Email .... scitor@systematix.com
Website .... www.systematix.com

Systematix Information Technology Inc. is a leading information technology consulting firm, currently working with over 500 IT consultants across Canada. There are 30 employees and consultants at the Toronto location. Systematix enjoys a good reputation with both consultants and clients. Graduates most likely to be hired at the Toronto location come from the following academic areas: Bachelor of Science (Computer Science), Bachelor of Commerce/Business Administration (Information Systems), Master of Business Administration (Information Systems) and Community College Diploma (Computer Science). In addition, Systematix typically requires consultants who have solid technical skills and experience in mainframe, mini, or PC environments. These graduates would occupy Programmer, Analyst, Project Leader, Network Analyst and Network Support positions. The most suitable method for initial contact by those seeking employment is to mail a resume with a covering letter. Contacts: Norbert Rozko, Lisette Silva or Jeannette Kalkounis.

SYSTEMATIX INFORMATION TECHNOLOGY INC.
10405 Jasper Avenue, Suite 120
Edmonton, AB T5J 3N4

Tel. 780-421-7767
Fax 780-428-1775
Email .... sciedm@systematix.com
Website .... www.systematix.com

Systematix Information Technology Inc. is a leading information technology consulting firm, currently working with over 500 IT consultants across Canada. There are 50 employees and consultants at the Edmonton location. Systematix enjoys a good reputation with both consultants and clients. Graduates most likely to be hired at the Edmonton location come from the following academic areas: Bachelor of Science (Computer Science), Bachelor of Commerce/Business Administration (Information Systems), Master of Business Administration (Information Systems) and Community College Diploma (Computer Science). In addition, Systematix typically requires consultants who have solid technical skills and experience in mainframe, mini or PC environments. These graduates would occupy Programmer, Analyst, Project Leader, Network Analyst and Network Support positions. The most suitable methods for initial contact by those seeking employment are to mail, fax or e-mail a resume with a covering letter, or by applying through the company's website. Contact: Janice Fernie, Manager, Consultant Resourcing.

TALISMAN ENERGY INC.
855 - 2nd Street SW, Suite 2400
Calgary, AB T2P 4J9

Tel. 403-237-1234
Fax 403-237-1601
Email .... tlm@Talisman-energy.com
Website .... www.Talisman-energy.com

Talisman Energy Inc. is a senior oil and gas company active both domestically and internationally. The company's head office is located in Calgary, Alberta. Talisman employs 650 people in Canada and a total of 950 people worldwide. Graduates most likely to be hired come from the following academic areas: Bachelor of Arts (Economics), Bachelor of Science (Geology), Bachelor of Engineering (Chemical, Civil, Mechanical, Environmental/Resources, Geological Engineering), Bachelor of Laws, Bachelor of Commerce/Business Administration (General, Accounting, Finance, Human Resources), Chartered Accountant, Certified Management Accountant, Certified General Accountant, Master of Business Administration (Finance), Master of Science (Geology) and Community College Diploma (Accounting, Secretarial, Automotive Mechanic, Engineering Technician). Effective communication skills, team player, good organization skills and independence are all listed as desirable non-academic qualifications. Company benefits are rated above average. The potential for advancement is listed as excellent. The most suitable methods for initial contact by those seeking employment are to mail or fax a resume with a covering letter. Talisman Energy Inc. does hire summer and co-op work term students. Contact: Mary Meenagh, Human Resources Advisor.

TAX COMPLIANCE GROUP
2700 Matheson Boulevard East, 8th Floor, West Tower
Mississauga, ON L4W 4V9

Tel. 905-624-2060
Fax 905-624-1077
Website .... www.taxprep.com

Tax Compliance Group develops tax software and related products for the accounting and bookkeeping professions. The company is the largest distributor of such software and as part of CCH Canadian Limited, Tax Compliance Group has the most complete variety of tax software and services in Canada. During the tax season, Tax Compliance's busy season, the group employs as many as 75 people. Graduates most likely to be hired come from the following academic areas: Bachelor of Science (Computer Science), Bachelor of Engineering (Computer Systems), Chartered Accountant, Certified Management Accountant, Certified General Accountant, Master of Business Administration (General, Accounting, Marketing), Community College Diploma (Accounting, Marketing/Sales, Office Administration, Secretarial, Computer Science, Electronics Technician) and High School Diploma. Graduates would occupy Inside Sales Representative, Administrative Assistant, Receptionist, Order Entry Clerk, Programmer and Quality Assurance Tester positions. The ability to work well with others and independently, confidence, promptness, happy, a healthy attitude and enjoy working in an office environment are all listed as desirable non-academic qualifications. Company benefits are rated above average. The potential for advancement is listed as being good. The average annual starting salary falls within the $20,000 to $45,000 plus range, depending upon the position being considered. The most suitable method for initial contact by those seeking employment is to mail a resume with a covering letter. Tax Compliance Group does hire co-op work term students for quality assurance and support positions throughout the year. Contact: Human Resources.

TECHNILAB PHARMA INC.
17800, rue Lapointe
Mirabel, QC J7J 1P3

Tel. 450-433-7673
Fax 450-979-6350
Email .... courrier@technilab.ca
Website .... www.technilab.ca

Technilab Pharma Inc. develops, manufactures and markets a broad range of generic prescription drugs and over-the-counter medications in a variety of dosage forms. Founded in 1974, the company's strong growth is attributed to research and its strategic development of new products. Technilab sells some 70 products to over 6,500 customers under its own trademarks as well as under private trademarks. The company also distributes, under exclusive licenses, drugs manufactured by other companies through its well established Canada-wide sales force. Headquartered in Mirabel, Technilab also maintains leading-edge research and manufacturing facilities. Technilab employs approximately 155 employees at this location and a total of 187 employees across Canada. Graduates most likely to be hired come from the following academic areas: Bachelor of Science (General, Chemistry, Computer Science, Pharmacy), Bachelor of Engineering (Chemical, Industrial Chemistry), Bachelor of Commerce/Business Administration (Accounting, Finance, Human Resources, Information Systems, Marketing), Chartered Accountant, Certified Management Accountant, Master of Science (Chemistry) and Community College Diploma (Accounting, Secretarial, Laboratory Technician). Graduates would occupy Laboratory Technician, Programmer Analyst, Medical Representative, Analytical Development Technician, Accounting Clerk, Secretary, Regulatory Affairs Director, Quality Assurance Director/Supervisor and Quality Assurance Technician/Inspector positions. Pharmaceutical experience is listed as a desirable non-academic qualification. Company benefits are rated as industry standard. The potential for advancement is listed as being good. The average annual starting salary falls within the $25,000 to $30,000 range. The most suitable method for initial contact by those seeking employment is to mail a resume with a covering letter. *Contact:* Human Resources Department.

TECK CORPORATION
1 First Canadian Place, PO Box 170
Toronto, ON M5X 1G9

Tel. 416-862-7102
Fax 416-365-7747
Email .... info@teck.com
Website .... www.teck.com

Teck Corporation is one of Canada's oldest mining companies and a leading mine development and operating company. The company began as a gold mine in 1913, with the Teck-Hughes gold discovery at Kirkland Lake, Ontario, and today produces gold, copper, zinc, lead, niobium, silver and metallurgical coal from 11 mines in Canada, Chile and Australia. Teck is the largest shareholder in Cominco Ltd., one of the world's leading producers of zinc. Most of these projects involve partnerships or joint ventures with other companies and the establishment of working relationships, with Teck in most cases being the builder and project manager. Operating partners include Aur Resources Inc., Cambior Inc., Cominco Ltd., Empresa Nacional de Mineria (ENAMI), Homestake Mining Company, Inversiones Mineras S.A., Minorco, Nissho Iwai, Noranda Inc., PacMin Mining Corporation Limited, Rio Algom Limited, Sumitomo Metal Mining America Inc., SC Minerals America Inc. and Western Copper Holdings Limited. Graduates most likely to be hired come from the following academic areas: Bachelor of Science (Geology) and Bachelor of Engineering (Mining). Applicants would be hired as Geologists or Mining Engineers. An interest in the outdoors and previous work experience are both listed as desirable non-academic qualifications. Company benefits are rated as excellent. The potential for advancement is listed

as being good. The most suitable method for initial contact by those seeking employment is to mail a resume with a covering letter (applicants should be able to furnish references upon request). Teck Corporation does hire summer students on a regular basis. (Vancouver Headquarters: 200 Burrard Street, Suite 600, Vancouver, British Columbia, V6C 3L9; Phone 604-687-1117; Fax 604-687-6100). *Contact:* Mr. B. D. Simmons.

TEKLOGIX INC.
2100 Meadowvale Boulevard
Mississauga, ON L5N 7J9

Tel. 905-813-9900
Fax 905-812-6272
Email .... hr@teklogix.com
Website .... www.teklogix.com

Teklogix Inc. is a leading worldwide supplier of wireless data communication systems designed specifically for industrial applications. Founded in 1967, the company's global operations are represented by 35 direct sales and support offices and 26 independent distributors. With over 5000 installations in 45 countries, the company's client list includes firms in all types of industries including: aerospace, automotive, pharmaceutical, furniture and textile manufacturing, as well as transportation and ports. Headquartered in Mississauga, Teklogix has 300 employees at this location, a total of 320 in Canada and a total of 600 employees worldwide. Graduates most likely to be hired come from the following academic areas: Bachelor of Arts (General, Economics), Bachelor of Science (Computer Science, Mathematics), Bachelor of Engineering (Electrical, Mechanical, Computer Systems, Industrial Engineering, Industrial Production/Manufacturing), Bachelor of Commerce/Business Administration (General, Accounting, Finance, Human Resources, Information Systems, Marketing), Certified Management Accountant, Master of Business Administration (General, Marketing) and Community College Diploma (Accounting, Business, Human Resources, Electronics Technician, Engineering Technician). Analytical, good problem solving skills, team player, excellent interpersonal skills, previous work experience and a high level of initiative are all listed as desirable non-academic qualifications. Company benefits are rated as industry standard. The potential for advancement is listed as being excellent. The average annual starting salary falls within the $40,000 to $45,000 range. The most suitable methods for initial contact by those seeking employment are to mail, fax or e-mail a resume with a covering letter, or via the company's website. Teklogix Inc. does hire summer and co-op work term students. *Contact:* Human Resources.

TEKNION FURNITURE SYSTEMS LIMITED
1150 Flint Road
Toronto, ON M3J 2J5

Tel. 416-661-3370
Fax 416-661-2647

Email .... jayne.canning@teknion.com
Website .... www.teknion.com

Teknion Furniture Systems Limited is an international designer, manufacturer and marketer of leading edge furniture systems, servicing an international client base. Established in 1981, Teknion employs 2,600 people worldwide and has more than 1.5 million square feet of facilities, including manufacturing plants, administrative offices and sales offices. Seven of the company's manufacturing facilities have been awarded ISO 9001 or 9002 designations. Teknion's corporate headquarters is located in Toronto. The company's U.S. headquarters is located in Marlton, New Jersey, and the European head office is based in London, England. In July 1998, Teknion completed a public offering of subordinate voting shares and is listed on the Toronto Stock Exchange under the symbol TKN. Teknion helps customers create workspaces that advance their strategic intent. As a customer centred organization, the company works with architects, interior designers, and facilities managers to develop valuable customer driven solutions. The company's superior products have won recognition around the world for innovation and excellence. Teknion's products unite simplicity with layered performance. They are designed to provide solutions for a business environment transformed by technology and new work styles. Teknion's international capabilities include a worldwide network of dealers and service providers that can help its customers define their needs, specify the products and create a work setting that will advance their business goals. The company's products are now sold in over 50 countries through a network of more than 400 authorized dealers. Teknion has a rapidly growing North American market presence and continues to expand into South and Central America, the Caribbean, Pacific Rim, Middle East and Europe. Graduates most likely to be hired come from the following academic areas: Bachelor of Engineering (General, Mechanical, Automation/Robotics, Industrial Design, Industrial Engineering, Industrial Production/Manufacturing), Bachelor of Commerce/Business Administration (Accounting, Finance, Human Resources, Information Systems, Marketing), Certified General Accountant and Community College Diploma (Accounting, Human Resources, Information Systems, Marketing/Sales, Graphic Arts, CAD/CAM/Autocad). Graduates would occupy Manufacturing Engineer, Production Supervisor, MRP Purchaser, CSR, Design Engineer, Industrial Engineer, Technical Support Specialist, Financial Analyst, Administrative Assistant, Accounts Receivable/Payable Clerk, Marketing Coordinator and Industrial Designer positions. Team player, good interpersonal and organizational skills, ability to multitask and computer literacy are all listed as desirable non-academic qualifications. Company benefits are rated as industry standard. The potential for advancement is listed as excellent. The average annual starting salary varies with the position being considered. The most suitable method for initial contact by those seeking employment is to fax a resume with a covering letter. Teknion Furniture Systems Limited does hire summer and co-op work term students. *Contacts:* Jacquie Little, Manager, Employee Relations or Jayne Canning, Recruitment Specialist.

TELEBEC LTEE
7151, rue Jean Talon Est
Montreal, QC H1M 3N8

Tel. 514-493-5394
Fax 514-493-5352
Email .... spotente@telebec.qc.ca
Website .... www.telebec.qc.ca

Telébec Ltée, a subsidiary of BCE Inc., is a telecommunications company operating wholly in the province of Québec. There are approximately 250 employees at this location, and a total of 960 employees throughout Québec. Graduates most likely to be hired come from the following academic areas: Bachelor of Arts (Economics, Journalism), Bachelor of Engineering (Electrical, Telecommunications), Bachelor of Commerce/Business Administration (Finance, Marketing), Chartered Accountant and Master of Business Administration (Finance, Marketing, Project Management). Graduates would occupy Marketing Analyst, Marketing Manager and a variety of positions in the engineering department. Team work, entrepreneurship, action-oriented, fast learner, excellent communication and interpersonal skills, innovative, and experience in pertinent field are all listed as desirable non-academic qualifications. Fluency in French is required. Company benefits are rated above average. The potential for advancement is listed as being good. The average annual starting salary falls within the $30,000 to $40,000 range for recent graduates. Those with related work experience can expect a higher starting salary. The most suitable methods for initial contact by those seeking employment are to mail, fax or e-mail a resume with a covering letter, or via the company's website. Telébec Ltée does hire summer and co-op work term students. *Contact:* Sandra Potente, Manager, Human Resources.

TELEFILM CANADA
600, rue de la Gauchetiere Ouest, 14e étage
Montreal, QC H3B 4L8

Tel. 514-283-0838 x2049
Fax 514-283-2043
Email .... laportd@telefilm.gc.ca
Website .... www.telefilm.gc.ca

Telefilm Canada is a federal cultural agency which fosters Canadian creative expression in the television, film and new media sectors using commercial and industrial means. Telefilm financially invests in both established and emerging talent to produce culturally relevant, high quality works, and ensures the widest possible distribution of such works in Canada and abroad. The talent from which Telefilm draws is diverse, representing Canada's official languages, multicultural and Aboriginal communities. The works produced define Canadian culture and are powerful conveyors of information, enlightenment and entertainment. Telefilm Canada employs 98 people at this location, a total of 142 in Canada and a total of 144 people worldwide. Graduates most likely to be hired come from the following academic areas: Bachelor of Arts (English, French, Journalism, Political Science, Film/Cinema Studies), Bachelor of Science (Computer Science), Bachelor of Engineering (Computer Systems), Bachelor of Laws, Bachelor of Commerce/Business Administration (General, Accounting, Finance, Human Resources, Public Administration), Chartered Accountant, Certified Management Accountant, Certified General Accountant, Master of Business Administration (General, Accounting, Finance, Human Resources, Public Administration), Community College Diploma (Accounting, Business, Communications/Public Relations, Facility Management, Financial Planning, Human Resources, Office Administration, Purchasing/Logistics, Secretarial, Journalism, Legal Assistant, Television/Radio Arts, Broadcasting, Computer Science, Electronics Technician, Information Systems) and High School Diploma. Graduates would occupy Counsellor, Analyst, Technician, Controller, Director, Specialist, Coordinator, Agent Writer, Assistant, Chief and Administrator positions. Team player, previous work experience, artistical sense, good interpersonal skills, analytical abilities, sense of prioritization, representation ability, strong ethics, pluridisciplinary, bilingualism and good negotiation skills are all listed as desirable non-academic qualifications. Company benefits are rated above average. The potential for advancement is listed as being good. The average annual starting salary falls within the $50,000 to $55,000 range. The most suitable method for initial contact by those seeking employment is to fax a resume with a covering letter. Telefilm Canada does hire summer and co-op work term students. *Contact:* Human Resources Department.

TELEGLOBE CANADA INC.
1000, rue de la Gauchetière Ouest
Montreal, QC H3B 4X5

Tel.	514-868-7272
Fax	514-868-8179
Website	www.teleglobe.com

Teleglobe Canada Inc. is a global North American-based overseas carrier whose capabilities can be accessed in virtually all countries. Teleglobe develops and provides overseas telecommunications services. It meets the global connectivity needs of established and emerging carriers around the world, as well as those of cable network operators, broadcasters and other large telecommunications services users, and is expanding to service select consumer markets. In key markets, the corporation establishes its presence through its own gateways. There are 700 employees at this location, a total of 850 in Canada and 1,100 employees worldwide. Graduates most likely to be hired come from the following academic areas: Bachelor of Arts (Economics), Bachelor/Master of Science (Computer Science), Bachelor of Engineering (Electrical, Computer Systems, Telecommunications), Bachelor of Laws, Bachelor of Commerce/Business Administration (Accounting, Finance, Human Resources, Information Systems, Marketing), Chartered Accountant, Certified Management Accountant, Certified General Accountant, Master of Business Administration (Accounting, Finance, Information Systems, Marketing), Master of Engineering (Electrical, Telecommunications) and Community College Diploma (Accounting, Administration, Business, Secretarial, Computer Science, Electronics Technician, Engineering Technician). Graduates would occupy professional positions such as Engineer, Accountant, Account Manager, Product Manager, IT Specialist, management positions such as Associate Director, Director, Technician and specialized Clerk positions. Team player, innovative, an ability to work in a changing environment, dynamic and bilingual are all listed as desirable non-academic qualifications. Company benefits are rated as excellent. The potential for advancement is listed as being good. The average annual starting salary falls within the $30,000 to $35,000 range. The most suitable methods for initial contact by those seeking employment are to mail or fax a resume with a covering letter, or via telephone. Teleglobe does hire summer and co-op work term students. *Contacts:* Carole Rhéaume, Senior Advisor, Human Resources or Danielle Monette, Senior Advisor, Human Resources.

TELEPHONE COMMUNICATORS CANADA LIMITED
106 Front Street East, Suite 303
Toronto, ON M5A 1E1

Tel.	416-367-5255
Fax	416-367-5999
Email	tcc@telefocus.com

Telephone Communicators Canada Limited is a marketing service bureau. The company plays the role of liaison between the client and the client's customers. Telephone Communicators employs more than 100 people. Post-secondary education is not a prerequisite for employment application. A strong command of the English and/or French languages, sense of humour, entrepreneurial in nature, good telephone manner, positive, team player and a customer service orientation are all listed as desirable non-academic qualifications. Applicants would occupy Telephone Communicator, Customer Service Representative, Account Manager, Supervisory and Assistant Supervisory positions. Company benefits are rated as industry standard. The potential for advancement is listed as excellent. The average annual starting salary falls within the $20,000 to $28,000 range and may be commission based depending upon the specific client. The most suitable methods for initial contact by those seeking employment are to mail a resume with a covering letter, or via telephone. Telephone Communicators Canada Limited does hire summer students. *Contact:* Human Resources.

TELESAT CANADA
1601 Telesat Court
Gloucester, ON K1B 5P4

Tel.	613-748-8700
Fax	613-748-8865
Email	t.mcguire@telesat.ca
Website	www.telesat.ca

Telesat Canada is a world leader in satellite communications and systems management. Created in 1969, the Company made history with the launch of Anik A1 in 1972 - the world's first commercial domestic communications satellite placed in geostationary orbit. Currently regulated by the Canadian Radio-television Telecommunications Commission, the Company's satellites carry television and radio broadcasting, voice and data communication networks. Poised to start offering its telecommunications and broadcast services internationally, Telesat is now finalizing plans for its next generation of fixed Service Satellites, and is investigating how best to provide interactive multimedia services to customers in Canada and beyond. This location is Telesat's headquarters, where the majority of its 500 employees are located. The remainder are located in sales offices and satellite communications centres across Canada, with several teams of employees on international assignment around the world. Graduates most likely to be hired come from the following academic areas: Bachelor of Science (Computer Science, Mathematics), Bachelor of Engineering (Electrical, Telecommunications, Aerospace), Master of Engineering (Electrical) and Community College Diploma (Electronics Technician, Engineering Technician). Graduates would occupy Engineer, Systems Engineer, Scientific Programmer, Programmer Analyst and Technologist positions. Good communication skills, flexible and team player are listed as desirable non-academic qualifications. Company benefits are rated above average. The potential for advancement is listed as average. The average annual starting salary falls within the $35,001 to $40,000 range, depending upon the position being considered. The most suitable method for initial contact by those seeking employment is to mail a resume with a covering letter. Telesat Canada does hire summer and co-op work term students. *Contact:* Staffing and Relocation Officer.

TELETECH CANADA
100 Sheppard Avenue East
Toronto, ON M2N 6N5

Tel.	416-228-7530
Fax	888-654-8525
Email	jamiea@teletech.ca.com
Website	www.teletech.com

TeleTech Canada is one of the leading tele-services firms in North America. The company provides all levels of inbound and outbound services including customer support, technical support, order taking, telesales and fulfillment. Teletech deals primarily with Fortune 500 clients and operates call centres around the globe. Graduates most likely to be hired come from the following academic areas: Bachelor of Arts (English, French, Languages), Bachelor of Commerce/Business Administration (Accounting, Finance, Human Resources, Information Systems, Marketing), Master of Business Administration (Finance, Human Resources, Information Systems, Marketing) and Community College Diploma (Business, Communications/Public Relations, Financial Planning, Human Resources, Marketing/Sales, Office Administration, Journalism, Television/Radio Arts/Broadcasting). Graduates would occupy Human Resources Administrator, Recruiter, Client Service Account Executive, Operations Management, Billing Coordinator, Accounts Payable, Warehouse Manager, Call Centre Associate and Technical Support Associate positions. Team player, initiative, adaptable, creative and innovative are all listed as desirable non-academic qualifications. Company benefits are rated as industry standard. The potential for advancement is listed as being excellent. The average annual starting salary falls within the $20,000 to $25,000 range. The most suitable methods for initial contact by those seeking employment are to mail, fax or e-mail a resume with a covering letter, or by applying in person. Teletech Canada does hire summer and co-op work term students. *Contacts:* Jamie Allison, Manager, Human Resources or Stella Kerrigan, Supervisor, Recruitment.

TELLABS COMMUNICATIONS CANADA LIMITED
2433 Meadowvale Boulevard
Mississauga, ON L5N 5S2

Tel.	905-858-2058
Fax	905-858-0418
Website	www.tellabs.com

Tellabs Communications Canada Limited is involved in the research and development, marketing, sales and service of telecommunications products. Tellabs Communications Canada Limited is a subsidiary of Lisle, Illinois based Tellabs Operations, Inc. Tellabs Communications Canada Limited employs 50 people at this location and a total of 70 people in Canada. Graduates most likely to be hired come from the following academic areas: Bachelor of Arts (General), Bachelor of Science (Computer Science), Bachelor of Engineering (General, Electrical), Bachelor of Commerce/Business Administration (Accounting, Finance, Marketing), Chartered Accountant (Finance), Certified Management Accountant (Finance), Certified General Accountant (Finance), Master of Business Administration (Accounting, Finance, Marketing, Management), Master of Science (Computer Science), Master of Engineering (Electrical, Technical) and Community College Diploma (Accounting, Administration, Marketing/Sales, Purchasing/Logistics, Secretarial, Human Resources, Computer Science, Electronics Technician, Engineering Technician). Graduates would occupy Intermediate Software Designer, Technical, Engineering and Business/Sales related positions. Applicants should

be motivated and maintain a positive attitude. Company benefits are rated as excellent. The potential for advancement is listed as being good. The average annual starting salary falls within the $35,000 to $40,000 range. The most suitable method for initial contact by those seeking employment is to mail a resume with a covering letter. Tellabs Communications Canada Limited occasionally requires temporary assistance that is clerical or warehouse related. *Contact:* Human Resources Supervisor.

TEMBEC INC.
Case Postale 3000
Temiscaming, QC J0Z 3R0

Tel.	819-627-4323
Fax	819-627-3946
Website	www.tembec.ca

Tembec Inc. is a leading integrated Canadian forest products company marketing its products in over 50 countries. Products include softwood, hardwood and pine lumber, hardwood flooring, laminated veneer lumber, oriented strand board, high-yield chlorine-free market pulps, specialty alpha and dissolving cellulose pulp, bleached kraft pulp, newsprint and publishing papers, coated paperboard and bristols, lignosulfonates, phenolic resins and ethanol. Tembec has grown from its original mill in Témiscaming to an integrated forest products company with over 6,875 employees. Most of the company's operations are centered in northwestern Québec and northeastern Ontario with additional facilities located in New Brunswick, Manitoba, British Columbia and France. Graduates most likely to be hired come from the following academic areas: Bachelor of Science (Chemistry, Microbiology), Bachelor of Engineering (Chemical, Environmental, Industrial, Mechanical), Chartered Accountant, Certified General Accountant, Master of Science (Pulp and Paper), Master of Engineering (Pulp and Paper), Community College Diploma (Electronics Technician, Pulp and Paper) and High School Diploma. Graduates would occupy Junior Engineer, Accountant and Labourer positions. Company benefits are rated above average. The potential for advancement is listed as excellent. The average annual starting salary falls within the $25,000 to $30,000 range. The most suitable method for initial contact by those seeking employment is to mail a resume with a covering letter. Tembec Inc. does hire summer students. *Contacts:* Yves Ouellet, Personnel Manager or Denis Lacourse, Personnel Supervisor.

TENAQUIP LTD.
20701 Chemin Ste-Marie
Ste-Anne-de-Bellevue, QC H9X 5X5

Tel.	514-457-7122
Fax	514-457-4815
Email	annie@tenaquip.com
Website	www.tenaquip.com

Tenaquip Ltd. is a national distributor of industrial equipment and supplies. The company was founded in 1968 as Canada's first catalogue distributor of material handling and storage products. Since then Tenaquip Ltd. has grown to become a major industrial products distribution company employing over 250 people and utilizing more than 210,000 square feet of office and warehouse space in Ste-Anne-de-Bellevue, Mississauga, Ottawa and Cornwall. Retail store locations at each branch serve local markets, while the warehouses in Ste-Anne-de-Bellevue and Mississauga ship products across the country. Tenaquip Ltd. is a privately held, 100% Canadian-owned company. Graduates most likely to be hired come from the following academic areas: Bachelor of Engineering (Industrial Production, Instrumentation) and Bachelor of Commerce/Business Administration (Accounting, Information Systems, Marketing, Purchasing). Graduates would occupy Inside Sales Representative, Customer Service Representative, Product Manager, Associate Product Manager, Accounting Clerk and Buyer positions. Team player, and excellent organization and communication skills are listed as desirable non-academic qualifications. Company benefits are rated above average. The potential for advancement is listed as being good. The average annual starting salary falls within the $30,000 to $35,000 range. The most suitable methods for initial contact by those seeking employment are to fax a resume with a covering letter. *Contact:* Annie Tashdjian, HR Manager.

TENNECO CANADA INC.
1800 - 17th Street East, PO Box 800
Owen Sound, ON N4K 5Z9

Tel. 519-376-9650
Fax 519-376-9656
Website .... www.tenneco.com

Tenneco Canada Inc., Owen Sound manufactures automobile ride control parts. The company employs 370 people at this location. Graduates most likely to be hired come from the following academic areas: Bachelor of Science (Computer Science, Environmental, Metallurgy), Bachelor of Engineering (Automation/Robotics, Mechanical, Industrial Design, Industrial Production), Bachelor of Commerce/Business Administration (General, Accounting, Finance, Human Resources, Information Systems, Marketing, Public Administration), Certified Management Accountant, Community College Diploma (Accounting, Administration, Business, Communications, Human Resources, Marketing/Sales, Secretarial, Journalism, CAD/CAM/Autocad) and High School Diploma. Company benefits and the potential for advancement are both rated as excellent. The average annual starting salary falls within the $35,000 to $40,000 range, and is subject strictly to each applicant's qualifications. The most suitable method for initial contact by those seeking employment is to mail a resume with a covering letter. Tenneco Automotive Inc. does hire summer and co-op students at the Owen Sound facility. *Contact:* Evan Ewasko, Human Resources Manager.

TENROX
5995, boul Gouin Ouest, Suite 302
Montreal, QC H4J 2P8

Tel. 514-336-4567
Fax 514-856-9997
Email .... jobs@tenrox.com
Website .... www.tenrox.com

Tenrox delivers powerful internet/intranet, client/server and multimedia software to corporations. Tenrox specializes in the development of complete software solutions from analysis, design, and implementation through debugging and testing. Graduates most likely to be hired come from the following academic areas: Bachelor of Engineering (Computer Systems), Bachelor of Commerce/Business Administration (Marketing) and Community College Diploma. Graduates would occupy Administrative Assistant, Marketing/Sales Representative, Tester (applicants with a DEC/Diplome d'études collegiales), Technical Support Engineer and Software Engineer positions. Previous work experience (primarily for engineering positions), team player, innovative and creative

are listed as desirable non academic qualifications. Company benefits are rated as industry standard. The potential for advancement is listed as excellent. The most suitable method for initial contact by those seeking employment is to e-mail a resume with a covering letter. Tenrox does hire summer and co-op work term students. *Contact:* Julia Abbruzzese, Human Resources Specialist.

TETRA PAK
10 Allstate Parkway, 2nd Floor
Markham, ON L3R 5P8

Tel. 905-305-9777
Fax 905-305-6901
Website .... www.tetrapak.com

Tetra Pak manufactures and supplies packaging systems and materials to the food and dairy industry. The company employs 220 people at this location, 300 across Canada and a total of 33,000 people worldwide. Graduates most likely to be hired come from the following academic areas: Bachelor of Arts (Economics), Bachelor of Science (Biology, Chemistry), Bachelor of Engineering (Pulp and Paper, Electrical, Automation/Robotics, Mechanical, Industrial Production), Bachelor of Commerce/Business Administration (Accounting, Finance, Human Resources, Marketing), Chartered Accountant, Certified Management Accountant, Certified General Accountant, Master of Business Administration (Accountant, Finance, Marketing) and Community College Diploma (Accounting, Business, Communications, Human Resources, Marketing/Sales, Electronics Technician, Millwright). Graduates would occupy Technician, Supervisor, Management, Development, Sales Representative, Sales Manager, Accountant and Controller positions. Flexible, comfortable in a fast paced environment, adaptable to change, team player and good decision making abilities are all listed as desirable non-academic qualifications. The most suitable method for initial contact by those seeking employment is to mail a resume with a covering letter. Tetra Pak does hire summer students. *Contact:* Human Resources Department.

THE LODGE AT KANANASKIS, CANADIAN PACIFIC HOTELS
PO Box 249, Kananaskis Village
Kananaskis, AB T0L 2H0

Tel. 403-591-7711
Fax 403-591-7770
Email .... rohearn@lak.cphotels.ca
Website .... www.cphotels.com

The Lodge at Kananaskis, a Canadian Pacific Hotel, is a modern alpine resort designed as a year round conference and vacation centre. Canadian Pacific Hotels is the largest owner-operated hotel company in Canada and one of the leading hotel companies in the world. Built for the 1988 Winter Olympics, The Lodge at Kananaskis is the closest mountain resort to Calgary. Situated in the heart of Alberta's Kananaskis Country, the resort is nestled in the majestic beauty and natural serenity of the Canadian Rockies. The Lodge at Kananaskis employs a total of 315 staff, dedicated to providing uniquely satisfying guest experiences and consistently exceeding guest expectations. Graduates most likely to be hired come from the following academic areas: Bachelor of Commerce/Business Administration (General, Hospitality/Food and Beverage Management), Community College Diploma (Hospitality, Travel/Tourism), High School Diploma and Bachelor of Arts (General). Graduates are hired to occupy a variety of positions from entry level to management, depending upon experience. Team player, dedicated, customer service oriented, positive attitude, and able to work in and enjoy a constantly changing environment are all listed as desirable non-academic qualifications. Company benefits are rated as excellent. Canadian Pacific Hotels is dedicated to promoting from within and has a successful internal promotion program in place called, The Pathfinder Program. Accordingly, the potential for advancement is also rated as excellent. The average annual starting salary is dependent upon the position being considered. The most suitable methods for initial contact by those seeking employment are to mail or fax a resume with a covering letter. Summer students are hired, primarily through hospitality management co-op placement programs. *Contact:* Human Resources Department.

THOMAS COOK GROUP (CANADA) LIMITED
100 Yonge Street, 15th Floor
Toronto, ON M5C 2W1

Tel. 416-359-3700
Fax 416-359-3671
Email .... resume@tcgamericas.com
Website .... www.us.thomascook.com

Thomas Cook Group (Canada) Limited provides retail travel services, retail travelers cheques, and retail/wholesale of foreign currency and precious metals. Thomas Cook Group (Canada) Limited is a member of the London, United Kingdom based Thomas Cook Group. The group's history dates back to 1841, and today is a leading international travel and financial services group with a worldwide network providing services to customers at more than 3,000 locations in over 100 countries. Thomas Cook employs more than 12,000 people around the world. Thomas Cook Group (Canada) Limited employs more than 500 people. Graduates most likely to be hired come from the following academic areas, Bachelor of Arts, Bachelor of Commerce/Business Administration, Chartered Accountant, Certified Management Accountant, Master of Business Administration and Community College Diploma (General/Related). Graduates would occupy Clerical, Supervisory, Junior Management and some Professional positions. Company benefits are rated above average. The potential for advancement is listed as being good. The average annual starting salary falls within the $15,000 to $20,000 range. The most suitable method for initial contact by graduates seeking employment is to mail a resume with a covering letter. Thomas Cook Group (Canada) Limited does hire summer students. *Contact:* Human Resources.

THOMPSON'S TRANSFER COMPANY LIMITED
PO Box 670
Middleton, NS B0S 1P0

Tel. 902-825-3929

Thompson's Transfer Company Limited is a freight haulage trucking company and moving company. Graduates most likely to be hired come from the following academic areas: Bachelor of Arts (English), Bachelor of Science (Computer Science, Mathematics), Bachelor of Engineering (Computer Systems, Mechanical), Bachelor of Commerce/Business Administration (Accounting, Finance), Master of Business Administration (General, Accounting, Finance, Human Resources, Information Systems, Marketing, Public Administration), Community College Diploma (Accounting, Administration, Advertising, Business, Auto Mechanic, Computer Science) and High School Diploma. Graduates would occupy Accounting, Clerical,

Mechanic and Truck Driver positions. Previous work experience (two years), computer skills, friendly, an ability to get along with others, motivated and an ability to work without guidance are all listed as desirable non-academic qualifications. Company benefits are rated as industry standard. The potential for advancement is listed as being good. The average annual starting salary falls in the $15,000 plus range. The most suitable method for initial contact by those seeking employment is to mail a resume with a covering letter. Thompson's Transfer Company Limited hires summer students for moving company activities. *Contact:* David Boran, Director of Safety and Personnel.

THUNDER CREEK SCHOOL DIVISION NO. 78
PO Box 730
Moose Jaw, SK S6H 4P4

Tel. 306-694-2121
Fax 306-694-4955

Thunder Creek School Division No. 78 operates elementary and secondary schools in the Moose Jaw area. Graduates most likely to be hired come from the following academic areas: Bachelor of Education (General, Early Childhood ECE, Primary Junior, Junior Intermediate, Intermediate Senior, Special Needs), Bachelor of Commerce/Business Administration (General, Accounting, Finance) and Community College Diploma (Accounting, Administration, Business, Communications, Secretarial, Auto Mechanic). The most suitable method for initial contact by those seeking employment is to mail a resume with a covering letter. *Contact:* Human Resources.

TIGER DRYLAC CANADA INC.
110 Southgate Drive
Guelph, ON N1G 4P5

Tel. 519-766-4781
Fax 519-766-4787
Email .... info@tigerdrylac.on.ca
Website .... www.tigerdrylac.on.ca

Tiger Drylac Canada Inc. is a privately owned company and manufacturer of powder coatings. Powder coating is one of the least expensive finishing methods available today, while also achieving savings in energy, labour, production and waste disposal. The first production of powder coatings began in 1968 at Tigerwerk Lack-u Farbenfabrik GmbH & Co. KG in Austria, and since that time has expanded from a single facility in Austria to world-wide locations, including seven in the United States and Mexico. The company established itself in the Canadian market in 1991, with a state-of-the-art facility in Guelph and a warehouse in Montreal. Tigerwerk received its ISO 9001 certification in 1994 and the Guelph facility received ISO 9001 certification in 1995. There are 47 employees at this location and a total of 50 employees in Canada. Graduates most likely to be hired come from the following academic areas: Bachelor of Science (Chemistry) and Bachelor of Engineering (Chemical, Industrial Chemistry). Graduates would occupy Lab Technician and Chemist positions. Previous work experience in colour matching, the ability to work independently, excellent written and spoken English language skills, and good supervisory, leadership and communication skills are all listed as desirable non-academic qualifications. Company benefits are rated as industry standard. The potential for advancement is listed as being good. The average annual starting salary falls within the $25,000 to $35,000 range. The most suitable methods for initial contact by those seeking employment are to mail, fax or email a resume with a covering letter. Tiger Drylac Canada Inc. does hire summer and co-op work term students. *Contacts:* Richard Wentzell, Quality Assurance Manager or Cindy Embro, Human Resources Representative.

TIP TOP TAILORS
637 Lakeshore Boulevard West, Suite 120
Toronto, ON M5V 3J8
Tel. 416-586-7314
Fax 416-586-7472
Email .... mwatson@dylex.com
Website .... www.tiptop.ca

Tip Top Tailors is a specialty menswear retailer with over 90 years of history in the Canadian retail industry. A division of Dylex Limited, Tip Top is a Canadian company headquartered in Toronto. Tip Top has over 100 stores from coast to coast and employs 2,500 people across the country. Graduates most likely to be hired come from the following academic areas: Bachelor of Arts (English, History, Journalism, Sociology), Bachelor of Science (Computer Science, Mathematics), Bachelor of Education (Adult), Bachelor of Commerce/Business Administration (Accounting, Finance, Human Resources, Information Systems, Marketing, Public Administration), Master of Business Administration (Accounting, Finance, Human Resources, Marketing) and Community College Diploma (Business, Communications, Facility Management, Financial Planning, Human Resources, Marketing/Sales). Graduates would occupy Clerk, Supervisory, Store Management, Department Management and Analyst positions. Team player, service driven, results oriented and a high energy level are all listed as desirable non-academic qualifications. Company benefits are rated above average. The potential for advancement is listed as being good. The average annual starting salary falls within the $15,000 to $20,000 range. The most suitable method for initial contact by those seeking employment is to mail, fax or e-mail a resume with a covering letter. Tip Top Tailors does hire summer students. *Contact:* Human Resources Area Partner.

TNL CONSTRUCTION LTD., INDUSTRIAL CONTRACTORS
7580 River Road, Suite 110
Richmond, BC V6X 1X6
Tel. 604-278-7424
Fax 604-278-7107

TNL Construction Ltd., Industrial Contractors is a heavy industrial construction firm. There are 15 employees at this location and a total of 600 employees across Canada. Graduates most likely to be hired come from the following academic areas: Bachelor of Engineering (Civil, Mechanical, Welding, Mining), Community College Diploma (Accounting, Purchasing/Logistics, Auto Mechanic, CAD/CAM/Autocad, Welding, Trades - Rigging, Millwright etc.) and High School Diploma. Graduates would occupy Project Engineer, Quality Control Field Engineer and Site Administrator positions. Mechanical aptitude, self-starter, independent thinking and previous work experience are all listed as desirable non-academic qualifications. Company benefits are rated as excellent. The potential for advancement is listed as being good. The average annual starting salary falls within the $35,000 to $40,000 range. The most suitable method for initial contact by those seeking employment is to mail a resume with a covering letter. TNL Construction Ltd. does hire summer students. *Contact:* Human Resources.

TOON BOOM TECHNOLOGIES
7 Laurier Street East
Montreal, QC H2T 1E4
Tel. 514-278-8666
Fax 514-278-2666
Email .... natacha@toonboom.com
Website .... www.toonboom.com

Toon Boom Technologies develops 2D animation software for the animation industry. There are 35 employees at this location and a total of 38 employees in the company. Graduates most likely to be hired come from the following academic areas: Bachelor of Science (Computer Science) and Bachelor of Commerce/Business Administration (General, Marketing). Graduates would occupy Software Developer and Sales positions. Team player, good communication skills, hardworking and a high level of initiative are all listed as desirable non-academic qualifications. Company benefits are rated above average. The potential for advancement is listed as being good. The most suitable methods for initial contact by those seeking employment are to mail, fax, or e-mail a resume with a covering letter. *Contact:* Natacha Menard, Human Resources.

TOROMONT CAT
3131 Highway 7 West, PO Box 5511, Building B
Concord, ON L4K1B7
Tel. 416-667-5511
Fax 416-667-5687
Website .... www.toromont.com/toromontcat

Toromont Cat is a heavy equipment dealership representing Caterpillar and other equipment lines, maintaining dealerships in Ontario, Newfoundland and Labrador. The company is dedicated to supplying new and good quality used Cat and competitive equipment to the markets it serves. Toromont offers the complete line of Caterpillar equipment as well as specialized attachments. Operational activities at this location involve sales, service and parts supply. Toromont Cat is a division of Toromont, a Canadian public company with over 1,900 employees throughout North America. In addition to representing Caterpillar and other equipment lines through Toromont Cat, the company is one of Ontario's premier construction equipment rental companies through Battlefield Equipment Rentals and is a North American leader in Industrial and Process Refrigeration through CIMCO Refrigeration. Toromont Cat employs approximately 650 people. Graduates most likely to be hired come from the following academic areas: Bachelor of Engineering (Electrical, Mechanical, Metallurgy, Mining), Chartered Accountant (Finance), Certified Management Accountant (Finance), Certified General Accountant and Master of Business Administration (Accounting, Marketing). Graduates are hired to occupy specific salaried positions. A high energy level, outgoing personality and good interpersonal and communication skills are all listed as desirable non-academic qualifications. Company benefits are rated above average. The potential for advancement is listed as being good. The average annual starting salary falls within the $25,000 to $40,000 plus range, depending upon the position being considered, and is commission based for sales positions. The most suitable method for initial contact by those seeking employment is to mail a resume with a covering letter. Toromont Cat does hire summer students. *Contact:* Human Resources.

TORONTO AMBULANCE
4330 Dufferin Street
Toronto, ON M3H 5R9

Tel. 416-392-2000
Fax 416-392-2039
Website .... www.city.toronto.on.ca

Toronto Ambulance is the government run municipal ambulance service for the city of Toronto. Toronto Ambulance provides 24-hour pre-hospital emergency and non-emergency care and transportation to and between hospitals for ill or injured individuals. The service also offers public education programs to promote rapid and appropriate use of emergency medical resources in time of need. Toronto Ambulance serves in excess of 2.4 million people in the Toronto area and is the largest municipal Emergency Medical Service (EMS) in Canada employing more than 500 people. Graduates most likely to be hired come from Community College Diploma programs in Ambulance and Emergency Care. Graduates are hired to occupy Ambulance Officer and Ambulance Dispatcher positions. Opportunities are also available for Clerical support and Maintenance staff. Employee benefits are rated above average. The potential for advancement is listed as being good. The average annual starting salary falls within the $35,000 to $40,000 range. The most suitable methods for initial contact by those seeking employment are to mail or fax a resume with a covering letter to City of Toronto, Corporate and Human Resources at 55 St. John Street, Toronto, Ontario, M5V 3C6 (Fax 416-397-9818). Toronto Ambulance is part of the new City of Toronto Works and Emergency Services Department. Contact: Corporate and Human Resources.

TORONTO ASSOCIATION FOR COMMUNITY LIVING
20 Spadina Road
Toronto, ON M5R 2S7

Tel. 416-968-0650
Fax 416-968-6463

The Toronto Association for Community Living provides residential, vocational and other support services for persons with developmental disabilities and their families. The association employs approximately 1,100 people. Graduates most likely to be hired come from the following academic areas: Bachelor of Arts (Social Work, Sociology, Social Services, Psychology), Bachelor of Education (Early Childhood Education, Special Needs), Master of Arts (Social Work, Psychology) and Community College Diploma (Social Work). Graduates would occupy Residential Counsellor, Instructor, Vocational Counsellor, Resource Teacher and Consultant positions. Previous work experience, and a positive, caring attitude towards persons with developmental disabilities are listed as desirable non-academic qualifications. Company benefits are rated above average. The potential for advancement is listed as being good. The average annual starting salary falls within the $25,000 to $30,000 range. The most suitable method for initial contact by those seeking employment is to mail a resume with a covering letter. The Toronto Association for Community Living does hire co-op work term and summer students for its Shadow Lake Camp Contact: Human Resources.

TORONTO COLONY HOTEL, THE
89 Chestnut Street
Toronto, ON M5G 1R1

Tel. 416-977-0707
Fax 416-585-3164

Website .... www.toronto-colony.com

The Toronto Colony Hotel is a superior quality hotel located in the heart of downtown Toronto. With a total of 717 guest bedrooms, the hotel employs a total of 364 people, and is part of a wider group that employs a total of 900 people in Canada, and 5,000 people worldwide. The Colony Hotel is located just blocks away from the city's main attractions such as The Eaton Centre, The Art Gallery of Ontario, City Hall, Skydome, and the CN Tower. The hotel hosts a variety of services including two restaurants, indoor and outdoor pools, 25 meeting rooms, a revolving Lakeview Room that offers spectacular city views, weight room, sauna, whirlpool, as well as other services. Graduates most likely to be hired come from the following academic areas: Bachelor of Arts (General, Criminology, Psychology), Bachelor of Engineering (General, Electrical), Bachelor of Commerce/Business Administration (General, Accounting, Human Resources, Information Systems, Marketing, Public Administration) and Community College Diploma (Accounting, Administration, Advertising, Business, Communications/Public Relations, Human Resources, Information Systems, Marketing/Sales, Secretarial, Electronics Technician, Engineering Technician). Graduates would occupy the entry level positions of Lobby Attendant and Waitstaff, as well as Clerk, Sales Person, Accountant, Receiver/Purchaser, Engineer, Human Resources Manager, Reservationist, Secretarial, Door/Bell Person, Front Desk Manager, Food and Beverage Manager, Security Officer, Payroll Clerk and Fitness Attendant positions. Outgoing, excellent people skills, professional demeanor, organized and conscientious are all listed as desirable non-academic qualifications. Company benefits are rated as industry standard. The potential for advancement is listed as being good. The average annual starting salary falls within the $25,000 to $30,000 range. The most suitable methods for initial contact by those seeking employment are to mail or fax a resume with a covering letter. The Toronto Colony Hotel does hire summer and co-op work term students. Contact: Shelley Edwards, Human Resources Assistant.

TORONTO COMMUNITY AND NEIGHBOURHOOD SERVICES
55 John Street, Metro Hall, 9th Floor
Toronto, ON M5V 3C6

Tel. 416-392-8665
Fax 416-397-9818
Website .... www.city.toronto.on.ca

Toronto Community and Neighbourhood Services Department provides a variety of social and educational services for the residents in the city of Toronto. The service divisions include Children's Services, Homes for the Aged, Hostel Services, Toronto's Non-Profit Housing Companies (Cityhome and The Housing Company), Social Development, Social Services, Library and Public Health Board. Graduates most likely to be hired come from the following academic areas: Bachelor of Arts (Family Studies, History, Economics), Bachelor of Education (Adult/Gerontology, Early Childhood Education), Master of Arts (Social Work) and Community College Diploma (Social Work). The majority of entry-level positions require some relevant work experience, attained through summer work, field placements or volunteer work. Also, some clerical and computer experience (eg. database, word processing) is desirable. Employee benefits are rated as excellent. The potential for advancement is listed as being good. The most suitable method for initial contact by those seeking employment is to mail a resume with a covering letter. Toronto Community and

Neighbourhood Services does hire summer students from designated programs of study. *Contact:* Staffing Coordinator.

TORONTO COMMUNITY CARE ACCESS CENTRE
250 Dundas Street West, Ground Floor
Toronto, ON M5T 2Z5

Tel. 416-506-9888
Fax 416-506-1629

The Toronto Community Care Access Centre is a non-profit organization that provides in-home health and support services. The centre serves people who are recovering from surgery or a hospital stay, are chronically or terminally ill, physically or mentally disabled or frail due to advancing years. The centre puts people in touch with a wide variety of professional, home support and personal care services, helping people of all ages and cultures receive help and care in their own homes instead of depending only on family members, hospital or nursing homes. In addition, the centre helps plan client's placement into long-term care facilities such as nursing homes and old age homes. Toronto Community Care employs a total of 300 people. Graduates most likely to be hired come from the following academic areas: Bachelor of Arts (General, Social Work), Bachelor of Science (Audiology, Nursing, Occupational Therapy, Physiotherapy, Speech Pathology) and Community College Diploma (Secretarial, Nursing RN/RNA, Social Work). Graduates would occupy Physiotherapist, Social Worker, Speech Pathologist, Care Coordinator, Clerical, Secretarial and Support positions. Knowledge of community health, and strong communication, assessment and organizational skills are all listed as desirable non-academic qualifications. Company benefits are rated as industry standard. The potential for advancement is listed as being average. The average annual starting salary falls within the $40,000 or $45,000 range. The most suitable method for initial contact by those seeking employment is to mail a resume with a covering letter. The Toronto Community Care Access Centre does hire summer and co-op work term students. *Contact:* Carol Boulding, Human Resources Associate.

TORONTO EAST GENERAL & ORTHOPAEDIC HOSPITAL INC.
825 Coxwell Avenue
Toronto, ON M4C 3E7

Tel. 416-469-6326
Fax 416-469-7982
Email .... hr@tegh.on.ca

Toronto East General & Orthopaedic Hospital Inc. is a 500-bed acute care community teaching hospital located in southeast Toronto. The hospital employs approximately 2,000 people. Graduates most likely to be hired come from the following academic areas: Bachelor of Science (General, Nursing, Physical Therapy), Bachelor of Education, Bachelor of Commerce/Business Administration, Master of Business Administration, Masters (Health Care/Nursing Administration) and Community College Diploma (Business, Laboratory Technician, Nursing RN/RNA). Applicants should have some familiarity with or working exposure to hospital operations. Company benefits are rated above average. The potential for advancement is listed as being good. The average annual starting salary falls within the $25,000 to $30,000 range, and is dependent upon the position being considered. The most suitable method for initial contact by those seeking em-

ployment is to mail a resume with a covering letter. *Contact:* Human Resources.

TORONTO FIRE SERVICES
4330 Dufferin Street
Toronto, ON M3H 5R9

Tel. 416-392-0162
Fax 416-392-0599
Email .... rbarrow@city.toronto.on.ca
Website .... www.city.toronto.on.ca/fire

Toronto Fire Services is the largest fire service in Canada and the fifth largest in the world. The service was created on January 1st 1998 when the six municipal fire departments of Metropolitan Toronto amalgamated. Toronto Fire Services currently employs 3,100 people. Applicants must be legally entitled to work in Canada, possess a secondary school diploma or have the equivalent combination of education and experience, understand and be able to communicate clearly in English under stressful conditions, and possess a pardon if previously convicted of a criminal offence. When applying, applicants must submit the following documents: an original and valid (conducted within 6 months of the application deadline) Occupation Specific Vision, Hearing and Fitness Assessment Certificate from York University, a copy of the current certification in Cardiopulmonary Resuscitation, Basic Rescuer Level 'C' (or approved equivalent), a copy of the current St. John Ambulance Standard First Aid (or approved equivalent), an original and valid Ontario driver's abstract (current within 30 days, showing not more than five demerit points and no unpaid fines). This standard must be maintained throughout the hiring process. At the time of the job offer, applicants must also present a valid Ontario Class 'D' licence (minimum), with a 'Z' air brake endorsement. Applicants are hired to occupy Probationary Fire Fighter positions. In addition to excellent physical fitness and strength abilities, a mechanical aptitude, ability to work shifts, and team player are listed as desirable non-academic qualifications. In the Fire Service teamwork is everything, since Fire Fighters depend on each other to successfully perform their duties. Company benefits are rated as excellent and include paid vacation, 11 designated holidays annually, sick pay, a comprehensive dental, prescription, and, supplemental hospital plan, life insurance, long-term disability insurance, uniform issue and cleaning allowance, and financial rewards for long service. The potential for advancement is also rated as excellent. The average annual starting salary falls within $40,000 to $45,000 range. Applicants are encouraged to attend one of the job orientation information sessions at the Toronto Fire Academy, 895 Eastern Avenue. Information about the sessions will be available on the recruitment hotline (416) 392-FIRE/392-3473, and in community newspapers. Initial contact may also be made by mailing or faxing a resume with a covering letter to Ron Barrow, Recruitment Officer at 895 Eastern Avenue, Toronto, ON, M4L 1A2 (Phone 416-392-0163). *Contact:* Recruitment Officer.

TORONTO HILTON
145 Richmond Street West
Toronto, ON M5H 2L2

Tel. 416-869-3456
Fax 416-860-6820
Website .... www.hilton.com/hotels/TORHITW

The Toronto Hilton is a major full-service hotel, located in the heart of Toronto's downtown. The Toronto Hilton employs a total of 350 people, and offers accommodation, recreation, restaurant and bar, and meeting facilities. Graduates most likely to be hired come from the following academic areas: Bachelor of Commerce/Business Administration (General, Human Resources) and Community College Diploma (Business, Human Resources, Hospitality). Graduates would occupy entry level Front Office, Guest Services Agent, Food and Beverage and Restaurant Supervisor positions. Previous work experience and a hospitality attitude are listed as desirable non-academic qualifications. The most suitable method for initial contact by those seeking employment is to mail a resume with a covering letter. *Contacts:* Director, Human Resources or Assistant Director, Human Resources.

TORONTO HUMANE SOCIETY

11 River Street
Toronto, ON M5A 4C2

Tel.	416-392-2273
Fax	416-392-9978
Website	www.humanesociety-ca.org

The Toronto Humane Society provides animal protection services. Operational activities include lost and found, adoption, vaccination clinic, spay and neuter clinic, emergency rescue for injured stray animals, and education/awareness programs on issues of animal exploitation and abuse. Founded in 1887, the Toronto Humane Society has the distinction of being Canada's oldest continuously operating humane society and is the largest in Canada in terms of membership and financial resources. The society has a staff of over 100 full-time and 25 part-time employees, as well as relying upon approximately 600 dedicated volunteers, who perform over 16,000 hours of work yearly. Graduates most likely to be hired come from the following academic areas: Bachelor of Arts (General, but prefer English, Sociology, Philosophy), Bachelor of Laws (Animal Rights), Bachelor of Education, Bachelor of Commerce/Business Administration, Community College Diploma (Animal Health) and Doctor of Veterinary Medicine. Bright, hardworking, reliable and a commitment to animal protection are all listed as desirable non-academic qualifications. Employee benefits are rated as excellent. The potential for advancement is listed as being good. The average annual starting salary depends on the position being considered. The most suitable method for initial contact by graduates seeking employment is to mail a resume with a covering letter. The Toronto Humane Society does hire summer students. *Contact:* Human Resources.

TORONTO HYDRO ELECTRIC COMMISSION

777 Bay Street, 4th Floor
Toronto, ON M5G 2C8

Tel.	416-599-0400
Fax	416-591-4721

Toronto Hydro Electric Commission provides electrical services within the city of Toronto. The commission employs approximately 1,400 people. Graduates most likely to be hired come from the following academic areas: Bachelor of Arts (Journalism), Bachelor of Science (Computer Science), Bachelor of Engineering (Architectural/Building, Electrical, Computer Systems, Telecommunications, Industrial Design), Bachelor of Architecture, Bachelor of Commerce/Business Administration (Accounting, Finance, Human Resources, Information Systems, Marketing), Certified Management Accountant, Certified General Accountant, Master of Business Administration (Accounting, Finance, Human Resources, Information Systems, Marketing), Master of Engineering and Community College Diploma (Accounting, Administration, Business, Communications, Facility Management, Financial Planning, Human Resources, Marketing/Sales, Purchasing/Logistics, Secretarial, Journalism, Architecture, Drafting, CAD/CAM/Autocad, Computer Science, Electronics Technician, Engineering Technician/Technologist, Welding). Graduates would occupy Clerical, Administrative, Technical and Field positions. Initiative, creativity, analytical skills, previous work experience, customer service orientation, strong verbal and written communication skills, team player and good interpersonal skills are all listed as desirable non-academic qualifications. Company benefits and the potential for advancement are both rated as excellent. Toronto Hydro Electric Commission does hire students for summer and co-op work terms. *Contact:* Personnel Services.

TORONTO LIFE MAGAZINE

59 Front Street East, 3rd Floor
Toronto, ON M5E 1B3

Tel.	416-364-3333
Fax	416-861-1169
Website	www.tor-lifeline.com

Toronto Life Magazine is a monthly city magazine concerned with business stories, citizen profiles, calendar events, and other articles which directly relate to Toronto. The magazine attempts to celebrate the city while featuring important articles that Torontonians would find relevant to their everyday lives, or may simply better inform them of the city in which they live. Toronto Life employs 50 people. Toronto Life is published by Key Publishers who are also publishers of TL Fashion, Canadian Geographic, Where Magazines, Wedding Bells, Owl & Chickadee, among others. Graduates most likely to be hired come from the following academic areas: Bachelor of Arts (Economics, English, History, Journalism, Political Science), Bachelor of Commerce/Business Administration (Marketing), Master of Business Administration (Marketing), Master of Arts (English, Journalism) and Community College Diploma (Graphic Arts, Journalism). Related work experience is a must. The amount of work experience required depends upon the department being considered. Graduates with the appropriate amount of work experience would occupy Copy Editor, Circulation Assistant, Sales Representative, Production Coordinator, Administrative Assistant, and Sales and Marketing Assistant positions. Other qualifications sought include the ability to work in a team environment, the desire to advance the magazine as well as oneself, a good sense of humour, and a strong belief and love for magazines and the industry. Toronto Life Magazine offers a relaxed and informal work environment and employees must feel comfortable with this style. Company benefits are rated above average. The potential for advancement is listed as average. The average annual starting salary falls within the $20,000 to $25,000 range. The most suitable method for initial contact by those seeking employment is to mail a resume with a covering letter. Toronto Life has Editorial Internships available year-round, including summer (these are not paid positions). *Contact:* Human Resources.

TORONTO MUTUAL LIFE INSURANCE CO.

112 St. Clair Avenue West
Toronto, ON M4V 2Y3

Tel.	416-960-3463
Fax	416-960-9927

Toronto Mutual Life Insurance Co. offers life, accident, and short term disability insurance products and services in most provinces within Canada. There are approximately 25 employees at this location. Graduates most likely to be hired come from the following academic areas: Bachelor of Arts (Social Sciences) and Community College Diploma (Business, Marketing). Graduates are hired for entry-level Clerk positions. Good customer service skills, successful completion of business related courses, excellent interpersonal skills and business related work experience are all listed as desirable non-academic qualifications. Company benefits are rated as industry standard. The potential for advancement is listed as average. The average annual starting salary falls within the $15,000 to $20,000 range. The most suitable method for initial contact by those seeking employment is to mail a resume with a covering letter. Toronto Mutual Life Insurance Co. does hire summer students on a regular basis. *Contact:* Geoffrey Harrison, Vice President & Secretary.

TORONTO REHABILITATION INSTITUTE
550 University Avenue
Toronto, ON M5G 2A2

Tel. 416-597-5111
Fax 416-597-6626
Website .... www.torontorehab.on.ca

Toronto Rehabilitation Institute provides a comprehensive range of inpatient and outpatient rehabilitation services and complex continuing care for adults who experience debilitating, often life-threatening, illness or injury. The institute is a tertiary care facility operating on five sites located in Toronto, including: 130 Dunn Avenue, 345/347 Rumsey Road, 520 Sutherland Drive, 47 Austin Terrace and 550 University Avenue. Patient care services are organized into six clinical programs: the acquired brain injury and stroke rehabilitation program, the cardiac rehabilitation and secondary prevention program, the complex continuing care program, the geriatric rehabilitation program and the spinal cord rehabilitation program. Toronto Rehabilitation Centre is a teaching hospital of the University of Toronto providing academic and practical training for students in a broad range of disciplines including dentistry, medicine, nursing, nutrition, occupational therapy, pharmacy, physiotherapy, psychology, social work, speech language pathology and therapeutic recreation. Graduates most likely to be hired come from the following academic areas: Bachelor of Arts (Recreation Studies, Social Work), Bachelor of Science (Computer Science, Nursing, Occupational Therapy, Pharmacy, Physiotherapy), Bachelor of Education (Adult), Bachelor of Commerce/Business Administration (Accounting, Finance, Information Systems), Chartered Accountant, Certified Management Accountant, Certified General Accountant, Master of Business Administration (Information Systems), Master of Social Work, Master of Science (Speech Pathology), Master of Education (Adult Education) and Community College Diploma (Accounting, Human Resources, Recreation, HVAC Systems, Mechanic, Dental Assistant, Laboratory Technician, Nursing RN/RPN, Radiology Technician, Rehabilitation Therapy). Graduates would occupy Staff Nursing, Nursing Management and positions related to the applicant's academic background. Organized, punctual, and excellent interpersonal and communication skills are listed as desirable non-academic qualifications. Employee benefits are rated as industry standard. The potential for advancement is listed as being good. The average annual starting salary falls within the $30,000 to $35,000 range. The most suitable methods for initial contact by graduates seeking employment are to mail or fax a resume with a covering

letter. Applications are encouraged from qualified women and men, members of visible minorities, aboriginal peoples and persons with disabilities. Summer positions are available for Nursing students only. *Contact:* Human Resources.

TORONTO REHABILITATION INSTITUTE
47 Austin Terrace
Toronto, ON M5R 1Y8

Tel. 416-537-3421
Fax 416-537-8628
Website .... www.torontorehab.on.ca

Toronto Rehabilitation Institute provides a comprehensive range of inpatient and outpatient rehabilitation services and complex continuing care for adults who experience debilitating, often life-threatening, illness or injury. The institute is a tertiary care facility operating on five sites located in Toronto, including: 130 Dunn Avenue, 345/347 Rumsey Road, 520 Sutherland Drive, 550 University Avenue and 47 Austin Terrace. Patient care services are organized into six clinical programs: the acquired brain injury and stroke rehabilitation program, the cardiac rehabilitation and secondary prevention program, the complex continuing care program, the geriatric rehabilitation program, the musculoskeletal rehabilitation program and the spinal cord rehabilitation program. Toronto Rehabilitation Centre is a teaching hospital of the University of Toronto providing academic and practical training for students in a broad range of disciplines including dentistry, medicine, nursing, nutrition, occupational therapy, pharmacy, physiotherapy, psychology, social work, speech language pathology and therapeutic recreation. Graduates most likely to be hired come from the following academic areas: Bachelor of Arts (General), Bachelor of Science (Health Sciences, Nursing, Pharmacy, Physiotherapy, Occupational Therapy), Bachelor of Commerce/Business Administration, Master of Science (Nursing), Community College Diploma (Accounting, Business, Secretarial, Human Resources, Food/Nutrition, Nursing RN/RPN, Pharmacy Technician, Central Supply Technician, Materials Management) and High School Diploma. Graduates would occupy Budget Officer, Accounts Receivable Clerk, Accounts Payable Clerk, Secretary, Health Records Technician, Health Records Manager, Director of Nursing Practice, Nursing Unit Manager, Nurse RN, Nurse RPN, Grad Nurse, Physiotherapist, Occupational Therapist, Central Supply Technician, Food Services Supervisor, Dietician, Pharmacy Technician, Pharmacist, Human Resources, Payroll Coordinator and Store Supervisor positions. Previous related work experience is listed as a desirable non-academic qualification. Employee benefits are rated as industry standard. The potential for advancement is listed as being good. The average annual starting salary falls within the $30,000 to $35,000 range. The most suitable methods for initial contact by graduates seeking employment are to mail or fax a resume with a covering letter. The most suitable method for initial contact by those seeking employment is to mail or fax a resume with a covering letter. Toronto Rehabilitation Institute, Austin Terrace site does hire summer students. *Contact:* Recruitment and Employee Relations.

TORONTO STOCK EXCHANGE / TSE
2 First Canadian Place
Toronto, ON M5X 1J2

Tel. 416-947-4700
Fax 416-947-4792
Email .... jobs@tse.com
Website .... www.tse.com

The Toronto Stock Exchange / TSE is Canada's number one marketplace for the trading of equities and related investments. The second largest exchange in North America, the TSE develops innovative derivatives, indices and information products to suit the needs of investors at home and abroad. The TSE also develops policies ranging from trading, corporate governance to telecommunications. The Toronto Stock Exchange employs 550 people. Graduates most likely to be hired come from the following academic areas: Bachelor of Arts (Economics), Bachelor of Science (Computer Science), Bachelor of Engineering (Computer Systems), Bachelor of Laws, Bachelor of Commerce/Business Administration (General, Accounting, Finance), Chartered Accountant, Certified Management Accountant, Certified General Accountant, Master of Business Administration (General, Accounting, Finance, Human Resources, Marketing) and Community College Diploma (Accounting, Administration, Business). The most suitable method for initial contact by those seeking employment is to mail, fax or e-mail a resume with a covering letter. The Toronto Stock Exchange does hire summer students. *Contact:* Human Resources.

TORONTO TRANSIT COMMISSION / TTC
1138 Bathurst Street
Toronto, ON M5R 3H2

Tel.	416-393-4564
Fax	416-397-8307
Website	www.ttc.on.ca

The Toronto Transit Commission / TTC provides public transit services for residents of the city of Toronto. This involves the maintenance and operation of transit equipment as well as associated services. The TTC is an equal opportunity employer, with approximately 10,700 employees in a variety of operational areas. Graduates most likely to be hired come from the following academic areas: Bachelor of Arts, Bachelor of Science (Computer Science), Bachelor of Engineering (Mechanical, Electrical, Structural, Architectural, Civil) and Community College Diploma (Business, Computer, Engineering Technician, Mechanic, Electrical Technician). Graduates would occupy Clerk, Technician, Tradesperson, Administrative Staff, Labourer, Professional and Driver positions. Applicants should be service oriented individuals. Company benefits and the potential for advancement are both rated as excellent (90% of promotions are internal). The average annual starting salary varies widely with the position being considered. The most suitable method for initial contact by graduates seeking employment is to visit the TTC Employment Office at this address. Summer job applications should be made between September and December for the following summer. The Employment Office is open Monday through Friday, from 7:45am to 3:00pm. *Contact:* Human Resources Department, Placement Services.

TORONTO WORKS AND EMERGENCY SERVICES DEPARTMENT
55 John Street, Metro Hall, 19th Floor
Toronto, ON M5V 3C6

Tel.	416-392-7729
Fax	416-392-0816
Email	works@city.toronto.on.ca
Website	www.city.toronto.on.ca

The Toronto Works and Emergency Services Department provides essential services that affect the day to day life of Toronto residents. The department provides water, wastewater, solid waste, transportation, fire and ambulance (see listings) services to residents and businesses in the city of Toronto. The department has approximately 9,300 employees, and has operations from Pickering in the east, to the border with Mississauga in the west, and from the shores of Lake Ontario to York Region in the north. Graduates most likely to be hired come from the following academic areas: Bachelor of Science (Surveying), Bachelor of Engineering, Bachelor of Commerce/Business Administration (Accounting) and Community College Diploma (Related Technical Programs). Graduates would occupy Administrative, Clerical and Technical positions. Initiative, creativity, a positive work attitude and good interpersonal skills are all listed as desirable non-academic qualifications. Company benefits and the potential for advancement are both rated as excellent. The average annual starting salary falls within the $15,000 to $35,000 range, depending on the position being considered. In order to be considered for employment graduates must complete an employment application form at City Hall. The Works and Emergency Services Department does hire summer students for positions related to their academic studies. *Contact:* Personnel Services Supervisor.

TORONTO ZOO
361A Old Finch Avenue
Toronto, ON M1B 5K7

Tel.	416-392-5900
Fax	416-392-5934
Website	www.torontozoo.com

The Toronto Zoo is responsible for zoo operations, operating through four operational goals, including recreation, education, conservation and research. The Toronto Zoo employs 250 full-time staff and over 130 seasonal staff (summer students). Graduates most likely to be hired come from the following academic areas: Bachelor of Science (Biology, Computer Science, Zoology, Nursing, Nutritional Sciences), Bachelor of Engineering (Civil), Bachelor of Commerce/Business Administration (Accounting, Human Resources), Chartered Accountant, Master of Business Administration (Public Administration) and Community College Diploma (Accounting, Advertising, Human Resources, Information Systems, Marketing/Sales, Secretarial, Graphic Arts, Hospitality, Journalism, Security/Enforcement, Travel/Tourism, Agriculture/Horticulture, Automotive Mechanic, Carpentry, Computer Science, Electronics Technician, HVAC Systems, Plumber, Welding, Animal Health, Dietitian/Nutrition, Laboratory Technician, Nursing RN). Graduates would occupy positions in the three main operational areas: Administrative & Site Services, Biology and Conservation, and Marketing and Communications. Positions include, Computer Services, Registered Nurse, Animal Keeper, Commissary Assistant, Project Management, Financial Services, Purchasing Agent, Personnel Clerk, Human Resource Officer, Building Trades, Public Relations and Animal Health Unit positions. Outgoing, customer service oriented, initiative and the ability to work with minimum supervision are all listed as desirable non-academic qualifications. Company benefits are rated as excellent. The potential for advancement is listed as being good. The most suitable method for initial contact by those seeking employment is to mail a resume with a covering letter. The Toronto Zoo does hire summer students. *Contact:* Human Resources.

TORONTO-DOMINION BANK / TD
55 King Street West, 14th Floor, TD Tower
Toronto, ON M5K 1A2

Tel. 416-982-8141
Fax 877-832-7759
Website .... www.tdbank.ca

The Toronto-Dominion Bank / TD is a recognized leader in the financial services industry. Employing 30,000 people worldwide, the TD offers customers a full line of retail, commercial, corporate, investment banking and treasury products and services. The TD actively seeks college and university graduates for their management development programmes across Canada. Graduates most likely to be hired come from the following academic areas: Bachelor of Arts (General, Economics), Bachelor of Science (Actuarial, Computer Science, Mathematics, Physics), Bachelor of Engineering (General, Computer Systems, Telecommunications), Bachelor of Commerce/Business Administration (Accounting, Finance, Human Resources, Information Systems, Marketing), Chartered Accountant, Certified Management Accountant, Certified General Accountant, Master of Business Administration (Accounting, Finance, Information Systems, Marketing) and Community College Diploma (Financial Planning, Marketing/Sales, Computer Science). Customer service skills, team player, motivation and a commitment to ongoing learning are all listed as desirable non-academic qualifications. Company benefits and the potential for advancement are both rated as excellent. The average annual starting salary varies significantly, based upon the experience and educational background of the applicant. The most suitable methods for initial contact by those seeking employment are to mail or fax a resume with a covering letter, or through the company's website. The Toronto-Dominion Bank does hire summer students. *Contact:* Manager, Recruitment.

TOSHIBA OF CANADA LIMITED
191 McNabb Street
Markham, ON L3R 8H2

Tel. 905-470-3500
Fax 905-470-3521
Email .... resumes@toshiba.ca
Website .... www.toshiba.ca

Toshiba of Canada Limited is a leading manufacturer and distributor of home entertainment, business and medical equipment. Established in August 1969, Toshiba of Canada Limited is a wholly-owned subsidiary of Toshiba Corporation, Tokyo, Japan. Toshiba is ranked as the 6th largest electronics equipment manufacturer in the world. Toshiba of Canada ranks in the top three in the high technology, office products and electronics markets in which it competes in Canada. In Canada, Toshiba offers its customers a diverse range of innovative products, systems and services, coupled with customer service, through four operating divisions: the consumer electronics group, the information systems group, the office products group and the medical systems group. Toshiba's Markham head office includes a research and development centre, product demonstration rooms, training classrooms, a technical support area and highly automated warehouse and distribution facilities. The company currently employs a substantial workforce across the country, primarily at its head office in Markham as well as in regional offices in Victoria, Vancouver, Calgary, Edmonton, Ottawa, Montreal, Quebec City and Halifax. Graduates most likely to be hired come from the following academic areas: Bachelor of Engineering (Electrical, Biomedical Electronics, Computer Systems), Bachelor of Commerce/Business Administration (General, Accounting, Human Resources, Marketing) and Community College Diploma (Accounting, Business, Communications/Public Relations, Marketing/Sales, Office Administration, Secretarial, Computer Science, Electronics Technician, Engineering Technician, Information Systems). Company benefits are rated above average. The potential for advancement is listed as being good. The most suitable methods for initial contact by those seeking employment are to mail, fax or e-mail a resume with a covering letter, through the company's website, or via campus career centres. Toshiba of Canada Limited does hire summer students. *Contact:* Human Resources.

TOTAL CARE TECHNOLOGIES INC.
1708 Dolphin Avenue, Suite 500
Kelowna, BC V1Y 9S4

Tel. 250-763-0034
Fax 250-763-0039
Email .... tctcareers@total-care.com
Website .... www.total-care.com

Total Care Technologies Inc. is a dynamic software development, marketing and services organization focusing on staff scheduling solutions for health care organizations. The company has become Canada's leading provider of innovative staff scheduling systems in the Canadian health care industry. Total Care has developed marketing initiatives with national and international business partners in Quebec, the United States and Holland, and has produced ESP (Environment for Scheduling Personnel), a world-class product installed in three languages, in three countries. Total Care has grown continuously to meet the needs of its expanding client base resulting in very high client satisfaction, and has twice won Science Council of British Columbia competitions for research and development. Graduates most likely to be hired come from the following academic areas: Bachelor of Science (Computer Science, Mathematics) and Bachelor of Engineering (Computer Systems). Depending upon the individual's education and experience, graduates would occupy various positions including: Software Quality Analyst, Applications Consultant/Instructor and Software Development positions. A positive attitude, team player, high standards, and strong technical and interpersonal skills are all listed as desirable non-academic qualifications. The most suitable methods for initial contact by those seeking employment are to e-mail a resume with a covering letter, or through the company's website. Total Care Technologies Inc. does hire summer and co-op work term students. *Contact:* Human Resources.

TOURISM YUKON, YUKON
PO Box 2703
Whitehorse, YT Y1A 2C6

Tel. 867-667-3009
Fax 867-667-8844
Website .... www.gov.yk.ca

Tourism Yukon is responsible for the development and marketing of tourism in Yukon. In addition, Tourism Yukon is responsible for historic site management, implementation of heritage specific land claim agreements, and scientific research, including archaeology and paleontology. There 45 full time employees, and 35 seasonal employees. Graduates most likely to be hired come from the following academic areas: Bachelor of Commerce/Business Administration (Human Resources, Information Systems, Marketing, Public Administration) and Community College Diploma (Marketing/Sales, Travel/Tourism). Graduates would occupy Marketing Manager, Marketing Officer, Finance and Systems Manager and Personnel Technician positions. Company benefits are rated as excellent. The potential for advancement is listed as average. The average annual starting salary falls within the $40,000 to $45,000 range. The most suitable method for initial contact by those seeking employment is to mail a resume with a covering letter. Tourism Yukon does hire summer students, generally students returning home to Yukon from university. *Contact:* Ms. C. Jenkins, Director, Corporate Services.

town✽shoes
THE SHOE COMPANY
A DIVISION OF TOWN SHOES

TOWN SHOES
44 Kodiak Crescent
Toronto, ON M3J 3G5

Tel. 416-638-5342
Fax 416-638-0639

Town Shoes is involved in the ladies, high fashion footwear and accessories business. Town Shoes consists of 14 retail stores and the head office location (this address). Stores are located in Kitchener, Ottawa, Toronto and vicinity. Town Shoes has been in business for over 45 years and today has approximately 900 employees in Canada. Town Shoes also operates The Shoe Company. This is a value oriented, assisted service operation which is being rapidly expanded across Canada, and presently consists of 33 stores. Graduates most likely to be hired come from the following academic areas: Bachelor of Arts (General, English, Fine Arts), Bachelor of Commerce/Business Administration (General), Master of Business Administration (General, Marketing) and Community College Diploma (Business, Fashion Merchandising, Graphic Arts). Graduates would occupy Executive Trainee, Management in Training (MIT) and Retail Sales Associate positions. Previous retail experience, a passionate interest in fashion and excellent people skills are listed as desirable non-academic qualifications. Company benefits and the potential for advancement are both rated as excellent. The average annual starting salary falls within the $20,000 to $25,000 range for sales representatives, and within the $25,000 to $30,000 range for trainee positions. The most suitable methods for initial contact by those seeking employment are to fax a resume with a covering letter, or via telephone. *Contact:* Ms Terry Tracey, Director of Recruiting.

TOYOTA CANADA INC.
1 Toyota Place
Toronto, ON M1H 1H9

Tel. 416-438-6320
Fax 416-431-1871
Website .... www.toyota.ca

Toyota Canada Inc. is a leading automobile manufacturer and importer, with dealers across Canada. The company purchases vehicles and auto parts from Japan and across North America. In turn, Toyota sells those passenger vehicles, parts, forklift vehicles and trucks, and distributes them to locations throughout Canada. This location is also active in the marketing of Toyota's products through-

out Canada. There are approximately 300 employees at this location. Graduates most likely to be hired come from the following academic areas: Bachelor of Commerce (Marketing) and Community College Diploma (Marketing, Human Resources, Auto Technician/Mechanic, Materials Management, Purchasing/Logistics). Graduates would occupy Automotive Technician, Marketing Coordinator and Analyst positions. Flexible, promotable and excellent communication skills are all listed as desirable non-academic qualifications. Company benefits are rated above average. The potential for advancement is listed as being good. The average annual starting salary falls within the $30,000 plus range. The most suitable method for initial contact by graduates seeking employment is to mail a resume with a covering letter. Toyota Canada Inc. does hire summer students. *Contact:* Human Resources Manager.

TOYS R US (CANADA) LTD.
2777 Langstaff Road
Concord, ON L4K 4M5

Tel. 905-660-2000
Fax 905-660-2022
Email .... helander2@toysrus.com
Website .... www.toysrus.com

Toys R Us (Canada) Ltd. operates retail toy stores across Canada following the warehouse store concept. Toys R Us (Canada) Ltd. is a subsidiary of US based Toys R Us, International, which operates 450 stores in 27 countries, including franchise stores. The parent company, Toys R Us, USA operates an additional 700 stores in the United States. Toys R Us (Canada) Ltd. employs 200 people at this location and a total of 3,000 people across Canada. Graduates most likely to be hired come from the following academic areas: Bachelor of Arts (Economics), Bachelor of Science (Computer Science), Bachelor of Education (Adult), Bachelor of Commerce/Business Administration (Accounting, Finance, Human Resources, Information Systems, Marketing), Certified Management Accountant, Certified General Accountant and Community College Diploma (Accounting, Facility Management, Human Resources, Marketing/Sales, Graphic Arts). At the head office, graduates are hired to occupy Accounting Clerk, Marketing and Advertising positions, and at store locations, graduates would occupy Management Trainee positions. Previous retail work experience, teamwork, and strong written and oral communication skills are all listed as desirable non-academic qualifications. Company benefits and the potential for advancement are both rated as excellent. The average annual starting salary falls within the $25,000 to $30,000 range. The most suitable methods for initial contact by those seeking employment are to mail, fax or e-mail a resume with a covering letter. Toys "R" Us (Canada) Ltd. does hire summer students. *Contact:* Randall K. Helander, Director of Human Resources.

TRANS CANADA CREDIT CORPORATION
3 Concorde Gate, 4th Floor
Toronto, ON M3C 3N7

Tel. 416-382-5314
Fax 416-382-5318
Email .... tccrecruit@sprint.ca
Website .... www.norwestfinancial.com

Trans Canada Credit Corporation provides a full range of financing services including consumer loans, mortgages, retail sales financing, leasing and private label credit card services to customers and retail customers across Canada. The company was incorporated in 1940 and since then has grown to a nation wide organization servicing 1.5 million customers and clients through a network of over 160 locations across Canada. Trans Canada Credit is part of San Francisco, California based Well Fargo and Company, which is a diversified financial services organization. Wells Fargo has been in operation for 100 years and currently has assets of over $200 billion and over 102,000 employees worldwide. Trans Canada Credit Corporation employs 300 people at this location and a total of 1,700 people across Canada. Graduates most likely to be hired come from the following academic areas: Bachelor of Commerce/Business Administration (General, Accounting, Finance, Information Systems, Marketing), Master of Business Administration (General, Accounting, Finance, Information Systems, Marketing) and Community College Diploma (Accounting, Advertising, Business, Marketing/Sales). Graduates would occupy Call Centre, Credit, Collections, Sales, Information Systems (PC/LAN) and Quality Assurance positions. Team player, good customer services skills and a sales orientation are listed as desirable non-academic qualifications. Company benefits are rated as excellent with the company offering a benefits program which is fully company paid and includes profit sharing, a non-contributory pension plan and a fully equipped fitness facility at its Don Mills location. The potential for advancement is listed as being good with Trans Canada Credit strongly committed to the development of its employees, providing extensive training through various in-house programs, external courses and an educational subsidy program. The company actively fosters promotion from within, and the majority of managers and senior executives have developed their careers from entry level positions within the company. The average annual starting salary falls within the $25,000 to $30,000 range. The most suitable methods for initial contact by those seeking employment are to mail, fax or e-mail a resume with a covering letter. *Contact:* Anne Bloom, Employee Relations Specialist.

TRANS MOUNTAIN PIPE LINE COMPANY LTD.
1333 West Broadway, Suite 900
Vancouver, BC V6H 4C2

Tel. 604-739-5000
Fax 604-739-5335

Trans Mountain Pipe Line Company Ltd. owns and operates a pipeline system for the transportation of crude oil and petroleum products from Edmonton to the West Coast and Washington State. At the U.S. border, the company's pipeline connects with a pipeline owned and operated by a wholly-owned subsidiary, Trans Mountain Oil Pipe Line Corporation, which delivers Canadian petroleum to refineries in northwestern Washington State. Another subsidiary, Trans Mountain Enterprises of British Columbia Limited, owns and operates a pipeline for the transportation of jet fuel to Vancouver International Airport. Graduates most likely to be hired come from the following areas: Bachelor of Arts (Economics), Bachelor of Science (Chemistry, Computer Science), Bachelor of Engineering (General, Environmental, Electrical, Mechanical, Metallurgy), Bachelor of Laws (Environmental), Bachelor of Commerce/Business Administration (Accounting, Finance), Chartered Accountant, Certified General Accountant and Community College Diploma (Purchasing/Logistics, Secretarial, Computer Science). Graduates would occupy Pipeline Engineer, Draftsperson,

Environmental Technician, Journeyman Electrician, H.D. Mechanic, Millwright, Instrumentation, Financial Analyst, Clerical and Accounting positions. Company benefits are rated as excellent. The potential for advancement is listed as being good. The most suitable method for initial contact by those seeking employment is to mail a resume with a covering letter. Trans Mountain Pipe Line Company Ltd. does hire summer and co-op work term students. *Contact:* Human Resources.

TRANSAMERICA LIFE INSURANCE COMPANY OF CANADA
300 Consilium Place
Toronto, ON M1H 3G2

Tel. 416-290-6221
Fax 416-290-2911
Website .... www.transamerica.com

Transamerica Life Insurance Company of Canada provides financial security services, innovative and affordable life insurance and annuity products. The company has operated in Canada since 1927 and and ranks among the top providers of life insurance in the country. In addition to providing term and universal life insurance, Transamerica provides a solid mix of investment products including segregated funds, guaranteed interest accounts, RRIFs/LIFs, RRSPs/LIRAs and annuities. Transamerica Life Insurance Company of Canada is a wholly owned subsidiary of San Francisco, California based Transamerica Corporation, one of the world's largest financial services companies. In Canada, Transamerica's life insurance and investment products are available to consumers through some 6,000 advisers located in all major Canadian cities, working through Transamerica's 92 general agencies, 13 brokerages, two branch offices and several members of the Investment Dealers Association. Graduates most likely to be hired come from the following academic areas: Bachelor of Arts (Economics, Psychology, General), Bachelor of Science (Actuarial, Mathematics), Bachelor of Commerce/Business Administration and Community College Diploma (Business, Communications, Graphic Arts). Graduates are hired to occupy a variety of positions including Customer Service Representative and Policy Accounting Clerk. Good communication skills, flexibility, customer service skills and computer literacy (e.g. word processing and spreadsheet applications) are all listed as desirable non-academic qualifications. Company benefits are rated above average. The potential for advancement is listed as average. The average annual starting salary falls within the $20,000 to $30,000 range. The most suitable methods for initial contact by those seeking employment are to mail or fax a resume with a covering letter. Transamerica Life Insurance Company of Canada does hire summer students on a limited basis. *Contact:* Human Resources.

TRANSCANADA
111 - 5th Avenue SW
Calgary, AB T2P 3Y6

Tel. 403-267-6100
Fax 403-267-8832
Email .... careers@transcanada.com
Website .... www.transcanada.com

TransCanada is a leading North American energy company. The company's operations are divided into five strategic business units: TransCanada Transmission, TransCanada Midstream, TransCanada Energy, TransCanada Power and TransCanada International.

These business units are active in the pipeline transmission business through to energy transmission, manufacturing and processing, as well as the marketing and trading of energy products and services across North America and around the world. With a $26 billion asset base, TransCanada's common shares trade under the symbol TRP, primarily on the Toronto, Montreal and New York stock exchanges. TransCanada employs a total of 6,500 people worldwide. Graduates most likely to be hired come from the following academic areas: Bachelor of Science (Chemistry, Computer Science), Bachelor of Engineering (General, Chemical, Civil, Electrical, Mechanical, Computer Systems, Industrial Design, Telecommunications), Bachelor of Commerce/Business Administration (General, Accounting, Finance, Human Resources, Information Systems), Chartered Accountant, Certified Management Accountant, Certified General Accountant, Master of Business Administration (General, Accounting, Finance, Human Resources, Information Systems), Master of Science and Master of Engineering. TransCanada employs creative and innovative people who are encouraged to realize their full potential. The company fosters a working environment that emphasizes teamwork, initiative, involvement, communication and continuous improvement. Accordingly, leadership, business acumen, customer focus, project management, team player, problem solving and good communication skills are all listed as desirable non-academic qualifications. TransCanada helps employees improve their performance by providing a wide range of internal and external training opportunities. The company sponsors memberships in professional associations and provides financial support to employees who wish to further their education in areas of benefit to the company. The most suitable methods for initial contact by those seeking employment are to mail, fax or e-mail a resume with a covering letter, or via the company's website. TransCanada does hire summer students (on a limited basis) and co-op work term students. *Contact:* Human Resources.

TRANSCANADA ENERGY
237 - 4 Avenue SW, Suite 3400
Calgary, AB T2P 5A4

Tel. 403-213-3100
Fax 403-213-3636
Email .... energy_careers@transcanada.com
Website .... www.transcanada.com

TransCanada Energy buys and sells energy commodities, including natural gas, natural gas liquids, crude oil and refined products, and provides a selection of supply, storage and transportation services to its customers. These services are provided in both Canada and the United States. TransCanada Energy is an operating business unit of Calgary based TransCanada. TransCanada is a world-class energy services company, with strategic business units active in the pipeline transmission business through to energy transmission, manufacturing and processing, as well as the marketing and trading of energy products and services across North America and around the world. TransCanada Energy employs a total of 450 people at this location. Graduates most likely to be hired come from the following academic areas: Bachelor of Arts (Economics), Bachelor of Science (Computer Science), Bachelor of Engineering (Computer Systems), Bachelor of Commerce/Business Administration (General, Accounting, Finance, Human Resources, Information Systems, Marketing), Chartered Accountant, Certified Management Accountant, Certified General Accountant and Community College Diploma (Facility Management, Office Administration, Secretarial, Computer Science, Information Systems). Company benefits are rated above average. The potential for advancement is listed as being good. The average annual starting salary falls within the $50,000 to $55,000 range. The most suitable method for initial contact by those seeking employment is to mail a resume with a covering letter. TransCanada Energy does hire summer and co-op work term students. *Contact:* Denise Paul.

TRANSCO PLASTIC INDUSTRIES
150 Merizzi
Montreal, QC H4T 1S4

Tel. 514-733-9951
Fax 514-733-5481

Transco Plastic Industries is a vertically integrated (extrusion/printing/converting) plastic bag manufacturer. The company employs approximately 140 people at this location and a total of 190 across Canada. Graduates most likely to be hired come from the following academic areas: Bachelor of Engineering (General, Electrical, Automation/Robotics, Industrial Production, Process), Community College Diploma (Electronics Technician, Engineering Technician), and High School Diploma. Graduates would occupy Trainee, Process Engineering, Clerical and General Production positions. Initiative, team player, and a minimum of two to three years work experience are all listed as desirable non-academic qualifications. Company benefits are rated above average. The potential for advancement is listed as being good. The average annual starting salary is dependent upon the position being considered. The most suitable method for initial contact by those seeking employment is to mail a resume with a covering letter. Transco Plastic Industries does hire summer students. *Contacts:* Human Resources or Michel Boulanger, Operations Manager.

TREBAS INSTITUTE
451, rue Saint-Jean
Montreal, QC H2Y 2R5

Tel. 514-845-4141
Website .... www.trebas.com

Trebas Institute is a private career college with campuses in Montreal, Toronto and Vancouver. Since 1979, Trebas has offered training programs in the digital media, including Interactive Multimedia, Film and Television Production, Music Business Administration, Audio Engineering and Recorded Music Production. There are 35 employees at the Montreal campus (head office), 90 in Toronto and 35 employees at the Vancouver campus. Those persons most likely to be hired for instructor positions come from backgrounds in Multimedia Development, 3D Animation, Digital Audio, Music Business, and Film/TV Production. Excellent communication skills, problem solving and analytical abilities are listed as desirable non-academic qualifications. Company benefits are rated as industry standard. The potential for advancement is listed as being excellent. The most suitable method for initial contact by those seeking employment is to mail a resume with a covering letter. Trebas Institute does hire summer students. (Toronto Location: 410 Dundas Street East, Toronto, ON, M5A 2A8, Phone 416-966-3066; Vancouver Location: 112 East 3rd Avenue, Vancouver, BC, V5T 1C8, Phone 604-872-2666). *Contact:* The Director.

TRENCH LIMITED
71 Maybrook Drive
Toronto, ON M1V 4B6

Tel. 416-298-8108
Fax 416-298-6290

Trench Limited designs, tests and manufactures high voltage electrical equipment. The company employs approximately 315 people at this location, and a total of 450 people in Canada. Graduates most likely to be hired come from the following academic areas: Bachelor of Arts (Economics, Geography, History, Languages, Music, Political Science), Bachelor of Science (Chemistry, Computer Science, Mathematics, Physics), Bachelor of Engineering (Industrial Chemistry, Materials Science, Electrical, Power), Bachelor of Commerce/Business Administration (General, Accounting, Finance, Human Resources, Information Systems, Marketing), Certified Management Accountant, Certified General Accountant, Master of Business Administration (General, Human Resources, Marketing), Master of Arts (Industrial Relations), Master or Engineering, Doctorate (Engineering), Community College Diploma (Accounting, Administration, Business, Human Resources, Marketing/Sales, Purchasing/Logistics, Secretarial, CAD/CAM/Autocad, Electronics Technician, Engineering Technician, Welding) and High School Diploma. Graduates would occupy Finance, Human Resources, Marketing, Sales, Engineering, Research and Development, Design, CAD Drafting, Industrial Engineering, High Voltage Testing, Quality Assurance and Production positions. A willingness to learn throughout career, good oral and written communication skills, team player, positive attitude, previous work experience (depending upon position) and an ability to get along with co-workers and supervisors are all listed as desirable non-academic qualifications. Company benefits are rated above average. The potential for advancement is listed as being good. The average annual, entry level salary for non-managerial positions falls within the $25,000 to $35,000 range. The most suitable method for initial contact by those seeking employment is to mail a resume with a covering letter. Trench Limited occasionally hires summer students, this varies from year to year. *Contact:* Katherine Jordan, Human Resources Manager.

TRILLIUM HEALTH CENTRE, MISSISSAUGA SITE
100 Queensway West
Mississauga, ON L5B 1B8

Tel. 905-848-7100
Fax 905-848-5598
Website .... www.trilliumhealthcentre.org

The Trillium Health Centre, Mississauga Site (formerly The Mississauga Hospital) is a diversified community hospital with over 400 beds. In 1998, The Mississauga Hospital and the Queensway General Hospital amalgamated to form the Trillium Health Centre. The Trillium Health Centre employs a total of 2,700 staff and 400 physicians. The Mississauga Site primarily serves the residents of the southern, central and eastern sections of Mississauga. Graduates most likely to be hired come from the following academic areas: Bachelor of Arts (General, Economics, English, Languages, Philosophy, Political Science, Social Work, Sociology, Psychology, Recreation), Bachelor of Science (General, Biology, Chemistry, Computer, Health Sciences, Mathematics, Microbiology, Nursing, Pharmacy, Physics, Psychology), Bachelor of Engineering (Systems, Electrical, Environmental, Industrial, Materials Science, Mechanical), Bachelor of Education (General, Adult, Childhood, Physical, Special Needs) Bachelor of Commerce/Business Administration (Accounting, Finance, Marketing, Information Systems, Public Administration), Chartered Accountant (Finance), Certified Management Accountant (Finance), Certified General Accountant (Finance), Master of Business Administration (Accounting, Finance, Marketing, Information Systems, Public Administration), Master of Science (Nursing), Master of Engineering (Biomedical Engineering), Master of Education (Adult Education), Doctor (Psychology, Pathology, Gerontology) and Community College (Accounting, Administration, Business, Communications, Facility Management, Secretarial, Cooking, Hospitality, Human Resources, Recreation, Photography, Social Work, Computer, Electronics, Engineering, Mechanic, Ambulance/Emergency Care). Maturity, reliable, motivated, good work ethic, excellent communication skills and leadership potential are all listed as desirable non-academic qualifications. The most suitable method for initial contact by those seeking employment is to mail a resume with a covering letter. Trillium Health Centre, Mississauga Site does hire summer students. *Contact:* O. Rita DoCanto, Human Resources Advisor.

TRIMARK INVESTMENT MANAGEMENT INC.
5140 Yonge Street, Trimark Tower, Suite 900
Toronto, ON M2N 6X7

Tel. 416-228-5785
Fax 416-590-0492
Email .... tmcarthr@trimark.com
Website .... www.trimark.com

Trimark Investment Management Inc. is a leading Canadian investment management company. Trimark provides a full range of investment products, including mutual funds, specialty GICs and segregated funds, as well as a variety of other financial services and products through Trimark Trust. Established in Toronto in 1981 with a staff of six, Trimark today has more than 850 employees across Canada. Graduates most likely to be hired come from the following academic areas: Bachelor of Arts (French, Journalism), Bachelor of Science (Computer Science), Bachelor of Education (Adult), Bachelor of Commerce/Business Administration (General, Accounting, Finance, Human Resources, Information Systems, Marketing), Chartered Accountant, Master of Business Administration (Finance) and Community College Diploma (Accounting, Administration, Advertising, Business, Communications/Public Relations, Financial Planning, Human Resources, Information Systems, Marketing/Sales, Secretarial, Graphic Arts, Journalism). Graduates would occupy Clerk, Customer Service Representative, Software Developer in Information Systems and Departmental Assistant positions in various departments including Accounting, Marketing, Human Resources, etc. Team player, positive attitude, initiative and the willingness to "go the extra-mile" are all listed as desirable non-academic qualifications. Company benefits are rated as excellent and include a full benefits package including vision care, dental and extended health, a no-commission group RRSP and employee stock purchase plan, matching of charitable donations plan, fitness memberships, and more. The potential for advancement is listed as being good. The average annual starting salary falls within the $30,000 to $40,000 range. The most suitable methods for initial contact by those seeking employment are to mail, fax or e-mail a resume with a covering letter. Trimark Investment Management Inc. hires a limited number of co-op work term students. *Contact:* Tracey McArthur, Human Resources.

TRIPLE-A MANUFACTURING COMPANY LIMITED, THE
44 Milner Avenue
Toronto, ON M1S 3P8

Tel. 416-291-4451
Fax 416-291-1292

The Triple-A Manufacturing Company Limited is involved in the manufacturing of a wide variety of storage systems. The company employs more than 50 people. Graduates most likely to be hired come from the following academic areas: Bachelor of Arts (General), Bachelor of Science (Computer Science), Bachelor of Engineering (Mechanical), Bachelor of Commerce/Business Administration (Accounting), Certified Management Accountant, Certified General Accountant, Community College Diploma (Accounting, Marketing/Sales, Purchasing/Logistics, Secretarial, Architecture/Drafting, Industrial Design CAD/CAM/Autocad) and High School Diploma. In addition to unskilled labour positions in the manufacturing plant, graduates would occupy Receptionist, Order Desk Clerk, Engineer, Estimator, Secretary, Clerical and Computer Operator positions. Company benefits are rated as excellent. The potential for advancement is listed as average. The average annual starting salary falls within the $20,000 to $25,000 range. The most suitable method for initial contact by those seeking employment is to mail a resume with a covering letter. The Triple-A Manufacturing Co. Ltd. does hire summer students. *Contacts:* Ms. D. Partridge or Mr. A. Lerman.

TRISTAN & ISEUT / AMERICA

20 des Seigneurs
Montreal, QC H3K 3K3

Tel. 514-937-4601
Fax 514-935-1233

Tristan & Iseut / America operates retail chain stores with boutiques in Quebec, Ontario and the United States. The head office is located in Montreal, complete with buying, design and production departments. There are 200 employees at this location, a total of 1,200 employees across Canada and an additional 200 employees in the United States. Graduates most likely to be hired come from the following academic areas: Bachelor of Arts (Languages), Bachelor of Science (Computer Science), Bachelor of Engineering (Computer Systems), Bachelor of Commerce/Business Administration (Accounting, Finance, Human Resources, Information Systems, Marketing), Chartered Accountant, Master of Business Administration (Accounting, Finance, Information Systems, Marketing), Community College Diploma (Computer Science) and High School Diploma. Graduates are hired to occupy Accounting Clerk, Accounts Payable Clerk, Data Entry Clerk, Import Clerk, Distribution Clerk and Receptionist positions. Previous work experience, alertness, good attention span, character, quickness and good references are listed as desirable non-academic qualifications. Company benefits are rated as industry standard. The potential for advancement is listed as average. The average annual starting salary depends upon the position being considered and the applicant's experience. The most suitable methods for initial contact by those seeking employment are to mail a resume with a covering letter, or through an employment agency. Tristan & Iseut / America does hire summer students at their boutique locations for Sales Staff positions. *Contact:* Connie Fuoco, Human Resources Director.

TRUSERV CANADA COOPERATIVE INC.

PO Box 6800
Winnipeg, MB R3C 3A9

Tel. 204-453-9616
Fax 204-453-9414

TruServ Canada Cooperative Inc. is an expanding wholesale distributor of hardware and general merchandise, serving a national chain of over 500 stores. Based in Winnipeg, TruServe is a cooperative owned by independent Canadian retailers. The cooperative employs 340 people at this location and a total of 360 people in Canada. Graduates most likely to be hired come from the following academic areas: Bachelor of Science (Computer Science), Bachelor of Commerce/Business Administration (Accounting, Finance, Human Resources, Information Systems), Chartered Accountant, Certified Management Accountant, Certified General Accountant, Master of Science (Computer Science), Community College Diploma (Accounting, Advertising, Human Resources, Purchasing/Logistics, Secretarial, CAD/CAM/Autocad, Computer Science) and High School Diploma. Graduates would occupy Programmer/Analyst, Technical Support (Retail Systems), Communications/Network Support, Controller, Assistant Controller, Human Resources Manager, Human Resources Administrator, Desk-Top Publishing, Accounting Clerk and General Clerical positions. Previous work experience, outside activities/hobbies and possessing future goals are all listed as desirable non-academic qualifications. Company benefits are rated above average. The potential for advancement is listed as average. The average annual starting salary for entry level clerical jobs falls within the $15,000 to $20,000 range. For other areas, the average annual starting salary depends upon the position being considered. The most suitable method for initial contact by those seeking employment is to mail a resume with a covering letter. TruServ Canada Cooperative Inc. hires summer students for entry level accounting and summer receptionist positions. *Contacts:* Karen Froese or Cathy Gamby.

TST OVERLAND EXPRESS

PO Box 3030, Station A
Mississauga, ON L5A 3S3

Tel. 905-625-7500
Fax 905-624-7010
Website .... www.tstoverland.com

TST Overland Express is a leader in high quality "time sensitive" North American transportation services. Established in 1928 and previously known as TNT Overland Express, the company became TST Solutions Inc. in 1998. TST Solutions includes TST Expedited Services and TST Overland Express. Within TST Overland Express there is Load Brokerage Services and TCEI, the truckload division. The company is the first North American wide carrier to achieve ISO 9002 registration. TST Overland Express is the Canadian member of ExpressLINK, a North American strategic alliance. ExpressLINK was formed in 1996 by TST Overland Express, Estes Express Lines of Richmond, Virginia, GI Trucking of La Mirada, California and Lakeville Motor Express of St. Paul, Minnesota. ExpressLINK combines the regional strength and quality of each member, all leaders in their respective markets, into a seamless direct service throughout North America. ExpressLINK employs more than 10,000 people across North America. TST Overland Express employs 1,200 people in Canada. Graduates most likely to be hired come from the following academic areas: Bachelor of Arts, Bachelor of Science, Bachelor of Commerce/Business Administration, Chartered Accountant, Certified Management Accountant and Community College Diploma (Transportation, Computer Science, Auto Mechanic, Secretarial). Graduates would occupy Clerk/Biller, Secretary, Dockworker, Driver, Dispatcher and Management positions. A sincere and intelligent interest in their work, responsible, mature and a willingness to learn are all listed as desirable non-academic qualifications. Company benefits are rated above average. The potential for advancement is listed as being good. The average annual starting salary falls within the $15,000 to $20,000 range. The most suitable method for initial contact by those seeking employment is to mail a resume with a covering letter. TST Overland Express does hire summer students, usually for clerical or dockwork positions. *Contact:* Human Resource Manager.

TUFF CONTROL SYSTEMS LTD.
5 Director Court, Unit 104
Vaughan, ON L4L 4S5

Tel. 905-850-8560
Fax 905-850-8577

Tuff Control Systems Ltd. provides security services, assisting retailers in controlling losses. There are a total of 65 employees in Ontario, located mostly in the greater Toronto area, but also in Windsor, London and the Ottawa areas. Graduates most likely to be hired are Community College graduates specializing in Security and Enforcement and High School graduates. Graduates would occupy Trainee Investigator positions. An outgoing personality, the ability to handle difficult situations with the public, responsible, good judgment, a mature attitude and good observation skills are all listed as desirable non-academic qualifications. In addition, applicants must not have a criminal record. Company benefits are rated as industry standard. The potential for advancement is listed as average. The average annual starting salary falls within the $15,000 to $20,000 range. The most suitable methods for initial contact by graduates seeking employment are to fax a resume with a covering letter, or via telephone. Tuff Control Systems Ltd. does hire summer, part-time and co-op work term students. *Contacts:* Debi Bellis or Chris Blake.

TVONTARIO
PO Box 200, Station Q
Toronto, ON M4T 2T1

Tel. 416-484-2600
Fax 416-484-2633
Website .... www.tvo.org

TVOntario (TVO) is an Educational Telecommunications Provincial Agency. TVO's primary objectives are the acquisition, production and distribution of programs and materials (teacher's guides) in French and English within the educational broadcasting field. TVOntario employs between 350 and 500 people. Graduates most likely to be hired come from the following academic areas: Bachelor of Arts (Fine Arts, Languages, Communications), Community College Diploma (Secretarial, Radio and Television Arts), Bachelor of Education (Adult, Childhood), Bachelor of Commerce/Business Administration and Master of Business Administration (Finance). Graduates are hired to occupy Technician, Production, Equipment Maintenance, Programming, Accounting, Clerical, Marketing and Public Relation positions. Bilingualism is a definite asset. Company benefits are rated as excellent. The potential for advancement is listed as average. The average annual starting salary falls within the $25,000 to $30,000 range. The most suitable method for initial contact by graduates seeking employment is to mail a resume with a covering letter. *Contact:* Human Resources Department.

UAB GROUP OF COMPANIES, THE
4300, rue Jean-Talon Ouest
Montreal, QC H4P 1W3

Tel. 514-735-3561
Fax 514-735-8439
Email .... uabØ98@attmail.com

The UAB Group of Companies is an independent adjusting firm and along with its subsidiaries provides full services to insurers and self-insured companies. This includes virtually all the underwriting and loss management services the group's clients require. UAB has 850 employees in 115 locations across Canada. Graduates most likely to be hired come from the following academic areas: Bachelor of Commerce, Bachelor of Business Administration and Community College Diploma (Insurance). Graduates are hired to occupy the position of Insurance Claims Adjuster. Autonomous, and self-starting are both listed as desirable non-academic qualifications. Company benefits are rated above average. The average annual starting salary falls within the $23,000 to $25,000 range. The most suitable method for initial contact by those seeking employment is to mail a resume with a covering letter. The Underwriters Adjustment Bureau Ltd. does hire summer and co-op work term students. *Contact:* Personnel Department.

UBI SOFT ENTERTAINMENT INC.
5505 Saint-Laurent Blvd., Suite 5000
Montreal, QC H2T 1S6

Tel. 514-490-2000
Fax 514-490-0882
Website .... www.ubisoft.qc.ca

Ubi Soft Entertainment Inc. handles every stage of the creation of new interactive software games, from their design and production to their distribution. These activities offer a wide variety of career opportunities to creative and innovative young graduates who are high-tech enthusiasts. Founded in 1986 and today a leader in the multimedia field, Ubi Soft is an international company employing over 1,400 people in 9 production studios and 16 subsidiaries located in Europe, North America and Asia. Presently, Ubi Soft distributes its catalogue of over 1,200 products in 50 countries in 22 different languages. Established in Montreal in July of 1997, Ubi Soft has over 400 employees at this location and is always seeking talented graduates eager to take on new creative challenges in the video games industry. Graduates most likely to be hired come from the following academic areas: Bachelor of Arts (Graphic Arts, Music), Bachelor of Science (General, Computer Science), Bachelor of Engineering (General, Computer Systems), Bachelor of Commerce/Business Administration (General, Accounting, Marketing), Chartered Accountant, Certified Management Accountant, Certified General Accountant, Master of Business Administration (Marketing, Management, International Business) and Community College Diploma (Animation, Audio/Visual Technician, Graphic Arts, Music, Computer Science, Engineering Technician). Graduates would occupy Marketing Manager and Project Coordinator positions. A bona fide video game enthusiast is listed as desirable non-academic skill. Company benefits and the potential for advancement are both rated as excellent. The most suitable method for initial contact by those seeking employment is to apply through the company's website. Ubi Soft Entertainment Inc. does hire co-op work term students. *Contact:* Human Resources.

UNI-SELECT INC.
170, boul Industriel
Boucherville, QC J4B 2X3

Tel. 450-641-2440
Fax 450-641-6566
Website .... www.uni-select.com

Uni-Select Inc. distributes automobile parts and supplies. There are 250 employees at this location, and a total of 847 employees in Canada. Graduates most likely to be hired come from the following areas: Bachelor of Science (Computer Science), Bachelor of Commerce/Business Administration (Accounting, Finance, Human Resources, Information Systems, Marketing), Chartered Accountant, Certified Management Accountant, Certified General Accountant, Master of Business Administration (General, Accounting, Finance, Human Resources, Information Systems, Marketing) and Community College Diploma (Accounting, Business, Purchasing/Logistics, Secretarial). Graduates are hired to occupy Clerk, Technician, Coordinator and Accountant positions. Team work, flexible, leadership skills, communicative, efficient, dynamic and previous work experience are all listed as desirable non-academic qualifications. The average starting salary falls within the $30,000 to $35,000 range. The most suitable methods for initial contact by those seeking employment are to mail or fax a resume with a covering letter. Uni-Select Inc. does hire summer students. *Contact:* Marie-Josée Ladouceur, Human Resources Coordinator.

UNION GAS LIMITED
200 Yorkland Boulevard
Toronto, ON M2J 5C6

Tel. 416-491-1880
Fax 416-496-5309
Website .... www.uniongas.com

Union Gas Limited is a major Canadian natural gas utility which provides energy delivery and related services to more than one million residential, commercial and industrial customers in over 400 communities in northern, southwestern and eastern Ontario. The company's distribution service area extends throughout northern Ontario from the Manitoba border to the North Bay/Muskoka area, through southern Ontario from Windsor to just west of Toronto, and across eastern Ontario from Port Hope to Cornwall. Union Gas also provides natural gas storage and transportation services for other utilities and energy market participants in Ontario, Quebec and the United States. The company's system is an important part of the delivery system which brings natural gas from western Canadian and US supply basins to eastern markets. Union Gas Limited employs 2,900 people and is a member of the Vancouver based Westcoast Energy group of companies. Graduates most likely to be hired come from the following academic areas: Bachelor of Arts (Economics), Bachelor of Engineering (Civil, Mechanical), Bachelor of Commerce/Business Administration (Marketing, Accounting), Certified Management Accountant, Master of Business Administration (Marketing, Accounting), Master of Arts (Economics) and Community College Diploma (Engineering Technician, Electronics Technician, Instrumentation, Secretarial, Human Resources). Co-op work experience is listed as a desirable non-academic qualification. Company benefits and the potential for advancement are both rated as excellent. The average annual starting salary falls within the $25,000 to $30,000 range. The most suitable method for initial contact by those seeking employment is to mail a resume with a covering letter. Union Gas Limited does hire summer students on a lim-

ited basis. (Head Office: 50 Keil Drive North, Chatham, Ontario, N7M 5M1; Phone 519-352-3100). *Contact:* Coordinator, Staffing and Training.

UNION PACIFIC RESOURCES INC.
425 - 1st Street SW, Suite 400
PO Box 2595, Station M
Calgary, AB T2P 4V4

Tel. 403-231-0111
Fax 403-231-0144
Email .... humanresources@upr.com
Website .... www.upr.com

Union Pacific Resources Inc. is one of North America's largest domestic independent oil and gas exploration and production companies. In addition, the company maintains operations in Latin America and hard mineral resource operations. The company has been the most active driller in the United States for the past seven years and is best known as the leader in horizontal drilling and applying technology to produce oil and gas at the lowest possible cost. Based in Fort Worth, Texas, Union Pacific Resources Inc. acquired Calgary based Norcen Energy Resources Ltd. in March of 1998. Graduates most likely to be hired come from the following academic areas: Bachelor of Science (Computer Science, Geology), Bachelor of Engineering (Chemical, Electrical, Mechanical, Petroleum), Bachelor of Commerce/Business Administration (Accounting, Marketing, Land Management), Master of Science (Geology, Geophysics) and Community College Diploma (Engineering Technician). Graduates would occupy Engineer-in-Training, Junior Geologist, Junior Geophysicist, Accountant-in-Training, and positions in the Business Training Program specializing in Accounting, Marketing and Land Management. A high level of initiative, enthusiasm, adaptability, flexibility and a demonstrated ability to work in a team environment are all listed as desirable non-academic qualifications. Company benefits and the potential for advancement are both rated as excellent. The average annual starting salary falls within the $30,000 to $35,000 range. The most suitable method for initial contact by those seeking employment is to mail a resume with a covering letter. Union Pacific Resources Inc. does hire summer students. *Contact:* Human Resources.

UNIQUE MOULD MAKERS LIMITED
1830 Ellesmere Road
Toronto, ON M1H 2V5

Tel. 416-289-6653
Fax 416-289-1830
Email .... resume@uniquemould.com
Website .... www.uniquemould.com

Unique Mould Makers Limited designs and manufactures high quality, high performance injection mould specifically for caps, closures and medical applications. In business for 30 years, the company is recognized as an international leader in packaging mould technology with current exports to twenty countries worldwide. Utilizing state of the art CAD technology, mould designs include prototypes, single face moulds and stack moulds, covering the food, beverage and pharmaceutical industries. All moulds are designed, built and tested in-house at the company's modern, 27,000 sq. ft. facility located in Toronto. In addition to this location, sales offices are located in Canada, the United States and the United Kingdom. The company employs a total of 87 people worldwide. Graduates most likely to be hired come from the following academic areas: Bachelor of Engineering (Electrical, Mechanical), Bachelor of Commerce/Business Administration (Accounting), Certified Management Accountant, Community College Diploma (Facility Management, Human Resources, Marketing/Sales, Purchasing/Logistics, Computer Science) and Related Trades, including Mould Making, General CNC and EDM skilled trade areas. Graduates would occupy Entry Level Apprentice/Trainee positions in all areas including general administration and skilled trades. Enthusiasm, team player, and good analytical and problem solving skills are all listed as desirable non-academic qualifications. Company benefits are rated as industry standard. The potential for advancement is listed as being average. The average annual starting salary falls within the $35,000 to $40,000 range. The most suitable methods for initial contact by those seeking employment are to fax or e-mail a resume with a covering letter. Unique Mould Makers Limited does hire summer and co-op work term students. *Contact:* Mark Todd, Human Resources.

UNISYS CANADA INC.
2001 Sheppard Avenue East
Toronto, ON M2J 4Z7

Tel. 416-495-0515
Fax 416-495-4495
Email .... marsha.terry@unisys.com
Website .... www.unisys.com

Unisys Canada Inc. is a leading provider of information technology products and services. Unisys Canada Inc. is a subsidiary of Unisys, a global company operating in more than 100 countries around the world. Unisys provides information technology services to leading financial services institutions, airlines, communications providers, commercial market leaders and government agencies around the world. Unisys employs more that 34,000 people worldwide. Unisys Canada Inc. employs more than 250 people at this location. Graduates most likely to be hired come from the following academic areas: Bachelor of Arts (General), Bachelor of Science (Computer Science), Bachelor of Engineering (Electrical), Bachelor of Laws, Bachelor of Commerce/Business Administration, Chartered Accountant, Certified Management Accountant and Master of Business Administration. Graduates would occupy Systems, Marketing, Sales, Finance and Administration positions. Company benefits are rated as industry standard. The potential for advancement is listed as excellent. The average annual starting salary falls within the $30,000 to $35,000 range. The most suitable method for initial contact by those seeking employment is to mail a resume with a covering letter. Unisys Canada Inc. does hire summer students on a limited basis. *Contact:* Human Resources Department.

UNITED GRAIN GROWERS LIMITED / UGG
PO Box 6600
Winnipeg, MB R3C 3A7

Tel. 204-944-5490
Fax 204-944-5477
Website .... www.ugg.com

United Grain Growers Limited / UGG is a recognized leader in the agri-source industry providing innovative, high quality services, products and programs that meet farmers' business needs. UGG's broadly based strategy is currently built around four core businesses, including: contracting, marketing and transporting grain to meet food industry requirements; retailing and distributing crop inputs to produce grain and forage crops; manufacturing and retailing feed and breeding stock used in livestock production; and providing knowledge-based services used in farm production and management. UGG's strategy is to integrate these commercial services and thus provide farmers with a 'pipeline' of goods and services, that help them through the stages of the production and marketing cycle in crops and livestock. Founded in 1906 and headquartered in Winnipeg, UGG is publicly traded on the Toronto Stock Exchange and the Winnipeg Stock Exchange under the symbol UGG. There are 350 employees at this location and a total of 1,500 employees in Canada. Graduates most likely to be hired come from the following academic areas: Bachelor of Science (Agriculture/Horticulture, Nutritional Sciences), Bachelor of Commerce/Business Administration (Accounting, Finance, Human Resources, Information Systems, Marketing), Chartered Accountant, Certified Management Accountant, Certified General Accountant and Community College Diploma (Accounting, Business, Human Resources, Marketing/Sales, Purchasing/Logistics, Agriculture/Horticulture, Information Systems, Animal Health). Sample positions that graduates would occupy include: Facility Manager, Sales Assistant, Production Assistant, Accountant, Customer Service Representative, Logistics Coordinator, Crop Production Services Assistant, Forage Seed Trader, Programmer Analyst, Information Centre Consultant and many more. Customer oriented, accurate, professional and well developed interpersonal and communication skills are all listed as desirable non-academic qualifications. Company benefits and the potential for advancement are both rated as excellent. The most suitable methods for initial contact by those seeking employment are to mail or fax a resume with a covering letter, or by contacting the Staffing Hotline at 204-944-2275. United Grain Growers Limited does hire summer and co-op work term students. *Contact:* Norma Guiboche, Staffing Supervisor.

UNITRON INDUSTRIES LTD.
PO Box 9017
Kitchener, ON N2G 4X1

Tel. 519-895-0100
Fax 519-895-0108
Email .... hr@unitron.com
Website .... www.unitron.com

Unitron Industries Ltd. is a global leader in hearing aid technology and manufacturing. Founded in 1964, the company has grown into one of the leading hearing aid manufacturers in the world. With ISO 9001 and CE designations, the company has manufacturing facilities and sales offices in Canada, the United States and Germany, Unitron serves customers in more than 70 countries around the world and exports over 75% of its product globally. Based in Kitchener, the company employs 210 people at this location and a total of 350 people worldwide. Graduates most likely to be hired come from the following academic areas: Bachelor of Arts (Economics), Bachelor of Science (Computer Science, Mathematics, Audiology), Bachelor of Engineering (Electrical, Mechanical, Computer Systems, Industrial Design), Bachelor of Commerce/Business Administration (General, Accounting, Human Resources, Information Systems),

Certified Management Accountant, Certified General Accountant, Master of Science (Audiology), Master of Engineering (Electrical) and Doctorate (Audiology, Electrical Engineering). Graduates would occupy Administrative Assistant, Human Resources Coordinator, Help Desk Administrator, Assembler, Technician, Technologist, Engineer and Audiologist positions. Team player, strong communication skills, creativity, enthusiasm and good organizational and communication skills are all listed as desirable non-academic qualifications. Company benefits and the potential for advancement are both rated as excellent. The average annual starting salary falls within the $30,000 to $35,000 range. The most suitable method for initial contact by those seeking employment is to e-mail a resume with a covering letter. Unitron Industries Ltd. does hire summer and co-op work term students. *Contact:* Manager, Human Resources.

UNIVERSAL FLAVORS (CANADA) LTD.
110 Vulcan Street
Toronto, ON M9W 1L2

Tel. 416-245-6610
Fax 416-245-6379

Universal Flavors (Canada) Ltd. is involved in the manufacture of food flavours and fruit preparations for all areas of the food industry. The company employs more than 50 people. Graduates most likely to be hired come from the following academic areas: Bachelor of Science (Chemistry, Microbiology, Food Sciences) and Community College Diploma (Science, Laboratory Technician). Graduates would occupy Product Development Technologist, and QC Laboratory Technician positions. A good work ethic, flexibility, and excellent communication skills are all listed as desirable non-academic qualifications. Company benefits are rated above average. The potential for advancement is listed as being good. The average annual starting salary is dependent upon the position being considered. The most suitable method for initial contact by those seeking employment is to mail a resume with a covering letter. Universal Flavors (Canada) Ltd. does hire summer students. *Contact:* Personnel Manager.

UNIVERSITY HEALTH NETWORK
101 College Street, CW2 - 335
Toronto, ON M5G 1L7

Tel. 416-340-4141
Fax 416-340-3476
Website .... www.uhealthnet.on.ca

University Health Network is one of Canada's largest acute-care teaching institutions with approximately 1,000 beds. Formerly The Toronto Hospital, University Health Network is made up of Toronto General Hospital, Toronto Western Hospital, Princess Margaret Hospital and Toronto Medical Laboratories. The Network employs more than 9,500 people. Graduates most likely to be hired come from the following academic areas: Bachelor of Arts (General, English, Psychology, Recreation Studies, Social Work, Sociology), Bachelor of Science (General, Biology, Chemistry, Computer Science, Environment/ Ecology, Microbiology, Physics, Dentistry, Nursing, Nutrition, Occupational Therapy, Pharmacy, Physiotherapy, Psychology, Speech Pathology), Bachelor of Engineering (General, Chemical, Civil, Electrical, Mechanical, Biotechnology, Computer Systems, Engineering Physics, Environmental/Resources, Telecommunications, Transportation), Bachelor of Education (General, Early Childhood, Adult, Special Needs), Bachelor of Commerce/

Business Administration (General, Accounting, Finance, Human Resources, Information Systems, Marketing, Public Administration), Chartered Accountant, Certified Management Accountant, Certified General Accountant, Master of Business Administration (General, Accounting, Finance, Human Resources, Information Systems, Marketing, Public Administration), Master of Science (General, Nursing), Master of Education, Community College Diploma (Accounting, Business, Communications/Public Relations, Facility Management, Human Resources, Office Administration, Secretarial, Cook/Chef, Child Care/Education, Security/Enforcement, Social Work, Carpentry, Computer Science, Electronics Technician, Engineering Technician, Information Systems, Plumber, Tool and Die/Machinist, Welding, Ambulance/ Emergency Care, Animal Health, Dental Assistant, Dietitian/Nutrition, Health/Home Care Aide, Laboratory Technician, Nuclear Medicine, Nursing RN/RNA, Radiology, Rehabilitation Therapy, Respiratory Therapy, Ultra-Sound Technician, Radiation Therapy) and High School Diploma. Graduates would occupy positions in areas relating to their specific area of study, including Administration, Technical (e.g.. MRI, Radiation Therapist), Nursing, Coordinator, Secretarial, Security, Physiotherapy, Occupation Therapy, Accounting, Laboratory, Clerical, IT, Maintenance, etc. Good communication and interpersonal skills, bilingual, organized, and the ability to work in a busy and stressful environment are all listed as desirable non-academic qualifications. Employee benefits are rated above average. The potential for advancement is listed as being good. The average annual starting salary falls within the $25,000 to $30,000 range. The most suitable methods for initial contact by those seeking employment are to mail or fax a resume with a covering letter. University Health Network does hire summer students. *Contact:* Staffing Solutions Department.

UNLEASH CORPORATION
5397 Eglinton Avenue West, Suite 210
Toronto, ON M9C 5K6

Tel. 416-622-7658
Fax 416-622-7631
Email .... lkistner@unleashcorp.com
Website .... www.unleashcorp.com

Unleash Corporation provides solutions integration of business computer systems, specializing in sales force automation, accounting and distribution systems. The company employs a total of 20 people. Graduates most likely to be hired come from the following academic areas: Bachelor of Science (Mathematics - UofW), Bachelor of Engineering (Computer Systems), Bachelor of Commerce/Business Administration (General, Accounting, Finance, Information Systems), Certified Management Accountant, Master of Business Administration (General, Accounting, Finance, Information Systems, Marketing), Community College Diploma (Accounting, Information Systems, Marketing/Sales, Computer Science), Microsoft Certified Systems Engineer (MCSE) and Microsoft Certified Solutions Developer (MCSD) accreditations. Graduates would occupy Junior Developer, Business Analyst and System Engineer positions. Team player and professional appearance are both listed as desirable non-academic qualifications. Company benefits are rated above average. The potential for advancement is listed as excellent. The average annual starting salary falls within the $30,000 to $35,000 range. The most suitable method for initial contact by those seeking employment is to mail a resume with a covering letter. *Contact:* Larry Kistner, President.

URBAN SYSTEMS LTD.
286 St. Paul Street, Suite 200
Kamloops, BC V2C 6G4

Tel. 250-374-8311
Fax 250-374-5334
Email .... kamloops@urban-systems.com
Website .... www.urban-systems.com

Urban Systems Ltd. is a multidisciplinary firm of engineers, planners and landscape architects located in six offices throughout British Columbia and Alberta. The company's clients include small municipalities, land developers, and First Nations. Urban Systems is a client focused organization rather than a project focused one. Graduates most likely to be hired come from the following academic areas: Bachelor of Arts (Geography, Urban Geography/Planning), Bachelor of Science (Geography), Bachelor of Engineering (Civil), Bachelor of Landscape Architecture, Bachelor of Laws (Local Government Consulting), Master of Engineering (Civil, Environmental, Hydrology, Transportation), Community College Diploma (Business, CAD/CAM/Autocad, Engineering Technician) and High School Diploma. Graduates would occupy Consulting Engineer, Planner, Landscape Architect, Local Government Consultant, Civil Engineering Technologist/Technician, Landscape Architect Technician, Administrative and Accounting positions. The company places a tremendous emphasis on the development of its staff, ensuring that they are challenged, stimulated and have the necessary tools to better serve clients. Urban Systems' work environment is informal and friendly, but intense. As a demanding business, the company stays competitive by seeking people that want to do challenging work as opposed to "doing a job". Urban Systems creates an environment of freedom and responsibility to provide every employee with the ability to manage their own career. Accordingly, enthusiasm, team mindset, responsible, hardworking and eager to learn are all listed as desirable non-academic qualifications. Company benefits are rated above average. The potential for advancement is listed as excellent. The average annual starting salary falls within the $35,000 to $40,000 range. The most suitable methods for initial contact by those seeking employment are to mail or fax a resume with a covering letter. Urban Systems Ltd. does hire summer and co-op work term students. Contacts: Shannon McQuillan, Staffing Resources Advisor or Trina Wamboldt, Office Administrator.

UUNET, AN MCI WORLDCOM COMPANY
20 Bay Street, Suite 1300
Toronto, ON M5J 2N8

Tel. 416-368-6621
Fax 416-368-6701
Email .... resumes@uunet.ca
Website .... www.uunet.ca

UUNET, An MCI WorldCom Company provides corporate level internet services to more than 80,000 companies in 114 different countries. Established in 1991, UUNET, was the first commercial internet access providers in Canada. The company controls its entire Canadian east-west DS-3/OC-3 (45 Mbps/155 Mbps) redundant backbone, providing its customers with a fast, reliable and available internet network across the country. Together with the worldwide UUNET operating companies, UUNET is the leading internet provider in the world. The company employs 125 people at this location and a total of 200 employees across Canada. Graduates most likely to be hired come from the following academic areas: Bachelor of Arts (General, Economics, English, Philosophy, Political Science), Bachelor of Science (General, Computer Science), Bachelor of Engineering (General, Civil, Electrical, Computer Systems, Engineering Physics), Bachelor of Education (General), Bachelor of Commerce/Business Administration (General, Human Resources, Marketing), Master of Business Administration, Master of Engineering, Community College Diploma (Accounting, Business, Human Resources, Marketing/Sales, Office Administration, Computer Science, Engineering Technician) and High School Diploma. Graduates would occupy NCC Specialist, Customer Service and Network Engineer positions. Team player, responsible and reliable are all listed as desirable non-academic qualifications. Company benefits are rated above average. The potential for advancement is listed as being excellent. The average annual starting salary falls within the $40,000 to $45,000 range. The most suitable methods for initial contact by those seeking employment are to fax or e-mail a resume with a covering letter. UUNET does hire co-op work term students. Contacts: Lenaee Coubrough or Lori-Lynne Viol.

UWI UNISOFT WARES INC. / UWI.COM
1095 McKenzie Avenue, Suite 400
Victoria, BC V8P 2L5

Tel. 250-479-8334
Fax 250-479-3772
Email .... jobs@uwi.com
Website .... www.uwi.com

UWI Unisoft Wares Inc. / UWI.Com, developer of the first internet forms software, is the leader in the internet forms market segment. The company's InternetForms System helps businesses develop cost-effective, internet based business forms that save both time and money over traditional paper forms. All products in the InternetForms System support the Universal Forms Description Language (UFDL), which describes InternetForms much like HTML describes web pages. UWI.Com offers UFDL to the public as a common, open standard for forms design. The company also offers organizations complete solutions in areas such as workflow, legacy and ODBC data access, and Palm Top integration with the enterprise. UWI.Com employs 30 people at this location and a total of 40 people worldwide. Graduates most likely to be hired come from the following academic areas: Bachelor of Arts (English, Fine Arts, History, Journalism), Bachelor of Science (Computer Science, Mathematics), Bachelor of Engineering (Electrical, Computer Systems, Microelectronics), Bachelor of Commerce/Business Administration (Accounting, Finance, Information Systems, Marketing), Master of Arts (English, Visual Arts), Master of Science (Computer Science), Master of Engineering (Computer Systems), Community College Diploma (Accounting, Administration, Advertising, Business, Communications/Public Relations, Financial Planning, Information Systems, Marketing/Sales, Secretarial, Animation, Audio/Visual Technician, Fashion Arts, Graphic Arts, Journalism, Computer Science) and High School Diploma. Graduates would occupy Technical Writer, Programmer, Marketing, Sales and Web Development positions. Hardworking, driven, creative and HTML experience are all listed as desirable non-academic qualifications. Company benefits and the potential for advancement are both listed as excellent. The average annual starting salary falls within the $30,000 to $35,000 range. The most suitable method for initial contact by those seeking employment is to e-mail a resume with a covering letter. UWI.Com does hire summer and co-op work term students. Contact: Human Resources.

VAN HORNE CONSTRUCTION LIMITED
3279 Caroga Drive
Mississauga, ON L4V 1A3

Tel. 905-677-5150
Fax 905-677-7291

Van Horne Construction Limited is a general contracting firm. The firm employs fewer than 10 people. Graduates most likely to be hired come from the following academic areas: Bachelor of Engineering (General, Industrial), Master of Engineering (Structural) and Community College Diploma (Engineering Technician). Graduates would occupy the positions of Estimator and Project Manager (Trainee). Company benefits are rated above average. The potential for advancement is listed as being good. The average annual starting salary depends upon the applicant's level of experience. The most suitable method for initial contact by those seeking employment is to mail a resume with a covering letter. *Contact:* Doug Lock.

VANCOUVER CITY SAVINGS CREDIT UNION / VANCITY
183 Terminal Avenue
Vancouver, BC V6A 4G2

Tel. 604-877-8298
Fax 604-877-8299
Email .... personnel_resumes@vancity.com
Website .... www.vancity.com

The Vancouver City Savings Credit Union / VanCity is a financial institution providing a full range of financial services. Since 1946, Vancouver City Savings Credit Union has grown to be one of the largest credit unions in the world with over 252,000 members and nearly $5.6 billion in total assets. Through the years, VanCity has become known as a progressive and caring employer and has been named as one of the best companies to work for in British Columbia and Canada. VanCity employs approximately 1,500 people in the province of British Columbia. Graduates most likely to be hired come from the following academic areas: Bachelor of Arts (Economics), Bachelor of Science (Computer Science), Bachelor of Commerce/Business Administration (Accounting, Finance, Information Systems, Marketing), Chartered Accountant, Certified Management Accountant, Certified General Accountant, Community College Diploma (Accounting, Business, Financial Planning, Information Systems, Insurance, Marketing/Sales, Purchasing/Logistics, Computer Science) and High School Diploma. Applicants should possess exceptional communication, relationship building, sales and service skills to apply towards VanCity's goal of building and maintaining financial relationships. Company benefits and the potential for advancement are both rated as excellent. The average annual starting falls within the $25,000 to $35,000 range, depending on the position being considered. The most suitable method for initial contact by those seeking employment is to mail, fax or e-mail a resume with a covering letter. VanCity does hire summer and co-op work term students. *Contact:* Personnel Department.

VANCOUVER HOSPITAL AND HEALTH SCIENCES CENTRE
899 West 12th Avenue
Vancouver, BC V5Z 1M9

Tel. 604-875-4111
Fax 604-875-4761
Email .... careers@vanhosp.bc.ca
Website .... www.vanhosp.bc.ca

Vancouver Hospital and Health Sciences Centre is an adult tertiary care, teaching and research facility. Originally founded in 1886, the Vancouver Hospital of today is comprised of five sites: Vancouver General Hospital, UBC Hospital, Mary Pack Arthritis Centre, G. F. Strong Rehabilitation Centre and George Pearson Centre. The hospital is the primary referral, teaching & research hospital in the province with strong links to the Faculty of Medicine at the University of British Columbia. The Vancouver Hospital and Health Sciences Centre provides a wide range of medical, surgical and psychiatric services and covers virtually every specialty except pediatrics and maternity. The hospital is one of North America's leading health care centres and Canada's second largest hospital with 1,900 beds and treating nearly 116,000 patients every year. Graduates most likely to be hired come from the following academic areas: Bachelor of Science (Audiology, Nursing, Nutritional Sciences, Occupational Therapy, Pharmacy, Physical Therapy, Psychology, Speech Pathology), Bachelor of Engineering (Electrical, Automation/Robotics, Biomedical Electronics), Bachelor of Commerce/Business Administration (Human Resources, Information Systems), Certified General Accountant, Master of Business Administration, Master of Health Sciences, Community College Diploma (Accounting, Human Resources, Purchasing/Logistics, Computer Science, Nursing RN, Radiology Technician, Respiratory Technician, Ultra-Sound Technician) and High School Diploma. Graduates would occupy positions relating directly to their particular academic background. A commitment to patient-centred delivery of care, and strong interpersonal and communication skills are listed as desirable non-academic qualifications. Company benefits and the potential for advancement are both rated as excellent. The average annual starting salary falls within the $30,000 to $35,000 range. The most suitable methods for initial contact by those seeking employment are to mail or fax a resume with a covering letter. *Contact:* Human Resources Office.

VAPOR CANADA INC.
10655, boul Henri-Bourassa Ouest
St. Laurent, QC H4S 1A1

Tel. 514-335-4200
Fax 514-335-4231

Vapor Canada Inc. designs and builds systems and subsystems for the mass transit industry. The company employs approximately 160 people. Graduates most likely to be hired come from the following academic areas: Bachelor of Engineering (Electrical, Computer Systems, Telecommunications, Mechanical, Industrial Design), Bachelor of Commerce/Business Administration (Accounting, Finance), Master of Business Administration (Finance), Master of Engineering (Electrical, Mechanical), Community College Diploma (Accounting, Administration, Business, Marketing/Sales, Secretarial, Drafting, CAD/CAM/Autocad, Computer Science, Electronics Technician, Engineering Technician, Technical Trades, Welding) and High School Diploma. Graduates would occupy Engineering Technician, Mechanical Engineering Technician, Electronics Technician, Electronics Technologist, Manufacturing Engineering Technician, Mechanical Engineer (Design), Electrical Engineer (Design), Software/Hardware Engineer, Reliability/Maintainability Engineer and Manufacturing Engineer positions. Creativity, initiative, team player, and good verbal and written communication skills are all listed as desirable non-academic qualifications. Company benefits are rated above average. The potential for advancement is listed as being good. The average annual starting salary falls within the $25,000 to $30,000 range. The most suitable method for initial contact by those seeking employment is to mail a resume with a covering letter. Vapor Canada Inc. occasionally hires summer students. *Contacts:* Manager, Human Resources or Manager, Engineering Department.

VAUGHAN ECONOMIC AND TECHNOLOGY DEVELOPMENT

2141 Major Mackenzie Drive
Vaughan, ON L6A 1T1

Tel. 905-832-8521
Fax 905-832-6248
Email .... ecdev@city.vaughan.on.ca
Website .... www.city.vaughan.on.ca

The City of Vaughan Economic and Technology Development Department is primarily involved in attracting and retaining commercial and industrial development. Operational activities include expediting the development process for developers, economic research activities, publishing city information, public relations and marketing the city to prospective firms and employers. The department employs approximately 15 people. Graduates most likely to be hired come from the following academic areas: Bachelor of Arts (Urban Geography/Planning, Journalism, Economics) and Bachelor of Commerce/Business Administration (Marketing). Graduates would occupy Economic Developer, Marketing and Communications Specialist and Economic Researcher positions. Employee benefits are rated as excellent. The potential for advancement is listed as being good. The average annual starting salary is $35,000 plus. The most suitable method for initial contact by those seeking employment is to mail a resume with a covering letter. The Economic and Technology Development Department does hire summer students for the collection of data. *Contact:* Manager.

VAUGHAN ENGINEERING

PO Box 2045, Station M
Halifax, NS B3J 2Z1

Tel. 902-425-3980
Fax 902-423-7593
Email .... corpserv@mgnet.ca
Website .... www.mgnet.ca

Vaughan Engineering is a multi-discipline professional consulting engineering company providing services to regional and international clients. The company specializes in project solutions which require integrating advanced engineering techniques with information technology and advanced materials. Vaughan is a member of the MacDonnell Group (MG) Limited, an alliance of companies and partnerships committed to world class technology and consulting solutions in the engineering, geomatics, environmental, computer graphics, and management consulting fields. Vaughan employs 45 people at this location, and a total of 110 employees in Canada. Graduates most likely to be hired come from the following academic areas: Bachelor of Science (Computer Science, Environmental), Bachelor of Engineering (General, Materials Science, Pollution Treatment, Civil, Architectural/Building, Surveying, Municipal, Ports and Marine Structures, Electrical, Instrumentation, Power, Mechanical, Industrial Design, Marine, Environmental), Master of Engineering (Advanced Composite Materials, Environmental), Doctorate (Advanced Composite Materials, Intelligent Structures) and Community College Diploma (Computer Science). Graduates are hired for a variety of positions relating directly to their educational background

and experience level. Previous consulting experience, computer literacy (essential) and the ability to work independently are all listed as desirable non-academic qualifications. Company benefits and the potential for advancement are both rated as excellent. Average annual starting salaries are above the industry average, and are dependent upon the qualifications and experience of the applicant. The most suitable methods for initial contact by those seeking employment are to mail, fax or e-mail a resume with a covering letter. Vaughan Engineering does hire summer students. *Contact:* Human Resources.

VAUGHAN HYDRO ELECTRIC COMMISSION

2800 Rutherford Road
Vaughan, ON L4K 2N9

Tel. 905-832-8371
Fax 905-303-2000
Website .... www.city.vaughan.on.ca

The Vaughan Hydro Electric Commission provides hydro electric services to the city of Vaughan. The commission employs approximately 150 people. Graduates most likely to be hired come from the following academic areas: Bachelor of Engineering (Electrical), Bachelor of Commerce/Business Administration, Chartered Accountant and Community College Diploma (Accounting, Business, Computer Science, Electrical, Drafting, CAD/CAM/Autocad). Graduates would occupy Engineer (in training), Technician, Draftsperson, Accounting Clerk, Billing Clerk, Revenue Clerk, Payroll Clerk and Financial Analyst positions. Employee benefits are rated as excellent. The average annual starting salary falls within the $30,000 to $35,000 range. The most suitable method for initial contact by those seeking employment is to mail a resume with a covering letter. The Vaughan Hydro Electric Commission does hire summer students. *Contact:* Recruitment Officer, Human Resources.

VAUGHAN RECREATION AND CULTURE DEPARTMENT

2141 Major Mackenzie Drive
Maple, ON L6A 1T1

Tel. 905-832-8500
Fax 905-832-5630
Website .... www.city.vaughan.on.ca

The City of Vaughan Recreation and Culture Department is responsible for the delivery of parks and recreation services, facility operations, administration, and the design and development of parks and heritage resources. The department employs more than 100 people. Graduates most likely to be hired come from the following academic areas: Bachelor of Arts (General, Fine Arts, History, Journalism, Psychology, Recreation, Sociology, Urban Geography), Bachelor of Science (Forestry, Geography), Bachelor of Education (Adult, Child, Physical, Special Needs), Bachelor of Landscape Architecture, Bachelor of Commerce/Business Administration (Marketing), Master of Business Administration (Marketing, Information Systems) and Community College Diploma (Facility Management, Graphic Arts, Recreation, Architecture/Drafting, Industrial Design). Graduates would occupy Programmer, Landscape Architect, Landscape Technician, Facility Operator, Food Services Technician and Administrative Assistant positions. Previous work experience or volunteer experience are listed as desirable non-academic qualifications. Employee benefits are rated as excellent. The average annual starting salary falls within the $30,000 to $35,000 range. The most suitable method for initial contact by those seeking employment is to mail a resume with a covering letter (no phone calls please). The Recreation and Culture Department does hire summer students. *Contact:* Human Resources Department.

VEBA OIL OPERATIONS B.V.
717 - 7th Avenue SW, Suite 1480
Calgary, AB T2P 0Z3

Tel.	403-263-2330
Fax	403-313-1001
Email	moreland@cadvision.com

Veba Oil Operations B.V. is a major oil company in Libya, with an average production of 120,000 barrels of oil per day. Veba Oil Operations B.V. is active in the exploration development and production of oil and gas. Graduates most likely to be hired are Bachelor of Engineering graduates specializing in Chemical, Mechanical and Petroleum/Fuels. Graduates would occupy Senior Engineer, Staff Engineer and Senior Staff Engineer positions. Company benefits are rated as excellent. The potential for advancement is listed as average. The average annual starting salary falls in the $60,000 plus range. The most suitable method for initial contact by those seeking employment is to mail a resume with a covering letter. (See also, listing for Moreland Resources Inc.). *Contact:* Kam Fard, P.Eng..

VELA INFORMATION MANAGEMENT CONSULTANTS
665 - 8th Street SW, Suite 720
Calgary, AB T2P 3K6

Tel.	403-263-2553
Fax	403-264-1179
Email	jobs@vela.ca
Website	www.vela.ca

Vela Information Management Consultants offers consulting services including systems analysis and design, client/server database development and internet integration. Vela is part of the Clifton group of companies, which include Clifton Associates Ltd., Vela, and Envista Technologies. Founded in 1988, Vela has offices in both Saskatchewan and Alberta employing a total of 30 professionals. Graduates most likely to be hired come from the following academic areas: Bachelor of Science (Computer Science), Bachelor of Engineering (General), Bachelor of Commerce/Business Administration (Information Systems), Master of Business Administration (Information Systems) and Community College Diploma (Computer Science). Graduates would occupy Programmer, Programmer Analyst, Business Analyst and Project Manager positions. Entrepreneurial, creative and able to work well in a team environment are all listed as desirable non-academic qualifications. Company benefits are rated as excellent. The potential for advancement is listed as being good. The average annual starting salary falls within the $35,000 to $40,000 range. The most suitable method for initial contact by those seeking employment is to mail a resume with a covering letter. *Contact:* Human Resources.

VELTRI GLENCOE LTD.
73 Main Street, PO Box 460
Glencoe, ON N0L 1M0

Tel.	519-287-2283
Fax	519-287-2285

Veltri Glencoe Ltd. produces metal stamping, automotive parts for both Tier 1 and Tier 2 automotive part suppliers. The company supplies to both North American and Japanese companies. The company employs approximately 215 people at this location, and a total of 600 people worldwide. Veltri Glencoe Ltd. is a registered QS 9000 company. Graduates most likely to be hired come from the following academic areas: Bachelor of Engineering (Automation/Robotics, Computer Systems, Industrial Design, Industrial Production), Bachelor of Commerce/Business Administration (Accounting, Finance, Human Resources), Chartered Accountant, Certified Management Accountant, Certified General Accountant and Community College Diploma (Accounting, Human Resources, Purchasing/Logistics, Secretarial, Engineering Technician). Graduates would occupy Tooling Engineer, Controller, General Accountant, Human Resources Generalist, Purchasing/Logistics and Office Administration positions. Team player, enjoy working in a fast paced environment and previous experience in the automotive industry are all listed as desirable non-academic qualifications. Company benefits are rated above average. The potential for advancement is listed as being good. The most suitable method for initial contact by those seeking employment is to mail a resume with a covering letter. *Contact:* Human Resources.

VILLA PROVIDENCE SHEDIAC INC.
PO Box 340
Shediac, NB E0A 3G0

Tel.	506-532-4484
Fax	506-532-8189

Villa Providence Shediac Inc. operates a nursing home. There are approximately 210 employees. Graduates most likely to be hired come from the following academic areas: Bachelor of Science (Nursing) and Community College Diploma (Nursing RN/RNA). Applicants should be able and like to work in an environment of physically and mentally handicapped people. Company benefits are rated above average. The potential for advancement is listed as average. The average annual starting salary falls within the $45,000 to $50,000 range. The most suitable methods for initial contact by those seeking employment are to mail or fax a resume with a covering letter. Villa Providence Shediac Inc. does hire summer students for student project work. *Contact:* Yvon Girouard, Human Resources Director.

VISTAR TELECOMMUNICATIONS INC.
427 Laurier Avenue West, Suite 1410
Ottawa, ON K1G 3J4

Tel.	613-230-4848
Fax	613-230-4940
Email	jobs@vistar.com
Website	www.vistar.ca

Vistar Telecommunications Inc. engages in technical innovation and systems development in the field of wireless and satellite communications and the integration of satellite and terrestrial communications networks. Vistar is a recognized leader in mobility systems and products, advanced multimedia, consumer infotainment, and consulting in marketing research. The company offers uniqueness in its products with technological, and cost advantage. Vistar employs approximately 60 individuals. Graduates most likely to be hired come from the following academic areas: Bachelor of Engineering (Electrical, Telecommunications), Master of Engineering (Electrical, Electronics), Doctorate of Engineering (Electrical, Electronics) and Community College Diploma (Electrical Technician, Engineering Technician). Graduates would occupy Hardware and Software Engineer positions, such as Satellite Systems Engineer, Digital Signal Processing Software Engineer, RF Engineer and Hardware Designer. Team player and dedication are both listed as desirable non-academic qualifications. Company benefits are rated as excellent. The potential for advancement is listed as being good. The average annual starting salary falls within the $45,000 to $50,000 range. The most suitable method for initial contact by those seeking employment is to mail, fax or e-mail a resume with a covering letter. Vistar Telecommunications Inc. does hire summer students. *Contact:* Dr. R.W. Breithaupt, Vice President, Technology.

VITANA CORPORATION
5470 Canotek Road, Unit 26
Ottawa, ON K1J 9H3

Tel.	613-749-4445
Fax	613-749-4087
Email	hr@vitana.com
Website	www.vitana.com

Vitana Corporation uses the latest technology to design, manufacture and market design kits, which in turn are used by other engineers in the design of their products. Vitana works extensively with semi-conductor manufacturers, showing-off the features of their chips. The company has targeted companies offering chip solutions in the following areas: USB, FireWire (IEEE 1394) CMOS Imagers, video/image processing, graphics, data communications, bus architectures, DSP, input/output and motion control. Vitana's work begins with hardware and software design, through to manufacturing and distribution of its kits worldwide. Founded in 1992, Vitana employs a total of 27 people. Graduates most likely to be hired come from the following academic areas: Bachelor of Science (Computer Science), Bachelor of Engineering (Electrical, Computer Systems), Certified Management Accountant, Certified General Accountant and Community College Diploma (Computer Science, Electronics Technician, Engineering Technician). Graduates would occupy Computer Engineer, Electrical Engineer, Junior Technician and Senior Technician positions. Team player, quick learner and enjoy challenges are listed as desirable non-academic qualifications. Company benefits are rated above average. The potential for advancement is listed as being good. The average annual starting salary falls within the $45,000 to $50,000 range. The most suitable method for initial contact by those seeking employment is to mail a resume with a covering letter. Vitana Corporation does hire students for summer and co-op work terms. *Contacts:* Marc Bisson, Director of Operations or Brigette Yachon, Director of Engineering Services.

VOLVO CANADA LTD.
175 Gordon Baker Road
Toronto, ON M2H 2N7

Tel.	416-493-3700
Fax	416-493-8754
Website	www.volvo.ca

Volvo Canada Ltd. is involved in the wholesale of automobiles for the Canadian market. The company employs 65 people at this location and a total of 250 people across Canada. Graduates most likely to be hired come from the following academic areas: Bachelor of Arts (Economics), Bachelor of Commerce/Business Administration (Accounting, Finance, Human Resources, Information Systems, Marketing, Public Administration), Master of Business Administration (Accounting, Finance, Human Resources, Marketing), Community College Diploma (Accounting, Administration, Advertising, Business, Financial Planning, Human Resources, Marketing/Sales, Secretarial) and High School Diploma. Graduates would occupy Accounting and Field Service positions relating to dealer support. Company benefits are rated as excellent. The average annual starting salary falls within the $30,000 to $35,000 range, and is dependent upon the position being considered. The most suitable method for initial contact by those seeking employment is to mail a resume with a covering letter. *Contact:* Anne Lake, Human Resources Administrator.

VON TORONTO
3190 Steeles Avenue East, Suite 300
Markham, ON L3R 1G9

Tel.	416-499-2009
Fax	416-499-8460
Email	vonmetro@direct.com
Website	www.von.ca

VON Toronto provides community nursing and related health services to clients, either through Community Care Access Centre referrals or direct, private fee for service. VON Toronto is the Toronto branch of VON Canada / Victorian Order of Nurses which is a national health care organization and a federally registered charity that has been caring for the lives and well being of Canadians in their homes and local communities since 1897. VON's more than 50 different home nursing, health promotion, support and other services are delivered to a million Canadians and their families every year through its network of 71 local branches, 8,000 health care providers and 10,000 volunteers nationwide. VON Toronto employs approximately 300 people. Graduates most likely to be hired come from the following academic areas: Bachelor of Science (Nursing, Nutritional Sciences, Physical Therapy, Speech Pathology), Bachelor of Commerce/Business Administration (Accounting, Finance, Human Resources, Information Systems, Marketing, Public Administration), Chartered Accountant, Master of Business Administration (Accounting, Human Resources), Master of Science (Nurse Practitioner), Community College Diploma (Administration, Business, Human Resources, Marketing/Sales, Customer Service, Public Relations, Fundraising, Dietician, Massage Therapy, Nursing RN/RNA, Community Nursing) and High School Diploma. Graduates would occupy Nursing, Dietician, Physiotherapist, Volunteer, Hospice/Palliative, Occupational Health and Safety, Training and Development, Information Systems, Programming, Secretarial, Customer Service, Fundraising, Public Relations, Accounting, Records Management and Purchasing positions. Creative, dedicated, highly professional, accurate, enthusiastic, continuous learner, self-motivated, problem solving skills, previous work experience, possess clinical work habits, confidence, and excellent interpersonal and communication skills are all listed as desirable non-academic qualifications. Company benefits are rated above average. The potential for advancement is listed as average. The average annual starting salary falls within the $20,000 to $25,000 range. The most suitable methods for initial contact by those seeking employment are to mail or fax a resume with a covering letter. VON Toronto does hire summer students, applications should be made prior to May 1st. *Contact:* Human Resources.

VOYAGEUR INSURANCE COMPANY
44 Peel Centre Drive, 4th Floor
Brampton, ON L6T 4M8

Tel. 905-791-8700
Fax 905-791-0669

The Voyageur Insurance Company sells travel insurance through retail travel agencies and airlines. In addition, Voyageur provides claims services to policyholders and a 24 hour assistance hotline to all policyholders while travelling. The company employs more than 100 people. Graduates most likely to be hired come from the following academic areas: Bachelor of Arts (General, Psychology), Bachelor of Science (Computer Science, Nursing), Bachelor of Engineering (Computer Systems), Bachelor of Commerce/Business Administration (Accounting, Finance, Information Systems, Marketing), Chartered Accountant (Finance), Certified Management Accountant (Finance), Certified General Accountant (Finance), Master of Business Administration (Accounting, Finance, Information Systems, Marketing, Public Administration) and Community College Diploma (Accounting, Administration, Advertising, Business, Insurance, Marketing, Purchasing/Logistics, Secretarial, Graphic Arts, Human Resources, Travel/Tourism, Computer, Emergency/Paramedic, RN/RNA). Graduates would occupy Programmer/Analyst, Project Accountant, Assistant Coordinator, Claims Examiner, Outside Sales Manager, Inside Sales Assistant, Human Resource and Clerical positions. Customer service oriented, organized, and excellent interpersonal and communication skills are listed as desirable non-academic qualifications. Company benefits are rated as excellent. The potential for advancement is listed as being good. The average annual starting salary falls within the $15,000 to $20,000 range. The most suitable method for initial contact by those seeking employment is to mail a resume with a covering letter. Voyageur Insurance Company does hire summer students. *Contact:* Human Resources.

WABASH ALLOYS ONTARIO
7496 Torbram Road
Mississauga, ON L4T 4G9

Tel. 905-672-5569
Website .... www.wabashalloys.com

Wabash Alloys Ontario is involved in the recycling of aluminium scrap for distribution to automotive industry diecasters. Wabash Alloys Ontario is a division of Wabash, Indiana based Wabash Alloys, LLC. Founded in 1958, Wabash Alloys, LLC has grown to become the world's largest producer of recycled aluminum casting alloys. Wabash Alloys Ontario employs more than 100 people at this location. Graduates most likely to be hired come from the following academic areas: Bachelor of Science (Metallurgy), Bachelor of Engineering (Industrial), Bachelor of Commerce/Business Administration (Marketing) and Community College Diploma (Metallurgy). Graduates would occupy Technicians, Management Trainees, Marketing Trainee and General Accounting positions. Company benefits are rated as excellent. The potential for advancement is listed as average. The average annual starting salary falls within the $30,000 to $35,000 range. The most suitable method for initial contact by those seeking employment is to mail a resume with a covering letter. *Contacts:* Peter Black, Vice President, Administration or Greg Fuller, Vice President, Manufacturing.

WACKENHUT OF CANADA LIMITED
332 Consumers Road
Toronto, ON M2J 1P8

Tel. 416-493-8119
Fax 416-493-6683
Website .... www.wackenhut.com

Wackenhut of Canada Limited is an international security firm providing guard services, alarm equipment and response services, patrols and inspections, access systems, canine security and upscale security services. Wackenhut's clients range from condominiums, to factories and parks. There are 350 employees at this location, a total of 1,000 in Canada, and a total of 50,000 employees worldwide. Graduates most likely to be hired come from the following academic areas: Community College Diploma (Accounting, Administration, Business, Marketing/Sales, Secretarial, Security/Enforcement, Private Investigations) and High School Diploma. Graduates would occupy Security Officer, Private Investigator, Patrol Driver, Supervisor, Dispatcher and Office Staff positions. Dedication, responsible, clean record, flexible, and able to work shift work are all listed as desirable non-academic qualifications. Company benefits are rated as industry standard, and include dental, medical and pension benefits. The potential for advancement is listed as excellent. The average annual starting salary falls within the $20,000 to $25,000 range. The most suitable method for initial contact by those seeking employment is to complete an application at this location. Wackenhut of Canada Limited does hire summer students. *Contact:* Tara H. Slade, Office Administrator.

WALBAR CANADA
1303 Aerowood Drive
Mississauga, ON L4W 2P6

Tel. 905-602-4041
Fax 905-625-8360

Walbar Canada manufactures turbine components, compressor airfoil and turbine parts for aircraft gas turbine engines and is a wholly-owned subsidiary of Walbar. In order to ensure precision manufacture, Walbar employs a range of equipment including CNC machine tools, Heat Treat and Coating Process, and E.D.M. (Electrical Discharge Machining). Walbar Canada employs approximately 200 people. Graduates most likely to be hired come from the following academic areas: Bachelor of Science (Computer Science), Bachelor of Engineering (Mechanical, Industrial Design), Bachelor of Commerce/Business Administration (Accounting, Finance, Information Systems, Marketing), Certified Management Accountant (Finance), Master of Business Administration (Accounting, Finance, Information Systems, Marketing), Master of Engineering (Industrial Design, Mechanical) and Community College Diploma (Accounting, Marketing/Sales, Purchasing/Logistics, Human Resources, Electrician, Engineering Technician, Industrial Design, Mechanic). Graduates are hired to occupy Manufacturing Engineer, Process Engineer, Industrial Engineer, Maintenance Mechanic, Electrician and Finance positions. An ability to handle multiple tasks, work under pressure towards deadlines, computer skills, and good interpersonal and communication skills are all listed as desirable non-academic qualifications. Company benefits are rated above average. The potential for advancement is listed as being good. The most suitable method for initial contact by those seeking employment is to mail a resume with a covering letter. *Contacts:* Director, Human Resources or Ramla Passi, Human Resources Administrator.

WANDLYN INNS LTD.
PO Box 430
Fredericton, NB E3B 5P8

Tel. 506-452-0550
Fax 506-452-8894
Website .... www.wandlyn.com/Fredericton

Wandlyn Inns Ltd. operates a chain of motor inns, including dining, lounge and convention facilities. The company is also involved in real estate sales and development. Wandlyn Inns Ltd. employs 50 people at this location and approximately 1,200 people across Canada. Graduates most likely to be hired come from the following academic areas: Bachelor of Commerce/Business Administration (Accounting, Information Systems, Marketing) and Community College Diploma (Accounting, Business, Purchasing/Logistics, Secretarial, Travel/Tourism). Graduates would occupy Clerical and Management Trainee positions. Hard working, an ability to deal with the public, strong personality and a professional appearance are all listed as desirable non-academic qualifications. Company benefits are rated as excellent. The potential for advancement is listed as being good. The average annual starting salary varies with the position being considered and the qualifications of the applicant. The most suitable method for initial contact by those seeking employment is to mail a resume with a covering letter. Wandlyn Inns. Ltd. does hire students for seasonal and part time employment. Contacts: Rick Draper, Director of Operations or Doug French, Comptroller.

WANG GLOBAL
150 Middlefield Road
Toronto, ON M1S 4L6

Tel. 416-298-9400
Fax 416-412-4834
Email .... canada@wang.com
Website .... www.wang.com

Wang Global is the second largest independent network and desktop integration services company in Canada (IDC, May 1998). The company is headquartered in Billerica, Massachusetts and has subsidiaries in over 40 countries, including Canada. As a leading international network and desktop integration and services company, Wang Global provides a comprehensive range of information technology services. The services provided are focussed on improving the reliability, availability and performance of companies' information technology infrastructures, helping to free those customers to concentrate on their core businesses. Wang Global employs a total of 20,000 people worldwide and the company's strategic relationships and alliances allow it to offer the best information technology solutions to customers. Key global alliances include Intel, Cisco and Dell. Other alliances include: Intel, Novell, Olivetti Computers Worldwide, HP, IBM/Lotus, SUN, 3Com, Cabletron, Netscape, Compaq, Motorola, Bay Networks, NEC Technologies and Viewsonic, as well as other industry leaders. Wang Global's commitment to quality service and customer satisfaction is backed by ISO9002 certification in Canada. In Canada, Wang Global provides coast to coast coverage through 400 employees nationwide, working from 30 direct service locations and through 100 service part-

ner locations. The company's depth and breadth of expertise is ensured by superior technical personnel who keep current with rapidly changing technology through frequent accredited training. Wang invests heavily to ensure it has the latest equipment and most up-to-date skill sets, as well as having the worldwide internal electronic computing environment to give staff online access to the latest technical and marketing materials. Graduates most likely to be hired are Information Systems and Computer Science graduates with a Community College Diploma. Graduates would occupy Field Technician Trainee positions. Good customer service skills, ability to work independently and previous work experience are listed as desirable non-academic qualifications. Company benefits are rated above average. The potential for advancement is listed as being good. The average annual starting salary falls within the $30,000 to $35,000 range. The most suitable method for initial contact by those seeking employment is to mail a resume with a covering letter. Wang Global does hire summer and co-op work term students. Contact: Human Resources.

WARNER-LAMBERT CANADA INC.
2200 Eglinton Avenue East
Toronto, ON M1L 2N3

Tel. 416-288-2200
Fax 416-288-2156
Website .... www.warner-lambert.com

Warner-Lambert Canada Inc. operates through four operational divisions, including Warner Welcome (OTC products), Parke Davis (pharmaceutical), Adams Brands (confectionery) and the Consumer Health Division (OTC products). The company employs more than 500 people across Canada. Graduates most likely to be hired come from the following areas: Bachelor of Arts (Psychology, Sociology), Bachelor of Science (General, Biology, Chemistry, Computer, Mathematics, Microbiology, Nursing, Pharmacy, Physics), Bachelor of Engineering (Chemical, Computer Systems, Electrical, Industrial, Materials Science), Bachelor of Education (General, Adult, Physical), Bachelor of Commerce/Business Administration (Accounting, Finance, Information Systems, Marketing, Public Administration), Chartered Accountant, Certified Management Accountant, Certified General Accountant, Master of Business Administration, Master of Arts (Psychology, Sociology), Master of Science (General, Biology, Chemistry, Computer, Mathematics, Microbiology, Nursing, Pharmacy, Physics), Master of Engineering (Chemical, Computer Systems, Electrical, Industrial, Materials Science), Master of Education (General, Adult, Physical) and Community College Diploma (Accounting, Graphic Arts, Human Resources, Journalism, Television/Radio Arts, Architecture/Drafting, Computer Science, Electronics Technician, Engineering Technician, Mechanic, Animal Health, Food/Nutrition, Laboratory Technician, Nursing RN/RNA, Radiology Technician, Respiratory Technician). Company benefits and the potential for advancement are both rated as excellent. The average annual starting salary is dependent upon the position being considered. Job hunters should research thoroughly and be creative when contacting Warner-Lambert, request an annual report and attempt to set-up an informational interview with the appropriate department. Summer students are hired for Sales and Marketing positions. Warner-Lambert is an equal opportunity employer. Contact: Joyce Spencer, Human Resources.

WCI CANADA INC.
866 Langs Drive
Cambridge, ON N3H 2N7

Tel.	519-653-8880
Fax	519-653-3189

WCI Canada Inc. (Fridgidaire/Eureka) is a major household appliance company. WCI Canada Inc.'s parent company is the Fridgidaire Home Products company based in Augusta, Georgia. Fridgidaire Home Products is one of the leading North American manufacturers of gas, electric and battery powered handheld outdoor power equipment, lawn mowers and lawn and garden tractors, as well as a significant producer of major appliances for the home including refrigerators, freezers, ranges, dishwashers, washers, dryers, room air conditioners and dehumidifiers. The company has eighteen locations in ten states and two provinces employing a total of 15,000 people. This location is primarily involved in the assembly, sales, marketing, and related administrative operations. There are 160 employees at this location and a total of 1,000 in Canada. Graduates most likely to be hired come from the following academic areas: Bachelor of Arts (Economics), Bachelor of Commerce/Business Administration (Marketing), Certified Management Accountant, Community College Diploma (Accounting, Advertising, Human Resources, Marketing/Sales, Secretarial) and High School Diploma. Graduates would occupy Administrative Assistant, Marketing Coordinator, Sales Administrator, Financial Analyst and Accounting Clerk positions. Team player and professionalism are both listed as desirable non-academic qualifications. Company benefits are rated as industry standard. The potential for advancement is listed as average. The average annual starting salary falls within the $20,000 to $25,000 range. The most suitable method for initial contact by those seeking employment is to mail a resume with a covering letter. WCI Canada Inc. does hire summer students. *Contact:* Human Resources Coordinator.

WEATHERFORD ARTIFICIAL LIFT SYSTEMS - COROD PRODUCTS AND SERVICES
2801 - 84 Avenue
Edmonton, AB T6P 1K1

Tel.	780-417-4800
Fax	780-464-5189
Website	www.weatherford.com

Weatherford Artificial Lift Systems - Corod Products and Services is a leading world class manufacturer and marketer of quality oil lifting equipment. The company has manufacturing facilities in Edmonton producing Progressive Cavity Pumps and a new plant producing Continuous Sucker Rods. In addition, the company operates a fleet of 37 company rigs throughout Western Canada and the United States, and several more in Venezuela. There are 200 employees at this location, and a total of 650 employees in Canada. Graduates most likely to be hired come from the following academic areas: Bachelor of Science (Computer Science, Metallurgy), Bachelor of Engineering (General, Mechanical, Metallurgy, Petroleum/Fuels), Bachelor of Commerce/Business Administration (Accounting, Finance, Human Resources), Chartered Accountant, Certified Management Accountant, Certified General Accountant, Community College Diploma (Accounting, Business, Human Resources, Office Administration, Secretarial, CAD/CAM/Autocad, Computer Science, Electronics Technician, Tool and Die, Machinist, Welding) and High School Diploma. Graduates would occupy Product Development Engineer/Technologist, Applications Engineer, Accountant, Controller, Payable/Receivable Representative, Administrative Assistant, Welder, Millwright, Heavy Duty Technician, Plant Operator, Test Bench Technician, Assembler and Warehouse positions. Excellent customer service skills, a combination of education and practical experience, superior verbal and written communication skills, a high level of initiative, team player, punctuality and a good attendance record are all listed as desirable non-academic qualifications. Company benefits are rated above average. The potential for advancement is listed as excellent. The average annual starting salary falls within the $40,000 to $45,000 range. The most suitable method for initial contact by those seeking employment is to mail a resume with a covering letter. Weatherford Artificial Lift Systems - Corod Products and Services does hire engineering students for summer and co-op work terms. *Contact:* Human Resources.

WEB OFFSET PUBLICATIONS LTD.
1800 Ironstone Manor
Pickering, ON L1W 3J9

Tel.	905-831-3000
Fax	905-831-3266

Web Offset Publications Ltd. is a commercial publication printer. The company employs more than 100 people. Very few post-secondary graduates are hired. Those most likely to be hired come from the following academic areas: Bachelor of Arts (General), Bachelor of Commerce/Business Administration (General, Finance), Certified General Accountant and Community College Diploma (Accounting, Administration). These graduates would occupy Clerk positions in the Accounting Department. High School graduates are also hired for printing press operations and would occupy Press Helper positions. Company benefits are rated above average. The potential for advancement is listed as being good. The average annual starting salary falls within the $15,000 to $20,000 range. The most suitable method for initial contact by graduates seeking employment is to mail a resume with a covering letter. Web Offset Publications Ltd. does hire summer students for the period between May and August. *Contact:* Human Resources.

WENDY'S RESTAURANTS OF CANADA
6715 Airport Road, Suite 301
Mississauga, ON L4V 1X2

Tel.	905-677-7023
Fax	905-677-5297
Website	www.wendys.com

Wendy's Restaurants of Canada is a major quick-service restaurant chain with over 270 locations across Canada and growing. Each restaurant location employs between 35 and 50 full and part-time staff, while Wendy's employs a total of 6,000 people in Canada. Graduates most likely to be hired come from the following academic areas: Bachelor of Arts (General), Bachelor of Commerce/Business Administration and Community College Diploma (Hotel/Food Administration, Tourism). Graduates are hired as Restaurant Management Trainees. The applicant should maintain a positive attitude, possess excellent interpersonal skills and an eagerness to work. Company benefits and the potential for advancement are both rated as excellent. The average annual starting salary for management positions falls within the $25,000 to $30,000 range. The most suitable methods for initial contact by those seeking employment are to mail or fax a resume with a covering letter. Wendy's Restaurants of Canada does hire summer students, in certain cases. Application for summer and part-time hourly employment should be made in person to the Manager at the desired restaurant location. *Contacts:* Sandra Lennon, Director of Human Resources; Julie Seguin, HR Manager Eastern Canada or Liz Volk, HR Manager Central Canada; Tracey Lahun, HR Manager Western Canada.

WEST END SYSTEMS CORP.
39 Winner's Circle Drive
Arnprior, ON   K7S 3G9

Tel. 613-623-9600
Fax 613-623-0989
Email .... bob_kedrosky@newbridge.com
Website .... www.utoronto.ca/~micronet/partners/
West_End.html

West End Systems Corp. is a leader in the telecommunications industry, providing business-smart innovative solutions to cable television operators. As a member of the Newbridge family of companies, West End Systems is uniquely positioned to deliver fully managed voice, data and LAN service access for wireline and HFC networks. Graduates most likely to be hired come from the following academic areas: Bachelor of Science (Computer Science, Mathematics), Bachelor of Engineering (Electrical, Telecommunications) and Master of Engineering (Electrical). West End offers an attractive compensation package and ample room for employees to demonstrate their full range of creative and technical capabilities. Correspondingly, company benefits are rated above average and the potential for advancement is listed as excellent. The average annual starting salary falls within the $40,000 to $45,000 range. The most suitable methods for initial contact by those seeking employment are to mail, fax or e-mail a resume with a covering letter, or apply through the company's website at www.westendsys.com/. West End Systems Corp. does hire co-op work term students. *Contact:* Bob Kedrosky, Manager, Human Resources.

WEST PARK HOSPITAL
82 Buttonwood Avenue
Toronto, ON   M6M 2J5

Tel. 416-243-3645
Fax 416-243-3422
Email .... hr@westpark.org
Website .... www.westpark.org

The West Park Hospital is a designated greater Toronto area rehabilitation and local complex continuing care facility. The hospital has approximately 320 beds and employs approximately 800 persons. The hospital operates with a program management organizational structure and responds to the needs of its communities with evolving, innovative programs based on best practice research. Interdisciplinary teams are to be found in the following service areas: respiratory, amputee, neurological and geriatric rehabilitation, mycobacterial lung disease, prosthetics, special care, multiple sclerosis, adult physically disabled, ambulatory care, post polio, seniors mental health, acquired brain injuries, and transitional living. Graduates most likely to be hired come from the following academic areas: Bachelor of Arts (Journalism, Psychology, Recreation Studies, Social Work), Bachelor of Science (Computer Science, Audiology, Nursing, Nutritional Sciences, Occupational Therapy, Pharmacy, Physio/Physical Therapy, Psychology, Speech Pathology), Bachelor of Education (Adult), Bachelor of Commerce/Business Administration (Accounting, Finance, Human Resources, Information Systems, Marketing), Certified General Accountant, Master of Science (Nursing), Master of Education, Community College Diploma (Accounting, Administration, Communications/Public Relations, Facility Management, Human Resources, Information Systems, Purchasing/Logistics, Secretarial, Journalism, Recreation Studies, Social Work/DSW, Computer Science, Health/Home Care Aide, Nursing RN/RNA, Respiratory Therapy) and High School Diploma. Graduates would occupy Physiotherapist, Occupational Therapist, RN, RDN, Respiratory Therapist, Recreation Therapist, Social Worker, Therapeutic Dietitian, Advanced Practice Nurse, Marketing Representative, Public Relations, Human Resources, Secretary, Personal Care Attendant, Organizational and Personal Development Consultant, Research Assistant, Information Analyst, Computer Support Specialist, Support Assistant and Client Care Attendant positions. Excellent interpersonal and organizational skills, reliable work habits, strong customer service skills, able to work in a transdisciplinary team environment and previous work experience in a hospital setting are all listed as desirable non-academic qualifications. Employee benefits and the potential for advancement are both rated as excellent. The most suitable methods for initial contact by those seeking employment are to mail, fax or e-mail a resume with a covering letter, or by applying in person at the hospital. The West Park Hospital does hire summer students. *Contact:* Employee Relations Department.

WESTBURNE INC.
505, rue Locke, bureau 200
Montreal, QC H4T 1X7

Tel. 514-342-5181
Fax 514-342-6347
Website .... www.westburnesupply.com

Westburne Inc. is a leading integrated wholesale distributor of electrical, plumbing, HVAC and industrial supplies. Westburne's customer base includes contractors in the residential, commercial and industrial construction industries, as well as to industrial and commercial enterprises, utilities and public sector institutions across North America. The company currently has 5,200 employees in North America, a third of whom are in sales serving over 100,000 customers in a network of branches extending from northern British Columbia to Newfoundland, and throughout the United States. Graduates most likely to be hired come from the following academic areas: Bachelor of Science (Computer Science), Bachelor of Engineering (General, Industrial), Bachelor of Commerce/Business Administration (Accounting, Finance, Information Systems, Marketing), Certified Management Accountant, Certified General Accountant, Master of Business Administration (Finance, Marketing) and Community College Diploma (Administration, Business, Marketing/Sales, Purchasing/Logistics, Human Resources, Electronics, HVAC Systems). Graduates are hired to occupy Sales Representative and Branch Management Trainee positions. Initiative, creativity, a team spirit, and good interpersonal and communication skills are all listed as desirable non-academic qualifications. Company benefits are rated as industry standard. The potential for advancement is listed as excellent. The average annual starting salary falls within the $25,000 to $30,000 range. The most suitable method for initial contact by those seeking employment is to mail a resume with a covering letter. Westburne Inc. does hire summer and co-op work term students. *Contact:* Human Resources.

WESTCOAST ENERGY INC.
1333 West Georgia Street
Vancouver, BC V6E 3K9

Tel. 604-691-5666
Fax 604-691-5868
Email .... humanresources@westcoastenergy.com
Website .... www.westcoastenergy.com

Westcoast Energy Inc. is a leading North American energy company active in natural gas gathering, processing, transmission, storage and distribution, as well as power generation, international energy businesses and financial, information technology and energy services businesses. Canadian owned and operated and headquartered in Vancouver, Westcoast Energy Inc. is a publicly traded company on the Toronto and New York stock exchanges. The company was established in 1957, and today employs 5,900 people. Graduates most likely to be hired come from the following academic areas: Bachelor of Engineering (Chemical, Systems, Environmental, Electrical, Mechanical), Bachelor of Commerce/Business Administration (Accounting, Finance), Chartered Accountant (Finance), Certified Management Accountant (Finance), Certified General Accountant (Finance), Master of Business Administration (Accounting, Finance), Community College Diploma (Accounting, Secretarial, Human Resources, Electronics Technician, Engineering Technician, Industrial Design) and High School Diploma. At the head office location, graduates would occupy positions in Engineering/Drafting, Administration, Accounting/Finance and Data Processing. In field operations, with locations throughout northern British Columbia, graduates would occupy positions in Telecommunications, Measurement and Engineering Technologies, Instrument and Electrical Technologies, Millwrights, Heavy Duty Mechanics, Pipefitting, Steam Engineering, Welding and Gas Processing. Company benefits are rated as excellent. The potential for advancement is listed as being good. The average annual starting salary falls within the $30,000 to $35,000 range. The most suitable method for initial contact by those seeking employment is to mail a resume with a covering letter. Westcoast Energy Inc. does hire summer and co-op work term students, primarily engineering and technology students. *Contact:* Human Resources.

WESTIN PRINCE HOTEL
900 York Mills Road
Toronto, ON M3B 3H2

Tel. 416-444-2511
Fax 416-444-9597

Westin Prince Hotel is a full-service hotel. The hotel employs approximately 315 people. Graduates most likely to be hired come from the following academic areas: Master of Business Administration, Community College Diploma (Accounting, Human Resources, Secretarial, Travel/Tourism) and High School Diploma. Graduates would occupy Accounting, Front Desk, Reservations, Human Resources and Secretarial positions. Work experience, positive attitude, personality and a professional appearance are all listed as desirable non-academic qualifications. Company benefits are rated above average. The potential for advancement is listed as being good. The average annual starting salary ranges from $15,000 to $22,000. The most suitable method for initial contact by those seeking employment is to mail a resume with a covering letter. The Westin Prince Hotel does hire summer students as required. *Contact:* Isobel Millar, Director of Personnel.

WEYERHAEUSER CANADA LTD.
1850 Mission Flats Road, PO Box 800
Kamloops, BC V2C 5M7

Tel. 250-828-7387
Fax 250-828-7567
Website .... www.weyerhaeuser.com

Weyerhaeuser Canada Ltd. is a major forest products company with lumber, pulp, paper and other diversified business interests across Canada. Weyerhaeuser Canada Ltd. is a wholly owned subsidiary of Tacoma, Washington based, Weyerhaeuser Company, one of the largest forest products companies in North America. Weyerhaeuser Canada Ltd. began operations in 1965, and has grown to become one of the largest forest products companies in Western Canada based on sales and assets. Today the company employs 5,800 people in operations in British Columbia, Alberta, Saskatchewan and Ontario. Graduates most likely to be hired come from the following academic areas: Bachelor of Science (Forestry), Bachelor of Engineering (Chemical, Electrical, Mechanical), Bachelor of Commerce/Business Administration (Finance) and Chartered Accountant (Finance). Graduates are hired to occupy Project Engineer, Electrical/Instrumentation Engineer, Process Engineer, Professional Forester and Corporate/Divisional Financial Manager positions. Team player, results oriented, and good problem solving, communication and coaching skills are all listed as desirable non-academic qualifications. Company benefits are rated as excellent. The potential for advancement is listed as being good. The average annual starting salary falls within the $30,000 to $35,000 range. The most suitable method for initial contact by those seeking employment is to mail a resume with a covering letter. *Contacts:* Vinotha Naidu, Pensions and Benefits Coordinator or Mike Rushby, Vice President, Human Resources.

WEYERHAEUSER CANADA LTD., DRYDEN MILL
175 West River Road, Mail Bag 4004
Dryden, ON P8N 3J7

Tel. 807-223-9281
Fax 807-223-9388
Website .... www.weyerhaeuser.com

Weyerhaeuser Canada Ltd., Dryden Mill produces a variety of papers including photocopier paper, commercial printing paper and business forms. The mill serves major markets located in the midwestern United States and in eastern Canada. Weyerhaeuser Canada Ltd. is a wholly owned subsidiary of Tacoma, Washington based, Weyerhaeuser Company, one of the largest forest products companies in North America. Weyerhaeuser Canada Ltd. began operations in 1965 and today employs 5,800 people in operations in British Columbia, Alberta, Saskatchewan and Ontario. The company acquired the Dryden Mill in 1999. There are approximately 1,000 employees at the Dryden location. Graduates most likely to be hired come from the following academic areas: Bachelor of Engineering (Chemical, Pulp and Paper, Architectural/Building, Instrumentation, Mechanical, Resources/Environmental), Bachelor of Commerce/Business Administration (Human Resources, Information Systems) and Certified General Accountant. Graduates would occupy professional positions in Engineering, Accounting, Information Systems, and a variety of office positions. An ability to work hard and use common sense and a proven work history are both listed as desirable non-academic qualifications. Company benefits are rated above average. The potential for advancement is listed as excellent. The average annual starting salary falls within the $40,000 to $45,000 plus range. The most suitable method for initial contact by those seeking employment is to mail a resume with a covering letter. Weyerhaeuser Canada Ltd., Dryden Mill does hire summer students. *Contact:* Human Resources.

WHISTLER AND BLACKCOMB MOUNTAINS
4545 Blackcomb Way
Whistler, BC V0N 1B4

Tel.	604-932-3141
Fax	604-938-7838
Email	bsehr@intrawest.com
Website	www.blackcomb.com

Whistler and Blackcomb Mountains is a major ski resort based in Whistler, British Columbia. Operational activities include retail, mountain operations, sales and marketing, food and beverage, finance, human resources, etc. The number of employees varies with the season. Graduates most likely to be hired come from the following academic areas: Bachelor of Arts (Recreation Studies), Bachelor of Education (Children), Bachelor of Commerce/Business Administration (Finance, Human Resources, Information Systems, Marketing), Community College Diploma (Accounting, Human Resources, Marketing/Sales, Secretarial, Graphic Arts, Recreation Studies) and High School Diploma. Graduates would occupy Kids Camp Child Care Worker, Accounts Payable/Receivable Clerk, Sales and Marketing, Graphic Designer, Receptionist, Administrative Assistant, Lift Maintenance Mechanic, Data Entry Clerk, Computer User Support, Human Resources, and Food and Beverage positions. Friendly, outgoing, team player, presentable and excellent customer service skills are all listed as desirable non-academic qualifications. Company benefits are rated as excellent. The potential for advancement is listed as being good. The most suitable methods for initial contact by those seeking employment are by calling the Job Line at (604) 938-7367, or via e-mail. Whistler and Blackcomb Mountains does hire students for the summer season (June 17 to September 4), and the winter season (November 22 to May 22). In addition, there are also a limited number of year round positions available. *Contact:* Human Resources.

WHITE ROSE HOME AND GARDEN CENTRES
4038 Highway 7 East
Unionville, ON L3R 2L5

Tel.	905-477-3330
Fax	905-477-1105
Email	hr@whiterose.ca

White Rose Home and Garden Centres is the largest retailer of nursery, home decor and craft related items in Canada. The company's stores are open seven days a week, every day except for Christmas and New Years. White Rose employs 100 people at this location, and a total of 1,900 people in Canada. Graduates most likely to be hired come from the following academic areas: Bachelor of Arts (General), Bachelor of Science (General, Agriculture/Horticulture, Biology), Bachelor of Commerce/Business Administration (General, Finance), Chartered Accountant, Certified General Accountant, Community College Diploma (Accounting, Advertising, Business, Retail, Communications/Public Relations, Facility Management, Human Resources, Marketing/Sales, Office Administration, Purchasing/Logistics, Secretarial, Graphic Arts, Interior Design, Journalism, Security/Enforcement, Agriculture/Horticulture, Computer Science)

and High School Diploma. Graduates would occupy Department Manager, Graphic Artist, Research Technician, Visual Services Clerk, Advertising Coordinator, Assistant Controller, Human Resources Manager, Executive Assistant, Merchandise Associate, Buyer, Payroll Administrator, Loss Prevention Officer and Media Researcher positions. The ability to learn and apply technical knowledge, work in a team environment and the ability to handle and resolve customer complaints are all listed as desirable non-academic qualifications. Company benefits and the potential for advancement are both rated as excellent. The average annual starting salary falls within the $25,000 to $30,000 range. The most suitable methods for initial contact by those seeking employment are to mail, fax or e-mail a resume with a covering letter. White Rose Home and Garden Centres does hire summer and co-op students, as well as requiring additional staff in the spring. *Contacts:* Cheryl Sproul, Human Resources or Shana White, Human Resources.

WHITEHORSE, CITY OF
2121 - 2nd Avenue
Whitehorse, YT Y1A 1C2

Tel.	867-668-8619
Fax	867-668-8384
Email	labour@city.whitehorse.yk.ca
Website	www.city.whitehorse.yk.ca

The City of Whitehorse provides municipal government services, including fire suppression and transit services, to a population base of approximately 23,000 people, spread over a wide geographical area. The City maintains a permanent workforce of approximately 200 people, plus a casual or seasonal workforce that will range between 10 and 50 employees. Graduates most likely to be hired come from the following academic areas: Bachelor of Arts (Geography, Recreation Studies, Urban Geography), Bachelor of Science (Biology, Computer Science, Environmental, Geography), Bachelor of Engineering (Civil, Resources/Environmental), Bachelor of Commerce/Business Administration (Accounting, Finance, Human Resources, Information Systems, Public Administration), Master of Business Administration (Accounting, Finance, Human Resources, Information Systems, Public Administration), Master of Engineering (Civil), Community College Diploma (Accounting, Administration, Business, Facility Management, Human Resources, Logistics, Secretarial, Recreation Studies, Travel/Tourism, Architecture/Drafting, CAD/CAM/Autocad, Computer Science, HVAC Systems) and High School Diploma. Graduates would occupy Planning, Engineering, Parks and Recreation, Community Services, Municipal Services, Human Resources, Accounting, and Administration positions. Previous work experience, good computer skills (word processing and spreadsheet applications), excellent oral and written communication skills, and good organization and interpersonal skills are all listed as desirable non-academic qualifications. Company benefits are rated as excellent. The potential for advancement is listed as being good. The average annual salary for a mid-range position falls within the $40,000 to $45,000 range. The most suitable methods for initial contact by those seeking employment are to mail a resume with a covering letter, or by responding to advertised positions. The City of Whitehorse does hire summer students, primarily for positions in the planning, engineering and recreation fields. *Contact:* Human Resources.

WIC RADIO, Q107/TALK 640
5255 Yonge Street, Suite 1400
Toronto, ON M2N 6P4

Tel. 416-221-0107
Fax 416-512-4810
Email .... webmaster@q107.com
Website .... www.wic.ca

WIC Radio, Q107/Talk 640 owns and operates radio stations Q107 (http://www.q107.com) and Talk 640 (http://www.talk640.com). Operational activities include on-air announcing, news production, creative writing, programming music, promotions, trafficking of commercials, engineering, computer operations, research, sale of airtime, accounting, human resources, reception and secretarial. There are more than 50 employees at this location. Graduates most likely to be hired come from the following academic areas: Bachelor of Arts (General, Journalism, Music), Bachelor of Science (Computer Science), Bachelor of Commerce/Business Administration (Accounting, Finance, Marketing), Chartered Accountant, Certified Management Accountant, Certified General Accountant (one or two accounting positions only), Master of Business Administration (Marketing), Community College Diploma (Accounting, Advertising, Business, Marketing/Sales, Secretarial, Television/Radio Arts) and High School Diploma. For broadcasting positions, talent and experience are the first and foremost qualifications overriding education in most cases. Company benefits are rated above average. The potential for advancement is listed as average. The average starting salary ranges widely with the position being considered, experience and talent and is commission based for certain positions. The most suitable method for initial contact by those seeking employment is to mail a resume with a covering letter. WIC Radio, Q107/Talk 640 does hire summer students. *Contact:* Human Resources Director.

WIC TELEVISION ALBERTA AND WIC PREMIUM TELEVISION
5325 Allard Way
Edmonton, AB T6H 5B8

Tel. 780-436-1250
Fax 780-438-8438
Website .... www.wic.ca

WIC Television Alberta and WIC Premium Television operates ITV in Edmonton, RDTV in Red Deer, CISA in Lethbridge, CICT in Calgary, pay and specialty television services and television production services. The company employs approximately 400 people. Graduates most likely to be hired come from the following academic areas: Bachelor of Laws (Corporate/Contract), Bachelor of Commerce/Business Administration (Accounting, Finance), Chartered Accountant, Certified Management Accountant, Certified General Accountant and Community College Diploma (Accounting, Administration, Communications, Human Resources, Marketing/Sales, Secretarial, Graphic Arts, Journalism, Television/Radio Arts, Computer Science, Electronics Technician, Engineering Technician). Graduates would occupy Accounting Clerk, Accounts Payable Clerk, Secretary, VTR Technician, VTR Editor, Audio Technician, Post Audio Technician, Maintenance Technician, Camera Operators (E.N.G., Studio, E.F.P.), News Reporter, Producer, Writer, Traffic Secretary, Editor, Television Host/Anchor, Computer Systems Technician, Television Assistant and Labourer positions. Company benefits are rated as industry standard. The potential for advancement is listed as average. The average annual starting salary falls within the $25,000 to $30,000 range. The most suitable method for initial con-

tact by those seeking employment is to mail a resume with a covering letter. WIC Television Alberta and WIC Premium Television does hire summer students. *Contact:* Human Resources.

WIC, WESTERN INTERNATIONAL COMMUNICATIONS LTD.
505 Burrard Street, Suite 1960
Vancouver, BC V7X 1M6

Tel. 604-687-2844
Fax 604-687-4118
Website .... www.wic.ca

WIC, Western International Communications Ltd. is an integrated Canadian communications, broadcast and entertainment company with its head office in Vancouver. WIC is the only Canadian broadcasting company operating in television, pay television, radio and satellite network services. WIC owns eight television and 12 radio stations across Canada and is a shareholder in the CTV Television Network. WIC employs 40 people at this location, and a total of 2,000 people across Canada. Graduates most likely to be hired come from the following academic areas: Bachelor of Arts (English, Journalism), Bachelor of Science (Physics), Bachelor of Engineering (Computer Systems, Telecommunications), Bachelor of Laws, Bachelor of Commerce/Business Administration (Accounting, Finance, Human Resources, Information Systems, Marketing, Public Administration), Chartered Accountant, Master of Business Administration (Accounting, Finance, Human Resources, Information Systems, Marketing, Public Administration) and Community College Diploma (Accounting, Administration, Advertising, Business, Communications, Marketing, Secretarial, Journalism, Legal Assistant, Television/Radio Arts). At the WIC Head Office, graduates would occupy Lawyer, Accountant, Public Relations, Secretarial and Legal Assistant positions. At Station locations, graduates would occupy Journalist, Promotions and Writer positions. Previous work experience, a willingness to learn and good references are listed as desirable non-academic qualifications. The most suitable method for initial contact by those seeking employment is to mail a resume with a covering letter (contact head office for a list of stations). WIC employs summer students at some of the television and radio station subsidiaries (contact station location). *Contact:* Human Resources.

WINNERS APPAREL LTD.
6715 Airport Road, Suite 500
Mississauga, ON L4V 1Y2

Tel. 905-405-8000
Fax 905-405-7581
Email .... winners@psinet.com

Winners Apparel Ltd. is Canada's leading off-price fashion retailer in men's, women's and children's wear. There are 180 employees at this location and a total of 2,800 employees across Canada. Graduates most likely to be hired come from the following academic areas: Bachelor of Commerce/Business Administration (Accounting, Finance), Certified Management Accountant, Certified General Accountant and Community College Diploma (CAD/CAM/Autocad). Graduates would occupy Clerk and Coordinator positions. Previous related work experience, team player and strong communication skills are listed as desirable non-academic qualifications. Company benefits are rated above average. The potential for advancement is listed as excellent. The average annual starting salary falls within the $20,000 to $25,000 range, varying with the position being considered. The most suitable methods for initial contact by those seeking employment are to mail or fax a resume with a covering letter. Winners Apparel Ltd. occasionally hires summer students. *Contact:* Human Resources.

WMA SECURITIES
5020 - 68 Street, Suite 4
Red Deer, AB T4N 7B4

Tel.	403-346-0095
Fax	403-346-0067
Email	Ivanabelar@usa.net
Website	www.wmas.com

WMA Securities is an international investment firm. The company specializes in helping clients reduce taxes, asset maximization, debt reduction, growth and withdrawal of investments tax-free. WMA Securities has openings in all major Canadian cities. There are 20 employees at this location, a total of 200 across Canada and 2,000 employees worldwide. Graduates most likely to be hired come from the following academic areas: Bachelor of Commerce/Business Administration (General, Accounting, Finance, Human Resources, Information Systems, Marketing, Public Administration, Management), Master of Business Administration (General, Accounting, Finance, Human Resources, Information Systems, Marketing, Public Administration) and Community College Diploma (Accounting, Advertising, Business, Communications/Public Relations, Facility Management, Financial Planning, Human Resources, Insurance, Marketing/Sales, Office Administration, Purchasing/Logistics, Real Estate Sales, Hospitality, Television/Radio Arts). Graduates would occupy Entry Level Investment Advisor (Trainee) positions. Team player, leader, people-person and hard working are all listed as desirable non-academic qualifications. Company benefits are rated as industry standard. The potential for advancement is listed as being excellent. The average annual starting salary falls within the $50,000 to $55,000 range and is commission based. The most suitable methods for initial contact by those seeking employment are to mail or fax a resume with a covering letter. WMA Securities does hire co-op work term students. *Contact:* Ivan Abelar, Associate.

WOMEN'S COLLEGE CAMPUS / SUNNYBROOK
76 Grenville Street
Toronto, ON M5S 1B2

Tel.	416-323-6050
Fax	416-323-6177
Website	www.sunnybrook.utoronto.ca

The Women's College Campus of Sunnybrook & Women's College Health Sciences Centre is a general teaching hospital with a focus on women's health, family and community medicine, dermatology and perinatal services. Women's College Hospital amalgamated in 1998 with Sunnybrook Health Science Centre and the Orthopaedic & Arthritic Hospital to form the Sunnybrook and Women's College Health Sciences Centre. Fully affiliated with the University of Toronto, the Women's College Campus employs more than 1,000 people. Graduates most likely to be hired come from the following academic areas: Bachelor of Science (Nursing, Health Sciences, Occupational Therapy, Physiotherapy), Bachelor of Engineering (Mechanical, Electrical), Certified Management Accountant and Community College Diploma (Nursing RN/RNA, Laboratory Technician, Radiology, Respiratory Therapy, Health Records/Administration). Graduates would oc-

cupy Registered Nurse, Health Records Technician, Respiratory Therapist, Radiology Technician and Accounting Clerk positions. Team player, and excellent communication and interpersonal skills are listed as desirable non-academic qualifications. Employee benefits are rated as excellent. The average annual starting salary falls within the $30,000 to $35,000 range. The most suitable method for initial contact by those seeking employment is to mail a resume with a covering letter. *Contact:* Human Resources.

WOODBRIDGE FOAM CORPORATION
4240 Sherwood Town Boulevard
Mississauga, ON L4Z 2G6

Tel.	905-896-3626
Fax	905-896-8592
Email	bob_connolly@woodbridgegroup.com
Website	www.woodbridgegroup.com

Woodbridge Foam Corporation is a major supplier of molded polyurethane foam products for automotive and commercial industries worldwide. The company manufactures foam seating components, energy-absorbing safety foams, acoustical foams, fabricated, slab and roll-goods foam products, foam-in-place seating products and offers assembly and sequencing services. Woodbridge also provides engineering, prototyping, development and testing for foam components and their manufacture. Headquartered in Mississauga, the company is a privately owned Canadian corporation with 42 locations in the United States, Canada, Mexico, England, Germany, Australia, Brazil, Venezuela, Egypt and Japan. There are 200 employees at this location, a total of 1,500 in Canada and a total of 4,500 employees worldwide. Graduates most likely to be hired come from the following academic areas: Bachelor of Engineering (Chemical, Electrical, Mechanical, Automation/Robotics, Instrumentation), Bachelor of Commerce/Business Administration (Accounting, Finance, Human Resources), Master of Business Administration, Master of Engineering (Chemical, Mechanical) and Community College Diploma (Purchasing/Logistics Engineering Technician, Information Systems). Graduates would occupy Process Engineer, Project Engineer, Engineering Technician, General Accountant, Financial Analyst and Human Resources Consultant positions. Excellent analytical and problem solving skills, a high level of initiative, persuasiveness, loyalty, entrepreneurial, innovative, and good listening, presentation and verbal communication skills are all listed as desirable non-academic qualifications. Company benefits are rated above average. The potential for advancement is listed as being excellent. The average annual starting salary falls within the $45,000 to $50,000 range. The most suitable methods for initial contact by those seeking employment are to fax or e-mail a resume with a covering letter. Woodbridge Foam Corporation does hire co-op work term students and occasionally hires summer students. *Contact:* Robert Connolly, Human Resources Manager.

THE DOCUMENT COMPANY

XEROX

XEROX CANADA INC.
5650 Yonge Street
Toronto, ON M5J 2J1

Tel. 800-ASK-XEROX
Fax 416-733-6802
Website .... www.xerox.ca

Xerox is a leading supplier of a broad range of highly competitive document processing products and services that focus on helping people and businesses be more productive in the creation, production and distribution of documents. Xerox Canada Inc. provides equipment, supplies and services that facilitate the six basic phases in the life cycle of a document: create, link, archive, process, distribute and output. In addition to technical support services, Xerox Canada offers a wide range of professional and consulting services that help businesses become more productive in the way they handle their documents, from in-house printing through to mail services. Headquartered in Toronto, Xerox Canada Inc.'s research and manufacturing facilities support Xerox services around the world. Xerox Canada maintains a global mandate for material based research in Mississauga, as well as a state of the art call centre facility in New Brunswick to service customers across the country. Xerox employs 550 people at this location, a total of 4,800 across Canada and a total of 80,000 people worldwide. Graduates most likely to be hired at Xerox Canada come from the following academic areas: Bachelor of Arts (Economics), Bachelor of Science (General, Biology, Chemistry, Computer Science, Mathematics), Bachelor of Engineering (General, Electrical, Mechanical, Computer Systems, Telecommunications, Systems Design Engineering), Bachelor of Commerce/Business Administration (General, Accounting, Finance, Information Systems), Master of Business Administration (General, Accounting, Finance, Information Systems, Marketing) and Community College Diploma (Business, Facility Management, Marketing/Sales, Graphic Arts, Electronics Technician, Engineering Technician, Information Systems). In the Sales Organization graduates would occupy Document Solutions Consultant and Systems Analyst positions. In the Administration Organization graduates would occupy Administration Representative and Business Support Representative positions. At the Corporate Head Office graduates would occupy Financial Analyst and Business Analyst positions. Volunteer work, sports involvement, team player, enthusiasm, an aptitude to learn and co-op work term experience are all listed as desirable non-academic qualifications. Company benefits and the potential for advancement are both rated as excellent. The average annual starting salary for service positions falls within the $25,000 plus range, for administration positions it falls within the $30,000 plus range, and for sales positions it falls within the $35,000 plus range. The most suitable methods for initial contact by those seeking employment are to mail or fax a resume with a covering letter, or by applying through the company's website. Xerox Canada Inc. does hire co-op work term students. *Contact:* Human Resources.

XEROX RESEARCH CENTRE OF CANADA
2660 Speakman Drive
Mississauga, ON L5K 2L1

Tel. 905-823-7091
Fax 905-822-6984
Website .... www.xerox.ca

The Xerox Research Centre of Canada is involved in fundamental studies in materials science, synthesis and materials processing technology and the development of materials for novel imaging processes. The centre employs 150 people, with Xerox employing a total of 4,800 people across Canada and 80,000 worldwide. Graduates most likely to be hired come from the following academic areas: Bachelor of Science (Chemistry, Physics), Bachelor of Engineering (Chemical, Industrial Chemistry, Materials Science), Master of Science (Chemistry, Physics), Master of Engineering (Chemical) and Doctorate (Chemistry, Physics, Chemical Engineering). Graduates would occupy Technical and Research positions. Team player, good communication and interpersonal skills are listed as desirable non-academic qualifications. Company benefits are rated as excellent. The potential for advancement is listed as being good. The average annual starting salary falls within the $30,000 to $55,000 range, and is primarily dependent upon degree equivalence. The most suitable method for initial contact by those seeking employment is to mail a resume with a covering letter. The Xerox Research Centre of Canada does hire summer students. *Contact:* Corina Cluteman, Human Resources Specialist.

YANKE GROUP OF COMPANIES
2815 Lorne Avenue
Saskatoon, SK S7J 0S5

Tel. 306-955-4221
Fax 306-955-5663
Email .... hr@yanke.ca
Website .... www.yanke.ca

Yanke Group of Companies is a privately owned Saskatchewan based international transportation company. The company has 7 separate operating groups, 1,400 pieces of equipment and 700 employees. Yanke has diversified to service customers that require expedited and non-expedited full truckload dry van, open deck, rail, freight forwarding, air cargo, ocean cargo and logistics management services. Guided by the company's mission, vision and core values, the Yanke Group of Companies are committed to delivering unequalled transportation solutions in partnership with their customers. Graduates most likely to be hired are those with a Degree, Diploma or Professional Accreditation specializing in the following areas: Administration, Finance, Accounting, Human Resources, Information Systems, Operations/Logistics, Risk Management/Loss Prevention, Sales/Marketing and Maintenance. Leadership abilities, transportation industry experience, and managerial and supervisory experience are listed as desirable non-academic qualifications. The ideal candidate can typically be described as a risk taker who is innovative, responsible, reliable and possesses a high level of energy. Company benefits and the potential for advancement are both rated as excellent. The average annual starting salary ranges widely, depending on the degree of responsibility, the level of authority and the complexity of the tasks to be undertaken as described in the work description. The most suitable method for initial contact by those seeking employment is to mail a resume with references, under a cover letter. Yanke Group of Companies does hire summer students on an "as required" basis. *Contact:* Human Resources Department.

YELLOWKNIFE, CITY OF
PO Box 580
Yellowknife, NT X1A 2N4

Tel. 867-920-5600
Fax 867-669-3463
Email .... cityhr@city.yellowknife.nt.ca
Website .... www.city.yellowknife.nt.ca

The City of Yellowknife provides municipal government services for the population of Yellowknife. As the capital city of Northwest Territories, Yellowknife has a population of over 18,000, and has continued to grow as a mining, transportation, communications and administrative centre. The city currently employs approximately 150 people. Graduates most likely to be hired come from the following academic areas: Bachelor of Arts (General, Criminology, Recreation Studies, Urban Geography/Planning), Bachelor of Science (General, Computer Science), Bachelor of Engineering (General, Civil, Computer Systems, Environmental/Resources), Bachelor of Commerce/Business Administration (General, Accounting, Finance, Human Resources, Information Systems, Public Administration), Master of Arts (Recreation), Master of Library Science and Community College Diploma (Administration, Business, Facility Management, Human Resources, Information Systems, Purchasing/Logistics, Secretarial, CAD/CAM/Autocad, Computer Science, Engineering Technician, Ambulance/Emergency Care). Graduates would occupy Clerk, Technician, Secretarial, Facility Maintenance, Engineering, Municipal Enforcement, Emergency Services, Recreation Programming, Urban Planner and Development Officer positions. Previous work experience, flexibility, team player, public relations skills and dedication are all listed as desirable non-academic qualifications. Company benefits are rated as excellent. The potential for advancement is listed as being good. The average annual starting salary falls within the $30,000 to $35,000 range. The most suitable method for initial contact by those seeking employment is to fax a resume with a covering letter. The City of Yellowknife does hire summer and co-op work term students. *Contacts:* Sheila Dunn, Human Resources Director or Kelly Arychuk, Human Resources Officer.

YORK SOUTH ASSOCIATION FOR COMMUNITY LIVING
101 Edward Avenue
Richmond Hill, ON L4C 5E5

Tel. 905-884-9110
Fax 905-737-3284

York South Association for Community Living provides residential and adult life skills programmes for people with developmental delays. The association employs approximately 125 people. Graduates most likely to be hired come from the following academic areas: Bachelor of Arts (General, Psychology, Recreation Studies) and Bachelor of Science (Psychology). Graduates are hired as Community Support Workers or Community Support Facilitators. Applicants should have a positive and pleasant personality, a good sense of humour and good team work skills. Applicants should also be willing to work shifts (weekends as well) with people who have developmental delays or physical handicaps. Company benefits are rated above average. The potential for advancement is listed as being good. The average annual starting salary falls within the $25,000 to $26,000 range. The most suitable methods for initial contact by those seeking employment are to mail or fax a resume with a covering letter. York South Association for Community Living does hire summer and co-op work term students. *Contact:* Erica Nielson, Administrative Assistant.

YWCA OF CALGARY
320 - 5th Avenue SE
Calgary, AB T2G 3E5

Tel. 403-263-1550
Fax 403-263-4681
Website .... www.ywcaofcalgary.com

YWCA of Calgary provides services for women and families, including housing, employment, health and fitness, and educational services. The YWCA employs more than 100 people. Graduates most likely to be hired come from the following academic areas: Bachelor of Arts (English, Psychology, Recreation Studies, Social Work), Bachelor of Science (Computer Science), Bachelor of Education (General, Early Childhood), Bachelor of Commerce/Business Administration (Accounting, Finance, Marketing), Community College Diploma (Accounting, Administration, Communications, Marketing/Sales, Recreation Studies, Massage Therapy, Social Work) and High School Diploma. Graduates would occupy Counsellor, Clerk, Teacher and Accountant positions. Team player, and good communication and supervisory skills are listed as desirable non-academic qualifications. Company benefits are rated as excellent. The potential for advancement is listed as being good. The average annual starting salary falls within the $15,000 to $20,000 range. The most suitable method for initial contact by those seeking employment is to mail a resume with a covering letter. The YWCA of Calgary does hire summer students. *Contact:* Verla Dowell, Executive Assistant.

ZEIDLER ROBERTS PARTNERSHIP / ARCHITECTS
315 Queen Street West
Toronto, ON M5V 2X2

Tel. 416-596-8300
Fax 416-596-1408
Email .... djefferies@zrpa.com
Website .... www.zrpa.com

Zeidler Roberts Partnership / Architects is a full-service international architectural practice with offices in Toronto (head office), West Palm Beach, London and Berlin. There are 95 employees at this location and a total of 120 worldwide. Involved in all aspects of building design, the firm lists an impressive portfolio of very significant buildings across Canada and around the world, including Canada Place-Vancouver, Toronto Eaton Centre, Media Park-Cologne, Ontario Place, National Trade Centre, Mississauga Living Arts Centre and Sick Children's Hospital, to name a few. A demanding office, with high expectations, but always seeking exceptional new talent, graduates most likely to be hired come from the following academic areas: Bachelor of Arts (Urban Geography/Planning), Bachelor of Engineering (Architectural/Building), Bachelor of Architecture, Bachelor of Landscape Architecture and Community College Diploma (Graphic Arts, Architecture/Drafting, CAD/CAM/Autocad). Graduates would occupy entry level Design, entry level Technical Document Preparation, entry level Construction Administration, Intern Architect and junior level Technologist positions. Additional academic and non-academic qualifications desired include: second language with preference to French, Spanish and Arabic, an ability and desire to travel, excellent verbal presentation skills, solid design and technical background, Autocad 14, and additional computer skills in word processing, spreadsheet, 3D computer graphic and manual graphic applications. Company benefits are rated as industry standard. The potential for advancement is listed as average. The average annual starting salary falls within the $25,000 to $35,000 range. The most suitable method for initial contact by those seeking employment is to mail a resume and sample portfolio (non-returnable - 81/2 x 11). Interviews are by appointment only, written references. Zeidler Roberts Partnership/Architects does hire summer and co-op work term students, these are limited to architectural and related fields (model building, drafting and general office duties). *Contact:* David Jefferies, BES, B.Arch., OAA, Director of Office Management.

ZENON ENVIRONMENTAL SYSTEMS INC.
845 Harrington Court
Burlington, ON L7N 3P3

Tel.	905-639-6320
Fax	905-639-1812

Zenon Environmental Systems Inc. is a world leader in providing advanced technology products and services in water purification, process separation and wastewater treatment and recycling. The company employs 200 people at this location, a total of 275 in Canada and 300 people worldwide. Graduates most likely to be hired come from the following academic areas: Bachelor of Science (Chemistry), Bachelor of Engineering (Chemical, Industrial Chemistry, Membrane Technology, Civil, Electrical, Mechanical, Industrial Design, Industrial Production, Resources/Environmental, Water Resources), Bachelor of Commerce/Business Administration (Accounting, Finance, Human Resources, Information Systems, Marketing, Public Administration), Doctorate (Chemistry) and Community College Diploma (Architecture/Drafting, CAD/CAM/Autocad, Electronics Technician, Engineering Technician). Graduates would occupy Environmental Technician, Engineer (All Types), Laboratory Technician, Chemist, Sales, Marketing, Finance, Administration, Accounting, Field Service Representative and Mechanical Technician positions. Company benefits are rated above average. The potential for advancement is listed as being good. The average annual starting salary falls within the $25,000 to $30,000 range. The most suitable methods for initial contact by those seeking employment are to mail or fax a resume with a covering letter. Zenon Environmental Systems Inc. does hire summer students. *Contact:* Human Resources.

ZIFF ENERGY GROUP
1117 Macleod Trail SE
Calgary, AB T2G 2M8

Tel.	403-265-0600
Fax	403-261-4631
Email	ziff@ziffenergy.com
Website	www.ziffenergy.com

Ziff Energy Group is the largest energy consulting organization in Canada providing a unique combination of corporate analysis, natural gas strategies and regulatory support for Canadian, American and international energy companies, government agencies and investors. The company's expertise and innovative approaches produce practical solutions for greater profitability for its customers. The group maintains offices in Calgary and Houston, Texas. There are 35 employees at this location and a total of 45 employees in the company. Graduates most likely to be hired come from the following academic areas: Bachelor of Arts (Economics), Bachelor of Science (Ge-

ology), Bachelor of Engineering (General, Computer Science, Geological Engineering), Bachelor of Commerce/Business Administration (General, Accounting, Information Systems), Certified General Accountant and Community College Diploma (Computer Science). Company benefits are rated above average. The potential for advancement is listed as being good. The most suitable methods for initial contact by those seeking employment are to mail or fax a resume with a covering letter. Ziff Energy Group does hire summer students. *Contact:* Human Resources.

ZTR CONTROL SYSTEMS INC.
PO Box 2543, Station B
London, ON N6A 4G9

Tel.	519-452-1999
Fax	519-452-7764
Email	hr@ztr.com
Website	www.ztr.com

ZTR Control Systems is involved in the design and development of monitoring and control system solutions for a number of different industries. The company has had a special focus on the railway, power generation and wastewater treatment sectors. ZTR integrates internally developed technologies with rugged off-the-shelf components when designing or enhancing control system solutions. Current products utilize PLC's and embedded microprocessors as the heart of the system. A graphical PC based application utilizing remote communications technology can also be implemented to provide customers with global access to their sites. With offices located in Canada and the United States, ZTR Control Systems is currently marketing and supporting products in North America and abroad. Graduates most likely to be hired come from the following academic areas: Bachelor of Science (Computer Science), Bachelor of Engineering (Electrical, Mechanical, Automation/Robotics, Computer Systems) and Community College Diploma (Computer Science, Electronics Technician). Graduates would occupy Electronics Technologist, Electronics Technician, Electrical Engineer, Controls Engineer, Applications Engineering and Software Developer positions. Co-op experience, leadership skills, team player, excellent written and verbal communication skills, and an understanding of basic business values such as honesty and trust are all listed as desirable non-academic qualifications. Company benefits are rated above average. The potential for advancement is listed as being excellent. The average annual starting salary falls within the $40,000 to $45,000 range. The most suitable methods for initial contact by those seeking employment are to mail, fax or e-mail a resume with a covering letter. ZTR Control Systems Inc. does hire summer and co-op work term students. *Contact:* Patricia Rossi, Human Resources Manager.

ZURICH CANADA
400 University Avenue
Toronto, ON M5G 1S7

Tel.	416-586-3000
Fax	416-586-3082
Website	www.zurichcanada.com

Zurich Canada is one of the country's leading providers of home, auto and life insurance products. Zurich Canada is a member of Zurich, Switzerland based Zurich Financial Services. The company is a leading internationally-recognized provider of insurance and financial services in non-life and life insurance, reinsurance and asset management. The group operates in 50 countries worldwide and employs a total of 47,000 people. Zurich Canada employs 800 people at this location and a total of 2,200 people across Canada. Graduates most likely to be hired come from the following academic areas: Bachelor of Science (Actuarial, Computer Science, Physical Therapy), Bachelor of Engineering (Civil, Mechanical), Bachelor of Commerce/Business Administration (Accounting, Finance, Human Resources, Information Systems), Certified Management Accountant, Certified General Accountant and Community College Diploma (Accounting, Administration, Business, Communications, Facility Management, Financial Planning, Human Resources, Insurance). Graduates would occupy Clerk, Trainee, Assistant, Programmer and Recruiter positions. Customer service skills, work experience and good time management skills are listed as desirable non-academic qualifications. Company benefits are rated as industry standard. The potential for advancement is listed as average. The average annual starting salary for entry level positions falls within the $15,000 to $20,000 range. The most suitable method for initial contact by those seeking employment is to mail a resume with a covering letter. Zurich Canada does hire summer students. *Contact:* Human Resources Manager.

Industry Index

COMMUNICATIONS: BOOK, MUSIC AND VIDEO PUBLISHING

COMMUNICATIONS: NEWSPAPER, MAGAZINE AND INFORMATION PUBLISHING

CONSUMER PRODUCTS AND SERVICES: AGRICULTURE

CONSUMER PRODUCTS AND SERVICES: AUTOMOBILE

CONSUMER PRODUCTS AND SERVICES: BREWERIES AND DISTILLERIES

CONSUMER PRODUCTS AND SERVICES: ENTERTAINMENT

CONSUMER PRODUCTS AND SERVICES: FOOD PRODUCTS

CONSUMER PRODUCTS AND SERVICES: HOUSEHOLD GOODS

CONSUMER PRODUCTS AND SERVICES: PACKAGED GOODS

HIGH TECHNOLOGY: BIOTECHNOLOGY AND PHARMACEUTICALS

HIGH TECHNOLOGY: COMPUTER SOFTWARE AND HARDWARE

HIGH TECHNOLOGY: COMMUNICATIONS AND TRANSPORTATION

HIGH TECHNOLOGY: ELECTRONICS

INDUSTRIAL PRODUCTS AND SERVICES: BUSINESS EQUIPMENT AND FORMS

INDUSTRIAL PRODUCTS AND SERVICES: CHEMICAL, PLASTIC AND PAPER

INDUSTRIAL PRODUCTS AND SERVICES: ELECTRICAL

INDUSTRIAL PRODUCTS AND SERVICES: ENGINEERING, ARCHITECTURE AND CONSTRUCTION

INDUSTRIAL PRODUCTS AND SERVICES: MACHINERY

INDUSTRIAL PRODUCTS AND SERVICES: METAL FABRICATION

INDUSTRIAL PRODUCTS AND SERVICES: STEEL

INDUSTRIAL PRODUCTS AND SERVICES: TRANSPORTATION EQUIPMENT AND AUTO PARTS

MERCHANDISING: HOSPITALITY, LODGING, FOOD AND RENTAL

TRANSPORTATION SERVICES

UTILITIES: HYDRO, GAS AND WATER

UTILITIES: TELEPHONE

Geographic Index

BRITISH COLUMBIA

ALBERTA

SASKATCHEWAN

MANITOBA

ONTARIO

QUEBEC

NEW BRUNSWICK

PRINCE EDWARD ISLAND

NOVA SCOTIA

NEWFOUNDLAND

NUNAVUT

NORTHWEST TERRITORIES

YUKON

Co-Op Work Index

Summer Job Index

Alphabetical Index

ALSO FROM THE PUBLISHERS OF THE CAREER DIRECTORY

Need to find a search firm or recruitment agency that specializes in your industry?

CANADIAN DIRECTORY OF SEARCH FIRMS (2000 EDITION)

Now in its fourth annual edition, the *Canadian Directory of Search Firms (2000 Edition)* is the most comprehensive guide to Canada's recruitment industry ever published. This authoritative trade reference provides detailed and up-to-date information on over 2,000 search firms and 3,500 recruiters across Canada. Each listing includes: key contact names, practice specialties, address, telephone/fax numbers, email addresses, websites, year founded, recruiters employed and fee information.

Best of all, none of the firms in the *Canadian Directory of Search Firms (2000 Edition)* charges job-seekers any kind of fee. All the firms are paid by employers to locate candidates for available positions.

Indexing Information: An easy-to-use **Occupational Index** lets you quickly locate firms specializing in over 70 industries. A detailed **Geographic Index** lets you discover all the search firms in cities and towns across Canada. A special **International Index** lists over 200 firms in the USA, Asia and Europe that actively recruit in Canada. And a giant **"Who's Who" Index** lists more than 3,500 recruitment professionals and their firms across Canada.

$44.95

Sold at bookstores across Canada. To order by credit card, call 1-800-361-2580 or (416) 964-6069. Credit card orders can also be faxed to (416) 964-3202. More information at http://www.mediacorp2.com/cdsf. ISBN 0-9681447-6-4.

ALSO FROM THE PUBLISHERS OF THE CAREER DIRECTORY

Need to find the top Canadian employers in your field?

5,000
Canadian Employers
Indexed by Occupation

WHO'S HIRING 2000

Now you can target your job search efforts on the employers hiring the most people in your field. This book brings you detailed information on Canada's top employers in 60 major occupations:

❑ Accounting	❑ Education	❑ Multimedia
❑ Actuarial	❑ Engineering	❑ Oil & Gas
❑ Administrative	❑ Finance	❑ Operations
❑ Advertising	❑ Forestry	❑ Packaging
❑ Aerospace	❑ Franchising	❑ Pharmaceutical
❑ Agriculture	❑ Geologists	❑ Plastics
❑ Apparel	❑ Govt./Nonprofit	❑ Printing
❑ Architecture	❑ Graphic Arts	❑ Public Relations
❑ Arts & Culture	❑ Health/Medical	❑ Publishing
❑ Automotive	❑ Hospitality	❑ Pulp & Paper
❑ Banking	❑ Human Resource	❑ Purchasing
❑ Bilingual	❑ Insurance	❑ Quality Control
❑ Biotech	❑ International	❑ Real Estate
❑ Clergy	❑ Law	❑ Retail
❑ Computing	❑ Librarians	❑ Sales
❑ Construction	❑ Logistics	❑ Scientific
❑ Consulting	❑ Management	❑ Telecom
❑ Design	❑ Marketing	❑ Trade Shows
❑ Direct Mktng.	❑ Metals	❑ Trades/Technicians
❑ Disabled	❑ Mining	❑ Transport

The 2000 Edition has been significantly expanded and features:

✓ **More employers...** Now includes <u>over 5,000 Canadian employers</u> that have advertised at least two new career opportunities in the last 12 months.

✓ **Expanded Listings...** Now <u>tells you what each employer does</u> and shows all the positions they advertised. Also features <u>expanded contact information</u> for each employer, including HR contacts, addresses, telephone/fax numbers, email addresses and websites.

✓ **More Occupations...** Now shows the top employers in <u>60 major occupational categories</u> so you can target your job search with more precision.

✓ **Special Geographic Index** ranks the top employers in cities and towns across Canada.

Don't waste a moment cold-calling employers that aren't growing — use this quality directory to find the top new employers in your field. 480 pages.

$29.95

Sold at bookstores across Canada. To order by credit card, call 1-800-361-2580 or (416) 964-6069. Credit card orders can also be faxed to (416) 964-3202. We accept Visa, MasterCard and Amex. More information at http://www.mediacorp2.com. ISBN 0-9681447-7-2.

ALSO FROM THE PUBLISHERS OF THE CAREER DIRECTORY

*Interested in discovering
Canada's best places to work?*

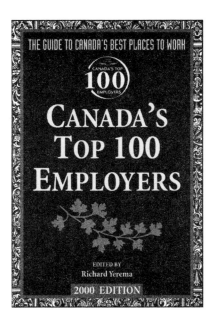

CANADA'S TOP 100 EMPLOYERS
(2000 EDITION)

New this year from Mediacorp is *Canada's Top 100 Employers (2000 Edition)* — an affordable pocketbook that surveys the best places in Canada to work.

This unique guide contains in-depth profiles of the companies and organizations (both large and small) that lead their industries in offering exceptional employee benefits, working conditions and interesting perks.

The book includes a wealth of information on each employer, including recent developments in their business, benefits offered, salary information and how to apply for job opportunities. Plus you get full contact information, including HR contacts, telephone/fax numbers, addresses, company websites and email addresses. 288 pages.

$17.95

Sold at bookstores across Canada. To order by credit card, call 1-800-361-2580 or (416) 964-6069. Credit card orders can also be faxed to (416) 964-3202. More information at http://www.mediacorp2.com. ISBN 0-9681447-9-9.

ALSO FROM THE PUBLISHERS OF THE CAREER DIRECTORY

*Need to find all the current
job opportunities in your field?*

Discover the newspaper that brings you all the current job opportunities in your field! Every week, *Canada Employment Weekly* brings you over 1,000 job opportunities from across Canada. No part-time, temporary or seasonal jobs — just full-time, salaried positions with companies and organizations that are succeeding in today's economy.

All the job listings in our newspaper are new every week. You get complete descriptions of each position, the qualifications required and valuable background information on the employer drawn from the proprietary databases we use to publish *The Career Directory*, *Who's Hiring*, the *Canadian Directory of Search Firms* and *Canada's Top 100 Employers*. And we show you how many other positions the employer has publicized in the past year, so you can tell if they're growing. Listings are indexed in 60 major occupational categories.

Canada's largest career newspaper is sold at thousands of newstands across Canada. The newsstand price is $4.65 per copy plus tax. You can also subscribe and have the paper delivered to you by first-class mail. To subscribe by credit card, please call:

1-800-361-2580

Or call (416) 964-6069. Credit card orders can be faxed to (416) 964-3202. Our subscription rates for 12 issues are as follows:

❏ **Canada** (except NS, NB and NF) $49 + $3.43 GST   ❏ **USA** $66.00 (or send US$44)

❏ **Canada** (NS, NB and NF) $49 + $7.35 HST   ❏ **Overseas** $103.50 (or send US$69)

ALSO FROM THE PUBLISHERS OF THE CAREER DIRECTORY

Need to see all the job listings in CEW, but can't wait for the mail?

Get your copy of CEW before it comes off the press!

CEWExpress is the fast new online version of *Canada Employment Weekly*. It features exactly the same content as the newsprint edition, but offers the following advantages:

- ✔ **Instant Delivery.** A new issue is available to subscribers every Tuesday at 4:30 pm (Toronto time) — a full day before the paper appears on newsstands.

- ✔ **Searchable Text.** Job listings are searchable by keyword, so you can quickly find new opportunities in your field across different occupational categories.

- ✔ **Apply Faster.** Job listings include built-in links to employers' websites and email addresses, so you can research hot prospects and apply for positions instantly.

- ✔ **Get Full Directory Listings.** Where an employer (or search firm) is also listed in *The Career Directory*, *Who's Hiring*, the *Canadian Directory of Search Firms* or *Canada's Top 100 Employers*, you can see their full listing from the relevant directory online.

Like the newsprint edition, job listings in **CEWExpress** are indexed in 60 major occupational categories, so you see all the vacancies in your field across Canada at once. And all the positions are new every week, so you don't waste a moment reading outdated information.

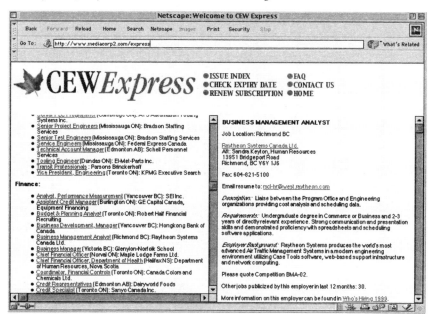

A 12 week subscription to CEWExpress costs $49 plus tax, regardless of where you live. To view some sample issues, point your browser to **http://www.mediacorp2.com** and follow the directions. <u>If you like what you see, complete the secure online subscription form.</u> You'll receive a password that lets you access current issues for the duration of your subscription.

ALSO FROM THE PUBLISHERS OF THE CAREER DIRECTORY

Need to find all the job opportunities published in your field in the last 12 weeks?

CEW SPECIAL REPORTS

Discover all the job opportunities in your field that have been published in the last 12 issues of *Canada Employment Weekly.* Now you can order a custom-made **Special Report** showing all the positions that have appeared in any of the newspaper's 60 occupational categories. The service is ideal for jobseekers who need to catch up on all the recent vacancies in their field. There's no better way to jump-start your job search!

When you order a **Special Report**, you'll receive a custom printout showing each job listing exactly as it appeared in *Canada Employment Weekly*, including the date of publication. Your **Special Report** is sent by Expressmail and delivered within 48 hours. (If you prefer, you can receive it instantly by E-mail instead.)

The price for one category is $39.95 (or order three categories for $59.95).

To order by credit card, call 1-800-361-2580 and indicate the category you require:

❏ Accounting	❏ Education	❏ Multimedia
❏ Actuarial	❏ Engineering	❏ Oil & Gas
❏ Administrative	❏ Finance	❏ Operations
❏ Advertising	❏ Forestry	❏ Packaging
❏ Aerospace	❏ Franchising	❏ Pharmaceutical
❏ Agriculture	❏ Geologists	❏ Plastics
❏ Apparel	❏ Govt./Nonprofit	❏ Printing
❏ Architecture	❏ Graphic Arts	❏ Public Relations
❏ Arts & Culture	❏ Health/Medical	❏ Publishing
❏ Automotive	❏ Hospitality	❏ Pulp & Paper
❏ Banking	❏ Human Resource	❏ Purchasing
❏ Bilingual	❏ Insurance	❏ Quality Control
❏ Biotech	❏ International	❏ Real Estate
❏ Clergy	❏ Law	❏ Retail
❏ Computing	❏ Librarians	❏ Sales
❏ Construction	❏ Logistics	❏ Scientific
❏ Consulting	❏ Management	❏ Telecom
❏ Design	❏ Marketing	❏ Trade Shows
❏ Direct Mktng.	❏ Metals	❏ Trades/Technicians
❏ Disabled	❏ Mining	❏ Transport

To order by credit card, call 1-800-361-2580 or fax your order to (416) 964-3202

COMMENTS & CHANGES

Please correct / add the following information in the next edition of *The Career Directory*:

_____

_____

_____

_____

_____

_____

_____

_____

_____

_____

_____

_____

NAME OF EMPLOYER

SUBMITTED BY (OPTIONAL)

DATE   TELEPHONE

Mail completed form to: The Career Directory, Mediacorp Canada Inc., P.O. Box 682, Station "P", Toronto, ON M5S 2Y4. Or fax to (416) 964-3202. You can also e-mail corrections to: ry@mediacorp2.com.

THE
CAREER
DIRECTORY

2000 EDITION

This directory is sold at major bookstores across Canada. You can also order directly from the publisher:

- ❑ **Telephone**. To order by credit card, please call 1-800-361-2580 or (416) 964-6069.
- ❑ **Fax**. Fax your credit card order to (416) 964-3202.
- ❑ **Mail**. Send this form and your cheque or money order (payable to "Mediacorp Canada Inc.") to the address below.

Total charges per copy ordered are:

Shipped to	Directory	Shipping	GST	Total
Canada	$27.95	$6.00	$2.38	$36.33
USA	27.95	9.91	0.00	37.86
Overseas	27.95	18.64	0.00	46.59

Charges shown are for delivery by first-class airmail. Shipments in Canada are sent via two-day Expressmail. FedEx delivery is also available on rush orders. All orders are shipped on the same or next business day.

ORDER FORM

GST # 134051515

THE CAREER DIRECTORY
2000 EDITION

Number of copies ordered: ▢

Method of Payment:
- ❑ Visa
- ❑ MasterCard
- ❑ Amex
- ❑ Cheque

NAME

ADDRESS

CITY   PROV.   POST. CODE

COUNTRY

TELEPHONE

CREDIT CARD NUMBER

EXPIRY DATE   SIGNATURE

Send or fax to

THE CAREER DIRECTORY
P.O. BOX 682, STATION "P", TORONTO, ON M5S 2Y4
TEL. (416) 964-6069 • FAX (416) 964-3202
TO ORDER, CALL TOLL-FREE 1-800-361-2580